A History of the Co-operative Movement in Israel

A History of the Co-operative Movement in Israel

A Source Book in 7 Volumes

by

HARRY VITELES

BOOK FIVE

Workers Producers Transportation and Service Co-operatives

LONDON
VALLENTINE · MITCHELL

SBN: 85303 013 8

First Published 1968 in Great Britain by
Vallentine, Mitchell & Co. Ltd.
18 Cursitor Street, London, E.C.4

Made and printed in Great Britain by Northumberland Press Limited
Gateshead

Foreword

The co-operative movement in Israel has exercised a considerable influence on the thought and imagination of people from other countries. To the settled countries of Europe and North America, the novel Israeli forms of co-operation may have been mainly a stimulus to intellectual curiosity, or at most to a meditation on basic social and economic theory. To many of the newly emerging countries, with an economy still to make, they present a much more practical challenge. Is or is not a system based on the kibbutz or the moshav the way forward for tropical agriculture emerging from tribal tenures and primitive techniques? Is the massive organization of the Histadrut, which combines in a single entity not only co-operative organization, but trade unionism, political power, capitalist enterprise and social security, a model which can be imitated in countries with limited political and industrial experience and even more limited capital resources? Such questions cannot be answered on a basis of superficial impressions, or the reading of what may be called the light literature of the co-operative movement. Only a detailed historical study of co-operation in Israel, its ideological drives and the material pushes and pulls to which it was subjected, can really explain how it came to be what it is and how relevant it is likely to be to the experience of others.

There is probably no one living better equipped to write such a book than Harry Viteles. He has worked with and for the Israeli co-operative movement for 35 years. He was General Manager of the Central Bank of Co-operative Institutions in Palestine from 1925 to 1946. He was the first to be appointed to the Chair of Co-operation at the Hebrew University of Jerusalem. He has an unrivalled collection of relevant documents and he has spent eight years extracting from them everything of interest and significance in the history of co-operation in Israel. His approach is scrupulously detached and impartial, an invaluable quality in the historian of a movement of great complexity and often subject to intense ideological debate.

A work in seven volumes is inevitably a source book for students rather than a simplified summary for the general reader. But in future there will be no excuse if the writer of a more condensed work makes an incomplete or partisan statement. Even if he has no Hebrew, he can now trace the progress of every organizational move, and track every doctrine back to its source or sources in Mr. Viteles' learned and comprehensive study. It is a worthy monument to two, if not three, generations of pioneers in Israel, and a clear exposition of a social and economic structure which has aroused lasting interest in many, all over the world, who have never been in Israel. They include those with problems of their own to solve as well as those whose studies lie in the field of social change and economic reorganization, and all will benefit from the devoted labours of this pioneer of Israeli co-operation.

MARGARET DIGBY

Preface

This is a series of seven* books about the Co-operative Movement in Israel, viz.:

The Evolution of the Co-operative Movement in Israel
The Evolution of the Kibbutz Movement
An Analysis of the Four Sectors of the Kibbutz Movement
The Moshav Movement (Co-operative Smallholders Settlements)
The Workers Producers Transportation and Service Societies
Central Agricultural Co-operatives
Consumers' Co-operatives

This series of books is intended for ordinary readers who do not have easy access to the source material (about 90 per cent in Hebrew), and also for those who wish to enquire further into the varied facets of the Jewish Co-operative Movement in Israel.

The Jewish Co-operative Movements in other countries were, and are, almost entirely confined to credit co-operatives. The relatively few Jewish consumers' workers producers and agricultural co-operatives, mainly in Eastern Europe, had a short and not too successful life. In Israel, the agricultural, consumers' and workers producers co-operatives constitute the largest numerical groups in the co-operative movement. The first consumers' and workers producers and service co-operatives in Palestine were established about the year 1910 as part of the incipient Jewish labour movement.

The first agricultural co-operatives in Israel were established at the end of the nineteenth century. These types of co-operatives were organized to meet a revolutionary change in the occupational stratification of the Jews; with emphasis on physical work, especially on agricultural work, rather than on commerce and finance.

The credit co-operatives have also played an important role in the economic integration of immigrants in the towns, villages, and rural communities in Israel. In Israel the credit co-operatives, unlike the Jewish

*** Another two books are planned: one on credit co-operatives and the banks which financed the co-operatives in Israel, and the second about housing societies, provident and pension funds, and audit unions.**

credit co-operatives in other countries, include a large number of rural credit societies whose members are mainly farmers. And all of the credit co-operatives in Israel, like Jewish credit co-operatives in the Eastern European countries, are of the Schultze Delitsch type with limited liability. They have a mixed occupational membership and do not confine their business to making loans.

Israel is not the birthplace of the communitarian settlements. This pattern of life, generally referred to as communistic and communitarian settlements, was found in Europe in the Middle Ages, and in the Eastern and North-Eastern United States in the eighteenth and nineteenth centuries. Today there are the Hutterite communitarian settlements in Canada and the United States; and the Bruderhoff communities in Paraguay, Uruguay and the United States. There were mobile and temporary communitarian groups (kibbutzim) in Palestine before 1910. The kvutza, Deganya Alef, established in the Jordan Valley in 1910, is generally considered the first settled communitarian group. Both in the past and in the present, the communitarian settlements outside Israel, with relatively few exceptions, are religious sects. In Israel the kibbutz movement is a secular movement but with a strong nationalist (the revival of the Jewish Nation) and political flavour. Even the religious kibbutzim (Hakibbutz Hadati), the smallest of the four kibbutz sectors in Israel, do not have a religious base in the same sense as the communitarian settlements referred to above.

Ein Ganim near Petah Tikva was probably the first moshav, a co-operative smallholders' settlement established in Palestine (1908). But the pattern of the moshav was found in Europe much earlier. There were the Dukhobor communities in Czarist Russia in the second half of the nineteenth century. And they emigrated from Czarist Russia, first to Cyprus and then to Canada in the last quarter of the nineteenth century.

The kibbutzim and the moshavim may be called the specialty of the Jewish Co-operative Movement in Israel. In no other country in the world, as far as I know, have there been as many kibbutzim and moshavim, and with as large a population, as there are in Israel.* Many people outside Israel, not excluding those especially interested in and concerned with Israel, are surprised that there are other types of co-operatives in the country. Visitors who come to Israel to study its Co-operative Movement, especially from Asiatic and African countries, are mainly interested in the kibbutzim and the moshavim. Some visitors are mainly interested in the workers producers and service co-operatives, especially the bus and trucking co-operatives, and in the central agricultural marketing societies.†

* The kolkhozim in the U.S.S.R. and in other European communist countries and the communes in Red China are neither kibbutzim nor moshavim. And the agricultural producers co-operatives in Red China and in other countries are not moshavim.

† The Histadrut (General Federation of Labour in Israel) has established in Tel Aviv an Afro-Asian Institute for Co-operation and Labour to help the development of co-operation in undeveloped countries. According to the Report of the

The material in this series of books is mainly a digest of the source material which the writer collected and used: books; reports of studies; minutes of the meetings of the Co-operative Council and of the governing bodies of the respective co-operative sectors; the registrar's reports, leaders and articles in the daily newspapers and in the periodicals of the main co-operative sectors; and special reports of enquiries made by and about the respective co-operative sectors, etc.

Since World War Two, and more especially since the establishment of the State, the various top governing organs, such as the councils and congresses of the four sectors of the kibbutz movement, have debated—almost ad nauseam—the various aspects of their central consumer services. The two books on kibbutzim include, generally as appendices, digests of articles, etc., and of the internal codes or regulations for the central consumer services which the kibbutz sectors have introduced. Though the internal codes of the four sectors of the kibbutz movement are very similar in content. These digests are supplemented by summaries of articles and of the discussions and decisions of the governing organs of the kibbutz sectors about their respective central consumer services. The articles and discussions are replete with similarities in argument.

Admittedly the personal element—evaluation—plays an important role both in the screening and in the analysis of the material. Though the digests of the material have been culled and considerably shortened, repetition is unavoidable.

A primary basic principle of co-operation is voluntary association. Co-operatives are intended for the masses, and are what is generally called a popular (folk) movement. Each group of co-operators is identified with and dedicated and determined to achieve its respective credo (ethos). The opinions of those at the meetings of the governing organs of their respective co-operatives and/or movements are important, even if they are the same. Because, in the last analysis, the decisions of a democratic regime are the summation of what most of the members consider as the necessary and/or desirable course of action at a given time, and under certain conditions. It is important to know how many members feel the same way about a certain question even if what they say is a repetition of what others have already said.

If I differ with a statement in any source, I express my opinion in a note and not in the text. And such opinions are generally based on 40

Registrar of Co-operatives* this Institute in 1963 arranged four courses in co-operation and labour. Two of these courses conducted in English had 78 students from 27 countries in Africa and Asia, including the Middle East. A third course given in French had 44 students from 11 countries in Africa and Asia. The fourth, a six-month course, was arranged for 13 workers in the printing trade from Kenya. Under the auspices of the International Institute for Co-operative Studies and Labour Problems for Latin-American countries, the Department for International Relations of the Ministry of Foreign Affairs jointly with the Political Division of the Histadrut arranged a four-month course in co-operative studies for 30 students from 11 Latin-American countries. Another similar ten-week course was arranged for 27 farmers from Mexico. (*Labour and National Insurance—Monthly Review of the Ministry of Labour—No. 7, 15 July 1964 (Hebrew) pp. 207-233.)

years' experience in, and knowledge about, the co-operative movement in Palestine and Israel as well as visits to the co-operative movements in other countries, and the relevant literature.

I thank those, too many to mention, who helped me to obtain the source material.

I especially appreciate the loyal co-operation of Mrs. Sylvia Farhi, of Jerusalem, who has typed and re-typed the handwritten and typescript drafts. And were it not for the encouragement of my late wife and of Dr. Joseph J. Schwartz, I might not have completed the seven books to which I have devoted all my time during the last eight years.

28 December 1964 Harry Viteles

TABLE OF CONTENTS

BOOK FIVE

Introduction

(WORKERS' PRODUCERS, TRANSPORTATION AND SERVICE SOCIETIES (WPSTS))

1. Factories; Workshops; and Labour Contracting societies (Commandites).
2. Consumer Services, i.e. hotels and restaurants, theatres, laundries, vendors of ice, meat, kerosene, etc.
3. Bus and transportation co-operatives.

These three types of WPSTS have the following characteristics:

(*a*) Only those working in the WPSTS are members, and the members may not engage in any other gainful employment. In the case of the Histadrut-sponsored WPSTS (90 per cent of all) the member must be a member of the Histadrut, the respective craft union, and also of Chevrat Haovdim.

(*b*) Every ordinary member participates with the same amount in the share capital of the respective co-operative and has only one vote. When a member leaves the society, a special committee estimates the value of the member's participation in terms of the purchasing or replacement price at the time. This is also the procedure in the event a member becomes incapacitated for work, or in the case of his death.

(*c*) The transportation co-operatives pay the same basic wages (including pay for overtime), fringe benefits and allowances for working clothes and education, etc., to all members, irrespective of the type of work; plus graduated allowances for seniority and dependents. Most of the other two categories of the WPSTS grade the basic wages according to skill and seniority. All WPSTS pay the respective trade union scale of wages and fringe benefits to their wage workers. (The workers' producers societies in England, France, Italy and other countries also use wage labour and apprentices.) The payments made to worker-members are not considered as wages but as advances which theoretically are payable only after a society has covered all other operational expenses—depreciation, wages for hired workers, etc. After the allocation of a percentage of the surplus for the reserves, part of the surplus, if any, is distributed, generally in equal shares, among the members. Some WPSTS distribute part of the surpluses also among the wage workers.

This book excludes the factories and workshops; processing food and packaging plants, etc.; which kibbutzim and a few moshavim, agricultural, and central and/or primary consumers' co-operatives own and operate. As in other countries, the workshops and factories owned and operated by the agricultural and consumers' co-operatives in Israel use non-member labour almost exclusively. The labour force of three large processing and canning factories—mainly citrus by-products and vegetables—owned by kibbutzim, is predominantly wage labour. And not a few workshops and factories in the kibbutzim and also factories owned by the respective kibbutz sectors (such as the starch and the brick factories owned and operated by Hakibbutz Haartzi and the plywood and insulation material plants of Ichud Hakvutzot V'Hakibbutzim) use wage labour—members of other kibbutzim and non-members. With few exceptions, the workshops and factories in the kibbutzim, and the transportation services (generally operated jointly by several kibbutzim) use some wage labour, i.e. non-kibbutz members. These transportation services are not legal entities, but are organic parts of the respective kibbutzim.

Also excluded are

(*a*) WPSTS contracting groups for all kinds of agricultural work, including harvesting, packing and grading of citrus and other fruits; agricultural technical services such as seed production; cattle breeding; and crop and cattle insurance; etc. Nearly all these services are registered under the Co-operative Societies Ordinance as agricultural co-operatives.

(*b*) Histadrut-sponsored factories, etc. which are not registered under the Co-operative Societies Ordinance. One school of Histadrut co-operators consider these plants and services "as co-operative" since, in principle, they are owned by and subject to the control and general authority of Chevrat Haovdim (see Book One), which was registered in 1924 under the Co-operative Societies Ordinance, largely because it was the most convenient and easiest procedure. According to a Report on the Labour Economy, 1959-62 (Economic and Social Research Institute Histadrut, Executive Committee, June 1963), the Histadrut at the end of 1960 had 389 industrial establishments in which it controlled fifty per cent or more of the votes. These workshops and factories each had a labour force of five or more. The total labour force was 23,977; their global business in 1960 was just under IL.453 million and their global business in 1961 was estimated at IL.563 million.

The 389 workshops include 133 Histadrut-sponsored workers' industrial co-operatives (transportation and service co-operatives are excluded) affiliated to Merkaz Haco-operatzia. These 133 had a combined labour force of 3,615 (members and non-members), and accounted for about IL.53 million or 11·6 per cent of the global 1960 business (IL.453 million) reported for all the 389 Histadrut-sponsored workshops and factories. Of the 133 industrial workers co-operatives, 43·7 per cent had labour forces of between five and 30 each (1,581 of the total labour force of 3,615) and accounted for IL.23 of the IL.53 million total business in 1960 of the 133 workers' industrial co-operatives. In 1960 the 133 workers' industrial co-operatives had an average labour force (members and non-members) of 27 and an average global business of IL.397 thousand per co-operative.

The Histadrut-sponsored agricultural colonization sector, according to the report on the Labour Economy, 1959-62, had 119 workshops and factories, each with five or more workers (no differentiation is made between kibbutzim and moshavim, but the moshavim and moshavim shitufiim had relatively few industrial plants). There was a labour force of 5,334 (members and non-members) in these 119 workshops and factories, and the global business in 1960 was over IL.94 million. About 23 per cent of the 119 had labour forces of between five and 30 (total 1,210) and 36 per cent with between 31 and 100 each (total 1,926). These two groups account for IL.19 million and over IL.34 million respectively of the total business in 1960 of more than IL.94 million. The average number of workers and the gross business in 1960 for each workshop and factory was IL.45 thousand and IL.793 thousand respectively.

CHAPTER ONE

Basic Principles

There are records of workers' producers co-operatives in France, Italy, England and in the United States of America (New England States). The largest number of such co-operatives, with the largest number of workers, members and non-members, and the place with the greatest interest in these, was in France and England, during the second half of the nineteenth and first two decades of the twentieth century. Social reformers, like the Christian Socialists in England and the French Utopians propagated, helped to organize, and tendered financial assistance to workers' producers, transportation and service societies (WPSTS). Between 1850-60 the Government in France gave direct and indirect assistance to workers producers societies. Some social reformers and utopians considered this aid the most effective means to combat unemployment and facilitate the psychological adjustment to large scale industrial concentration and mechanization.

In Israel most of the workers producers co-operatives are workshops and factories. But the three Histadrut-sponsored bus co-operatives, owned and managed by the members, account for two-thirds of all the workers, members and non-members in the WPSTS. With relatively few exceptions, all the WPSTS are Histadrut-sponsored.

Some Histadrut-sponsored workers' producers co-operatives, jointly with Histadrut-sponsored bodies such as Kupat Haco-operativim, the financial organ of the Merkaz Haco-operatzia, the central organ of Histadrut-sponsored WPSTS, jointly own the actual plant which is registered under the Companies Ordinance. Most of the workers' producers co-operatives have non-member workers and apprentices who are referred to as wage workers.[1]

There is no objection in principle to co-operatives, other than integral co-operatives and WPSTS, using wage labour. In fact, it is difficult to visualize how credit, consumers, marketing and supply co-operatives (referred to as indirect co-operation) could operate without non-member personnel. In a co-operative democracy such as that envisaged by Sidney and Beatrice Webb, Charles Gide and Ernest Poisson, all consumers are members of consumers' co-operatives. They own the source of raw materials, and the factories which produce the goods sold by them. Therefore, the factories, under this scheme, employ only members of the consumer co-operatives. The protagonists of co-operative commonwealths are not very clear to what extent, if any, those employed in the factories should actually run them. Only a relatively small and not a very influential minority in the consumers' co-operative movement in Europe and in the Americas favour giving the workers even an advisory voice in the management of factories, plantations, warehouses, cold storage plants, etc., which the consumers' co-operative own and operate.

The WPSTS, like the integral co-operatives (communitarian or socialistic communities) combine co-operative ownership of all property, production, and consumption. They are opposed to any form of exploitation, i.e. direct or indirect profit from the work of others. The introduction of wage labour is generally accepted as one of the most important reasons for the failure of such a large percentage of the WPSTS in Israel and also in other countries. Integral co-operation, unlike indirect co-operation (such as consumers, credit, housing and to an appreciable extent agricultural) is predicated on the maximum blending and harmonious relationship of the members who spend most of their working hours together and in close personal contact. Generally speaking, the use of non-members affect basic attitudes of human relationship and introduce the element—probably unconscious at first—of differentiation between employer and employee and between more difficult and less difficult types of work.

Dr. Ferdynand Zweig in his book "The Israeli Worker" writes[2]:

> "The myth of co-operative industry at one time was very strong in Israel. It was regarded as the key to a new socialist type of society which would do away with hired labour. The co-operative system seemed ideally suited to the character and habits of the Israeli, to his quest for independence and freedom. This myth is now subsiding and one rarely hears nowadays expressions of such high hopes." (p. 223.)
>
> "There are many reasons for this development, some external and some internal. . . . Working capital seems to be their Achilles' heel. . . . But even more serious are the internal handicaps . . . linked mainly to the unusual mixture of co-operative ideology and individualistic psychology of the membership." (pp. 233, 234.)
>
> ". . . This not only complicated the running of the enterprises but also considerably strained their internal structure. The workers were divided into first and second class personnel. The members were expected to work harder and better, to set a good example to the hired labour. But in fact this was not so. The members claimed the easy, or supervisory jobs, often without proper qualifications, and they claimed other privileges as well.
>
> "But in times of crises . . . It was often reported to me during my visits to such enterprises . . . the members were put on part pay, while the employees had to be paid fully, or when arrears in wages were inevitable, those who suffered most were more often members than employees." (p. 234.)

"Social relations between the two groups of workers in most enterprises are tense and strained at best, and irritating and troublesome at worst. . . . The crux of the relationship can best be expressed in the phrase often heard among the employees 'Too many bosses around'." (p. 235.)

"In some of the co-operatives which I visited the usual arrangements (i.e. for employees) did not come up to the social standards set up by agreement between the Histadrut and the Manufacturers Association . . . the wage system was based on piecework, while there was no Joint Production Committee as required in such cases . . . the relationship of the members to the co-operative itself is . . . an even more important drawback. The fact is that members frequently do not regard the co-operative as the final stage of their journey towards independence. While working in the co-operative they look around for an opportunity to jump out of the business and start a workshop of their own . . . the co-operative loses its best members. . . . I heard a number of stories which were actually cases of complete crippling of the co-operative's chances of existence." (p. 235.)

"The principle of full equality in pay for all members does not work out as expected, especially in larger co-operatives . . . the individualistic spirit reasserts itself. 'Why should I work harder for the same money?' a member will ask himself, and a certain tendency towards low scale performance sets in . . . an atmosphere of grievance and frustration gets hold of members and the standard of performance decreases." (p. 236.)

". . . Management structure—often lacks experience and expert knowledge. Experts are rarely invited, as there is no money for such matters, and their advice is subject to the agreement of the members concerned. The best men are reluctant to take on managerial positions which are difficult, even more difficult than in private enterprise, as they, i.e., those in managerial posts, are more often open to criticism from all sides, while being virtually without any reward." (p. 236.)

". . . The responsibility of management is always collective. There is hardly a single general manager with central authority . . . and 'meeting sickness' is a real handicap to decision and responsibility. . . .

"Cliques and coteries are formed, some belonging to the 'Government party', some to the opposition. . . .

"The Israeli experience has proved once more that the success of the co-operative enterprise is primarily not a question of equipment, technique, capital structure . . . but of morale and psychology. . . .

"It seems that the co-operative form is more suited to agriculture, consumers needs, etc., etc. . . . than to direct industrial enterprises . . ." (pp. 236-37.)

Mr. Ermano Mondini in January 1957, writes[3]

"Amongst the inhabitants of Israel . . . Co-operation is looked upon as a definite moral standard, a way of life . . . we are face to face with the 'Co-operative State'.

"When I visited Holon (south of Tel Aviv) I was impressed by another printing and binding co-operative society—'Hakoreh', composed entirely of war disabled and the Society itself is housed in the Co-operative House, a building which belongs to the Union (Merkaz Haco-operatzia).

"The Hamlachim Metallurgic Co-operative of Petah Tikva—had a difficult history. . . . In 1934 when the Society had been in existence for four years, the Central Union made it compulsory for all employees to become members of the Society. . . . The fusion of the old and new members was not successful, probably because a common co-operative spirit was lacking and because the attitude of the new members did not harmonize with that of the original members. In consequence the Co-operative disintegrated and a private firm specializing in ironwork construction took over. The Central Union—renewed its efforts—provided equipment and promoted a new co-operative which was expected to reach a very high level of technical skill and, provided that adequate finance was available, it could become a well established productive society.

"The Maalith Elon Society—builds elevators (maalit) and moving staircases—has 40 workers and six engineers." Members and private sources each contributed half its capital.

"The Palceramique Co-operative, Haifa—produces all types of pottery from the most ordinary to the most artistic—has a splendidly equipped modern oven and has a special section for hand painted pottery. Shares are divided equally between members and private persons.

". . . For the first time in Israel at this Society there was a tendency to oppose any increase in the membership,[4] which in 1948 was 16 and is now only 21. . . . My impression is that such a development is nothing more than a manifestation of a restricted idea of co-operation and of the true nature of Workers' Producers' Societies. Workers' Producers' Societies should not be regarded as an antidote to unemployment and under-employment. . . . They should be regarded as a way of life (in the economic sense) and prejudice has to be overcome so that when the first stage of liberation from want has been achieved co-operatives should be able to look further ahead and visualize what else co-operation has to offer, resisting the short-sighted impulse to keep what they have acquired . . . in Israel. . . . Co-operatives are organically part of the . . . Histadrut which completely monopolizes every aspect of the worker's life . . . there is no Trade Union which merely fights for an increase in salaries whilst the co-operative movement seeks to overcome the class trouble."

Early Days

The need to compete with cheap unorganized labour, mainly Arab, stimulated the Jewish workers in Israel to establish the first jointly owned and managed workshops. The literature about the beginning of the pre-World War One WPSTS movement in Israel refers to "two groups of seamstresses" in Jaffa and Jerusalem, each organized by the two main labour parties, "Poalei Zion" and "Hapoel Hatzair". A group of draymen and another of tailors in Jaffa formed commandites. An Achdut printing shop was started in Jerusalem in 1910 and a shoemakers' co-operative was organized in Tel Aviv shortly after. A co-operative machine shop and a co-operative joinery were started in Haifa.

According to Mr. Lush's article[5] written in October, 1955, some bakers in 1919 organized "Maafiyah Amamit" (popular bakery); another group established Omanut (ladies' custom tailoring) and a third group united into the Nagariya Shitufit (co-operative carpentry). He notes that a post-World War One movement for the organization of WPSTS in Israel was especially noticeable during the period 1918-20. Three of the seven WPSTS established during these years were in Tel Aviv. Several tens of mobile groups for building and for constructing roads were operating in 1921, most of them organized and employed by Misrad L'Avodot Tziburiyot (the public works department of Histadrut) and its successor, the co-operative Solel Boneh. The fourth Aliya (1924-28) gave a further impetus to the establishment of WPSTS and 52 were started during the years 1925 and 1926.[6]

The combine of the owners of small passenger cars (from surplus stock of the First World War) that established routes in Tel Aviv and Jaffa, probably was the first effort to organize a passenger transportation co-operative. These car owners agreed to take passengers in rotation, "first in line is first to take passengers". However, they rejected the initial suggestion to combine and to replace the small cars with a jointly owned bus. One of the owners of a small car purchased a bus and then leased it to "Galei-Aviv", a loose group of owners of small passenger cars. This was the impetus for other owners of small cars to organize a savings group for the purchase of buses. Galei-Aviv jointly with another group, Hamaavir, whose main function at the time was the centralized printing of bus tickets, organized the company Galei Hamaavir. The group 'Galei-Aviv disappeared, but Hamaavir continued and registered under the Co-operative Societies Ordinance in 1928.[7]

The Histadrut, which held its first (founders) Congress in December (Chanuka), 1920, replaced the labour political parties which, during the periods immediately preceding and immediately following the First World War, played an important role in the organization of WPSTS. WPSTS were sponsored for the economic integration of mass immigration, especially during peak unemployment periods in the pre-State period, and again during the first five years of the post-State period between 1948 and 1952 and again from 1958 to 1960. In the early days, the Histadrut left the actual organization and supervision of the WPSTS to a committee appointed and sponsored in 1922 by the Tel Aviv-Jaffa Labour Council.[8] Heterogeneous groups were organized and their members knew very little, if anything, about either the theory or practice of WPSTS.

It was later decided that the co-operative division of the Tel Aviv-Jaffa Labour Council should also deal with WPSTS. One objective was to diversify the WPSTS, which at this time were mainly concentrated in building trades and ancillary branches (such as the manufacture of building materials). A special effort was made to organize WPSTS suitable for women, such as tailoring establishments, laundries and restaurants. On the advice of the co-operative division of the Tel Aviv-Jaffa Labour Council, the Histadrut appointed Vaadah Merkazit LeCo-operatzia (a central committee for co-operatives) attached to Vaad Hapoel (Histadrut Executive Committee).

Merkaz Haco-operatzia (the central organ and audit union for the Histadrut-sponsored WPSTS) was organized in January, 1928, and in accordance with the following decision of the Third Histadrut Congress in 1927:

"The Third Congress of the Histadrut (July 1927) expresses satisfaction with the multiplication of WPSTS in the towns and villages in recent years. The Congress considers the expansion of the WPSTS movement, which creates employment opportunities, as one of the important Histadrut activities. Of especial importance, is that this activity (establishment of WPSTS) helps in the revival of Jewish labour on a healthy co-operative basis. The Congress directs Histadrut organs (mosadot) to pay special attention to and to concern itself with the development of this activity."

A census was taken in July 1926, by the central co-operative Committee[9] of Four, appointed by the Tel Aviv-Jaffa Labour Council. It covered 76 Histadrut-sponsored WPSTS with 835 workers, including 49 apprentices and 73 temporary wage workers, all women primarily engaged in the clothing, printing and laundry co-operatives. Thirty-nine of the 76 WPSTS with 561 workers (members and non-members) were in Tel Aviv-Jaffa. Five of the 39 WPSTS in Tel Aviv accounted for 210 of the 561 workers. Mr. A. Dickenstein, a member of the Committee of Four, notes that "in spite of the appreciable number of WPSTS there were no inter-co-operative relationships." There were nine WPSTS with 81 workers in Jerusalem, and 10 with 92 in Haifa. The co-operative Committee of Four concluded that "many of the WPSTS (in Tel Aviv) would have done better had they been established in other places. Recently the WPSTS did not have employment for all their workers (members and non-members. . . . Work and revenue were distributed equally (among the workers)—this included work which WPSTS members obtained through the employment exchange, and turned over their earnings to the co-operative."

The 76 Histadrut-sponsored WPSTS had LE.18,000 capital and reserves and reported a monthly business of LE.13-14,000. The report on the 1926 census draws attention to:

(*a*) The large disparity in the participation of the members of the 76 WPSTS in the share capital of their respective societies.

(*b*) The managers of the WPSTS spend so much of their time in untangling the finances ("exchange of promissory notes") and making "combinations" that they had to neglect such problems as productivity, quality of goods, etc.

(*c*) WPSTS were not legal entities (i.e. they had not yet been registered under the Co-operative Societies Ordinance of 1920), and very few enjoyed banking facilities.

(*d*) Thirty of the 76 WPSTS reported equal emoluments for all members. This, Mr. Dickenstein attributes to the fact that most of the WPSTS were founded by workers having the same degree of skill. Twelve WPSTS used the craft union scale of wages; 10 paid the same basic wage to all members, plus family allowances on the basis of the number of dependents; 15 others combined the craft union scale with family allowances and nine used the contract system (piece work).

None of the WPSTS then, or now, guaranteed full-time employment. The Committee found that in slack times the printing co-operatives permitted their members to accept "odd and casual employment." The WPSTS required their members to work only for the WPSTS and do such work as the respective management or works committee decided. Probationers generally received lower wages than the permanent members. When admitted as members the probationers shared in the divisible surpluses on the same basis as the older members.[10]

At the end of 1929 the unregistered Merkaz Haco-operatzia reported 42 affiliated WPSTS with 506 member and 199 non-member workers. The 42 WPSTS, nearly all registered under the Co-operative Societies Ordinance of 1920, included 10 transport co-operatives with 252 members and 37 wage workers. The following decision, which was never implemented, of the First Congress of the unregistered Merkaz Haco-operatzia at the end of June 1930, in which representatives from 37 WPSTS participated, is of interest:

"The Merkaz in the future should approve only such new WPSTS which are built on a healthy economic basis in which the human material of the founders has been carefully screened. Among the problems of the WPSTS with which Merkaz Haco-operatzia had to deal were the conflicts of the WPSTS with the Histadrut. The WPSTS should admit as members only those who have the requisite technical qualifications and 'trouble makers' should be expelled, and the WPSTS must understand that the Merkaz 'cannot manage the individual co-operatives.'"

Merkaz Haco-operatzia attributed the failure of most of the WPSTS organized prior to 1925 to the fact that

"the members themselves (of the WPSTS) actually were not the creators and the owners of the undertakings; their responsibilities were very limited and there was a lack of concern about the consolidation and the improvement of the relationship between members; they were not successful in the selection of managers; the quality of the product was bad; and the movement leaned too much on the Kupat Poalei Eretz Yisrael (Palestine Workers Fund, KAPAI). If it (i.e. KAPAI)[11] could not invest additional funds and provide for the payment of wages to members, the WPSTS were faced with dissolution."

Between 1921-32 the WPSTS constituted about 17 per cent (68) of the (393) societies which were registered under the Co-operative Societies Ordinance. The first WPSTS were registered in 1923. At the end of 1932 the WPSTS accounted for about 17 per cent of the active registered co-operatives, i.e., still on the register. Eleven of the 67 WPSTS registered during this period were transportation co-operatives. The Registrar's Report does not differentiate between passenger and goods transport co-operatives. The Gdud Haavoda (Labour Battalion), the first WPSTS to register (1923) under the Co-operative Societies Ordinance of 1920, was struck off the register in 1928 (see Book One). The Registrar's Report describes the Gdud Haavoda as "a novel organization of a group of Jewish labourers in various occupations—its objects were to contract for all kinds of manual labour and to pool the earnings amongst its members. The members lived in communal camps, ate in communal kitchens and generally aimed at the establishment of a complete communistic society (social-economic and not political) in miniature." The literature about the Histadrut-sponsored WPSTS not infrequently claims that Israel was the first to introduce bus and road haulage co-operatives and that there is no other country which has so many transport co-operatives.[12]

Merkaz Haco-operatzia's Report noted that the Jewish drivers of the bus co-operatives participated in the general strike of all drivers, Jewish and Arab, on 3 November, 1931, against the Mandatory Government.[13] The Jewish bus co-operatives

> "could not disassociate themselves from the general problems of the industry. Its secretary, jointly with the representatives of the Arab drivers, discussed with the Mandatory Government the bus drivers' complaints against the respective Government departments, and especially the Railway authorities who were pressing the Government for 'legislation which would restrict the development of this branch (road transport)'."

The same report singled out the following as the "two outstanding achievements" in 1931: the many small and competing bus lines in Jerusalem were united into a single intra-bus passenger co-operative "Hamekasher" (the link); and the arrangements made it possible for Hamekasher and other bus co-operatives to plan to purchase large, modern and comfortable buses. These achievements made it possible to reduce the fares. But the report cautioned the bus co-operatives against excessive borrowing, which would stimulate uncontrolled and chaotic competition between the co-operatives and a crisis, which could not be quickly resolved.

The organization of road haulage co-operatives had been less successful than that of the bus co-operatives, the report noted. And the co-operative garages, owned and managed by Jewish mechanics, had not yet gained the confidence of the owners of the vehicles.

There was a special reason, occasionally mentioned in pre-State co-operative literature, for organizing the bus and road haulage co-operatives, viz., security. Most of the members of the bus and road haulage co-operatives were part of the self-defence organization, Hagana. Communication had to be kept open between the towns in which the preponderant majority of the Yishuv lived; and between those towns and the old moshavot and the new agricultural settlements which were being established.[14]

Merkaz Haco-operatzia was deeply concerned lest the WPSTS would become workshops jointly owned by artisans, lacking "any personal attachment of the members to their respective enterprises." It was also apprehensive that since the members of the WPSTS had permanent employment on favourable conditions, the ties between these and the other members of the Histadrut would become tenuous. The report urged the secretariat and management of Merkaz Haco-operatzia to intensify and extend its programme of co-operative education.

The bus co-operatives were small, loose organizations from a co-operative point of view, and inter-bus competition within the same area was not unusual.[15] Members retained both the *de jure* and the *de facto* ownership of their vehicles. The main function of the first bus co-operatives was to allot the work in rotation between members. Every member retained the proceeds from and paid all the expenses for his own vehicle.

Members of the road haulage co-operatives arranged the contracts and distributed the work among the members on a mutually agreed basis. But an appreciable number of the drivers who owned their vehicles did not join the road haulage co-operatives. The report noted that the amalgamation of these small loosely knit road haulage co-operatives was a slow and difficult process which the Merkaz Haco-operatzia pursued arduously.

In 1929 some of the WPSTS affiliated to Merkaz Haco-operatzia were not satisfied with the Mashbir's purchasing and marketing services (see Book Seven). They wanted to establish their own organ for the purchase of raw materials and the sale of their finished merchandise. *Inter alia*, the disgruntled WPSTS accused the Mashbir of giving preference to imported and to local non-co-operative merchandise. But the more successful WPSTS which had no difficulty in disposing of their products, such as bedsteads, plumbers' equipment and installations, on the local market, were not interested in establishing central purchasing organs.

The report noted that though the problem of wage labour was serious only in two or three WPSTS affiliated to Merkaz Haco-operatzia, "we cannot close our eyes to the hidden potential social dangers to the WPSTS".

Generally speaking, the Merkaz Haco-operatzia Report considered that "the period is too short for any conclusions about the achievements of the WPSTS . . . the Histadrut has not sufficiently grasped the value of the accomplishments in this short period. . . . Most of the WPSTS have consolidated their position and the conditions of work for their members are better than those in parallel non-co-operative branches."

Relationship Between the Histadrut and Merkaz Haco-operatzia

Zvi Lieberman, Nahalal, who was a member of the management of "Mashbir" in 1931, gave three reasons for what he considered the failure of WPSTS in Israel.

"1. Insufficient working capital.
2. Failure to produce good quality products and lack of technical experts.
3. Unsatisfactory internal relationship and lack of attention to organization. There was too much haste in creating the WPSTS and insufficient care in screening the suitable human material, which later precipitated internal disputes."[16]

N. Verlinsky in the same issue of "Co-operatzia" attributed the birth and the evolution of the WPSTS to:

1. The absence of large capitalists in Israel during the first quarter of the 20th century.
2. The predominance of light industry organized in small units, most of which employed fewer than twenty people.
3. The ideology of the Histadrut.

According to Mr. Verlinsky, the Histadrut considered WPSTS as an important socialist lever in building the country on a solid socialist foundation. But it was a mistake to exaggerate the extent of the socialist aspirations found in the WPSTS. The Histadrut's influence was only "ideological" and "the WPSTS are not prepared to surrender their practical interests." He did not think that there was much difference between the so-called socialist WPSTS and the bourgeois credit co-operatives; in both cases the materialistic aspect had priority over co-operative ethos. This materialistic approach explains why most of the WPSTS, and even the most consolidated WPSTS, employed wage workers. Merkaz Haco-operatzia and the Histadrut committees and organizations had not influenced the WPSTS to admit the wage workers as members.[17]

The Fourth Histadrut Congress in January 1933, appealed to Merkaz Haco-operatzia and to the members of its affiliated WPSTS and explicitly directed that it was in the interest of the future of Israeli Histadrut-sponsored co-operation, to safeguard and preserve the principles of the Histadrut; to avoid the use of wage labour and also any tendency for closed co-operatives which could lead to the degeneration of co-operation.

"The Congress recognizes the urgent need for the establishment of a central organization for Histadrut-sponsored WPSTS whose functions should be to ensure the uninterrupted basic development of co-operative workshops and factories in all branches; continuous guidance and supervision; and also to deal with the organizational, social and economic problems of WPSTS. The Histadrut Council will decide on the composition of this Centre (i.e. Merkaz Haco-operatzia).

"The Congress considers that it is essential to draw up obligatory uniform rules (Takanon) for all Histadrut-sponsored WPSTS. And

Merkaz Haco-operatzia should submit a draft of such rules to the next meeting of the Histadrut.

"The Congress considers as an urgent need the creation of a special fund attached to the Workers' Bank for the expansion and consolidation of WPSTS. To this fund, the Histadrut should allocate part of the funds which it collects abroad annually (contributions) and the Palestine Zionist Executive should use for this purpose part of the funds which it allocates to its labour and urban colonization departments. The fund, on the advice of Merkaz Haco-operatzia should make loans through the Workers' Bank, Ltd., and investments in WPSTS.

"The Congress also asks Mashbir to make a special effort to sell the merchandise produced by the Histadrut-sponsored WPSTS and to purchase the raw materials which these need."

"Merkaz Haco-operatzia L'mlacha Haroshet V'sherutim Tziburiim Brith Pikuah" (Centre for Co-operative Industry and Public Service Audit Union), organized in 1928, was registered on 18 June, 1931, under the Co-operative Societies Ordinance of 1920. As a condition for its registration, Merkaz Haco-operatzia had to agree that its member co-operatives would also be audited by Government-licensed auditors.[18] The Vaad Hapoel (Executive Committee) of the Histadrut appointed the first Management Board of Merkaz Haco-operatzia, three Histadrut representatives and two from the rank and file of the 52 affiliated WPSTS. "Brith Pikuah" (Audit Union) was added to the name in 1934 when Merkaz Haco-operatzia was re-registered under the new Co-operative Societies Ordinance (1933) and Regulations (1934), which exempted registered co-operatives that were members of audit unions from audits by Government-licensed auditors. The Co-operative Societies Ordinance, 1933, & Regulations, 1934, authorized the Registrar of Co-operatives to issue special auditing licences only to the Audit Union's staff (See Book One).

The first formal Annual General Meeting of Merkaz Haco-operatzia on 30 November, 1934, (followed on 1 December, 1934, by the Third Congress of the WPSTS) decided that every affiliated WPSTS must pay to Merkaz Haco-operatzia an annual levy equal to one per cent of its total wage bill for member and non-member workers. The principal speaker, Y. Brudni* (later known as Bareli) (joint manager of the Workers' Bank Ltd.) told the first General Meeting of Merkaz Haco-operatzia that the Jewish co-operative movement in Israel would have no *raison d'être* unless it were welded to the implementation of Zionism.

"We are proud that we made co-operation an important factor in carrying out this task. Histadrut-sponsored co-operation is not just a legal pattern, but it is a way of life for a member for all his life. Co-operation considers itself tied to the new social order . . . it fights intermediaries and all and any form of exploitation. And it is inconceivable that within our orbit there will be bodies that are established on foundations foreign and contrary to the basic principles of the Labour Movement."

Mr. Brudni urged Merkaz Haco-operatzia not to confine itself to audit and instructions. Rather, it should consider as its main task the cementing of inter-WPSTS relationships and also of bonds between its affiliated WPSTS and with the Histadrut. The success of the WPSTS movement depended on a strong ideological and organic contact with the Histadrut. He added, that it was especially important to establish an organic relationship between the WPSTS movement and the Histadrut-sponsored consumers co-operative movement. Because "in this field there is an extensive pasture for activity for which there are good prospects."[19]

Mr. Brudni referred to the danger of the WPSTS becoming closed private partnerships; and that the use of "wage labour could not be permitted".

The first circular letter of Merkaz Haco-operatzia to its affiliated WPSTS outlined a seven point programme:

(*a*) Establish a special fund for WPSTS.
(*b*) Prepare a detailed plan for consolidating the existing WPSTS.
(*c*) Arrange suitable financing for the WPSTS.
(*d*) Expedite the registration of all affiliated WPSTS under the Co-operative Societies Ordinance.
(*e*) Draft a code with regard to such problems as assignments and wages of members; use of surpluses; the purchase of raw materials, and the marketing of the finished products.
(*f*) Prepare a uniform accounting system for all affiliated WPSTS.
(*g*) Make a basic study of the possibilities of expanding and developing WPSTS in Israel.

During the early years, Merkaz Haco-operatzia also helped its affiliated WPSTS to obtain work and orders, especially from Histadrut-sponsored institutions and co-operatives.

The Histadrut Executive Committee appointed an *ad hoc* committee to enquire into the status and the problems arising out of the social aspects of WPSTS. The committee's conclusions were submitted to the Sixth Histadrut Congress in January 1945. Here are the observations of two speakers at the Congress:

Mrs. Golda Meyerson (who became known as Mrs. Meir and was Foreign Minister from 1956 to 1966) praised the unique achievements of the bus co-operatives, which she described as one of the three most important economic branches in the Yishuv. The Congress discussed the question of wage labour in the WPSTS, and appealed to the members of WPSTS not to betray their brilliant past and destroy what they had created. Wage labour in the bus co-operatives had increased in recent years. Originally, the use of wage labour was on a small scale and it was thought that it was only a temporary phase which would pass. "I am sure that nobody thought of introducing wage labour . . . as a permanent feature." The basic principle of the Histadrut is that every member must live from his labour and not exploit the labour of his neighbour. When this principle breaks down, the whole Histadrut collapses.

Y. Chazan (a leading theoretician of Hashomer Hatzair and of its sponsored kibbutz movement, Hakibbutz Haartzi (Book Three Section Three) expressed his

> "unequivocal confidence in the Histadrut-sponsored WPSTS." And "my confidence was reinforced after my meetings with the members of the bus co-operatives, at the meetings of the committee, which were difficult and at times very painful. Because I acquired the highest respect for these members who knew how to establish this economy (i.e. bus services) and because of their unflinching devotion to and bonds with it . . . it would be a calamity for all of us, and more especially for the Histadrut, if we did not find a suitable remedy for the problem of wage labour in the co-operative sector (WPSTS) . . . a tragedy for the members . . . because they are an inseparable part of us (Histadrut), mortals of our own flesh."

The Sixth Histadrut Congress (January 1945) decided that it could not tolerate in its midst members who exploited wage labour. The Congress instructed the Histadrut Executive Committee to eliminate all wage labour in accordance with its previous publicized decisions. Any Histadrut-sponsored WPSTS that continued to ignore the Congress decisions would have to face the consequences.

Post-State Developments

During 1949, Merkaz Haco-operatzia organized 190 new WPSTS, 70 more than the total number of WPSTS affiliated to it at the end of 1948. The average membership of the new WPSTS was nine. In organizing such a large number of WPSTS, Merkaz Haco-operatzia, *de facto*, put into cold storage the policy of screening the applicants for membership and the branches of industries for which workers' producer societies were organized. Also, it practically disregarded the problem of the availability of adequate financing.

The focal point of the general debate in the Government Co-operative Advisory Council about WPSTS was whether their main purpose was to facilitate and expedite the economic integration of immigrants. Most of the Council's discussions about WPSTS took place between 1949 and 1951, the years of the largest absolute and relative expansion, and again between 1954 and 1956, the period of the largest absolute and relative failure of WPSTS. The Director-General of the Ministry of Labour summed up the post-State situation as follows: "This is the hour for action and it is difficult to be too punctilious about the social and economic fundamentals. . . . Do not interfere with the general activity out of a concern about the first steps. . . ."

Those members of the Co-operative Advisory Council who were critical of and opposed the too rapid expansion of the WPSTS movement did not underestimate the past achievements of the WPSTS in spite of the relatively large rate of failures. Generally, the larger absolute and relative failure of WPSTS than of any of the other types of co-operatives was attributed to internal rifts. They argued, however, that it was a short-sighted policy to sacrifice co-operative content and over-indulge in deviationism for the sake of temporary advantages. Public funds and other outside sources were used for equipping most of the new WPSTS. Yet the members of many of these WPSTS considered everything as their property and thought that they had the unqualified right to dispose of the assets when they considered the time propitious from a financial point of view. Equally serious was the tendency of not a few WPSTS to become closed bodies, using wage labour and requiring new members to pay excessive entrance fees and participation in share capital. The minority group in the Co-operative Advisory Council underlined that if almost all the WPSTS' own funds were proscribed as non-refundable to members leaving, this would reduce defections. Members would be reluctant to surrender their share in these funds if, in the event of liquidation, the assets of the respective WPSTS exceeded their liabilities.

The Co-operative Advisory Council thought the authority of Merkaz Haco-operatzia in its affiliated WPSTS could be increased by expanding its educational, instructional and supervisory activities. The emphasis would be on inculcating the members of the WPSTS with an appreciation of the social aspects so that they would not consider their co-operatives only as a source of livelihood. By proper selection of skill and fields of activity, the WPSTS would also help to reduce the State's dependence on imports.

During 1952 there was a decrease in the number of WPSTS, from 393 to 349, affiliated to Merkaz Haco-operatzia, and in their total labour force, from 13,131 to 12,203, a drop of 928, compared with 1951. The number of members decreased from 8,127 to 7,842; wage workers from 4,258 to 3,694 and apprentices from 746 to 667.

During the second half of 1952, the WPSTS, especially those organized in the post-State years, found it very difficult to accommodate themselves to the Government's new economic policy introduced in February of that year. There was a sharp restriction in allocations of raw materials and the WPSTS, particularly the younger ones, did not have any stocks.

During 1953 there was a further decrease in the number of WPSTS (by 15) affiliated to Merkaz Haco-operatzia and of their total labour force (by 363). Almost the entire increase in the gross turnover in 1953 of the affiliated WPSTS, compared with the turnover in 1952, is ascribable to the 30 per cent increase in prices during 1953. As in 1952, the industrial workers' co-operatives suffered the largest number of casualties (13). And the road haulage co-operative reported the largest decrease in the total labour force (268).[20]

In 1953 Merkaz Haco-operatzia secretariat reported[21] that none of its affiliated WPSTS, that had started operations in the previous year, could be considered "as a corner stone for the WPSTS movement," and "the problem of the WPSTS does not exist" as far as the Government, the colonization institutions and the Histadrut are concerned. Merkaz Haco-operatzia secretariat pointed to the increased tendency of the consumers' co-operatives to establish their own bakeries as evidence of a concerted effort to stunt the growth of the WPSTS movement, and more especially to destroy its affiliated co-operative bakeries. Histadrut-sponsored consumers' co-operatives were also developing other manufacturing branches which were in competition with parallel Histadrut-sponsored WPSTS.

The first joint mutual aid project of the 65 co-operative bakeries affiliated to Merkaz Haco-operatzia was the financing of a co-operative bakery in Eilat (on the Red Sea) in November 1953. All the 65 affiliated co-operative bakeries contributed IL.3,000.

Since there were few who wanted to learn the trade, there were only apprentices among the 400 wage workers, some of the co-operative bakeries affiliated to Merkaz Haco-operatzia introduced mechanization, and some of the smaller bakeries amalgamated. As soon as the Government abolished the linking of bakeries with flour mills, the affiliated co-operative bakeries planned to start the central purchase of flour, which they hoped would improve the quality of the bread and reduce the cost of flour.

In 1953 a brief summary was published of a meeting[22] between road haulage co-operatives affiliated to Merkaz Haco-operatzia and kibbutzim that did an appreciable amount of haulage for others. It was reported that 3,550 lorries, representing 80 per cent of the tonnage in Israel, were idle, and that many drivers did not renew their licences. Unlike the bus co-operatives, which acted together in negotiations with the Government, the road haulage societies were not united and, therefore, the Government and others did not comply with their requests.

This meeting decided jointly to:

(*a*) fix the rates for road haulage;
(*b*) share to the maximum extent the available work; and
(*c*) ask the Ministry of Transport and the public institutions not to raise the licence fees; to authorize an immediate increase in the scale of charges for haulage; not to obligate, directly or indirectly, the public to give preference to the railway or any other Government transportation facilities; to issue import licences only for the renewal of lorries; to revive the Citizens' Advisory Committee of the Ministry of Transport.

Yisrael Maliskovitz in 1953, writing about the economic position of the bus co-operative Egged (Eshed),[23] also deals with the attitude of the Histadrut towards the bus co-operatives. Because the Histadrut institutions did not help, Egged's difficulties were increased in its negotiations with governmental and other agencies about economic questions. He cites as one example the Histadrut's hostile attitude to the request of the bus co-operatives for an increase in bus fares. In August 1952, a Histadrut committee favoured a 25 per cent increase in the bus fares; one quarter of the increase was intended for the reduction of an accumulated operational deficit. A Histadrut representative asked for only a 20 per cent increase, though "according to the calculations, which time has proven correct, a 70 per cent increase in bus fares was needed".

Mr. Maliskovitz also referred to the constant criticism by the Histadrut press, and he cited in particular "a vicious attack on our establishment which was completely untrue" (in Davar of 8 March, 1953), (Chapter Four). He described the statement as "smear and lies".

> "I cannot come with any complaints of the writer of the article, Mr. Shabatai . . . since after all this is his livelihood. And what does one not do to earn a livelihood, especially a journalist who wants to be popular as a specialist about everything. The editor of Davar, who has to bow to the authority of Histadrut, should have at least simultaneously asked for and published our comments on the article as you do in other cases such as complaints about Tnuva and other bodies," Mr. Maliskovitz wrote. He asked the editor: "Why did you refuse to publish the comments of our members who objected to your mutilation of the contents?"

A. Hochman, writing[24] about the second anniversary of Egged (Eshed) in 1953, included the following paragraph about the Histadrut's attitude towards this co-operative:

> "Our relationship with the Histadrut is a long and difficult chapter, with many obstacles and crises. In the earliest stages of the discussion about the fusion of the bus societies into one co-operative, the bus co-operatives accepted the control and authority of the Histadrut. . . ." The difficulties started "at the moment when they (the Histadrut) started to interpret in practical language the conception of and how to apply control and authority. The source of these difficulties was in reservations which the co-operatives made 'about certain points' and on the other hand, the undue suspicions which the Histadrut showed in the course of the negotiations."

The reservations of the bus co-operatives may be attributed to the difficulties of a transition from "a way of life", to which they had been accustomed for years, to an appreciably more restricted "way of life", which constrained the freedom and autonomy of their activities and their desire for "a maximum clarification of every point in order to avoid misinterpretations and misunderstandings in the future. It is my opinion that the reservations did not conflict with or deviate in any way from their (i.e. the bus societies) agreement in principle to the control and authority of the Histadrut." Those representing the Histadrut in the negotiations seem to have been unduly influenced by the general attitude and suspicions of the Histadrut of the intentions of the bus co-operatives. This affected the degree of the Histadrut's flexibility and understanding, which the bus co-operatives expected, since this would minimize

> "the many complications and crises, and expedite the establishment and the activation of the new society (Egged (Eshed)). . . . We have the right to insist on the understanding and confidence of the Histadrut; the linking of control with education and guidance which should be

simultaneously supplemented by the Histadrut's help to safeguard our rights and the possibilities of the existence of the undertaking."

The following is a summary of a one-page unsigned leader (in 1953) about the bus co-operatives in the bi-monthly, Hameshek Hashitufi, of the consumers' co-operative movement. The leader admits[25] that it cannot judge the accuracy of the report that normal co-operation between Merkaz Haco-operatzia and the bus co-operatives continues. Inasmuch as the differences within and between the bus co-operatives on the one hand, and those between the bus co-operatives and the Histadrut organs (including Chevrat Haovdim) on the other hand have not improved, it would be unexpected that the relationship between "the bus co-operatives and Merkaz Haco-operatzia were normal". If the bus co-operatives were to substitute action for declarations of intentions, there would be no need to press for the immediate implementation of all the changes which the Histadrut and Chevrat Haovdim suggested. Merkaz Haco-operatzia and the bus co-operatives argue that the Histadrut-sponsored agricultural settlements also have deviated from "economic principles and co-operative organization". Even if there were a modicum (atom) of truth in this allegation, the article noted, it would not justify "the de-co-operatization of the bus co-operatives. It is clear to everybody that all the patterns of Histadrut-sponsored agricultural settlements are closer and more loyal to the basic values of the Labour Movement than are the bus co-operatives. . . ." It was alleged further that the bus co-operatives were no longer an example of the co-operative socialization of large transportation systems as defined by Bernard Lavergne.[26] The most urgent necessity was said to be that "the needs of the consumers should receive the maximum consideration. There must be an end to the monthly and daily increase of bus fares; the question of wage labour in the bus co-operatives must be settled and the . . . authority of Histadrut over all questions which are not within the scope of the Government's authority must be widened." As matters now stand, the Histadrut and Chevrat Haovdim cannot even give their moral support to the bus co-operatives in their negotiations with the Ministry of Transport. It is regrettable that the Ministry of Transport had to intervene because the Histadrut was unable to arrange for the bus co-operatives to consider "the interests of the public". It was an open secret that the "Minister and the Director-General (of the Ministry of Transport) are not among the friends of the Co-operative Movement (Histadrut-sponsored) as a whole and of the bus co-operatives in particular. . . ."

According to this leader, the average annual gross emoluments per member and non-member (including apprentices and seasonal wage workers) respectively in the affiliated WPSTS for 1952 were IL.2,654 and IL.1,942.[27]

According to an article in 1954, "Basic Problems of Road Haulage Co-operatives"[28] by D. Carmel, lorries carried 80 per cent of the volume of goods in 1952, compared with 65 per cent in 1951. Because of the rigid curtailment of imports and the steep decline in immigration the total volume of freight[29] hauled by all road transport was reported to have decreased by about 40 per cent. There was a further drop (extent not given) during 1953-54 because there was

1. a decrease of licences for imports;
2. an increase in competition with the railway and other Government carriers; and
3. the Israel Fuel Company introduced its own tankers for haulage.[30]

Mr. Carmel concluded that even if the Government approved the increased rates, the general position of road haulage would not be consolidated. The road haulage industry, co-operative and non-co-operative, was doing very little to counteract the Government's efforts to stimulate the increased haulage by rail, which he personally considered less efficient than road transport. He agreed that haulage by rail saved an appreciable amount of foreign exchange. Mr. Carmel quoted the following reply to his letter to the Minister of Transport (who at the time was not a member of the Labour party) that transport by road is more efficient than by rail:

> "It is true but it is impossible to rely only on the non-Government sector. An additional transportation system must be maintained over which the public has full control and that is the railways."

The closing paragraph of the Minister's letter to Mr. Carmel stated: "In my opinion there is room for more efficiency of the branch (i.e. road haulage). The principal stumbling block is psychological and it is not easy to change the habits of the haulers."

In the autumn of 1954 Shituf[31] carries very brief reports about the regional meetings of WPSTS in Jerusalem (6 July, 1954), Rishon Le-Zion, Tel Aviv, Haifa (May to July) for members of management committees of the WPSTS in the respective districts that were affiliated to Merkaz Haco-operatzia.[32] According to these reports, it seems that Merkaz Haco-operatzia used those regional meetings to sell

(*a*) the idea that the purpose of the WPSTS is to provide a secured place of employment and that they are not a source for personal enrichment; and

(*b*) the plan of the secretary of Merkaz Haco-operatzia about the structure of the share capital of the WPSTS, viz. that every member of a WPSTS affiliated to Merkaz Haco-operatzia should hold one voting share. But a member may subscribe to an unlimited number of non-voting dividend-paying shares.

Those opposed to the plan argued that it created two types of members, those who could afford to acquire only one share and those who acquired many shares. This would increase internal conflict. There was also the potential danger of requests for appreciable redemptions of the dividend-bearing shares which the societies might not be able to meet. Finally, that it is an innovation for co-operatives in Israel to pay dividends on common stock, which in the long run, might do more harm than good.

The speakers at the meetings also referred to the decline in the number of WPSTS, members, and total labour force; the problem of closed co-operatives and the corollary questions of the participation of new members in the respective society's capital and the need to minimize the danger that the younger and/or newer members would take over the management and the assets which the older members had accumulated. Wage workers earned more or as much as members, without having to invest or assume any financial or other responsibilities. Therefore, the wage workers refused to become members even when the participation was fixed as low as IL.1,500-IL.2,000 ($900-$1,200).

Some speakers at the regional conferences attributed the crisis in the movement to the establishment of too many WPSTS in the same branch (especially food processing), without considering whether there was a need for them. Fewer WPSTS would have been liquidated had Merkaz Haco-operatzia acted sooner and with a firmer hand when internal disputes arose.

The report of the co-operative department for 1954 notes that "it would have been possible to have stabilized an appreciable number of WPSTS whose liquidation has been started, if there had been sufficient contact between the WPSTS and the consumer co-operatives which . . . should be important clients of the WPSTS."

Some speakers considered the imposed double loyalty on the members a disadvantage, i.e., loyalty to their respective co-operatives and to the Histadrut (respective craft union).[33] There were also complaints (but without giving any examples) that Histadrut institutions purchased inferior quality goods from non-co-operatives. As a result WPSTS could not dispose of their products and had to be liquidated.

Other participants suggested that the liquidation of the obsolete societies and the amalgamation of the smaller co-operatives would make it possible for WPSTS to acquire additional and newer equipment. The younger members wanted the system of equal remuneration replaced either by piece work or by the same minimum emoluments for all plus incentive bonuses.

At the regional conferences of management committees during the second half of 1954, Merkaz Haco-operatzia was asked to devise a procedure which would foster the election of the best qualified members for the technical jobs and business and administration of the WPSTS.

In 1954 the situation in the co-operative sweets and soap factories was reported satisfactory. The return to free trading made it possible for these WPSTS again to use their trade marks. And they acquired a fixed custom by

> "improving the quality and reducing the prices. The members willingly accepted a reduction in remuneration in exchange for a good name in the market. The demand exceeds the supply and the co-operatives could use additional financing for equipment and for the bulk purchase

of raw materials and to help them carry large stocks and to give more liberal credit facilities."

Another article in the same issue of Shituf by a member of a small co-operative printing shop notes that the distribution of administrative functions in the small WPSTS is generally a question of chance and that training and the aptitude of those elected, generally speaking, is not a consideration. A small group becomes entrenched and the rank and file members develop a fear psychosis that changes in management may result in a business recession of the respective WPSTS. The members are convinced that nobody else can fill the jobs in which the old timers are entrenched. The final result is invariably contraction, degeneration, economic insecurity, financial instability, and decreased competitive power. Such WPSTS try to save themselves by increasing the use of wage workers who, on the one hand are less expensive to employ and easier to handle than members, and on the other hand create a chasm between the members of the respective co-operatives as the owners of the property, and the wage workers. There is a tendency for the members to shift to administration and to jobs which require a minimum of physical labour, and for the wage workers to become the producers. Yet another manifestation is that the wage workers press for expansion, while the members are apprehensive about the increased responsibility which expansion involves. The next step, according to the writer of this article, is the conversion of the WPSTS into a non-co-operative pattern which permits an unrestricted use of wage labour.

APPENDIX

STATISTICAL DATA

(DATA FOR 1948-62 EXTRACTED FROM SHITUF—MAY/JUNE 1962 (pp. 16-19))
Amounts in IL.000

Year	No. of WPSTS	Members	Wage Wkrs and Apprentices	Total Labour Force	Capital and Resrvs[b]	Gross Turnover	Emoluments to Mmbrs & Non-Mmbrs
1938	72	1,931	1,130	3,061	—	—	—
1943	115	3,733	1,160	5,346	—	—	—
1948	150	4,186	1,831	5,564	1,975	9,749	4,531
1949	236	4,689	2,281	6,970	4,089	15,777	7,320
1950	368	6,021	3,506	9,527	2,838	27,199	11,483
1951	391	6,380	5,098	11,478	7,577	42,680	22,277
1952	383	6,136	5,585	11,721	7,272	58,926	28,994
1953	349	5,737	4,941	10,678	8,549	70,087	32,169
1954	293	6,973	4,937	11,910	9,575	77,178	29,360
1955	250	6,480	5,038	11,518	12,321	83,818	31,547
1956	235	6,689	5,594	12,283	13,840	106,317	44,433
1957	237	6,655	6,014	12,669	13,085	126,733	52,737
1958	226	6,674	5,881	12,555	15,378	140,755	52,351
1959	219	6,879	6,462	13,341	19,856	156,068	61,948
1960	203	7,073	6,651	13,724	13,328[a]	170,066	65,044
1961	204	7,502	6,998	14,500	13,877[a]	192,133	70,574
1962	201	7,741	6,948	14,689	25,926[c]		

[a] Capital and Reserves was used in 1960 and 1961 to cover the Balance Sheet Operational deficit.

[b] Distribution of Capital and Reserves According to Sectors of WPSTS (in IL.000).

Year	Industrial Workers Co-operatives	Transportation (Passngr & Goods)	Service
1954	2433·0	6494·0	648·0
1957	3590·0	8891·0	1605·0
1958	3814·0	10100·0	1464·0
1959	3902·0	14760·0	1816·5
1960	4681·7	6624·2	2022·4
1961	6084·1	5520·9	2272·3

[c] The own funds of the WPSTS increased by over IL.12 million or by 90 per cent. Most of this increase, or IL.10 million, was reported by the WPSTS in the metal and electrical branch. Most of the IL.10 million was reported by Haargaz industrial workers co-operative, owned jointly by Kupat Haco-operativim and the labour contracting society of workers in Haargaz, as a result of the revaluation of Haargaz assets.

WPSTS AFFILIATED TO MERKAZ HACO-OPERATZIA

(Tables taken from Shituf, March 1963, and May-June 1963)

Year	Industrial Workers Co-operatives: No. Soc.	Industrial Workers Co-operatives: Total Labour Force (Members and Non-Members)	Transportation (Bus and Passenger) Co-operatives: No. Soc.	Transportation (Bus and Passenger) Co-operatives: Total Labour Force (Members and Non-Members)	Service Co-operatives: No. Soc.	Service Co-operatives: Total Labour Force (Members and Non-Members)	All Affiliated WPSTS: No. Soc.	All Affiliated WPSTS: Total Labour Force (Members and Non-Members)
1948	75	2,092	24	3,028	16	444	115	5,564
1950	286	2,424	30	4,184	45	919	368	9,527
1960	123	3,394	27	8,758[a]	53	1,572[a]	203	13,724
1961	122	3,688[a]	27	9,240	55	1,568	204	14,500
1962	117	3,568	26	9,465	58	1,656	201	14,689

Type of Workers	1960: Members	1960: Non-Members	1962: Members	1962: Non-Members	1960: Main Branch	1960: Total Labour Force (Members & Non-Members)	1962: Main Branch	1962: Total Labour Force (Members & Non-Members)
Producers Co-operatives								
Industrial Workers	1,449	1,945	1,455	2,113	Metal & Electrical	904	Metal & Electrical	1,116
Transportation	4,729	4,029	5,375	4,090	Bus Co-ops.	7,471	Bus Co-ops.	8,073
Service	895	677	911	745	Restaurants and Hotels	262	Restaurants and Hotels	233
Total	7,073	6,651	7,741	6,948				

[a] Does not include non-member labour force in Tel Aviv Co-operative Restaurant.

Item	Industrial Workers Co-operatives							
Average[a]	1948	1951	1954	1957	1958	1959	1960	1961
1. No. of Co-operatives	75	296	219	170	158	138	123	122
2. No. Workers per Co-operative[a]	28	17	20	23	24	25	130	30
3. Average Turnover (IL.)								
(a) Per Co-operative	46,120	44,760	124,260	267,420	300,210	360,616	431,500	468,680
(b) Per Worker	1,653	2,622	6,119	11,510	12,548	14,690	15,700	15,504
4. Average Capital & Reserves per Co-op. (IL.)			11,001	21,001	24,001	28,300	38,100	49,900
5. Percentage Relation of Wages Paid (members & non-members) to Gross Annual Business.	38·6	41·7	30·1	27·2	27·8	26·3	25·3	24·8
6. Average Wages per Worker IL.								
(a) Actual IL.	639	1,093	1,839	3,128	3,491	3,863	3,981	3,847
* (b) Index—1950=100	100	127	213	362	405	210	217	209
* (c) Consumers Price Index —1950=100	100	110	250	300	310	125	129	138
* (d) Real Wages—1950=100	100	115	85	121	131	168	168	152

Note a Members and Non-members.
* For 1959, 1960 and 1961 the Index is 1954=100.

Transportation (Bus & Road Haulage)[b]

Average[a]	1948	1951	1954	1957	1958	1959	1960	1961
1. No. of Co-operatives	**24**	40	26	24	28	324	27	27
2. No. Workers per Co-operative[a]	126	133	244	316	274	311	324	342
3. Average Turnover (IL.)								
(*a*) Per Co-operative	235,750	651,150	1,764,000	2,993,600	2,851,970	3,286,141	3,632,220	4,250,200
(*b*) Per Worker	1,869	4,889	7,232	9,481	10,406	10,560	11,198	12,420
4. Average Capital & Reserves per Co-op. (IL.)			249,800	370,500	360,700	546,200	245,300	204,400
5. Percentage Relation of Wages Paid (members & non-members) to Gross Annual Business.	53·2	60·5	55·1	52·1	45·2	44·4	46·3	43·6
6. Average Wages per Worker IL.								
(*a*) Actual IL.	993	2,956	3,982	4,941	4,703	5,165	5,204	5,416
* (*b*) Index—1950=100	100	177	239	296	282	130	131	136
* (*c*) Consumers Price Index —1950=100	100	110	250	300	310	125	129	138
* (*d*) Real Wages—1950=100	100	161	96	99	91	104	102	99

Note a Members and Non-members.

b Grouping passenger & road haulage co-operatives gives an inaccurate and distorted picture. The Tables in the Report on Activities of Merkaz Haco-operatzia, 1948-1961 from which the data were extracted do not differentiate between the bus and road haulage co-operatives.

* For 1959, 1960 and 1961 the Index is 1954=100.

Service Societies

Average[a]	1948	1951	1954	1957	1958	1959	1960	1961
1. No. of Co-operatives	16	55	48	43	40	305	30	29
2. No. Workers per Co-operative[a]	28	20	24	27	28	29	305	29
3. Average Turnover (IL.)								
(*a*) Per Co-operative	39,500	61,560	85,440	219,190	336,660	337,726	363,680	367,230
(*b*) Per Worker	1,424	3,084	3,626	8,260	12,230	11,321	12,260	12,881
4. Average Capital & Reserves per Co-op. (IL.)			13,500	37,300	36,600	33,600	38,200	41,300
5. Percentage Relation of Wages Paid (members & non-members) to Gross Annual Business.	28·7	29·7	43·1	31·2	22·8	30·5	30·9	31·4
6. Average Wages per Worker IL.								
(*a*) Actual IL.	408	915	1,562	2,577	2,787	3,521	3,789	4,046
* (*b*) Index—1950=100	100	121	207	341	369	225	243	259
* (*c*) Consumers Price Index —1950=100	100	110	250	300	310	125	129	138
* (*d*) Real Wages—1950=100	100	110	93	114	119	188	138	188

Note a Members and Non-members.
* For 1959, 1960 and 1961 the Index is 1954=100.

CHAPTER TWO

Organizational Structure

Analysis of Minutes of Governing Bodies and Reports on the Activities of Merkaz Haco-operatzia and Miscellaneous Sources

A member of the Merkaz (Central Committee) of Merkaz Haco-operatzia suggested to the Third Congress in November 1934 (date not given) that the overriding authority of a WPSTS should be transferred from the general meeting to a managerial group or to experts. "General meetings, especially of co-operatives having 150 or 200 members, are no longer able *de facto* to control the affairs . . . in a WPSTS, which has to compete with well-equipped private capitalist enterprises. . . ."

One of the participants in the general debate criticized the secretary of Merkaz Haco-operatzia because the report about the increase of the labour force in the WPSTS did not differentiate between member and non-member workers. This information was especially desirable about the increase by 350 workers in the transportation co-operatives. "We decided at the last meeting that the use of wage workers was prohibited," he said.

A member delegate from a small road haulage co-operative in one of the larger villages, demanded that Merkaz Haco-operatzia should have unlimited authority "in its war against the sinners (the bus co-operatives)." He argues that the WPSTS movement as a whole and the Histadrut will be blamed for the failure of any WPSTS. Therefore, Merkaz Haco-operatzia is duty bound to root out the lust of the bus-co-operatives for riches derived from speculation and that it must safeguard the purity of the WPSTS movement. Only such a decision can justify the fact that this Congress devoted most of its time to the bus co-operatives.

Some member delegates were extremely disturbed by the fact that Merkaz Haco-operatzia had failed to arrange facilities for central purchasing. This was attributed to "the open and subversive opposition of the managers of the WPSTS," or to the fact that Merkaz Haco-operatzia "did not know how to explain the position to the members or to the WPSTS", or to "the weakness of the inter-co-operative relationship;" or because "there is no feeling of belonging to one large co-operative family".

The manager of the Egged bus co-operative said that the WPSTS did not feel the need for their own central purchasing organ because there was an abundance of commercial credit facilities. Therefore, the WPSTS did not sufficiently feel the need to economize in interest and other expenses.

Some of the speakers suggested that the Merkaz Haco-operatzia's scale of levies should not be fixed as a percentage of the wage bill or of the business done by the respective affiliated WPSTS. They suggested a fixed annual amount for each member of every affiliated WPSTS.

Most of the participants in the general debate complained that Merkaz Haco-operatzia had neglected the road haulage co-operatives. This was reflected in the following unsatisfactory position:

(*a*) Only 20-25 per cent of the lorry drivers were organized into road haulage co-operatives compared with 80 per cent of the bus drivers.

(*b*) The Mandatory Government's regulations for road haulage were much looser than those for passenger transport, "except for reports for every minor transgression." Therefore, there were more lorries than were needed.

(*c*) Cut price warfare in the road haulage branch was reflected in the average monthly earnings of LP.10-12 ($40-48) for a 10-12 hour day, and often a seven-day week.

The secretariat explained that the Merkaz Haco-operatzia department for road haulage co-operatives was discontinued because the affiliated road haulage co-operatives had not contributed towards its upkeep. The department had made little headway in reducing the competition between the affiliated road haulage co-operatives. Furthermore, the road haulage co-operatives, organized by the kibbutzim, also competed with the affiliated road haulage co-operatives.

One member delegate of a road haulage co-operative in Haifa referred to a kibbutz whose competition destroyed road haulage co-operatives. He criticized Merkaz Haco-operatzia's failure to intervene with the Histadrut, which did more for its sponsored non-co-operative road haulage units than it did for its sponsored road haulage co-operatives.

> "I know of cases where Histadrut-sponsored financial institutions were stricter with road haulage co-operatives than were the private banks." He said.

The Third Congress, of November 1934, instructs Merkaz Haco-operatzia to pay special attention to the consolidation of the existing industrial workers co-operatives. And when establishing new industrial workers co-operatives, Merkaz Haco-operatzia should aim for joint ownership of the plant by co-operatives of the workers (commandites) and the Histadrut (through one of its sponsored economic bodies).

The Third Congress is of the opinion that in view of the difficult position of the road haulage co-operatives, Merkaz Haco-operatzia should take special measures to improve the position of those existing and it also should organize new ones.

A few speakers in the general debate asked why there were only 20 industrial workers co-operatives with a total labour force of 424 (members and non-members). They did not consider the ten workshops, with 155 workers, for building materials and concrete water pipes, or the four bakeries, with 40 workers, as industrial workers co-operatives.

The three members of the Merkaz Haco-operatzia secretariat and of the Central Committee (Merkaz) tried to explain away the unsatisfactory position of co-operative factories and workshops. One member of the secretariat referred to the "appreciable amounts" which the American Jewish Joint Distribution Committee (Joint) and the Jewish Colonization Association (I.C.A.) had invested in fostering WPSTS in Poland, all of which failed. If Merkaz Haco-operatzia had received only a small part of the funds which these two organizations had given to the WPSTS in Poland, "it would turn over the world." He admitted that Merkaz Haco-operatzia had not yet found the correct approach and that the failures exceeded the successes of WPSTS in Israel. He urged that the industrial workers co-operatives and the Histadrut should establish joint enterprises.

The confusion about the scope and purpose of co-operative education was reflected in the delegates' comments about the demarcation between the Histadrut cultural department and Merkaz Haco-operatzia. Some of the speakers thought of co-operative education in terms of lectures and these were not to be confined to co-operation; others spoke of co-operative education only in terms of training of staff and leaders (members and non-members).

A member of an inter-urban bus co-operative told the Third Congress that unless Merkaz Haco-operatzia assumed the full responsibility for co-operative education the entire work would be jeopardized.

A member of the Merkaz Haco-operatzia Central Committee said: "We must find the proper way to organize educational activity; to find an approach to those in the WPSTS and where there is a wide field of dormant initiative in local management."

Another delegate thought that the simple solution was to arrange the types of lectures which would draw the members of the WPSTS. The Histadrut's function was "to spread the co-operative and socialist principles in our midst." Yet another delegate wanted to confine the educational programme to lectures on the philosophy of the WPSTS ethos, since most of the members of the WPSTS had no idea about or any orientation for co-operative life.

The opening address by one member of the Central Committee at the Fourth Congress of 16 June, 1938, asked the Congress to:

1. take stock of both the achievements and the weaknesses of the WPSTS movement since the Third Congress in November 1934;
2. seek ways and means to bolster the Merkaz Haco-operatzia's financial instruments established in previous years;
3. explore the possibilities of improving co-operative education within the WPSTS, both affiliated and non-affiliated.

Referring to his second point he said:

"There is no hope of expanding, strengthening and widening the existing and establishing large new enterprises unless we know how to strengthen and improve the instruments (organizations) with whose help we function."

He deplored the fact that so many of the WPSTS

"are only technical organizations. I do not feel that the co-operative ideal has resounded (rung) in their midst. The *petit bourgoisie* tie is too strong. It seems to me that as the economic aspect strengthens, the social aspects are mutilated to the same degree. . . . We cannot build and develop the co-operative workshops, factories and consumer services . . . unless . . . the members are bound together by social and idealistic motives. This is missing. We cannot integrate the diverse elements in our midst, especially from among the new immigrants, most of whom are strangers to our aims. We still stand at the beginning of this task."

S. Gorochowsky (Goren) reported that Merkaz Haco-operatzia appointed a special tribunal to deal with

"the many complaints which were filed against affiliated WPSTS that did not carry out the terms of the agreement. In some cases we requested, and in some instances received, authority to expel the guilty societies from Merkaz Haco-operatzia and the members of these societies from the Histadrut . . . but this court was discontinued in September 1935, when the Italian-Abyssinian war started and it has not yet been reconvened. Merkaz Haco-operatzia Central Committee discussed this question at many meetings. As a result of considerable efforts, the Histadrut Executive Committee also considered the problem. But the discussions were interrupted in the middle and were not renewed."

Mr. Gorochowsky noted that Merkaz Haco-operatzia was fully aware of the defects of its supervision and that its audits uncovered irregularities *post facto*. The minutes of the meetings for the last two years showed that Merkaz Haco-operatzia Management Committee appreciated the need of, but had not yet found the money to pay for a roving auditor or inspector for surprise checks of the WPSTS. In spite of the fact that an auditor was stationed in Haifa for six to seven months a year, the WPSTS in Haifa were as dissatisfied as they were when the Third Congress was held in November 1934. He asked whether the affiliated WPSTS were prepared to increase the budget for these activities.

He also noted that there were not enough WPSTS or a large enough volume of business to warrant the organization of central purchasing agencies similar to the NOA, a subsidiary of the Merkaz Haco-operatzia, which serviced the affiliated transport co-operatives. The efforts to do this for the co-operative restaurants were unsuccessful.

Mr. Gorochowsky noted that mutual aid was a by-product of the proper kind of co-operative education. One cannot create this by directives from the top or by resolutions from the bottom. He cited as an example the request, especially from the transport co-operatives, for a central economic committee. But Merkaz Haco-operatzia had not found "the members . . . prepared to give their time" to the work.

Some of the 20 delegates who participated in the general debate criticized Merkaz Haco-operatzia for not circulating its reports before the Congress met and complained about the generalities in the secretary's address.

The secretary explained that the circulation of the reports before the opening would have delayed the Congress for which they had only three weeks to prepare.

One delegate noted that

> ". . . here at the Congress we (WPSTS) are one family, but *de facto* we are competitors day in and day out. It should be a function of Merkaz Haco-operatzia to eliminate this. If there were any justification for not having convened a Congress for nearly four years, there was none for the infrequent meetings of the Council of Merkaz Haco-operatzia. If the members of the WPSTS had had the opportunity of discussing the agenda of the Congress before it met, their delegates would have come with instructions, and the general debate would have been fruitful. Merkaz Haco-operatzia management committee did too much on its own and its contacts with the member societies are too nebulous."

A delegate from an inter-urban bus co-operative suggested that more consistent and persistent supervision by Merkaz Haco-operatzia would minimize the need

> "to ask us to mend mistakes which were made a year ago. The co-operatives should be given the opportunity to know as much about the activities of Merkaz Haco-operatzia as the latter knows about the internal operations of its affiliated WPSTS. While WPSTS have their internal bulletins, Merkaz Haco-operatzia does not have its own publication. Affiliated WPSTS in Tel Aviv receive much more attention and service than those in Haifa and elsewhere. Every WPSTS makes its own Sabbath."

A delegate, an ex-member of a moshav ovdim who joined a bus co-operative "five years ago", was surprised by the apathetic attitude of members. He said that the lack of confidence and the failure of the members to carry out directives had its roots in Merkaz Haco-operatzia.

> "We are not interested and do not desire to foster WPSTS that *de facto* are only coincidental unions of so many people for assuring a livelihood for their members, though this is an important aspect of life. . . .
>
> "True, we have built a co-operative (collective) economy and have raised the man . . . from the dunghill of exploitation and made of him a worker standing on his own feet, upright and free; but . . . the aim of the WPSTS movement is to establish and maintain a constantly

increasing number of broad and expandable economic undertakings on the basis of self-labour, their own capital and mutual aid. . . . Our ultimate aim is to make the country an all inclusive Jewish labour commonwealth.

"The member WPSTS use Merkaz Haco-operatzia as a façade whose instructions are to be obeyed only when convenient. . . ."

The members of the bus co-operatives constituted 45 per cent of the membership of all the affiliated WPSTS. Yet, Merkaz Haco-operatzia devoted more than 45 per cent of its staff, time, and effort to these WPSTS.

A manager of a co-operative joinery whose business was with other WPSTS suggested that

"there should be a regulation that affiliated WPSTS use only other affiliated WPSTS and the Merkaz Haco-operatzia should set up a committee to deal with and have the authority to adjudicate these questions."

Another delegate added that

"there is the fear of one affiliated WPSTS kidnapping customers from the other. If a WPSTS invents something of importance and which eases its work and could facilitate the work of others, he keeps this (invention) a secret from all other WPSTS." He suggested that Merkaz Haco-operatzia should furnish information to its affiliated WPSTS about "technical and administrative innovations (improvements)."

A member delegate noted that

"Unlike those admitted into the kibbutzim, those who joined WPSTS have not received any co-operative education or indoctrination. They join the WPSTS as a way out or by accident when looking for a steady job. . . . This . . . creates a pattern of WPSTS in which the social aspect of co-operation has no place."

An ex-farmer now a member of a WPSTS, added that when joining an agricultural co-operative

"I knew who I was and why I was obliged to do so and so in the co-operative. But as a member of a WPSTS, I do not feel this obligation. The Histadrut is responsible for this."

He noted the lack of an inter-co-operative spiritual unity and mutual aid and the lack of any provision for the dependents of deceased members.

A delegate member from the bus co-operative for Tel Aviv and its suburbs (in which 40 of the labour staff of 250 were non-members, but none of these 40 were drivers), attributed the unsatisfactory inter-member relationships and other social aspects within the WPSTS to their bad economic position. He asked for evidence to support the charges of mismanagement.

The Congress of 16 June, 1938, asks Merkaz Haco-operatzia to arrange for joint inter-WPSTS marketing of their products, mutual aid and reciprocal relations; and that Merkaz Haco-operatzia should not accept new WPSTS that would compete with its affiliated WPSTS.

The delegates' criticism at the Fourth Congress of 16 June, 1938, of Merkaz Haco-operatzia educational activities was that there was too much national and party indoctrination by half-a-dozen organizations, and there was practically no co-operative education about such aspects as equitable distribution of work and the fruits of one's labour.

A delegate from a WPSTS in Haifa referred to the secretary's report that the Merkaz Haco-operatzia educational department had arranged 500 lectures in Tel Aviv and many other good activities. According to his information, which many others confirm, a representative of Merkaz Haco-operatzia visited the affiliated WPSTS once to explain the need for educational activities.

The member delegate from the co-operative restaurant in Jerusalem said that the educational activity of Merkaz Haco-operatzia on their behalf was "a trip to the Dead Sea." Most of our members do not know the meaning of co-operation.

A delegate of a WPSTS with a predominantly non-European membership asked for a weekly or monthly periodical with articles of a more popular character than those in Hameshek Hashitufi (the organ of the Histadrut-sponsored Consumers' Co-operative movement). Merkaz Haco-operatzia should also arrange, preferably in a village, throughout the year intensive short courses adapted to the needs of the varied membership in its WPSTS. It should not, it was urged, postpone the plan to develop a uniform technical Hebrew terminology, especially for the bus co-operatives.

A member delegate of the bus co-operative in Haifa disagreed with the criticism that the lectures delivered at the Merkaz Haco-operatzia course on co-operation

> "were a duplication of material found in Hameshek Hashitufi . . . they also included those problems which this Congress was discussing. And since tens of listeners attended these courses regularly, it was essential to continue them."

He suggested that the lectures should be printed and circulated among the WPSTS members.

S. Gorochowsky (Merkaz Haco-operatzia secretariat) admitted the shortcomings of its educational programme and agreed that it should do its best to meet the request of its affiliated WPSTS. But affiliated WPSTS also should share in the responsibility.

The Fourth Congress approves and expresses much appreciation for the extensive educational (cultural) work of Merkaz Haco-operatzia and of the Histadrut. And it notes the important achievements of the course on co-operatives held in Tel Aviv and recommends that similar courses should be repeated in Tel Aviv and arranged in Haifa and, if possible, also in Jerusalem.

The Merkaz Haco-operatzia report on activities between 1938 and 1942 noted that the Fourth Congress (16 June, 1938) elected a Council of 24 and the Council at its third meeting on 2 March, 1939, added five more. The Council also met on 20 November, 1939, and on 27 January, 1941. The Council considered the reports in which the Merkaz Haco-operatzia secretariat submitted and discussed *inter alia* the following problems: Inter-WPSTS relations, such as mutual aid; the expansion of the WPSTS movement; supervision and audit of the affiliated WPSTS; wage labour; the activities of its subsidiaries (NOA) the Merkaz Haco-operatzia central purchasing agency, and of Kupat Haco-operativim, its financial organ. Detailed minutes of the Council meetings were sent to all the WPSTS affiliated to Merkaz Haco-operatzia.

The Fourth Congress had decided there should be a congress at least once every two years. The Second World War and other circumstances made it impossible to carry out this decision. The majority of the Council at its third meeting on 27 January, 1941, rejected the suggestion of Merkaz Haco-operatzia secretariat

> "to decide on convening a Congress . . . in the nearest future" and instructed Merkaz Haco-operatzia to fix the date after again reviewing the situation. "In the meantime the situation on the Egyptian front deteriorated and the tension and strain in the country increased. After that there was the preparation for and the elections to the Histadrut Congress . . . and after that it was decided to convene the Congress without any further delays."

In December 1935 Merkaz Haco-operatzia organized a special department for bus co-operatives. The secretariat reported that Chevrat Haovdim had not exercised its right to appoint two of the members of the Management Committee of the department. One of the main functions of the department was to represent the bus co-operatives in negotiations with the Mandatory Government's central and district transport committees and authorities and in the negotiations for contracts with municipalities and other local authorities. This department also dealt with geographical boundary disputes between the bus co-operatives, a most contentious problem. The department did very little (reasons not given) to carry out its plan to deal with the general question of wage labour in the bus co-operatives. But it devoted considerable time to the problem of labour relations between the bus co-operatives. Both parties were satisfied with the results.

One of the reasons for the unsuccessful and short life of the pool of road haulage co-operatives, the report notes, was that the representatives of Merkaz Haco-operatzia and of Chevrat Haovdim on the Management Committee of the pool were a minority. Therefore, they could not resolve "the differences between the (road haulage) co-operatives, most of which basically were imaginary." Yet another cause of friction was the fact that the pool included the road haulage co-operatives which the kibbutzim had organized. These were smaller and their interests were not the same as those of the affiliated road haulage co-operatives.

The secretariat's report for 1939-42 created the impression that the bus co-operatives, particularly during 1940 and 1941, showed considerable concern for the interests of the consumers and the general economy of the country. Before implementing the authorization to increase their bus fares by 20 per cent, the bus co-operatives gave very long and careful consideration to the fact that this "would be followed by increases in many other fields and that in this way the (bus) co-operatives would still further complicate the economic life of the country . . . and consequently the fares, for some routes, were not changed for some time."

The report for 1938-42 noted that Merkaz Haco-operatzia was unable to carry out the suggestion made at the Fourth Congress on 16 June, 1938, to centralize the purchases for WPSTS other than for the transport co-operatives, since there were no customers for large quantities. Merkaz Haco-operatzia, according to the report, made a few centralized purchases for service and industrial workers co-operatives "with much success".

The secretariat of Merkaz Haco-operatzia reported that it was unable to carry out the resolution of the Fourth Congress on 16 June, 1938, nor that of the first Council meeting, "to widen the chain of WPSTS . . . in order to meet the needs of an increased immigration". The day to day activities and problems left no time "to engage in the building of co-operation and adding bricks, tiers and floors". Priority had to be given to the organization of more and more training and refresher courses for drivers, printers, bakers and locksmiths. The demand for these courses which were well attended, was increasing. The managers of transport co-operatives and engineers gave most of the lectures, and the stenographic reports of the courses were circulated.

During the transport exhibition from 9 May to 22 May, 1940, which was arranged jointly by the Jewish Agency and the Merkaz Haco-operatzia transport divisions, lectures illustrated by demonstrations were given about technical and road safety problems.

The report also noted that a representative of the Merkaz Haco-operatzia secretariat was very active on the occupational hygiene and social committee which the Histadrut sponsored. However, this committee, when visiting the WPSTS affiliated to Merkaz Haco-operatzia reported that these neglected and were not concerned with the health of their members and employees. The report[34] in a special study, drew attention to the unsatisfactory health of the drivers, and Merkaz Haco-operatzia was gravely concerned that it might be necessary to make attendance at special courses obligatory.

The reports of the auditing department cover the accounting and the commercial aspects of all WPSTS affiliated to the Merkaz Haco-operatzia.[35] This department made and submitted reports on 276 special investigations carried out during the period between 1938 and 1941. It was the opinion of the auditing department that only the participation of a

Merkaz Haco-operatzia representative in the daily management of the WPSTS could assure effective and preventive supervision.

The report noted that because of the Arab disturbances (1936-39) and the Second World War, the Merkaz Haco-operatzia secretariat had to postpone the expanded programme for co-operative education and to carry on with the old programme of "hundreds of lectures on political economy and co-operative, literary and technical subjects; organizing sightseeing trips, especially for the children and of parties for members and their families; the collective purchase of books; and assistance to six of the larger WPSTS to establish libraries. There were a few technical seminars for regional managers and cultural committees. The report notes that in spite of the pressure "that there should be only one Histadrut co-operative journal (platform) for all of the Histadrut-sponsored co-operatives, everything was ready for the first issue of a monthly journal (Shituf) for WPSTS".

All lectures and lecturers had been arranged for a seminar in June 1941. This seminar was cancelled because very few of the WPSTS evinced any interest or willingness to free some of their members for these courses. And none of the kibbutzim in the South and in Emek Hefer (Lower Shomron) could allocate the accommodation which was needed for the lecturers and students.

The general course in Tel Aviv on co-operation was continued, but on a reduced scale, between December 1938 and March 1939, and for one month in the year 1939-40. Lectures during most of the year of 1941 were not given, but were resumed in December 1941. It was expected that they would continue until March 1942. But the report noted that strictly speaking there were no courses on co-operation; half or more of the lectures covered problems of the Histadrut, Government and municipal administration and general economics.

The secretariat of Merkaz Haco-operatzia was of the opinion that unless the managers and leaders of the affiliated WPSTS displayed more interest in co-operative educational activities, there was little hope of any progress in this field.

The report noted that human relationships within the affiliated WPSTS varied from a many faceted pattern of mutual assistance to what could be called impersonal attitudes, i.e. the members considered their respective WPSTS as only legal partnerships for earning a living. The only inter-WPSTS examples of mutual aid, which the report cited, were the Merkaz Haco-operatzia financial subsidiary Kupat Haco-operativim and the central purchasing subsidiary NOA; and a few scattered instances of temporary arrangements for pooling and exchanging resources and for financial and technical help to WPSTS in trouble. The chapter in the report relating to mutual aid concluded in a pessimistic strain, both as regards achievements and practical potentialities.

The report for 1938-42 also referred to a suggestion that the Histadrut-sponsored consumers' co-operatives should establish their own bakeries. Merkaz Haco-operatzia insisted that WPSTS bakeries should supply bread for the consumers' co-operatives and others (See Book Seven). It was disappointing, the report added, that the co-operative bakeries were not providing a better quality bread with a guaranteed weight at a lower price than that charged by the private bakeries. This would have been possible had the bakeries not disbanded, six months after its establishment, the efficient and useful joint laboratory for testing bread and the ingredients used.

The secretariat's report to the Fifth Congress of 7 to 9 April, 1949, anticipated the adverse criticism of the shortcomings of the educational activities of Merkaz Haco-operatzia and pleaded guilty to the charge. It placed the blame on the unsuitable personnel, but added that most of the WPSTS did not ask for educational programmes and that "less than a minyan" (ten) attended the lectures by important lecturers. Merkaz Haco-operatzia had prepared a varied educational programme, including vocational education.

The manager of a metal workers co-operative, who was also a member of Merkaz Haco-operatzia's Management Committee, said that very few members of the affiliated WPSTS really knew what a co-operative was. If a real effort had been made to explain in detail the social and economic problems of WPSTS, the members would not have become only "screws in the co-operative machine".

A member of the Histadrut Executive Committee told the Fifth Congress that unless the WPSTS movement were more active in the field of trade education there was a real danger that WPSTS of certain branches, such as the printing industry, would disappear. The assumption that WPSTS were intended for only those between the age of 35-45 years old was both erroneous and dangerous. He asked why members of the WPSTS did not send their children to trade schools and why they failed to recruit from abroad some of the young skilled craftsmen urgently needed by the WPSTS. "The fate of trade education and of the WPSTS are joined."

One of the founders of the second largest and oldest printing co-operatives noted that he did not recall that their co-operative or Merkaz Haco-operatzia had arranged "any discussions with the members about co-operative questions and principles; or procedure, particularly about the practices in the country. . . . There should be a code (shulchan aruch) about day-to-day life, suitable as a guide for both the old and new WPSTS, but which will not interfere in the development of a WPSTS".

A few member delegates complained that except for its auditors, Merkaz Haco-operatzia representatives had not visited their respective societies for two or three years. The old WPSTS also need direction and advice.

A few member delegates accused Merkaz Haco-operatzia of favouritism and pursuing a policy of "divide and rule". A member delegate of a bus co-operative demanded that Merkaz Haco-operatzia should discontinue its direct negotiations with several of its affiliated bus co-operatives about the amount of financial participation of new members and about their amalgamation into one country-wide bus co-operative. "I call on the secretariat not to put into effect any agreement or to continue any conversations and/or to close any negotiations, which have not been first discussed with the central bus transportation office," he said.

The delegate from Haifa WPSTS, which in 1948 accounted for 25 per cent of the WPSTS movement (it is not clear whether the speaker referred to numbers of co-operatives and/or members) complained that they had to go to Tel Aviv for decisions and that, generally speaking, they were treated as "step children". He suggested that an adequately staffed branch of Merkaz Haco-operatzia should be opened for the Haifa district.

The delegates of the affiliated WPSTS in Jerusalem noted that because Merkaz Haco-operatzia representatives in Jerusalem had to refer to Merkaz Haco-operatzia in Tel Aviv all applications for loans and relief, WPSTS in Jerusalem had lost business. They asked that the Merkaz Haco-operatzia office in Jerusalem should have more authority.

S. Goren admitted that "even the special circumstances do not justify the interval (of eleven years) between the Fourth and Fifth Congress. We need this indirect contact with the community more than you do."

Replying to the questions about integration, he noted that a more detailed plan than that published in Shituf and mentioned by Professor Benenson, was not available. The practicability of even the draft submitted depended on tying it in with the general integration plan. He agreed that the negotiations about the capital participation by new members accepted must be direct with the respective WPSTS. But the focal aim, integration of the immigrants, was common for all WPSTS.

He explained that the staff of Merkaz Haco-operatzia was "tired", their load was too heavy. It was difficult to get a suitable and adequate staff without an increase in the budget. Therefore, the affiliated WPSTS should continue to press the Histadrut for a subsidy to Merkaz Haco-operatzia, a justified demand especially today, "since we are dealing with the establishment of WPSTS for immigrants".

The delegate from an engineering (metal work) workers' co-operative criticized the Merkaz Haco-operatzia's secretariat for suggesting partnerships between WPSTS and private capital. The private shareholders were said to be interested in maximum prices which is generally tied up with a limitation in production, while the WPSTS were primarily interested in maximum employment and production. The result was persistent conflict. He also advised the Merkaz Haco-operatzia secretariat to discontinue its propaganda about socialism being the ultimate goal of co-operation. "Co-operation is a movement of and for labour, this is its function. Only by impregnating the WPSTS with the Histadrut spirit in their daily life, can we resolve their problems."

The delegate of the workers co-operative in Hamalchim considered as unsatisfactory the arrangement with the previous owner who continued as an equal partner. For instance, the partners' object to equal emoluments for all members of the co-operative, and this is a more difficult question than is the question of wage labour. He said:

"And we should not be ashamed to admit (say) that this arrangement gives the members of the co-operative the opportunity to hide behind the backs of the partners for not accepting the demand of the wage workers. I do not say that this is so in our case, but theoretically this is possible. And, therefore, I do not think this is the right method and it should be re-examined. . . ."

The speaker admitted that the partnership saved "members" who had been working there for seventeen years. . . ." But the undertaking was in difficulties because the partners wanted to pull out some of the capital instead of increasing their participation for expanding the plant. Merkaz Haco-operatzia did not support the view of the co-operative of workers because it did not wish to antagonize the Manufacturers Association and discourage other investors from entering into partnership with WPSTS.

The delegate of a large metal workers WPSTS agreed with this criticism of joint ownership by industrial workers' co-operative and private capital. In their case, the plant could accept 30 additional members if the partner agreed to provide his half of the additional investment capital needed.

The delegate of a young co-operative for ceramic products, which accepted a partner in 1948 when times were at their worst, reported that the first year's experience was successful from every point of view. Their partner was prepared to invest his share of the funds needed to double the membership, but the co-operative of workers could not raise its share.

A delegate of a diamond co-operative[36] alleged that

(*a*) their partners did not provide sufficient operating capital and
(*b*) the prices which they realized were much lower than those which the non-co-operative diamond cutters obtained.

The secretary of the federation of the Histadrut-sponsored diamond cutting industry replied that breaking through the monopoly of the private diamond industry was a long and expensive procedure. He admitted that they had underestimated the capital investment per worker needed, and had made inadequate reserves for the abnormal fluctuations (periodic crises) of the diamond industry. But, he considered that the organization of twelve co-operatives with 400 diamond cutters and polishers was an achievement, considering the obstacles which the industry placed in their way. They had not yet found a method to minimize the large differences in earnings between the workers which induce internal disputes in the co-operatives.

Several delegates criticized Merkaz Haco-operatzia and Kupat Haco-operativim for encouraging diamond co-operatives because this was too risky and because it was a "capitalistic" industry. They referred to IL.30,000 lost in financing one of those co-operatives.

S. Goren said that joint ownership of factories and workshops by co-operatives of workers and private capital was not a matter of choice or ideology but one of practical necessity. Though each party had one-half of the votes and shares, *de facto* the respective co-operative of workers had the decisive voice because it supplied the labour. Until such time as the

Histadrut could replace private capital, such partnerships would increase.

M. Weisbrot (Egged) said, that while he agreed in principle to the amalgamation of the bus co-operatives, either into one body or into two bodies, one each for intra and for inter-urban bus transport, the time was not yet ripe for this major operation.

A member delegate to the Congress, who was a member of the "Dan" bus co-operative in Tel Aviv for twenty years, argued that amalgamation was tantamount to the liquidation of the bus co-operatives. The pride of ownership, responsibility for management and the active participation in planning would disappear if all the bus co-operatives were amalgamated into one large national co-operative. He asked whether the advantages of one central bus organization should be considered as more important than the sense of responsibility and of independence which smaller bus co-operatives engender among their members. He thought that the following five main reasons why the Histadrut favours amalgamation were equally good reasons for retaining individual bus co-operatives.

(*a*) Direct elections are more likely to improve the social aspects of co-operation than impersonal representation through regional meetings which is unavoidable in a co-operative with 1,000-1,500 members.

(*b*) One country-wide bus co-operative is not a guarantee for better and more efficient use of equipment, since it destroys a member's pride and sense of responsibility for his bus. Members are more likely to make temporary sacrifices to enable a small co-operative to acquire new equipment than are the members of large impersonal co-operatives.

(*c*) There cannot be more public supervision than that which Chevrat Haovdim appointees are authorized to exercise over the Histadrut-sponsored bus co-operatives. Effective internal control by members decreases in direct ratio as the membership grows.

(*d*) The superiority of large bodies to integrate immigration is not an iron rule. For instance, the large kibbutzim did not integrate relatively more people than the smaller kibbutzim. Not size, but a sense of equity and of loyalty to the labour ethos is the decisive factor for the degree of integration. Only the Government can cover the unavoidable operating losses resulting from rapid and unregulated large scale integration. Reducing the participation of new members in a co-operative's capital is not a solution for the integration of immigration. And, generally speaking, smaller units require a relatively larger labour force than do large central bodies and therefore their integration potentialities are greater.

(*e*) Merkaz Haco-operatzia erroneously thinks that the inter-co-operative jurisdictional disputes about the boundaries is the main cause for the unsatisfactory service. Israel wants and needs direct connection between every village and every town. Empty and over-crowded buses on the same route at the same time are relatively few. In normal times every route is sure of an almost guaranteed load and no route can depend on casual "pick ups" on the road. A rigid timetable is a condition *sine qua non.*

Members of the Merkaz Haco-operatzia secretariat described the arguments against immediate amalgamation as "vacuous rationalization". They argued that there is one over-all reason for a central bus co-operative, viz. ". . . the interests of the development of the country. And Merkaz Haco-operatzia must consider this . . . as one of its urgent and immediate tasks."

Prof. M. Benenson, a well known social insurance actuary, and an active member of the Merkaz Haco-operatzia Management Committee for many years, referred to a detailed but imperfect plan for the integration of the immigrants into the various sectors of the affiliated WPSTS. Though the WPSTS were asked to comment on this plan, not "a single suggestion for changing it (the plan) has been advanced. . . . No economist can guarantee with complete certainty that this or another way is the best way . . .".

Referring to the debate about large versus small undertakings, Prof. Benenson said that "the social-economic structure of the present immigration is unsuitable for large undertakings". The financing of these, also, is much more difficult and he is "pessimistic about the possibility of getting help from the Government which compliments us (WPSTS) but will not give us any priority (special rights)".

According to Prof. Benenson, one of the important advantages of co-operative production is that it is not bound to a particular procedure and has always accommodated itself to realities. WPSTS start small and grow gradually; they can enjoy the advantages of being small and yet work together as large undertakings. For example, the metal industry WPSTS lack modern technical apparatus, particularly for the finishing processes. These co-operatives together could and should establish one central casting or pouring plant (for moulds), jointly employ one or more engineers to assist in planning and making estimates, etc. He also refers to the decision in principle of the co-operative bakeries to establish a central flour mill and begin joint purchases, etc.

Professor Benenson stated that the only justified claim for income tax exemptions is for new and small WPSTS during the first few years.

A delegate of WPSTS in the metal branch endorsed Professor Benenson's suggestion for joint ownership of specialized machinery. It is more important and urgent for Merkaz Haco-operatzia to press for this kind of fusion than for the amalgamation of the bus co-operatives.

The Fifth Congress, 7-9 April, 1949, asked Merkaz Haco-operatzia to renew and to expand the scope of its co-operative educational and vocational training activities without which "we will not succeed in becoming a large popular movement . . . for the building of the country and for establishing within it a co-operative regime". The Congress also asked the Ministry of Education to include co-operation in the curriculum of the schools (the resolution did not specify whether the plan was intended for primary or secondary) and to establish a Chair on Co-operatives in the Hebrew University.[37] In addition:

1. The Congress instructed Merkaz Haco-operatzia to encourage projects jointly owned and managed by co-operatives of labour and private capital in important industries, provided that the autonomy of the respective co-operative of workers and the expansion of the respective project were ensured; and that the Chevrat Haovdim were able to exercise such control over the respective co-operatives of workers as would safeguard the social aspects.
2. It instructed Merkaz Haco-operatzia to issue a directive that the annual accounts of the WPSTS, which its auditing department prepared and certified, must reflect the real position of the respective societies. It directed the WPSTS to submit regularly to the auditing department of Merkaz Haco-operatzia their monthly trial balance-sheets and within three months after the close of their respective fiscal years their annual accounts for auditing. The Council was authorized to prepare and to enforce a detailed plan for putting into effect these instructions.
3. It renewed its previous decision that the Congress should be convened every two years. Postponement of a Congress required the approval of the Council by a two-third majority.
4. It elected a Council of 72 members that included all the 32 members of the Merkaz Haco-operatzia Central Management Committee. The Council by a two-thirds majority could co-opt additional members and replace members. The Council met not less than once every four months and was the highest authority in the interval between Congresses.
5. It asked all affiliated transport co-operatives to centralize all their purchases with the Merkaz Haco-operatzia subsidiary NOA and requested all other affiliated WPSTS to concentrate their purchases and marketing with the special department for these purposes, which Merkaz Haco-operatzia had organized. The Congress instructed this department to co-operate with the Council of Histadrut-sponsored industries with the ultimate aim of centralizing the purchases of and sales within this department.
6. It considered that the amalgamation of the bus co-operatives into one body was a step in the right direction. The Congress also instructed Merkaz Haco-operatzia to direct its efforts to the amalgamation of industrial workers' co-operatives in the respective industrial branches of industry into larger plants, and to find a way for the Histadrut-sponsored agricultural settlements and the Histadrut-sponsored WPSTS to establish joint projects.

The secretary told the Council Meeting on 14 July, 1949, that Merkaz Haco-operatzia was doing its best to counteract the very bad press about the bus co-operatives, which reflected the growing dissatisfaction of the public. The bus societies' explanations about their sacrifices during the war and the difficulty of getting new vehicles, was countered by an allegation that the members had emptied the coffers of their co-operatives. The secretary of Merkaz Haco-operatzia denied the allegation that bus fares had to be increased because the members of the bus co-operatives were drawing excessively high wages and fringe benefits in "various ways".

Little progress had been made in the renewal of educational activities, and attendance at lectures and informal forums had been disappointing. Merkaz Haco-operatzia was now thinking about introducing short seminars for the active leaders of the WPSTS. There was also a suggestion to send a group to the U.S.A. "to study all fields which interest us".

J. Baniel*, head of the auditing department of Merkaz Haco-operatzia, reported that since the Mandatory Government regulations and controls and income-tax were introduced in 1942, the affiliated WPSTS delayed unduly the submission of their annual accounts for audit. Some WPSTS had specific reasons "but this is not the place to describe them". Accounting became complicated and the WPSTS got into the habit of postponing the closing of their books and not keeping their books *au jour*. Most of the affiliated WPSTS no longer submitted monthly trial balance-sheets to the auditing department or details for their annual accounts. By the end of June 1949, only ten WPSTS, all small co-operatives, had submitted their annual accounts for auditing. The larger WPSTS submitted their accounts for auditing fifteen months and more after the close of their respective fiscal years. Under these conditions, systematic and useful auditing became almost impossible. He added: "Our situation at present (mid-July, 1949) is bad in every respect." The audit of the annual accounts of only 20 of the 130 affiliated WPSTS had been finished and the annual accounts of 30 others were being audited. Not a few affiliated WPSTS had not submitted their 1947 annual accounts for auditing. In 1950 the annual accounts of 300 affiliated WPSTS had to be audited. By mid-1949, it was estimated that the auditing of the annual accounts in mid-1949 would be two years or more in arrears.

Merkaz Haco-operatzia hesitated to ask the Registrar of Co-operatives to apply sanctions (fines) in the case of about 100 affiliated WPSTS that had not submitted their annual accounts for auditing within three months from the end of their financial years, as prescribed by the Regulations to the Co-operative Societies Ordinance, 1933. Such action would lower the prestige of Merkaz Haco-operatzia, which was the Audit Union, and the WPSTS and others would consider Merkaz Haco-operatzia as "a branch of the Government investigation department and it would no longer be a federation of WPSTS, united voluntarily for the idealistic purposes of developing co-operation, mutual aid and self supervision...."

Mr. Baniel urged the affiliated WPSTS to be frank and to say "we wish to abolish the audit department of Merkaz Haco-operatzia". He urged the WPSTS that it is in the best interests of the country to accept and loyally carry out the Government price control and income-tax regulations of

"their own elected Government. And everybody who fails to report part of the revenue in order to conceal part of the income of the member, is contravening the law and ethics. While we were not appointed as guardians of the morale (of the WPSTS and their members) or as agents of the Government treasury, we should not tolerate in our midst any law breakers. We will not approve any balance-sheet which we suspect is based on fraud. . . . We are one family and the sins of the one fall on the whole family."[38]

Referring to Mr. Baniel's report, a Council member representing the bus co-operatives, attributed the delay in the submission of annual accounts for auditing to inadequate guidance by Merkaz Haco-operatzia and to its inadequate auditing staff.

The Council member, representing the diamond workers co-operatives, asked whether the funds available could not be better used for establishing export producing WPSTS instead of co-operative bakeries. Unless Merkaz Haco-operatzia shows a more positive attitude to the financial needs of the diamond cutting co-operatives it would be better "to throw them out" and for "their members to transfer to another branch. . . ."

A second Council member from the diamond workers' co-operatives drew attention to the large number of immigrants and war veterans integrated by their co-operatives, compared with those integrated by the co-operative bakeries.

A member of the Merkaz Haco-operatzia secretariat, replying to the complaints of the diamond cutters co-operatives, assured the Council of the unequivocal impartiality of Merkaz Haco-operatzia towards the various types of WPSTS.

The secretary of Merkaz Haco-operatzia assured the diamond workers co-operatives "that there was not another branch in which Merkaz Haco-operatzia had devoted so much time and effort and such a large proportion of its money. This was the only type of industrial workers co-operative for which Merkaz Haco-operatzia has established a separate department. But the secretariat cannot remain indifferent to the fact that certain of its affiliated diamond co-operatives have contravened Merkaz Haco-operatzia's decisions.

Referring to the delay and/or non-submission of annual accounts, the secretary of Merkaz Haco-operatzia proposed to enlist the assistance of the Registrar of Co-operatives because "he uses Merkaz Haco-operatzia as his instrument and we consider the Co-operative Department as ours."

The Council Meeting on 14 July, 1949, authorized Merkaz Haco-operatzia to warn all members of its Managing Committee that failure to attend two consecutive meetings without a good and acceptable reason would be followed by automatic cancellations of membership on the Committee.

The Council insisted that all the affiliated WPSTS should submit their monthly trial balance-sheets by the 15th of the following month; and that they should send in their annual accounts for auditing not later than three months after the end of their fiscal year.

The secretariat's report[39] to the Council Meeting of 24-25 May, 1950, noted that the negotiations for amalgamating the five bus co-operatives with their 2,050 members took into account the "reform" measures to reduce wage workers. The problem was how to reconcile the large (IL.3000 and more) participation in the share capital and entrance fees, which the bus co-operatives were asking from new members. In addition, the Histadrut requested that the bus co-operatives "should admit hundreds of war veterans as members". Merkaz Haco-operatzia wanted the bus co-operatives to minimize the amount which new members are asked to pay. It is also pressing the bus co-operatives to amend their rules to enable them to accept Chevrat Haovdim as a special member with special rights, but without any financial obligations. Merkaz Haco-operatzia, subject to confirmation by the Histadrut Executive Committee, had agreed to accept the following "reform" which the bus co-operatives made about May 1949, and which Chevrat Haovdim had approved. The bus co-operatives would

(*a*) distribute among their respective members the difference between the old and revised evaluation of their assets (mainly of equipment and of immovables), since this would reduce their share capital, and the bus co-operatives could fix the amount which new members had to pay at about IL.1,500;
(*b*) amend their rules to provide a special status for Chevrat Haovdim.

But the Histadrut Executive Committee disapproved the "reform" because this "would destroy the economic foundations and withdraw funds required for the vital current needs. . . ." The Histadrut Executive Committee appointed a special committee to

1. thoroughly discuss all the aspects of the "reform" and
2. find a way to vitalize and develop bus transport.

But the bus co-operatives did not postpone the implementation of their "reform".[40]

Merkaz Haco-operatzia in 1950 again tackled the general problem of the vehicles of the bus co-operatives, which were inadequate and unsuitable. The general state of nerves induced by rationing, inflation, price control, rigid curtailment of imports and the shortage of supplies, accentuated and intensified the cold war between the bus co-operatives and the rest of the community.

The secretariat's report to the Council Meeting of 24-25 May, 1950, also noted that the Histadrut did not support the proposal of some of the bus co-operatives to establish one national bus company in which the Jewish Agency, the Histadrut and municipalities together would hold half the voting shares (in such proportion as those bodies jointly would decide). All the bus co-operatives would amalgamate into one central co-operative which would hold the other half of the voting stock.

The representative of a bus co-operative in Haifa accused "Merkaz Haco-operatzia of not being sufficiently persistent in its support of amalgamation".

Mr. I. Kitzis, member of the Secretariat of Three of Merkaz Haco-operatzia (Messrs. Goren and Ritov were the other two), summarized the problems of the bus co-operatives as follows:

"We can follow one of three procedures:

1. Equalize the conditions, wages and supplemental payments and settle the jurisdictional (boundary) disputes;
2. accept nationalization; and
3. amalgamate all bus societies into one body.

Under our conditions, fusion seems to us to promise more than the others. We always have said that it is impossible to impose a fusion, and it is for the general meetings of the respective bus co-operatives to make the decision. But if the question were in my hands, I would impose the fusion, not because I wish it, but because 1,400 members of the bus co-operatives voted for and 700 against fusion. Today the matter can be arranged with honour; but if the solution will be imposed from above, we could not propose what we consider reasonable conditions. This arrangement (fusion) also buries the problem of reform."

A member of a bus co-operative in Haifa made the following observation in the general debate:

"The allegations made against us with regard to the 'reform', which we carried out seem strange since we were told to go ahead. . . ."

The representative of the bus co-operatives in Tel Aviv stated that Merkaz Haco-operatzia implemented the "reform" with the full approval of Chevrat Haovdim. "I participated in the meetings and was present when they (Chevrat Haovdim) approved this." And a member of the Merkaz Haco-operatzia Secretariat confirmed this member's statement that the bus co-operatives executed the "reform" with the approval of Chevrat Haovdim.

A representative of an intra-urban bus co-operative, which rejected amalgamation, asked why the most experienced member of the Secretariat who had devoted two decades to bus co-operatives did not sit on the central transport committee.

Only one of the six representatives of the bus co-operatives who participated in the debate agreed with Mr. Kitzis's suggestion for an imposed fusion. The other five called for patience and urged Merkaz Haco-operatzia to try to convince the members of the bus co-operatives who opposed union.

M. Davidson (Drom Yehuda) said:

"The Council should not take any decision on this question (fusion) because this would force the two recalcitrant bus co-operatives to draw their own conclusions. I believe that the fusion will be established but you are stimulating a battle against it. Therefore I advise against impetuosity. You always stressed the importance of democracy of the general meetings and now Mr. Kitzis wants an imposed fusion. Go to the meetings of bus co-operatives, explain and convince them" (the members).

Zeev Onn, of Chevrat Haovdim, regretted:

> "that the reform had been carried out in spite of the unequivocal opposition of the Histadrut Executive Committee. This seriously affected our long existing intimate relationship. And I do not know how this will end. A sub-committee of the Histadrut transportation committee is investigating this question. . . ."

The Histadrut now, as in the past, considered that it is its responsibility to see to it that bus transport would serve the best interests of the community. Therefore, it considered amalgamation as the best and most effective method for the exploitation of the transport economy in the interests of the country.

The co-operative pattern of bus transport could be retained only if there were only one bus co-operative for the entire country, which would operate in the interests of the entire community. He regretted the ineffectual control by the Histadrut and the Government in the past and warned the bus co-operatives that the

> "*status quo* cannot continue. The Histadrut and the Government consider that the interests of the community must have precedence over those of a few hundred members of the bus co-operatives. . . . There is no reason or justification for turning the clock back. If a way will not be found which is both in the interests of the community and of the members of the bus co-operatives, then we will decide in accordance with the best interests of the community."

Practically all the speakers at this Council Meeting of 24-25 May, 1950, agreed that nationalization of bus services would be bad, both for the consumers and the Government, and that it would destroy the co-operatives.[41] A member of the largest bus co-operative in Haifa said: "I do not consider that it would be a calamity if all the transport workers would become Government employees overnight, but it is clear that this would be a great loss for the Co-operative Movement."

A Council member of the bus co-operative in Tel Aviv, referring to the suggestion for placing the bus services under municipal control, noted that the operating costs of such bus services abroad were higher than those privately or co-operatively owned. The fusion of all the bus co-operatives into one national system was the only solution.

An influential minority wanted the Histadrut to compel the intra-urban bus co-operatives to amalgamate with the three inter-urban bus co-operatives, which already had fused into Eshed. Complete fusion was the only way to attain uniform conditions of work and the maximum productive and efficient use of the equipment and labour force, members and non-members. Jurisdictional differences between bus co-operatives would disappear and it would be possible to open the 150 routes which are now under dispute and therefore not operating.

Those opposed to compulsory fusion thought that while in the long run the fusion plan would materialize, it could be expedited and facilitated by "softening the dissenters and making them understand".

Another group asked the Council "to obligate the bus co-operatives to amalgamate along the lines approved by Chevrat Haovdim and Merkaz Haco-operatzia secretariat. The institutions concerned are requested to take the measures necessary to carry out this decision as soon as possible and also to communicate the decision to the Minister of Transport."

The Council approved on 25 May, 1950, the following resolution:

> "The Council is deeply concerned about the difficulties which have developed in the field of bus transportation and about the parting of ways with which the bus co-operatives are confronted.
>
> "The Council empowers Merkaz Haco-operatzia and its secretariat to proceed in their unequivocal determination to strengthen the bus transportation by expediting the establishment of one bus co-operative for the entire country, which will be subject to the instructions and supervision of the Government and the Histadrut."

The secretariat's report to the Council Meeting on 24-25 May, 1950 also noted that the jurisdictional dispute between the Histadrut-sponsored consumers co-operatives and the Histadrut-sponsored WPSTS about bakeries was acute. Merkaz Haco-operatzia insisted that since the consumers co-operatives did not produce the agricultural goods which they market, there was no reason why they must bake the bread which they sell. The consumers co-operative movement had not accepted the proposal that the consumers co-operative societies and the WPSTS bakeries should jointly and as equal partners establish bakeries and that Chevrat Haovdim should adjudicate any differences. According to the same report, the 51 co-operative bakeries, scattered in nearly every section of the country, have 434 members and are "among the most successful" co-operatives within the WPSTS movement. The bakery division of Merkaz Haco-operatzia was doing everything to ameliorate, modernize, and mechanize the equipment; improve the quality of the products; centralize purchases of flour; and raise the standard of skill of the members. A chemical engineer directed the testing of the flour and other materials, and supervised the sanitary and other aspects which affect the bread.[42] ". . . it has now become the ambition of this engineer, Merkaz Haco-operatzia and the co-operative bakeries to achieve leadership in quality and in correct weight of the bread and fair price".

The report also referred to the full co-operation between the co-operative bakeries and the Government departments which "controlled their (the co-operative bakeries) accounts and mixture of flour".

Representatives of the co-operative bakeries on the Council referred to the declaration of the head of Chevrat Haovdim, Mr. Zeev Onn, at the Fifth Congress, 7-9 April, 1949, that the consumers' co-operatives were entitled to establish their own bakeries.

"It is clear that we will be unable to compete if we do not soon arrange for new equipment, especially in the towns. The co-operative bakeries account for 30 per cent of all workers in the bakeries in Haifa. With the opening of a large bakery in Haifa, in which LP.75,000 was invested, there is no possibility of competing, without new equipment."

The representatives of the co-operative bakeries also complained that the Government in allocating foreign currency for equipment had favoured Hamashbir Hamerkazi and non-co-operative bakeries to the co-operative bakeries. They agreed with Chevrat Haovdim that

> "the increase of productivity was needed to give a new content to co-operation and that it would also be in the interests of the State as a whole because it will help reduce prices for the consumers and improve the workers' standard of living."

If the Histadrut Executive Committee wishes to prevent the intensification of a quarrel between brothers "it must act immediately". They agreed with the secretariat's statement that the bakeries which the consumers co-operative movement proposed to establish would fail ". . . if this will be done without the co-operation of the co-operative bakeries." They criticized the Histadrut and the Government because the bakers' delegation to the United States to study productivity had only one representative from the co-operative bakeries. All the others were members of the secretariats of the craft union for bakers.

The secretariat told the Council of Merkaz Haco-operatzia on 12 September, 1951, that inter- and intra-co-operative differences had held up implementing the decision to fuse the three inter-urban bus co-operatives into one bus co-operative Egged (Eshed). A special *ad hoc* committee, dealing with the evaluation of property of the new society and the respective participation in its capital by each of the three bus co-operatives, was also looking into the question of the deterioration in public relationship which had become a most serious problem.

S. Goren, opening the Fourth Council Meeting of Merkaz Haco-operatzia on 8 May, 1957, explained that the Council Meeting was not intended as a substitute for the Sixth Congress of WPSTS to be held shortly. He explained that

> "many who had been elected members of the Council by the Fifth Congress . . . have left the WPSTS movement or died. Therefore other affiliated WPSTS were given the right to elect representatives on the Council to replace these. . . ."

Y. Ritov told the Council that the internal reorganization of Merkaz Haco-operatzia into four departments, each with its own management and enjoying considerable autonomy, had taken a year. Old WPSTS, now more alive and aware of their own strength and powers, were seconding their best people to help organize and guide the new WPSTS. He warned against the repetition of the mistakes made in the mass production of

WPSTS in 1950 and 1951 and that Merkaz Haco-operatzia should not again

> "build on sand or water or depend on more promises (i.e. of funds). Come what may, definite undertakings must replace promises. It requires actual cash investments to create every single employment opportunity."

The prospective members must be conditioned for their work and for the Histadrut. Merkaz Haco-operatzia must revive, but on a wider scale, its technical department and expand and reorganize the auditing and control departments and the educational and public relations activities. Thus far, they have acted on the decision to co-opt two members each from the transportation and from the industrial workers co-operatives for Merkaz Haco-operatzia Secretariat. But only one of the four invited to join the secretariat responded. Mr. Ritov also referred to a plan for Merkaz Haco-operatzia, jointly with other Histadrut-sponsored organs, to organize an investment company as a subsidiary of Kupat Haco-operativim.

He told the Council that Merkaz Haco-operatzia could improve its services if its affiliated WPSTS would:

1. double the budget of Merkaz Haco-operatzia and their participation in its financial subsidiary, Kupat Haco-operativim;
2. second many more people to help organize and guide the new WPSTS for immigrants; and
3. not confine their acceptance of Merkaz Haco-operatzia's authority "to lip service", and understood that Merkaz Haco-operatzia does not ask for and does not wish dictatorial powers.

M. Weisbrot regretted the failure of Merkaz Haco-operatzia to submit a report on its activities. Without help from national and other funds, the affiliated WPSTS could not integrate many new immigrants.

D. Reznick (Hanamal Hachadash Road Haulage Co-operative) criticized the persistent decline of guidance to its WPSTS, which was so important, both from an "economic and social point of view". He asked how the road haulage co-operatives could integrate new members if Merkaz Haco-operatzia could not help them retain their places of work.

A. Tzwick warned the WPSTS that improvements could not be decreed. They must first admit the need for improvement and also voluntarily accept the authority of the Histadrut and of Merkaz Haco-operatzia. He wanted Merkaz Haco-operatzia to impose its authority on those affiliated WPSTS that disregard the basic principles of their ethos.

Zeev Onn stated that Chevrat Haovdim had approved the reorganization of Merkaz Haco-operatzia which provided for three autonomous divisions: transport; industries and workshops; and consumer services, and that

> "the Government and the Histadrut are prepared to give practical assistance provided that the WPSTS movement expand the Kupat Haco-operativim . . . provide an adequate number of qualified organiz-

ers and advisers for the new WPSTS; and prescribe special rights (ownership) of Chevrat Haovdim in the respective WPSTS in which public funds have been invested."

Mr. Singer regretted that, *de facto*, there were affiliated WPSTS and their members who did not consider themselves a part of the WPSTS movement (i.e. Merkaz Haco-operatzia).

M. Sternberg (Haargaz) attributed this to the insufficient communication between Merkaz Haco-operatzia and the managements and members of its affiliated WPSTS.

Mr. Feintel (Co-operative bakery—Aharon) noted that the position was much better when it was possible for an individual member of a WPSTS to talk things over with the heads of Merkaz Haco-operatzia.

The Council meeting on 8 May, 1957, instructed Merkaz Haco-operatzia to submit to the next Council meeting a detailed budget which would provide for additional staff.

S. Goldman in 1957 writes that the reorganization of Merkaz Haco-operatzia into four divisions could serve a useful purpose only if supplemented with "technical organs which have their own staffs". Merkaz Haco-operatzia assumed

> "functions and obligations which neither the theoretical nor co-operative aspects require. And if it rendered these services in another form, their importance and usefulness probably would be greater than they are now . . . if Merkaz Haco-operatzia introduces changes its prestige will not be blemished. . . . Other institutions and bodies after tens of years of experience and work are now taking stock daily, if not hourly. They are sending groups abroad for study; they are inviting experts from abroad; they are employing research and efficiency staff in their offices and undertakings . . . are looking for new ways and new forms for their work."

If introduced, the new scientific approach should be used for all new WPSTS and for those old WPSTS that accept additional members.

> "In recent years important institutions have integrated an appreciable number of members from the ranks and from the managements of the WPSTS movement, whose aptitudes the WPSTS and Merkaz Haco-operatzia did not uncover, employ and exploit. . . . Merkaz Haco-operatzia still does not have internal regulations which clearly define the scope of the functions, authority, and responsibilities of its staff."

Normalization (stability) of the WPSTS movement requires new regulations which are attuned to the new realities of the country. The WPSTS should begin to breathe the new air and apply themselves to broader and new outlooks, and pay due regard to the "co-ordination of the theory and practice".

Shalom Black[43] writes

that there is need for an effective application of a three-point programme:

(*a*) "guidance and practical help in the administration of the affairs of the WPSTS;

(*b*) "persistent supervision of the economic and social aspects of the WPSTS and

(*c*) "ensuring daily contact between the WPSTS and Merkaz Haco-operatzia, which depends on 'the moral and practical help of the economic subsidiaries of Merkaz Haco-operatzia' and on the attitude of the WPSTS".

A third, and unsigned article, written in early 1958, noted that Merkaz Haco-operatzia "has cast off its old form and dressed itself in a new pattern."[44] This marks the beginning of a new era, the departmentalization of Merkaz Haco-operatzia's activities, federated into one central organ for joint and common services. Elected members from the WPSTS will constitute half the management committees and the secretariats of the respective divisions; Chevrat Haovdim will appoint the other half. The Chevrat Haovdim secretariat will have the decisive vote in adjudicating differences between the two groups on the management committees and on the secretariats.

> "The intention is not just simple election as a cloak for democracy. The affairs of the co-operatives within the respective divisions will be managed by the joint practical and active participation of the representatives of the WPSTS affiliated to the respective divisions. There will be no WPSTS movement unless genuine co-operators will stand at the head of the respective divisions, and there is a genuine mutuality within the camp; co-operative helping co-operative; branch helping branch; unit helping unit; a pioneer spirit for the guidance of weak and/or new WPSTS; co-operative ideological indoctrination and the raising of a new generation to carry on."

Without a movement there can be no WPSTS and there can be no co-operation without a unique ethos which is not confined to the narrow personal interests of the member. This reorganization of Merkaz Haco-operatzia is a genuine attempt to reinvigorate the WPSTS movement.

On 28 January, 1958, the Central Committee of Merkaz Haco-operatzia approved the decision of Chevrat Haovdim of 15 January, 1958, about the changes in the organizational structure of Merkaz Haco-operatzia. But the Committee would not accept those provisions in the reorganization plan, which limited the executive functions of Merkaz Haco-operatzia and its secretariat.

The report of Merkaz Haco-operatzia for 1948-58 insisted that the preservation of the complete organizational and administrative structure of its affiliated WPSTS required that the management of the three divisions and also the management of the new company, Teeus,[45] should be concentrated under the roof of Merkaz Haco-operatzia. The reorganization would be carried out within the present legal framework (rules) of Merkaz Haco-operatzia. This reorganization would have to be supplemented by increasing the authority of Merkaz Haco-operatzia and bolstering its financial resources.

At the outset, the affiliated WPSTS were not too happy with the reorganization plans of the Merkaz Haco-operatzia and most of the members of management objected to

> "the complete separation between the three divisions, and the elimination of the Merkaz Haco-operatzia Central Committee and the watering down of the authority of its secretariat. This weakens and may ultimately lead to the liquidation of Merkaz Haco-operatzia". There is a "natural and necessary" inter-relationship between the three main categories of WPSTS since unlike consumers' co-operatives, all the WPSTS are "the source of livelihood for every member and his family—material and spiritual—and in this respect there is no difference between a bus co-operative, an industrial workers co-operative and a service society. Their joint activity within their own chosen and one single centre . . . has strengthened and consolidated the WPSTS movement . . . without this it will crumble and crash."

But the reorganization plan was accepted and put into operation. The secretariat of Merkaz Haco-operatzia continued as the "roof management and co-ordination committee of the three divisions". And Merkaz Haco-operatzia continued to act as the audit union for all the WPSTS affiliated to the respective divisions. It also carried on the departments for organization and integration; legal advice and arbitration; education and culture, including the issue of Shituf and other publications; statistics; insurance; finance and accounting; and administration and technical questions.

The first meeting of the Management Committee of the division for transport co-operatives on 25 February, 1958, decided that the secretariat of the division should include four members appointed by Chevrat Haovdim; two by Merkaz Haco-operatzia and five by its affiliated transport co-operatives. Of these five, one each were to be appointed by Egged (Eshed) and by the road haulage co-operatives jointly. The secretariat of the division for transport co-operatives would meet weekly and its Management Committee monthly.

Y. Ritov told the Fifth Council of Merkaz Haco-operatzia, 2 March, 1958, that in many ways the ten-month period since the Fourth meeting of the Council on 8 May, 1957 was one of the most important in the life of Merkaz Haco-operatzia. After heated discussion at two sessions, the Merkaz Haco-operatzia Central Committee approved the reorganization plan "with certain reservations". It also asked Chevrat Haovdim to:

(*a*) Make concrete suggestions to strengthen and expand the WPSTS movement;
(*b*) pattern the new plants set up by the Industrial Development Company after industrial workers' co-operatives, and
(*c*) insist that the department in Merkaz Haco-operatzia for industrial

workers' co-operatives must deal with all new societies of this type, and increase the personnel of this sector.

Mr. Ritov explained that the number of members of the Management Committee (22) and of the secretariat (11) of the transportation division of Merkaz Haco-operatzia was larger than the parallel bodies of the divisions of industrial workers' co-operatives and for the service societies. In addition to the three bus co-operatives (Egged (Eshed), Dan and Hamekasher) the transportation division included 21 road haulage co-operatives (of which 11 were owned by kibbutzim), one taxi and one sea transport co-operative. While the bus co-operatives *de facto* were monopolies, the road haulage co-operatives

"(did) not enjoy a too large share of this business and the percentage (was) declining. There still is the difficult problem of bringing into the co-operative sector the private unorganized road haulage operators, many of whom are members of the Histadrut."

He wanted the Histadrut-sponsored non-co-operative road haulage sector to be fused with Merkaz Haco-operatzia transportation division.

Zeev Onn expected each of the three divisions to explore immediately the possibility of creating a form of mutual assistance between their respective WPSTS, such as the interchange of labour during certain seasons, which would reduce the need for even seasonal wage labour and a mutual aid fund to take care of slack times, which could become an inter-division mutual aid fund.

S. Goren thought that the success of the new organizational structure of Merkaz Haco-operatzia, which some members of its Central Managing Committee did not whole-heartedly support, depended entirely on loyal inter-division co-operation and on the unequivocal co-operation of the three divisions with Merkaz Haco-operatzia.

M. Lavi submitted Merkaz Haco-operatzia's 1958 budget of IL.440,000. (In 1957 the actual revenue and expenditure was IL.402,000 and IL.429,000 respectively). The organization of additional WPSTS required more instructors. New WPSTS were not assessed during their initial period. The cumulative operational deficit of Merkaz Haco-operatzia at the end of 1958 was estimated at IL.150,000. The affiliated WPSTS were expected to cover a part of the deficit over a period of three years. And Merkaz Haco-operatzia subsidiaries—viz. NOA, Kupat Haco-operativim, the Central Provident and Pension Fund Magen, etc., were asked to provide IL.30,000 for the 1958 budget. It was estimated that the increased membership in the existing WPSTS would increase the proceeds from the levies by IL.10,000. Mr. Lavee also expected an increase in commission on insurance which the affiliated WPSTS would place through the insurance division of Merkaz Haco-operatzia, and the more efficient collection of fees payable by new co-operatives for organizational and registration services. Finally, the income from special service fees would increase.

A. Davidson insisted that the affiliated WPSTS representatives should hold the majority of places on the Management Committees of the respective divisions.

A. Hochman considered the reorganization of Merkaz Haco-operatzia as both "a natural and logical by-product" of the developments during the last few years. However, the procedure imposing the reorganization from the top, was wrong. "But Merkaz Haco-operatzia and we, and not the Histadrut and Chevrat Haovdim, are to be blamed, for this since we permitted too many things to slip out of our hands." To prevent a repetition of these mistakes, the authority and functions of every division must be clearly defined. The divisions should take over only "the good that has accumulated in dealing with the co-operatives" and must avoid institutionalization. Merkaz Haco-operatzia must remain "the roof for all its affiliated WPSTS", but its authority and scope of activities must not in practice nullify the three autonomous divisions.

S. Goren stated that they are still dealing with the problem of the composition of the Management Committees for the three divisions. In the case of the division for industrial workers' co-operatives, it would be very difficult to apportion representation both on the basis of industrial branches and of regions.

Y. Ritov stated that since the Merkaz Haco-operatzia Central Management Committee freely and without instructions from anybody approved the reorganization plan, there seemed to be no need to submit the plan for the Council's confirmation. There was a direct relationship between the reorganization plan and the establishment of the necessary contacts with the company for industrial development.[46]

The Fifth Council on 2 March, 1958, approved and confirmed

(*a*) the reorganization of Merkaz Haco-operatzia;
(*b*) the budget of Merkaz Haco-operatzia with one change—viz., that the affiliated WPSTS would cover the operational deficit of Merkaz Haco-operatzia within five and not three years.

The Council directed the division of transport co-operatives to negotiate with all the respective parties concerned with a view of finding a positive solution for the difficulties resulting from the rupture of relations between the Histadrut and Egged (Eshed).

The Council decided that the Sixth Congress of WPSTS should be held during the second half of 1958. And it directed Merkaz Haco-operatzia to appoint a special committee to arrange a joint celebration of the fiftieth anniversary of the WPSTS movement in Israel; the thirtieth anniversary of Merkaz Haco-operatzia and the tenth anniversary of Shituf, the monthly organ of Merkaz Haco-operatzia.

A. Frumerman asked the First Meeting of the management committee of the division for industrial workers' co-operatives, on 4 March, 1958:

(*a*) what will be the role of Kupat Haco-operativim in the contacts between the new company, Teeus, and the respective WPSTS;

(b) at which stage will the contact be between the company, the division for industrial workers co-operatives and the integration division of Merkaz Haco-operatzia;
(c) who in the division for industrial workers co-operatives will be responsible for the co-ordination of the activities of the old and the new industrial workers co-operatives respectively.

S. Goren replied that the Merkaz Haco-operatzia secretariat would include members of the secretariats of the three divisions and that it would be responsible for the expansion and consolidation of Kupat Haco-operativim and for all the WPSTS affiliated to Merkaz Haco-operatzia. Every new WPSTS would be attached to one of the three divisions. In the case of a co-operative of workers in an administered factory, a representative of the division to which the respective commandite was attached would be co-opted to the active non-technical management of that plant. In the case of those new plants which the Teeus Company would set up without the co-operation of workers, the local workers councils would be empowered to select workers, who from the point of view of their technical and social aptitudes, were suitable material when the time came for change-over into a co-operative. The participation of a member in the capital of workers commandites would not exceed the equivalent of two months' salary and it would be payable in instalments.

S. Goren's opening address at the Sixth Council Meeting of Merkaz Haco-operatzia on 12 January, 1959 referred to the decision of the Fifth Council, 2 March, 1958, to establish within Merkaz Haco-operatzia three divisions, one each for industrial workers, transport, and service co-operatives. The co-operative restaurants were included within the division for service co-operatives.

Y. Ritov spoke about the activities of the division for bus and road haulage co-operatives. He also dealt with those "general problems of Merkaz Haco-operatzia which are common to all three divisions", such as the activities of its auditing division, which in September 1958 was from six to 24 months in arrears in the preparation of the audited annual accounts for 200 affiliated WPSTS. During the last quarter of 1958 the auditing department completed and dispatched to 101 affiliated WPSTS their audited annual accounts; completed the audit of the annual accounts of another 17, and the annual accounts for another 49 were in the process of being checked. Each of the 20-25 auditors in the auditing division were responsible for a group of affiliated WPSTS and submitted periodically to the respective divisions a report on the state of the auditing of their respective affiliated WPSTS.

M. Lavi considered that the 1959 budget proposed for Merkaz Haco-operatzia to be too heavy a burden. The rate of levy on the bus co-operative was 29 per cent higher than on the other affiliated WPSTS and 10 per cent higher than it was for 1958. In accordance with the decision of the Fifth Council Meeting, on 2 March, 1958, the affiliated WPSTS were obligated to cover the accumulated operational deficits of Merkaz

Haco-operatzia for previous years. He asked Merkaz Haco-operatzia to press the many affiliated WPSTS to settle their arrears and to pay their dues punctually.

Y. Ritov told the Seventh Council on 3 September, 1959, that the secretariat still opposed the demand of the Histadrut central auditing service that the auditing division of Merkaz Haco-operatzia be organized into a separate audit union. He complained that the Ministry of Transport refused to introduce joint activity and consultation with Merkaz Haco-operatzia of the kind and extent desirable.

A. Hochman (Egged (Eshed)) regretted the lack of progress in resolving questions which were raised ten years ago at the Fifth Congress, on 7-9 April, 1949. Except for the bus co-operatives, the integration of new immigrants by the affiliated WPSTS had been insignificant. During the last decade the question, "Are we a movement" had been raised repeatedly. He considered the "200 apprentices" in Egged (Eshed) as the future garin (kernel) for this co-operative. To ensure their continuity the other WPSTS should adopt this procedure. He repeated the suggestions made to, but not acted upon, by the Sixth Council of 12 January, 1959, to appoint a Committee made up only of members from the WPSTS, to enquire into and report on all aspects of all internal and external problems. He did not want representatives of Merkaz Haco-operatzia on this committee "because . . . we are drowned in the sea of the current questions."

M. Lavi stated that the affiliated WPSTS contributed IL.325,000 for the budget of Merkaz Haco-operatzia; they could not pay more. There was an accumulated operational deficit of IL.125,000. He thought that the Histadrut was under an obligation to cover the budget of Merkaz Haco-operatzia since its functions were similar to those of the craft unions. He refuted the allegation "that the number of WPSTS does not increase because of a lack of plans. The truth is that there are plans but these cannot be carried out with empty hands."

Zvi Lehman (Merkaz Haco-operatzia) attributes the critical position of the WPSTS movement to:

- (*a*) The fact that the WPSTS, as such, is a complex economic-organizational pattern that is always confronted with serious dangers.
- (*b*) Merkaz Haco-operatzia is unsuitable, organizationally and otherwise, to the present needs.
- (*c*) The fact that the available funds are insufficient for Merkaz Haco-operatzia to carry on the necessary economic-financial and social organizational activities.

Even some of the oldest WPSTS were said to be in "a critical condition". If the movement is not to disappear the affiliated WPSTS should take over the management of Merkaz Haco-operatzia. The basic foundation of the WPSTS sector is healthy; if only they would develop it.

Zeev Onn refuted the allegation in Mr. Ritov's article, "Yesterday", in Davar (date not given), that "the colonization and all other Histadrut-sponsored economic projects were organized from the 'top'". True, the Zionist Organisation, the Israeli Government and the Histadrut helped. But "without the voluntary choice of the 80,000 members in the kibbutzim and moshavim ovdim, there would have been no Histadrut-sponsored agricultural colonization". Referring to Mr. Goren's statement that Merkaz Haco-operatzia does not have a budget for co-operative educational work, Mr. Onn asks whether they have instructors. Will the WPSTS second at least fifty of their members for this work? A temporary leave of absence of a year or two does not destroy a member's link with his WPSTS which he will still regard as "his home". (Call from the audience: "I doubt whether it will be possible to find members to accept the appointments."). While appreciating the importance of those members who have been pensioned, Mr. Onn doubts whether these alone can carry the full or even main burden of the educational work.

S. Hadari (Ofir—the only boat haulage co-operative) considered it harmful for a WPSTS to have outside bodies, co-operative or non-co-operative, as partners. Since their co-operative had dissolved the partnership with the Zim Shipping Company, Ofir has improved. The difficulties of Hamalchim were induced not only by wage labour but by its partnership with Hamashbir Hamerkazi. Such a partnership may be "justified for a transitory period and until the co-operative is on its feet (consolidated). But experience has shown that such a permanent partnership invariably has an unhappy ending."[47]

Zeev Onn urged the Council to expand their educational activities among the rank and file of all their WPSTS before they convened their Sixth and long overdue Congress. He cautioned them that their approach (style) "of previous years is unsuitable for the last quarter of 1959". He referred to the three-fold purpose of the Government-Histadrut company Teeus: industrialization; the geographical distribution of the population; and the establishment of workers industrial co-operatives, in the development zones. The company started with IL.4 million and appeared to be certain of at least another IL.16 million. While the pivotal concern was the expansion of the industrial integration capacity of the country, Israel as "a democratic State does not wish to impose any particular pattern from the top". True, there is not a single industrial workers co-operative included in the ten undertakings, which the company already has established, or in the fifteen other projects in preparation. This is "your responsibility. You have not created the ties. I ask—why?"

Mr. Onn said that he is certain that the forthcoming Ninth Mapai Congress will call on the 80,000 members of the youth movement, Hanoar Haoved, to join WPSTS and also Histadrut-sponsored colonization groups. The call for the younger members of the WPSTS to volunteer to help to organize and direct the activities among Hanoar Haoved, Mr. Onn considers, as evidence of the Histadrut's positive and co-operative attitude towards the WPSTS sector. And he hopes that "within a few years the public administrative form of Histadrut-sponsored industry will be changed and that these will be operated in accordance with the wishes of the workers and the general desires of the Histadrut".[48]

The standing committee for the Sixth Congress of Merkaz Haco-operatzia appointed by the Eighth Council of 29 September, 1959, issued the following statement.

Merkaz Haco-operatzia received a request, dated 11 February, 1960, from the secretariat of Chevrat Haovdim to postpone the Sixth Congress of WPSTS convened for March 1960. This report notes that the national federations of building workers and of office personnel will meet early in March. Every Congress, "and more especially yours (Merkaz Haco-operatzia), which is convening after an interval of eleven years, is a public event both for the delegates to the Congress and for those who are not in the movement, and should be ensured of a befitting response". Chevrat Haovdim, supported by the general secretary of the Histadrut, suggested postponing the Sixth Congress of Merkaz Haco-operatzia to the end of April or early in May 1960. "In the light of the importance which we attach to your Congress, we suggest that your Committee (i.e. the preparatory committee for the Sixth Congress) should use the intervening time to prepare the plan for the consolidation and expansion of the WPSTS sector, and to co-opt from the ranks of its WPSTS new forces for the activities of Merkaz Haco-operatzia and of its ancillary organs."

S. Goren explained that the Ninth Council Meeting of 4 May, 1960, was convened because the Sixth Congress was cancelled 96 hours before the date fixed, 25 April. The new date for convening the meeting may be fixed only after conferences with those who insisted on the postponement. The Council therefore must decide on some of the proposals which "we had planned to bring to the Congress".

Y. Ritov reports that all the preparations "in every detail" had been completed for the Sixth Congress and that invitations were sent to the delegates and guests. On 21 April, 1960, "we received a request from Chevrat Haovdim to postpone the Congress". Merkaz Haco-operatzia secretariat discussed with the standing committee for the Sixth Congress the Chevrat Haovdim's request. A tense and stormy session decided to comply with Chevrat Haovdim's demand. This incident radiated considerable tension in the standing committee and within the affiliated WPSTS.

He refuted the allegation in the press that the postponement was requested because the preparation for the Congress was considered inadequate. A standing committee, consisting mainly of members from every category of affiliated WPSTS, made more than adequate preparations for the Sixth Congress. The three sub-committees of the preparatory committee dealt with every aspect of Merkaz Haco-operatzia and its subsidiary bodies. The sub-committees visited many affiliated WPSTS of all categories; and met and discussed with the Chevrat Haovdim secretariat and with the co-ordinating committee of the Histadrut Executive Committee all their claims and counter-claims. The request of Merkaz Haco-operatzia for a direct meeting with the Histadrut Executive Committee was granted after considerable delay. The secretariat, jointly with the standing committee, had three meetings with the Chevrat Haovdim secretariat. Chevrat Haovdim repeatedly postponed the final and fourth joint meeting which was to summarize the discussions. And the fourth meeting held on 21 April, 1960, "was very short" and "stormy". The Merkaz Haco-operatzia secretariat and the standing committee for the Sixth Congress left the meeting with a feeling that "the question of the postponement already had been decided".

Zeev Onn confirmed the correctness of Mr. Ritov's chronological report, and read to the Council the decision of Chevrat Haovdim's secretariat at its meeting on 21 April, 1960. "In the light of the discussions it was decided to ask Merkaz Haco-operatzia to postpone the Congress which will enable the Histadrut governing bodies about to be elected (the co-ordinating committee and secretariat of Chevrat Haovdim) to discuss and to define their stand on the problems with which the Histadrut-sponsored WPSTS are confronted." This decision, he explained, seemed advisable because the proposals for Merkaz Haco-operatzia activities during the next four years, i.e. between the Sixth and Seventh Congresses, which the Sixth Congress would be asked to approve, "seemed to us inadequate as a basis for resolving the basic problems of the WPSTS". They considered that it was their duty to ask the co-ordinating committee of the Histadrut Executive Committee, the secretariat of Chevrat Haovdim, and perhaps also the Histadrut Executive Committee, to express their views. On the same day (that is when the resolution to ask for a postponement of the Congress was taken) "I met several tens of members of the WPSTS and was told that . . . the purpose of the Congress is . . . also to submit proposals for resolving the crisis of the WPSTS because you (i.e. Merkaz Haco-operatzia) were not prepared". Mr. Onn advised Merkaz Haco-operatzia "to open a new page" (in preparation for the Congress) and to start on an extensive educational campaign among the rank and file of its affiliated WPSTS about their problems. He hoped that simultaneously the Chevrat Haovdim secretariat and the co-ordination committee of the Histadrut Executive Committee also would formulate their proposals to the Sixth Congress.[49]

Mr. Onn considered the question of wage labour as "a problem about a basic principle". The wage workers in the WPSTS justly demanded "a theoretical and practical solution of their status". The stark truth was that only 60 or 62 per cent of the labour force in the WPSTS were members.[50] Speaking personally and not for the Histadrut, he found the proposals of Merkaz Haco-operatzia about wage labour, in spite of the sharp condemnation, were *de facto* a request for the Congress to approve perpetuating wage labour in the WPSTS. He referred to Haargaz, which had a remarkable record from many points of view, and had accumulated "millions". Yet Haargaz had not distributed its reserves among the members; the company Haargaz, of which the co-operative with its 104 members was an equal partner, had 600 or 700 wage workers. Hundreds of these workers justly demanded to be admitted as members. And in spite of their agreement of 19 January, 1952, with the Histadrut, the three bus co-operatives still had 2,000 wage workers.[51] Mainly because of differences about the admission of the wage workers as members, "the relations between the bus co-operatives and the Histadrut have not been normal" during this interval of eight-and-a-half years.

Mr. Onn then referred to the request that Chevrat Haovdim should decrease its participation to less than 50 per cent on the Management Committees of Merkaz Haco-operatzia and of its three divisions. He added that people appointed by Chevrat Haovdim should act in their personal capacity. Mr. Onn wanted the WPSTS to elect the Management Committee and the secretariats of their respective divisions, and that the three divisions should appoint the Merkaz Haco-operatzia secretariat and not *vice versa*. Finally, he suggested that Chevrat Haovdim should designate its representatives to the secretariat of Merkaz Haco-operatzia which the three divisions had appointed. The proposal, which the preparatory committee had prepared for submission to the Sixth Congress, *de facto* left everything as it was ("it is the same woman with a different coat") and did not in any way "whatsoever" democratize the WPSTS movement. According to Mr. Onn, it was not improbable that after the reorganization of Merkaz Haco-operatzia, the difference between the divisions might increase and even become more serious. But this did not frighten the Histadrut, provided that each of the WPSTS divisions would be on their own and carry the responsibility, in the same way as the Histadrut-sponsored consumers and other types of co-operatives.

He then notes that Merkaz Haco-operatzia's proposals to the Sixth Congress omitted any mention of the decision of the last Histadrut Congress that Hanoar Haoved should be conditioned for the WPSTS. This required that Merkaz Haco-operatzia, jointly with Hanoar Haoved, should carefully map out a detailed plan of action and then submit concrete proposals to the Sixth Congress. "Either you did not think of it or you thought that the matter will take care of itself." He also warned the affiliated WPSTS against utopian demands such as asking for colonization loans similar to those given to Histadrut-sponsored colonization sectors. He favoured the establishment of a special fund to give loans repayable in two or more years (but not as long as 15 or 20 years) for the consolidation of 120 of the 140 industrial workers co-operatives. The Histadrut insurance and pension funds, jointly with the Ministry of Commerce and Industry, were each to provide two million pounds within a year or two for this purpose. This special fund was to be administered jointly by the Government, Chevrat Haovdim, the Workers Bank Ltd., and representatives of the WPSTS affiliated to the division of industrial workers' co-operatives of Merkaz Haco-operatzia.

A. Hochman, a member of the preparatory committee for the Sixth Congress, considered Mr. Onn's action unfair, and his explanations, though presented "elegantly" on two occasions, as unconvincing. He characterizes the postponement of the Sixth Congress as an "unprecedented act of contempt for thousands. In the preparatory conversations we were subjected to insults and threats, without cause from any point of view." The question of wage labour cannot be resolved by even the most carefully phrased resolutions of a Congress. If the Congress is to be convened only "after things have changed", this is a *de facto* postponement "for at least two or three years". He asks how Mr. Onn reconciles his declaration about "self-determination of the WPSTS" with his demand to postpone the Congress of Merkaz Haco-operatzia.

A. Tzwick noted that "those who set the tone in the Histadrut and consider wage labour as inexcusable in WPSTS, not too long ago all but forced the Histadrut-sponsored settlements to use wage labour".[52] He was not reconciled to wage labour. If he were absolutely certain that the Histadrut's underlying motive was the elimination or an appreciable contraction of the use of wage labour by all WPSTS, he would have taken the remarks of the Chevrat Haovdim's representative more seriously. Chevrat Haovdim "has the key for the solution in their hands". But *de facto* Chevrat Haovdim, which is a partner of the Haargaz Company (through Kupat Haco-operativim), seems less concerned with wage labour in Haargaz than in the bus co-operatives. That the majority in the Histadrut "no longer believe" in bus co-operatives is evident by its acceptance of the conclusions of the "Khoushi" and "Meshel" Committees (See Chapter Six) which, *de facto*, are a death sentence for the co-operative pattern of bus transport. He asked Mr. Onn how he reconciles his allegation that the Histadrut-sponsored WPSTS have unquestionably deviated from the social aspects of co-operation and from the Histadrut "course" and his insistence for unequivocal freedom for all the WPSTS sectors to carry on "as the spirit moves them".[53]

S. Stenger (Chevrat Haovdim) noted that Merkaz Haco-operatzia and its leaders, consciously or unconsciously, ignore the basic problems of the affiliated WPSTS on which the future of the WPSTS movement depends. A Congress, convened merely "for formal reasons", and confining itself to "beautiful declarations" which are not supplemented by action, would only increase the disappointment. The focal point of the Congress should be the future of the industrial workers co-operatives, which is threatened. A debate on wage labour in the bus co-operatives "would throttle the discussion of the problem of industrial workers co-operatives". Mr. Stenger suggested the following pre-Congress programme for Merkaz Haco-operatzia:

(*a*) The mobilization of more members from the affiliated WPSTS for its activities, such as organization, instruction and supervision of new WPSTS; the appointment of a full-time worker for the indoctrination of Hanoar Haoved.

(*b*) The setting up of several new industrial workers' co-operatives in the development zone which would take over plants established by the industrial development company Teeus.

(*c*) The preparation of a practical plan for integrating wage workers in the existing WPSTS as members.

(*d*) The promotion of a IL.4 million combined fund of the Ministry of

Commerce and Industry, Chevrat Haovdim, the Bank Israel-America,[54] plus the proceeds from the participation of the new members in the capital of the respective WPSTS.

(*e*) The delineation in detail of the relationship between the WPSTS and Chevrat Haovdim, and the extent of the participation of Chevrat Haovdim in Merkaz Haco-operatzia organs.

Mr. Hendel did not believe in the possibility of a "once and forever" solution for wage labour, which Mr. Onn suggested, or for any other questions except extinction (death). For life constantly creates new problems. He asked whether it was only a coincidence that the chairman of the Histadrut *ad hoc* committee on wage labour was an undisguised representative of the craft union and that the committee did not include any representatives of the bus co-operatives. Were the real reasons for postponing the Merkaz Haco-operatzia Congress given by Mr. Onn? He urged the Council to fix at once a new and early date for the Sixth Congress.

B. Lin (Histadrut) said that he participated in the meetings and shared the responsibility for the decision of the Chevrat Haovdim secretariat to postpone the Sixth Congress of Merkaz Haco-operatzia which he considered "as the lesser of two evils". "And were I a representative of a WPSTS or a member of the Council I certainly would have expressed my embitterment about this further postponement." He noted that for the first time Merkaz Haco-operatzia gave, and the Chevrat Haovdim secretariat had an opportunity to discuss in advance of the Congress, the text of the proposals prepared by the preparatory committee. There were serious differences of opinion between the secretariats of Merkaz Haco-operatzia and of Chevrat Haovdim about some of the major proposals, such as those relating to the authority of the respective divisions in Merkaz Haco-operatzia and the appointment of its secretariats; and who should set up the new joint fund for the consolidation of WPSTS. If Chevrat Haovdim and Merkaz Haco-operatzia appeared as a divided house at the Sixth Congress, this would have sparked long and useless debates "which would not be a blessing for the WPSTS movement". Finally, there was no need to postpone the Sixth Congress for more than two or three months.

S. Goren did not accept Mr. Onn's explanations why the Sixth Congress must be postponed. "No Congress can resolve or liquidate wage labour." He, too, thought that the preparatory committee's suggestions to a Congress can only lay down the general principle of procedure. Referring to democratization, he noted that the representatives of the WPSTS constituted half of all the Merkaz Haco-operatzia organs; 85 per cent of the Management Committee of the division for bus and road haulage co-operatives, and the majority of the Management Committees of the other two divisions. The Management Committee of each division would elect its secretariat and its delegates to the Congress of Merkaz Haco-operatzia.

Only direct action by the Histadrut could influence some of Hanoar

Haoved to join the WPSTS. Even the most qualified member from any Histadrut-sponsored WPSTS would have no influence.

He supported the resolution proposed that the Sixth Congress of Merkaz Haco-operatzia be convened within a maximum period of three months.

Zeev Onn suggested that the Council instruct Merkaz Haco-operatzia to arrange for a series of general meetings of its affiliated WPSTS to discuss in advance the problems which the Sixth Congress would consider.

Y. Ritov replied that the general meetings which Mr. Onn requested had been held. Three issues of Shituf also were devoted mainly to the background material for the Sixth Congress. Merkaz Haco-operatzia had done more educational work in advance of its Sixth Congress than the Histadrut had done for its last Congress.

Zvi Lehman was convinced more than ever that there was no good reason for Chevrat Haovdim to order the postponement of the Sixth Congress. He thought that self-determination meant the right of every co-operative to exercise its own opinion and to maintain its self-respect.

He agreed that the modernization of the workshops of the industrial workers co-operatives should have a prior claim on "the limited resources which we can mobilize". In addition to the 60 industrial workers co-operatives which "we have consolidated" there were another 70 which could be changed into vital and efficient undertakings only if they were first consolidated financially.

M. Rolnik (Namlit—Building Materials) alleged that the unfriendly attitude within the Histadrut impaired the continuity of the WPSTS movement. He referred to an important Histadrut-sponsored undertaking that was putting up a plant for building materials which would compete with and "destroy our co-operative".

Accepting wage labour as a permanent feature admittedly was a deviation from the co-operative pattern of the WPSTS. But economic considerations, especially the need to expand, made it essential to adopt a more flexible attitude towards this question. Since kibbutzim also used wage labour, why censure only the WPSTS about this "guilt".

Z. Weiser (Egged (Eshed)) ascribed the postponement of the Sixth Congress to the desire of the Histadrut Executive Committee to complete the formulation of a policy statement on wage labour in the bus co-operatives.

> "The conditions of the wage workers in Egged (Eshed), Dan and Hamekasher are better than in any other enterprises in the country, including those sponsored by the Histadrut. A wage worker in Egged feels better than does one in Solel Boneh."

And the bus co-operatives will not discontinue the "sin" of equal reward for every member.

S. Goren's closing remarks noted that those who incorrectly stated that the industrial workers co-operatives faced collapse had done them a disservice. Though the situation was difficult and required action "they will not collapse tomorrow".

The Ninth Council of 4 May, 1960, protested against the order of the Chevrat Haovdim secretariat to postpone the Sixth Congress, given four days before the date fixed for its opening, 25 April, 1960. The Council demanded that the Sixth Congress should be convened within a maximum period of three months and asked the Histadrut organs concerned to expedite the completion of their discussions relating to this Congress.

Zvi Lehman at the meeting of the division for industrial workers co-operatives of Merkaz Haco-operatzia, 21 May, 1960, urged Merkaz Haco-operatzia to establish a special export division to further and foster exports by industrial workers co-operatives. He regretted that budgetary difficulties had delayed the establishment of a department to advise the co-operative workshops on production problems, cost accounting, etc. The division for industrial workers co-operatives could meet the requests of

"many of its affiliated co-operatives who are seeking technical managers for guidance and without which a new undertaking is doomed to failure. Many liquidations during the last two years could have been avoided if they had double the present staff of six instructors for 140 affiliated industrial workers co-operatives."

The Tenth Council of Merkaz Haco-operatzia on 27 June, 1960, was informed that a budget committee made up of representatives of Merkaz Haco-operatzia and its three divisions had previously approved the 1959-60 budget of IL.625,000 for gross expenditure and IL.522,500 for gross income. This committee recommended an increase of the levy on the affiliated WPSTS sufficient to cover the estimated deficit of IL.103,000.

The treasurer, on the advice of the Merkaz Haco-operatzia secretariat, asked the Council to increase the budget to IL.736,000, i.e. by IL.111,500, and "to supplement and expand its cultural, organizational and other services". This increased the estimated deficit for 1960 to IL.214,500.

Zvi Lehman spoke at some length about the expansion of the economic guidance service and the fostering of exports. He suggested an increase of the budget to a million pounds; introduction of a system of progressive levies on the affiliated WPSTS, and that every opportunity be given to the Histadrut to participate actively in the spending of the budget.

The proposals were very sharply debated by fourteen speakers in the debate, but the observations of the speakers were not included in the published summary of the proceedings. The debate revealed that the annual levy amounted to IL.40-IL.50 per member for the small and medium-sized WPSTS and to less than this for the larger affiliated ones. The representatives of the smaller and medium-sized WPSTS insisted on a uniform levy per member for every affiliated WPSTS; others pressed for a progressive levy based on the "means test". The debate also revealed that the Histadrut returns to Merkaz Haco-operatzia 30 per cent less of the gross amount of dues, etc., which the members of all the affiliated WPSTS pay, than the amount which the Histadrut refunds to Hamerkaz Hachaklai of the gross amount which its members pay. This gap should be corrected without delay.

Y. Merom (Histadrut Central Auditing Department) urged that the auditing department of Merkaz Haco-operatzia should become an autonomous audit union "in every respect" and should have its own budget. This recommendation tied up with a previous suggestion that Merkaz Haco-operatzia should differentiate between the general levy which it collected from all affiliated WPSTS, and the charges for specific services such as the auditing and certification of the annual accounts; assistance in import and export transactions, and technological guidance.

The Tenth Council, of 27 June, 1960, confirmed the original budget which the budget committee had approved, viz., expenditures IL.625,500; revenue IL.522,500 plus another IL.103,000 to be raised by increasing, retroactive to 1 January, 1960, the general levy by 25 per cent for the three bus co-operatives and by 20 per cent for all other affiliated WPSTS. Should this increase prove to be inadequate to cover the additional IL.103,000, this special levy should be further increased to the extent necessary to cover the difference.

The Council demanded that the Histadrut increase by at least IL.100,000 the refunds of the taxes which it collected from the members of affiliated WPSTS. This would enable Merkaz Haco-operatzia to supplement its educational, cultural and instructional activities for both old and new affiliated WPSTS.

The Council instructed Merkaz Haco-operatzia immediately to prepare the 1960-61 budget. The estimated revenue should differentiate between the proceeds from a progressive levy payable by all affiliated WPSTS, and the proceeds from the fees for such services as auditing and certification of annual accounts; special investigations, etc. The budget committee was instructed to submit the draft 1960-61 budget for the Council's approval before the end of 1960.

Y. Ritov reported to the Eleventh Council of Merkaz Haco-operatzia on 12 December, 1960, that the Merkaz Haco-operatzia secretariat suggested that the Sixth Congress should meet on 20-21 February, 1961. The secretariat would submit orally supplemental data to its report on the activities of Merkaz Haco-operatzia prepared for the Sixth Congress, which was to have met on 20-24 April, 1960. The agenda of the Sixth Congress had yet to be completed.

The Eleventh Council approved the secretariat's proposals.

M. Ben-Tzur, legal adviser of Merkaz Haco-operatzia, submitted to the Eleventh Council orally the draft rules for an arbitration tribunal which were to be attached to Merkaz Haco-operatzia. If approved by the Council, the rules would also require "the formal approval of our Congress and of the Histadrut Executive Committee". In drafting the rules for this arbitration tribunal, due consideration was given to the rules of the Histadrut arbitration tribunal and to the State's laws about arbitration procedure. Criminal cases were excluded from the competence of the proposed arbitration tribunal and its rules were not intended to replace the prescriptions of the Co-operative Societies Ordinance or the rules of the respective WPSTS affiliated to Merkaz Haco-operatzia. Appeals from the decisions of the arbitration tribunals of the respective WPSTS might be referred to the arbitration tribunal, which was an adjunct of Merkaz Haco-operatzia.

The Eleventh Council approved the rules of the Merkaz Haco-operatzia arbitration tribunal.

According to a summary (Shituf, March 1962, pp. 46-48) of the minutes of the first meeting of the Management Committee of the autonomous auditing division of Merkaz Haco-operatzia Services, on 27 February, 1962, Chevrat Haovdim decided on this arrangement on 26 September, 1961. Merkaz Haco-operatzia, on 21 November, 1961, elected the Management Committee. Although the department had an autonomous management it was considered as an organic part of Merkaz Haco-operatzia which continued as the authoritative organ for all Histadrut-sponsored WPSTS except auditing. There was a delay in convening the first meeting of the Management Committee because of a difference of opinion between the secretariat and the co-operative division of Chevrat Haovdim, whether the Management Committee should include two members of the management of the Workers Bank (or of any other Histadrut-sponsored body) that did business with WPSTS affiliated to Merkaz Haco-operatzia. According to Mr. Lavi, the chairman of the Management Committee, this question has not been resolved. He stated that this meeting was convened and the two members whose membership was questioned were not invited. The secretary-general of the Histadrut was advised to this effect. The auditing department services 205 WPSTS and 25 WPSTS Provident Funds that were also affiliated to Merkaz Haco-operatzia.

On the assumption that the accounts of all affiliated WPSTS, other than the bus co-operatives, will be checked bi-monthly, four full-time auditors would be used, and another six or seven full-time auditors were required in addition to those presently concerned with the industrial workers and service co-operatives. It would not be easy to find the people qualified and to resolve the budgetary problems. They should also tighten the control and audit of the accounts of those undertakings, wholly or partially owned by WPSTS which were registered as companies. A special department to keep the accounts of the existing and any new small WPSTS, especially those in the development zone, should be established. Mr. Lavee reported that Merkaz Haco-operatzia not only had approved the budget for the additional manpower needed to carry out the aforementioned purposes but had also assumed the full responsibility for collecting the fees for the auditing departments. The auditing division would concentrate on the current services and not on "archaeology" (i.e. raking up the past). All the decisions of its Management Committee are strictly internal and its members must not communicate these to anybody.

Summary of Decisions of the Sixth Congress of 15-16 July, 1962.

1. The Congress elected a Council of 119 members, inclusive of a 59-member Merkaz (Central Committee) that the Congress elects. The Council meets annually and more frequently at the request of not less than one-third of its members or of the secretariat of Chevrat Haovdim.
2. The Merkaz meets quarterly and as and when requested by not less than one-third of its members or of the secretariat of Chevrat Haovdim. The Merkaz elects from its members an active secretariat, the principal administrative organ.
3. The Congress directs the Merkaz to examine, and if necessary, introduce changes in the classification of the WPSTS and their affiliation with the respective three departments (industrial workers; transport; and services) of Merkaz Haco-operatzia co-operatives. After the Merkaz has introduced the changes in the classification, the delegates of the three types of WPSTS who have participated at this Congress will meet and elect the managements of the respective three divisions, and the management of every division will elect its secretariat. The Merkaz (Central Committee), in co-ordination with the Management Committee of each of the three divisions, shall define the authority and functions of the respective divisions.
4. The Merkaz shall define the tasks, authority and the scope of activities and the procedure of the secretariat of Merkaz Haco-operatzia and of the managements of the respective divisions.
5. The Congress expresses its regret about the failure to comply with the decision of the Fifth Congress to convene the Congress bi-annually, and it decides that the Congress shall be convened tri-annually and sooner if the Council so decides. The Council will define the regulations for the election of delegates to the respective Congress.
6. The Congress expresses its satisfaction with the steps taken to establish co-operative committees in the towns and villages made up of representatives of the WPSTS and labour councils in the respective communities. And these joint committees could become an effective factor for the supervision and development of WPSTS and for forging stronger ties between the WPSTS and the other Histadrut bodies and activities and spread the co-operative doctrine among the workers.
7. The Congress establishes a panel of 66 arbitrators to deal with intra-member differences in the WPSTS and with differences between members and their respective WPSTS.
8. The Congress hopes that the co-operative division of Chevrat Haovdim will evolve into a central and principal organ for all Histadrut-sponsored co-operatives and act as the central organ for their economic and social activities, co-ordination, co-operative education and public relations.

APPENDIX ONE

"Hamalchim" Co-operative Society

Chaim Zackai's article* about the affair (parasha) of "Hamalchim and its meaning" is a concise factual summary about the genesis and demise of the industrial workers co-operative, "Hamalchim", established in 1947 when the workers purchased a half-interest in the plant, which was on the verge of bankruptcy. "The workers wished to save their place of employment and livelihood." The proceeds from the sale of half the Company's shares "covered only part of the plant's debts and the fate of the undertaking revolved around the problem of working capital". In 1949, those who held the other half interest decided to sell their shares to the members of the co-operative. Kupat Haco-operativim not only helped "Hamlachim" to acquire these shares but also to purchase a 50 dunam building site on which a new plant was erected and equipped with modern machinery. In 1951, Hamashbir Hamerkazi acquired half of the shares in "Hamalchim" at the book value, which was based on the actual cost of the plant, equipment, etc.

Hamashbir Hamerkazi's participation in the day-to-day administration of "Hamalchim" through its representatives on the society's management was only *pro forma*, and the entire *de facto* management remained in the hands of the co-operatives. "And in this both sides sinned." Though the managers, members of the co-operatives, had grown up in the plant, they were not equipped to deal with and to resolve the serious and complicated problems of "Hamalchim". Non-member managers were appointed but these were frequently changed. The undertaking did not have the

> "technical know-how and the considerable experience required for its complicated construction and the casting of metal. There also were frequent strikes since the shortage of working capital made it impossible to pay wages regularly and fully. The extraordinary efforts of Merkaz Haco-operatzia, and more especially of Kupat Haco-operativim, failed to ameliorate the difficulties, which were accentuated by destructive elements among the members . . . whose activities demoralized the discipline and the normal operations."

Kupat Haco-operativim supplied the money needed for refunding the capital participation of fifteen members who were eased out of "Hamalchim". But the society also had to borrow on the private market at usurous interest rates. While "emoluments had to be paid punctually, the co-operative had large arrears in income tax, national social insurance."

The annual accounts for 1955 showed an accumulated operational deficit of IL. 250,000. An arbitration committee† recommended appreciable cuts in fringe benefits, discontinuance of the payment of a thirteenth month's salary, and other economies. Furthermore, the members' accounts were to be debited "with half the amount, which the arbitrators decided the members had not been justified in withdrawing, even though this was done in accordance with the decision of the Management."

* Shituf, January-February 1960, p. 18.

† The members of the Arbitration Committee were Messrs. S. Goren (Merkaz Haco-operatzia) and Y. Efter (Hamashbir Hamerkazi).

The members were embittered and there was a decline in their work morale; most of the wage workers in the smelting department were discharged because their productivity was very low.

In 1958 a second committee, made up of representatives of Hamashbir Hamerkazi and Merkaz Haco-operatzia, was appointed "to define ways for ameliorating the position of "Hamalchim". The secretariat of Chevrat Haovdim approved the report of this Committee. The new Management of "Hamalchim" which was established included representatives on a *pro rata* basis of the shareholders. Hamashbir Hamerkazi's appointee replaced the manager of "Hamalchim," "but the management continued to be top heavy; new funds were not provided and the members did not raise their productivity. The abolition of automatic bonuses aroused bitterness."

Unauthorized strikes were called, even though the general meeting of "Hamalchim" decided "that those members, who were not prepared to accept the changes, may leave the co-operative".

A third committee appointed "with unlimited authority" to decide on the future of "Hamalchim" unanimously submitted the following plan:

1. (*a*) Kupat Haco-operativim transfers the shares—12½ per cent of the total—to Hamashbir Hamerkazi and the latter will then have 62¼ and the co-operative of workers 37¾ of all the shares.
   (*b*) Hamashbir Hamerkazi takes over the entire administration of the plant and also must arrange for adequate financing, including working capital; ensure normal production and punctual payment of wages and the other obligations of "Hamalchim."
2. Hamashbir Hamerkazi appoints the general manager. The management of three will include two representatives appointed by Hamashbir Hamerkazi and one by the co-operative of workers.
3. Any member of the co-operative who disagrees with the reorganization plan, in full or in part, and expresses his desire to leave will receive IL.2,000-IL.2,500 as payment for his share in the society's participation in "Hamalchim's" capital.
4. The scale of remuneration and conditions of work now prevailing in the Koor* undertakings also will apply to all workers, members and non-members of "Hamalchim." And the remuneration will be graded on the basis of skill. Special grants may be paid to the members of the co-operative only if and when a dividend is declared and paid on the preference shares of "Hamalchim".
5. The expeditious and unequivocal implementation of the plan makes it necessary to postpone for one year the arbitration of the differences between Hamashbir Hamerkazi and the co-operative of workers in "Hamalchim".

Mr. Zackai writes that the members of the co-operative apparently did not have "the social stamina to fight out their problems. They were shortsighted and negligent . . . and they used a subjective approach towards the cardinal problems."†

A large number in the co-operative of workers in "Hamalchim" disregard the organizational discipline and the problems of productivity. They are the ones

* Koor is the holding Company for the Histadrut-sponsored Solel Boneh and its subsidiaries.

† Is this not generally true of all individuals in all walks of life and in all patterns of economic undertakings, co-operative and non-co-operative?

who decided its fate (i.e. of "Hamalchim"). This incident according to Mr. Zackai sheds light on the pattern of relationships which are basic in any partnership between a co-operative and external forces, public or private. It demonstrated that equality of compensation for all members of a co-operative is an obstacle which destroys the main incentive for advancing one's skill and raising the productivity.* The members may share equally only in such part of the profits which it is permissible to use for this purpose. Premiums must be linked directly to production in excess of the fixed norms for a particular branch or product.

APPENDIX TWO

Background Material about the Postponement of the Sixth Congress of Merkaz Haco-operatzia

The following note† on behalf of the editors of "Shituf" introduces a special section, "The Members Have the Floor" ("Reshut Hadibur L'Chaverim").

> "We present the proposal and suggestions for a free expression of views received in connection with the Sixth Congress of the WPSTS which had been convened for 22 April, 1960.

Less than a dozen replies are published in the January-February and May-June, 1960, issues of Shituf.‡ Most of the replies published are from the same people who do most of the speaking at the meetings of Merkaz Haco-operatzia Council; the Central Management, and the Congresses. Generally speaking, these communications are a repetition of shibboleths, complaints, etc., and include very few constructive or instructive suggestions. This is equally true of the few short articles published in the two aforementioned issues of Shituf.

The leit-motiv of most of the published replies is that "co-operative education is the most neglected field . . . *de facto* there is none". One member writes:

> "In the course of years I have come to the conclusion that the tottering cultural and educational status is the main cause . . . which brings a WPSTS to the brink of crisis and which ends in its liquidation. . . . The WPSTS could have avoided liquidation and overcome economic and administrative difficulties . . . if the members had really been co-operative conscious and if there had been intra-member relationship. It seems that it is easier and more convenient to uncover economic-financial difficulties . . . in a WPSTS than to uncover and to admit a lack of co-operative consciousness, and abnormal intra-member-relationships. It is these which really are the road blocks. . . . While it may be possible to put the blame on higher bodies for the economic-

* There are not a few WPSTS in Israel and commandites in France where this is not the case. And this is certainly not the case of a large number of the members of the kibbutzim, where they all enjoy the same standard of maintenance. That the vatikim in kibbutzim have higher standards of housing is not necessarily a contradiction to the principle of an equitable standard of living for all unless one quibbles about the meaning of equitable.

† Shituf, January-February 1960, p. 10.

‡ There is nothing to indicate whether Shituf published all or only some of the replies and if the latter, what was the basis of selection.

financial deficiencies . . . we (the members) are primarily to blame for the lack of a co-operative consciousness and social complications. . . . All investments for the establishment of a new WPSTS, unless simultaneously supplemented with practical steps, to indoctrinate the members with a co-operative consciousness . . . can be considered as wasted. It is doubtful whether all devotees who work with the co-operatives really believe in the organic relationship between the economic and the social-educational aspects. While all agree in principle about the need for social-cultural activities, not all of them believe that social-educational activity is economically essential."

Another general criticism is the inadequacy of the contact between "Merkaz Haco-operatzia and the rank and file of the members". The contact with the madrich (counsellor) from Merkaz Haco-operatzia is by its very nature limited to the day-to-day problems which the co-operative encounters. The respondents suggest meetings at fixed intervals, semi-annually or more frequently, between the members of the governing organs of Merkaz Haco-operatzia and the members of a WPSTS, to discuss general co-operative problems and not only economic problems. . . . This would widen the horizon of the members and create a feeling of sharing a joint fate."

Some of the respondents mention the need for more and better facilities for consultation about technical problems and about such problems as how to expand exports.

The Sixth Congress could be the turning point for the WPSTS to emerge from their years "of stupor" and decline and, in the course of time, they may even succeed in becoming a movement. One should search inside and not outside the WPSTS for those factors "which will determine the future of the WPSTS." Another member urged Merkaz Haco-operatzia

"not to start any activity for the expansion of the framework until they have completed its internal house cleaning". Much depends on whether the WPSTS "will succeed in raising the level of the humdrum traditional discussions" and in "consolidating the appreciable hidden (stored) forces for a renewed effort to carry out important missions".

The following statement by a member with thirteen years' seniority in an industrial workers' co-operative, about the importance of intra-member (social) relationships and adequate inter-kibbutz mutual aid, represents the views of all those correspondents who referred to these aspects in their replies.

"I have come to the conclusion that all depends on the attitude of the members towards their respective WPSTS and on the relationship between themselves. This stamps the pattern of the co-operative and its future, and will serve the WPSTS in times of crisis and prevent deviations and defilement in times of prosperity."

The main or only concern of a number of the respondents was that the Sixth Congress must take measures to preserve the existing pattern and entity of the bus co-operatives. These "have demonstrated their organizational and technical efficiency only because every member felt that he was part of the enterprise and not a wage worker".

A few replies note that during the interval of eleven years since the Fifth Congress the number of members in the age group 50 and over had increased to such an extent as "to bring to the foreground (precipitate) without doubt, economic and social problems in all the WPSTS". This problem must not be confused with the much discussed question of integrating the wage workers as members.

> "I refer to those WPSTS, though few in numbers, such as the distributors of ice and paraffin, whose scope of activities, because of objective conditions, has and will continue to decline." There are "some hundreds of members, of an average age of 50-55, in these WPSTS. The main question is what to do with them until they will be eligible for pensions in 10-15 years. These WPSTS should 'establish ancillary undertakings'."

For this the WPSTS need the effective assistance of the other WPSTS and also from Government and Histadrut bodies, especially about the problem of suitable occupations for the older age groups.

One of the oldest members of the oldest printing co-operative attributed the difficulty of recruiting new blood for the WPSTS to the large amounts which the respective WPSTS ask all new members to pay into the capital and that the prevailing wage rates (includes fringe benefits, etc.) of experienced skilled workers is at least as much as the gross emolument which the members with the same skills receive.

> "On the other hand, the WPSTS cannot lower the technical standard of their plants by accepting unskilled or semi-skilled members." The same respondent also feels that the WPSTS sector cannot hope to expand without having its own bank, "which will not think of us only in terms of clients . . . whether credit-worthy or not . . . and it . . . will adopt a more liberal attitude about collateral than do other banks. All this would encourage the existing sound WPSTS to expand their framework and to integrate new members and would also make it possible for new WPSTS to arrange their affairs at a more leisurely pace."

A number of the correspondents, who stressed the organizational aspects and adequate supervision of the daily activities of the WPSTS, generally speaking supported the need for increasing the supervision and guidance by Merkaz Haco-operatzia and that the latter should have a permanent representative in every affiliated WPSTS—"large and small" who also would guide and supervise the intra-member relationships and the ideological and educational aspects. The members of the WPSTS should be encouraged

> "to express their views at the general meetings of their respective co-operatives and not to be frightened by the differences of opinions prevailing among them".

APPENDIX THREE

Attitude of Histadrut

A leading article in Shituf (February 1960, p. 1) quotes the resolution of the first session of the Histadrut Congress of February, 1960.

1. "The Congress enjoins the Histadrut to strengthen the activities of industrial workers co-operatives; to expand the existing WPSTS in various branches and to establish new co-operative workshops adapted to the needs of the immigrants."

2. The Congress confirms the demand made on the bus co-operatives that are performing an important function in the life and economy of the country, to admit their permanent wage workers and employees as members.
3. The Congress resolves that the establishment of industry and of industrial workers co-operatives in the development zones should help to expand the employment opportunities.
4. Efforts should be made to develop in the ranks of labour youth (Hanoar Haoved) garinim for industrial producers co-operatives.

The leading article in Shituf complains that all references to the service co-operatives were consciously omitted in the above quoted resolutions:

> ". . . there is no mention of the Government Co-operative Advisory Council". And also notes that "it would be desirable for the Congress (i.e. the second session of the Histadrut Congress to be convened at a later date) to define in details the role which WPSTS can play and the kind and the extent of the help which the Histadrut should make available. . . ."

Shituf, July-August, 1960, (pp. 1-2) refers to the two meetings which the Merkaz Haco-operatzia secretariat had with the full secretariat of Chevrat Haovdim, with the General Secretary of the Histadrut presiding. In these discussions about the social and economic problems of the Histadrut sponsored WPSTS

> "the tenseness of the atmosphere was apparent. But, to be frank, both sides had one common interest, viz. the consolidation and expansion of WPSTS by eradicating wage labour". Basically the plan of Merkaz Haco-operatzia for the elimination of all wage labour within the next four years was accepted. "In spite of all of the difficulties encountered in the negotiations about the elimination of wage labour in the bus co-operatives the path already has been measured and the road prepared for changing the status of *hundreds* (original underlined) of wage workers to that of members in the bus co-operatives".

This leading article in Shituf notes that the admission of hundreds of wage workers as members will require the expansion of equipment and buildings and an increase in working capital.* Many of the wage workers can pay in cash only a small part of their participation in the capital of the bus co-operatives, and arrangements must be made that credit facilities will be available to help provide the wage workers with the balance. Chevrat Haovdim must be ready to join with other bodies in establishing a special fund of IL.4 million for the aforementioned purposes, and a second of IL.5 million for the new WPSTS that will be established outside the development zones.

At these joint meetings of Chevrat Haovdim and the Merkaz Haco-operatzia Secretariat, the Chevrat Haovdim Secretariat asked "to what extent will Merkaz Haco-operatzia be able to influence its affiliated WPSTS to admit the wage workers as members?" Merkaz Haco-operatzia replied that that would require appreciable financial assistance from the Histadrut and that "the amount cannot be fixed in advance." Its affiliated WPSTS cannot supply the money for additional organizational and supervisory staff which Merkaz Haco-operatzia needed.

* This is true only to the extent that the admission of the wage workers as members actually increases the total labour force of the respective WPSTS.

CHAPTER THREE

General Economic Statistical Data

Analysis of Minutes of Governing Bodies and the Reports on the Activities of Merkaz Haco-operatzia and Miscellaneous Sources

The Secretariat's report to the Third Congress of November 1934, noted that seven new and eleven old WPSTS already operating were registered under the Co-operative Societies Ordinance (1933) and three "financially unsound" WPSTS were liquidated. During the year the total labour force, members and non-members, increased from 1,475 to 2,178. The 26 bus and road haulage co-operatives accounted for 1,209 or about 55 per cent of this labour force.[55] The capital and reserves of the affiliated WPSTS almost doubled during the year (from LP.105,000 to LP.200,000) and their total business had increased by 60 per cent (from LP.575,000 to LP.900,000).

S. Gorochowsky (Goren) told the Fourth Congress on 16 June, 1938, that some of the bus co-operatives did not use the surpluses for consolidating and strengthening their position but distributed them among their members. Therefore, the bus co-operatives were in an unsatisfactory financial position. "We did what we could; we cautioned them at dawn and in the evening, but this did not help."

Y. Ritov reported that in spite of the general unfavourable conditions engendered by the prolonged Arab disturbances (which started in the spring of 1936), "the WPSTS . . . stand firm". Though there were "liquidations and bankruptcies in the (non-co-operative) printing trade almost every day, the two printing co-operatives in Tel Aviv continued and two new printing co-operatives, one each in Jerusalem and Haifa, were developing satisfactorily".

Most of the work of the printing co-operatives was obtained from the private trade and not from the Histadrut and/or public and national bodies. The co-operative printing workshops could compete with the other printers because they had superior equipment and their members agreed to a reduction of emoluments. Mr. Ritov also reported the growing antagonism of the rank and file of the proletariat to the bus co-operatives which "was apparent everywhere . . . in the Histadrut Congresses and Councils and in the Party (MAPAI). . . . They do not consider us an organic part of the labour movement; they look upon us as the arrogant and exploiters".

S. Gorochowsky supplemented Mr. Ritov's report with a detailed analysis of the three groups of WPSTS and a more cautious evaluation of their achievements and present status. "We still have a long way to travel and much to add and to learn. And if our co-operatives thought that they have reached the height of their development they have had to wake up to the stark realities that there are still many obstacles to clear."

He noted that as a result of "the contraction in building and increased competition, the members' emoluments have decreased appreciably" in the building materials co-operatives. The Arab disturbances also made it difficult to operate the silicate brick factory which the Histadrut, in March 1936, had helped a workers industrial co-operative to acquire from the creditors. Two or three co-operative carpentry shops were closed because building had declined and the transport of materials by road was difficult. The co-operative Haargaz switched to the manufacture of steel furniture because the demand for bodies for buses and lorries had slackened considerably.

> "The banks are still competing for their (bus co-operatives) custom. The transportation co-operatives showed considerable initiative in making economies and in rearranging their debts and credits; and the members became adjusted to the new conditions of work and reduced their emoluments. . . . The endurance of the driver on this front has sealed a bond (brith) between the drivers, the labour community and the defence (Haganah) of this country."

A member of the co-operative silicate brick factory referred to by Mr. Gorochowsky absolved Merkaz Haco-operatzia of any responsibility for their present difficult position. The Arab disturbances and an almost complete stoppage of building when the factory was purchased (at a cost of LP.17,000) could not be foreseen.

A delegate from the largest bus co-operative in Haifa said that it was a crude mistake to consider the Histadrut "as the rich uncle. The Histadrut has only what we give to it; the WPSTS should first give before they go to the Histadrut with demands. The WPSTS should first create their own financial instrument, Kupat Haco-operativim".

A member of a road haulage co-operative of the kibbutzim in the Jordan Valley told the Congress that they must consolidate their inter-co-operative relationships (such as inter-co-operative mutual help), especially between the co-operatives of the same branch, before they can expect more recognition and help from the Histadrut. He cited as an example that road haulage co-operatives should jointly engage technical assistance; share work and rolling stock; and fix prices.

A member of the Haifa labour co-operative committee said that the members of the WPSTS had withdrawn from the daily life of the Histadrut and were rarely seen in the crafts unions. The WPSTS did not provide workers for the Histadrut-sponsored public activities. "A worker joining a WPSTS meets the other members for the first time and therefore his reaction to a member is the same as that to a private employer."

A member of the bus co-operative in Tel Aviv who is on the Management Committee of Merkaz Haco-operatzia replied to the Haifa delegate:

> "If we admit that we sinned and also that we are to blame for the wall between ourselves and the labour councils, this, however, does not free the Histadrut governing organs, and more especially its Council, from the responsibility of breaking down this wall. The lack of understanding, I do not want to say hatred, shown by the labour councils, is inexcusable."

A vatik of the WPSTS movement described an article in Hameshek Hashitufi (details not given) about the WPSTS as harsh and unfair. He considered it as part of "a campaign against the WPSTS as such . . . and this type of criticism is very widespread. At all kinds of meetings, celebrations, etc.; in every place they turn us inside out and search out our blemishes". He also allegedly said that "the labour council has been pressing our fourteen year old co-operative to join a syndicate with private manufacturers of tiles who wish to maintain high prices. This is a problem that not only his co-operative has encountered".

A delegate drew the attention of the Congress to the increase in the number of workshops, transportation and service undertakings which the kibbutzim were establishing. Though the WPSTS affiliated to Merkaz Haco-operatzia will be the first to be "hurt", for various reasons (reasons not given) they cannot publicly oppose this development. But it would be a mistake "to close one's eyes to the potential dangers" and Merkaz Haco-operatzia should be on guard lest this "boring" will destroy the existing WPSTS.

A delegate from a building materials co-operative noted that the Jewish Agency and other national bodies help and support kibbutzim but the WPSTS have to fend for themselves.

A vatik of the WPSTS movement would make it obligatory for all the workshops in the kibbutzim to affiliate to Merkaz Haco-operatzia.[56] This would make it easier for co-operative industry to compete with private industry. And it would eliminate competition between the kibbutz workshops and the industrial workers co-operatives.

This speaker also suggested that the representatives of Merkaz Haco-operatzia should sit on the management of such Histadrut-sponsored bodies like Solel Boneh, Yael road haulage company and Hamashbir Hamerkazi Co-operative Wholesale Society (see Book Seven).

A member of the Histadrut upper hierarchy questions "the moral and practical value of a Histadrut representative, uninformed and really not concerned with any WPSTS' troubles, appearing once or twice a year with the rights of a policeman. An honest man will refuse to judge the affairs of co-operatives after an annual visit to a general meeting".

He thinks that a decision of WPSTS to distribute the profits resulting from the use of wage labour is anti-co-operative and *de facto* vitiates the decision to eliminate all wage labour. WPSTS must be encouraged to plough in their profits. On the other hand, if WPSTS are obliged to distribute part of the profits to wage workers who have no liability for losses, the WPSTS probably would choose to operate as marginal concerns. Histadrut participation as partners in WPSTS will not help to eliminate wage labour and may even be harmful since the wage workers would not consider the Histadrut as a neutral party. The Histadrut's focal goal is to own and/or control factories and other economic undertakings. Therefore, it is not much less interested in changing wage workers into owners than in changing the owners of the WPSTS into wage workers in the Histadrut-sponsored undertakings which serve the interests of all workers.

> "The Histadrut together with the WPSTS, and also *vice versa*, jointly constitute a productive entity . . . they are linked organically, spiritually, economically and socially, this is the guarantee for . . . the ultimate creation of the Jewish Labour Commonwealth (Chevrat Haovdim)."

He did not object to the workshops etc., which kibbutzim establish, provided that reasonable precautions are taken against unnecessary duplication and competition, such as establishing competing bus and/or road haulage services on the same route.

And this speaker also accepted the principle that "every co-operative and every other Chevrat Haovdim affiliate (co-operative and non-co-operative) should give priority to WPSTS. But the WPSTS have to bear in mind that the Labour Councils in Haifa, Jerusalem and Tel Aviv must also look after the organized workers in the non-co-operative enterprises. There is no room for any monopoly. A WPSTS is or should be more than a partnership of workers; it is *de facto* an instrument of Chevrat Haovdim. And if, for instance, the labour force, members and non-members, in a certain WPSTS constitutes approximately twelve per cent of all organized labour in a respective industry, he thought that the respective WPSTS was entitled to, say, 25 per cent of the work in such an industry which the Labour Councils were in a position to distribute.

The secretary of the Histadrut's sponsored co-operative committee in Haifa objects to the labour council's bias in favour of organized labour outside the WPSTS and to the labour council's pressure on the co-operative tile workshop to join a cartel. He did not object to an agreement between WPSTS and other producers about quality, prices, and the elimination of destructive competition. But he was opposed to any combine which threatened the autonomous existence of a WPSTS.[57]

A member of Merkaz Tnuva's Central Management thought that the Histadrut (Chevrat Haovdim) should supplement its formal right to cast half the votes and its other rights at general meetings of WPSTS, with financial aid for co-operative education of the members and for training leaders, instructors, etc. Even if the Histadrut had the resources, he was opposed to the Histadrut taking over and changing the members and the non-member wage workers of the WPSTS into Histadrut personnel. Histadrut should activate its formal rights by appointing a qualified representative to participate in the daily management of Merkaz Haco-operatzia.

A Histadrut veteran notes that the labour movement in Israel, unlike the pre-World War Two labour movement in Germany, Austria and Italy, but like the labour movement in Belgium, established its own economic enterprises. First the Histadrut sponsored the kibbutzim and moshavim ovdim and later its own industries. This policy, he considered essential for the "establishment of a home for the Jews in accordance with the ideology of the Socialist-Zionist Labour Movement".[58]

A delegate representing a WPSTS in Haifa compared the suggestion that Chevrat Haovdim or another Histadrut-sponsored body should own all the WPSTS and that the members of the WPSTS should become wage workers, to the transfer of a patient from one bed to another as a means of curing him. The shortcoming of the WPSTS, including the use of wage labour, could be minimized if the Histadrut would require all of its sponsored WPSTS to join Merkaz Haco-operatzia and to carry out the latter's recommendations.

Another delegate said that

> "it would be more accurate to say that there are no relationships between the co-operatives and the Histadrut than to say that such relationships are bad. The WPSTS do not enjoy the rights of citizenship in the Histadrut. Tel Aviv is the host for the Congress, yet not even one representative of its labour council appeared at our Congress, yesterday or today. And I would be prepared to free them from participation here if they would only participate in our work, day in and day out."

Yet another delegate pointed out that since the conditions of work and the fringe benefits in the WPSTS were so much better than in the private sector, the Histadrut should show "understanding and appreciation and not confine itself to complaints that our affairs are not in order." Such criticism may be in place and even justified, if the WPSTS received from the Histadrut more than they gave to it.

A vatik in the Histadrut-sponsored co-operative movement said that resolutions cannot create co-operation or correct unco-operative practices or

> "force the early coming of the Messiah. . . . It would be possible to screen the types of WPSTS which should be established and the conditions for membership, if the resources (financial) were available. . . . But in Israel we are not in a position to do this. The urge to establish WPSTS came and must continue to come from within, from a desire to establish employment opportunities. The kibbutz also was created not because their members refused to be exploited by the farmers of Petah Tikva and Hadera, but because the farmers of Petah Tikva and Hadera did not wish to employ the Jewish workers. . . ."

All talk about Histadrut help for the WPSTS is theoretical because it does not have the several hundred thousand pounds which is required for this purpose.

A member of the labour sponsored co-operative committee in Haifa said that Merkaz Haco-operatzia did not initiate the organization of new WPSTS but were confronted with *faits accomplis*. "We only had to approve them and in some cases not willingly. When several WPSTS were established in the same branch, the market would not absorb the increased production of the particular products. Merkaz Haco-operatzia should have done more to co-ordinate and to prevent competition between WPSTS in the same branch."

The Fourth Congress of 16 June, 1938, directs Merkaz Haco-operatzia to continue its efforts to enlist the co-operation of the kibbutzim, moshavim, Histadrut-sponsored contracting institutions and consumers co-operative movement for the co-ordination of their factories with the WPSTS.

The Fourth Congress demands priority within the Histadrut economy and also insists that immediate measures should be taken to eradicate the hostile attitudes of some of the labour councils to the WPSTS.

The Report on the Activities, 1938-42, of Merkaz Haco-operatzia noted the expansion of the WPSTS movement except for the bus co-operatives which lagged behind the "needs of the Yishuv and of the labour community". The total labour force of the affiliated WPSTS, members and non-members, at the end of 1940 was somewhat less than at the end of 1937, 3,073 and 3,095, respectively. But non-member workers, 1,092, exceeded by 100 their number at the end of 1937. The bus and road-haulage co-operatives accounted for nearly the entire increase, while the industrial workers co-operatives reported a decrease of wage workers (from 320 to 214).

The secretariat hoped that this failure to grow did not reflect any tendency for the WPSTS to become closed co-operatives or that internal decadence had started, or that the WPSTS movement in Israel, like that in other countries, did not have good prospects. Were it not for the support of the Histadrut, the bus co-operatives, which *de facto* have a monopoly of the bus services, could not have become "a vital factor in the Yishuv".

Merkaz Haco-operatzia succeeded in its efforts to amalgamate into one bus co-operative the three affiliated and also the three non-affiliated and smaller bus co-operatives servicing Haifa. Seven inter-urban bus co-operatives, that were servicing nineteen routes in southern Israel, amalgamated into Drom Yehuda, which had been affiliated to Merkaz Haco-operatzia since 1935 and had joined the Histadrut in 1939. The Histadrut special transportation committee could only minimize but not eliminate the cut-throat competition between the bus co-operatives for Army contracts. Some members who left Egged and other bus co-operatives organized companies which competed with the bus co-operatives.

The report notes that in spite of the favourable conditions in Israel, such as good roads and inadequate railway freight facilities, the road haulage co-operatives, which at the end of 1940 were numerically the largest group of WPSTS affiliated to Merkaz Haco-operatzia, have not achieved a pivotal position and were the weakest group. They suffer "most from the cut-throat competition and inability to defend themselves". The report ascribes this unsatisfactory position to the following circumstances:

1. The country has more lorries than it can normally use. Vested interests, especially the sales agencies (most of which are non-Jewish), have thwarted all efforts to bring lorries within the regulations (i.e., subject to the same type of control) prescribed for bus routes.
2. The considerable difference in the standard of living between the Jewish and the Arab drivers.
3. The Histadrut-sponsored central transport office (Hamerkaz L'Hovala) includes also the road haulage service of kibbutzim and moshavim and individual drivers with their own lorries. It does not give special consideration to the road haulage co-operatives. Therefore, nobody found it advantageous to join the existing or to organize new road haulage co-operatives that paid their share of the budget and obeyed the decisions of the central transport office. A reorganization committee made up of representatives of the trucking co-operatives, Histadrut-sponsored agricultural settlements and Histadrut employment offices in Haifa and Jerusalem, recommended the Histadrut to sponsor the organization of a road haulage company in which Chevrat Haovdim would hold 51 per cent of the voting stock. This company would admit only organized co-operatives and other groups, and such individual haulers who organize co-operatives, or have joint offices for the distribution of work. According to the report, this recommendation was not accepted because there was a sellers' market. Furthermore, the road haulage co-operatives affiliated to Merkaz Haco-operatzia could not resolve their internal differences and present a united front.
4. Citrus exports had to be discontinued during World War Two.[59] Lorries were used for transporting half the crop of the groves to the railway stations and/or to Haifa, Jaffa and Tel Aviv ports. There also was an appreciable decrease in imports, which lorries transported from the ports to the internal markets. Road haulage co-operatives servicing the ports suffered most by the decline of imports and exports.

During the four years since the Fourth Congress in June 1938, there was no progress in re-establishing the co-operative restaurants which had been closed, mainly in the larger moshavot, because the settled labour force was too small. And the co-operative restaurants also could not give the same liberal credit facilities as the private restaurants. The report suggests that Merkaz Haco-operatzia, jointly with the labour contracting co-operatives and companies, must assume the responsibility for the re-establishment of the co-operative restaurants for which considerable capital is needed.

According to the report, the three co-operative restaurants, one each in Jerusalem, Haifa and Tel Aviv, "excel in the quality, freshness, purity and cleanliness of the food and low prices". And these play an important role in the feeding of the labour sector and the "wide masses".

The restaurants had unequivocally accepted the Histadrut's authority but this had not affected the autonomy of the respective co-operatives.

The restaurants in Haifa and Jerusalem, both organized in 1929, having labour forces (members and non-members) of 155 and 53 workers respectively, have expanded and modernized their facilities and improved their financial position. But the co-operative restaurant in Tel Aviv (organized in 1927) with a labour force (members and non-members) of 155 had to be liquidated and reorganized on different lines. The crisis through which this co-operative passed "was very severe if not the most severe in the history of the Jewish Labour Movement".

> "We (Merkaz Haco-operatzia) erred and it was a basic mistake to have been influenced by the boom atmosphere of 1934 and to have built and invested in the expectation that the boom would continue. We should not have permitted investments disproportionate to the capital and reserves of the co-operative restaurant. Basic improvements, interior and exterior, were essential, but there was no justification for such a big jump at one time."

Therefore in 1938, Merkaz Haco-operatzia decided that the co-operative restaurant in Tel Aviv had to be liquidated and immediately to register a new co-operative, "Workers Kitchens, Tel Aviv".[60] With the approval of the creditors to whom the assets were charged, the co-operative building, equipment, etc. were transferred to the new body. The report adds:

> "To our joy the new co-operative is developing very satisfactorily. We changed the administration and set up a new management which is subject to our direct instructions and supervision. There are grounds to hope that the new co-operative will atone for all its previous mistakes and stumbling blocks."[61]

The report notes that the secretariat was unable to exercise the authority which Chevrat Haovdim vested in Merkaz Haco-operatzia to appoint representatives on the management of its affiliated WPSTS. There were few volunteers for these appointments and only one of these who

> "considered this as an important function on behalf of the Histadrut and . . . is rendering valuable service". Merkaz Haco-operatzia Secretariat therefore must conclude that only full time paid staff can accept the responsibility to direct and to instruct the WPSTS in the spirit of the Histadrut and its sponsored co-operative movement. This would require an appreciable increase of the budget of the Merkaz Haco-operatzia.[62]

The report refers to an enquiry committee which the Histadrut appointed in April, 1940, to itemize all the Histadrut-sponsored industries; suggest measures for co-ordination and financing; and advise the Histadrut which industries the WPSTS should amalgamate, etc. Certain difficulties (no details given) made it impossible for the committee fully to carry out its terms of reference. When the Histadrut opened its central office for Histadrut sponsored industries on 15 December, 1940, which the committee suggested, it assumed that this office in the course of its actual work and experience would define its functions. The Secretariat of Seven of this central industrial office included three appointees of Chevrat Haovdim and two each from Merkaz Haco-operatzia and Hamerkaz Hachaklai. According to the report for 1938-42, the central office did not establish any new Histadrut-sponsored industries; or do much about centralized purchasing of raw materials and the marketing of the finished products; or carry out the decision to establish a fund of LP.10,000 for financing existing and new industries. The only practical accomplishment of the central office, according to this report, was the organization of a consortium of three Histadrut-sponsored financial institutions for financing industries. Up to the end of 1941 the consortium had advanced about LP.10,000.

The secretariat's report to the Fifth Congress of Merkaz Haco-operatzia, 7-9 April, 1949, notes that between July 1938 and March 1948, the number of its affiliated WPSTS increased from 72 to 150. And 112 of the 150 were registered during this period (71 since 1946). The membership of affiliated WPSTS increased from 1,931 to 4,186 but the number of wage workers employed remained practically static, 1,130 and 1,160 in 1938 and 1948, respectively. The shortage of manpower during World War Two, 1939-45, and the first few post-war years, and the increased pressure by the Histadrut, engendered a more liberal open-door policy by the affiliated WPSTS. Inflation accounts for part of the increase in capital and reserves (from IL.1.4 to IL.3 million) and in the annual business of the WPSTS[63] (from IL.451 thousand in 1938 to nearly IL.4 million in 1948).

After describing the development of the various types of its affiliated WPSTS in the different branches of industry the secretariat's report deals with the activities of Merkaz Haco-operatzia, department by department. A special department had arranged 20 new WPSTS for 300 veterans of World War Two and the War of Liberation, and for the admission of 300 war veterans into existing WPSTS. It also explains at some length, and emotion, why the special department of Merkaz Haco-operatzia, which started in 1949 to deal with the post-State immigrants (predominantly non-European), could not follow the usual procedure and screen the prospective members. And also why it could not investigate the need for and the probability of success before organizing a WPSTS in this or that locality.

"We are organizing manpower who have neither money, equipment or housing; or even a common language or other ties; and most of them have no trade. For instance we approved three co-operative joineries for new immigrants in Jaffa without having investigated whether Jaffa needs these. But we had to hurry and put these three groups to work to counteract apathy, discouragement and degeneration. We started three instead of one co-operative because . . . it is impossible to unite different ethnic groups into one society. Though immigrants from

> Poland and Yemen have lived in one community (in Israel) here for tens of years, there is still an impregnable wall between them." "Though fully aware of the fact that a certain locality is suitable for the marketing of the product of a certain type of co-operative, yet we have to establish this society in another place which is suitable . . . since the overall consideration had to be the backgrounds (needs) of the members. . . ."

The secretariat's report ends with the warning that if the Histadrut, the Government and the Jewish Agency will not demonstrate their interest in a practical way and provide most of the "millions which will be required . . . we will not accomplish the task". The secretariat's report also notes that all its affiliated WPSTS submitted for adjudication to a special department of Merkaz Haco-operatzia differences between their members; inter-society jurisdictional and other differences; and differences between WPSTS and third parties. The secretariat advises that these activities should be transferred either to a "permanent arbitration tribunal or to another body of this kind or to include these within the legal division about to be set up".

A delegate from a bus co-operative told the Congress that the relationship between the members of WPSTS and the Histadrut could be improved if the WPSTS movement had a seat on the Histadrut Executive Committee and also was represented on other Histadrut policy-making bodies that define "attitudes". Merkaz Haco-operatzia and others are pressing the bus co-operatives to amalgamate. It would facilitate matters if the bus co-operatives participated on those bodies which fix major policies and decide about their future.

S. Goren (Secretariat) at the second session of the Congress proposed that new and old WPSTS should integrate another 25,000 workers; of these, 5,000 members during the next two years to be distributed equally between existing and new WPSTS. He estimated the cost at IL.3 million. The 5,000 immigrants would contribute a maximum of IL.750,000; the WPSTS and Chevrat Haovdim IL.250,000 within two years (three-quarters and one quarter respectively) by increasing the capital of Kupat Haco-operativim by IL.1 million. The Government, the Jewish Agency and others must find the other IL.2 million. He asked the WPSTS to follow the example of the kibbutzim and the moshavim ovdim, and to provide the organizers, instructors, and supervisors who should volunteer for six months to a year. The new WPSTS must include some partnerships between co-operatives of workers and Histadrut-sponsored organs which should provide at least half the investments for each undertaking. Experience demonstrated the advantages of Kupat Haco-operativim, acting as the trustee for the Histadrut's participation.

A delegate of the Histadrut spoke at some length at the fifth session of the Fifth Congress on 9 April, 1949, about the unsatisfactory attitude of the Government towards the co-operative movement, and yet labour was the dominant and decisive sector in the Government. The Government's hesitant attitude is reflected in the platonic confused text of the several references to co-operatives in the draft constitution for the State of Israel.[64]

A member of Merkaz Haco-operatzia's Haifa regional office described the proposals for increasing the membership of WPSTS as impetuous and unplanned. It was not based on the premise that

> "opening the gates of WPSTS for the integration of immigrants is a duty which they owe to themselves and not to the new immigrants. . . . Accepting immigrants cannot be thought of as a contribution to somebody but as one of the principal means for safeguarding the status of the WPSTS sector in the country. Only if we use all possible means to expand the WPSTS sector can we safeguard the old and consolidated WPSTS." He warned the old and consolidated WPSTS not to be so arrogant and so sure that nothing will happen to them. At the same time he advised the WPSTS "to take the offensive and not to be satisfied with the scope of activities which they already have achieved".

A delegate from Haargaz asked if there was not a contradiction in the request to integrate immigrants and to increase the productivity per man hour simultaneously. The new immigrant is not technically qualified to match the productivity per man-hour of an old worker. It was suggested that a special fund, and not the respective WPSTS, should cover the appreciable potential operational losses which the marked differences in productivity between the old and new worker would engender, certainly during the initial period. He doubted whether the skilled workers would be attracted to the WPSTS if they had to accept the same pay as the new unskilled workers and the apprentices.

This speaker also noted the negative attitude of labour councils and asked whether other Histadrut bodies, co-operatives, the Government, the Jewish Agency and Solel Boneh would do business with WPSTS. Haargaz had found that although "the bus co-operatives" enjoyed a monopoly they were the most difficult customers. They were the first to oppose Haargaz, the only plant of its kind (bodies for buses, lorries, etc.). And Merkaz Haco-operatzia was alleged to be passive when the bus co-operatives "encouraged the establishment of a private firm" for the manufacture of bodies, and the labour council in Petah Tikva circularized all the transportation co-operatives to patronize this private firm.

A delegate of one of the largest co-operative joineries complained that Histadrut-sponsored bodies, like Kupat Cholim and Tnuva, did not give preference to WPSTS, even though their terms were as favourable as those of the private sector.

All delegates who referred to the question of the integration of additional members agreed that the WPSTS should do their share. On the other hand, they agreed with the view of the delegate from the road haulage co-operative in Haifa that "membership in a co-operative (WPSTS) is not a simple matter. This requires a considerable aptitude of adaptability."

A delegate from a co-operative carpentry said that the increased revenue of the bus co-operatives came from the 200,000 new immigrants. The same applied to those bus co-operatives with routes to the former Arab regions which had been converted into immigration communities.

A. Shatman (road haulage co-operative Emek Hefer, all of whose members are kibbutzim) urged that the main consideration should be the long range point of view and not immediate "profit and loss" resulting from the integration of immigrants.

M. Weisbrot replied that the security of the present members in a WPSTS must be assured. Since in the last analysis the WPSTS movement is responsible for every unit, WPSTS, it should decide whether to expand this or that WPSTS, and/or to establish additional WPSTS in a particular branch. It is unlikely that the WPSTS movement will approve expansion if the long range effect will be to endanger an existing WPSTS. Internal discipline within the WPSTS movement and within the component WPSTS must be strictly enforced. The individual member of a WPSTS must enjoy a reasonable standard of living, social insurance, security of employment, etc., but the WPSTS movement should decide on the disposition of all surpluses which are "holy and useful for the expansion. And under no circumstances should accumulated surpluses, reserves, etc., be distributed among the members." He favoured exempting WPSTS from income tax provided that the money be used for the integration of immigrants, etc.

The manager (member) of Achdut printers co-operatives considered it highly unfair to deprive the vatikim of their savings. He gave the following example. Two equally skilled printers arrived in Israel in 1923; one accepted employment in a large private press, "Haaretz", and the other joined the co-operative Achdut. The wages of the first were fixed according to his skill and he was "boss" of his pay. The printer who joined a co-operative received during most of the years only 60 per cent of the fixed wage because the co-operative needed money for new equipment, building and for other common purposes. The cumulative effect of these investments was to increase the real value of the share in the printing co-operative's capital. Why should not the co-operative distribute part of the increased value among the members.

A number of other delegates endorsed this view and suggested that the differences between the real (replaceable value) and the balance-sheet value of the shares should be credited to those members who "were the initiators and in a measure had risked their money." But a member may withdraw such credit balances only if and when he leaves or is expelled from the society.

> "While I am duty bound to make it possible for a new member to enjoy the same conditions of work as does an old member, I have no obligations to share with him the surpluses which I have accumulated during the several decades I have worked in the co-operative."

Several delegates at the Fifth Congress thought that Merkaz Haco-operatzia could point to relatively few achievements during the eleven-year interval since the Fourth Congress. The increase in affiliated WPSTS from 72 to 150 included nearly fifty societies that were six months old or less.

The delegate from Handasa (engineering) Co-operative asked why WPSTS account for only "several hundred of over 10,000 people employed in the metal industry in Tel Aviv?' And if the integration of immigrants is the overall plank, Merkaz Haco-operatzia should concentrate on organizing large well equipped and efficiently administered co-operative factories rather than small plants. He agreed, however, that it is more difficult to deal with membership problems in large industrial workers' co-operatives.

R. Shenkar, a Histadrut representative on the Merkaz Haco-operatzia Central Management Committee, suggested that it would be

> "more constructive to establish hundreds of WPSTS in the next two or three years than to continue the discussion about the social aspects of co-operation. . . ." He believed that "the time and the prevailing conditions will determine the role of WPSTS in building the country". He was sure that since private capital seemed afraid of industry, as it was of agriculture, that industry would develop co-operatively. And both from an ideological and practical point of view there is no place for another pattern.[65]

A delegate from Shachar (a bus co-operative servicing Haifa and the suburbs) considered it unfair to ask the WPSTS to carry the financial responsibility for integrating immigrants. This is the responsibility of the Government and the Jewish Agency. Is not a WPSTS more like a moshav than a kibbutz? he asked. But he had not heard that "a farmer in Nahalal or in Kfar Yehoshua has been requested to share his house with an immigrant.[66] The WPSTS also were ready to contribute their services as instructors etc., as do the members of moshavim. But they cannot assume the financial burden".

A delegate of an inter-urban bus co-operative who had served in North Africa during World War Two and in the conquest of the Negev during the War of Liberation, criticized the tendency to speak of the non-European immigrants as a lower species of humanity.

> "I have seen them in important posts as privates and officers in the Army. A couple of Moroccan companies participated in the conquest of Beersheba and lost half of their men. They wanted to remain in Beersheba and organize a WPSTS. But they could not achieve their purpose and they remained as wage workers and were exploited by the private contractors who established the undertaking which they (the Moroccan war veterans) wished to set up."

The speaker asked why Merkaz Haco-operatzia did not help in this instance and also in the case of an abandoned textile factory in Beit Dagon.[67]

Another delegate, from a war veterans metal workers co-operative, considered most of the talk about integration of immigrants as "double talk". He compared the attitude of the WPSTS to the bus passenger who shouts to his friend: "no more room". There was a decision that the affiliated WPSTS should accept war veterans up to 15-20 per cent of their total labour force (members and non-members). According to the secretariat's report, the WPSTS integrated only 300 war veterans.[68]

A member of a new WPSTS who arrived in Israel "a few months ago" and who spoke in Yiddish asked Merkaz Haco-operatzia "what it has actually prepared for the new immigrants already here, and for those who will arrive in Israel, to root them to the life of the country. . . ."

The most important need was for "one or two (people) to guide and to help new WPSTS to get on their feet". He also thought that at least part of the proceedings should have been translated into Yiddish.

A vatik replied that the immigrants who arrived during the first three decades found still fewer facilities. There was no Merkaz Haco-operatzia; the Histadrut was still young; employment opportunities were fewer, etc.

The head of the Jerusalem office of Merkaz Haco-operatzia felt that Merkaz Haco-operatzia was over-estimating the integration potentialities of the bus co-operatives and that it was not doing enough to foster the expansion of other WPSTS.

A. Reiss (Chevrat Haovdim) told the second session of the Fifth Congress that the Histadrut's domination of the WPSTS would destroy their autonomy. This was the main, if not the principal, stumbling block in the negotiations about the seven-point and later the four-point programme. He divided WPSTS into two groups. First are those that stress the

> "efficient organization of work and maximum profits . . . and have some members who are not even from the labour movement. Such WPSTS do not perform a public function and have no relationship to the labour movement and its goals". This approach is "to the disadvantage of the members because it does not engender a friendly attitude of the public to the WPSTS, which is so essential for their development".

The second group are WPSTS affiliated to Chevrat Haovdim, whose goal is similar to that of the labour movement, viz., to establish

> "a working people in our country and the Histadrut-sponsored WPSTS serve as an instrument . . . for the creation of a working people whose aim is to achieve . . . socialism. This approach enables the WPSTS movement . . . to serve the interests of the labour movement and to establish complete harmony . . . with the Histadrut. . . ."

Mr. Reiss did not understand "the apprehension . . . that the Histadrut wished to dominate the co-operatives' property". He asked them to give one example where the Histadrut, even in those undertakings in which it was a large shareholder and investor, had demanded profits or asked that standards of the working conditions of the workers should be lowered. But "on the other hand the Histadrut must be sure that the WPSTS movement will be one of the instruments . . . of the labour sector . . . for achieving the genuine independence of the worker out of conviction and not because of political considerations. . . ."

M. Weisbrot noted that the Histadrut had treated members of the bus co-operatives as "second class" members. More recently the attitude had improved and the general atmosphere was less hostile. He hoped that the concurrent supervision by Chevrat Haovdim would make special enquiries "from time to time" unnecessary. The staff of Merkaz Haco-operatzia are loyal to the Histadrut, probably the most loyal within the Histadrut, and it should be able to keep the Histadrut fully informed about the bus co-operatives. Since the WPSTS are as trustworthy as the members of other Histadrut-sponsored co-operatives, they, therefore, should enjoy equality with the other Histadrut co-operators." It was generally not accepted that those who organized and developed the bus transport system were just as idealistic and made as many sacrifices as had the "chalutzim" who "went to the village (agriculture)".

B. Lin (Chevrat Haovdim) noted that the natural desire to extend routes will continue to be a source of inter-bus co-operative conflict; the only solution is one central transport body. It does not necessarily follow that if the transport system were nationalized, the bus fares would be higher. The public will not accept the *de facto* monopoly over a public service, which the bus co-operatives enjoy, unless there is rigid public control over them.

He accepted in principle the need for the type of Histadrut supervision which Mr. Reiss of Chevrat Haovdim described, since this would minimize the potential failure of the existing WPSTS and contribute to the success of new WPSTS and their immigrant members. The supervision by the Chevrat Haovdim through its representative must be as legally binding on the WPSTS as it is for the other Histadrut-sponsored co-operatives. "I want, for example, that Chevrat Haovdim should appoint as its representative on the 'Dan' Management a member of this co-operative. If the representative is not a member of a bus co-operative, then he must study the problems of transportation."

The majority of the delegates, who referred to the problem of Chevrat Haovdim supervision, agreed with the formulation by the manager of "Dfus Hapoel Hatzair" (the second largest printing co-operative), who was also a member of the Merkaz Haco-operatzia Management Committee. He noted that the Histadrut has not yet acknowledged "the value of our movement". But now that the WPSTS understand that they and the Histadrut share common interests, tension between the WPSTS movement and the Histadrut has decreased. The main difference between a WPSTS of non-Histadrut workers ("not necessarily capitalists") and one of Histadrut members is that the Histadrut-sponsored WPSTS must and do accept public supervision. But the Histadrut-sponsored WPSTS cannot accept the unlimited authority of the Histadrut since this would destroy the *raison d'être* why they prefer to work as a WPSTS, i.e. "to live an independent life", based on practical mutual help and understanding; and receive reasonable emoluments plus maximum social security while working and later when on pension. The WPSTS can accept in principle the Histadrut proposal to reduce the entrance fees for new members (including participation in the respective WPSTS capital). But they cannot accept a directive which would deprive the *vatikim* of their rights to the savings (reserves) which a WPSTS has accumulated over a period of many years.

A small minority of the participants in the general debate supported the view of "give and take" proposed by the delegate of a war veterans metal co-operative who also was a member of the Merkaz Haco-operatzia Management Committee. The WPSTS ask the Histadrut for financial help (loans); for subventions to enable Merkaz Haco-operatzia to expand and intensify its activities, etc., and that the Histadrut should intervene with the Government about the income taxes which WPSTS are asked to pay. On the other hand, the Histadrut-sponsored WPSTS must accept real and effective Histadrut supervision. While acknowledging the contribution of the bus co-operatives during the difficult periods with the Arabs, World War Two and the War of Liberation, he asked the bus co-operatives not to forget that they have the Jewish Agency, the Histadrut and the Government to thank for the monopoly which they enjoy.

Another speaker noted that in those undertakings jointly owned by the co-operative of workers and a Histadrut-sponsored organ, there was friction between the old and the new members of the co-operative, and between the members of the workers co-operative and wage labour. That these conflicts have frequently resulted in "a crisis", he attributed to the fact that the fringe benefits of the wage workers were not as good as those for the members of the co-operative (commandite). There should be equal fringe benefits for all, but on the other hand the differential wage according to skill, etc., should be retained.

A delegate from Haargaz replied that there was no differentiation in fringe benefits as between members of the workers co-operatives and the wage workers. He considered a partnership between a co-operative of workers and the Histadrut ("through its sponsored institutions") "as the only equitable solution for the social aspects of co-operation, especially for WPSTS with hundreds of members . . . it was the only way for the development of industry and services on a co-operative basis worthy of the name. . . ."

He also gave the following reason why so few members of the WPSTS send their children to secondary trade schools. "Most of the members are only concerned with the financial position of their respective WPSTS and that they should receive a respectable severance allowance. They are not concerned with co-operation as a unique sector (cell) in the economic life and they do not worry about who will carry on after them. . . ."

A. Zabarsky (Chevrat Haovdim representative on the Merkaz Haco-operatzia Central Management Committee) admitted that except for the bus co-operatives the growth of the WPSTS movement was unsatisfactory. The situation could be improved only by replacing small WPSTS with undertakings owned jointly in every respect by a co-operative of workers and the Histadrut. This would ensure the position of the worker as an active partner and the "possibilities of developing both as a worker and as a manager". This also should make it easier to enlist the financial support of the Government and others interested in the integration of the immigrants.

The secretary of Merkaz Haco-operatzia in his closing remarks[69] forecast that the WPSTS movement would double both in the number of societies and in membership. He asked the WPSTS to use "Shituf" as their forum. The Council, a new body, should meet at least once every four months and serve as a good sounding board. In Israel, as in other countries, it is exceptional that those who organize new ventures do not lose their money. The undertakings pass through several hands before they become profitable. He noted that if funds had been available they could have acquired several large factories and converted these into co-operatives or into partnerships between private capital and co-operatives of workers.

The Fifth Congress, of 7-9 April, 1949, asks for the early enactment of the new Co-operative Societies Ordinance[70] and it is of the opinion that the obligatory affiliation of every registered co-operative to an audit union is basic to co-operation.

The Congress notes that it is the duty of every affiliated WPSTS to integrate its respective quota of new immigrants, and of war veterans, viz. not less than 25 per cent of the present membership. Members of the affiliated WPSTS are requested to volunteer as instructors in economic and social questions for the new WPSTS.

It asks the Co-operative Department to press for the immediate reintroduction of the income tax exemptions which WPSTS enjoyed up to 1944.

The Congress decides to refer the suggestion about the special privileges of Chevrat Haovdim in the WPSTS to the Merkaz Haco-operatzia Central Committee for discussion.

The secretary of Merkaz Haco-operatzia reported to the first meeting of the Council on 4 July, 1949 (elected by the Fifth Congress (7-9 April, 1949)), that most of the "80 new co-operatives having 800 members (immigrants and war veterans) already had been registered (report does not state during which period). There are under consideration proposals for the establishment of another 126 WPSTS. Merkaz Haco-operatzia had added a technical division, headed by an experienced engineer, and a statistical department, and it will establish a department for co-operative restaurants and hotels.

The negotiations with the Government about a special fund of half a million pounds for the expansion of WPSTS were without results so far, and there was practically no hope of obtaining any money from the Jewish Agency. The average participation of a new member in the capital of a WPSTS was IL.800-IL.1,000. Of this amount, average cash participation of a member was IL.150-200; Kupat Haco-operativim (from a fund of IL.100,000) advanced new members loans of IL.300-350 cash. This was inadequate and there was a real danger that an appreciable number of the new WPSTS might die of undernourishment. Until now, not one member of the old WPSTS had volunteered his services as an instructor for new WPSTS.

The secretary's report also referred to a decision of the road haulage co-operatives to establish a national federation to co-ordinate activities and decrease their rates, "even though from the point of view of maintaining a decent standard of living for their members this course was not simple". The road haulage co-operatives agreed to Government control and hoped that it would help them to acquire new lorries and equipment. The secretary also told the Council that Merkaz Haco-operatzia had resolved the jurisdictional differences between Egged and Hamekasher to their mutual satisfaction. Dan (Tel Aviv) was the only bus co-operative that had asked for help to carry out the reform programme which the Histadrut had suggested for increasing the membership (see Chapter Two).

The first speaker in the general debate expressed disappointment that Government and public institutions had not contributed their share to the special fund of Kupat Haco-operativim for the integration of immigrant and war veterans. Several Council members complained that the amount which the new members paid from their own resources into their respective WPSTS capital, plus the loans which the WPSTS received, covered only half the cost of the equipment which was actually needed for the additional members. Therefore, the WPSTS could not acquire all the equipment required for their integration.

The Council member from Haargaz thought that if the limited funds available were used for expanding older WPSTS, the amount needed per new member for equipment would be reduced and the WPSTS could integrate a relatively larger number of new immigrants.

The secretariat's report had not been circulated before the Second Meeting of the Council.

Y. Ritov reminded the meeting of 24-25 May, 1950, that the Fifth Congress (7-9 April, 1949) had approved a five-year plan for integrating another 25,000 members into new and old affiliated WPSTS at an estimated total cost of LP.15 million, exclusive of the participation of the new members. The quota for 1949 and 1950 was 5,000 each, and this first stage required IL. 3 million.

During the 17-month period since the end of 1948, the number of affiliated WPSTS had increased from 111 to 375 (in 55 localities) and the labour force, members and non-members, from 5,230 (3,810 members) to 9,330 (7,010 members). Of the 3,200 increase in members the post- and pre-State affiliated WPSTS account for about 2,200 and 1,000 respectively. Half the 3,200 new members were post-State immigrants; and the other 1,600 included 160 invalided and semi-invalided war veterans "who could not have been integrated into other work". Mr. Ritov told the Council that the WPSTS movement in Israel enjoys a

> "special distinction in the world co-operative movement" and "arouses astonishment and emotion because, unlike the WPSTS in other parts of the world, it has justified the many hopes that were placed in it . . . we now see with greater clarity, and have greater hope, that our WPSTS

in villages and in towns are advancing towards a socialist regime in Israel". The report emphasized that they are striving not for a communist world but for a socialist world which will give them "democratic and completely free democracy. . . . We see the development in our country only in terms of socialism. The aridness of our country, the intake from the diaspora (galut), the poverty of the community and because the country is still very young, compels us to be dependent to some extent on capitalist methods. But our clear aim is the elimination of capitalism. With all that is good and positive in communism we do not want a communistic regime which in practice has shown that it does not guarantee the freedom of the individual or of society."

S. Goren reported that the 3,200 new members in the pre- and post-State WPSTS paid in about LP.750,000 into the capital of their respective WPSTS. And three special funds granted loans amounting to LP.750,000-IL.800,000. The banks and the Histadrut-sponsored and other credit co-operatives were the major participants and the Government and Kupat Haco-operativim were the minor participants in these special funds. Mr. Goren noted that 95 per cent of the WPSTS that received loans from the special funds were meeting their obligations punctually and that tens of thousands of pounds already had been repaid. Because there was a delay of several months in establishing the second and third funds "many plans for establishing new WPSTS did not materialize. Some new WPSTS were destroyed during this interlude and still other groups who had organized WPSTS cancelled their plans."

In the general debate a member of the secretariat of the Haifa branch of Merkaz Haco-operatzia said "the resources of the funds have been used up three or four months ago. This has precipitated the discouragement which prevails among those who still wish to organize WPSTS and who in planning their budget considered this help."

The terms of the credits from these funds were the same as those of bank credits and the WPSTS ask for changes. These special funds did not grant facilities for raw materials, advances against stocks and for working capital.

The general trend of discussion was that the secretariat's plan to add 25,000 workers in the Histadrut-sponsored WPSTS movement within five years was "imaginary". Some questioned whether the WPSTS would integrate even 2,500 additional members annually, because the rate of immigration had dropped. ". . . It is not easy to combine those from the West with those from the East into WPSTS worthy of their name."

The secretariat's report referred to the impressive growth of co-operative metal and electrical workshops. For over a period of years these were unsuccessful and now they were "making a reality of a dream . . . to establish a position in this basic industry. . . . But they were just at the beginning of the long and difficult road."

Some of the largest of these metal and electrical workshops are jointly owned by Histadrut-sponsored companies and co-operatives of workers.

Merkaz Haco-operatzia was about to take over from the owners one of the largest plants for the manufacture of fittings, metal pipes, etc., and also was negotiating the purchase of one of the larger factories producing motors. An autonomous department within Merkaz Haco-operatzia looks after the technical problems and training, the purchase of raw materials and the marketing of finished goods, etc.[71]

The report classifies 12 WPSTS as co-operative restaurants and hotels.[72] The eleven affiliated co-operative footwear workshops with 109 members included the largest shoe factory ("Naalei Artzeinu") in Israel at the time (May 1950).[73]

Because of a slump in the diamond industry generally, the report noted that not all the co-operatives for cutting and polishing industrial diamonds with a total of 236 members were operating in April, 1950. The Histadrut was useful in taking over the diamond business since the co-operatives used a relatively large percentage of wage labour.

Since early 1950, the Government started to curtail severely all imports, including raw materials and equipment of all kinds. This threatened the existence of some of the WPSTS. The report wanted the Government to consider that the WPSTS, unlike many private enterprises, did not use devious methods to get imports. It also noted that the WPSTS were overlooked in the allocation of loans from the 20 million dollars earmarked for factories and workshops out of the first American Export-Import Bank loan of $100,000,000.[74] Therefore, they were considering sending a mission to try and raise money in the U.S.A.

The Secretariat's report also noted that the 25 affiliated road haulage co-operatives had 799 members. Nine of these 25 were road haulage co-operatives whose members were members of kibbutzim and moshavim ovdim. "Tachbura" is the central organ for these, while "Shelev" co-ordinates the activities of the seven largest inter-urban road haulage societies. Merkaz Haco-operatzia hoped that one central organization would ultimately replace these two and take over the distribution of the work between all Histadrut-sponsored road haulage co-operatives.

A representative of "Shelev" complained about the "anarchy" in road haulage generally. The customers fix prices, there is no effective control of spare parts and the supervision of the Merkaz Haco-operatzia subsidiary purchasing company, NOA, is both limited and weak. There is "no address" to which complaints can be sent. The Histadrut Executive Committee, he said, is no longer interested in the road haulage co-operatives.

A representative of Chevrat Haovdim described the statement of the secretary (Mr. Y. Ritov) that the WPSTS are one of the "foundations of the socialist society in the country as a wish and not a fact". He had not found in the WPSTS even a desire to assume this function.

> "At the Congress of consumers co-operatives I stressed the need for a more effective relationship between consumption and production, a relationship between purchaser and the seller." A WPSTS is not only "a place of employment" but is a "better and fuller way of life for the

worker . . . where he can benefit from the fruits of his labour", it is also "the duty of every member of the WPSTS to increase and improve the quality of his productivity and reduce the price of the commodities to their true value. The WPSTS must become laboratories for finding ways and means to carry out these reforms . . . set an example of reforms to the entire Histadrut-sponsored industry and the craft unions must learn from them. . . . A co-operative movement which cannot answer this call and carry out this task is far from being a basis for a socialist society."

A member of a bus co-operative regretted that the representative of the Chevrat Haovdim joined the chorus of accusers who have adopted extreme tactics (a campaign of exaggeration). The bus co-operatives have acquired their rights by their efforts and they started "in time of great stress".

Another member of a bus co-operative asked why the differences between the Histadrut and its sponsored bus co-operatives were considered more serious than similar differences which at one time existed between the Histadrut and its sponsored agricultural labour sector. He asked ". . . what are the obligations which we have not fulfilled? If there is a shortage of tomatoes, is the entire blame laid on the kibbutzim? And why do they blame us for the shortage of buses?"

The Second Council Meeting on 25 May, 1950, noted that some WPSTS had not integrated their quota of new members prescribed by the Fifth Congress, and ordered these WPSTS to do so immediately. All WPSTS were asked to keep their doors open for the integration of additional members.

The Council decided to study further the question of compensation for members and submit its conclusions to the next meeting of the Council.

The Council instructed Merkaz Haco-operatzia to make it obligatory for its affiliated WPSTS to comply with a request to second members as instructors for new WPSTS.

The secretariat's oral report to the Third Council of 12 September, 1951, noted that "there were sufficient reasons which forced us to postpone convening the Council . . ." and promised to convene a number of meetings in the next few months.

The 398 affiliated WPSTS in 63 localities had 8,019 members, 3,390 wage workers and 727 apprentices. Their global business in 1950 was IL.23 million, of which the post-State WPSTS accounted for IL.5 million. The business of the pre-State WPSTS in 1950 was double that for 1948. The oral report attributed the increase in the turnover mainly to inflation and a seller's market.

Since the Council Meeting of 24-25 May, 1950, Merkaz Haco-operatzia had organized and registered 92 and had liquidated 69 WPSTS. Another 20 WPSTS were in the process of registration. Some of the WPSTS were amalgamated "with the blessing of Merkaz Haco-operatzia".

"It was clear at the outset that many of the large numbers of WPSTS

> registered during a short period would fall. There are those who think that the percentage of liquidations are below the expected minimum when one considers the human material, the inadequate equipment and technical training of the new members."

The growing shortage of financial resources and of suitable quarters for the new WPSTS added to the difficulties.

The decision of the Fifth Congress of April 1949, to add 25,000 members to the WPSTS movement within five years, by a 25 per cent annual increase in membership, was now considered as unrealistic. In the 15 months since the Second Council Meeting of 14 July, 1950, the pre- and post-State WPSTS integrated only 800 new members. This included 650 probationers in the bus co-operatives whose final confirmation was uncertain. According to the Secretariat's oral report the greatest difficulty was the

> "fantastic amount for entrance fee . . . and share capital which the bus co-operatives ask members to pay. And the younger WPSTS are more extreme than are the older WPSTS about the high standards of skill they require etc. Our movement will reach a breaking-point, and the closed co-operatives will blow it up."

The report also noted that many WPSTS do not welcome the audit of Merkaz Haco-operatzia and frequently conceal information from the auditors.

The oral report also stressed the following developments in the affiliated WPSTS:

1. The conversion of the largest of the co-operative metal smelting workshops, Hamalchim, into a co-partnership co-operative productive society; Chevrat Haovdim, Kupat Haco-operativim and the co-operative of workers are equal partners (Appendix One, Chapter Two).
2. With the improvement generally of the market, the position of the seven co-operative diamond cutting and polishing workshops with 245 workers improved. These co-operatives found the visit to Israel of a delegation from the International Union of Diamond Workers as very useful.
3. A company was registered to centralize and market the finished goods from most of the industrial workers co-operatives and of some of the medium size private factories.

The Histadrut is again trying to establish a central purchasing and marketing body for all Histadrut-sponsored industrial undertakings—co-operative and others. The company organized for this purpose, "Hameshavek" (the marketer), and owned jointly by Chevrat Haovdim, the WPSTS and the kibbutzim workshops, was unsuccessful allegedly because it was too limited in scope.

Y. Ritov considered the Fourth Meeting of the Council of Merkaz

Haco-operatzia, of 8 May, 1957, as a continuation of the meeting of the leaders of the Tel Aviv and Haifa regions held on 15-16 February, 1957, which discussed the future of the WPSTS movement. The theme of his address to this Council Meeting was "Signs of a New Epoch" for the WPSTS. The secretariat did not submit a detailed report on the activities of Merkaz Haco-operatzia during the last few years, since this would detract attention from the focal theme: the developments of the WPSTS movement in the light of renewed immigration which has bolstered "their feeling that the movement is coming out of its depression". During the last few months, the liquidation of WPSTS was no longer an infectious and contagious disease and had dropped "to a more or less normal rate". While most of the WPSTS were consolidated and strengthened, there were still "weak and shaky WPSTS that require both internal and external bolstering. . . . Some of these may have to be liquidated." It was also probable that the Government, the Jewish Agency, the Histadrut and other public bodies would now grant the financial assistance which the WPSTS for some years have been asking. "This change is spurred by the realities which makes it obligatory to direct many immigrants to WPSTS, and not because their (the institutions, etc.) attitude has changed."

Mr. Ritov told the Council that because Merkaz Haco-operatzia had not yet defined the procedure for fixing the minimum amount which new members had to pay into the capital of the respective societies to which they are admitted, the WPSTS have not opened their doors to new members. "The isolationism is the greatest danger for the WPSTS, especially since this is tied up with the aging of the present members of the WPSTS and of their institutions. . . ."

Y. Eraz (Etziyon—Joinery, Jerusalem) reported that his co-operative was a successful amalgamation of three co-operatives, and other WPSTS could usefully follow this example. But the new co-operative cannot fully use their technical people and all the existing opportunities for work because they do not receive enough help from Kupat Haco-operativim.

S. Hadari (Ofir) thought that if the WPSTS had a greater say in the activities of Kupat Haco-operativim, this would facilitate the sale of its shares.

E. Hendel (Egged (Eshed)) reported that more recently they integrated 250 new members, and desired to accept more members. Chevrat Haovdim confirmed the amount which new members should pay into the co-operative's capital, but objected to defining such amount as the equivalent of so "many months emoluments paid to members". The Histadrut had not yet approved the procedure which Egged (Eshed) had fixed for increasing the efficiency of the driver and of the bus. On the other hand, the Ministry of Transport's subsidies to cover the operational losses were conditional on the bus co-operatives continuing with the present system of work.

A. Arazi (Choma)[75] thought that WPSTS could exploit the difficulties of many private undertakings if they could demonstrate their aptitudes to reduce production costs and to increase the productivity p.m.h. Choma is now in the final stages of converting several large undertakings into joint undertakings. The fate of thirty WPSTS is still in the balance. He warned against under-estimating the difficulties of influencing immigrants who were members of WPSTS abroad, mostly in Poland, to join WPSTS here, because these people are accustomed to the Government supplying the means of production and raw material, etc., and also assuming the responsibility for marketing. Therefore, these immigrants may be frightened by responsibility.

> "We must learn to understand them; get accustomed to them and to educate and to mould them to the conditions in Israel. They should be asked to assume the responsibility for management of the enterprise gradually. New organizational methods will be necessary."

He suggested integrating these immigrants into the existing WPSTS, large and small, and that these should be moved from the towns to the villages. New garinim for WPSTS should be directed to border settlements.

M. Shimonovitz (inspector of WPSTS—Co-operative Department) told the Council that on the basis of his enquiry about the liquidation of WPSTS, it appeared that about a hundred WPSTS could have been saved if they had been helped in time. Some of the relatively large number of liquidations of WPSTS were caused by:

(*a*) Inadequate attention by Merkaz Haco-operatzia to the organizational and social aspects;
(*b*) lack of co-operation and co-ordination between the WPSTS and the consumers co-operative movements, which led to the establishment of too many plants for the manufacture of the same commodities;
(*c*) the Histadrut not having insisted on co-ordination between Solel Boneh and WPSTS, thus competition in the manufacture of building materials developed;
(*d*) the Government's failure to help weak WPSTS. Some paid 30 per cent p.a. interest for working capital facilities.

Y. Borowsky (Egged (Eshed)) noted that the bus co-operatives successfully met the serious competition of the railways and the inter-urban taxi service because they

(*a*) pay equal basic emoluments to all members;
(*b*) have a considerable degree of internal democracy and
(*c*) have persistently integrated new members.

If the affiliated WPSTS had a well equipped financial organ, fewer WPSTS would have been liquidated. Therefore, the WPSTS should increase their financial participation in Kupat Haco-operativim by a IL. million. He would make it obligatory for all vatikim in the WPSTS to serve as instructors for young WPSTS.

Y. Maliskovitz (Egged (Eshed)) reported that because the operational costs have increased, the bus co-operatives persistently have operational deficits. The increase of the debts of the bus co-operatives by IL.5 million in the course of two years could be attributed to the admission of new members. Though the Government Development Department turned down their request for a loan of IL.5 million, the bus co-operatives built stations for the new settlements and admitted immigrants as members.

The Council Meeting of 8 May, 1957, decided to ask all affiliated WPSTS to admit the maximum number of new immigrants as members. And it insisted that Government, Zionist and Histadrut-sponsored institutions should make available to the WPSTS financial resources. The Council directed Merkaz Haco-operatzia to appoint a competent committee to study the integration capacity and to fix the quota of immigrants which every affiliated WPSTS should admit as members. It again called on the vatikim and other experienced members of the affiliated WPSTS to volunteer to act as advisers to new WPSTS.

Y. Ritov told the Fifth Council Meeting of Merkaz Haco-operatzia, of 2 March, 1958, that Egged (Eshed) now *de facto* has no contacts with the transportation division of Merkaz Haco-operatzia. For some years the Histadrut fixed, and the Ministry of Finance then accepted, the scale of emoluments for the members of the bus co-operatives. Unlike the position in other branches, Mr. Ritov alleged that the basic wages have not been increased "for a long time", and that this was really the cause "for the big strike in 1956" of the bus co-operatives. The bus co-operatives, and more especially Egged (Eshed) continued to press the Histadrut to approve an increase in the basic wages for members. Pinchas Lavon, the general secretary of the Histadrut, sent a cordial but very firm warning to Egged (Eshed) not to carry out an internal decision "to increase the basic emoluments of members if its requests are not approved" by the Histadrut. Egged (Eshed) Council "unexpectedly decided not to wait any longer" for the report of a new enquiry committee which the Histadrut proposed to appoint and on which the bus co-operatives would be represented. Egged (Eshed) and the other bus co-operatives had the right to appeal through the accepted channels against the committee's decisions. Nevertheless the Egged Council ignored a second warning from the Histadrut general secretary and all the warnings by Merkaz Haco-operatzia, and decided "on an immediate increase of basic emoluments" for its members. The Histadrut countered by carrying out the warning that it "cannot deal with any matters pertaining to Egged (Eshed)". Mr. Ritov noted "this lack of normal contacts between us and the Egged . . . from a long range point of view is potentially dangerous to all of the bus co-operatives . . . and, therefore, the conflict must be quickly settled." He said that the exclusion of Egged from the Histadrut's jurisdiction *de facto* "has destroyed every tie between it and the public". And the new transport authority[76] which must replace that of the Histadrut "will not be any better for Egged (Eshed) and for the other bus co-operatives in general."

A. Davidson doubted whether the other WPSTS if they had been treated like Egged (Eshed) and had been waiting two years for a positive answer to their request for an increase in the basic emoluments, would have acted any differently. Referring to the oft repeated allegation that the bus co-operatives enjoy a *de facto* monopoly, Mr. Davidson stated that their inter-urban bus co-operatives have a monopoly only on those routes which are unprofitable and which others do not service. On other routes, they have the competition of the railways and of limousine services.

A. Hochman wanted the Council "to decide whether Egged (Eshed) is wrong or right". And the Histadrut also must decide either to expel Egged (Eshed) or give the co-operative its full rights.

> "We want to respect the Histadrut and we do not wish to compel it to take a certain action. Other groups within the Histadrut—nurses, doctors, engineers—have 'sinned' but they were not excommunicated." Even allowing for their sins, the positive aspects of the bus co-operatives exceed the negative ("the light exceeds the shade"). "This gives me and the other members certain rights; one of them is the right to sin."

Zeev Onn asked to be considered only as a participant *a persona*, for he was not attending the Council Meeting "to impose the views of the Histadrut Executive Committee."

Mr. Onn described himself as a "chasid" of the bus co-operatives. He asked Mr. Hochman how one can establish a criterion for sinning. And how could Egged simultaneously pay retroactively an additional IL.50 a month to its members, and at the same time plead that it was incurring operational losses? There was never any talk about expelling the Egged (Eshed) members from the Histadrut. The only threat was that the Histadrut would discontinue all contacts with Egged (Eshed).

Mr. Onn also told the Council that WPSTS have and can play an important role by co-operating with the company for industrial development in which Chevrat Haovdim and the Government each invested IL.2 million and which, it was hoped, would attract another IL.20 million in loan capital. In particular, he called for "the goodwill and the unequivocal co-operation and understanding" of the bus co-operatives. Unless they make full amends for having defied the Government, the Histadrut, Merkaz Haco-operatzia and its transportation division (by paying to all their members a retroactive supplement) Egged (Eshed) and other bus co-operatives would be confronted with a serious crisis.

Y. Ritov noted that prior to the decision of the Council of Egged (Eshed) to increase retroactively the wages of their members, the co-operative's representatives declared that they would accept the decision of the public enquiry committee provided they would have the right of appeal. The night before the meeting of its Council, Messrs. Lifshitz and Onn of Chevrat Haovdim advised Egged (Eshed) representatives:

> "We will set up the committee. But we have to submit the question for a formal decision. And we assure you that this will be done."

This notice did not deter the Egged Council from making its decision. The enquiry committee was set up and Egged had the opportunity of getting out of the difficulty in an honourable way, by giving this committee its blessing; cancelling its Council's decision and discussing its claims with the public committee. Egged remained loyal to its tradition of disregarding authority and discipline.

Levy Kantor (Histadrut) disagreed that Egged (Eshed) had a right to sin and noted that none of the Egged participants in the debate referred to the suggestions made to them on how "to resolve the crisis". He refuted even the suggestion that the delay in appointing a committee to study the question of basic wages was due to "dilly dallying". Egged (Eshed) was fully aware of the debates and the differences within the Histadrut Executive Committee about this question. And Egged could not justify its decision to act on its own; especially since the Histadrut's general secretary had advised Egged about the appointment of the enquiry committee. What was being questioned was not the amount of the increase (IL.50 a month) but the act.

Y. Melamed called on the Histadrut, Chevrat Haovdim and Merkaz Haco-operatzia to bring Egged back "within the fold" so that they can "get on with their daily chores" of putting into effect the "reforms which Chevrat Haovdim in consultation with us has prepared".

I. Kitzis asked Egged to apply in writing for a joint meeting with the Histadrut Executive Committee and Chevrat Haovdim. Since the representatives of Egged admitted making mistakes, "it should be easier to find a way of settling the differences".

Y. Ritov told the Council that the Polish immigrants expect to receive at once permanent and furnished housing; employment in a factory or if in a WPSTS, they insist that their participation in the capital of the respective WPSTS should be the equivalent of only one month's salary and payable in 30 monthly instalments, as it was in the WPSTS in Poland. These immigrants do not wish "to hear about co-operation; they no longer believe in co-operation and generally speaking are "intractable".

It has been impossible to get any part of the million pound fund which Mr. Ritov insists the Government, the Jewish Agency and the Histadrut promised to set up to help immigrants to join WPSTS. The cost for integrating a member, Mr. Ritov estimated at IL.8-10,000. The joint fund would give a maximum loan of IL.1,500 for any individual on the unconditional guarantee of co-makers and provided that the borrower could match this amount. Under these conditions it required superhuman efforts to start 20 new WPSTS.

Mr. Ritov also told the Council: "Actually we have not advanced one step in expanding our network of WPSTS throughout the country. And we are in a much more difficult position today than we had anticipated." Unlike most other WPSTS "the bus co-operatives all these years admitted new members". Egged and Dan are enforcing Chevrat Haovdim's decision about the amount of the participation of new members in the share capital. (Mr. Ritov did not give details.) Hamekasher appealed against the decision. Two other old WPSTS—the Hapoel Hatzair printing works and a building materials plant (not identified) accepted ten and twelve new members respectively. "The fate of WPSTS which do not accept new members must be death."

S. Goren referred to the organization of commandites to assume the technical responsibility for the work in the plants which the industrial development company (and/or others) will own, manage, and assume the financial and commercial responsibilities. The immigrants from Poland and other communist satellite countries prefer this pattern because they wish to limit their financial participation and their responsibilities in general to a minimum. Mr. Goren added that he is not interested in the nuances of patterns. "We want to build a labour economy in which the workers will do the work and get the full fruits of their work and will manage and assume the responsibility for its growth."

He considered it as most unsatisfactory that the affiliated WPSTS integrated only 100 of the 71,100 new immigrants who arrived in 1957. The WPSTS have a real but last opportunity to participate in carrying out the plan to establish 600 new factories and workshops in the development zones, in which IL.500-600 million will be invested and which are expected to provide between 50,000 and 60,000 jobs. The first and unconditional requirement is that the affiliated WPSTS must translate into action the call of the preceding Council Meeting for vatikim in affiliated WPSTS to volunteer as full-time leaders of new WPSTS to be established in the development zones. "This decision must not become a fraud."

Mr. Lavi hoped that the efforts to organize new WPSTS in the development zones would not result in the neglect of the existing WPSTS, especially the medium size WPSTS "that are struggling for their existence and whose members are prepared, if necessary to forgo their salaries to prevent their co-operatives from disintegrating."

He asked that some of the new WPSTS be located in the Haifa and Jerusalem corridors and in Tiberias, Safed and Acre.

A. Razi, a new member of the management of the new Government-Histadrut industrial development corporation for development zones, suggested that the WPSTS

(*a*) must follow the general trend and start plants which require a minimum of 15-20 workers;
(*b*) accommodate themselves to the fact that the new immigrants include very few skilled people; and
(*c*) remember that the main reason why so many WPSTS disappeared was inadequate financing, short and long term.

D. Resnik attributed the present unsatisfactory status of the road haulage co-operatives to:

(*a*) Unfair competition of the railways which have a monopoly of all Government work. The road haulage co-operatives could accept these contracts at lower prices.

(*b*) The privileged status of Tovala which enjoys specially favourable conditions as regards foreign exchange for new equipment, etc., prices and credits.
(*c*) Lack of credits for longer periods than for 30 months, which the road haulage co-operatives need to change over to diesels. They were not asking for subsidies.
(*d*) Unlike the position in 1950-51 when the participation of a new member covered the full cost of a lorry, today the new members, especially immigrants, pay so little, that it takes the combined participation of six to cover the cost of only one.

Mr. Shimonovitz (Co-operative Department inspector for WPSTS) refuted the allegation that the main reason for the liquidation of such a large percentage of the WPSTS organized since 1952 was the unsuitability of the immigrants for co-operation. Inadequate direction and supervision by Chevrat Haovdim, Merkaz Haco-operatzia and the Co-operative Department, under-capitalization and insufficient financial assistance, were the main reasons. Compounded high interest rates probably would destroy many more, especially the small WPSTS. He also pointed to the lack of co-operation and co-ordination between the Histadrut's other sponsored economic undertakings and the WPSTS. He alleged that Solel Boneh *de facto* boycotted the industrial workers co-operatives for building materials and that Hamashbir Hamerkazi practically ignored the co-operative bakeries and the co-operative food processing projects. He asked what was the use of auditing the annual accounts for 1955 in 1958?

I. Rolnik (Namlit cement products) gave a warning against establishing new WPSTS in those branches where the existing societies had marketing difficulties. Generally speaking, competition between WPSTS in the same branch was undesirable.

L. Ezroni (Rases in the Negev) complained that this co-operative did not enjoy any advantages by being in the development zone. There should be instructors on the spot to teach the new immigrants, most of them from North Africa, the elements of co-operation. He asked were suitable methods used to attract people? The WPSTS of which he is a member, should have "40-50 members", and not six who are also having a hard time. The members do not even have a common language and need an interpreter. He asked why new and unneeded co-operative carpentry shops were organized in the towns, while there were many places in the Negev without any carpenters.

Y. Borowsky (Egged), and a member of Merkaz Haco-operatzia Central Management Committee, thought that the Histadrut's threat to expel the bus co-operatives and the reorganization imposed on Merkaz Haco-operatzia was wrecking the WPSTS movement. He noted that

(*a*) the representatives of Chevrat Haovdim on the Management Committee of Merkaz Haco-operatzia rarely attended its meetings.
(*b*) The dedication of their leaders had weakened. They belittled the achievements which, in spite of the "mistakes", were significant.

"Why have none of the old WPSTS become the mentors of one or more new WPSTS?"

(c) The rank and file of members of the WPSTS were inactive.

Y. Kretchmer (Dfus Achduth) noted:

1. Merkaz Haco-operatzia, like the different sectors of the kibbutz movement, should have an active and efficient planning department, to prepare a plan for every new WPSTS. Otherwise the WPSTS movement will be unable to exploit fully the financial and other assistance from the new industrial development company.
2. There was no useful purpose in organizing additional WPSTS since the continuity of the existing WPSTS is very doubtful because they were closed co-operatives.
3. The Histadrut department of dues and levies had allocated only IL.85,000 for Merkaz Haco-operatzia and larger amounts for other organizations whose members pay a much smaller global amount in dues and fees, relatively speaking, than do the members of the WPSTS affiliated to Merkaz Haco-operatzia.

S. Goren, the chairman of the division of industrial workers co-operatives of Merkaz Haco-operatzia, explained to the First Meeting of its Management Committee on 4 March, 1958, that the division would consider and decide all questions relating to the affiliated industrial workers' co-operatives and that these would have the right of appeal against any decisions of the division to the respective Histadrut organs. He referred to the Government-Histadrut-sponsored company, Teeus, for industrial development in development zones (of which he is general manager) and its impact on industrial workers co-operatives. In a large measure, the development and fate of co-operative workshops and factories depended on whether these can and will accommodate themselves to such changes in their pattern which the company may require.[77]

A. Tzwick told the Management Committee that Merkaz Haco-operatzia decided to support the establishment of the new company because they thought that this "would strengthen the WPSTS". Since this company no longer had its office in the Merkaz Haco-operatzia building he was worried that in the course of time the bonds between the WPSTS and the company would "become loose". He was also apprehensive that most of the projects which the company proposed to establish would be "administrative" undertakings, owned and run by the company or by one of its subsidiaries or by a partnership.

A. Razi noted that it was possible to change the administrative undertakings into co-operatives, as and when this was feasible and practical. It should be relatively easy to organize groups of workers within the respective undertakings into commandites.

M. Yavnieli believed that in the course of a year or two it should be possible to define the pattern of an industrial workers co-operative most suitable to the needs of Teeus.

H. Goldberg thought that one of the ways of promoting close liaison with Teeus was to second vatikim from the WPSTS to the company's projects in the "development zones", and for Kupat Haco-operativim and the new company to finance jointly all new co-operative undertakings.

B. Giladi had no apprehensions that "the company's activities will impair the WPSTS movement". But the WPSTS movement could disintegrate if it continued to display lack of initiative and did not take advantage of financial possibilities which the Teeus offers.

A. Levin thought that while it might be possible to recruit some vatikim in the WPSTS to work in the development zones, very few, if any, of the well established WPSTS would be willing to move to and/or start from scratch in the development zones. Financing was needed to bolster the pre-State and the new WPSTS in the cities and in the moshavot.

Mr. Benvowitz thought that some ex-members of WPSTS that were liquidated because of "social or economic difficulties" still "yearn" for co-operation and would be ready "to try their luck a second time in co-operative workshops in the development zones".

S. Goren noted that the Histadrut acquiesced to the request of the Minister of Commerce and Industry that the company's offices should not be in the Merkaz Haco-operatzia building.

The Teeus Management Committee of ten includes an equal number of Government and Chevrat Haovdim representatives. Since it is not the company's intention to establish only large plants and/or basic industries, there is no reason why existing industrial workers co-operatives, if they do not wish to move, cannot establish branches in the development zones.

S. Goren's opening address at the Sixth Council Meeting, 12 January, 1959, notes that "the skies of the bus co-operatives have darkened" and there is a question as to whether "in the light of the changes we will succeed in preserving the co-operative foundation. This depends on many factors and I do not know whether we can direct and define these."

Y. Ritov reported that 1958 was a critical year for the road haulage co-operatives; there was a shortage of work because of the increased competition with the Government-owned railways and the semi-Government road haulage company (mainly for hauling phosphates from the Negev). The affiliated road haulage co-operatives had difficulties in repaying short term loans which they had used for the purchase of new equipment. On the other hand, in 1958 there was a very marked improvement in the services of the bus co-operatives and there were very few complaints about queueing, delays, and the control of traffic.[78] He draws attention to the increase and improvement of bus stations, of the seating capacity of the new modern equipped buses, and most important the improvement in the relationships between the passengers and the drivers.

Mr. Ritov referred to the decision of the Mapai Congress in April 1958, about the changes in the ownership of the bus transportation services and to a later but similar decision by Chevrat Haovdim. The majority of an *ad hoc* committee appointed by Chevrat Haovdim, which included representatives of all political parties, supported the recommendation of the

Mapai representatives on the committee. The then Minister of Transport suggested that the implementation of the recommendation should be postponed for two years. If, during this respite, efforts to obtain an agreement for more public control of the bus co-operatives prove unsuccessful, the committee will resume its deliberations "along the lines of the Khoushi Committee's discussions" (see Chapter Five).

On 8 January, 1959 (i.e. four days before this meeting), Mr. Ritov noted, that the plenary session of the Histadrut Executive Committee reviewed the decisions of its small Executive Committee to confirm the Khoushi Committee's recommendations. The Government still had to decide whether it would take a 50 per cent interest in the proposed inter-urban Bus Transportation Company for the entire country. The municipal and other local authorities had not yet decided to participate in the two public bus transportation companies of the respective regions. What, he asked, will be the fate of the recommendations if the bus co-operatives reject the plan?

A. Tzwick noted that for some time the atmosphere in the Histadrut was not such as to encourage co-operation. "We have reached a low level in . . . our co-operation (WPSTS). . . . If we do not find ways and means of expanding and developing—complete degeneration is to be expected." He cited as an example of the negative WPSTS atmosphere in the Histadrut, the spirit of the discussions about the fate of the bus co-operatives, viz. that "if it is impossible to overcome the social and economic obstacles in the WPSTS movement, then we will liquidate it. . . ." While not denying apprehension about the many economic and social defects of the bus co-operatives he disagreed sharply with those who thought that the "excessive use of wage labour" was responsible for the Histadrut decision to abandon the bus co-operatives. He thought they could still successfully combat the plan.

A. Hochman insisted that only the members, and not outsiders who do not and are not obliged to know all that goes on within the WPSTS, can decide about their fate. The council is duty bound to advise the Histadrut that it is unequivocally opposed to the decision of Chevrat Haovdim.

B. Roznik criticized the Histadrut and the Government for having established the semi-Government transport company "Tovala" for hauling the phosphates from the Negev mines which has crippled several road haulage co-operatives, some of them operating "tens of years". Had the Government or some other body given some modicum of assistance to "Yael", the first road haulage co-operative to haul the phosphate, there would have been no need for Tovala.

I. Kitzis was certain that the Histadrut, if requested, would decide to postpone action and re-examine the question of the reorganization of the bus services. Otherwise it would be suicide and could not be mended later.[79] But the appeal to the Histadrut is conditional on the Council's unanimous decision to reject the Histadrut Executive Committee's decisions.

Y. Maliskovitz thought it unreasonable that the Histadrut's strained relationships with Egged should continue. Egged had repented and had undertaken to repair the mistake.

He asked the Council to confirm its determination to continue the practice of equal emoluments for all affiliated WPSTS, irrespective of type of work, etc. and not to permit the Histadrut to interfere with this policy.

A. D. Lichtman (Hamekasher) admitted that the Histadrut had justified complaints against the bus co-operatives. But it should "not throw out the baby with the bath water." A joint committee of representatives of the bus co-operatives and the Histadrut should clarify and take action against co-operatives that disregard the Histadrut's authority.

Zvi Lehman supports the suggestion to ask the Histadrut to postpone a final decision for "a year or two" about the reorganization of the bus co-operatives. But at the same time the Council, and in the first place the members of the bus co-operatives, must ask themselves "where do we go from here?" It is not enough to say "no" or to decide "to continue with the existing state of affairs". They must submit a constructive alternative proposal.

E. Hendel asks whether Egged "was the only body which has not accepted the unrestricted authority of the Histadrut?". And what has this to do with changing the co-operative structure. The Khoushi Committee discussed the question "how to change and not whether to change the pattern. How is it possible to discuss this question without first consulting us?"

The Sixth Council of 12 January, 1959, is strongly of the opinion that there is a real danger that the Histadrut Executive Committee's decision about the bus transportation system will create confusion in the entire Histadrut-sponsored co-operative movement in the State. Therefore the Council urges the Histadrut Executive Committee not to make any decision for the present about the reorganization of bus transportation, since all the possibilities of finding a solution acceptable to the WPSTS, and to the bus co-operatives in particular, have not yet been fully explored.

The council insists that the WPSTS should open their gates to new members. And it instructs the Merkaz Haco-operatzia secretariat to fix an obligatory quota of new members to be admitted by every affiliated WPSTS and to make sure that these quotas are filled.

S. Goren reported to the plenary session of the management committee of the division for industrial workers societies on 19 January, 1959, that in 1958 the division mobilized about IL.1·5 million from two banks and approximately another IL.60,000 from the Government Development Budget for "additional equipment" and other purposes required for the expansion of eleven industrial workers co-operatives. In 1959 they expected to mobilize about IL.600-750,000 from the Histadrut provident and pension funds, and to continue their efforts to increase from IL.145 to IL.160 million the working capital facilities for all the division's affiliated co-operatives.

He explained that during the three years between 1956 and 1958, the Government was interested in creating competition with the hope that the strong will survive. On the other hand, the Government during these years also approved practically all applications from bakeries for loans since it was interested in forestalling an increase in the price of bread.

Mr. Goren thought that the obligatory quotas of new members which Merkaz Haco-operatzia fixed for every WPSTS in line with the decision of the Sixth Council (12 January, 1959) were too small. He noted that every WPSTS is free to fix the amount and other conditions for the initial payments which new members have to make.

P. Globovitz noted the difficulties of integrating new members without precipitating "internal shocks". He suggested consideration of the question of new members after the immigrants have been integrated into the life of the country. "There are not a few instances of WPSTS which were destroyed because they had not carefully screened the applicants." Because industrial workers co-operatives "wish to avoid annihilation, we will object, even if sanctions are applied against us. Wage labour should be reduced but there is no need for a threat of sanctions."

N. Fein noted "that it is immoral not to admit as a member, a wage worker who has worked for the co-operative for ten years, and for the co-operative to continue on the basis of wage workers".

But it is essential to differentiate between integration of members and integration of immigrants. It is easier to establish new WPSTS for new immigrants than for the existing WPSTS to admit immigrants as members.

D. Kretchmer was disturbed with Mr. Globovitz's preference for sanctions to the admission of immigrants, especially since the continuity of the existing WPSTS depended on the admission of new members. But without the help of Merkaz Haco-operatzia the WPSTS cannot resolve the question of the initial financial participation by new members.

Y. Cohen considered the debate futile because "without the help of the Histadrut and the respective craft union we will not succeed" in integrating additional members.

S. Goren noted that on the basis of thirty years' experience with WPSTS, he had come to the conclusion that a large co-operative with many members does not crumble, while small WPSTS disappear. Merkaz Haco-operatzia can and will help and direct immigrants who wish to join WPSTS where they can get the financial assistance which they may need for their initial payment to the different WPSTS.

Zvi Lehman reported that one of the difficulties was that in the opinion of the Ministry of Commerce and Industry, about two-thirds of the 160-170 affiliated industrial workers co-operatives are producing commodities which are in "over supply" (such as clothing, shoes and packaging of foodstuffs). They are, therefore, not eligible for loans from Government development funds and/or the Bank of Israel. The division is examining 55-60 applications (other than from printing co-operatives) for about IL.1 million of loans. He noted that it was unfortunate that the co-operative printing shops, bakeries and workshops for building materials had not used the facilities for equipment which the Government offered some years ago.

D. Kretchmer replied that the Government did not approve the applications for credits from the printing co-operatives. He wanted a planning department to study and pass on all plans, including those which two printing co-operatives had submitted. Because the clients pay with six month promissory notes, the printing co-operatives urgently required additional working capital.

S. Bloch (co-operative joinery) complained about the Government's refusal to qualify the co-operative joineries for work on the low cost housing projects.

A. Frumerman (co-operative bakery) complained about the cancellation of an allocation of $80,000 which had been approved for their society. Yet, the metal co-operatives were eligible for capital investment loans from the Government development fund, though there is an over-supply of metal goods.

On 24 February, 1959, the division for bus and road haulage co-operatives of Merkaz Haco-operatzia convened a special meeting of its affiliated road haulage co-operatives to discuss "the crisis" described as mainly "financial". These co-operatives had used short loans for the purchase of new equipment to replace old vehicles, most of them dating from 1942 and 1943. The road haulage co-operatives need "a minimum two years extension" for their debts of IL.2·25 million to four financial institutions. Three years ago the Ministry of Finance approved a working capital credit of a half million pounds for the road haulage co-operatives on condition that they would not press their demand for an increase in rates. This credit will not be renewed and the road haulage co-operatives are now permitted to increase their rates. But in view of

(*a*) the keen competition for business, and
(*b*) the intention of the railways to reduce their rates on long hauls by 20 per cent and more, the road haulage co-operatives dare not increase their rates.

It was also reported that the Government-sponsored road haulage company Tovala and the Government railways, in complete disregard of the accepted ethics for competition, were expanding their penetration into the fields of the road haulage co-operatives. If the Government also carried out its plan to increase the price of fuel and licence fees for diesel lorries, this could lead to the collapse of the road haulage co-operatives. The Government was reported to have threatened to discontinue their direct credit of IL.500,000 unless the road haulage co-operatives agreed to the issue of the loans through the banks and linked to the cost of living index or in some other way.

"This demand is absolutely contrary to the character and purpose of the credit."

Mr. Shamgar reported that "for some reasons" the Minister of Transport had not approved the recommendations of an *ad hoc* Citizens' Enquiry Committee of the road haulage branch.

Y. Ginzberg complained that the Government encouraged them to introduce diesels and then decided to increase the price of fuel and double the licence fees (from IL.750 to IL.1,500) for diesel lorries.

Mr. Eshed noted that the Government rejected their proposal to appoint a standing public committee on road haulage.

D. Halprin suggested the appointment of two internal committees, one to try to minimize the competition between road haulage co-operatives and road haulage firms and between the affiliated road haulage co-operatives; a second for direct negotiations with the authorities in order to safeguard the interests of the road haulage co-operatives.

S. Peri attributed the difficulties of the road haulage co-operatives to the failure to organize the entire road haulage business, the Histadrut-sponsored and non-Histadrut within one framework. They should insist on the Histadrut

(*a*) taking immediate measures along these lines, and
(*b*) inviting the representatives of the road haulage co-operatives to any discussions relating to their interests.

E. Lifshitz noted that because of the competition in this branch, any threat of a stoppage of work is unimplementable. They should submit a memorandum to the Government asking it, *inter alia*, pending an interview, to postpone any new measures or restrictions. They also should issue a statement to the Press about the plight of the road haulage co-operatives.

The division for bus and road haulage co-operatives of Merkaz Hacooperatzia, on 24 February, 1959, appointed a committee of seven to meet and make representations to the Government authorities. If new indirect taxes (increased licence fees) were imposed the division should call a special meeting of the road haulage co-operatives.

S. Goren told the Seventh Council Meeting of 3 September, 1959, that since the Sixth Council meeting of 12 January, 1959, the number of industrial workers co-operatives had decreased from 153 to 137. In contrast, the labour force increased by 147 and was now about 4,200. Eleven industrial workers co-operatives were transferred to the division for service co-operatives; eight were liquidated and three new industrial workers co-operatives were established.

> "We were anticipating a large emigration from Rumania. We hoped that we would integrate many workers who would consider the co-operative way as a basis for their life in the country. Regretfully our hopes did not materialize. And we must take cognizance also of the appreciable change in our economy (i.e. of Israel). Realistically speaking the establishment of a factory requires an investment of from IL.7,000 to IL.10,000 per worker and we do not have such means."

Since the Sixth Council they had obtained IL.1·75 million, nearly all from the Development Fund and the Histadrut-sponsored industrial "Israel-American Bank". While "we obtained suitable financing for every plan for additional equipment and buildings, we have not resolved the problem of working capital".[80] Mr. Goren drew special attention to the very critical position of "one of our largest co-operatives, Hamalchim", which was one of the best for many years. Chevrat Haovdim asked Hamashbir Hamerkazi to take over the participation of Kupat Haco-operativim in Hamalchim and to become the majority partner and shareholder and to assume the management. This co-operative's membership decreased from 290 to 55.

Y. Ritov told the Seventh Council of the division for bus and road haulage co-operatives that

> "this year has been the most stormy and active in the life of both the bus and road haulage co-operatives. This is the only sector in the co-operative movement in Israel for which an external body fixes the emoluments for the members, i.e. *de jure* the Chevrat Haovdim Executive Committee and *de facto* the Ministry of Transport. The prevailing conception in the public and also within the (Histadrut) institutions about the earnings of members of the bus co-operatives are distorted. . . ."

The Ministries of Finance and of Transport, dissatisfied with the findings of the Chevrat Haovdim *ad hoc* committee and also the Bar Tal wage committee (see Chapter Five) appointed a new *ad hoc* committee (Solomon Committee) which, after many months of deliberations, recommended a graded scale of emoluments for the members of the bus co-operatives. Merkaz Haco-operatzia and the Ministry of Transport may audit, control, and check separately and/or jointly, the cost calculations of the bus fares, a most troublesome question which led to a complete stoppage of bus services (except Jerusalem) three years ago. Because Government subsidies cover the difference between the official and the actual bus fare, the bus co-operatives seem indifferent to the cost calculations and complained "that the subsidies are demoralizing for the members". But there was a potential danger of a serious crisis when the Government discontinued its subsidies. It would also be difficult to increase appreciably the bus fares at one time.

Because of the high rate of traffic accidents in the country,[81] the insurance companies increased the rates for third party insurance. Therefore, the Egged (Eshed) and Dan bus co-operatives jointly arranged their own internal third party insurance. The preliminary reports indicate that thus far the costs were lower than the scale of premiums which the insurance companies charged.

Y. Ritov noted that, generally speaking, there is complete anarchy in the road haulage co-operatives, intensified by the introduction of very large lorries, including three of 40 tons, and also by the increased competition of the Government railway system, and of the semi-Government road haulage company, "Mifalei Tovala". Allegedly, this company had priority for the import of the best lorries on the most convenient terms. Mr. Ritov also referred to the competition with citrus growers, who either use or hire out their lorries during the summer for general haulage. Other "industrialists" including Solel Boneh, also used their lorries for general haulage. Unlike the bus services, there were no regulations about routes, etc. for the road haulage services. Immigrants brought their capital to Israel in the form of lorries and then used these to earn their livelihood. Mr. Ritov noted that the one ray of light was the decision of the banks to prolong by four years the amortization period of about IL.3 million of debts of the road haulage co-operatives. He was optimistic about getting some relief for the road haulage co-operatives from the recent increases in direct and indirect Government taxes.

M. Steinberg (Haargaz) wanted a thorough study of the reasons for the failure of Hamalchim. The use of wage labour could not be the main or only reason since other WPSTS used wage labour without this affecting their economic and financial position. In spite of the modern buildings, equipment and a plentiful supply of work, the productivity of Hamalchim was very low. He was sure that this fall in productivity had developed gradually, but the group dealt with the manifestations too late.

M. Lavi (Merkaz Haco-operatzia) reported that during the last two years the number of lorry drivers in Israel had increased to 18,000. Anybody with IL.1,500 could start a road haulage business. "Tovala (a semi-Government road haulage company) receives unlimited import licences and foreign exchange for the import of new lorries. Though these are intended for transporting the products of the mines in the Negev . . . we know only too well that Tovala also is increasingly penetrating into the general field of road haulage."

He wanted Israel to introduce licensing for commercial road transport similar to that in the U.S.A.

S. Goren, opening the Eighth Council, of 29 September, 1959, noted that most of the WPSTS did not qualify for help from the Government Development Fund because they were not on the list of eligible branches. "Most of our industrial workers co-operatives still are small and medium size workshops." Only Kupat Haco-operativim, which during the last year received only IL.72,000 from the Histadrut, could help these. He reiterated that the Histadrut did not keep its promise to match pound for pound subscriptions for share capital which Kupat Haco-operativim would raise. The Histadrut subscribed only IL.10,000 against the IL.300,000 which Kupat Haco-operativim raised in the last few years. And he confirmed that they cannot find the new immigrants to organize WPSTS that would qualify for loans from the new Government-Histadrut industrial development company. When this company was organized,

> "I asked for a list of ten WPSTS that were 'choked' because they had insufficient funds and that were ready to move to the development zones. There was one response and even in this case the members changed their minds." (Zvi Lehman intervened and said that Teeus, the Government-Histadrut-sponsored company for industrial development, changed its mind). "Give us the garinim and Teeus will supply the means," Mr. Goren replied.

The company was also prepared to turn over the enterprises which it had established and which were more or less consolidated, to Histadrut-sponsored and non-sponsored WPSTS.

I. Kitzis reported that the attitude of some people in Chevrat Haovdim towards WPSTS had improved. But the staffs of the Histadrut and of the local labour council still did not consider the WPSTS as "an integral part of the Histadrut economy and enjoying the same status as the other Histadrut-sponsored co-operative sectors".

M. Weisbrot (Teeus) noted that the moment the Histadrut was asked to translate lip service for the WPSTS into action, "their attitude and opinion immediately changes".

D. Reznick complained that the Histadrut no longer gave the road haulage co-operatives the same degree of help, and generally "treats the WPSTS as step-children".

Y. Antin (Hanamal Hachadash) described the discussions at Council meetings as a continuous round of "vicious circles". There seemed to be no time for a thorough discussion of the pivotal question of how to achieve co-operation.

Y. Ben-Dror (Co-operative Department) noted that the research department of the Ministry of Labour had been requested "to analyse the economic, social and organizational reasons which spurred the liquidation of WPSTS".

The council, on 29 September, 1959, demanded the Government and/or the Histadrut organs to refrain from introducing changes in the activities and management of the bus co-operatives without the full co-operation of the respective bus co-operatives and of Merkaz Haco-operatzia.

The Council called on the authorized Government and Histadrut bodies to take immediate measures to improve the state of the road haulage branch "and to direct its future development on healthy foundations".

S. Goren opening the meeting of the division for industrial workers co-operatives of Merkaz Haco-operatzia, of 21 May, 1960, stressed the importance of raising the standard of productivity of the industrial workers co-operatives to that accepted in the country. As a first step, the equipment of the co-operative workshops must be as good as that of the "private and of the Histadrut-sponsored industry. . . . In the last two years Merkaz Haco-operatzia actually had to force the industrial workers co-operatives to raise their technological standards. Long term financing was available but not a few of the affiliated industrial workers co-operatives . . . ignored (evaded) the directive about this question."

One of the conditions of those providing capital investment funds was that the respective co-operatives must provide part of the investment funds by increasing their capital. This intensified a member's interest in higher productivity and improved quality. Mr. Goren thought that the use of wage labour also was closely related to the question of modernization and to stimulating a member's consciousness of productivity. The contraction of wage labour must be a condition for the approval of long term consolidation and modernization loans.

Zvi Lehman considered the recent increase of joint labour-management production councils in the Histadrut-sponsored administrated industry as a "decisive step in the direction of the co-operative horizon". Barring the lack of financial assistance it would be possible to consolidate most of the industrial workers co-operatives that have attained a standard of productivity at least equal to that of non-co-operative industry in the country. And "sometimes we are called on to save private undertakings which have collapsed because of bad management and low productivity. And we have proved in certain cases (names given) that we reorganized these into industrial workers co-operatives, whose management progressively improved." The consolidation of existing industrial workers' co-operatives will stimulate their expansion and encourage them to accept as members their senior wage workers, immigrants and youth.

Mr. Meduyak (book binding co-operative) said that he cannot understand why some Histadrut-sponsored bodies preferred to use and buy from non-co-operative undertakings. He suggested that Chevrat Haovdim designate one organ to centralize orders for merchandise, which the Histadrut and its sponsored organizations required, and distribute the orders among Histadrut-sponsored undertakings, including co-operatives.

M. Ofner said that the lack of interest in WPSTS is in line with the "times". Merkaz Haco-operatzia and others could do nothing to counter the stark reality "that it is difficult to carry on economic experiments on a co-operative basis. I doubt whether a steel rolling mill or a new Solel Boneh can be established on co-operative principles."

Y. Winterstein (Oz-On—metal and electrical co-operative) reported that their co-operative had increased its turnover to half-a-million pounds. But it could not obtain sufficient working capital because it was unable to meet the banks' conditions about collateral security. He cited another co-operative whose imminent bankruptcy could be prevented if other WPSTS would buy from this co-operative its finished products which they need.

Zvi Lehman reported that during 1958-59 the division arranged long term loans of over IL.2·6 million for some of the affiliated workers co-operatives that invested IL.1·5 million of their own resources. Practically every industrial workers co-operative that submitted "a reasonable plan" received the necessary finances. The division saved affiliated bakeries and food products co-operatives from collapse. Were it not for the modern equipment which the division helped the printing co-operatives to acquire, these would have become "second or third rate plants". Mr. Lehman gave several examples of industrial workers co-operatives that had become leaders in their respective branches. On the other hand "not a few industrial workers co-operatives were weakened and then liquidated because they did not have managers or efficient management".

Most industrial workers co-operatives had not yet realized that modernized management is as important as money, equipment and raw materials. He cited several co-operative workshops that received very adequate financial help but failed because their management was unsatisfactory.

Mr. Lehman also reported that the annual business of the affiliated industrial workers co-operatives in 1960 would amount to about IL.57

million, an increase of IL.6-7 million over 1959. According to accepted standards, an industrial workers co-operative needs a working capital equivalent to two months' turnover. Actually, the affiliated industrial workers co-operatives had only 20-25 per cent of the amount which they need for working capital. "The stringency in working capital is endangering the existence of several plants and preventing many from achieving profitability. . . . We must find a remedy for this problem."

Y. Yudelevitz (Choma, building materials) reported that they have been using their new machine for only eight months. Yet, to be competitive, they ordered a new type of machine which, with the same labour force in the same number of hours, produced double the quantity as their present equipment. And "we have no other recourse than to pay usurious interest rates" for loans to purchase the new machines. Members had to increase their working day to twelve hours in order to pay the interest and amortization charges.

Arieh Tzwick on 6 June, 1959, reported that at the end of 1959 the division for service co-operatives, encompassed 54 consumer service co-operatives with 923 members and 629 wage workers and apprentices. The two largest groups of service co-operatives were

(*a*) twelve societies for the distribution of meat, ice and paraffin, which had 354 members and 46 wage workers and apprentices;

(*b*) eight societies, for the excavation and distribution of gravel and loose earth, etc., had 196 members and 105 wage workers and apprentices.

Three co-operative restaurants had 181 wage workers, and only 50 members. Mr. Tzwick noted that "recently, a number of service co-operatives received loans from the Histadrut-sponsored Industrial Bank Israel-America, and from other financial bodies". But, generally speaking, in the allocation of loans for consolidation and expansion, the bias against the service co-operatives continued. The division held applications for IL.750,000 from 16 service co-operatives for consolidation and expansion, and he anticipated applications from 30 more affiliated service co-operatives for IL.750,000.

During the last year the division arranged for twelve conferences and 92 general meetings, and made "hundreds of visits" to its affiliated co-operatives. The division continued to urge its service co-operatives to admit more members and "to eliminate all wage labour". He hoped for a further improvement in social cohesion and internal member relationships, which to no small degree depended on an improvement of their unsatisfactory economic position.

M. Lavi thought that the service co-operatives more than the industrial workers co-operatives needed advice on how to improve management and how to increase their efficiency and productivity.

S. Stenger (Chevrat Haovdim) said that Chevrat Haovdim, jointly with the Ministry of Commerce and Industry, the Histadrut-sponsored Industrial Bank Israel-America and the WPSTS, would establish a joint fund for the consolidation of all types of WPSTS. This, he hoped, would "facilitate the admission of wage workers as members of service co-operatives".

S. Goren added that the new joint Government-Histadrut Industrial Development Fund excluded service co-operatives such as distributors of paraffin, meat and ice. While Kupat Haco-operativim would continue to help all types of WPSTS, "we are unable to retain WPSTS in which the wage workers exceed the number of members".

D. Lipman (Chof-Yam, excavation and distribution of gravel, etc.) pleaded for assistance for the renewal of their licences and concessions for excavation. The co-operatives were told that the source of gravel is "thinning out". On the other hand concessions were awarded to "newcomers" in this branch.

A. Yerushalmi (Imun—Tel Aviv-Jaffa port tally clerks) wanted a more aggressive and active Management Committee elected for the division for service co-operatives.

A. Grunwald (Delek—distribution of paraffin) told the meeting that in spite of their extraordinary efforts, the society could not consolidate its position or expand unless Merkaz Haco-operatzia helped them to obtain adequate financing.

The division for service co-operatives on 6 June, 1960, instructed the Secretariat of Merkaz Haco-operatzia to work for an increase in the capital of Kupat Haco-operativim and also to establish as a subsidiary or ancillary to Kupat Haco-operativim a special fund earmarked for increasing the membership of the existing service co-operatives and for increasing the number of service societies. The industrial workers and the service co-operatives should mobilize IL.250,000 for this special fund and this would encourage Chevrat Haovdim and others also to participate.

The division for service co-operatives instructs its Management Committee to redouble its efforts to expand this sector and to enlist the help of Government and Histadrut-sponsored bodies, such as the Workers' Bank and the Israel-America Bank. The division demands that in the allocation of funds for consolidation and expansion, its affiliated co-operatives should enjoy "a status equal to that of the industrial workers co-operatives".

Zvi Lehman (Shituf, January-February 1961, pp. 12-13) wrote about the consolidation during the three years from 1958 to 1960, of 89 or two-thirds of all affiliated industrial workers co-operatives. These 89 provided between 30 and 60 per cent of the capital investments required for their new equipment, the expansion and improvement of existing accommodation and the construction of new quarters, improving the quality of products, and increasing their exports. The 89 industrial workers co-operatives borrowed IL.4·8 of about IL.9·5 million which they invested in these three years. Of this IL.4·8, IL.1·7 million was borrowed from Chevrat Haovdim sponsored organs, and IL.3·1 million from the Government. About 40 industrial workers co-operatives have not received any help, "and their future is doubtful. . . ."

According to Mr. Lehman the question of wage labour in the co-operative workshops and factories was basic and not transitional or seasonal. The Histadrut was especially concerned with the difference in the working conditions between the employers (members) and wage workers in its sponsored WPSTS. This difference created a "barricade" between the members and the wage worker.

> "And there is no doubt that a member of an industrial workers co-operative is more painstaking about the maintenance and maximum exploitation of the equipment than is the wage worker. . . . Yet there are not a few of the good members, especially vatikim, who have their reservations about the (above) logical conclusions. These members have aged and are tired, it is easier and more convenient to continue with the past (practice) than to start the revolution. . . ."

The WPSTS movement must continue to press for the mechanization and modernization of the existing co-operative workshops and simultaneously press the Histadrut to increase the number of co-operative plants and their "economic help" for these.

Abraham Daniel (Shituf, January-February 1961, pp. 14-15) writes that the department for service co-operatives in Merkaz Haco-operatzia was fully alive to the potential effects on their affiliated co-operatives of the following two conflicting and contradictory trends. With the expansion of the State economy, new and modern services had sprouted, such as public relations, mechanization of offices, etc. Co-operative services societies that were not attuned to these developments had disappeared. Co-operatives' servicing of the ports, mechanization of office procedure, and art and education accounted for the slight increase in the affiliated service co-operatives during the last two years. On the other hand, a number of the old service co-operatives, especially those for the distribution of meat and gravel, had been seriously impaired and there was a real danger that they would disappear. The organization and establishment of the new type of service co-operatives "is not a bed of roses". The department has had to take over the administration of some of the new service co-operatives because they

> "have not yet learned to stand on their own feet" and require more than the usual (customary) attention. And "it is with regret" that he notes the fact that "an appreciable number of the members" of the service co-operatives have not yet recognized the need and importance of specialization and of improvement of the services which the new era requires.

Mr. Daniel noted that the affiliated service co-operatives had about 1,000 members and 500 wage workers; "from the point of view of numbers, wage labour is not a serious problem". But the wage workers preferred to push their claims for higher wages rather than their admission as members. Because of the unique character of the different kinds of service co-operatives, he thought that they must deal with the question of wage labour "on a case to case basis". But the only way to counter the aging of the members in the service co-operatives was to integrate new members.

The financial institutions appeared very apprehensive and uncertain about "the vital need of the service co-operatives". It was thought that these had more financing difficulties than the other types of WPSTS. "About 80 per cent of their requests are for financing expansion and consolidation and 20 per cent are for working capital.

APPENDIX ONE

Kupat Haco-operativim

ANNUAL AUDITED BALANCE SHEET 31 DECEMBER, 1963.

Assets		IL.
Cash and Banks		29,890
Bills Receivable		48,540
Accounts Receivable (includes IL.24,141 from subsidiaries)		255,307
Loans, Discounts and other Accounts		
WPSTS and others	1,670,154	
Affiliated Companies	259,922	1,930,076
Investments and Fixed Assets		
Subsidiaries	241,711	
Haargaz (includes additional evaluation of shares IL.4,695,000)	5,384,000	
Affiliated Companies & others	454,337	
Securities	180,826	
Land (jointly with others)	3,700	
Payments & participation in a Building	59,306	
F. and F.		6,317,891
Expenses in Advance		87,760
Guarantees Outstanding		3,266,760
Total Assets		11,936,224
Liabilities		
Share Capital (Fully Paid)		1,421,336
Payments a/c Shares Subscribed		135,102
Revaluation of Haargaz Shares		5,140,000
Reserve Fund		8,605
Other Funds		93,033
		6,798,076
Debits & Losses Carried Forward		
Loss for BG. 31 December 1962	108,041	
Profit for 1961	16,969	91,072
		6,707,004
Loan for Earmarked Deposits		1,919,102
Guarantees		3,266,765
Demand Liabilities		43,258
Total Liabilities		11,936,229

APPENDIX TWO

NOA Ltd.

At the Fourth Congress on 16 June, 1938, the transport co-operatives expressed dissatisfaction with the company, Noa, Ltd., which they and Merkaz Haco-operatzia had established in 1934 for the centralized purchase of fuel, tyres and spare parts. Some delegates said that Noa had contracted for purchases "without adequate detailed investigation and sufficient know-how". Some of the transport co-operatives had not honoured their undertakings, and this was detrimental to the prestige of the WPSTS movement.

Another delegate replied that centralized purchasing can succeed only if the transport co-operatives purchase large quantities and unequivocally honour their undertakings and are loyal to their company, Noa. The critics forgot or disregarded the difficulties in organizing Noa and that the affiliated WPSTS object to and resist the use of force or even of pressure.

The delegates of the co-operative bakeries alleged that Merkaz Haco-operatzia considered as "unrealistic" (imaginary) the proposal to centralize the purchase of flour, which accounted for 60 per cent of the costs for all of its affiliated bakeries. This was an inexcusably short-sighted approach.

The report of Merkaz Haco-operatzia for 1938-42 noted that Noa, the central purchasing organ for the affiliated transport co-operatives, continued to contract for petrol and oil and to act as their purchasing agent for equipment, tyres and spare parts, which the co-operatives ordered. In the autumn of 1939, Noa placed a large order for spare parts which the transport co-operatives wished to stock. These paid 15 per cent cash when ordering and the balance was to be paid on delivery. Because Noa also stocked spare parts which the transport co-operatives did not specifically order, the report notes, "there were doubters because they (i.e. the transport co-operatives) thought that they would be compelled to buy . . . spare parts which they did not need and to pay more than the market prices". The report (for "various reasons") has no data about the extent of Noa's business. And the reader is asked to judge the volume of business done from a table giving the expenditures of the transport co-operatives during each of the years 1934-42 for fuel, oil, spare parts, tyres and equipment. The total was over LP.217 million. "Psychological obstacles" are mentioned as the principal reason for the relatively static volume of the company's business during the first six of the eight years. Petrol accounted for LP.1·8 million and equipment about three-quarters of a million pounds of Noa's business.

Noa thought that it would be possible to purchase equipment direct from the manufacturers instead of through their agents in Israel, provided it could centralize relatively large orders and reduce the number of makes of buses, lorries and cars to five or six. All preparations had been completed for Noa's agent to proceed to the U.S.A. to meet manufacturers when World War Two started. The report notes that it was "a stroke of luck" that the Government decided to become the importer of all equipment.

A member of the Merkaz Haco-operatzia Secretariat told the council of Merkaz Haco-operatzia on 14 July, 1949, that Noa had started to act also for affiliated WPSTS other than the transport co-operatives. Hamashbir Hamerkazi would sell the merchandise to WPSTS and agreed to limit its write-up to a maximum of seven per cent plus warehousing and also to grant three months' credit without interest. (Noa also acted as the purchasing agent for all the equipment which the Histadrut-sponsored transport co-operatives purchased with the allocations from the American Export Import Bank Loan (1951)).

The council member who represented the printers co-operatives said that he was dissatisfied because Noa had not yet centralized the purchases of the co-operatives other than transport co-operatives. He described the arrangements with Hamashbir Hamerkazi as inadequate, and added that little had been done to bolster the bonds between the WPSTS and the Histadrut-sponsored consumers co-operative movement.

The Secretariat's Report to the Fifth Congress, 7-9 April, 1949, noted that prior to 1948 the transport co-operative used Noa, as their purchasing organ, to a relatively small extent. The Government in 1949 introduced import quotas on the basis of past trade, and allotted to Noa a fourth of the amount which it needed. It was also decided, at the time, to increase Noa's capital from IL.60,000 to IL.100,000.

The failure to implement "the decision of the Fourth Congress 16 June, 1938, to establish a company to centralize the purchases of all WPSTS," the secretariat's report ascribed to the lack of a mutual business language and the prolonged negotiations to make Noa the central purchasing organ for all Merkaz Haco-operatzia affiliated WPSTS.

The Secretariat's Report to the Council, of 25-26 May, 1950, noted that Merkaz Haco-operatzia was not happy with the marketing agency "Shivuk" in which Merkaz Haco-operatzia and its affiliated co-operative workshops had 25 per cent each and Chevrat Haovdim the other 50 per cent interest and also the authority to adjudicate any differences. Since Merkaz Haco-operatzia was apprehensive that both it and its affiliated co-operative workshops would not be permitted to function as an equal partner with Chevrat Haovdim in "Shivuk", it proposed that its affiliated WPSTS should have their own purchasing and selling organ.*

> "We are not merely a melting pot of so many clients interested in providing their marketing requirements. As a movement, it is our duty to build up the economy, to expand the financial potentialities, in various directions (of the affiliated WPSTS). We want a genuine partnership with Chevrat Haovdim—as an equal with equals . . . though Chevrat Haovdim would have the decisive voice.† Without a genuine partnership, the problem (marketing) cannot be solved and we cannot compromise merely for the satisfaction of doing something. . . ."

The representative of Chevrat Haovdim told the council meeting that just as Tnuva marketed all the agricultural produce from all the Histadrut-sponsored agricultural settlements, the Histadrut wanted one sponsored marketing organ to service all Histadrut-sponsored workshops, including those in the kibbutzim,

> "and if you so desire it can become a large body not only to help the producer to market but also . . . to purchase and finance raw materials and production

* In 1951 Merkaz Haco-operatzia registered a special company Shatef, with a capital of IL.10,000 for the purchase of supplies and the marketing of the merchandise of industrial workers co-operatives. Up to the end of 1960 the company had done very little business.

† Is it not contradictory for one of two equal partners to have the decisive vote?

. . . of high quality merchandise which will be able to compete with the products of the private sector. . . . In the name of Chevrat Haovdim I inform you that Hameshavek is a partnership of Chevrat Haovdim, Histadrut-sponsored agricultural settlements and yourselves, and that you are an equal partner with all others. . . ."

The Report of Merkaz Haco-operatzia for 1948-58 noted that Noa, Ltd., had a share capital of IL.200,000. Noa's reserves amounted to about a million pounds. In 1958 there was a drop in the total business compared with 1957, IL.250,000 and IL.5,148,000 respectively.*

Noa is a shareholder and its representatives are on the management board of the Alliance Tyre Factory (in Israel) and in the Government-controlled Israel (Fuel) Company, Delek. At the end of 1961, Noa held 82,741 shares in the Alliance Tyre Factory. Of these, 36,592 belonged to the transport co-operatives that are shareholders in Noa. The report notes that "according to the information submitted, the Alliance Tyre Company has a total of 532,268 shares." And Noa holds (including those held for the transport co-operatives) about 18 per cent of all shares in the Alliance. Noa's holdings plus the shares belonging to the transport co-operatives, represent 25 per cent of all of the shares of the Alliance Tyre Company (and Koor the holding company of Solel Boneh holds another 25 per cent). There is a voting agreement between these two—Koor and Noa†. Noa had 379,536 shares in the Israel Fuel Company Delek, valued at IL.1 each. Of these, 48,440 belong to the transport co-operatives, 44,200 to Kupat Haco-operativim and 186,887 to Noa.‡

Noa increased its representation of foreign concerns during the period under review, which *inter alia*, include G.M.C. (Buicks); Pontiac cars; C.W.S. Manchester, and "several agencies from countries on the American continent and in Europe for lorries and buses; spare parts, and accessories for machines; and fuel and oils for cars, buses and lorries. Noa continued to expand its purchases from the direct sources which reduced the costs for the WPSTS and also helped to stabilize prices.

Noa had the agency for the Alliance Tyre Plant in Israel, in which it had

* The Report of Merkaz Haco-operatzia for 1949-58 states that in 1951, the industrial workers co-operatives established their own purchasing and marketing agency Shatef. In 1954, Shatef set up a subsidiary company, Shatef Exports. The two companies were making an effort to supply raw materials, and other commodities, technical equipment and tools for about 120 industrial workers co-operatives affiliated to Merkaz Haco-operatzia. Its total annual business dropped to IL.166,000 in 1958, compared with IL.360,000 and IL.903,000 in 1957 and 1956 respectively. The report attributed the marked decline in business during the last year to the Government's more liberal import policy "in recent years". The industrial workers co-operatives, especially those with insufficient working capital, preferred to make their purchases in the open market in small quantities, as the need arose. The WPSTS do not mind paying higher prices because the merchants give them liberal credits on convenient terms. Shatef had to insist on large orders and, since it lacks working capital, could not grant liberal terms of payment.

The report also noted that the Histadrut-sponsored consumers co-operatives do not yet make any purchases from the Histadrut-sponsored industrial workers co-operatives, even when the quality of the merchandise and the prices and terms of payment are as good as those prevailing in the non-co-operative sectors. It would be difficult to make any further progress unless and until the Histadrut prepared to impose its authority on its sponsored consumers co-operatives and its other economic undertakings which are purchasers.

† Noa in 1961 sold to Koor (Holding Company of Solel Boneh) 9,559 of its Alliance shares for nearly IL.217,000.

‡ The Market value of Noa's holdings is given as IL.467,216.

25 per cent of the company's IL.3 million common stock. It also held 17·5 per cent of the IL.4 million common stock of the Histadrut-sponsored Delek Fuel Company, of which it was one of the initiators and founders.

The following data were extracted from the detailed report prepared by the audit department of Merkaz Haco-operatzia.*

Noa's paid up capital at the end of 1961 was nearly IL.399,000 compared with over IL.206,000 at the end of 1960. The three bus co-operatives (Egged (Eshed), Dan and Hamekasher) held over 62 per cent (Egged (Eshed) having a share of over 41 per cent); the road haulage co-operative over 26 per cent (of which over 16 per cent belonged to TACHBURA); and various institutions 8·33 per cent (Merkaz Haco-operatzia accounting for 7·16 per cent). Chevrat Haovdim held one founders' share.

Noa also has 20,000 shares in the Rubber Products plant Hamegaper (IL.1 value per share).

Noa purchases the fuel for the bus co-operatives Egged (Eshed) and Dan and the road haulage co-operative Shelev (the second largest of the road haulage co-operatives affiliated to Merkaz Haco-operatzia) and charges these a nominal commission for its services.

† The following table shows the value of the shares held by Noa (*exclusive* of the shares which it held as trustee for the Histadrut-sponsored WPSTS and for Kupat Haco-operativim).

Company	Actual Value	Accretion in Value	Total
Alliance Tyre Co.	IL.859,437	214,145	1,073,582
Delek (Israel Fuel Co.)	IL.186,887	280,329	467,216
Hamegafer (Rubber Products Co.)	IL.20,000	49,722	69,722
Others	IL359	8,641	9,000
Total	IL.1,066,683	552,837	1,619,520

Noa also centralizes the purchase of spare parts for the transport co-operatives on a commission basis (4 per cent compared with between 7·5 and 10 per cent charged by other agents).

"More recently these purchases have been very limited because the co-operatives (transport) had very little cash available. Noa is trying to overcome this difficulty and is negotiating with foreign investors a credit for the co-operatives. The customs authorities have also been asked to recognize Noa as a bonded warehouse. And if this plan succeeds . . . Noa could relieve the co-operatives (transport) of the need to keep large stocks. This would reduce the prices and decrease the expenses in maintaining stocks and also improve their financial liquidity."

The following is a statement of Profit & Loss for the four years from 1957 to 1960.‡

* According to this report the bus and road haulage co-operatives in 1960 spent over IL.8 and IL.4 million for spare parts and tyres respectively.

‡ Compiled from Schedules 9 to 12 and p. 5 and 6 of the text of the report of the auditing division of Merkaz Haco-operatzia.

NOA LTD.

	(1)	(2)	(3)	(4)	(5)	(6)
Year	Gross Revenue	Dividends Included in (1)	Gross Expenditures	Interest Included in (3)	Gross 1-3 Prior to Provisions for Income Tax	Surplus after Income Tax & Allocations to Reserves & Dividend
	IL.	IL.	IL.	IL.	IL.	IL.
1957	277,929	9,008	255,224	79,757	22,705	−1,237
1958	331,158	69,021	270,258	72,700	60,900	−30,851
1959	426,844	125,787	293,451	88,300	133,393	7,628
1960	557,017	208,766	331,997	110,052	225,020	22,805

The report notes that Noa did not pay any dividends during the three years from 1955 to 1957. The transport co-operatives (shareholders of Noa) decided to use IL.143,000 or most of the net surpluses for rebates and discounts on their purchases of spare parts, and this amount was then used for the acquisition of additional Noa shares. It also notes that Noa's "investments in the Alliance Tyre Company and in the fuel company, Delek, account for a large part of Noa's profits. And in 1961 the company decided to transfer IL.104,163 or about 25 per cent of its gross profits for the three years from 1958 to 1960 (IL.419,313) to general reserves and to use IL.37,840 for payment of dividends.

On the basis of the audited annual balance-sheet as of 31 December, 1960, the Audit Union's report gives the following summary of Noa's financial position.

Assets	IL.000	Liabilities	IL.000
1. Fixed Assets	2,155·2	4. Paid-Up Capital & Other Funds	2,290·9
2. Stocks on Hand	903·8	5. Long Term Loan	678·0
3. Accounts Receivable and other Liquid Assets (after rebate of IL.772,838 of the transport co-operatives for fuel & tyres)	225·3	6. Accounts Payable	315·4
	3,284·3		3,284·3

The report notes that Noa's financial position is less favourable than that reflected in the above statement, since the stocks on hand, *de facto*, are not a liquid asset because the velocity of the movement of most items is very low. Noa buys most of the items abroad and has to pay for these in advance. Most of the Accounts Payable are one-month credits and Noa is under persistent financial pressure. The transport co-operatives complain because the terms of its credits are less favourable than those generally prevailing "in this branch". The indebtedness of the transport co-operatives to Noa for spare parts etc. at the end of 1960 was about IL.116,000, the equivalent of two months' credit (annual turnover is about IL.626,000). Therefore the transport co-operatives must occasionally purchase on credit from suppliers whose prices are higher than those charged by Noa.

NOA—AUDITED ANNUAL BALANCE-SHEET AS OF 31 DECEMBER, 1960

Assets			IL.
1. Fixed Assets (less Depreciation)			
(*a*) Office Building			61,839
(*b*) Land			7,296
(*c*) Machinery			8,393
(*d*) Furniture & Fixtures			16,318
Total			93,846
2. Investments in Companies			
(*a*) Shares (at cost) in Companies			1,359,694
(*b*) Bonus and other Premium Shares			553,814
(*c*) Loans			15,769
(*d*) Payment a/c of subscription of Shares in Oil Refinery			77,605
(*e*) Government Securities (at cost)			36,246
(*f*) Other securities			5,390
Total			2,048,518
3. Liquid Assets			
(*a*) Stocks at cost or less than cost (including stocks on order)			903,846
(*b*) Documentary Credits			32,625
4. Accounts Receivable			
(*a*) Clients, etc.	916,714		
(*b*) Promissory Notes & Undertakings	33,678		
Total	950,392		
Less Doubtful Accounts	5,000	945,392	
5. Interest in Advance		9,479	954,871
6. Cash		765	
Banks		9,865	10,630
7. Expenses in Advance			12,812
Total Assets			4,057,148

Liabilities		IL.
8. Fully Paid Up Shares		206,165
9. Subscriptions for Shares		26,767
10. Reserve Capital		5,666
11. Other Funds		627,972
12. Profit & Loss Carried Forward		423,792
(8)+(9)+(10)+(11)+(12)		1,290,362
13. Third Party Funds Earmarked for Investments		847,520
14. Long Term Loans		
(*a*) Koor (Linked)	317,500	
(*b*) American-Israel Bank (Linked) (Secured by Securities—Floating Charge etc.)	267,944	
(*c*) Gemul (Linked)	60,937	
(*d*) Miscellaneous	31,631	
Total 14		678,012
15. Loans—Amortization Period not Fixed		
(*a*) Bank Overdrafts	13,806	
(*b*) Short Term (Linked)	200,516	
(*c*) Bills Payable	6,451	
(*d*) Supplies; Accounts Payable, etc.	1,010,481	
Total 15		1,231,254
Total Liabilities		4,057,148

Guarantees

(*a*) Bills Turned over to Third Parties as Security.	IL.1,212,216
(*b*) Guarantees to Third Parties.	IL.402,000
(*c*) Documentary Credits.	IL.149,003

NOA LTD.
PROFIT & LOSS FOR 1960

	IL.
1. Gross Profit	335,195
2. Less Expenses	218,389
3. Net Profit	116,806
4. Dividends Received; Rent, etc.	95,323
(3)+(4)	212,129
5. Miscellaneous—Profit on Sales of Shares, etc.	124,753
(3)+(4)+(5)	336,882
6. Financing Expenses Less Interest & Commission	112,865

7. Profit Prior to Income Tax	224,017
8. Less Income Tax	35,000
9. Net Profit for 1960	189,017
Profit & Loss 31.12.1959	246,647
Plus Net Profit for 1960	189,017
Total	435,664
Less Allocated Income Tax for Previous Year	11,872
Profit and Loss Carried Forward	423,792

APPENDIX THREE

Mutual Insurance and Central Pension Fund

The Report of Merkaz Haco-operatzia for 1938-42 notes that the Fourth Congress of 16 June, 1938, unanimously decided that Merkaz Haco-operatzia should establish a department for all kinds of insurance—fire, burglary, third party, etc., for its affiliated WPSTS. This allegedly would reduce the premiums which its affiliated WPSTS pay. Experience would demonstrate the possibility of collective insurance for total coverage for the individual members of the affiliated WPSTS. The larger co-operatives opposed the plan because they did not wish to share with the smaller affiliated WPSTS the special premiums and other advantages which they already enjoyed.

The Council Meeting on 2 March, 1939, confirmed the resolution of the Fourth Congress and also decided to make it obligatory for all affiliated WPSTS to arrange their insurance of property only through the insurance department of Merkaz Haco-operatzia with the understanding that the premiums will not be higher than those which the respective WPSTS paid prior to the centralization of the insurance. The Council also decided to prepare and to submit to the next Council meeting a detailed plan for comprehensive collective personal insurance.

"A number of co-operatives refused to turn over their insurance to the department and have urged its abolition", the report notes. Inasmuch as Merkaz Haco-operatzia has not disciplined its affiliated WPSTS for more serious intransigences, it is not surprising, notes the report, that it did not do so in this instance of open disregard of the Congress and Council decisions about the insurance. Because the larger WPSTS were not interested in the plans for comprehensive social insurance, Merkaz Haco-operatzia has postponed but has not given up the plan.*

* From a co-operative point of view it is questionable whether co-operatives should be compelled to arrange their insurance through Merkaz Haco-operatzia which was organized and registered as a co-operative for non-financial activities, such as audit and supervision. There is also some doubt whether a strict interpretation of the Co-operative Societies Ordinance 1933 permits an Audit Union to engage in such activities.

Evaluating the activities of the insurance department of Merkaz Haco-operatzia in the decade since its establishment, the secretariat's report to the Fifth Congress, 7-9 April, 1949 notes that "we have tried but we have not succeeded" in centralizing the insurance of all types of all of the affiliated WPSTS. The large WPSTS in particular, "hurt (weakened) the department and also themselves". The report adds that it is not clear whether and to what extent the insurance department of Merkaz Haco-operatzia will continue to favour the Histadrut-sponsored insurance company, "Hassneh", and whether this was advantageous or disadvantageous.

The report considers that the main achievement of the insurance department was that it made the WPSTS more insurance conscious; it obtained a general reduction in premium rates by all insurance companies; it was one hundred per cent successful in the claims which it handled; and it helped to establish and manage the emergency insurance funds during World War Two and the War of Liberation.

The Fifth Congress, 7-9 April, 1949, reconfirmed the previous decision that it was obligatory for all affiliated WPSTS to arrange all their insurance through the insurance department of Merkaz Haco-operatzia unless Merkaz Haco-operatzia approves other arrangements for respective affiliated WPSTS. The Congress empowered Merkaz Haco-operatzia to establish a special management committee which would deal with all questions directly related to the insurance department, and specified that the insurance department of Merkaz Haco-operatzia should continue to give the Histadrut-sponsored "Hassneh" Company priority over all other insurance companies.

The secretary of Merkaz Haco-operatzia told the Council on 14 July, 1949, that the advantages of centralizing insurances are seriously impaired because many of the affiliated WPSTS do not place their insurance through its insurance department. This refusal to use the insurance department is a deviation from the co-operative principle of self-help and mutual help.

Prof. M. Benenson reports about the activities of the two committees, one on general insurance and the other on social insurance, which the Fifth Congress (7-9 April, 1949) appointed. He estimated that the WPSTS affiliated to Merkaz Haco-operatzia annually pay a quarter of a million pounds in premiums for insurance of property, fire accident, etc. The committee on general insurance feels that at the outset it would be preferable for Merkaz Haco-operatzia, as agent for its affiliated WPSTS to act jointly with a consortium of insurance companies and should not immediately rely only on internal insurance. He asks the Council also to decide on the action to be taken against those affiliated WPSTS that have refused to show their insurance policies to the Insurance Committees of Merkaz Haco-operatzia.

Prof. Benenson also told the Council on 14 July, 1949, that the committee on social insurance must proceed cautiously. Thus far it has sent to the road haulage and bus co-operatives draft regulations (CHUKA) for old age pension funds. And it suggests that every transport co-operative should establish a co-operative provident and pension fund which would be under the guidance and control of a central co-ordinating committee. He notes that further study and more statistical data are needed before the committee on social insurance can make recommendations about the social insurance for the industrial producers and service co-operatives. But these should begin immediately to withhold 34 per cent of the gross wages for a pension fund, the WPSTS should pay 17 per cent and all their respective members 17 per cent of their emoluments.

A delegate, representing the bus co-operatives, suggested postponing the question of social insurance for a year.

A representative of Egged (Eshed) thought that centralized insurance would benefit only the smaller WPSTS that are affiliated to Merkaz Haco-operatzia and should be used only for these. He opposes centralization of any kind, including a consortium of insurance companies which the committee on general insurance suggested "because it will not be advantageous". It will be cheaper if Merkaz Haco-operatzia made direct arrangements with the respective insurance companies that have given satisfactory services to the WPSTS. And he was sure that every affiliated WPSTS would accept the authority of Merkaz Haco-operatzia with regard to insurance.

A third Council member, representing the bus co-operative (in Haifa), opposed the delaying tactics.

> "It is time for action in terms of the future. One should think in terms of large amounts, of the possibilities and of the advantage if we centralized in our hands large amounts. The insurance companies are not losing money."

He recommends that the Council should instruct Merkaz Haco-operatzia immediately to change its insurance department into an autonomous corporate body. Several other speakers supported this view.

The Council of Merkaz Haco-operatzia, on 14 July, 1949, authorizes Merkaz Haco-operatzia to carry out the decisions of the Fifth Congress (7-9 April, 1949):

(*a*) that it is obligatory for all affiliated WPSTS to place their insurance through the insurance department of Merkaz Haco-operatzia, and
(*b*) to organize a provident fund and a pension fund for every affiliated WPSTS.

One of the speakers at the Council Meeting of 24-25 May, 1950, stated that because the Merkaz Haco-operatzia Secretariat has become excessively involved with the bus co-operatives, it has neglected the more important question of provident and pension funds.

> "We will be confronted with surprises and serious disillusions when all the members of the WPSTS will become of pensionable age within a relatively short time."

Another Council member (Dan Bus Co-operative, Tel Aviv) thinks that all the WPSTS could follow the example of his co-operative and arrange for retirement pensions at 62.

According to the Secretariat's oral report to the Council of Merkaz Haco-operatzia, on 12 September, 1951, only 576 members of the affiliated WPSTS were covered by the "Hamagen" Central Pension Fund sponsored by Merkaz Haco-operatzia and an affiliate of Chevrat Haovdim, which started operations on 1 January, 1950. There was a decision that it was obligatory for all the members of all affiliated WPSTS to join Hamagen. The failure of the bus co-operatives to join Hamagen, notes the report, is "a disappointment".

Hamagen has no share capital and the liability of a member is limited to one pound. Every member contributes 12 per cent of his gross emoluments (including cost of living and fringe benefits) for an eight-hour day. But the management of any WPSTS may change the amount of a member's contribution. Hamagen ensures a pension equivalent to 60 per cent of a member's wages when pensioned, and the pension is linked to the cost of living index.

The insured elect their delegates to the general meetings of Hamagen, WPSTS with 20 members or less may elect one delegate for every ten members, and those WPSTS with over 20 may elect one additional delegate for every 30 members in excess of the first 20, provided that no WPSTS may send more than 10 delegates to a general meeting. Every delegate has one vote.

Hamagen's Management Committee of not less than five members meets not less than once a month. Half of the members of the Management Committee must be from the candidates nominated jointly by Chevrat Haovdim and Merkaz Haco-operatzia. The Council of Hamagen includes all the members of the Management Committee, and the General Meeting of Hamagen elects the other members of the Council. The total number of Council members is twice the number of the members on the Management Committee at the time. The Council meets quarterly.

The representatives of Chevrat Haovdim and of Merkaz Haco-operatzia each have the right to participate at all the General Meetings of Hamagen, and these may each cast a number of votes equal to five per cent of all the votes of all the delegates present at the respective General Meeting.

The Council of Merkaz Haco-operatzia, of 8 May, 1957, calls on every affiliated WPSTS to join Hamagen. And the Secretariat of Merkaz Haco-operatzia, jointly with managements of Hamagen and of other funds (presumably pension funds), will co-ordinate their investments in the respective affiliated WPSTS.

The Report of Merkaz Haco-operatzia for 1948-58 notes that Hamagen can offer the affiliated WPSTS the choice of eight pension plans, which provide pensions varying from 25 to 85 per cent of a fixed basic emolument, from IL.60 to IL.120 a month linked to the official cost of living index. According to the report, the "Hamagen Pension Fund is one of the important achievements of the WPSTS in the field of mutual help and social insurance".

H. Goldberg (Hamagen) reports to the meeting of the division for service co-operatives of Merkaz Haco-operatzia on 6 June, 1960, that only 29 of its 54 affiliated service co-operatives have joined Hamagen; and negotiations for the admission of 10 more are progressing. The division for service co-operatives is asked to prompt the remaining 15 of its affiliated service co-operatives that have not shown much interest in joining Hamagen.

Mr. Giladi's opening address at the Eleventh Annual Meeting of Hamagen (of 9 August, 1961*) notes that Hamagen is the smallest of Histadrut's seven sponsored Pension Funds.† On 1 July, 1961, Hamagen had 2,200 members (9,000 people including families) and its own funds (capital, reserves and various funds) amounted to just over IL.5·1 million. The insured may arrange for a minimum monthly pension of IL.60 and a maximum of IL.80. About 41 per cent and 38 per cent of the insured will receive a monthly pension of IL.60 and IL.80 respectively

"both very much smaller than the actual earnings of the insured . . . and

* Shituf, August-September 1961, pp. 66-74.

† The Registrar of Co-operatives reports that at the end of 1962 the 271 Provident Funds and Four Pension Funds registered under the Co-operative Societies Ordinance had resources amounting to IL.293 million. Of this, Hamagen accounts for IL.8 million.

the amount needed for a reasonable standard of living. They must do everything possible to convince members to increase the amount of their cover. A second real problem is to initiate action to bring within Hamagen the permanent wage workers in the WPSTS which would be an important incentive to the fund and appreciably increase the number of insured."

During 1960 Hamagen advanced IL.450,000 and IL.180,000 to affiliated WPSTS and to their members respectively. The management recommends that the entire surplus of IL.144,000 should be allocated to the three special reserves.

Zeev Onn (Chevrat Haovdim) was specially gratified with the increase of Hamagen's capital. But he noted that

> "only 2,200 of the 14,000 members* of the WPSTS affiliated with Merkaz Haco-operatzia had joined Hamagen. Egged (Eshed) and the Dan bus co-operatives have their own Provident Funds . . . every effort must be made to attain complete fusion of the WPSTS Pension Funds which would embrace all the members and wages workers of all the WPSTS. . . . Every Pension Fund of every WPSTS, including those to be established, must automatically join Hamagen."

He notes that in accordance with the agreement with the Ministry of Finance, half the resources of Histadrut sponsored pension and provident funds must be invested in Government securities and half in Histadrut-sponsored economic projects.

E. Hendel insists on abolishing the minimum cover of IL.60 "which today is unrealistic". And Hamagen, together with other financial bodies, should initiate the establishment of joint funds for the integration by the WPSTS of additional members.

D. Ginzberg notes that the changeover to a higher minimum cover is made difficult by the condition for retroactive linking of the payments (premiums).

Y. Cohen (and other speakers) supported Mr. Ginzberg's view, and pressed for immediate enforcement of the provision about the obligatory fusion of the provident and pension funds of all affiliated WPSTS and all their respective members and wage workers, not excluding Egged (Eshed) and Dan bus co-operatives.

M. Lavi (Merkaz Haco-operatzia) while agreeing that IL.60 cover is inadequate, notes that "there are WPSTS that are unable (financially) to insure their members for higher amounts".

N. Shelev thinks that the small membership does not jeopardize the future of Hamagen. "Let us not forget that in the beginning we had only about 500-1,000 members."

B. Halevi-Vernikov asks that those negotiating with WPSTS about the increase of the minimum cover should be more flexible. And he also asks for an arbitration tribunal to deal with appeals of individual members.

The Eleventh Annual General Meeting decided, *inter alia,* to accept the management's suggestion about the distribution of the surplus for 1960 and the amendments to the rules; and to accept the wage workers within Hamagen.

* At the end of 1961 the 204 WPSTS affiliated to Merkaz Haco-operatzia had 7,446 members and 7,050 wage workers and apprentices, or a total labour force of 14,496. Mr. Onn probably refers to the total labour force. At the end of 1962 the 201 affiliated WPSTS had 7,471 members and 6,948 wage workers.

STATUS OF THE MAGEN CENTRAL PENSION FUND ON SPECIFIED DATES

	1952	1954	1956	1958	1960
(*a*) Number of WPSTS affiliated	28	49	62	82	122
Members in the affiliated co-operatives	1,031	1,393	1,499	1,770	2,146
Number of people in the families of the insured	4,052	5,752	5,996	7,080	9,000
(*b*) Funds in IL.000					
Old Age	262·0	582·0	1,051·1	1,766·9	4,725 (Old Age, Widows & Orphans, Disabled)
Widows & Orphans	22·3	122·8	296·3	543·8	
Disabled		41·3	106·8	188·9	
Reserves			20·0	76·5	
Capital	289·9	780·6	1,563·4	2,696·0	4,152
(*c*) Investments in IL.000					
Not linked	47·2	179·9	287·2	598·4	876
Linked		100·0	825·6	1,516·1	4,263

Average age of the people at the end of 1961 was about 44 years.

On 1 July, 1962, Hamagen had 2,579 insured members (exclusive of 350 wage workers, all from Haargaz). At the end of 1961 the old age, widows and orphans and the disabled funds exceeded IL.5·7 million, and it is estimated that it will increase to IL.7·5 million by the end of 1962. And the paid-up capital of Hamagen at the end of 1961 was IL.5·2 million, an increase by one million over that at the end of 1960. About 83 per cent of its capital was invested in linked securities (compared with over 70 per cent at the end of 1950).

Decisions of the Sixth Congress of Merkaz Haco-operatzia, of 15-16 July, 1962 Proceedings.

1. The Congress recommends the amalgamation of the pension funds of Egged (Eshed) and Dan with Magen in such manner as will ensure the special interests of these two pension funds.
2. The Congress notes with regret that some of the WPSTS affiliated to Merkaz Haco-operatzia have not yet arranged social insurance and therefore have not ensured the minimum social security for their members and their families when the members for some reason must discontinue their work.
3. The Congress decides to require all affiliated WPSTS to join Magen and to require every new WPSTS to join Magen as a condition for admission to Merkaz Haco-operatzia.
4. Merkaz Haco-operatzia, jointly with the management of Magen, will decide about Magen's credit policy.
5. The Congress directs the management of Merkaz Haco-operatzia and Magen's management jointly to enquire into the possibilities of establishing a special fund to assist in financing the arrangements for the insurance of those members of WPSTS who do not have the resources to pay the retroactive premiums.

APPENDIX FOUR

MERKAZ HACO-OPERATZIA—BUDGET—AMOUNTS IN IL.000

	1959-60 Budget	1959-60 Spent	1960-61 Budget	1960-61 Spent	1961-62[a] Budget
Revenue					
1. Insurance Commissions & Membership Fees Participation	431·5	403·0	377·0	412·0	475·0
2. Kupat Haco-operativim (Financial Organ of Histadrut-sponsored WPSTS)	19·7	19·7	19·5	11·0	19·5
3. Noa, Central Purchasing Organ	6·0	6·0	6·0	6·0	6·0
4. Shatef Marketing, local and export	6·0	6·0			
5. Magen—Mutual Insurance & Pension Fund	5·4	5·4	5·5	6·0	6·0
6. Merkaz Movement (Central Organ for Restaurants, Hotels, etc.)	2·9	2·9	4·0	8·0	8·0
7. Joint Undertakings (with Chevrat Haovdim)			5·5	4·0	
8. Teeus Industrial Development Company for Development Zones			12·0	12·0	6·0
9. Advertisements in monthly journal, Shituf	5·0	5·0	14·0	6·0	5·0
10. Service Charges for Liquidations	5·0	5·0	3·5	9·5	3·0
11. Other Internal Sources	2·4	4·5	3·5	1·0	2·5
12. Histadrut-sponsored Insurance Co. Hassneh) Commission)	17·0	17·0	20·0	23·0	25·0
13. Histadrut Central Dues Department (from proceeds received from WPSTS members)	95·5	95·5	100·0	106·0	115·0
14. Ministry of Labour grants and Chevrat Haovdim grants			14·0	17·0	
Total	596·4	570·0	584·5	621·5	671·0
Operational Deficits for Previous Years	29·0	64·0	110·5	83·0	42·0
Grand Total	625·5	634·0	695·0	705·0	713·0[a]

(a) On the basis of the activities up to 1 June, 1962, the operational deficit for 1961-62 is almost at IL.42,000, plus another IL.30,000 to cover the salary increases prescribed by the audit union. The global operational deficit at the end of 1961-62 will amount to IL.190,000 to which IL.30,000 has to be added, making a total of IL.220,000 accumulated operational deficits. They will have to implement the decision of the Council meeting of 27 June, 1960, and of the Secretariat of the division for transport co-operatives of 27 June, 1961, and increase the participation of the aforementioned transport co-operatives by IL.20,000 annually. To ask the other affiliated WPSTS to increase their participation.

The gross annual revenue of the 200 affiliated undertakings is IL.200 million with a total labour force of 15,000. And the total annual wage bill is IL.70 million.

The following table shows the expenditures of Merkaz Haco-operatzia for specified years.

	1959-60		1960-61		1961-62(a)
Items	Budget	Spent	Budget	Spent	Budget
1. Wage Plus Fringe Benefits(c)	420·0	418·0	499·0	490·0	530·0
2. General Expenses	130·0	147·5	140·0	142·0	125·0
3. Consolidation of Debts	24·0	24·0	24·0	30·0	42·0
4. Amortization of Mortgages	19·0	19·0	11·0	11·0	11·0
5. Congresses (includes preparatory costs)	7·5	2·0(a)			5·0
6. Shituf—monthly journal	5·0	7·0	(b)	(b)	(b)
7. Cultural and Educational Activities, Organization and Education	20·0	16·6	21·0	32·0	
Total	625·5	634·1	695·0	705·0	713·0

(a) Congress postponed to 1962 a few days before date for which it was called.
(b) Included in general expenses.
(c) Increase due to a larger staff and not to increase in salaries. The Merkaz Haco-operatzia staff of 70 includes 21 in the auditing division which has its own management board.

CHAPTER FOUR

Bus Co-operatives

The main purpose of the first road built from Jaffa to Jerusalem in 1869 was to enable the people attending the opening of the Suez Canal to visit Jerusalem. Construction of highways on a relatively large scale was started after the British occupation of the Holy Land in 1919, and in 1921 there were already about 800 kilometres of roads, half of these all-year roads.

Mr. S. Etington writes ("Overland Transportation", The Economic Quarterly, October 1954), that the first section of the railway system in Israel, a ninety-kilometre run from Jaffa to Jerusalem, was opened in 1892. This was followed in 1908-14 by trunk lines connecting Acre, Haifa, Tzemach-Tulkarem with the Hedjaz line to Medina via Damascus which was started in 1905. A small branch line to connect Nahal Sorek, Beersheba and El Hafir with the Suez Canal was built during World War I and was dismantled immediately afterwards. The main 420-kilometre Kantara-Haifa network via Rafa, Gaza and Lod was constructed by the British Army 1915-18. The branch line, Gaza-Beersheba, which was built simultaneously with the Kantara-Haifa line, was dismantled in 1922.

During 1941-42 (World War II) the British Army constructed another 38 kilometres from Haifa, through Acre, to connect at the Palestine-Lebanon boundary (Rosh Hanikra) with the 200-kilometre line constructed simultaneously through Beirut and Tripoli in Lebanon. In other words, Mr. Etington notes, practically the whole of the railway system was built with an eye for tourists and pilgrims or for military purposes. The commercial and industrial requirements of the country were at best a secondary consideration.

The Yishuv favoured and pressed for the priority of the highway system which it considered essential for its physical and economic security. The State of Israel acquired, according to Mr. Etington, "a rundown railway with inadequate and unsuitable equipment, roughly handled by the Government and by Arab and Jewish saboteurs during the War of Liberation" 1947-48. In 1950 only 121 kilometres of the railways were in condition to be used, and most of the 52 locomotives dated from 1918. There were 38 usable carriages for passengers and 2,400 goods wagons of all sizes and types for various gauge railways. Since only 500 of the 7,000 pre-State railway workers remained, the State had to begin training new employees. The situation was specially difficult with regard to the shortage of maintenance staff.

About 950 kilometres of roads were added during the five-year post-State period, from 1949 to 1953, increasing the total to 2,550 kilometres. All-weather roads were increased from 1,380 to 2,150 kilometres.

Mr. Etington thought that investments to reactivate and improve the railways were unavoidable. The distances within the country were increasing as the country developed. The cost of transporting by rail a commodity like potash over long distances was 50 per cent cheaper than by road. The joint operation of railway and road transport was both possible and obligatory. In the final analysis, both systems had one common aim; the provision of an efficient service for the economic requirements of the country.

The Histadrut took an active interest in road transport from the beginning.

An account of the early days of the co-operative passenger service may be found in the story about the Dan bus co-operative and in that of about thirty years of bus transportation in Israel. From 1909 to about 1922, stage coaches were used between Tel Aviv and Jaffa and Petah Tikva and between Tel Aviv and Jaffa and Jerusalem. In 1920 "a number of box cars", each with six places for the passengers and one for the driver were introduced. And in 1922 some second-hand Sunbeam buses (each with 14 seats), purchased from the British Army, were run between Tel Aviv and Jerusalem and between Tel Aviv and Jaffa and on two internal routes in Tel Aviv.

Mr. Moshe Zvi Glusman, one of the organizers of the co-operative Regev, describes the early days of the bus service between Tel Aviv and the first suburbs on the Tel Aviv and Petah Tikva road. Nine families who had emigrated from Canada started Ramat Gan (then called Ir Ganim) on Pesach (March) 1922 on land adjoining the Histadrut-sponsored suburb, Shchunat Borochov. The latter was started about the same time with 22 families, all employed in Tel Aviv. A few months later these two suburbs, Ramat Gan and Shchunat Borochov, tied up with

> "a driver in Tel Aviv who put two buses, each with six places, at their service. With the increase of families in 1923 to forty in Shechunat Borochov and of twenty-eight in Ramat Gan 'two more small buses were added and driven by the local residents'. The trip was very slow and full of misadventures "because the road (really a path) was so bad. Not a few of the passengers got off the buses and walked most of the way, and quite a few helped the drivers in the repairs, changing and mending tyres, etc." The drivers divided the work between themselves and were on duty 'from early morning to late at night'."

In 1924, eight Ford buses, each having 13 places, replaced the old ones. The new buses also serviced the orthodox suburb Bnei Brak contiguous to (really a continuation of) Ramat Gan, which at the time, had twenty families. A good part of the revenue from fares was used for repairs and replacing tyres. The life of a tyre was a maximum of two months; and the buses were in the garage for repairs and servicing most of the time. The drivers were constantly quarrelling about the division of the proceeds between themselves and about the costs of the repairs. Some would not leave unless and until their buses were full. The passengers became very annoyed with the regular service and some made arrangements with two more drivers who had acquired new vehicles. This led to irresponsible price cutting and hawking for fares; services deteriorated and became still more irregular; and sabotage by the competing groups increased the danger of travelling. This undesirable state of affairs continued until the Ramat Gan local Council at the end of 1925 arranged for the two new drivers and their cars to join the older groups. The united group was given a *de facto* concession for these routes and an orderly service was introduced. The final decision, in 1928, to organize the co-operative Regev was prompted by the desire to minimize the strife between the drivers about the division of the revenue from the fares and other irksome difficulties. This fusion into one co-operative also made it possible to reduce the work-day and introduce one free day and an annual holiday for all their drivers. The pooling of vehicles made it possible to arrange a more regular service and this increased the number of passengers. The early days of the bus co-operative Regev were very difficult, mainly because of a lack of administrative experience and inadequate financial resources.

Moshe Parkul, a "chronic" zealot for order and co-ordination, was one of the founders of Galei-Aviv which served several routes in Tel Aviv. He has written a vivid description of the period from 1924 to 1926. When large middle class emigration from Poland (the fifth aliya) started early in 1924, most of these immigrants settled in and around Tel Aviv. The 1924-25 building and business boom left its impression on the passenger motor transportation business. The older generation of this fifth aliya "bought and sold building sites and houses, opened stores, etc., and the younger adult generation went into motor transport". It was comparatively easy to get both a driver's licence and a car licence for the entire country. There were no restrictions about the frequency of services and routes.

According to Mr. Parkul, young people as well as older people having "appreciable amounts", would invest in a thirteen-seat (exclusive of driver) bus and in a small shed where the passengers assembled, and start running on the Tel Aviv-Jaffa route. Those having only LE.25-30 would invest in a seven-seat "box bus" and work on the internal routes in Tel Aviv. Buying and selling of buses was a lucrative business. Drivers' wages were LE.4-5 a month. The demand for bus transport exceeded the buses available and not infrequently the service was delayed by the passengers who would "rush" the bus when it arrived and quarrel about their rights to get on. But the gross revenue for a day from 5 a.m. to midnight was LE.3 ($15) and barely covered the operational costs. Because of the bad condition of the streets the buses required frequent major repair. Mr.

Parkul also referred to "the plague of police reports, which sucked one's blood".

Without notice ("almost overnight") a real danger appeared, viz., the over-supply of vehicles. Three drivers (including Mr. Parkul) made the following proposal to a meeting of all the drivers in Tel Aviv:

(*a*) They should join forces into one company which should register with an official name.
(*b*) Elect a committee to look after their affairs.
(*c*) Issue tickets for twelve journeys and charge 50 Egyptian mills (\$0·25). In this way the passengers would be linked to the drivers from whom they bought these tickets. And "it was certain that 90 per cent of the passengers would buy these tickets" because there could be a saving of 20 per cent.
(*d*) The driver would have to turn in the stubs from the new cheap tickets.
(*e*) Every driver would be responsible for the maintenance of his car.

The majority favoured the plan, but some objected to the appointment of a committee and still others considered a discount of 20 per cent on the twelve journey ticket excessive. The discount was the equivalent to the cost of "a tin of petrol" (four gallons). The plan for joint action was forced on the drivers by another set of circumstances. At the end of 1924, at the height of the boom, complaints from many passengers reached Mr. Dizengoff, the 'mayor' (chairman of the Municipal Council) of Tel Aviv, and he wrote to the Governor of Jaffa. About the middle of 1925, the Mandatory Government directed that all cars were to be tested. This forced the owners of the cars "to spend tens of pounds" for basic repairs. Immediately afterwards all the drivers, without exception, were ordered to appear simultaneously in court on speeding summonses. The Mayor of Tel Aviv and the local senior police officer were present at the hearing. After a roll call of all the drivers, the Mayor "delivered a sharp rebuke" in Russian so that all could understand. He accused the drivers of endangering the lives "of his children" and warned them that their licences would be revoked if there was no improvement. "Since you derive (eat) your bread from the client, you also must be respectful to him. This also should be the practice in the relationship between yourselves." The Judge then fined each of the accused drivers (between LE.2 and LE.5), with a stern warning that if this occurred a second time, their driving licences would be withdrawn. This incident was used to bring up for approval proposals for a united body, 'and it was decided that a meeting for this purpose should be called immediately. All the drivers attended the meeting and unanimously approved the plan to establish one united body and to call it Galei-Aviv. The meeting rejected the bitter opposition to the 20 per cent discount on 12-journey tickets; decided to mark every vehicle of every member with the name Galei-Aviv plus a serial number; to publicize an explanation of their position; and to require every driver to pay a monthly membership fee of 150 Egyptian mills (\$0·75) to the new body. Mr.

Parkul noted that the public gladly accepted the new organization and that 90 per cent of the passengers bought the cheap tickets. The senior police officer's greetings to the meeting included a promise (which he kept) that "the reports would certainly stop if the relationship between the drivers and the public improved". But the committee which the meeting elected was unable to improve the internal discipline since every member "worked on his own vehicle and on his own account". A new member would be accepted only if he bought his car from a member who was withdrawing. Mr. Parkul noted that as a result of persistent efforts, both the external and internal relationships improved. The example of Galei-Aviv influenced the drivers on the Tel Aviv-Jaffa route to organize and register Hamaavir, and it also introduced the cheap ticket.

As the city extended and the population grew and new roads were constructed, the public insisted on more and better vehicles, and a reliable timetable of bus service. There was also some agitation for granting a concession to "a capitalist" who was prepared to establish a modern bus transport system in Tel Aviv. Galei-Aviv also decided to use the proceeds from the monthly membership fee of a half LE. and other funds to build a new bus which would increase the seating capacity from six to thirteen. The construction of the first three new bodies took "a long time" because there were no experts in this branch. And it was not easy to find three members who would agree to use the new bodies for their buses. The meeting which finally settled this question also admitted a new member on condition that he paid an entrance fee of LE.50 and also agreed to accept the fourth body for a thirteen-seat bus which was on order. According to Mr. Parkul, the public immediately reacted favourably to the larger buses and preferred to wait for these buses which ran only from 8 a.m. to 8 p.m.

Towards the end of 1925 the Histadrut had to intervene in a jurisdictional dispute between Galei-Aviv and Hamaavir about a new route which was also accompanied by a price-cutting "war". Neither side would make any concessions, and the Histadrut arbitrators' award that both organizations jointly operate on the new route was delayed for "some time". The award also prescribed that since Hamaavir had a larger number of members it should provide 60 per cent of the vehicles, etc. and receive 60 per cent of the gross revenue from this joint route. Galei-Aviv, the minority partner, "was completely dissatisfied and its rancour increased".

In the second half of 1925, the economic and financial crisis was accompanied by relatively large-scale emigration from Israel back to Poland. The gross intake from fares decreased by fifty per cent. Accordingly, some of the members could not continue to operate their vehicles because they were unable to pay the charge for the annual testing of the car, the costs of petrol, tyres, etc. As the economic condition further deteriorated those who continued to run their buses were on their last legs in spite of the reduced competition. Mr. A. Dickenstein, of the co-operative division of the Histadrut, renewed a suggestion which he had made earlier in 1925 at the beginning of the depression, that:

(*a*) Some of the buses should be put in "moth balls". This would eliminate the costs for the annual test and licences, repairs, etc.
(*b*) All members should pool all their revenue.
(*c*) Every member of the organization (pool) should work two full and four half-days a week; and when necessary they should work overtime, but without pay.

The members accepted the following compromise plan for a six-month trial period, which an elected committee of five would put into operation. Every member would run his own vehicle and would turn into the pool his entire intake less an agreed amount for depreciation. The pool paid all expenses except for tyres and repairs for which the owner would use the depreciation allowance.

"It was very difficult (for the members) to accommodate themselves to the idea that the receipts of one member from bus fares should be given to others. Furthermore, the member was subjected to restrictions and supervision . . . no committee in the co-operative movement in Israel has had to overcome so many obstacles . . . there were many cases of orders issued one day and withdrawn the next day.

"Within a short time we were confronted with the worrying fact that, since the initiative was in the hands of the arbitrators and the responsibility for the funds rested with the cashiers, the members became completely indifferent to their work. Even those who had been the most diligent . . . became robots. . . . The committee, to combat this harmful development . . . had to impose a minimum discipline, otherwise there would be no work at all. One of the most difficult tasks of the committee was to introduce and to maintain the five-minute schedule for the buses. The marked increase in the revenue of those routes which had previously operated with deficits was the most effective and convincing way of winning over the members."

During the six-month trial period of the aforementioned compromise plan the members had accommodated themselves so completely to the pooling of revenues that they forgot the expiration date. Mr. Parkul attributed this favourable change mainly to the fact that the member received his pay on time and did not have to worry about settling the accounts for petrol and oil, repairs, spare parts, etc. Another favourable factor was the increase in business resulting from the first Near East Fair in mid-1926. About the time the Fair was closed, at the end of 1926, Mr. Dickenstein first suggested the amalgamation of Galei-Aviv and Hamaavir. But the reaction was not favourable. Hamaavir's routes were more lucrative than those of Galei-Aviv, and the weekly remuneration of Hamaavir members was LE.2 compared with LE.1½ paid to Galei-Aviv members. Hamaavir vehicles carried thirteen passengers each while the "box cars" of Galei-Aviv (except for the "six red buses") carried seven each. In mid-1927 both groups agreed to draft the text of an agreement for a merger. The most serious obstacle in coming to an agreement was the pooling of the buses. Every member had to pay in cash an entrance fee of LE.25. A committee valued every member's vehicle, and those members whose bus was valued at less than LE.25 had to pay the difference in cash. Those members, whose vehicles were valued at more than LE.25, received the difference in cash.

Extracts from a report, "The Relation between the Co-operative Form Monopoly and Social Control" by Avner Hovne, 1951: [82]

The Report of the Investigating Committee of the Jerusalem Municipality in 1951 mentions, among the services of "Hamekasher", the intra-urban bus co-operative established in 1930, the following: It helped to create a Jewish community out of the varied elements of the Yishuv; in the 1936 disturbances (Arab disturbances 1936-39) it carried on its regular services plus additional duties assigned it by Haganah (Self-Defence); it contributed to the expansion of the Jewish community by extending the lines of its service; it continued operating through all the difficulties imposed by World War II and later by the Mandatory Government; in the siege (of Jerusalem) of 1948 it supplied ambulances, fuel and bread distributors; before and during the War of Liberation (1947-48) it operated its regular lines under the most dangerous circumstances and carried out special and dangerous tasks of supply and evacuation.

Mr. Goren, a member of the Secretariat of Merkaz Haco-operatzia since its inception, and who made a notable contribution to the organization of bus and road haulage co-operatives, stated in the Knesset:

The pre-Israel bus driver was one of the ideal types of pioneering Palestine, as portrayed in newspapers, the play of children and the reports of community officials.

Absence of large-scale capitalist organization is a condition, but not an explanation of the rise of public service co-operatives. The explanation is to be sought in specific aspirations and tensions. These were in the case of the bus co-operatives:

1. the tension between the national interest and foreign regime, i.e. the Mandatory Government, and
2. the aspiration of a self-conscious Labour Movement, operating in an undeveloped but dynamically expanding economy.

In 1950 the ratio of passengers to buses in inter-urban services was more than seven times the ratio of passengers for the railways. Of 1,295 buses licensed in 1950 (excluding from consideration 14 which were owned by institutions not engaged in hire transport traffic), 1,291 were owned by five bus co-operatives and by a private bus company. More than 30 per cent of lorries used in commercial hauling and 10 per cent of the taxis were owned by co-operatives.

In almost every country, concentration is far more advanced in bus transport than in road haulage. When an organization is free of effective competition and it also supplies a basic need, then the only real protection of the community lies in exercising administratively the controls which in a capitalist society, are generally exercised by competition. The bus co-operatives had succeeded as early as 1937 in eliminating "competition on the line". First, there is the need for control in deciding how the integrated market shall be divided. The enterprise may find certain routes unprofitable and decide to discontinue them, even though the continuation of those routes or the establishment of new, unprofitable routes, may be required by social policy.

In one field, statistics and book-keeping, lack of efficiency and clarity may actually benefit the enterprise at the expense of the public, since it makes effective social control impossible. One of the major elements in public utility regulations in other countries is usually a detailed prescription on the preparation and publication of accounts. The key questions are: How is a fair return to the members to be determined? How are the members' incomes to be limited to this? The virtues of the co-operative form are, in part, dependent on control of the co-operative exercised by outside and Governmental bodies. The claim is that central co-operative institutions and special co-operative laws make this control easy. The question is: How appropriate are the regulations and the laws and how effectively are they enforced?

Paragraph 8 of the Transportation Regulations (Routes and Tariffs) 1934, gives the Road Controller the right to cancel a licence for operating passenger services, according to his discretion, for any of the following reasons:

(*a*) If the services do not take into account the requirements of the public.
(*b*) If the licence holder contravenes any of the conditions specified in the licence and such contravention appreciably affects the possibility of the licensee giving the service.
(*c*) If in the opinion of the licensing authority the renewal of the licence is not in the interests of the public or the renewal of the licence does not tie in with the transport service programme.
(*d*) At any time during the period of the validity of the licence, the licensing authority may cancel the licence for such period as he deems fit and for the same reasons as the law permits him to refuse the renewal of a licence.
(*e*) The licensee may appeal against the decision of the licensing authority to the High Commissioner and his decision shall be final.

Perhaps because the regulation of bus fares preceded the general regulation of prices, bus fares were not included in later anti-profiteering legislation. The Defence (Prevention of Profiteering) Regulations, 1944, apply to road haulage and to taxis but not to buses. This is a source of weakness, since the anti-profiteering regulations contain a more flexible range of powers than do the Road Transport Regulations.

For the purpose of making general changes in rates, the Minister of Transport appoints *ad hoc* interdepartmental committees, which hear evidence, direct enquiries and make recommendations. Minor adjustments in rates are made by the Controller. Currently (1951) the Controller's role in allocating tyres, buses, and parts also enables him to gain compliance with his orders. In practice, this flexible power is today more useful than the drastic threat to suspend operations. The controller's assistant is specially responsible for supervising the bus co-operatives, but has no special staff for this purpose.

Regarding dissolution (of co-operatives): Under the Co-operative Societies Ordinance & Regulations, 1933-34, section 46, subsection 1, states:

> "If the Registrar, after an enquiry has been held under section 43 . . . is of the opinion that the society ought to be dissolved, he may order the society to be wound up, and shall publish his order in the Gazette."

The Municipalities' representatives may sit on rate-fixing committees, the Municipalities conduct investigations of rates and make recommendations to the Minister of Transport and the municipal authorities are in touch with the Controller's offices on day-to-day problems.

The Municipalities also enter into agreements with the bus co-operatives on the terms of services. However, since the Municipalities lack legal control in this area, the accommodation some of them reach with the co-operatives are little more than gentlemen's agreements.

The law assigns no rights of control of the bus co-operatives to the Histadrut. The agreements between the co-operatives and the Histadrut are like those reached with Municipalities, viz. "gentlemen's agreements" without legal sanction. The Histadrut, being a voluntary association, has the power to deny the co-operative members membership in the Histadrut, while the Municipalities have no comparable power. In addition, the agreements with the Histadrut are embodied in the rules of the co-operatives and may be enforced by the Registrar of Co-operative Societies.

The powers of either the Registrar or the Controller are sufficient to gain complete control over the co-operative (bus), but neither has the staff for the job. Further, there is a division of interest between them; the Registrar is interested in the co-operative character of the enterprise, the Controller of Road Transport is interested in the public service aspects. There is no regular contact between these two officials. This organizational defect enables key problems to "fall between the stools".

There are two major series of official reports by the bus co-operatives to the public authorities, both supplied by the Co-operative Centre (Merkaz Haco-operatzia). The first includes an annual report, a balance-sheet, a profit-and-loss account, the auditors' comments and a statistical summary supplied to the Registrar. The second is a monthly operating report, containing statistics on the vehicles, use, routes, journeys, wages, passengers carried, income, etc., submitted to the Controller of Road Transport. The two reports do not give a clear picture about the income of co-operatives; the cost of operation for various lines, per bus kilometre or per passenger kilometre; actual amounts invested in vehicles; or total payments paid to the members.

The most thorough appraisal of the problem of reporting by the bus co-operatives so far made is that of a sub-committee of the Inter-departmental Committee for determining Transport Rates, 1949-50 (hereinafter referred to as the Inter-departmental Committee).

The absence of a uniform accounting and statistical system for all the (bus) transport co-operatives made it difficult to control and to compare the accounts of the societies. The accounts are not *au jour*, and in some cases they are four months in arrears. This is unsatisfactory in a business whose accounts should give a current picture of the position. The Inter-departmental Committee recommended that the above deficiencies should be corrected at once.

So long as over-all income and detailed costs of the bus enterprises are not accurately known, the controlling of rates must be guess work. If their costs are not met the buses will not run, but if they are more than met, given the present system of handling and reporting finances, the error becomes a profit or bonus for the members.

Technically, cost accounting in bus services is generally far simpler than in the case of the railways or the road haulage services. There is no high fixed cost (charges), as there is in a railway system (tracks, locomotives) which it is difficult to apportion to specific runs. The major costs of buses, viz. labour, fuel and upkeep, vary directly with the service. Additions to the service can be made in small units, one more bus, one more driver. And unlike road haulage services, the character of the freight (passenger load) and of the runs is highly constant.

In regard to the revenue of the co-operatives, the sub-committee reports that the system of accounting for the sale of bus tickets, which accounts for nearly all their revenue, does not make possible a complete check. The sub-committee recommends an inclusive, clear, and open uniform system for the sale of bus tickets.

In regard to the costs of operation, the Committee had estimates of the revenue and expenditures per kilometre-tonnage, and these should be considered only as examples.

The current regulations do not require the bus co-operatives to show on their annual accounts the actual cost of their equipment (vehicles, etc.). The Regulations of the Co-operative Societies Ordinance (1934) require only that for "machinery, plant and implements" as a group the value on the last balance-sheet was to be shown and the value of acquisitions during the current year (less depreciation for the current year). The auditor is asked to state: "Have you satisfied yourself that the valuations of movable and immovable property shown on the balance-sheet represent the current value of actual costs, whichever is lower?" (Schedule 2, Item 16.) The 1950 amendments to these regulations require a detailed list of fixed assets, showing changes in the value of each.

Knowledge concerning the actual cost of each type of property gives an opportunity to judge the adequacy of the amounts set aside for depreciation which have to be covered by the fares. It also provides important information for determining the fair interest and fair profits of the investors and fair compensation in the event of public purchase.

All five (bus) co-operatives show the amount paid for vehicles in the year under review, but no one shows the amount paid, or even the amount paid plus renewal outlays in respect of buses bought previously. In the case of "Hamekasher", there is no trace of these vehicles in the latest balance-sheet; the only official hint of their existence is an item under "Expenditures" in the profit and loss account; "Rental of vehicles from Hamechabar" Inc. The report for the year 1949-50 to the Registrar of Co-operatives contains no further information concerning "Hamechabar". However in the report for the previous year, we learn in a note of the auditor that Hamechabar is a co-operative whose membership is made up entirely of the members of Hamekasher, but we are not told anything further.

In "Egged" and "Drom Yehuda" and "Dan", the vehicles are also owned by "subsidiaries": "Yania, Inc."; "Hamadrim, Inc."; and "Nahar, Inc." (respectively). In the case of "Dan" the latest balance-sheet carries a veiled reference to the cost of the vehicles, by way of listing the lump sum value of the shares of "Nahar" as assets of "Dan" and this value, as the auditor states, covers "the property and goodwill' of Nahar. We must assume that the buses are included in the property.

The way of learning how much has been spent on buses currently in use is to reconstruct the whole history, including:

1. a summary of the records of purchases from year to year over a period of many years (more than one-fifth of the buses currently in use were bought more than 16 years ago);
2. determining the outlays for renewal of vehicles for the same period; and
3. determining what part of the gross original cost plus renewal is represented by vehicles or parts of vehicles no longer in use.

This last sum must be subtracted from one and two. Calculations worked backwards is the shortest way to evaluating the original cost of vehicles currently in use. But there seems no way of doing this through the official financial reports alone.

Shachar, bus co-operative in Haifa, is in a separate category and its balance-sheet shows that it owns buses. For 1948 the value of these buses was shown at "cost minus depreciation". This, for a public utility, is not adequate, since we do not know if the "cost" is the original cost and "depreciation" is not shown separately. For 1949, Shachar shows the buses at "market value"; the auditor explains that the management of the co-operative decided to increase the book value of the vehicles in order to offset the increase in the value of the members' shares (prior to the distribution of capital which was connected with the "reform").

In no report of any of the bus co-operatives is the total monthly or annual income per member stated, nor are the components of the total income presented in such a form that the total may easily be calculated. It is customary for the bus co-operatives to pay the Histadrut tax, income tax, and contributions to charities for their members, over and above their wages. Yet we cannot tell from the report whether all or part of item I is indeed a part of the member's income.

Wages data are included in the monthly operating statements to the Controller and the information about members is clearly separated from that for non-members. Furthermore, there is a breakdown by occupation and the number of hours worked is also shown. However, the report of the Inter-departmental Committee raises doubts about their accuracy. The reports are not filled out in a standard way by the five bus co-operatives. They specifically exclude payments to members and non-members aside from salary and overtime and therefore supplied no direct answer to the question: How much do the members take out of the enterprise?

There is also the special payments made to members, such as occasional distribution of capital. In the balance-sheets for 1949, the auditors pointed out in special notes which assets of the various co-operatives had been increased in value "by decision of the management". In several cases the auditors also identified specifically, among the liabilities, a special fund which had been set up from which payments were or will presumably be made to members. The actual payments made from these funds and the conditions under which payments could be made are not stated.

There are four categories of workers in the bus co-operatives: Old members; new members; permanent hired workers; and temporary hired workers.

In 1950, the hired workers in three of the five bus co-operatives (Egged, Drom Yehuda and Dan) constituted 37 per cent to 38 per cent; in Hamekasher 31 per cent and in Shachar 19 per cent of the total labour force.

One in five among the hired workers of the bus co-operatives is an apprentice. Nine-tenths of the apprentices are garage workers, the other tenth are office workers.

Severance allowances are paid only to hired workers. Seniority supplements, formerly paid only to certain hired workers, are being paid also to members. All members receive equal (basic) pay. Hired workers are paid according to an occupational scale.

Though it is a practice for the bus co-operatives to carry some members without the obligation of work, those who have been incapacitated in service and also the widows of members, this is not revealed in the annual financial reports of the co-operatives.

Sons and sons-in-law of members have preference when candidates are selected for membership. This has been a part of the rules of the (bus) co-operatives for many years. It represents a continuation of a long established owners' psychology and not the rise of nepotism. However, now that the co-operatives are large important public utilities, the effect of this practice is unfair discrimination.

The rule which fixes the age of new members as 32 or less also applies to "permanents".

The sub-committee of the Histadrut Executive which negotiated the merger of the three bus co-operatives, Shachar, Egged (Eshed) and Drom Yehuda, in 1951 reported: "We suggested that the membership in the merged co-operative should be all inclusive, i.e. include drivers, skilled workers, porters, cleaning staff, workers in the garage and office employees.

The members decided that, as in the past, only drivers should be eligible. This has a social aspect because then the same wage is paid to all (members). If the other proposals had been accepted the wage scale would have been guided by skill."

Paragraph 65 of the Co-operative Societies Ordinance, 1933, includes, *inter alia*, the subjects concerning which the Minister, under whose jurisdiction the co-operatives may be at any time, may make regulations.

(*d*) Prescribe the conditions to be complied with by persons applying for admission or have been admitted as members; provide for the election and admission of members, and the payment to be made and the interest to be acquired before the exercise of the right of membership.

(*m*) Prescribe the extent to which a society may limit the number of its members.

(*p*) Provision for the share capital of any society to be variable in such a way as may be necessary to ensure that shares shall not appreciate in value and that the necessary capital shall be available for the society as required.

(*q*) Provision for persons qualified under the rules of the society not to be excluded from membership without due cause.

In practice the Registrar has intervened very little in these matters and even then not on the basis of his legal powers.

The 1950 Regulations (to the Co-operative Societies Ordinance, 1933) ask the auditor of producers' co-operatives (WPSTS) to report to what extent hired labour is used and if the practice is in accordance with the co-operative's rules. In practice this area is left to the Histadrut.

The members have two claims against the assets of the co-operative in the event of the sale or liquidation of the society: To divide up the reserves and redeem the shares at face value (if there is sufficient money after prior obligations have been discharged).

PLAN FOR EVALUATING SERVICES AND PAYMENT FOR MEMBERS OF BUS CO-OPERATIVES

Period	*What they give*	*What they get*
(A.) Monthly	Labour Management Use of Capital	Wages and overtime—social benefits and payments in kind. Undefined insurance rights.
(B.) Occasionally	Risk of Capital	Bonuses
(C.) Possibly once	Surrender of future claims.	Redemption of "shares" Division of reserves.

In the debate in the Histadrut Executive Committee, the bus co-operatives demanded 25 per cent of their monthly wages as a bonus for management services. The Histadrut fixed a range of 15 to 20 per cent to be finally settled later. Calculated on a IL.100 monthly wage, this is a payment for management services of IL.15 to IL.25 per member.

If the bus co-operatives devoted a sum equal to 25 per cent of their monthly wages to this purpose, they could employ one manager for every four members or, assuming a much higher rate of pay for managerial services than for bus driving, one manager for every eight members.

The investment of the members in the share capital of their respective bus co-operatives is today (1951) uniformly valued at IL.1,500 each. The Co-operative Societies Ordinance specifies a maximum annual dividend of 6 per cent of the value of the share, IL.7·5 per month.

The purpose of the "reform" was to make it possible to meet the need for expanding employment in the bus co-operatives by introducing a maximum of members and a minimum of hired labour. Most of the candidates for membership were ex-service men and they could not afford to pay the high prices being charged for membership shares, which ranged up to more than IL.3,000. With the reform, the price of shares was lowered to IL.1,500. This was the purpose of "the reform".

Before they lowered the cost of the share which a new member must henceforth pay, the members withdrew from the capital of the bus co-operatives and distributed the amount withdrawn among themselves as one-time bonuses, and partial compensation for their past labours and for self-restraint in not withdrawing all the surplus.

In Hamekasher and Shachar the intangible values, which were added to the assets by the decision of the management, were immediately and specifically balanced by the setting up of a special fund as a liability from which the members were to withdraw their bonuses. The path from the added intangible asset to the added liability to the pocket of the member is not clear from the official financial statements.

The procedure in Hamekasher is the most clear.

In the balance-sheet for the year ending 31 March, 1949, an item of IL.117,000 is listed on the assets side as "addition to the value" of the land and building "according to the decision of the management". The auditor states in a footnote on this balance sheet:

"The price of the fixed property was determined, according to the statement of the management, on the basis of their value in the market. The sum added to the value of the fixed property is carried over to a fund for enlarging the members' shares. This question is being discussed by the Histadrut."

On the liabilities side, we indeed find an item "Fund for increasing members' shares", IL.117,000.

In the following year, the new fund again appears on the balance-sheet but reduced to IL.82,000. Members are withdrawing their *pro rata* shares from the fund in three equal annual payments. A total of 114 members are reported on the 1949 balance-sheet; therefore the IL.117,000 of intangible value provided a IL.1,000 bonus for each member (over a period of three years).

Shachar: IL.994,000 (called "Adjustment Fund for transfer of value added") was divided among 393 members or an average IL.2,225. However a comparison with Hamekasher's IL.1,000 bonus is not correct. Shachar had no subsidiary company which owned its buses like the other four co-operatives, including Hamekasher. The subsidiaries are possible sources of "reorganization" bonuses.

In the case of Drom Yehuda, IL.189,000 was added to the value of the fixed property, this is a bonus of IL.1,000 for each of the 188 members. The shares held by the members were increased not by IL.1,000 but by IL.1,275.

Egged did not add the intangible value on the balance sheet. . . .

The vehicles (buses, taxis, etc.) belong to its subsidiary the "Yania" Co-operative and Egged rents the property from it. In the balance-sheet for 1951 an item, added value, was entered for the vehicles, according to the decision of the management. The procedure in Egged appears to have been very similar to that in Dan. In both cases the "reform" bonus appears to be intimately (organically) intertwined with a "reorganization bonus".

In 1947 two bus co-operatives, Hamaavir and Ichud-Regev, were amalgamated to form Dan. Separate corporate entities were formed, a drivers' co-operative, Dan, with no transport equipment, whose membership shares were nominal; and a bus renting company, Nahar, to which was assigned all the transport equipment formerly owned by the two bus co-operatives. Every member of the new bus co-operative, Dan, held IL.1,000 shares in Nahar.

The licences to operate bus services had been obtained in the name of Nahar rather than in the name of Dan. This was a means for lowering tax obligations to the Mandatory Government and it may also have been intended as a measure to avoid supervision by the Histadrut, particularly in the matter of hired labour. Unlike the bus owning subsidiaries of Hamekasher (Hamechabar), Egged (Yania); and Drom Yehuda (Hamadrim), Nahar was set up as a company and not as a co-operative. The Histadrut insisted that Nahar, though formally a limited company, also was subject to the audit of the Co-operative Centre (Merkaz Haco-operatzia).

Since Hamaavir, one of the two amalgamating co-operatives which merged to establish Dan-Hamaavir, was much better equipped than Ichud Regev, a member of Hamaavir received IL.1,000, while a member of Ichud Regev received IL.275.

The 1949 bonus in the case of Dan was combined with a sale of the shares of Nahar, owned by Dan members as individuals, to the co-operative Dan. Formally, this converted Dan into a producers co-operative, owning the producing instruments with which it worked—or nearly so. Nahar still existed, though its only apparent effect was to add confusion to the accounting reports.

In the balance-sheet of Nahar of 31 March, 1949, there is a new asset—"Goodwill" IL.532,000 and also three separate items under three types of property, each labelled "Addition of differences in evaluation", totalling IL.630,000. The total of these two tangible values, IL.1,162,000, is set up as a reserve fund under liabilities, an average of IL.2,200 for each of the 525 members (of Dan). In the balance-sheet of Dan for the same date, the assets include "purchase of all the shares of Nahar at cost", IL.1,582,350. Over four-fifths of this purchase price, i.e. IL.1,162,000, was for the tangible assets which had just been created. There are hints, but no complete answer as to how the intangible assets were transferred to the personal accounts of the members.

A second item in the liabilities of Dan for 1949, IL.68,000 "Provident Fund for members of Dan and Nahar", increased by IL.590,000. The balance-sheet has a note that IL.480,000 of the Provident Fund is "to be paid in monthly payments during a period of five years beginning 2 February, 1950". This appears to be a part of the channel from the "goodwill" etc. of Nahar to the housing of the members of Dan.

At the time of the organization of Dan, the bonus of 1949 was paid (simultaneously) with the sale of Nahar to Dan. In this period a business evaluated at IL.560,000 was sold for IL.1,580,000 or at a profit of more than IL.1,000,000 or 200 per cent—IL.2,200 profit on IL.1,050 invested by each member.

The process in Egged was similar to that in Dan. A previous investigator states that the Egged property was revalued and IL.723 was distributed to each member. However, there is no information about the bonus paid with the resale of the property of Yania back to Egged. Egged has a second subsidiary called Nitzah for holding real estate. The investigator indicated that in 1945 Egged members each paid IL.325 for their shares in Nitzah which then bought the real estate from Egged. In 1947 Egged bought these shares for IL.840 each, i.e. reacquired its own property from its members at a profit of IL.515 per member.

In the debate on the "reform" in the Histadrut Executive, the sum withdrawn from the co-operatives and divided among the members was stated to have been IL.3,000,000. A spokesman for the co-operatives disputed certain details but not the statement, which is either accurate or an understatement. These bonuses, together with all other past bonuses, are considered as compensation for risking the capital which the members supplied over the years.

A bonus of IL.2,200 paid in 1949 would be equivalent to a 10 per cent profit on an actual investment of IL.1,000 over a period of some 15 years. Actually, investments made in 1934 were not (the equivalent of) one-fourth of IL.1,000 and in 1937 the shares "in societies for the transportation of passengers" were IL.30 to IL.250 each. In 1935 the total number of members in the bus co-operatives was only half the number at the time of the "reform". The bonus of 1949, if considered as an accumulated profit dividend, reflects an annual return of over 25 per cent.

In the early years of the bus co-operatives there was a real risk of the members losing their investment. But as the co-operative enterprises became consolidated, they lost their speculative character.

As a possible justification for the size of the bonus, the changes in the purchasing power of money could be considered. The value of the shares was increased from IL.250 or less in 1937 to IL.500 in 1949. This increase was far more than the increase in the index of retail prices. Since the nominal value of the members' shares was increased without requiring additional investments on their part (i.e. the members) the original equity of the members was fully protected and there was no need for special bonuses for this purpose.

The similarity of "stock watering" to the "reform" bonus lies in the fact that both achieve profit for the original owners through the adjustment of book values.

The Co-operative Ordinance of 1933 states:

S.30 1. No part of the funds of a registered society shall be divided by way of bonus or dividend or otherwise among its members at a rate exceeding that prescribed in the regulations.

The relevant Regulations read:

S.39 10 (*a*) A dividend on share capital shall only be paid by registered societies with limited liability and shall not exceed six per cent. No bonus based on shares shall be distributed to the members.

The co-operatives did not call the payments a "bonus based on shares". The account of each member was credited and the members were able to withdraw this sum at certain intervals.

The reform was decided upon during 1949, before the annual profit-and-loss accounts were prepared. Drom Yehuda and Shachar showed operational losses for the year of the reform.

Logically the source of the payments was either surplus (the net results of the activities of the current year) or reserve (the accumulation of previous years). Concerning surpluses, the Regulations prescribe:

S.39 4. The reserve fund shall be indivisible and no member shall be entitled to a specific share in such fund, save in the case where a registered society is in liquidation or is being wound up. In such case that portion of the reserve fund left over after all liabilities have been met shall, except where the rules of the society otherwise provide, be divided among the members in such proportion as the share capital or interest of each member bears to the capital of the registered society.

On paper, the Histadrut would appear to have been empowered to prevent the "reform". For example, Section Vav (six), Para. 4 of the Rules of Dan, approved on 21 September, 1945, gave Histadrut delegates two rights:

(*a*) Participation in general meetings of the co-operative; and
(*b*) postponement of action by a general meeting on any proposal which, in their opinion, was contrary to the labour co-operative principles in Israel.

The issue was to be dealt with by arbitration between the bus co-operative and the Histadrut, and if a decision was not reached within a month, the co-operative was free to act. According to the amendments to these provisions in 1949, the rights of the Histadrut were to be exercised by the Co-operative Centre (Merkaz Haco-operatzia).

The report of the Executive Committee of the Histadrut, of 21 December, 1950, published in June 1951, summarizes the attitude of the Histadrut Executive Committee about "reform". In December, 1949, the majority of the Histadrut opposed the "reform", tried to stop it, but felt powerless to do this. This feeling of powerlessness in face of decisions of the bus co-operatives had already found clear expression a year earlier. In December 1949, the idea of demanding that the money be returned was debated but rejected as impracticable.

In 1949, Mr. Pinchas Lubianiker (who later became known as Lavon) then secretary of the Histadrut, called for bus services to be taken out of the hands of the co-operatives. Faced with this demand, the bus co-operatives needed the support of the Histadrut. The Histadrut was reluctant to continue carrying responsibility without increased supervision over their activities. Out of these circumstances arose a 12-point decision of the Executive Committee, dated 21 December, 1950, and 7 January, 1951, which was accepted, with some reluctance, by Shachar, Egged and Drom Yehuda as the basis for their merger into one bus co-operative, Egged (Eshed).

Point 10 of this decision details the four areas in which Egged (Eshed) co-operative cannot act without the prior approval of the Histadrut—mortgage, sale, transfer or lease of property. The details given will be defined when the rules of Egged (Eshed) will be prepared; Chevrat Haovdim must give its decision within 20 days of the receipt of the request; and the whole of Point 10 will be included in the Rules of Egged (Eshed).

Point 9 (of the 12 points) forbids the distribution of "funds" in the event of a formal liquidation of the co-operative and forbids in general, distribution from "established funds" without Histadrut approval. However, these provisions go little further than Regulation 39 (4) of the Co-operative Societies Ordinance, 1933, quoted earlier; if there is a legal loophole in the one, it exists also in the other. When Shachar added an intangible value to her assets and balanced this value with a special fund from which members could draw bonuses, it may be claimed that the money never was in an "established fund" and therefore its distribution was not prohibited. Yet the intention of the Histadrut Executive was to prevent future "reforms".

Points 5, 10 and 11 (Administrative Relations of the Histadrut and the Co-operatives)

Following a brief experience in which the Co-operative Centre (Merkaz Haco-operatzia) had exercised the rights of the Histadrut in all direct supervisory relations with the bus co-operatives, its Executive Committee decided that Histadrut representatives are to participate not only in general meetings of the co-operative (as formerly) but also are to be members of the Secretariat—one delegate during a one-year experiment will only attend meetings; the second delegate will have an active role in the regular affairs (Management) of the co-operative.

In defining the subjects in which the Histadrut is to have "rights", a list of 14 subjects replaces the general provisions in the 1945 Rules of Dan. In place of the right of the Histradut representative to postpone decisions of the general meeting, action may not be taken by the co-operative without prior Histadrut approval for the transfer of a lease of property; making mortgages; for making large loans; and concluding an agreement or partnerships with outside bodies.

Points 6 to 9 of the Histadrut Executive Committee's decision deal with members' wages, reserve funds, the order (i.e. the priority) of various claims out of revenue and the distribution of reserves and other funds in the event of dissolution. Only in the event of an actual dissolution as approved by the Histadrut or necessitated by nationalization of the enterprises, may these (i.e. reserves and other funds) be distributed among the members.

Regular returns to the members which must not be increased are:

(*a*) monthly wages, class aleph-aleph (AA), now to be classed only as "aleph";
(*b*) social rights (not defined, but presumably those now enjoyed); and
(*c*) 15 per cent to 25 per cent of the monthly salary for "effort and self-direction (i.e. management) of the enterprise".

The payment for "effort and self-direction", previously included in the salary, is now to be added to the salary. These changes together may add up to between IL.20-IL.40 per month to the member's emoluments. Payments must also not be increased from the distribution of 50 per cent of the surplus profits, after the deduction for depreciation and for payment of income tax, half of which is collectable only when a member leaves the co-operative. The remaining 50 per cent of the surplus is to be divided as follows: 45 per cent to reserve funds and 5 per cent to the Histadrut (Chevrat Haovdim). The auditor's report on Egged for the year ending 31 March, 1950, notes: "For the past two years the co-operative has not paid the Histadrut part of its profits as required by the rules".

Discontinuance of future bonuses to the members appears to be compensation (i.e. a counter measure) for raising the level of the regular payments. The new level is more specifically defined than before and only the administrative alertness of the Histadrut representatives can be an outside check on the possible emergence of new "social benefits".

Point 12 of the decision of the Histadrut Executive Committee establishes machinery for adjusting the differences between Egged (Eshed), Dan and Hamekasher about spheres of operation, their bonuses, etc.

The prohibition of future bonuses may have had another unfortunate effect, in driving a wedge between the interests of the war veterans who had benefited from the "reform" bonuses and the new members. Possibly some of these (i.e. new members) felt that when they were buying membership, they were acquiring, among other rights, the right to participate in future bonuses. It remains the view of the bus co-operatives that their property is simply the private property of its members. Once this fact is grasped, the "reform" bonus becomes quite understandable from their viewpoint.

Mr. Weisbrot of Egged stated at the meeting with the Histadrut Executive Committee in December 1950: "I do not know what has caught hold of these members (of the Histadrut Executive) who wished to condemn us because of the 'reform'. There are those who know how to value the members' activities; there are times when you praise us for the great deeds of the transport workers in difficult times. And those members after years of great suffering have acquired houses with 'reform' money. Among them are members who still owe not small amounts; instead of the Histadrut condemning them, she should give additional loans to (these) members. If the members (i.e. of the Histadrut Executive Committee) would overlook small matters, there would be an entirely different mutual feeling."

The Histadrut Executive in continuing to condemn the "reform" bonus publicly was basing itself on the view that the property of the bus co-operatives is not the private property of its members. One member of the Histadrut Executive Committee referred to the use of "the funds of the community" for private needs. Another referred to the extraction of vast sums from the transport system for distribution among members as "almost the action of a man who handles a matter of community character as if it were solely his own."

"Members of the co-operatives should not see themselves as owners of the transport enterprise but as workers in them in the service of the public. . . ."

Mr. Davidson, of Drom Yehuda, stated that the co-operatives have made great concessions on the assumption and belief that the Histadrut "sees the enterprise not as community (public) enterprise, but as one created and built by the members, who will continue to be its owners and continue to give of their best for the good of the community.

The real question is not whose property the "reform" disposed of, but did the disposal of it exceed the legal and moral rights of the co-operative members? The bus co-operatives are bound by one morality and legal structure by virtue of being co-operatives, and to another by virtue of being public utilities.

The title to the property was with the co-operative members but the disposal appears to have run counter to co-operative law and morality and the public utility morality. One of the tasks now facing the community is to give effective legal expression to the public utility morality. The alternative may be to rely on the co-operatives to continue giving of their best for the good of the community."

The level of Bus Service

The Controller of Road Transport confirms that the bus co-operatives turned down no opportunity to purchase buses. Several members of the Histadrut Executive Committee felt that had the will to acquire buses in the interest of the national need been strong enough to overcome the "selfish interests of the members," a way could have been found to convert the large sums which were distributed to members in the "reform" into buses. The co-operatives emphasize the objective difficulties which were very real; their critics emphasize that had they (i.e. the bus co-operatives) been imbued with the right spirit, they might have overcome the objective difficulties.

Even a private corporation might under these circumstances have preferred to save its reserves, rather than distribute them, in view of the rising cost of buses and the future need for a large number of buses. Histadrut critics want the co-operatives to act not according to standards of privately owned corporations but according to pioneering standards; and are attempting now to impose this by direct Histadrut supervision of their (i.e. the bus co-operatives) activities. However, there is a third kind of standard: a public utility standard, which can take on meaning only through effective public control. Perhaps the lack of buses is basically ascribable to the absence of effective public control, both over the purchasing programme of the co-operatives and the use of their reserves.

For many years there was an element of social control by the Jewish community over the rates (fares) charged by the co-operatives. Before the birth of the State, they voluntarily submitted the scale of fares to the Jewish Agency for approval. In spite of this, setting the fares is still a matter of bargaining based on estimates and not of public decision based on established principles and detailed and objective information. What is needed is a mechanism by which the citizen-rider can put his view effectively before the proper authority and get a real answer, i.e. changes in practice. A third factor had to be considered; the quality of social control, exercised on both the co-operative form and its public utility functions. Only with social control can the public utility function be guaranteed (i.e. the co-operative form may be adapted to serve the needs of transportation).

The technique by which co-operative capital was distributed among members was accompanied by a slight rise in the hired worker ratio. The distinction between members and hired workers is based on an occupational differentiation. The contrast in income between the members and workers is very sharp. The relations between the members and the workers have taken the form of relations between independent employers and organized employees.

The members have held fast to a number of basic co-operative principles and established co-operative practices. All members work. Shares and votes are equally distributed among members (i.e. one vote per member). The emoluments of members are equal. The Management is elected by and decisions are brought before general meetings.

Income and rights of the hired workers are far inferior to the members. The profit motive has a very important place in the bus co-operatives.

These may be considered a "business partnership in which the partners who comprise two-thirds of the workers, are organized as a co-operative".

The co-operatives have failed to give a basis for social control and wilfully or carelessly provide with considerable delay, confusing and incomplete information about their activities. They have refused on many occasions to deal with the public with a minimum of courtesy and consideration. They have treated themselves with extremely generous regular incomes and have on occasion voted themselves generous bonuses, at the expense of the service and minimal comfort of the ordinary citizen and worker. (Situation has much improved.)

The co-operatives are acting as they did when a bus co-operative consisted of a handful of men who pooled their resources to establish a three-bus co-operative to ply between a colony and a city in Mandatory Palestine 25 years ago. The property was theirs; no one else contributed to it and no one guaranteed that they would not lose it. They were fulfilling their public responsibility by keeping their line operating. Among their major virtues were their self-dependence and independence. Since the bus co-operatives arose in response to a certain set of conditions, which we may designate roughly as pre-capitalistic, and since our society has now moved into a new period, which we may designate as capitalistic, this form has become anachronistic and constitutes an impediment to progress.

The actual practices to which the co-operatives resort to press their claim for increased fares, etc., can be considered as no more proof that co-operatives are today inappropriate than as proof that the co-operative members are morally retrograde. The undesirable practices of the co-operatives are no more inevitably implicit in the co-operative idea than they are completely attributable to personal evil. They may be considered the result of known social pressures against which no adequate social counter-pressure has been reared.

It was the co-operative's attempt to expand membership, which, in the light of their insistence on protecting their traditional "property rights", gave (i.e. gave birth to) the peculiar co-operative form of a "reform" bonus which in other countries was done by "stock watering". The insistence on equal pay to all members leads to a rejection of the Histadrut proposal of differential pay and thereby crystallizes the "unco-operative" differences between the members and the hired workers.

The co-operative representatives have made clear that the co-operative members identify themselves as members of the Histadrut. The participation of the Histadrut may be considered not the intervention of an outside body, but as the creation of better conditions for the adaptation of the co-operative to current public needs. Yet there can be no doubt that this is a step towards the protection of co-operative principles and the co-operative future.

The Controller of Road Transport has the authority to grant or withhold licences at his discretion but not to commit the Government to the granting of an exclusive licence. The "rights of the co-operatives to the 'lines' they control are based solely on custom but not on law".

The anachronism lies rather with the system of social control over the co-operatives. The laws which give the basis for controlling them did not visualize co-operative monopolies, but deal separately with co-operatives in general and the transport services; they reflect Mandatory conditions 20 years ago (i.e. 1931). The manner of the administration of the laws has not been such as to bridge the gap; in many respects it is still more attuned to the pre-State Yishuv need of co-operative independence than to the present requirements of co-operative responsibility.

The Histadrut has come to play a key role as the representative of the public interest in supervising the bus co-operatives. The problem is: how much of its responsibility to see that this utility functions in the public interest can the Government delegate? It is a truism that internal relations are best handled if possible on an internal basis. The reticence of the Registrar of Co-operative Societies to exercise his legal powers in this area must be considered only wise.

In certain aspects of the services, particularly routing, scheduling, and public relations, more direct intervention by the Government than in the past is needed. In the area of financial control, the need for direct and immediate Government control is still clearer. Effective responsibility is inseparable from the control not only of fares and accounting but also of the costs on which the fares are based, and of saving and investment policies. The social control over the co-operative character of the enterprises requires

(*a*) prevention of speculation and excessive profits and
(*b*) reduction to a minimum of hired labour.

The first need is obviously met by those financial controls which would be instituted from a public utility viewpoint; that is, the measures taken to protect the passengers would automatically ensure the non-exploitative (co-operative) character of the enterprise *vis-à-vis* the public.

The great difference between the payments to members and the wages of their hired worker makes it desirable for the co-operatives to take on hired workers. With adequate financial control, the difference would be radically reduced and the need for direct intervention in the use of hired labour by anybody outside the co-operative would be greatly reduced, and to the extent it (control) was needed it could best be exercised by the Histadrut.

Transferring the bus co-operatives to public ownership would replace producer-owned organization by a consumer-owned organization. Many advantages are believed to flow from the elimination of the owners' interest, such as

(*a*) the problem of protecting the public from exploitation in fixing bus fares;
(*b*) orientation of the service to social rather than to business objectives; and
(*c*) improving labour relations.

The "line" form is used to refer to any organization in which authority "flows from the top to the bottom, without those on the bottom having the right to determine the selection of management, the planning of operations, the assignment of duties, or the division of income". This form, most clearly exemplified in the Army, is also common to the Civil Service and to private corporations. From this point on, "line" form will be used interchangeably with "private corporation" form, because this is the real alternative to the co-operative form for the organization of the bus enterprises. Under private ownership this would surely be true; it is almost as certain under public ownership.

Consideration should be given to the technical character of bus operation. The drivers may be subject to time tables, reporting requirements and spot checking; but unlike factory workers, their work is not done, generally, under direct supervision. This is less true of intra-urban than of inter-urban routes; it is very true of both at a time of special transport needs or emergency. In the light of these considerations, it might be unfortunate to abandon the co-operative form, so long as the possibility remains to adjust it to the overriding need for effective social control. Such adjustment requires that the ownership rights of the members, if not eliminated, must be greatly curtailed.

Thought is being devoted in co-operative and Histadrut circles in Israel not only to the need and possibility of limiting emoluments of members and eliminating the payments from the division of reserves, but also to the setting of general, over-all limits of members' income so as to protect the labour character of these organizations. However, there is a danger that such practices, if applied to bus co-operatives, might undermine the feeling of independence and the initiative which are the soul of the co-operative form. The emoluments of members should vary within reasonable limits and reward efficiency and penalize inefficiency while guaranteeing a decent livelihood under any circumstances.

The Regulating Commission of the Public Board could determine in advance the "planned" passenger kilometre cost of pre-determined routes. Factors beyond the control of the co-operative management would have to lead to a reconsideration of the plan. (An example of such a factor is a change in the cost of fuel.) However, savings from the planned cost which could be ascribed to the efforts of the management and workers could be distributed in part, among them. Such distribution could be of two sorts: a workers' bonus, equal for all workers whether members or not; and a members' bonus to members only.

Within the framework of effective social control, the nationwide bus co-operative may prove to be not only a form unique to Israel, but outstanding in the level of transport service it gives. The first stage recommended:

1. A special officer for financial and statistical reports of the bus co-operatives should be appointed.
2. Changes in the categories and rates of emoluments of members

should be temporarily subjected to prior Governmental approval.

3. Passengers' councils, to serve as advocates of the passengers, should be established in the three major cities.
4. Preparations should be made for an informed debate and decision on the future form of bus ownership and control by preparing recommendations of desirable alternative forms.

The reporting officer should have the use of all the powers for obtaining the financial and statistical reports which the law today gives to the Minister of Labour, the Minister of Transport, the Registrar of Co-operative Societies, and the Controller of Road Transport. It would be best to have an outside specialist, with the Controller and the Registrar acting as advisors.

Three weak points in the current reporting practices would have to be improved.

(*a*) Uniform reliable data on total emoluments and operating costs must be supplied.

(*b*) A comprehensive analysis must be made of members' total emoluments of all types from the co-operative.

(*c*) A breakdown of the reported value of vehicles and fixed property into original cost, renewal outlays (not including ordinary maintenance), and value added by administrative decisions, all these minus depreciation.

(Generally speaking these suggestions have been accepted.)

Passengers' Councils should be established

The present regional organization of the Controller of Road Transport should be paralleled by independent passengers' councils. They might include the municipality, rural communities in the area, the Histadrut and other economic and social groups with a direct interest in passenger service. The councils would hear complaints from individuals and groups and attempt to secure redress directly from the bus co-operative; and failing this, it (i.e. the regional passenger council) would attempt to obtain redress from the local (i.e. the regional) controller, and if necessary, from the Minister (presumably the Minister of Transport).

Alternative Permanent Form is regulation by a commission of a united national bus co-operative. The commission would be an integrated body, and would differ from the present regulatory structure, in which supervision of the bus co-operatives is divided between several bodies. It (i.e. the commission) would retain overall national responsibility, but it would delegate responsibility to regional offices, either its own, or those set up by the municipalities. The "reporting officer" would be part of its staff. The commission would be responsible to the people and to the Government for the efficiency of bus transport in Israel. The law establishing the commission would define in principle the new rights and duties of the members of the co-operative.

A public board could be established and the co-operative could operate the system for the board. The public board would differ from the regulatory commission in that it would not merely supervise the bus enterprise but would be directly responsible for administering it. With this added responsibility would go added powers. For example, it would have to be able not only to levy disciplinary fines, but, subject to due process, to make disciplinary dismissals. The general structure of the public board might resemble that of the Commission. Under the board, there would be no owners' incentive, because the shares would have been acquired by Government and the members (of the bus co-operatives) would no longer be owners. The board, unlike the Commission, would not merely approve the level of reserves and the investment programme, but also would determine them (i.e. fix the amounts). Rate fixing would be still simpler for the board than for the commission, because the scope and the power of the co-operative would be much less (i.e. contracted).

The central problems in determining the final form of organization of the bus enterprise is to get adequate control while providing the greatest possible amount of independence.

SUMMARY OF EIGHT ARTICLES ON BUS CO-OPERATIVES BY K. SHABATAI, 1953, AND REACTIONS TO THESE ARTICLES[83]

Mr. Shabatai (in his seventh article) writes that

"I told somebody who knows the bus services in the country that I plan to meet with the Eshed people; the man laughed and said 'this will not be one of your easiest assignments. They will come to you with praises and battle. . . . They are not afraid of anything; . . .'

"In spite of the warnings, I was surprised. I have seen much in my life; but the conversation with the Eshed spokesman was my first experience of its kind. I asked for information, the Torah which I should study. And they assaulted me with arguments instead of replies to questions; they showered me with such questions as 'why do I think that I must have these and those data which is an internal matter?' 'Why does this question interest me since the public is not at all interested in it? And why am I enquiring into and investigating a polemic question?' To put it bluntly they wanted to decide the questions which I should ask; this you may ask and this you may not ask. Admittedly I did not get much; their replies were either evasive or they did not reply at all."

He cites two examples: To his question whether they did or did not have a monopoly, Eshed answered: "The co-operative is not the only means of overland transportation. Everyone who wants to travel can use the train, taxi, truck, tender, etc." Mr. Shabatai then asked about the gross emoluments which a member receives. The reply was that even if Mr. Shabatai will report "the truth and only the truth" about the emoluments of the Eshed people, it will still be a smear. The Eshed spokesman asked "why don't the press write how much 'A' earns in the Histadrut; 'B' in Davar and 'C' in another place of employment?"

Mr. Shabatai then pressed the Chevrat Haovdim representative on the Eshed management since early 1952, to answer questions.

"You are the Histadrut trustee, the representative of the public in this sensitive artery of the life of the State and of the Histadrut and I am yours and the public's representative. . . . After some thought, Mr. K. replied, 'ask'."

Mr. Shabatai then asked Mr. K. that since Eshed claims that they operate with a deficit, how can they justify the fact that every Eshed member received the salary of a grade AA driver, irrespective whether or not he is entitled to this on the basis of skill. Eshed also pays every member a management supplement of 20 per cent and other fringe benefits which no other institution in the country pays. Is this possible, Mr. Shabatai asked, because Eshed has a monopoly. "If Eshed paid every worker according to his work . . . would not the operational deficit be smaller by as much as several thousand pounds?"

Mr. K. replied that he had used the same arguments with Eshed and its stock answer is: "We are all equal." This can be interpreted as "equal reward for all at the highest possible standards". But Mr. K. added there was an aspect which preceded the question of remuneration of members, viz. "the considerable waste apparent in all the activities. . . . On the basis of any economic calculation this must be a good business. . . . They (Eshed) earn a monthly surplus of IL.300,000. . . . There is no doubt that the purchasing procedure is not in order and . . . that the control should be increased. . . ."

At a later date Mr. K., replying to Mr. Shabatai's question whether there is hope that the position will improve, said: "I have come to pessimistic conclusions. The organization (i.e. Egged (Eshed)) is so hopeless and so out of line with the co-operative way, that only emergency measures can bring Eshed back on the right course. . . . I believe that the Histadrut can succeed only if it will exert all its authority. . . . And if you ask me how it is possible to do this, I say that the decision is in the hands of the Histadrut Executive Committee and is not in my hands."

In the first article, Mr. Shabatai notes that in Israel, bus transport and Eshed buses are synonymous terms. He describes the unspeakably bad bus service and the unfriendliness and insulting attitude of the Eshed drivers and also of other (bus) co-operatives as the most serious drawback in Israel. He then quotes a tourist as having said: "Were I not a Jew, I would say that your transport and its co-operatives and the socialism all together are nothing but Jewish deceit." Mr. Shabatai adds that he can no longer distinguish between good and bad, truth and untruth, justice and injustice, in the complaints about the transport and that "he must cultivate complete amnesia and start as a new born babe with a clean slate".

Generally speaking, Mr. Shabatai writes, that in most countries it is a basic principle that transport is "a public service of supreme importance for all and that it must be subject to control". He then notes that while waiting in a long queue, he asked one of his compatriots why so many half empty buses, relatively empty by Israeli standards, and travelling in the same direction, pass without stopping.

> "You apparently are new is Israel," answered his neighbour. "This is an 'Eshed' queue and it is in the Dan territory." I asked who gave Dan this monopoly. The answer—the "Histadrut." Another man in the queue intervened; "What do you mean the Histadrut gave it to her ('Dan'). When I wanted to pay the fare to Holon (adjoining Tel Aviv) the driver answered that the bus went only to Tel Aviv and that I would have to buy another ticket on a second bus. And when I expressed astonishment that such a small country with such small distances has such a complicated transportation arrangement, my neighbour said "you will find many more difficult and complex things. And all of this is done with one object—viz. that the members of the bus co-operative can fill their pockets with gold and build themselves palaces."[84]

Mr. Shabatai reports a second conversation with a bus driver who told him to buy a ticket at the ticket office. The driver's reaction to Mr. Shabatai's plea that he could not comply with the instruction since he had been standing a long time in the queue and was tired (late afternoon) was: "All this does not concern me. You were told to go to the ticket office. Don't you understand Hebrew?"

The reaction of one of the senior Histadrut economists to the aforementioned conversation was, according to Mr. Shabatai, that the bus co-operatives are continuing to do as they please.

> "The co-operative cannot operate in such a manner (an atmosphere) and the future is bound to react against them." This is a general reaction from "Dan to Beersheba", adds Mr. Shabatai, and among the old-timer and the immigrant . . . in the ranks of the coalition and of the opposition; among the extreme fanatical orthodox group and those who pray for the coming of Comrade Malenkov; the aged and infants; man and woman. . . . The opposition to the bus co-operatives seems to be the only thing which unites the community in Zion."

He then proceeds to analyse the "sins and sinners" and to enquire what are the remedies. The Registrar of Co-operatives is reported as having replied with the following analogy to Mr. Shabatai's question as to what can be done to remedy such an untenable position. "The only thing which can be done for a twisted foot is to wear a curved shoe; you cannot put a regular shoe on a crooked foot. It is not my intention to compare our State with a crooked foot. On the contrary, there is every foundation to assume that it (the State) is healthy and that its task is to straighten out the foot. And that its deformity is an inheritance."

The Registrar is also reported by Mr. Shabatai to have said that there was no other country which had an organization similar to Eshed.[85] Mr. Shabatai then quotes the following from an unidentified writer "who has investigated this problem" about the origin of the bus co-operatives in Israel:

> "The conditions under the Mandatory regime necessitated a transportation service entirely in the hands of the Jews. This accounts for extensive development of the bus co-operatives and their conversion in the course of time into monopolies of the lines of communication in the country. We preferred a Jewish monopoly to a Mandatory ownership. which was inimical to us (Jews) and such a tool in its (Mandatory Government) hands could endanger the lines of communication between the Jewish communities. But it would be wrong to conclude from this that everything proceeded in an equitable way and that the Yishuv was satisfied with the transportation services. It forgave their weakness and did not bring the case to the attention of foreign judges (i.e. Mandatory Government judges). And it was then equally important not to permit competition within the Jewish transportation system which would have only benefited the Mandatory Government which was developing the railways, not as a means of serving but rather of isolating the Jewish communities. The Histadrut encouraged the establishment and unification of the bus co-operatives. This would increase the membership of the Histadrut. The State inherited the transportation system together with its ailments."

Mr. Shabatai then proceeds to enquire why Israel, unlike most countries in Europe and in North America, did not try to free itself from its complete dependence on the non-Government transportation system. He finds that the first mistake was that everybody concerned "made a fashion out of the troubles. . . . The bus-co-operatives are the product of certain economic and transportation policies, born out of rape. The new creature, though born out of rape, wishes to live its own life."

The State, Mr. Shabatai notes, should have pondered on how to convert a co-operative bus system, "a product of rape and war", into a normal healthy and low cost (cheap) transportation service—with railways, trams, buses or a combination of all, and to free itself from the bus co-operatives which are cumbersome, tiresome and abnormal under the existing conditions.[86]

Mr. Shabatai writes that according to the published and unpublished reports of the open and closed sessions, the Histadrut Executive Committee considered "the sick leg" as a "unicus" and a "treasure which only Israel had . . . this leg had become the property of the members of the Histadrut . . . and must be guarded, and should stand on its deformed leg ('crookedness') against any cure, God forbid". During the five post-State years the Histadrut has exercised no end of patience in endless negotiations with the bus co-operatives to safeguard for itself "the leg which is deformed (not straight)".

The second mistake, according to Mr. Shabatai, was that the Histadrut and others forgot that the basic purpose of co-operatives was to make it possible for the small man not to be swallowed by large capitalist combinations or trusts. The State of Israel, and in particular the Histadrut, tried to marry the two opposites "co-operatives and monopolies; water and fire; day and night. And yet we are surprised that it has not advanced (gone forward) in accordance with our spirit, in accordance with the Histadrut and co-operative spirit."

Mr. Shabatai proceeds to test the validity of the Eshed contention that "it is unlike other monopolies because it is under very strict Governmental and Histadrut control." In Israel today, as in the pre-State period, there are only two concessions, one for the development of the Dead Sea and a second for electric power. Mr. David Weinstein, the legal adviser of Chevrat Haovdim, according to Mr. Shabatai, replied in the affirmative to the question whether the Government "could legally issue new licences for existing routes or for new routes", and that "the co-operative would not have a legal case against the new bodies". Mr. Zeev Onn, who on behalf of the Histadrut committee of three on road transportation, had carried on most of the negotiations with the bus co-operatives, agreed with Mr. Weinstein's replies and added that

> "there was not and there is not such a monopoly (i.e. for transportation). . . . At one period in the course of the negotiations, Egged and Drom Yehuda opposed while the other three bus co-operatives, Dan, Hamekasher and Shachar were for a union of all bus co-operatives. . . . We told the opponents that the Government would issue to the new body licences for their routes. It is true that there is no concession or monopoly. But there is something worse than that, viz. Chazakah" (rights of presumption or squatter rights). Jews are prone to turn worlds upside down for this cause (of Chazakah), to shed blood, to descend into the land of others."

According to Mr. Shabatai, a member of the Secretariat of Merkaz Haco-operatzia, (Y. Ritov), agreed that there was no monopoly and allegedly said: "The feeling of having a monopoly is not less serious than having a monopoly. . . . A Jewish group organized a transportation company, purchased automobiles and obtained licences for them. But the drivers of our buses cut the tyres of the new vehicles and caused the liquidation of the new company." A member of the Management Committee of Eshed replying to the question as to who gave them the monopoly said: "We conquered the country. The Histadrut gave it to us."

Mr. Shabatai notes that everybody agreed that the members of the bus co-operatives showed no evidence of grasping the fundamental truth that the transportation of passengers is a key public service which belongs to the people. The members of a bus co-operative did not seem to realize that there is a very basic difference between a co-operative of tailors or of shoemakers and a bus co-operative. This failure to understand that the transportation of passengers is a public service, is reflected in the attitude of the driver who tells the passenger: "I don't like you (you don't find favour in my eyes); don't travel with me." The driver ignores the fact that the "undesirable passengers" have no other means of transportation. Furthermore, the bus co-operatives refuse to accept the fact that the same public who entrusted to them the means of internal communication can also take it away from them. Even if the bus co-operatives hold a Government monopoly or a concession, these are revocable under certain circumstances.

Lastly, writes Mr. Shabatai, the bus co-operatives do not appreciate the fact (reality) that there is a basic difference between a private business and a co-operative,[87] and that the social aspects of co-operation cannot be ignored. Unlike the owners or partners of a non-co-operative organization, the members of co-operatives "may not do as they please". The Co-operative Societies' Ordinance and Regulations spell out what a co-operative may or may not do. The Registrar of Co-operatives, writes Mr. Shabatai, noted three anti-co-operative practices of the bus co-operatives, viz. the use of wage labour; withdrawal and distribution among their members of considerable funds from the coffers and the excessive emoluments which they pay to their members.[88] The Registrar of Co-operatives, according to Mr. Shabatai, evaded a direct reply to the two questions:

1. Have the bus co-operatives broken the law, and
2. whether, according to the Co-operative Societies' Ordinance and Regulations, it is the Registrar's duty to liquidate these bus co-operatives.

The Registrar's reply could be interpreted that: It is not a question of law but rather whether anybody would dare to liquidate the bus co-operatives. And the bus co-operatives, Mr. Shabatai writes, know this. On the other hand, the bus co-operatives persisted in saying "that it was absolutely untrue" that they were a public service or that they had sinned.

The control by the Ministry of Transport, according to Mr. Shabatai, has not improved the quality of the bus services. The five-year-old directive that standing in the buses was prohibited on the forty-mile route between Tel Aviv and Jerusalem is not enforced. It is still impossible to buy a through ticket if one has to use more than one bus. And when he referred to overcrowding on the intra-bus lines, the Minister of Transport, according to Mr. Shabatai, said: "There is overcrowding and overcrowding. Calculation of bus fares assumes a certain degree of overcrowding, but not to the extent to which the travellers are now subjected."

Generally speaking, Mr. Shabatai concludes that the Government was more effective in planning for the improvement and expansion of the railways than it was for the bus services. He writes:

> "I waited in vain for a hint by the Minister and the officials of the Ministry of Transport that they intended to look for ways how to re-

organize the co-operative bus transportation . . . to convert it into an instrument for the benefit of everybody." He was warned that the present Minister of Transport, a General Zionist (and not a Mapai member) will give them (the bus co-operatives) everything which they will ask and certainly will not do them any harm. "With us political consideration rules as a dictator." The Minister of Transport said: "I do not see any blemish in the co-operative pattern as such."

Mr. Shabatai's fifth article, "Comedy Instead of Control", notes that Eshed maintains that since it is subject to Histadrut control they cannot be considered a monopoly as the term is generally understood. He questions the possibility of effective control over a body which *de facto* is a monopoly and which argues that since it is prepared to carry out expeditiously every wish of the public, there is no need for any other similar service. Mr. Shabatai replies that: "Since the monopoly is clothed with a robe of righteousness and friendliness and with good relationship to the public . . ." it is all the more necessary to find out whether the Histadrut really uses its authority over the bus co-operatives. In the past, and especially in 1949 during the so-called "reform" period, experience demonstrated that if there was any control, it was ineffectual from every point of view. Merkaz Haco-operatzia, writes Mr. Shabatai, actually told the bus co-operatives that they may distribute resources among their members which were not even available (i.e., they were book-keeping assets) on condition that the co-operatives "would open their doors a bit to new members and accept 'control the size of an olive'."

The bulletin, "Histadrut", No. 44 (date not given), according to Mr. Shabatai, describes the character of the Histadrut control before and after the "reform". Mr. I. Kitzis of Merkaz Haco-operatzia Secretariat, allegedly said at a meeting of the Histadrut Executive Committee (date not given) that he considered the financial aspect (i.e. of the reform) as less important than the control which the Histadrut, Merkaz Haco-operatzia and the Government would exercise in the future, viz. ". . . that in the future . . . everything will be open and above board and certain matters will not be covered up . . . this is the essence of concurrent and effective control".

At the aforementioned meeting other members of the Histadrut Executive Committee allegedly pointed out that the Histadrut had not exercised strict and thorough control, and that therefore "reform" again appeared. Mr. Zeev Onn is reported as having said that "this is a bitter fact but, the bus co-operatives and their 1,500 members are not to be blamed", since the bus co-operatives, at the outset, did not want the "reform" because it was tied up with an agreement to accept new members. Then "we (i.e. the Histadrut) agreed to the 'reform' as the price for a little bit of control over the co-operatives".

Mr. Onn explained to the Histadrut Executive Committee the technique of the "reform":

First the members' participation in the co-operative's capital was credited with the difference between the replaceable and the balance-sheet value of the societies' assets. Merkaz Haco-operatzia and others had approved this action in principle.

Second, the bus co-operatives also credited the accounts of every member's participation in the refundable reserves with an additional amount of IL.1,000. This second transaction was discovered "en passant".

Mr. Shabatai estimates that this second part of the "reform" cost the consumers about IL.1½ million (1,500 members times IL.1,000). Mr. Onn argued that the "reform" also stimulated the bus co-operatives to introduce amendments in their rules which assured the Histadrut more effective control through the active participation of the Chevrat Haovdim representatives to the daily management of the bus co-operatives. The amendments also prescribed that the bus co-operatives must seek the approval of Chevrat Haovdim for any further amendments to their rules. Mr. A. Reiss (a member of the Histadrut committee of three on bus transportation), a supporter of the "reform" as a *quid pro quo* for control, is reported to have said: "We felt that the co-operatives needed public control. . . . I can justify the existence of the bus co-operatives only if they will be subject to public control."

The representatives of Mapai, Mapam and all other parties on the Histadrut Executive Committee allegedly were reported to have been of one mind about the prime importance of Histadrut control which the bus co-operatives had fought in the pre-State era. Mr. David Remez, the first Minister of Transport and one of the staunch supporters of WPSTS movement during the pre-State days, forgave the bus co-operatives for all but one of their sins, viz., their refusal to accept the Histadrut's authority to control their accounts. He described the primary purpose of the subsidiary corporates (co-operatives and companies), which the bus co-operatives had organized, as "veils to hide the profits derived from and the exploitation of public property." Mr. Remez is reported as having said that the refusal to accept the Histadrut's authority, reminded him of the refusal of *The Times* of London to accept an advertisement from a certain Jewish institution because it had no assurance that the funds which the institution was soliciting would be used for the purpose for which they were collected.

Mr. Shabatai's fifth article includes the following quotation from the minutes of the aforementioned Histadrut Executive Committee.

> "Mr. B. Lin moves that the Executive Committee should not associate itself with (acknowledge) the action taken without its approval and asks that the implementation should be stopped." Mr. Pinchas Lavon suggested deleting the last part about stopping the implementation, "not because I am for its implementation but because I do not wish the Histadrut Executive Committee to be in an untenable position (in an undignified position).[89]

Mr. P. Lavon summarized the character of the Histadrut control as follows:

"The Histadrut does not own the service and enjoys only a modicum, very small indeed, of control, which the co-operatives have acceded. If I am the owner of an undertaking and you do not have either ownership or any legal rights, then you must accommodate yourself more to the owner's wishes rather than impose your wish."

Mr. Shabatai accepts this interpretation subject to the following amendment:

"For years, the Histadrut has been in this untenable or uncomfortable position, and the bus co-operatives were aware of and fully exploited this state of affairs for their own interests and dragged the Histadrut after them. They (bus co-operatives) compelled the Histadrut against its wishes to say "amen" after everything which they did. . . . This is the history preceding the Histadrut's approval of the 'reform' as the price of a modicum of control" over the bus co-operatives.

An influential section of the Histadrut leadership noted that the first concession, i.e., the agreement of the bus co-operatives to admit new members, was unnecessary since the co-operatives needed new members to cope with the rapid expansion of the use of the bus services which followed the mass immigration.

In December 1949, six months after the "reform" Mr. Onn is reported to have said that the "reform assured (i.e. the members of the bus co-operatives) high wages plus premiums for effort, and participation in the management and in the risk . . . but the bus co-operatives did not accept our proposal".

According to Mr. Shabatai, the bus co-operatives were able to achieve their aims by a persistent policy of delaying tactics ("dragging out the question") and by "exalting control in their throats with the sword of monopoly in their hands". The bus co-operatives introduced an emolument system for members which included liberal fringe benefits. The end result was an excessive increase in bus fares without providing the "merchandise" (i.e. better bus service).

He compared the tactics of the bus co-operatives to "peace-mongers with swords in their hands ready for battle". The bus co-operatives in accepting "control" asked for clear and acceptable definitions. The negotiations also were overcast with the persistent threat of divorce.

When they were told that "your agreement to accept the decision of the Executive Committee were only words" the bus co-operatives had a standard reply: "We protest; it is not so." At one of the meetings, Mr. M. Namir (who at the time was general Secretary of the Histadrut) said: "You assured us that you consider the public interests as of primary importance." And the co-operatives' spokesman replied: "I do not accept this. Convince me why?" When an Eshed spokesman was asked what they proposed to do about the growing antagonism of the public, he answered that he had letters from passengers, "including important people, praising the politeness of this and that driver". While the Histadrut Executive Committee was unanimous in condemning the past of the bus co-operatives, they could not agree whether to "use drastic measures" or "less drastic measures with the hope that they (the co-operatives) will be good children". Mr. Namir told the bus co-operatives that co-operatives are becoming more hated than capitalism and that "you are the principal cause" for this. The bus co-operatives replied, and only indirectly, to this accusation with the counter-allegation that the Histadrut is the guilty party since it "does not deal with them properly" (according to the rules of the game). The Histadrut Executive Committee then were inclined to agree with the member who noted that "the biggest inequity" which the Histadrut had committed was "that all these years it rejected the proposal to annul her marriage with the bus co-operatives".

One of the serious ailments of the co-operative pattern of bus transport, according to Mr. Shabatai, is the "blurring of boundaries", i.e. confusing the functions with the social philosophy of co-operation (such as the use of the terminology, a co-operative monopoly). He illustrates this allegation with the following examples. Generally speaking in every country, irrespective whether the bus services are owned and/or administered by the State, municipalities or capitalist companies, a passenger can expect a reasonable equitable consideration of his complaint. In Israel when a member of the bus co-operative who also is a driver, considers the passenger's complaint against a fellow driver, the defendant and the judge are *de facto* one and the same. Mr. Shabatai also cites the system of the adjudication of differences between the Histadrut as controller and the bus co-operative as the controlled.

The Eshed spokesman always refers to "Both of us". (i.e. the Histadrut and the bus co-operatives). Mr. Shabatai writes that according to one who is well informed

> "the bus co-operatives in the management of their affairs have a medieval approach. Their conception of co-operation, the problems of equality and the question of socialism is childish, naive, laughable, simple . . . , and the business management of the bus co-operatives is comparable to that of the medieval age. They withdraw the last penny from the business. They have no understanding for the need of reserve funds. And they are persistently wrangling with the Histadrut, which insists that the rules should prescribe for obligatory reserves, and that these will not help it (transport co-operation) or the Histadrut or anybody. . . . They (bus co-operatives) do not have suitable records nor accounting systems from which it is possible to obtain information without delay. The accounts of the co-operatives not only are always six months or more in arrears but also are unclear and ambiguous. This (state of affairs) is ridiculous, irritating and really medieval."

The representative of Chevrat Haovdim on the daily management of Eshed (previously quoted) attributed the purchasing and other difficulties mainly to the organizational structure of the co-operative pattern.

"To his great regret the management's approach is political." This gives the tone to the administration of the undertaking. . . . In my opinion the second undesirable (bad) root in the co-operative organization is excessive democratization. They either are on the verge of elections or have just finished elections. That is to say, all the activities are directed and planned (with an eye) on the elections. And there are two factions, the older and the younger members, with conflicting interests, quarrels and collisions. And everyone wishes to be boss ('to sit on the chair'). And this precipitates heaps and heaps of failures, conflicts, waste, unnecessary expenses and all sorts of plagues. An end must be put to this, once and for all. Otherwise it is impossible to believe in the success of co-operative activities."

Mr. Shabatai's last of the eight articles enquires into the possibilities and probabilities of improving the services of the bus co-operative. Pivotal is the "burial of the medieval administration. It is possible to mend a tottering organization and to convert it into an efficient organization; similarly it is possible to revive a non-profitable business into new blooming ventures. . . . The central question is what is the root of the evil; whether it is organic or only a minor and curable ailment. . . ."

According to Mr. Shabatai, some blame the unsatisfactory status to lack of control; others insist that it is a social problem, while still others think it is the "pursuit of unjust gains by any means". He thinks that the situation is the by-product or a back wash from the 1930s. It is his opinion that the first problem is that every member of a bus co-operative, irrespective of his qualifications, type and expertness of work receives the salary of a driver classified as AA. This Mr. Shabatai describes as unfair to all other workers in other services and factories who are not members of bus co-operatives and also to all those who have to use and to pay for bus services. Mr. Shabatai ascribes this conception of equality to an erroneous definition of the conception of "equitability" and of "socialism". Mr. Shabatai asked Eshed whether there is not a contradiction between their claim that they are socialists who practise a form of complete equality and the fact that they draw interest on their investments in the society's capital. Eshed spokesmen replied that the supplement to which Mr. Shabatai refers is remuneration for self-administration, a return on investments. Mr. Shabatai notes that "they (bus co-operatives) dance simultaneously at two weddings", and a member from time to time can "decide whether it is in his interest to be a socialist or a capitalist", therefore a member may work by the hour or on a point system or on the basis of a combination of the two. It is possible for a member to get a full day's pay for 4½ hours' work, even though Eshed had accepted the Histadrut's directive for a 7-hour work day for those on the intra-urban and 7½ hours for those on the inter-urban routes. The bus co-operative legally evades the directive by considering 30 minutes for the drivers and 50 minutes for the garage staff as a legitimate break for lunch or supper; another 20 minutes for cleaning up; and allowing as much as 1½ hours as travelling time to and from place of work for "the hundreds of members who live in the suburbs, etc." And for all members over 50 years of age, the work day is 6½ hours gross. Mr. Shabatai explains the point system for calculating time. For instance, a journey from Tel Aviv to Haifa is considered as x points. If a member does the journey in x minus y points, the difference is considered and the member is paid for that much overtime. And there are "heaps upon heaps" of ways of receiving overtime pay for x hours and actually working only $x-y$ hours.

When it approved the "reform", Chevrat Haovdim guaranteed that the members would receive reasonable fringe benefits. Mr. Shabatai writes that Mr. S. Goren, of Merkaz Haco-operatzia, stated that the fringe payments which Eshed paid to its members, for instance, were only a few per cent more than the 30-35 per cent (of basic remuneration which Solel Boneh pays). Mr. Shabatai replies that standards cannot be measured by percentages. If the members of bus co-operatives withdraw the absolute maximum from the bus co-operative and as a result the members enjoy even a higher standard of fringe payments than do others (i.e. Solel Boneh workers), it is absurd to speak about "a reasonable scale of social insurance".

Mr. Shabatai writes that he tried unsuccessfully, to obtain a clear picture of the gross emolument of a member because Eshed considered this as a top secret. "Even the auditing department of Merkaz Haco-operatzia could not furnish me with reliable data about this." The senior auditor of this Department told him that

> "up to the end of 1952 they (the bus co-operatives) did not carry out the Histadrut's directives (wishes) about remuneration. Now the remuneration of members is in accordance with the Histadrut decision. But I do not know whether this is also true about the fringe payments. . . . Everybody laughed (at me). Everybody sent me to somebody else. . . . Those who know the co-operative (Eshed) inside and outside told me that my searching for reliable data on how to improve the economy so that the co-operative would show profits instead of losses, were in vain. They (Eshed) will always distribute what they have and even more. . . . The talk about operational deficits is an optical illusion."[90]

The following are extracts from the closing paragraphs of the eighth and the last of Mr. Shabatai's articles on 7 August, 1953.

> "Mr. Namir defined Eshed's attitude to the transportation business as follows: 'They (the members) consider themselves as wage workers and enjoy the conditions of nobles.'" Mr Shabatai accepts this definition subject to the addition "as nobles who have a monopoly. . . . who are assured of a high remuneration under any and all conditions.
>
> "Mr. Onn said that the two years since the signing of the agreement (between the Histadrut and Eshed, 9 January, 1952) was the last experiment to win the confidence of the public. . . . This experiment has failed most miserably. . . . Histadrut control (over the co-operative) is only imaginary. Drivers are openly speaking about a new reform. New

members are paying higher admission fees than the Histadrut has fixed. It is the same in every field. . . .

"Replying to the question about the future, the Registrar of Co-operatives was very cautious . . . he was dejected; he hammed, hawed and was silent, etc. and finally said that there is a Russian saying: a stamp without glue, you place the stamp, press it with your hand and for one moment you think it will stick; but it does not stick. And it will not stick.

"This is the position. The 'stickers' have laboured in vain. The following question is crystallizing among those who are most concerned with the issue. Can the Histadrut continue to work with Eshed? Or, more accurately, when will the Histadrut say 'enough'. And this should not be confined to the Histadrut. The Government also must know that it is impossible to continue as at present. And what about tomorrow? It is a general principle that everybody, the individual or the community, must do his best and be upright and worry about himself only on the morrow, i.e. the interests of the community should take precedence over self-interest."

The following message to the members from the management of Egged (Eshed) is found in L'Chavereinu, August 1953, p. 2 (the periodical of Egged (Eshed).

"We note with satisfaction that more recently the relationship between ourselves and the Government, particularly the Ministry of Transport, has been normalized. Through their daily contact with us, our occupational difficulties have become clear to them. And they also know how to appreciate our efforts to maintain orderly and efficient transportation for the benefit of the public." This note also commends the recent appointment of regional transportation committees whose representatives visited "many places of our work, both in the north and south". These committees are reported to have submitted favourable reports about the co-operative's (Eshed (Egged)) activities and these also "were turned over to the Ministry and also to the Minister of Transport."

The aforementioned issue of L'Chavereinu also included the full text of a letter signed "Ben Yabil, a member of Egged (Eshed) and a vatik in the Histadrut"—which Davar declined to publish. Mr. Yabil refers to the almost daily appearance in Davar over a period of months of letters which are so different, both in content and spirit, from those which Davar carried during the formative and early period of the bus co-operatives. The sharp differences of opinion, which also existed at that time, were not publicly aired and used

"to incite the public against the transportation workers. . . . There are few kinds of work which upset the nerves of the workers as much as transportation, therefore the conditions of the transportation workers cannot be compared with those in other undertakings. . . ." It is not surprising that the managements of the bus co-operatives, in view of

> "the constant increase of sick members with all kinds of ailments, had to introduce obligatory internal measures for the preservation of the human assets as well as for the material assets, (such as higher standards of social insurance)." The Histadrut Executive Committee should be proud of these and should not use these as a tool "for inciting the public against us. . . . Most of the Yishuv is now made up of new immigrants who are not *au courant* about or interested in the past. Is it right to exploit their lack of knowledge for inciting them against workers who have attained their present status through hard work, etc. . . . Since when do the honourable members of the Histadrut Executive Committee consider social fringe benefits as additional remuneration. . . . Do you also propose to consider as additional salary the allowances for entertaining, travelling, maintenance of cars of thousands of employees in other institutions which add up to considerable amounts."

Another article signed X in the August 1953, issue of L'Chavereinu (pp. 23-25) about Histadrut control refers in particular to the appointment of Histadrut representatives "to all the management bodies of the new co-operative (i.e. Egged (Eshed)) that will start operations after the liquidation of Egged, Drom Yehuda and Shachar".

This article also notes that the rules of Egged (Eshed) were only recently approved. Pending the formal election of the management and governing bodies of Egged (Eshed), the Histadrut agreed that only one of its representatives on the temporary governing bodies would participate in the meetings of the Society's management, secretariat and financial committee. This Histadrut representative would also have the right to sign cheques, letters, etc., and therefore he should be able to keep an eye on everything which goes on in the co-operative.

The anonymous writer then refers to Mr. Shabatai's articles (three already had appeared) and to the 22-item questionnaire which Mr. Shabatai sent to Egged (Eshed) after the publication of his first article. This questionnaire clearly indicated that Mr. Shabatai had received

> "instructions . . . from a few people who are interested in smearing and making us odious to the public". He (the anonymous writer) then cites two of the 22 questions which deal with alleged "fantastic hours of work" and anybody "who knows anything about the affairs of the co-operative could easily identify the prompter as being no other than our Histadrut controller. Therefore we must ask for his immediate withdrawal and his replacement, the sooner the better".

The issue of L'Chavereinu, September 1953, p. 3, refers to two meetings between Egged (Eshed) and the editors of Davar about Mr. Shabatai's "perversive and denunciatory articles . . . which poison the public's mind (air) about a Histadrut-sponsored co-operative". It seems that the "editors also understand that a serious mistake was made and injustice done towards our people and that they (Egged (Eshed)) should be given the opportunity to reply (react) to the scurrilous articles. They also agreed that an apology was due for the false charges which border on criminal accusations against Egged (Eshed) and some of its members. The management of Egged (Eshed) has submitted to its legal counsel the question of bringing legal action against Mr. Shabatai".

A second article in the September, 1953, issue of L'Chavereinu, signed Asher Karni[91] asks why Mr. Shabatai wrote the series of articles in 1953 and not in 1951-52 when it was the fashion to smear bus co-operatives. He quotes from an explanation by one of the editors of Davar to one of the members of the bus co-operative secretariat:

> "The public wants this. The subject of bus transportation is still topical with the public. It is still a choice evening delicacy with which to amuse the public." It is a pity that Mr. Shabatai, a stylist and literary journalist, "wishes to become an economist and express an opinion and to issue conclusive judgments about a technical subject which does not need his illumination. . . ." It is true that Mr. Shabatai seems to have consulted all possible sources even "the Encyclopedia on Social Sciences and a book on transportation by three professors. . . ."

Mr. Karni adds that there is no doubt that Mr. Shabatai in the course of his research could not himself dig up (obtain) all the material in the eight articles. He received much of the data from those who advised him on the compilation of his 22-item questionnaire prepared after his first article appeared. Especially objectionable, writes Mr. Karni, are the last two articles in which Mr. Shabatai presumptiously criticizes the maintenance of the equipment, business procedure, accounting system, and the management of Egged (Eshed). "But even in these aspects (here) Mr. Shabatai does not feel sufficiently firm on his feet and resorts to the assistance of Mr. K. who was encouraged to resign. . . ."

Referring to his persistent efforts to obtain from Egged (Eshed) management a detailed breakdown of members emoluments, Mr. Karni asked Mr. Shabatai:

> "Why write about this, why don't the newspapers report how much Mr. X. earns in the Histadrut; Mr. Y. in Davar and Mr. Z. in another place of employment?
>
> "The question of the wages of the workers in the Histadrut, Davar and in other places are settled on the basis of their work and not on consideration, calculations and conditions not arising from their work."

The November 1953 issue of L'Chavereinu reprints the notice "in a remote place of the paper" which the Davar editorial staff published about Mr. Shabatai's articles (date of publication of this notice not given). The aforementioned notice also includes Moshe Levita's comments on the editor's notice. The obscure notice in Davar referred to the following statement in Mr. Shabatai's article of 6 August, 1953,

> "that *inter alia* one of Eshed members told him that many among us deal with purchases (i.e. of supplies for Egged (Eshed)) and many were

prepared to forego their wages if only they also could do part of the purchasing". The editorial staff expresses their regret "that when editing the article we failed to notice the above sentence which could be interpreted as a slur on the morals of Eshed members who do the purchasing. The editors had no grounds for this accusation and there was no intent to show disrespect towards them".

Mr. Levita compares the above notice to a story about a warden (gabbai) of a synagogue, who told the congregation that the half of those in the synagogues are horses. And when the rabbi asked the "gabbai" to retract, the gabbai arose and declared that of course half of those in the synagogue are not horses. If the management of Egged (Eshed) agreed "to this form of apology then it (the management) also should declare whether the false charge quoted in the apology was the only smear against them and without any foundations. . . ." Mr. Levita describes the cancellation of their subscription for Davar by some members (of Egged (Eshed)) "as an impetuous and illogical reaction".

The November 1953 issue of L'Chavereinu carries also an article by Chaim Baer,[92] dated Tel Aviv, 29 August, 1953, which answers some of Mr. Shabatai's technical criticisms, such as why Egged (Eshed) intra-urban buses can pick up passengers only at specified points; and why the passengers must buy their tickets before they get on the bus, etc.

According to Mr. Baer the "bus co-operatives were pressurized by outside forces to accept the "reform", and that it is not true that there was more than one reform. Why should those who had worked for twenty or thirty years be asked to surrender their property to others without compensation. Immigrants living in the country only four years receive housing. Why then is it wrong for members of a bus co-operative with 20-30 years' seniority to buy their housing on credit. The article doubts whether it is possible to have a bus co-operative without equal basic wages. "And the institutions (i.e. Histadrut bodies), and not we, fix the scale of wages." He counters Mr. Shabatai's criticism of "medieval administration", by referring to but not quoting Mrs. Golda Meir, Minister of Labour (who was subsequently Minister of Foreign Affairs 1956-66) and to Dr. Boris Stern who is reported to have "stressed that the bus co-operatives . . . are doing a good enough job in managing the transportation". A special department in Egged (Eshed) deals "thoroughly" with all passengers' complaints and the members against whom the complaints are made are brought before internal adjudication tribunals and if found guilty are punished.

L'Chavereinu of November, 1953, also includes

(*a*) the full text of an article by Akiva Handler which Davar on 6 September, 1953, had published with changes and deletions;[93] and
(*b*) an undated open letter from Eliahu Weitzer to Mr. Shabatai.

Mr. Handler notes that Mr. Shabatai uses the well-known trick of the debaters and writers who first present the non-controversial points and then "proceed to pour out their heart", etc. Mr. Handler takes exception to the anonymity of most of the people quoted by Mr. Shabatai and also notes that the quotations are distorted and removed from their context and, therefore, create an erroneous impression. Referring to Mr. Shabatai's criticism that Egged (Eshed) delayed accepting the Histadrut's amendments to its rules, Mr. Handler asks how could the management accept such unco-operative suggestions as the participation of an outside body, Chevrat Haovdim, in the daily management, fixing the members' remuneration and in other internal administration questions of Egged (Eshed). The society had to seek the agreement of its members at a general meeting. With regard to paying all members with the basic wage equivalent to AA drivers, Mr. Handler writes that only three per cent of the members do not have the certificates of AA drivers and that these are specialists who could command a higher salary than the emolument which they receive from Egged (Eshed). These include first class mechanics, electricians, etc., and supervisors over wage workers. Member drivers also are used

> "as the need arises, as works managers, supervisors, etc., which are as important as that of driving buses. And that it would be inequitable to reduce their wages. . . . And does Mr. Shabatai refer to members who after tens of years of service are unable to continue driving". Mr. Shabatai either is ignorant of or prefers to disregard the "many efforts made in the country to increase productivity; inviting experts from abroad; establishing productivity institutes and production councils. . . . Why is it wrong (for Egged (Eshed)) to pay an incentive bonus to those who exceed the norms, and the norms are periodically reviewed in the light of the changes which have taken place in the work. . . . Overtime is unavoidable . . . and the co-operative is trying to minimize this. And the Society has fixed a maximum overtime with pay for any members. . . ."

In the closing paragraph of his article, Mr. Handler notes that he does not claim "that everything is in order, that we have reached perfection. There is still much which needs mending."

Mr. Eliahu Weitzer's letter[94] accuses Mr. Shabatai of having stooped even lower than the well-known editor of an evening paper, in the use of demagogic and banner headings calculated to attract and arouse the anxiety and to sharpen the impatience of the reader to read the next article. He invites Mr. Shabatai to visit one of their central garages, in order to remove his mistaken ideas that the co-operatives are not doing enough to ameliorate the transportation conditions.

> "The combinations to which we have to resort in order to adjust old spare parts even if these will be good for only a few days. . . ." the Government still does not make available enough foreign exchange for the import of essential spare parts. ". . . and you know that we were compelled to make our recent purchase of White buses through an inter-

mediary and pay a high ransom tax to an important institution in the State because this was the only way of getting these transferred to us."

Mr. Shabatai's articles also prompted an exchange of letters between Mr. Y. Ritov of the Merkaz Haco-operatzia secretariat and[95] Yitzchak Hadar, a veteran in bus co-operatives. Mr. Ritov starts his letter with the following quotation from Mr. Hadar's letter (about Merkaz Haco-operatzia):

"The pattern of the bus co-operative has had opponents since it was organized; and what is the share of Merkaz Haco-operatzia, the prostrate body, in this? Though I think the leaders of this body (Merkaz Haco-operatzia) have always undermined us, (Egged (Eshed)), we continue to participate in it. Among the rank and file there is a feeling that this body, Merkaz Haco-operatzia, creates dissension, antagonism, and strife instead of serving as a co-ordinating and unifying centre."

Mr. Ritov considers this quotation "not merely as words, but as the view of the Egged (Eshed) management".

The introductory sentence of Mr. Ritov's reply is

"This is what the members of Egged (Eshed) are being taught and told about the content and pattern of Merkaz Haco-operatzia."

He then proceeds to deal with Mr. Hadar's allegation that Merkaz Haco-operatzia was a "prostrate body". How is this possible for an organization that has been functioning for 25 years, he asked, and has 349 WPSTS affiliates in addition to Egged (Eshed). Merkaz Haco-operatzia has organized, shaped and helped to expand all the bus co-operatives and most of the other affiliated WPSTS. Merkaz Haco-operatzia is responsible for the organization of NOA and Kupat Haco-operativim and it has introduced and taught many of its affiliated WPSTS the rudiments of accounting, and has audited their accounts, etc. In 1932 Merkaz Haco-operatzia under the active leadership of S. Goren, initiated the general strike of all Jewish and Arab buses, which forced the Mandatory Government to recognize the routes of the respective bus co-operatives as concessions. It was Merkaz Haco-operatzia that mediated the acute jurisdictional quarrels among Jewish bus co-operatives. Who dealt with problems of relationship between the WPSTS and wage workers; life insurance and pensions for the members of the affiliated WPSTS and for the care of their widows and orphans? And when rationing and price control were introduced it was Merkaz Haco-operatzia that ensured fair play for the WPSTS. It established normal relationships between the bus co-operatives and the Mandatory Government in the entire country and, since the establishment of the State, with the Ministry of Transport, and with local authorities. The recent strained relationships between Merkaz Haco-operatzia and the bus co-operatives have their roots in a large measure in the unsatisfactory relationship between the bus co-operatives on the one hand, and the Government bodies, the municipalities and other local authorities, and the Press and the public, on the other hand. This strained relationship is a serious threat to the bus co-operatives primarily because

"the entire debate about the bus co-operatives has been perverted and does not penetrate into the roots of the problem . . . the great anxiety (nervousness) of the public; the hatred and envy . . . traceable, in not a small extent, to the internal confused procedure of the bus co-operatives . . . (which) have not excelled in management, organization, public relations, and the maintenance of equipment. They also have not displayed any aptitudes in their relationship with Merkaz Haco-operatzia. . . ."

Mr. Yitzchak Hadar's reply[96] to Mr. Ritov includes the following major complaints:

1. That the Histadrut Central Committee and not Merkaz Haco-operatzia, the "spinal cord of the WPSTS", dealt with the problem of the bus co-operatives. Was 25 years not a long enough period for Merkaz Haco-operatzia to mould (shape) the bus co-operatives and why was there a need for a "higher power to impose its authority on us (Egged (Eshed))? Are we less loyal than any other body in the Histadrut?"
2. Why has not the Histadrut imposed the sacred principle of self-labour on the kibbutzim? The bus co-operatives were asked to examine the immigrants' technical proficiency in various fields. But the bus co-operatives were not permitted to retain these (immigrants) as wage workers, which is so important if their garages are to put the maximum number of buses on the road. The conditions of work (i.e. for the wage workers) in the bus co-operatives are superior to those in other undertakings. And what did Merkaz Haco-operatzia do about this prejudiced and biased attitude towards the bus co-operatives?
3. Why did not Mr. Ritov write an article in Davar to counteract the malicious and untruthful accusations in Mr. Shabatai's articles.[97]

Mr. Hadar ends his reply to Mr. Ritov with the declaration that the bus co-operatives will remain loyal and insist on having the concessions for the unprofitable routes to the scattered settlements on the borders and to other very sparsely inhabited districts.

"As in the past, the members of the bus co-operatives will assume any task which the State or the movement will assign to them. We will help the Government with all our heart and strength to realize its great mission. But where are the leaders who will inspire us with the vision and the idealism?"

Egged (Eshed)

On 21 December, 1950, the Histadrut Executive Committee approved a resolution to the effect that the bus co-operatives must fuse into one countrywide organization. The *de facto* merger of the three inter-urban bus co-operatives (Egged, Drom Yehuda and Shachar) was consummated in November 1951 when they commenced to work together as a registered partnership, "Eshed". Though each co-operative retained its legal identity under the Co-operative Societies Ordinance, the three bus co-operatives pooled practically all their property, personnel, routes, managements, etc. All financial and other transaction from that date were in the name of "Eshed".[98]

On 16 January, 1952, "Eshed" wrote to the Histadrut Executive Committee that they accepted the decisions about merging ("Ichud"), and Histadrut control ("pikuach") from "then on and afterwards". The last sentence of this letter notes that the rules for the merger of the bus co-operatives will become operative after the general meeting approves the final draft.

The three bus co-operatives that merged into the partnership "Eshed" continued to pay their members the maximum emoluments, including fringe benefits. During this period of delaying tactics, "Egged" and "Drom Yehuda" carried out a "second" but smaller "reform"; Egged paid IL.900 each to most of its members and Drom Yehuda paid IL.600 to every member through their subsidiary co-operatives. This action probably prompted the resolution of the *ad hoc* Histadrut Committee of Three on Bus Transportation (31 October, 1951) which the Histadrut Executive Committee (of 2 November, 1951) confirmed, condemning the three partners in Eshed for changing their minds and insisting on Chevrat Haovdim modifying the extent of its control.[99]

> "The Histadrut asked all the bus co-operatives to unite into one body, which would be subject to the authority and control of Chevrat Haovdim; such a merger of the bus co-operatives it considered a blessing. But the Histadrut does not support the present action of Eshed, viz. to exploit the merger of the routes for the private interests of the bus co-operatives and to evade Histadrut control and to disregard the wide interests of the public, the Histadrut and the State.
>
> "Therefore, in view of Eshed's refusal to implement the Histadrut's instructions, the committee dealing with the questions of bus transportation at yesterday's meeting decided:
>
> 1. "to discontinue all negotiations with the 'Eshed' representatives and not to renew these until the bus co-operatives will accept the resolutions which the Histadrut Executive Committee adopted about bus transportation questions and the decisions of the Committee arising from these.
> 2. "to withdraw the participation of the Histadrut Executive Committee's representatives on the committee for effecting the merger of all bus co-operatives.
> 3. "to officially notify the Minister of Transport that the Histadrut does not 'stand behind' and is not responsible for the activities of Eshed.

4. "the Histadrut will not consider the appeal of 'Eshed' to the *ad hoc* committee that dealt with the jurisdictional conflict between Eshed and the bus co-operative Hamekasher" (in Jerusalem).

Since the completion of all the technical, legal and financial arrangements for merger is a long process, a Histadrut representative explained that in the public interest, it pressed the bus co-operatives to expedite the establishment of a temporary "Ichud". The first deadline was the end of July 1951; this was extended to the end of August and then to the end of September. Reluctantly, a Chevrat Haovdim representative, acting for the Histadrut, agreed to meet the preparatory committee and the lawyers acting for "Eshed" and its component bus co-operatives, and put the final touches to the rules of the new co-operative, which would be registered and would replace the partnership Eshed. Eshed and Chevrat Haovdim had previously approved the draft of the rules which were now submitted to Chevrat Haovdim for confirmation.

When the jurisdictional dispute started between the bus co-operative "Hamekasher" and the partnership "Eshed" about their respective areas of operation, Chevrat Haovdim agreed that "Eshed" should commence operations without delay on the basis of a temporary agreement which had been initialled four months before. "Eshed" then submitted a draft contract which included, *inter alia*, the following major changes about which neither the Histadrut nor Chevrat Haovdim had been consulted.

> First, the secretariat of Eshed was increased from eight to seventeen members, but the number of Chevrat Haovdim representatives on the secretariat remained at two. Second, the liquidation of the temporary partnership "Eshed" and its conversion into a permanent corporate body was subject to a simple majority of the members of each of the three bus co-operatives that had agreed to merge. The decision would not be subject to the confirmation of Chevrat Haovdim. Eshed also wished to evade accepting as members "several tens of the 90 permanent wage workers who have ten or more years' seniority".

To prevent the distribution by the bus co-operatives of any more of their assets in the future, an *ad hoc* committee was appointed, which included a representative of bus co-operatives. This committee was to arrange for the transfer from the partnership Eshed to Egged (Eshed), which was to be registered as a co-operative, of all the property of the three bus co-operatives on such terms as would protect the interests of the respective members of the co-operatives that were merging. This decision was stillborn. Furthermore, no steps were taken to deal with the problem of the emoluments for members which the bus co-operatives had increased.

In view of the aforementioned developments, Chevrat Haovdim considered it important "to finish within a few weeks" the final draft rules of the co-operative Egged (Eshed) and to resolve the outstanding problems. The negotiations were further protracted because the Histadrut insisted that the bus co-operatives should accept a seven-hour work-day for intra-urban routes and a seven-and-a-half-hour work-day for inter-urban routes.

The partnership Eshed on 1 November, 1951, issued a press release giving its version of the events. *Inter alia,* this release referred to the following decisions at the end of 1950:

(*a*) The establishment of "Eshed".
(*b*) The undertaking of the three bus co-operatives that formed the partnership Eshed to accept the authority of the Histadrut.
(*c*) The decision of a meeting on 30 October, 1951, at which the representative of the Histadrut was present, which reaffirmed that the three bus co-operatives would loyally carry out the decisions of the Histadrut Executive Committee and of the Histadrut *ad hoc* Committee of Three on Bus Transportation which the Histadrut Executive Committee had confirmed.

But the three bus co-operatives refused to discuss the more recent differences of opinion which they ascribed "to a misunderstanding". Except for a few minor details, Eshed's version of the negotiations about

(*a*) the temporary agreement which the three bus co-operatives had initialled and
(*b*) the drafting of the rules for the new co-operative Egged (Eshed), which would replace the partnership Eshed, agreed with the statements of the Histadrut *ad hoc* committee referred to in the preceding paragraphs.

Since "another month or two were needed" to draft the rules of Egged (Eshed) in final form, the three bus co-operatives back-tracked to the temporary agreement.

The Eshed press release, however, denied having introduced any radical changes in the draft rules. It explained that the increase of the secretariat from eight to seventeen was necessary because the secretariat would have to carry a heavy load. The secretariat would include members from all three bus co-operatives. And the press release also notes that Eshed suggested an increase from two to three of Chevrat Haovdim representatives on the Secretariat of Seventeen. It denied, however, the accusation that Eshed did not want Chevrat Haovdim to have the final say about the liquidation of the temporary partnership Eshed. But, it did suggest that the decisions of the Management Committee should be by a 75 per cent majority and not by unanimous agreement, provided the 75 per cent majority included the representatives of Chevrat Haovdim on the Management Committee. Allegedly Chevrat Haovdim did not ask Eshed to explain the amendment.

The three bus co-operatives, with the knowledge and consent of the Histadrut, set up an internal committee of three to appraise all their property. The report on this internal committee's valuation was submitted to Chevrat Haovdim, through the joint committee, which included a representative of Chevrat Haovdim, appointed to examine the appraisal. The Eshed press statement expressed the hope that "a way will be found to clear the misunderstandings and to establish desirable relationships with the Histadrut".

On 9 January, 1952, the three inter-urban bus co-operatives (Egged, Shachar and Drom Yehuda) signed the formal agreement which the Histadrut had approved. The last sentence of the preamble of this contract reiterates "the demand for including the bus co-operatives Dan and Hamekasher in the merger". Section one of this agreement prescribes that "the merger of the bus co-operative shall be built on self-labour . . . and. . . the integration of additional members in accordance with the needs of the economy". Section three of the formal agreement of 9 January, 1952, like the rules of the new co-operative Egged (Eshed), prescribes priority for membership for the sons and sons-in-law of all members and recognizes the principle of equal pay and equal fringe allowances for all members. A joint committee made up of representatives of the Histadrut, Merkaz Haco-operatzia and Egged (Eshed) will deal with the question of the integration of wage workers as members or their employment in accordance with the Histadrut decisions of 1946.

Sections 14 and 15 of the agreement of 9 January, 1952, prescribes that on or before 31 January, 1952, the members may decide about the liquidation of the temporary partnership Eshed, by a three-fourths majority vote of the entire membership of the three bus co-operatives (and not only of those members who attended the meeting at which the decision was taken), provided that all the representatives of Chevrat Haovdim on the Management voted for such liquidation. On the liquidation of the temporary partnership Eshed, all its assets would be transferred to its successor Egged (Eshed), irrespective when the latter would start operations. Section 16 of the agreement of 9 January, 1952, prescribes that the full text of the decisions of the Histadrut Executive Committee and of Chevrat Haovdim of 21 December, 1950, and of 7 July, 1951, which are attached as an appendix, are to be considered as an inseparable part of the agreement of 9 January, 1952, and are binding on the Management Committee and on the secretariat of Egged (Eshed) co-operative registered on 14 April, 1953. The rules of Egged (Eshed) embody practically all the provisions of this contract of 9 January, 1952, and its appendices.[100]

The following are the main provisions of the rules of Egged (Eshed). These rules are very similar to those of the other bus co-operatives and also to the model rules for the Histadrut-sponsored WPSTS.

> Egged (Eshed), affiliated with Merkaz Haco-operatzia, accepts as members only those who are members of the Histadrut. Applicants have to submit, together with their applications, the written approval of Merkaz Haco-operatzia and the latter first seeks the agreement of the respective local labour council of the community in which the applicant is a permanent resident, to the effect that the "applicant is qualified to be a candidate for membership". Egged (Eshed) may not accept any applicant to whom Chevrat Haovdim objects. . . . And any member of Egged (Eshed) who ceases to be a member of the Histadrut also

ceases to be a member of the society. Sons and sons-in-law of present and of future members enjoy first priority and non-member drivers working for Egged (Eshed) second priority over all other applicants provided that these two special categories of applicants also are subject to all other conditions for membership which its rules prescribe.

At least twice every year the Management Committee of the Egged (Eshed) decides whether and how many new members are needed. In the event of any differences of opinion on this question, Chevrat Haovdim is the adjudicator and its decision is final. All applicants who are accepted within three months from the date of the registration of the rules, including all members of the three bus co-operatives at the time of their merger, must be 18 and not over 32 years of age and hold a bus driver's licence. Applicants who are not members of Chevrat Haovdim (i.e. the Histadrut) may be accepted if recommended by the Management Committee of the Egged (Eshed) and by Chevrat Haovdim. Every candidate must undergo a medical examination by a team of doctors of Kupat Cholim (the Histadrut Workers Sick Fund). The management of the society also may require a medical examination of the applicant by one or more doctors it will appoint. The Management Committee may reject the applicant if it considers him unsuitable for the society's activities.

After the first probation period of six months, the Management Committee may decide not to permit the applicant to start the second probation period of twelve months and it is not required to give the reason for its decision. During the initial six-month probation period, the probationers receive the same wages as the society pays to wage workers. After that the probationer is on an equal footing with the members, except that the probationer

(*a*) is not entitled to any part of the surplus earned during his second probation period of 12 months unless he is accepted as a member before the expiration of this period;
(*b*) may not vote or be elected to any governing bodies of the society.

Two months before the end of the second probation period, unless otherwise notified, the probationer may consider himself a member. If at the end of the second probation period he is not accepted as a member, the probationer may appeal to the Council of the society which by a two-thirds majority of those present at the meeting may overrule the negative decision of the Management Committee. On the Management Committee's recommendation the Council by a three-fourths majority of those present at the meeting may admit a probationer who has served less than the prescribed probation period and/or applicants over the age of 32 and/or applicants who do not hold a bus driver's licence.

Members may be expelled for reasons prescribed in the society's rules and by a three-fourths majority vote of those participating in the Council meeting. A member expelled may appeal to the Merkaz Hacooperatzia before his case is referred to the society's council. And Merkaz

Haco-operatzia also may decide to review the charge and to ask the society to reconsider its decision. Under this procedure a four-fifths majority of those present at the respective council meeting is required for expulsion.

Only Chevrat Haovdim may authorize the temporary employment of non-member drivers, but such employment may not exceed six months and the number of the temporary drivers at any one time may not exceed five per cent of the entire membership of the society at that time. If the society needs additional permanent drivers, it must admit as members some of the drivers who have worked for six months or more for the society, provided these meet the conditions for membership which the rules prescribe. This priority applies also to those temporary drivers who worked for the society not less than four months and who were then released, and provided further that the need for additional drivers arises within two months after the society has released the respective drivers. With the prior approval of Chevrat Haovdim the society may also employ non-member skilled personnel, such as chief accountants, engineers, porters and cleaners; and the society may also accept as apprentices members of Hanoar Haoved. The respective craft unions will fix the conditions for the employment of apprentices. In the acceptance of apprentices, as in the case of the acceptance of new members, the children of those already members of the society have first priority provided the respective children have completed at least eight years' education and provided further that in the opinion of the Management Committee, they are suitable for the vacancies. The children of members who have not yet benefited from this privilege of priority enjoy priority over the children of those members whose children already have benefited from this priority.

Subject to confirmation by Chevrat Haovdim, the society's Management Committee, from time to time, fixes the amount which every member must contribute to the society's capital. The society is obligated to pay to a member withdrawing, or in the case of death of member, to his estate, the respective member's participation in the society's capital, and also the respective member's share in the society's divisible reserves and any other amounts standing to the credit of the respective member less any amounts due to the society from the respective member.[101]

Section D(3) of the rules prescribes the rights of members to

(*a*) work in the society;
(*b*) participate in all the benefits which the society provides for its members;
(*c*) receive, in addition to the basic emolument which is the same for all members (including allowances for cost of living, seniority and family status), a supplement of not less than 15 and not more than 25 per cent of the monthly basic emolument for his efforts and responsibility for the administration of the society.

Chevrat Haovdim is the final adjudicator of any differences of opinion about members' salaries and rights which may arise between the Management Committee of the society and the special Histadrut committee.

Egged (Eshed) rules prescribe that 25, 20 and five per cent of the surplus must be allocated to the reserves, depreciation funds, and Chevrat Haovdim respectively; 25 per cent is distributed among all members within three months after the approval of the audited annual accounts and the balance, i.e. 25 per cent, is transferred to a special divisible reserve account. Every member on leaving has a right to his share in this divisible fund and the amount of the respective member's share is calculated on the basis of the member's seniority in the society.[102]

Without the prior written approval of the Chevrat Haovdim Egged (Eshed) may not increase bus fares; establish any subsidiary, or participate in any enterprise or dispose of any of its property in any manner; or amend its rules. Amendments to rules also require the approval of Merkaz Haco-operatzia.

Section E. of the society's rules prescribes the governing bodies; how they are constituted; and their respective authorities. Notices of all general meetings and their agendas must be published in a Histadrut daily and sent to Merkaz Haco-operatzia and to Chevrat Haovdim. Every member has one vote and proxies are not permitted. Every member may submit to the election committee nominations for the council. The list of the nominees must be posted seven days before election day. No appeals are allowed from the results of the elections which are posted and signed by the chairman of the election committee. Elections of the Management Committee and other governing bodies must be held within fifteen days from the day when elections to the council are posted. The procedure for the election of the Management Committee is the same as that for the council.

The council has no less than 51 nor more than 71 members and Chevrat Haovdim appoints 15 per cent of the members of the council. Members of the council serve two years and are eligible for re-election. The council meets no less than once every three months and no less than 60 per cent of its members constitute a quorum. Decisions are by simple majority of those present. The powers of the council are the same as those prescribed for general meetings, other than the Annual General Meeting.

The Management Committee of Egged (Eshed) has no less than 19 members, all of them members of the council, and Chevrat Haovdim appoints three of the 19. Members of the Management Committee serve for two years with a right of re-election. The council may decide to increase the membership of the Management Committee provided the proportion between the number elected and the number appointed by Chevrat Haovdim is maintained (16:3). The Management Committee may delegate some of its day-to-day authority to Regional Committee(s) and elects between seven and nine of its members as the society's secretariat which must include two of the Chevrat Haovdim representatives appointed to the Management Committee. The secretariat acts in the name of the Management Committee and carries out the policies which the Management Committee fixes. A Control Committee of Three or more members elected annually concurrently "controls the management of the society's affairs, looks into members' complaints, examines the accounts and checks the cash". The Control Committee may request the Management Committee to convene special meetings of the society's council.

The quorum for the Management Committee, which meets at least once every two weeks, is 60 per cent of its members. All its decisions are by simple majority. The Management Committee must submit quarterly a report to Merkaz Haco-operatzia with a copy to Chevrat Haovdim.

A decision for the liquidation of the society requires a majority of four-fifths of the members present at a Council meeting called for this purpose and its decision is subject to the approval of Chevrat Haovdim. The society, after meeting all its obligations, may, with the authority of Chevrat Haovdim, distribute the balance of the assets among those who are members of the society at the time of liquidation.

Section F(3) of the society's rules lists the special rights of the Chevrat Haovdim and of Merkaz Haco-operatzia, in addition to those prescribed in the other sections (and mentioned in the preceding paragraphs). Chevrat Haovdim, though a member of the society, has no financial responsibilities; the society must obtain the prior approval of Chevrat Haovdim to pledge any of the society's property in any form and for a loan in excess of IL.50,000. A difference between the society and Chevrat Haovdim about matters which may affect (negatively) the general principles of Histadrut-sponsored labour co-operation in Israel, or may endanger the existence of the society, shall, at the request of the Society or of Chevrat Haovdim, be referred to an arbitration committee, to which the society and the Histadrut Executive Committee shall appoint one member, and these two appoint the third arbitrator. If the two arbitrators cannot agree on the third arbitrator, the Histadrut Executive Committee in consultation with the society's management, appoints the third arbitrator. The decision of the majority of the arbitration committee is binding on both sides.

Representatives of Chevrat Haovdim participating in any General Meeting of the society or any meeting of the council, may, at the next meeting of these representative bodies, ask for a reconsideration of a decision of any subject which already has been debated.

The Management's report to the first session of the meeting of the Egged (Eshed) Council (19 and 21-22 September, 1955) noted that Egged (Eshed) had overstepped by IL.6,603 per month the budget fixed; but for the four months between April and July 1955, revenue exceeded the expenditures by over IL.344,000. No conclusions were drawn from these favourable results because the revenues usually decreased during the winter months. "Yet it may be assumed that it will be possible to balance the budget and also to realize everybody's hope about refunding the amounts withheld...." The Government has decided to continue its monthly subsidy of IL.207,000 after 1 September, 1955, and up to 15 October, 1955. Thereafter, unless the Government decides to continue its subsidies, Egged (Eshed) is authorized to raise bus fares by 10 per cent.

A. M. Weisbrot notes that the Government and the Histadrut authorize Egged (Eshed) to raise by IL.25 a month the present basic emolument of members which has been the same for four years. In view of the favourable financial results anticipated by the end of August "there is no reason why the members will not get back the five per cent withheld. . . . And the Management thinks that it also will return the quarter of an hour daily and discontinue the five per cent withholdings."

The Management also advised the Government that Egged (Eshed) was unable to make the down payment of 25 per cent in cash on the 300 new buses to be purchased in England and the balance within 30 months. It still had another six monthly instalments to pay on account of the previous purchase of buses and had to arrange the financing for the bodies, etc., of the new buses, which amounted to between IL.12,000 and IL.13,000 for each bus (40 per cent of the cost of a bus). Egged (Eshed) awarded to the Histadrut-sponsored construction company the million-pound contract for the central garage in the north, though that company's "bid was among the higher ones but not the highest". This award was subject to the company agreeing that it would not charge more than "the market price" and accepting payment of IL.250,000 in cash and the balance, IL.750,000, in three annual instalments. There were reasonable prospects that Egged (Eshed) would receive loans for the garages from the Government Development Fund through the Ministry of Transport. Egged (Eshed) applied for IL.2 million on account of IL.3½ million which it invested in buildings (exclusive of cost of office buildings). Egged (Eshed) was also promised a loan of IL.250,000 for the equipment of the garages.

Mr. Weisbrot, referring to the increase of the book value of the members' financial participation in the co-operative from IL.5,000 to IL.8,000, notes that there is also a decision to review such revaluation annually. If there is an emergency devaluation, the evaluations of the member's financial participation in the co-operative will be reviewed every six months. He reports that Chevrat Haovdim refused to approve the recommendation of Merkaz Haco-operatzia to fix the value of the participation of a new member as the equivalent of a member's gross emolument for 28 months at the time when admitted. This would obviate perennial discussions of this question. A new member will pay part in cash on admission and the balance in monthly instalments.

Eliahu Rozen reports that the revenue from "specials" (i.e. buses hired for sightseeing and for the elections) account for nearly all the surplus. He asks why the excess expenditures (over the estimated amount) exceed the excess over estimated revenue. During this period the remuneration for overtime exceeded the withholdings (five per cent) of their "regular emoluments".

Mr. Aidleen asks why, in view of the decision to minimize the use of outside garages, IL.200,000 of repairs for equipment were contracted out to these garages. He also cites the serious shortage of all kinds of spare parts, the irregular check-up of the equipment and the delay in removing tyres for vulcanization.

The management's report notes that after a relatively quiet period of normal relationships between Egged (Eshed) and the Histadrut, the decision of the three bus co-operatives (that merged) to distribute certain pension and provident funds among its members has been headlined in the press. The report asked why those who disagreed with this action, which was neither illegal nor harmful to the public's interests, did not express their views to Egged (Eshed) direct or through Histadrut authorized bodies.

U. Weisbrot notes that the three bus co-operatives—Egged, Drom Yehuda and Shachar that were merged into Egged (Eshed)—are in the process of voluntary liquidation. Therefore, the respective provident funds of these three bus co-operatives in which the member's participation was voluntary, also have to be liquidated. The three bus co-operatives decided to refund to their respective members, including past members, their participation in the share capital plus the amount standing to their credit in the provident funds of the respective bus co-operatives. The members of the three bus co-operatives then paid their participation in the share capital of Egged (Eshed). The resources of the three provident funds were deposited with and pledged as security for credits which Egged (Eshed), when in process of registration, received from banks and credit co-operatives for the purchase of equipment and for making loans to individual members. The banks insisted that the resources of the provident funds remain on deposit with them as security for the debts of Egged (Eshed) on the following conditions:

(*a*) The banks would credit every member with his share in the provident fund of the respective bus co-operative in eight semi-annual instalments in the course of four years.

(*b*) Members would be permitted to withdraw their funds during this four-year period provided they were not indebted to the respective banks.

(*c*) Interest at the rate of 7⅓ per cent p.a. would be paid on such amounts which the respective members did not withdraw.

Mr. Weisbrot explains that the moneys of the three respective provident funds were not transferred to the new provident fund of Egged (Eshed) because "we did not wish to mix the old and new provident fund; a provident fund may not accept deposits". The new provident fund, which started operations on 1 April, 1954, undertakes to link compensation to a member's last salary.

The new provident fund, on the advice of Mr. S. (joint General Manager of the Workers Bank Ltd.), invested IL.700,000 in linked shares of the Israel Electric Company (in which the Government is the majority share holder) and IL.500,000 as a linked loan to the Jewish Agency. According to Mr. Weisbrot, they were advised that the investments would facilitate the negotiations of Egged (Eshed) for a Government credit for the purchase of 300 buses 'since the credit would come from Jewish Agency resources". The press, especially the Labour press, "showed a lack of confidence in us and in the information". The Labour press severely castigated Egged (Eshed) for withdrawing funds from Histadrut-sponsored financial bodies. But Egged (Eshed) could not act on the Histadrut suggestion to cancel the entire arrangement. He hoped that the question would soon be resolved.

M. Gelbard (Chevrat Haovdim) notes that Chevrat Haovdim is authorized to cast half the votes in the new provident fund (of Egged (Eshed)) and that none of this provident fund's decisions may become operative unless its representatives on the Management participate in such decisions. He regrets that Mr. Weisbrot did not mention that the Histadrut representatives on Egged (Eshed) management were not told about the arrangements made about the provident funds.

(*a*) He learned about the decision from "Maariv" (the evening non-Labour daily) which carried Mr. Weisbrot's story. "Twenty minutes after the meeting of the secretariat, the publication of Egged (Eshed) L'Chavereinu also carried the report."

(*b*) Mr. Weisbrot also failed to mention that the voluntary liquidation of the three bus co-operatives was only a formality which the Regulations of the Co-operative Societies Ordinance prescribed. Since the three co-operatives voluntarily decided to merge, it was logical to assume that their respective provident funds also would be merged and would continue as the provident fund of Egged (Eshed).

(*c*) Mr. Weisbrot ignored the other two interested parties in the provident fund, viz., the Histadrut and the public.

"All three (i.e. the Histadrut, Egged (Eshed) and the public) are the owners of the large glass house Egged (Eshed). . . . It has been said that an individual has three faces:

(*a*) the face which the public sees;
(*b*) the face as the individual sees himself and
(*c*) the face as he really is.

This can also be applied to Egged (Eshed). . . . This body must accommodate itself to the public interests, as well as to those of its members. The Government must be able to reply to the public.

Mr. Gelbard further noted that the publication of the story in Davar was not the source but the result of the problem. Those who acted without the knowledge of the management and considered "the arrangement as good" erred and cheated. The investment in Israel Electric Corporation shares was a good one. But it was not made in a "befitting way and those who did so did not think the problem through to the end". A member, for instance, who is entitled to IL.800 from the provident fund of one of the three bus co-operatives that merged will receive this money in eight semi-annual instalments.

"This will neither enrich the member nor bring any significant benefits. It would be much better if he has this IL.800 in a reliable institution from which, in case of need, he can borrow the IL.800 to add a room to his house or apartment; improve the furnishings, etc. . . . And in the long run, when because of a dispute or old age, incapacity or for any other reason, he (the member) has to leave Egged (Eshed), he can get back his entire participation. From an actuarial point of view, using an average age of all members, young and old as the base for the calculations, it was wrong to turn over the accumulation of 20 years' service in the old bus co-operative and to start a new participation in the new provident fund as from 1 April, 1955, because their potential period of productivity in most cases will be for a shorter period than that which has already passed. Egged (Eshed) must correct its mistake."

Mr. Eliahu Rozen attributed the misfortunes to the unsatisfactory relationships between Egged (Eshed) and the Histadrut. In the future, as in the past, in its negotiations with the Histadrut, Egged (Eshed) will come away with empty hands. The same can be expected in the current negotiations with the Histadrut about the provident fund.

"I think it is always a mistake to accept arbitration. Perhaps for once, the management will have the courage (enough guts) and first carry out its plans. . . . At some time we must come to the conclusion that we should not always behave like obedient (good) children, especially as regards the Histadrut. I have never seen the Histadrut worry about us, its most loyal workers, as much as it does about the other workers."

Samuel Zachrin describes the Histadrut's publicity about the distribution of the provident fund moneys as a deliberate action "to disrupt us and to forestall our requests in the near future". Therefore, he proposes a resolution "censoring the Histadrut for the publicity in its press about the provident funds".

Mr. Eliahu Elkalai opposes Mr. Zachrin's suggestion because in spite of the considerable misunderstanding which still exists between themselves and the Histadrut, the latter's "representatives who sit and discuss matters with us are in order", though it is not certain whether the Histadrut representatives on the management of Egged (Eshed) have done enough to obtain favourable Histadrut decisions.

Zvi Lehman (Chevrat Haovdim) asks whether anyone really believes that the Histadrut consciously wishes to prejudice the rights and benefits of members of provident funds. Formal explanations as to which was the competent body to decide on the use of the resources of the provident funds do not interest the Histadrut or the public. The significant issue is that action was taken "behind our backs and this we consider a serious breach of trust which the Histadrut and its representatives had placed in the society". Members of Egged (Eshed) should at least have known that it was advantageous to consult the Histadrut. A joint committee is seeking to resolve the question of the provident funds to the satisfaction of the Histadrut and of the members of Egged (Eshed).

The keynote of A. Hochman, a member of the management, closing the general debate of the Egged (Eshed) Council, was that a large, dispersed, complex and dynamic organization like Egged (Eshed) cannot guarantee that "there will be no mistakes or defects in the future". He reminded the members that during the last three difficult and bitter years

> "they had to proceed step by step, from crisis to crisis from every point of view . . . those in and those out know that the co-operative cannot continue indefinitely to operate with deficits. . . . I think that no other owner of an undertaking would have stood up to the difficulties which we were up against. And our main strength is the organizational pattern of the co-operative. Our (the management's) report stresses neither the rosy nor the black, but only the realities as they are."

There is no question of trying to cover up or retreat from a previous stand. The Minister of Transport had agreed on an alternative plan for balancing the budget. But in view of the complexity of the situation, Mr. Hochman asked the council to leave this matter in the hands of the co-operative's management. As an example, he cited the difficulties in timing accurately when it was possible to reduce manpower because "there are conditions in the State which make it necessary to withdraw at one time tens of members from work". Such conditions require flexibility and a quick adjustment.

With regard to anti-Egged publicity in Davar, Egged (Eshed) asked the Histadrut to define its policy clearly. "We should have told the Histadrut that we do not ask that it should always accept our view; we wanted only one thing—if we erred, punish us at home. Make another suggestion—inside (in the house)—attack us—but not in the street and in the press".

Mr. Hochman, generally speaking, agreed with the criticism of the accounting department of Egged (Eshed). Summing up the short period of the present management committee's activities, he said: ". . . I repeat what we said in the conclusion of the written report; we have not yet brought about the redemption. But there are encouraging signs. These oblige us and justify that we should continue with the same means as those with which we started."

The council on 22 September, 1955, called on the management of Egged (Eshed) to redouble its efforts and to continue with those measures which lead to efficiency, economies and orderly and normal work in the various branches.

The Minister of Transport when presenting his 1958-59 budget to the Knesset (March 1958) demanded that Egged (Eshed) and Dan require their members to repay such amounts as these two have distributed, without his authority. Government supervision, administrative, financial and economic, over the bus co-operatives during the last few years had increased, and an *ad hoc* committee was preparing special regulations. The printing of all fare tickets under Government supervision, beginning 14 May, 1958, should enable the Ministry of Transport to control the revenue of the bus co-operatives. The Minister of Transport mentioned that "Egged (Eshed) approved increases in the monthly emoluments to its members which were appreciably larger than the Government had authorized." Dan had increased the fringe benefits to members "by several tens of pounds per member" per month and had used for this purpose revenues from fares and Government subsidies which had been earmarked for renewal of equipment and the improvement of the services.

P. Lavon, the Secretary-General of the Histadrut, and Egged (Eshed) exchanged letters about the unauthorized payments which the bus co-operative Egged (Eshed) made to its members. Letter of 7 July, 1958, to Egged (Eshed) from Mr. P. Lavon:

"In accordance with our conversation today we herewith advise you of our conclusions.

(*a*) In accordance with the exchange of correspondence between us and on the basis of your unequivocal written undertaking of 5 May, 1958, we again note that the arrangements for the refund of the IL.54 per month which was paid to the members from December, 1957, to April, 1958, are subject to the arrangements which the Secretariat of Chevrat Haovdim and its organs will define.

(*b*) Should the Ministry of Transport require from you an undertaking with regard to any other amounts which you paid to your members, similar to the undertaking which the Dan co-operative has given, the Histadrut will insist that you should comply with such a request.

(*c*) The Histadrut does not consider itself obligated to request the Ministry of Transport to make available any funds other than the subsidies which have been allocated.

If you will accept our conclusions, then your representatives Messrs. A. Davidson and I. Duchovni may return to and participate in the Histadrut committee which is dealing with the problems of the structure for the emoluments (remuneration) of members.

(Signed)
P. Lavon."

Letter from Egged (Eshed) to Mr. P. Lavon, 30 July, 1958.

"Replying to your letter of 7 July, 1958, and in continuation of our conversation of even date, we confirm receipt of your above mentioned letter and its contents.

With regard to the IL.54 per month paid to the members from December 1957, to April 1958, we accept Mr. Lavon's conclusions that the amount paid should be deducted in twelve monthly instalments from the emoluments to members beginning 1 October, 1958.

In reply to paragraph (b) (of your letter), we have reached an agreement with the Ministry of Transport to make only such payments to the members as the Ministry of Transport will agree.

We will freeze and discontinue paying to the (Egged (Eshed)) members the IL.26 per month as a bonus for their participation in the co-operative's capital and for their responsibility for management and for overtime; and also IL.9 per month paid as the members' participation in the provident fund; total of IL.35 per month.

We have taken note that these arrangements became effective on 1 August, 1958.

(Signed)
Egged (Eshed)."

Letter from the Histadrut to the Egged (Eshed) Management, 30 July, 1958.

"We acknowledge with satisfaction the contents of your letter of even date. We also have noted the arrangement which you have made with the Ministry of Transport with regard to paragraph (b) of our letter of 7 July, 1958.

(Signed)
Z. L. Lifshitz."

EGGED (ESHED)—INTER-URBAN BUS CO-OPERATIVE
COMPARATIVE DATA FOR 1951 AND 1963[(a)]

				Increase 1951-63	
	Number of	1951	1963	Absolute	Percentage
1.	Buses[(c)]	960	1,484[(d)]	524	54
2.	Seating Capacity	33,500	66,655	33,155	98
3.	Members	1,710	3,237	1,527	89
4.	Wage Workers (inc. apprentices)	955	1,685	730	75
5.	Total Labour Force (3+4)	2,665	4,922	2,257	84
6.	No. of kilometres covered (in millions)	55·5	117	61·5	110
7.	Localities Serviced	650	1,050	400	60
8.	Routes	480	730	250	52
9.	Length of Routes (kilometres)	14,068	20,000	5,932	42
10.	Fares (millions of pounds)[(c)]	112	273	161	143
11.	Journeys (millions)[(c)] (no. fares)	3	6·1	3·1	100
12.	Passenger Sheds[(b)]	315	1,045	730	230
	Aver. No. of kilometres per bus	57,812	97,500	39,688	66
	Aver. No. fares per bus	116,600	227,500	110,840	94

(a) Table from Page 6 of Stencilled Pamphlet (November 1963) by Egged (Eshed) to commemorate the twelfth anniversary of the merger of the Bus Co-operatives Egged, Drom Yehuda and Shacher. Egged had been using electronic calculating machines, etc., for seven years. They are continuing to expand their electronic equipment to help resolve their problems.

(b) Egged (Eshed), in addition to the covered sheds for passengers, had 13 well equipped bus stations, two more were in course of construction (at the end of 1963), two more were to be built, and five more were planned.

(c) Egged has a "Department for Sightseers" which has "tens of specially equipped buses" and licensed guides who regularly attend Egged refresher courses. These buses have been used for over a million sightseers—local and foreign, in every part of Israel.

(d) At the end of 1961, 1,202 of their 1,349 buses were Diesel. Of the 1,202, a total of 702 were Royal Tigers Mark 2; 105 were Royal Tigers Mark 1; and 118 were Leylands. A total of 134 of the 138 petrol buses were White Supers. The average age of their 1,349 buses was six years (compared with an average age of 14½ years of their 949 buses in 1957).

EGGED (ESHED) BUS TRANSPORTATION CO-OPERATIVE IN ISRAEL LTD.
AUDITED ANNUAL BALANCE-SHEET FOR YEAR ENDING 31 MARCH, 1961
(IN IL.)

Liabilities		
1. Own Funds		
(*a*) Share Capital*		6,147,500
(*b*) Admission Entrance Fees		3,447,526
(*c*) Fund for Renewal of Inventory		2,770,848
(*d*) Profits on Sales of Property		707,344
(*e*) Accretion in Value of Spare Parts		534,778
(*f*) Total (*a*) to (*e*)		13,607,996
(*g*) Less Members' Debts a/c Share Capital		309,813
(*h*) (*f*) minus (*g*)		13,298,183
(*i*) Less Operational Deficits Previous Years		14,949,240
(*j*) Deficit in 1.		−1,651,057
2. Payments by 254 Probationers a/c Share Capital and Entrance Fees		2,291,260
Own Funds deficit 2. minus 1.(*j*)		640,203
3. Bank Loans (includes IL.702,132 linked to U.S. $		
(*a*) Payable in one year	5,498,396	
(*b*) Payable by end 1964	2,163,724	
	7,662,120	
4. Loans from Members	3,326,576	
5. Total 3+4		10,988,696
6. Accounts Payable		
(*a*) Banks	184,897	
(*b*) Suppliers	2,319,209	
(*c*) Members	2,543,485	
(*d*) Wage Workers	367,027	

(*e*) Reserve for Holiday and Severance Allowances	1,483,764	
(*f*) Members' Provident Fund	1,245,983	
(*g*) Miscellaneous	5,738,441	
(*h*) Total 6.		13,882,806
7. Bills Payable		
(*a*) Within one year	2,112,810	
(*b*) By October 1967	65,487	
(*c*) Total		2,178,297
8. Cheques drawn on Banks not presented		1,018,098
9. Income in Advance		175,291
10. Total Liabilities		28,883,391
11. Conditional Liabilities		1,645,761
Assets		
11. Capital Investments		
(*a*) Immovables		5,005,255
(*b*) Equipment		10,832,770
(*c*) Investments in Subsidiaries etc.		2,303,887
(*d*) Various Investments		985,709
(*e*) Other		1,434,470
(*f*) Total (11)		20,562,091
12. Liquid Assets		
(*a*) Stocks on Hand (fuel, spare parts, tyres, etc.)	3,662,127	
(*b*) Advance Payments for spare parts and tyres ordered	529,164	
(*c*) *Accounts Receivable* (clients includes IL.1,725,717)	2,436,671	
(*d*) Expenses in Advance	1,187,140	
(*e*) Bills for Collection	52,284	
(*f*) Cash and at Bank	453,914	
(*g*) Total (12)		8,321,300
Total Assets		28,883,391

Dated 9 July, 1962.

* 2,459 members. The Management decided that members admitted after 17 November, 1960, have to pay IL.2,500 share capital and IL.10,000 entrance fee.

INCOME & EXPENSES FOR YEAR APRIL, 1960 TO MARCH, 1961
(In IL.)

Income			
1. Fares (after deducting stamp duties; commissions; fees for rented vehicles)			49,658,305
2. Special journeys and Sightseeing (after deducting discounts, etc.)			6,805,161
3. Parcel & Messenger Service			1,067,999
4. Miscellaneous			243,157
5 Total Income			57,774,622
Expenditure			
6. Emoluments			
(*a*) Members	20,859,751		
(*b*) Wage Workers	6,556,866		
(*c*) Total		27,416,617	
7. Fringe (Social) Benefits			
(*a*) Members	5,349,765		
(*b*) Wage Workers	1,727,463		
(*c*) Total		7,077,228	
8. Fuel (after deducting IL.92,750 subsidies on petrol)		5,163,903	
9. Maintenance of Equipment		7,719,677	
10. Parcel Service Expenses (includes IL.199,692 Commission to Agents)		217,114	
11. Servicing Costs		3,635,126	
12. Insurance and Property Taxes		1,830,304	
13. Administration (Includes Financing)		2,930,922	
14. Amortization (Depreciation)			
(*a*) Equipment	4,050,684		
(*b*) Workshop Equipment	461,203		
(*c*) Other Property	144,313		
(*d*) Total		4,656,200	
15 Total Expenses		60,647,091	60,647,091
16. (*a*) Operational Deficit (15 minus (5))			2,872,469
(*b*) Losses from Cancellation on Concessionary Routes			127,499
(*c*) Gross Deficit			2,999,968
(*d*) Less Profit on property sold			28,526
17. Operational Deficit			2,971,442

DAN BUS CO-OPERATIVE, TEL AVIV[103]

Two bus co-operatives were operating in Tel Aviv, Hamaavir (315 members) and Ichud Regev (144 members). These amalgamated and registered a new bus co-operative—Dan—on 4 December, 1945.

During the Arab disturbances, 1936-39, the need to increase and to modernize the equipment and to expand the routes became clear. With the continuous expansion of the Tel Aviv boundaries, the jurisdictional disputes between the two bus co-operatives Hamaavir and Ichud Regev about routes increased. This sparked the merger of the two bus co-operatives into one co-operative "Dan"—with a joint membership of 459 and combined total of 233 vehicles between them.

When the two bus co-operatives were merged, their respective provident funds were liquidated and the assets and liabilities were transferred to a new provident fund which was registered under the Companies Ordinance as Kupat Hatagmulim (Provident Fund) for the members of Dan and Nahar, the latter was the holding company for Dan property.

Hamaavir bus co-operative was among the first to introduce a provident and pension fund. In 1938 it started to make allocations to a provident and pension fund "without knowing what its ultimate fate would be". In spite of the "financial panic" created by the beginning of World War Two in September 1939, "we acquired the land for building a garage and houses for the members". Though the situation became more critical when France collapsed (1940) and Italy entered the War (1941) and when the German Army was at Alamein (1941), Hamaavir carried out its plan and acquired a second site for a garage and for members' houses.

Mr. Aryeh Tager who was chairman of the manpower committee of Hamaavir when it merged with Ichud and registered as Dan, on 1 December, 1945, gives a succinct summary about the differences in the character of the members and in the traditions of the two bus co-operatives which merged into Dan. He describes the attitude to Ichud Regev by its members as that of an individual towards his own business. "He travelled when he wished; stopped work when he felt there was a need for it and changed work with other members by mutual agreement." The work in Ichud Regev was less strenuous than it was in Hamaavir. On the other hand, Hamaavir Bus Co-operative which always had insufficient members and inadequate equipment, maintained a strict time table for practically every branch of service.

A co-operative continuously strives for a maximum of equity in every respect for all its members. Dan had both intra-urban and inter-community routes, therefore, a difference in the conditions of work was unavoidable. Members on the routes in Tel Aviv complained about the weight of the buses for the towns and about having to travel so far from their homes. They were convinced that the inter-urban work was easier. Arrangements were made for members to alternate semi-annually on intra and inter routes; the members learned to know each other. An obligatory annual weekend at a rest house, at the co-operative's expense, helped to cement friendships between the members. Arrangements for annual vacations; fixed timetables for work; and the recording of all work helped to maintain the discipline and understanding by "an appreciable number of the members." But Mr. Tager complained that the system of annual elections "destroys any possibility of realizing even the minimum of planning", the reason being that the new people elected either ignore or upset completely what their predecessors introduced.[104]

Mr. Aryeh Maziar, describing the "wastefulness" of the annual elections, notes that

> "these are no longer suitable for a co-operative as large as ours with a modern economy, a large labour force and a complexity of problems. All who are familiar with the problems our co-operative has been grappling with in the last few years know that the bad blood of extreme democracy is in our veins and that the time has come to deviate from the archaic practice which directly hurts our co-operative and indirectly hurts the standard of our service to the public. . . . I know in advance that the suggestion to replace the annual elections with bi-annual elections will create a sharp difference of opinion among many members; the time is ripe to take the risk and to air this proposal. . . . Go out and see (for yourselves) how many conceptions and practices have outlived their usefulness (aged) in the course of several tens of years. And we continue to preserve an anachronism as if the world, society as a whole and our co-operatives are standing in the same place as thirty years ago. Are we a philanthropic society or an exclusive club or a *landsmanschaft* that retains annual elections in order to elect a management whose only function is the distribution of grants or to arrange Chanuka and Purim parties or to arrange an annual memorial." Certainly the members understand that it requires more than a few months to delve into and to understand the management "of such a complex co-operative as ours, with 950 members (men), whose management is bound up with problems and difficulties which one cannot learn quickly ("on one foot").

Mr. Maziar writes that it takes three months to distribute the functions and to set up a new management. Only five months remain for concentrated work because the last four months of the year are used for arranging the new elections; thus "a third of the year is wasted on politics".

Mr. Maziar attributes the lag between the rate of increase of passengers, and the rate of increase of populations in the localities which Dan services, to the inadequate public relations and contact with the public, and especially with members of the working class. An increase in the number of buses alone cannot narrow this gap. They must know more about the feelings of those who use the buses. True, no country is free of overcrowding (standing) during the rush hours. But measures must be taken to minimize overcrowding, queueing and walking. And above all "we should train our drivers always to remember that they are responsible for the good name of the co-operative as well as for the steering wheel".

Yitzchak Gluzman discusses ways and means of overcoming difficulties in a co-operative with hundreds of members in which the family atmosphere has disappeared. There is no longer a unity of interest and of action;

every member approaches the problems and the solutions from his own personal point of view. As a result internal antagonism becomes the main item at the general meetings. The vatikim more than others, who always believed

> "in the superior equity of the co-operative pattern and in its power to overcome obstacles, now think that the co-operative pattern is unsuitable because the times have changed. This change can also be attributed to the disappearance of the chalutz glamour since the establishment of the State . . . either the State or private enterprises should take over the bus services and in either case the rights of the workers must be fully secured."

Another school thought that if the rules of the co-operative were adapted to the appreciable increase in the number of members and the change in their character since the establishment of the State, it would then be unnecessary to abolish the co-operative pattern. One of the main causes for the constant ferment and instability which interferes with

> "the normal functioning of a co-operative and creates difficulties for the management, are the annual election of officers, management, etc. Office seekers spend considerable time and effort during the entire year building up goodwill for themselves among the members. This strain and unrest could be considerably minimized if biennial and triennial elections were arranged. If this change were combined with a change-over to regional elections, the . . . dangers of over-centralization and of managerial control would be minimized. The members in the respective regions would elect their representatives on the co-operative's governing bodies, etc. In a large co-operative one does not know his neighbour."

Mr. Gluzman also suggested that experts should be imported and members should be sent abroad to widen their knowledge and training. He also noted that the Histadrut, which contributed so much to the early development of their co-operative, had become a "stepmother". During its growing up stage, there were times when Dan needed but did not get moral support from the Histadrut. The members of the bus co-operatives should have their own and separate craft federation and it should be affiliated to the Histadrut. This would enable the members of the bus co-operatives to discuss and resolve their problems and would obviate the need of having to accept orders and/or to confirm agreements which others have made on their behalf. "A community of drivers roam the country like a herd of sheep without a shepherd. A basic change is unavoidable". Mr. Gluzman considers wage labour as most untenable, "and inequitable both from a social and moral point of view". At best it (i.e. wage labour) should be permitted only under "exceptional (rare) circumstances".

Akiva Friedman—one of the founders of Hamaavir—writes about "Blemishes and Correctives (Remedies)":

> "Twenty-three years ago I looked on the co-operative 'Hamaavir' as one

family, orderly and disciplined, in which peace and dedication were deeply rooted and the concern of every member for his neighbour and the mutual concern of all for the individual was predominant. I made a considerable effort to become a member and was very happy when I succeeded. At that time applicants were carefully screened. But once accepted your worries become everybody's worries; they gave him (i.e. the new member) the maximum help and participated in his joys.

"To my regret . . . the intimate family life of former days has completely disappeared. There is no concern about the co-operative or for the member's family. The young generation hold important administrative posts . . . instead of choosing talented people suitable to fill these posts, and who could ensure discipline, order and further growth . . . quick and comfortable service for the population and who would remove those who are stealing our bread. . . .[105] Because our living depends on the public who hate us . . . everything must be done to improve their attitude . . . the people will respect us if we will respect them. . . ."

Mr. Zeev Dagani frankly explains that Hamaavir and Ichud Regev merged and organized the Dan bus co-operative for purely commercial reasons and these considerations continue. There were no social ties (i.e. social aspects of co-operation) or "the element of public-national feelings or perceptions". Therefore, one cannot expect to find solidarity in Dan, that is, personal mutual identification.

He also explains that the original plan for the merger of all the Histadrut-sponsored bus co-operatives in Israel into one bus co-operative included also the Dan bus co-operative and Hamekasher of Jerusalem. It is not improbable that Dan would have been included if it had "fought for its rights". Dan was too quick to accept the decision to be excluded because its members did not at the time visualize the advantages of such a merger. If the question were reopened today, Dan would insist on being included. He considers the tenth anniversary of Dan as a minor holiday; the establishment of one country-wide bus co-operative that will include both Dan and Hamekasher will be the big holiday.

Mr. Dagani is convinced that Egged (Eshed) has demonstrated that a country-wide bus co-operative is preferable both in the interests of the public and of the individual. And he notes that the activities of the bus co-operatives

"already are completely encompassed by the Merkaz Haco-operatzia and the influence of the public authorities. . . . Because of this increased pressure, both our economic and administrative independence is declining and losing its meaning. . . . In being deprived of our autonomy, we are losing one of the distinguishing marks of this pattern (i.e. co-operative). It is not worthwhile looking for a repellent against the increased but natural onslaught of the public influence within its own (Dan's) institutions, because there is none. This development came as the public institutions became more mature and stronger and should not be attributed to the fact that "we failed." The fact that this influence emerged only recently and did not accompany our activity since its (Dan's) foundation, is due either to the fact that these institutions did not have the necessary strength to do so or that they did not consider this necessary."

Furthermore, this kind of influence can prove dangerous if it oversteps itself and becomes purely a matter of "meddlesomeness", or if we "adopt a disdainful attitude towards it". There is evidence that this weaving of the web of influence has very far-reaching arms. Therefore, the greater the need for action before it becomes too late. He thinks that only the organization of one country-wide bus co-operative can help.

Yisrael Savorai wants a clear unequivocal decision that the Management Committee and/or Council of Dan may not overrule a medical report about a candidate's unfitness for membership. He also seeks the opinion of the Management Committee and of the members about giving candidates psychotechnical tests. Every member who already fills or wishes to fill a managerial post, must have at least some elementary training and also take a refresher course in the respective branch of work. It was regrettable that Dan did not encourage nor made it possible for members with inventive aptitudes to improve their technical knowledge and to work on their ideas.

Moshe Rosenzweig, one of the younger members of Dan bus co-operative, writes that intimate family relationships of the members of Hamaavir both at work and during their leisure attracted him to the co-operative. "But since joining the co-operative (Dan) I was disillusioned, not in a small degree." He found that Dan was rife with and dominated by cliques with conflicting views. Unless this is uprooted "it will consume us. This (the co-operative) is not a political party of the Knesset. And the orators would do more good if in the first place they served as a good example in their work at the wheel and not in handing out jobs (patronage)." While Dan has increased its membership and expanded its economic activities "the spiritual life has congealed" and inter-member intimacy has disappeared.[106] While he appreciated the difficulties of arranging social evenings, etc., for such a large membership, he nevertheless deprecated the infrequency and the sterility of the general meetings. He suggested that Dan should have an informative internal monthly bulletin which could also serve as a forum.

Zvi Soslik's article "A Generation Goes and a Generation Comes"[107] notes that participation in Dan's capital gives the new members "all the material rights" but does not buy vetek (seniority),

> "the years of suffering and hardships, strife and blood . . . years of hard toil from morning until night under inhuman conditions . . . and money cannot replace the broken body and spirit of those who paved the way for the others who were handed a *fait accompli* . . . money cannot eradicate the writing engraved by the hand of time or reduce high blood pressure, bolster a weak heart, cure ulcers or decaying eyes, or straighten a misplaced vertebra". Yet the vatikim work, side by

> side, with the young on the same hard labour, ploughing new routes, and also frequently with "more devotion and responsibility". It may seem absurd to an outsider (non-member of a co-operative) to see somebody who has put in many years in managerial work "back at the wheel". He considers it "ridiculous to compare the co-operative (Dan) with one large family".

He pleads that Dan, following the example of Egged (Eshed), prepare and give the older members priority for administrative and managerial posts. The older members are entitled to the same consideration and care which is given to the maintenance of the equipment.

Mr. Soslik considers "cliques" which crop up in every conversation—"A plague not mentioned in the Bible except in the section on curses."[108] The existence of many parties and factions in the Histadrut and in the State does not justify the fragmentation of the members in a co-operative into groups such as the faithful, ex-service men, and the founders, with each group having a different goal. Do any of those groups deny that the interests of the co-operative Dan should have priority and that the co-operative Dan also must consider the interest of all its members? This does not mean that all members must think alike, since only people who have no opinions have no preferences. Members insist that those chosen should be leaders of the co-operative and not leaders of cliques. "And you should love your co-operative like yourself; this should be the entire Torah . . . and this credo should be the guide for the elections and for our life." Provided there are good reasons, he is not opposed to changes in the leadership and management. But he does object to changes which are intended only as a means of replacing the vatikim with younger people.

> "Why should we not understand that all of us—young and old—have our bad days and nobody wants to be considered as a dependent, eating bread of kindness". His closing paragraph reads: "Men do not become wise men merely by experience; but only to the extent that they have the aptitude to acquire the experience and to adapt their experience to their needs."[109]

Mr. Aaron Davshi writing on the society's cultural activities during the decade 1945-55, notes that Dan started to operate immediately after World War Two (early 1946) when it was essential to concentrate on such problems as readjustment of the tens of members who were being discharged from the Army and the admission of war veterans. In mid-1947 the Arabs started their revolt which led to the War of Liberation (in 1948-49) and there was need to concentrate on further readjustment afterwards, such as the repair of the equipment, etc. which was badly damaged during this period of unrest. He considers extra-curricular activities as one of

> "the important foundations for building up the social aspects of co-operation and a brotherhood of members within it". The first step was to bring together the members and their families at evening socials and

parties. "And to our regret the management and the members did not always show a full understanding for these activities. They considered our work as a waste of time. . . ." Most of the get togethers (parties) were arranged on religious and national holidays, and these always included an artistic programme by guest artistes, which had some bearing on the respective holiday. "During the ten years since the amalgamation there were tens of parties, some more successful than others, but most of them were acclaimed by the members as successful. There also were special parties for the children and youth in whom we tried to impregnate the feeling that they belonged to the one big family called Dan."

The one and two-day sight-seeing excursions had the double purpose of bringing the members and their families into the open country and also to give them the opportunity of getting to know the country and the life of the other sectors of the population. Groups of adults and of the young generation were encouraged to participate in practically every branch of sport, soccer, tennis, basketball, rowing, swimming and diving. Of special importance were the circulating libraries with thousands of books, and the rooms for adults and children. Mr. Davshi regrets that the plan for an internal news sheet did not materialize and that only two numbers were issued. He considers this as a vital necessity, no less for the management than for the thousand members. The members lost interest in the band which was taken over from Hamaavir and also in the chamber string orchestra that followed but dispersed within a relatively short time. Special courses in Bible, literature, languages and technical and other courses are becoming increasingly popular.

A Report on Public Transportation—Dan Bus Co-operative—Tel Aviv-Jaffa, by S. Kliyoski, submitted in August 1953.

Mr. Kliyoski's general conclusions are:

1. Dan bus co-operative has a genuine desire to serve the public to the best of its ability, to the extent that it is possible without the co-operative incurring operational deficits.
2. The co-operative pattern is not, in my opinion, the desirable structure for a public bus transportation system, because a co-operative is at considerable disadvantage in arranging the work and in the maximum exploitation of its resources.
3. More recently, the traffic management of Dan paid more attention and displayed goodwill to follow the suggestions which the municipal traffic committee made for improving the services.

Dan serves Tel Aviv-Jaffa, Ramat Gan and the small town of Petah Tikva (12 miles from Tel Aviv) and the maabarot in the environs. Dan carries 550,000 passengers daily. Every bus in operation carries 1,600 passengers daily which "is more than three times the average found in other countries". The over-crowding, especially in the difficult climatic conditions during eight months of the year, is unhealthy and also increases the tension between the drivers and the public. The driver of a bus also serves as a "ticket seller and information bureau; he maintains order within the bus; and opens and closes the doors of the bus". Dan has neglected public relations. A more accommodating attitude of the drivers "could win the sympathy of the public". If more efforts were made to keep the public informed about routes, time tables, etc., the services could be considerably expedited.

Between 1948 and 1952 the number of routes which Dan operated increased from 21 to 50; the number of fares per year more than doubled (from 84 to 170 million) and the number of buses during this period increased by only 50 per cent. In 1952, the Dan buses covered 19 million kilometres. On the average only 350 of Dan's 418 buses were usable daily. Thirty-six per cent of Dan's buses have been in use from eight to 20 years. Only 41 per cent of the buses have been in service four years or less. In other countries, according to Mr. Kliyoski, the average life of a bus is eight years and only an average 15 per cent of the buses are idle daily.

In support of his conclusion that the co-operative pattern is not suitable for public bus transportation, Mr. Kliyoski mentions the following: Dan has difficulties in arranging the plan of work because the traffic management has to deal with special requests of the members. Members with "ulcers" insist on assignments to routes which will enable them to eat at home in accordance with their eating schedules; some members cannot accept routes with too many turns; and still others can work only during certain hours, etc.

> "The traffic managers have to spend much of their time and their energy in debating personal problems with their members and therefore cannot devote enough time and energy to the technical problems. In preparing a plan of work, the needs of the transportation and of the public should be considered and not the convenience (requests) of the drivers."

It required considerable time and energy to get the Dan management to accept the fact "that there was no need for excessive secrecy", and to understand the economic importance of having and making available reliable data; to study concurrently the specific problems of the respective routes. Mr. Kliyoski ascribes the change in "the attitude of the traffic management towards scientific methods" to the financial advantages resulting from the improvements introduced.

It is relatively easy to explain to Dan's management that only a bus in use produces revenue; but it is very difficult to convince the members that they should reduce their rest periods at the terminal stations; discontinue one terminal station on each route; and to have short routes lengthened, and that these changes increase the efficiency of the service and decrease queueing.

The observations on Mr. Kliyoski's report, which the Dan bus co-operative released early in January, 1953, note with pride that when planning routes, timetables, etc., it considers the needs and conveniences of the members, because, generally speaking, this is advantageous rather than injurious to the services. In no other pattern of public transportation are the workers so careful in looking after the property or have such a high sense of personal responsibility for the vehicles and other equipment. There is no need for the management to worry about strikes and other "interruptions". The co-operative stresses that as in non-co-operative undertakings, only those (members) with between 20 and 25 years seniority and who suffer from chronic ailments are and should be given special consideration.

Dan doubts whether overcrowding can be appreciably reduced without additional buses and an increase in fares, and Dan refutes the charge that "the average load per (Dan) bus exceeds the accepted average". With the introduction of the sale of bus tickets by special employees in and outside the buses, the delays and the period for the turn round will be reduced. Overcrowding could be reduced if it were possible to stagger the starting and finishing times of the workers at their places of employment.

Haaretz (7 November, 1953) reports that on 6 November, 1953, the Minister of Transport discussed with the deputy director-general of the Ministry of the Interior and the representatives of the local authorities of the smaller communities the practical possibilities of converting Dan into a joint service owned by all the communities which this co-operative serves. Most of those at the meeting reacted favourably and suggested that a joint committee should prepare a practical plan. In March 1954, the Tel Aviv municipality decided to make a thorough investigation and to seek the help and co-operation of all the parties with which this study was concerned. Haaretz further reports that according to its sources of information, Dan would not oppose the plan provided that the rights of its members would be safeguarded.

Haaretz (26 November, 1953) published a note from Dan about an article "Revolution in Transport" by Mr. Machov, which Haaretz had published in its issue of 15 November, 1953. Though informed about the plan, Dan denied that its representatives participated at the meeting with the local authorities. Since it was not given the opportunity of examining the proposal, the Dan bus co-operative refused to comment on that part of Mr. Machov's article which dealt with the plan. If Dan was expected to take a stand on this question, it should have the opportunity of expressing its opinion. For three years Dan had been discussing with the Tel Aviv Municipality "with mutual sympathy" a plan which was based on an equal partnership of ownership and management. Dan would not consider a partnership with any party on any other basis.

Haaretz (9 December, 1953) reported that Dan rejected the suggestion for converting the co-operative into a public utility corporation in which Dan and all the communities which it served, would each hold 49 per cent of the shares and the Government two per cent. Dan insisted on a half interest in the ownership in the new corporate body, and that the public corporation management should have the deciding vote. The co-operative also wanted a "realistic appraisal" of its assets; that such an evaluation must include an allowance for goodwill; and that the new corporate body was to pay in cash for half the total appraised value of all Dan's assets. Furthermore, Dan would continue as a closed co-operative and the new corporation would fix emoluments in accordance with the method which Dan used and not in accordance with the method which the Ministry of Transport suggested.

DAN PUBLIC SERVICE CO-OPERATIVE LTD., TEL AVIV
AUDITED ANNUAL BALANCE SHEETS FOR YEAR ENDING 31 MARCH, 1962
(in Round Figures)

Liabilities		
1. Own Resources		
(*a*) Share Capital*	1,857,000	
(*b*) Admission Fees	3,756,035	
(*c*) General Reserves	7,034	5,620,069
Less:		
(*d*) Operational Loss (Current Year)	3,870,327	
(*e*) Previous Years	2,926,761	6,797,088
		1,177,019
Plus:		
(*f*) Payments to be made by 278 Probationers a/c of (*a*)+(*b*)		3,386,462
		2,209,443
(*g*) Less Amounts due a/c (*f*) (Bills to be Collected)		933,699
	Total (1)	1,275,744
2. General Reserves for Additional Fringe Benefits		
(*a*) Members	763,835	
(*b*) Wage Workers	297,986	1,061,821
3. Internal Insurance (Premiums Payable for Reinsurance)		678,045
4. Shareholders (all are Dan members) of Subsidiary Nahar		328,351
5. Miscellaneous Loans		1,378,987
6. Accounts Payable		
(*a*) Members+Probationers	587,918	
(*b*) Wage Workers Provident Fund	319,682	
(*c*) Wage Workers	577,630	
(*d*) Suppliers	570,430	
(*e*) Bank Overdraft (Secured by Chatel Mortgages)	617,396	
(*f*) Pre-Dated Undertakings	185,560	
(*g*) Miscellaneous	3,084,332	5,942,948
Total liabilities		10,665,896

* Paid by 1,238 members (IL.1,500 each).

Assets			
7. Capital Investments			
(*a*) Subsidiary Nahar (186,203 shares)		1,582,350	
(*b*) Current Accounts		6,240,704†	7,823,054
(*c*) Noa (Subsidiary of Merkaz Haco-operatzia)		179,046	
(*d*) Shares etc. in financial institutions		68,967	248,013
(*e*) Other			98,473
Total (7)			8,169,540
8. Members			
(*a*) Special Interest Free Loans (including IL.235,273 without fixed repayment date)		426,891	
(*b*) Members' Debts		164,584	
(*c*) Loans to Members	232,200		
Less Members' Deposits for Making Loans)	208,214	23,986	615,461
9. Stocks (fuel, tyres, etc.) per management's declaration			135,006
10. Accounts Receivable			
(*a*) Members and Probationers		103,269	
(*b*) Clients		89,694	
(*c*) Suppliers and Miscellaneous		126,714	319,677
11. Ministry of Finance—Subsidies to cover operational deficits			1,000,000
12. Expenses in Advance			207,488
13. Cash and Banks			218,724
Total Assets			10,665,896

There is a note on the balance-sheet that the Co-operative has additional potential liabilities of IL.6,819,253.

DAN BUS CO-OPERATIVE

INCOME AND EXPENDITURES FOR YEAR APRIL 1961, TO MARCH 1962

Income	IL.
1. Fares (less stamp duties; commission on sale of tickets)	30,289,320
2. Special Journeys (less discounts, etc.)	715,467
3. Publicity services (Advertisements in Buses)	54,600
4. Miscellaneous	65,582
5. Total Income	31,124,969

† Probably includes all equipment, immovables, etc. which Dan transferred to and leases from its subsidiary Nohar.

Expenditures		
6. Emoluments (including overtime, etc.)		
(*a*) Members[b]	11,589,237	
(*b*) Hired Labour (including first-year probationers)	4,021,374	
(*c*) Total		15,610,611
7. Fringe Benefits		
(*a*) Members	3,414,789[a]	
(*b*) Wage Workers	885,703[b]	
(*c*) Total		4,300,492
8. Fuel		2,728,720
9. Maintenance of equipment		8,542,935
10. Servicing Costs		1,979,725[c]
11. Insurance and Property Taxes		836,256
12. General Expenses		996,557[d]
13. Total Expenditures		34,995,296
14. Operational Deficit for Year (13 minus 5)		3,870,327
(*a*) Includes participation in members' provident fund (a subsidiary Co. Chavera)		IL.1,040,827
(*b*) Includes participation in employees insurance		IL.226,499
and provident fund		IL.39,893
(*c*) Includes concession payments to local authorities		IL.532,000
Licences for equipment and driving licences for members		IL.532,124
(*d*) Includes interest and commission		IL.279,993

HAMEKASHER BUS CO-OPERATIVE, JERUSALEM[110, 111]

Summary of a Report by an enquiry committee, August 1950, "Bus Transportation in Jerusalem".

On 9 January, 1950, the Municipal Council of Jerusalem fixed the following terms of reference for the enquiry committee.

> "To enquire into the complaints against Hamekasher; discuss how the services should be carried on, bus fares, conditions, equipment, etc., and the services for the suburbs. And if it (the committee) will find this necessary, to establish contact with the management of Hamekasher and representatives of the suburbs; centralize the material and submit a documented recommendation to the (Jerusalem) municipal council on how to remedy the situation."

In view of the terms of reference, the committee was uncertain whether it was within its competence to deal with accusations about the past. But after examining the deficiencies of the bus services which need rectifying, the committee decided that a study of the co-operative Hamekasher which has a virtual monopoly on the intra-urban routes in Jerusalem, was unavoidable. The committee expressed indignation at Hamekasher's complete indifference and opposition to the enquiry. Hamekasher's co-operation was limited to a statement acknowledging the Municipality's authority to look into the problems of transportation. Such information which Hamekasher submitted already was public property and it could have been obtained from other sources. In the summary of its findings the committee refers to the inaccurate data which Hamekasher submitted.

> "We have no doubt that the lack of reliable statistics . . . makes impossible the rational and maximum exploitation of the commercial potentialities. In our opinion, a basic reorganization is needed of this statistical department, whose chief should have wide economic knowledge. . . ."

The report notes that the enquiry committee selected

> "two or three of the many complaints about the behaviour of the drivers (one of which was signed by two members of the municipal council) about which Hamekasher had not yet made an internal investigation. But the co-operative refused to permit the respective drivers to appear before it." (i.e. the enquiry committee). The committee could not accept Hamekasher's declaration that "since Jerusalem was part of the State of Israel, only the Israeli Government had the right to ask for the figures and that the Jerusalem public, represented by the municipality, was not entitled to any explanations about the fares which it was asked to pay, or to express an opinion or to decide whether or not these are reasonable (acceptable)."

Hamekasher strongly resented the appointment of a committee to look into transport since similar action had not been taken with regard to other (public) undertakings. "The Jerusalem population and their representatives in the municipality had other ways of clearing up questions. . . . Hamekasher did not admit the extent of the ill feeling and complaints about the transport system which have been made to the municipality, in the press, at public protest meetings, etc."

During the second half of 1949, the Jerusalem Post published 25 letters of complaint about the buses, drivers' behaviour, Hamekasher, etc., and the public resentment over the fact that Hamekasher, except for one or two equivocal replies, did not answer but treated the public with contempt.

Chapter eight of the report describes the structure, administration and activities of Hamekasher and the attitude of its drivers to the public.

More serious, in the enquiry committee's opinion, were the complaints about the contemptuous attitude of the drivers to the public. The increase of and the change in the character of the population probably were responsible for the disappearance of the friendly relations between the drivers and the public which had existed for many years. There may have been objective causes such as overcrowding, the after-effects of the strain of two wars (i.e. World War Two and the War of Liberation), and the difficulty of the immigrants to adjust themselves to the different and more exacting set of standards.

"But," notes the committee, "we absolutely deny that the excessive strained relations during the last year between the passengers and some of the drivers of Hamekasher were unavoidable and that there is no cure . . . most of the witnesses differentiated between the old and the new drivers, though there were also some complaints about the old drivers. . . . The driver's behaviour also depends on his temperament and on the fact that he has to perform multiple duties. . . ."

The enquiry committee does not consider IL.2,000 which Hamekasher requires new members to pay into its capital (IL.1,500 by war veterans) as excessive "even if only the equipment and other movable property (of Hamekasher) are considered". The committee could not find out how many of the 167 members at the end of July 1950 were probationers. The wage workers "whose number is not small . . . seems to vary". The committee assumed that Hamekasher for economic reasons employed wage labour for unskilled work and also for work "requiring special skill (expertness)".

"These facts make it doubtful whether the co-operative is the suitable pattern for an undertaking like Hamekasher. Since Hamekasher members received fixed emoluments, there is practically no difference between a co-operative and another corporate form. . . . Most companies, like co-operatives, also require the approval of the management committee for all transfer of shares."

The committee notes that the Companies Ordinance makes it possible for the Government and the public to exercise more effective control than is possible under the Co-operative Societies Ordinance.

According to the report of the enquiry committee Hamekasher was

"ironically referred to as the monopoly to smash the rule of the public . . . a monopoly of the chosen ones, of strong armed men who spread terror". To be called a monopoly, is a social stigma. Denying this, Hamekasher argued that there are other means of transport such as taxis and private cars and the committee notes that Hamekasher forgets "that the overwhelming majority of the public are now dependent on the buses. Arab buses are no longer running". Therefore, concludes the committee, "Hamekasher has a *de facto* monopoly of the transport service for the masses in Jerusalem. This bus co-operative, to all intents and purposes, has the power to fix the conditions of the services because it knows that she (the municipality) needs and cannot obtain this service to any appreciable degree, from others."

The municipality, unlike municipalities in other countries, cannot even collect any taxes, licence fees or any other fees from Hamekasher.

According to the report, Hamekasher was "contemptuous" of the letters to the press and answered very few. The society did not even acknowledge the letters from the suburbs.

"We saw copies of the communications sent to the management of Hamekasher which were not even acknowledged. . . . We can quote from the evidence . . . which refers . . . to letters reaching Hamekasher which are either filed or thrown into the waste paper basket! When a Hamekasher representative was asked why he did not acknowledge the letters, he is reported to have replied 'because they seemed to him as idiotic'."

One member from Hamekasher's secretariat and two from its traffic committee each devote 20 hours a week to supervision; the rest of the time they work as drivers. There are also a few members who spend two hours a week on each route checking traffic and a few others who control the payment of fares in the buses. The committee found that some routes and buses had not been checked for a year. As a result there is laxity, especially with regard to the timetable about which there is considerable complaint. The punctuality of the drivers, such as reporting on time for work, is a special problem in the bus co-operatives. Yet the commercial success of the bus co-operative depends on punctuality. Though the committee was unable to obtain any data about the extent to which the (bus) co-operative used the sanction clause of its rules in order to maintain discipline, it seemed "that recently there was an improvement in this respect".

The enquiry committee notes that Hamekasher's management relies entirely on

"common sense and that they lack even a semblance of expertness and are working without a technical library".

The management of Hamekasher did not attend even short refresher courses. There was a feeling of "self-satisfaction" about everything. The section of the report which gives the summary of the findings closes with the following statement:

"In principle we favour the idea of transferring the ownership (of the bus transport system) to the municipality. But under no circumstances are we prepared, at this stage, to recommend the transfer of this undertaking to the municipality or to open negotiations for its purchase. Not only because the municipality does not have the resources required for this, but, primarily, because we know that the productivity in our public institutions has not reached that standard which is needed for the profitable administration of a business so varied as municipal bus transport."

Six pages are then devoted to a summary and to the recommendations about the amendments of the legislation which are urgently needed to enable the municipalities to exercise some control over the local transport system.

HAMEKASHER CO-OPERATIVE SOCIETY LTD., JERUSALEM
AUDITED ANNUAL BALANCE-SHEET FOR YEAR ENDING 31 MARCH, 1962
(in IL., round figures)

Liabilities		
1. Own Funds		
(*a*) Share Capital	354,000	
(*b*) Fund from Entrance Fees	363,473	
(*c*) (*a*) plus (*b*)	717,473	
2. Reserves		
(*a*) General	18,400	
(*b*) Renewal of equipment, etc.	330,031	
(*c*) Fund for garage	240,000	
3. (1) plus (2)		1,305,904
4. Less		
(*a*) Operational Deficits in previous years	1,703,174	
(*b*) Cancellation of balance of credits from previous years	1,603,230	
	99,944	
(*c*) Operational deficit for Year Ending 3 March, 1962	683,435	
(*d*) Total (4)		783,379
5. (3) minus (4)		522,525
6. Payments by 34 Probationers		448,068
7. (5) minus (6)		74,457
8. General Reserves for Additional Fringe Benefits		
(*a*) Members	296,778	
(*b*) Wage Workers	53,810	
(*c*) Total (8)		350,588
9. Loans from Banks and Others†		
(*a*) Payable within one year	606,945	
(*b*) Payable within more than one year	466,290	
(*c*) Loans from members	567,063	
(*d*) Total (9)		1,640,298
10. Accounts Payable		
(*a*) Supplies	338,610	
(*b*) Members	310,488	
(*c*) Wage Workers	117,238	
(*d*) Members' Provident Fund	37,708	
(*e*) Miscellaneous (includes IL.167,349 Hamekasher Development Company)	911,905	
(*f*) Total (10)		1,715,949
11. Bills Payable	1,301,843	
12. Miscellaneous	469,829	1,771,672
13. Total Liabilities		4,550,964

Assets		
14. Capital Investments		
(*a*) Immovables	96,282	
(*b*) Vehicles	1,914,951	
(*c*) Advances Paid for vehicles ordered	299,200	
(*d*) Equipment and F. & F.	68,877	
(*e*) Investments in NOA; Delek; and Alliance Tyre Co.	33,524	
(*f*) Others	35,664	
(*g*) Total (14)		2,448,498
15. Liquid Assets (Allowance made for Depreciation in Value)		
(*a*) Stocks on hand (spare parts; fuel; tyres, etc.)	785,487	
(*b*) Payments for spare parts etc. ordered	123,347	
16. Accounts Payable		
(*a*) Clients	182,649	
(*b*) Accountant General Subsidies	440,400	
(*c*) Miscellaneous	260,507	
(d) Members (4,038) and Wage Workers (1,516)	5,194	
17. Expenses in advance	213,784	
18. Bills for collection	670	
19. Cash and Banks	90,428	2,102,466
20. Total Assets		4,550,964
21. Conditional Liabilities		73,106

Dated 7 January, 1964.

INCOME AND EXPENDITURES FOR YEAR APRIL 1961, TO MARCH 1962
(in IL.)

Revenue			
1. Fares (less stamp duty and commission paid on ticket sales)			6,454,471
2. Special journeys (less commission)			484,761
3. Miscellaneous			12,175
4. Total			6,951,407
Expenditure			
5. Wages			
(*a*) Members	2,257,705		
(*b*) Wage Workers	1,152,647		
(*c*) Total		3,410,352	
6. Fringe Benefits			
(*a*) Members	715,942		
(*b*) Wage Workers	302,042		
(*c*) Total		1,017,984	
7. Fuel		596,850	
8. Maintenance of vehicles		979,053	
9. Services		362,958	

† Amounts Linked to Cost of Living Index and/or U.S. $ are not shown in Balance-Sheet.

10.	Insurance and Property Tax	323,323	
11.	Administration (includes financing)	364,185	
12.	Depreciation of vehicles, equipment of garages, etc.	722,250	
13.	Allocation for garage building	60,000	
14.	Total		7,836,955
15.	Operational Loss (14 minus 4)		885,548
16.	Government Subsidies	200,000	
17.	Profits from Sale of Property	27,113	227,113
18.	Loss Carried Forward on balance-sheet		658,435

CHAPTER FIVE

Public Enquiry Committees About Bus Co-operatives

The following is the full text of a press release which Egged (Eshed), Dan and Hamekasher jointly issued on 11 January, 1954.

"Dr. Avniel's statement to the Knesset on 6 January, 1954, and the reply of the Minister of Transport as reported in the press of 7 January, 1954, include the following sentences: 'The emolument of members of the bus co-operatives for a six to seven-hour work day is IL.350 a month plus IL.36 management fee, plus overtime pay, plus etc., etc.' And Dr. Avniel, *inter alia*, also allegedly said that the gross emolument of the members of the bus co-operatives is about IL.500 a month.

"And here are the true facts as confirmed by the Ministry of Transport in their letter of 31 December, 1953, to the bus co-operatives.

"A total of IL.225,200 was paid to the members of the bus co-operatives for April, 1953, and this includes basic emolument; seniority and family allowances; cost of living allowance and supplement for participation in the administration. Since April, 1953, an increase in the cost of living supplement which had been approved for the entire country has increased the total emoluments. The members also receive fringe benefits primarily in kind, such as vacations in rest houses, sick leave, etc., and pay for overtime, which amount to forty per cent of the emolument, in accordance with the craft union scale. There is a seven-hour work-day for those on the intra and seven and a half for those on the inter-urban services.

"It is clear that all the fringe benefits paid to the members of the bus co-operatives are the same which every institution and every employer pays. Therefore the considerable discussion about the fringe benefits to the members which the bus co-operatives pay is astonishing and presents an inflated picture of wages.

"We also are astonished at Dr. Avniel's assertion that the planning of the bus transportation was in the hands of men who were not experts. Foreign experts who examined the bus transportation services in the country have never expressed such an opinion. We doubt whether Dr. Avniel investigated the matter thoroughly; whether he is qualified to express an opinion about the expertness of those who are dealing with bus transportation in the country."

"Al Hamishmar" (the economic page), of 5 March, 1954, carries an article by Yedial Levin on "The Organizational Structure of the Transport Administration in the Country" (Israel). He attributes the unsatisfactory position of bus transportation to the fact that the organizational structure of the bus co-operatives is combined within the same framework ". . . by the interests and functions of the owners of the capital and of the employers; and those of the managers of the administration and of labour. . . . But (bus) co-operatives that employ a relatively large number of wage workers and enjoy a monopoly . . . can seriously exploit the . . . passengers. . . ."

The article notes that the present economic and financial conditions in the country and the condition of the bus service as such cannot be considered as auspicious for the transfer of this service to Government ownership. It is not the financial difficulties which interfere with the transfer of the ownership and management from the (bus) co-operatives to the Government. The Government does not have to purchase the transport services but can pay a fixed interest to the members on their investments in the bus co-operatives. But, there is no guarantee that State ownership and direct Government administration will assure a better and more efficient service and lower fares than those now prevailing.

Mr. Levin suggests that a body similar to the London Passenger Transport Board be set up in Israel. The main advantage of this form of administration is that "those providing the capital at a guaranteed fixed interest rate have no say in the management. It is not a Government department and it is administered on co-operative principles since the passengers(?) receive part of the surplus. But they do not share in the management of the services. . . .

"While it is impossible to use for Israel exactly the same public organizational set up as that of the London Passenger Transport Board, many of its structural principles are both possible and desirable in the reorganization of the bus transport service in the country.

"In Israel it is also possible to differentiate between ownership and administration. The real (replaceable) value of the property of the bus co-operatives can be fixed and the members can be given preferred shares or bonds for their respective *pro rata* share (calculated on replacement value) bearing a reasonable interest which would be included in the calculations of the fares. The interest would be a first charge, like wages, on the gross revenue . . . it would be only fair to distribute such shares or bonds also to the wage workers of the co-operatives on the basis of seniority of service. These shares or bonds would be transferable and negotiable in the open market. . . ."

Mr. Levin suggests that the Israeli passenger transport board should have three partners,

1. the Government and the local authorities;
2. Chevrat Haovdim; and
3. employees of the bus transport system.

On 25 November, 1954, the Minister of Transport appointed[112] a public committee to enquire into the problems of the road transport services (bus services), with Judge Zohar, the President of the Haifa District Court, as chairman. Of the other eight members, six were non-official. The other two were the directors-general of the Ministry of Finance and of the Ministry of Transport. The terms of reference embodied in the letters of appointment, authorized this committee of nine to enquire into and to report on:

1. The quality and efficiency of the existing bus service.
2. The organizational structure of the services and to what extent the existing legislation about the arrangements of the bus services met the needs of the public and of the State.
3. The influence of the present financial and economic conditions of the bus services on the quality and efficiency of the services.
4. The standard of bus services which could be expected under the existing economic administrative potentialities of the State and its population.
5. Procedure (principles) for calculating bus fares.[113]

The Minister of Transport had promised the bus co-operatives that the question of bus fares would have priority. The enquiry committee was unable to submit by 15 March, 1955, a report on all five points included in the terms of reference, of 21 February, 1955, and it decided to submit its conclusions and recommendations about the procedure for calculating bus fares. Presumably the chairman of the committee signed this report[114] on behalf and with the approval of the entire committee. The report refers to public and closed meetings of the committee.[115]

Shortly after the committee began work and before it had started a thorough examination of the material which it had obtained from diverse sources, the bus co-operatives asked for an immediate increase in bus fares by 40 per cent over those then in force. The co-operatives' request was predicated on the following:

(*a*) The increase in costs of the main items of expenses which had been used in calculating the costs when the Government had authorized an increase in bus fares in February 1954.[116]
(*b*) The need to cover current expenses and the accumulated operational deficits.
(*c*) Renewal of equipment, etc., could not be delayed.
(*d*) Obligatory surplus required.

The representatives of the bus co-operatives repeatedly declared that they could not accept "as a reliable (trustworthy) basis for the present or future calculations the system of calculating fares which the Ministry of Finance had fixed". Therefore, the enquiry committee felt that it was justified in considering its primary function to spell out the basis for calculating bus fares—a "bus transportation basket".

The estimated budgets which the enquiry committee recommended for the year April 1955 to March 1956, were calculated on the basis of the reports which the bus co-operatives had submitted about their respective actual expenditures for the previous years, and other data to which the committee had access. It also allowed for the increase in the costs of certain items. In estimating the revenue for 1955-56, the committee used the monthly reports which the bus co-operative submitted to the Ministry of Transport from February to October 1954. Allowances were made for the seasonal decrease in revenue during the winter months.

The committee's unanimous conclusion was that if the bus co-operatives put into effect its recommendations (given below), the gross revenue of Egged (Eshed) and of Dan would each be increased by six per cent and that of Hamekasher by nine-and-a-half per cent over the actual revenue which these respective bus co-operatives reported. The committee assumed that the bus co-operatives would put into effect its recommended "transportation basket" on 15 February, 1955, and that they would use it in April of each year when the fares, barring the unforeseen, would be reviewed.

This Citizens' Enquiry Committee of Nine recommended the bus co-operatives to adopt the following:

1. Introduction of a 44-hour week for the drivers on the intra-urban routes and 48 hours for those on the inter-urban routes and for all other staff.
2. Overtime for all kinds of work to be reduced as much as possible. Drivers should work overtime only where absolutely necessary, such as on long routes, and in Haifa on Saturdays. In the case of all other routes, overtime for drivers was permissible only on Saturday evenings and on the evenings of the official holidays. In the case of official holidays of a longer duration than one day, overtime for the drivers was permissible only in the evening of the last day of the official holiday.
3. Introduction of the regulations which Chevrat Haovdim prescribed (in its letter of 29 June, 1954) about payment of an extra month's salary every year (thirteenth month); sick leave with pay; annual holidays with pay; allowances for seniority and for dependents.
4. A maximum allowance of IL.6 a month for each member for clothing.
5. Payment of daily allowances (for food and lodging) only to drivers on routes where it was necessary to eat meals and to sleep away from home. The Committee submitted a schedule of allowances for these purposes.
6. Abolition of the point (premium) system.
7. Introduction of other economies, such as reduction in expenditures for entertaining, presents, etc.; decreased allowance for losses from

1½ to ½ per cent on sale of tickets and this allowance should be paid only to drivers, ticket sellers and cashiers who sell tickets;" and generally to eliminate all unnecessary general expenses.

8. Overtime should be paid by the hour at the normal rate of the basic emolument plus allowances for seniority, dependents, and an increase in the cost of living index. Members of Egged (Eshed) at that time were permitted to work a maximum of 40 hours overtime per month. There was no maximum for overtime for wage workers. Not all the members availed themselves of the right to work overtime because such overtime was done mainly on Sabbaths or on long routes. "But it (Egged (Eshed)) refused to furnish data about the number of members who do overtime."

The enquiry committee's report included the following observations about the economies which it recommended:

1. The bus co-operatives should set up a special reserve to cover any unforeseen needs which may arise in the next two years as a result of the reduction of allowances for overtime, bonuses, etc.
2. The bus co-operatives now pay to their members, in addition to basic emolument, special allowances, cost of living, etc., an "administration" fee. The enquiry committee's report notes that "the exact meaning and what this includes is still not clear to them". And it recommends that this administration fee should, for the time being, be fixed at IL.450 per year per member and "should not be considered as part of the emolument" or linked to the cost of living index or to the fringe benefits.
3. A preliminary condition for increasing the efficiency and improving the services of the bus co-operatives is that the number of types of buses used should be decreased; the buses in use should be reconditioned, and additional buses should be acquired immediately. For this purpose the committee included in the estimated budget for 1955-56 an equipment fund of IL. one million for "Egged (Eshed)"; IL.462,000 for "Dan" and IL.75,600 for "Hamekasher". The bus co-operatives should be required to pay every week a specific amount to this equipment fund allowing for depreciation which the Enquiry Committee included in the recommended budget for 1955-56. It also thinks that in addition to the depreciation, the bus co-operatives should use for improving and enlarging their vehicles and equipment, and for building and the liquidation of debts, the proceeds from the sale of such property which is not considered as absolutely vital and also special payments which the present members will make and the money which new members will be required to pay.
4. The enquiry committee also included in the estimated budget for the bus co-operatives, reserves for unforeseen expenditures such as abnormal increases in the cost of living index or an unforeseen decrease in gross revenue. The enquiry committee insists that all amounts in excess of the estimated revenue should be allocated to the afore-

mentioned fund for equipment, buildings, etc. But in the case of the surpluses which result from "efficiency" and economies in excess of the amounts fixed in the budgets, one half should be divided equally between the members and one half should be paid in to the special fund for equipment.

The enquiry committee gives the following reasons why it did not endorse the request of the bus co-operatives that the Government or some other third party should assume responsibility for any part of their accumulated operational deficits (IL.6 million for Egged (Eshed) and IL.2-2½ million for Dan and Hamekasher).

1. After deducting the debts incurred as a result of operational deficits (shown on their balance-sheets) the real or replaceable value of the property of the bus co-operatives still exceeds the actual amounts of the members' participation in their respective share capital and other own funds.
2. The bus co-operatives, in permitting the operational deficit to grow from year to year, "acted as if it was not their property and their concern ('worry')."
3. With "a minimum of goodwill the bus co-operatives" over a period of years and "without difficulty should be able to amortize their accumulated operational deficits in monthly instalments".

The enquiry committee further recommends that it should be made abundantly clear to the bus co-operatives that they and their members will have to bear the full responsibility for all operational deficits, present and future. It also concluded that the members were not justified in withdrawing funds from their respective bus co-operatives. It is immaterial whether the sources used for these payments are the entrance fees paid by new members or the revaluation of assets.

EXTRACTED FROM TWO SCHEDULES ATTACHED TO THE REPORT OF THE ZOHAR PUBLIC ENQUIRY COMMITTEE ABOUT CALCULATION OF BUS FARES

(Amounts in IL.)

	Monthly Emoluments per member—Expressed in IL. Paid by Co-op—Dec. '54			Recomnd by Enq. Comtee for 1955/56 (April-May)		
	Egged (E'd)	Dan	Hmksr	Egged (E'd)	Dan	Hmkshr
1. Basic Emolument (*a*)	125	127	127	122	123	123
2. Allowance for Participation on admin. of co-op.	48	48	48	38(*l*)	37(*l*)	37(*l*)
3. C.o.L. allowances	115	115	115	114(*f*)	114(*f*)	114(*f*)
4. 1+2+3	288	290	290	274	274	274
5. 13th Month Emolumnt(*b*)	24	24	24	20(*d*)	20(*d*)	20(*d*)
6. Vacation	8	8	8	7	7	7

	Monthly Emoluments per member—Expressed in IL. Paid by Co-op—Dec. '54			Recomnd by Enq. Comtee for 1955/56 (April-May)		
	Egged	(E'd) Dan	Hmksr	Egged	(E'd) Dan	Hmkshr
7. Clothing	10	10	5	6(*g*)	6(*g*)	6(*g*)
8. Provident fund (*b*)	38	39	39	31(*e*)	32(*e*)	32(*e*)
9. Daily allowance	25	19	19	10(*h*)		
10. Allowances for losses (on tickets sold to passengers)	10	16	14	(*k*)	(*k*)	(*k*)
11. Bonuses for drivers (*c*)	20	19	—		abolished	
12. Newspapers & books	5	5			abolished	
13. Total of items 5 to 12	140	140	109			
14. Item 4 plus item 13	428	430	399			
15. Pay for overtime work	90	59	75	(*j*)	9(*j*)	(*j*)
16. Item 14 plus item 15	518	489	474			
17. Dues to Histadrut				9(*i*)	7(*i*)	9(*i*)

(*a*) Includes seniority and family allowances. The committee suggested abolishing the uniform basic emolument (exclusive of seniority and family allowances) and introducing a graded scale of emoluments according to skill, etc. But the committee had no objection to the co-operative dividing equally among all the members the gross amount of emoluments fixed for the budget year 1955-56 (April-March).

(*b*) Calculated on basis of items 1 plus 2.

(*c*) Allowance ½-hour daily for obtaining the bus tickets which drivers sell to passengers.

(*d*) 1/12 of items 1 plus 3.

(*e*) 13·3 per cent of items 1 plus 3.

(*f*) The committee used the cost of living index (228) of 15 December, 1954.

(*g*) Based on quantities of certain items of clothing which Chevrat Haovdim fixed for everybody based on prices early in 1955. The committee included this item in the 1955-56 budget as a lump sum under general expenses and not in the budget for payments to members.

(*h*) Allowance is not to be paid to members on vacation, sick leave, the eve of Saturday and Holidays. The committee allowed for food IL.100 a month for all members

(*i*) Included as a lump sum on the basis of 2·7 per cent of salary, plus overtime, plus pay for thirteenth month.

(*j*) The committee suggested an increase in work hours per week and that overtime pay should be the same as for the regular working hours and not at time-and-a-half.

(*k*) The committee recommended a decrease of allowance from 1½ to 1 per cent of revenue from fares. This budget includes a lump sum but the losses are expected not to exceed ¼ to ⅓ of one per cent.

(*l*) The committee recommended that IL.450 per member per year should be set aside and to be considered as interest on the members' investments and should not be linked to the cost of living index or fringe benefits.

Reactions to Zohar Committee's Report

A leader in Shituf (February 1955—pp. 1-2) referred to the general storm aroused by the publication of the Zohar Committee's recommendation to increase by six per cent the fares of Egged (Eshed) and by 9½ per cent those of the bus co-operatives Dan and Hamekasher. It may have been a mistake that Shituf's first leader on this subject did not oppose the inclusion as members of the enquiry committee the directors-general of the Ministries of Transport and of Finance. Prior to the appointment of the enquiry committee, the aforementioned had considered and then denied the requests of the bus co-operatives to increase their bus fares. And since these two were included, why was a representative of Merkaz Haco-operatzia barred? This leader in Shituf also noted that the enquiry committee did not call on the Government-accredited auditors in the auditing department of Merkaz Haco-operatzia and of the bus co-operatives, or the auditors of the Co-operative Department of the Ministry of Labour for any assistance or advice. The sub-committee which dealt with cost accounting, the method for calculating bus fares, included one member of the enquiry committee and one member each from the staffs of the Ministries of Finance and of Transport. This leader in Shituf concluded that the recommendations seemed to be only a bad compromise between the demands of the bus co-operatives and the Government's declarations during the negotiations.

LeChaveireinu (periodical of Egged (Eshed)) of 14 February, 1955, pp. 3-18, published an article "February of Prices". The introductory paragraph refers to the "Unhappy (unfortunate) February", (1955) compared with February 1954, which is described as the beginning of the stabilized era of organizational operation of Egged (Eshed). (The co-operative *de facto* started operations in November 1951, as a partnership. It was registered on 14 April, 1953, as a co-operative and in February, 1954, attained effective unity and stabilization.)

> "After stormy debates (with the Histadrut) which continued for years... we finally arrived at the satisfying (enriched) moment when the new rules (of Egged (Eshed)) were finally confirmed and . . . its new management . . . was elected. The annual report of the first elected management of Egged (Eshed) (LeChaveireinu, No. 14, February 1955, pp.1-2) notes "that . . . it is natural that the realities are slightly darker than the dream . . . the realities demand sacrifices . . . *de facto* this is the first year during which the activities of its governing organs did not have to deal with conflicts and antagonisms of the various groups. Some members were found unsuitable for the posts for which they were elected. Their unsuitability can be attributed to "local patriotism" in pressing their candidates. There is still much to be done to simplify the process of carrying our decision'."

The article also notes that the management of Egged (Eshed) knew that a public enquiry committee could do very little. But on the other hand, it had to consider the possibility that if we "turned up our nose" the "infatuation" for such a committee would increase. And if the bus co-operative rejected the proposal, this would further intensify the suspicions against it.

> "And you are well aware how great are these suspicions." The press reported that soon after the enquiry committee was appointed, an Egged (Eshed) representative appeared before it and told the members: "Though you were appointed by the Minister of Transport, we (i.e. Egged (Eshed)) were the ones who asked for the establishment of the committee. Members, this was a 'play of words'; we were ordered to say this. It was better, the moment the committee was appointed, that we should say we also asked for this." Actually, the Histadrut decided on the make-up of the committee.

But Egged (Eshed), the article continued, had its doubts because its members were not

> "neutral objective people. It included the ex-manager of the old Egged. And a second member (name not given) who, though he is from our camp . . . cannot be considered objective . . . because he is the representative of the Ministry of Finance (on the committee) and will do everything possible, directly or indirectly, in order to convince the public that the increase (of bus fares) is unjustified. He has to consider the question of the cost of living index."

Egged (Eshed) Management Committee, according to the above article, reacted to the pressure of its internal opposition group, and because it considers that it would "be in vain" to dissent. It accepted the proposed composition of the enquiry committee. An official committee can by a court order force Egged (Eshed) to submit the material it wanted.

> "If 'God forbid' we were dissatisfied with the committee's findings, then we could have the opportunity of disassociating ourselves on the grounds that the composition of the public enquiry committee was not 'objective'." The article (in LeChaveireinu) adds that the findings are not good. "The conclusions of the committee's report will not be those we need."

The article also notes that the rules of Egged (Eshed) bind it "hand and foot" to the Histadrut with whom it must maintain normal relations. It attributes the several months' old break with the Histadrut to the personality of the Histadrut's representative on the Egged (Eshed) management who is unsuitable for this task. The new representative appointed by Chevrat Haovdim on the management of Egged (Eshed) "is performing his duties loyally and objectively". He is also considered as the adviser to Histadrut on Egged (Eshed) and tries his best "to understand our conditions and is accompanying us on our difficult path (road)".

Six semi-official committees and a number of licensed auditors enquired into and submitted reports about the bus co-operatives during the period 1951-54. These investigations probably were precipitated by seven requests from the bus co-operatives for a 15-25 per cent increase in fares, and all were accompanied with threats of a general stoppage of all bus services. The Government's first reply to all seven applications was "no", and then it later approved about half of the increase requested. When approving the seventh award (August 1954) the Government, instead of authorizing a direct increase in fares, decided to refund to the bus co-operatives the equivalent of the last increase in the price of fuel, which became effective on 23 February, 1954. The refund was equivalent to a subsidy of IL.60,000 a month to the bus co-operatives. The bus co-operatives, dissatisfied with the award, again threatened a general stoppage of buses.

Haaretz (28 February, 1955) reports that the chairman of the enquiry committee at his press conference on 27 February, 1955, appealed to the press and to the public not to emphasize only the negative aspects of its conclusion and recommendations and the statistical material. The enquiry committee planned to renew its activities shortly and to prepare a general report about the bus transportation system, which also would deal with the competition of the buses with taxis, especially in Tel Aviv, and with the railways. The mayors of the municipalities and of the villages would be asked to appear before the committee.

An unsigned article in Shituf, March-April 1955, p. 18, objected mainly to the committee's conclusions that the bus co-operatives alone were responsible for their critical financial and generally unsatisfactory position and that the excessive emoluments paid to the members were the principal cause of the lack of liquidity. It also noted that there was no precedent for the enquiry committee's recommendation that the bus co-operatives drastically cut the emoluments, including the fringe benefits.

The bus co-operatives, on the other hand, urged that if a practical "transportation basket" were fixed it would make it unnecessary to have to appeal to an adjudication tribunal, from time to time, about bus fares. The Histadrut Executive Committee suggested that the bus co-operatives participate in the committee which would fix the "transportation basket".

Haaretz (27 April, 1955) published the reply of the public relations department of Egged (Eshed) to an article on the calculation of bus fares by Y. Amitai which it had published. This article noted that Egged (Eshed)

(*a*) includes items which are not an equitable charge for calculating bus fares;
(*b*) allocates excessive amounts for depreciation; and
(*c*) pays to its members excessive allowances for clothing; books; holidays; participation in management and return on their participation in the Society's capital.

The article also noted that Egged (Eshed) members

(*a*) work only seven-and-a-half hours daily compared with eight hours by wage workers; and (*b*) receive a basic remuneration and fringe benefits in excess of those paid to wage workers of equal skill and seniority.

The reply of Egged (Eshed) notes that the conclusions of the report of the enquiry committee

> "have not contributed anything to the solution of the transportation problems and tried to lower standards of the working conditions of the members . . . it recommended an eight-hour day whereas in the whole world the labour day is shorter for transport workers than for other branches. The work day of the Government, municipal staff and staff of other public services is shorter than that of drivers. The only effect of lowering the standards of working conditions would be an appreciable decrease of productivity p.m.h. . . . Egged (Eshed) is prepared to serve anybody who has a real desire to learn or investigate the problem (bus transportation) and to place at his disposal all the material because we are interested in the public knowing everything."

Shituf, May 1955, pp. 23-24, carried a note, Transportation, "The Co-operatives Continue in their Struggle". The representatives of Chevrat Haovdim and the Management Committees of Egged (Eshed), after thoroughly investigating the position of the bus co-operatives, recommend to the Histadrut committee of three on bus co-operatives an increase of bus fares by 10·6 per cent. The committee of three then recommended that the Histadrut Central Committee should urge the Government to increase its subsidy to the bus co-operatives by 9·5 per cent. The bus co-operatives also asked the Ministries of Finance and Transport to reject the conclusions and recommendations of the Zohar Committee since the enforcement of their recommendations would result in a *de facto* lowering of the standard of living of the members of the bus co-operatives. The Enquiry Committee recommended an increase in hours of work and a reduction of allowances for clothing, holidays, and of payment for overtime.

This note in Shituf adds that the committee of the ministers dealing with economic questions favoured postponing the decision about an increase in bus fares until the public enquiry committee had studied the observations of the bus co-operatives to its recommendations. The relationship between the Ministry of Transport and the bus co-operatives was very strained. Only the Histadrut's intervention prevented a general strike of the bus co-operatives which had been fixed for 18 April, 1955. The Ministries of Transport and Finance decided to recommend an additional credit of IL.600,000 for eight months and to refund to the bus co-operatives IL.100,000-IL.150,000 of the increase in the duties on fuel.

The opening paragraph of the first article by Ben Moshe (head of the Public Relations Department of Egged (Eshed)) in L'Chaveireinu, p. 20, 28 May, 1955, refers to Mr. Y. Amitai's article and to the Haaretz economic editor's note introducing the article (Haaretz, 27 April, 1955) about calculation of bus fares. Mr. Ben Moshe writes that it is his purpose to point out Mr. Amitai's mistakes. But most of the first article (pp. 20-22) deals with Mr. Amitai's misconceptions and misinterpretations of terminology. The bus co-operatives do not accept and have submitted an appeal to the Minister of Transport about "the calculations of the Public Enquiry Committee" (on which Mr. Amitai's article is based). Mr. Ben Moshe writes that the Minister admits errors in the Committee's conclusions. He considers Mr. Amitai's definition of "social insurance", at least "several years behind the times". The members of Egged (Eshed) receive fringe payments which the Histadrut and the respective craft unions prescribe. The work day is seven-and-a-half hours for members and eight hours for non-members. Mr. Ben Moshe justifies the higher emolument to members because the members (drivers) receive overtime pay only for a maximum of forty hours a month and other members for twenty-five a month. And "the members frequently work more than the prescribed maximum" hours of overtime.

Mr. Ben Moshe disagrees with Mr. Amitai's contention that the supplement for management is really a dividend or interest payment and as such should be limited to six per cent on the member's participation in the co-operative's capital and calculated on the revalued ("reform") and not the actual amount which the members had paid in. Egged (Eshed) argues that this supplement, paid to old and new members, falls within the Histadrut definition of bonuses "for effort and self-management" and should be equivalent to 20 per cent of the basic emolument plus supplements for seniority, dependents and cost-of-living allowance. Mr. Ben Moshe adds: "We also pay a supplement of 15 per cent to permanent wage workers who have worked a number of years, though these do not participate in the management and have not invested in the co-operative's capital."

Furthermore, only some members work overtime and it was wrong for Mr. Amitai to include overtime pay in the calculations of members' gross monthly emoluments.

Mr. Ben Moshe also questions Mr. Amitai's statements that

(*a*) "depreciation" is really "profit" since this item is generally an allocation from "gross surplus";

(*b*) Egged (Eshed) is not entitled to charge "depreciation" on such items as spare parts which it manufactures.

Mr. Ben Moshe refutes Mr. Amitai's statement that since the bus co-operatives did not question the fairness of the public enquiry committee's conclusions when they were published, the bus co-operatives should now explain why they cannot implement them.

". . . the co-operatives, at a news conference called immediately after the publication of the conclusions, and also in their appeal to the Minister of Transport, pointed out that the enquiry committee's conclusions contained many mistakes. And that its conclusions could not be carried out because these assume a lower standard of working conditions for the members and also do not make any contribution to resolving the bus transportation problems."

Mr. Ben Moshe repeats the arguments of the bus co-operatives that bus fares in Israel are lower than in other countries and that "the work day in bus transportation services in the whole world is less than in other occupations." However Government and municipal employees work fewer hours than do the members of the bus co-operatives.

L'Chaveireinu (May 1955) reprints a note in Haaretz (11 May, 1955) weekly economic supplement signed with the initials B.B. which, *inter alia,* criticized the excessive dividend (interest) paid to its members on their actual participation in the capital of Egged (Eshed). The note in Haaretz also stated that the sub-committee of the Cabinet, made up of all the Ministers dealing with economic questions, had approved and published increases in bus fares which were higher than those which the public enquiry committee had initially recommended. Since the new schedule of bus fares was subject to review in February 1956, the writer of the note (B.B.) considered that "while the debate is still fresh, it is worth while to clarify certain questions of principle". B.B. then proceeded to deal with the two principles about which Messrs. Amitai and Ben Moshe exchanged views, viz.:

1. The gross monthly emoluments to members, more especially the fringe payments which only Egged (Eshed) members enjoy.
2. The question of depreciation.

B.B. noted that the other items in the calculations were costs which could be determined by actual facts and not questions "of expression of opinion". Also the public enquiry committee did not check the accuracy of the data which Egged (Eshed) submitted, such as allowances for spare parts. The data of the bus co-operates were uniform and sufficiently clear for the purpose of fixing an equitable fare. Only closer supervision by Governmental or "by another public body" could ensure uniform and clear accounting systems, wrote B.B. It is not difficult to calculate the return of the member on his investment and the rate of depreciation.

Mr. Amitai, on the basis of the data which the bus co-operatives submitted to the public enquiry committee, reached the conclusion that the gross monthly emoluments (exclusive of allowances for clothes and overtime) of a member and non-member are IL.462 and IL.274 respectively. The higher annual emolument by IL.1,800 (average) for a member compared with a non-member may be considered the dividend on the member's investment in Egged (Eshed). According to the accounts which Egged (Eshed) submitted to the public enquiry committee, the average monthly fringe payments to members and non-members were IL.113 and IL.41 respectively.

B.B. notes that the monthly fringe benefit of IL.113 per member is exclusive of the extra pay for time exceeding seven-and-a-half instead of the eight hour work day, the allowance for clothing and shoes, and the extra pay for participation in management and the incentive premiums. According to the accounts submitted to the public enquiry committee, the premium amounts to an average of nearly IL.48 per member per month and an average of less than IL.3 per non-member. Only 100 of the 1,303 non-members, receive the aforementioned incentive premium which all members receive.

B.B. thinks that a co-operative, like any other form of business, should earn enough to pay an equitable return on share capital. According to the accounts which the co-operatives submitted to the public enquiry committee, in connection with the fixing of bus fares, Egged (Eshed) asks for an annual interest of IL.3,423 per year per member on the IL.1,500 which a member paid into the co-operative's share capital. Assuming that the present purchasing power of the aforementioned IL.1,500 is IL.6,000, Egged (Eshed) is asking for an annual return of 57 per cent on the member's participation in the co-operative's share capital. This payment would further increase the difference between the maximum gross emolument of a member and a non-member.

Finally B.B. considers it improper to include in the cost accounting of bus fares both the IL.1·9 million for depreciation and the million pounds "to expedite the renewal of vehicles". However, it is desirable to set up a special fund to ensure a reasonable standard of (bus) transportation provided, however, that the members would not receive, directly or indirectly, any return from this special fund. B.B. challenges the IL.4·2 million or IL.5,400 per bus which Egged (Eshed) is asking for its 783 buses (of which 397 are Diesel buses).

> "In our opinion the calculation as such is not correct. Under no circumstances may the co-operatives insist that the public should pay for the exchange of all the buses into the most modern type. The value of the 386 Ford petrol 50-place buses, doing 35-40 kms. per hour, cannot be compared with the money value of the . . . Diesel doing '60 and more kilometres per hour'." (The present replaceable cost of a Ford bus is IL.15-20,000 less than the cost of a Diesel. Why should this difference of IL.20,000 be given as a present to the bus co-operatives, asked B.B.)

Mr. Ben Moshe's reply to B.B. explains why the insistence of Egged (Eshed) for a monthly allowance for spare parts of IL.240,000 instead of IL.200,000 proposed by the public enquiry committee is justified:

(*a*) the frequency of the replacement increases as the age of the bus increases; and

(*b*) the cost of spare parts for the new buses has increased considerably during the six months since the public enquiry committee started its enquiry.

Mr. Ben Moshe describes B.B.'s comparison of the average monthly gross income of members and non-members as "fallacious" since all the 1,943 members of Egged (Eshed) hold "AA" grade drivers' licences (recognized by the craft union) while the 1,333 non-member workers are of different grades, porters, janitors, etc. It is misleading to apply an average to the whole group. He writes that B.B.'s statement that "the wage workers are engaged in the same types of work as the members" is incorrect. The 1,333 wage workers include 300 apprentices, messengers, and 'several hundred cleaners, porters, etc.; a small number of white collar and an annual average of 150 drivers'."

According to Mr. Ben Moshe "in the opinion of experts" the depreciation period should be seven years. Since vehicles must be renewed, depreciation at that rate must be included in the current expenses. On the basis of a bus costing IL.35,000 and the acquisition of 10 new buses every month or 120 a year, the monthly depreciation is IL.350,000. "For a number of years the use of the depreciation funds have been subject to the joint supervision of representatives of the Ministry of Transport and the management of Egged (Eshed)."

Members cannot in any way benefit from this fund. And Egged (Eshed) has 1,150 and not 783 buses. The maximum speed of the Ford is much higher than that of the Tigers (a Diesel bus) and not *vice versa* as B.B. writes. And Mr. Ben Moshe asks "who benefits from the better buses, the drivers or the passengers?" Is there any doubt that the public would prefer better (more expensive and more comfortable) buses, which have a larger seating capacity?

On 29 June, 1952, Chevrat Haovdim communicated its decisions (given below) to the management of Eshed, the temporary partnership after the merger of the three bus co-operatives. This letter refers to "the calculation of the maximum emolument and the fringe benefits for Eshed members", which the Histadrut suggested to the Minister of Transport as a basis for fixing the bus fares. Paragraph (2) of the aforementioned letter notes that "the possibility of paying the members the remuneration plus the fringe benefits . . . depends on the gross revenue of Eshed; efficient management; productivity; self-administration; the effort made in the work; and the management's sense of responsibility".

(*a*) The basic monthly remuneration of a member whose skill is graded as "AA" is IL.100 plus IL.20 for those members with a seniority of at least ten years. Ten years at the rate of IL.2 per month is the maximum allowance for seniority.

(*b*) IL.5 allowance for a wife and IL.5 for every dependent child (under eighteen).

(*c*) Cost of living allowance, i.e., 100 per cent of the cost of living allowance fixed on 15 May, 1952, plus any additions which the Histadrut, in accordance with the prevailing practice, may approve from time to time.

(*d*) Supplement of twenty per cent of basic remuneration plus cost of living allowance. This also is considered as basic remuneration for the members' participation in the responsibility for the management.

(*e*) A thirteenth month remuneration to be paid in two instalments, at Passover and New Year.

(*f*) An amount equivalent to eleven per cent of the monthly emolument is to be paid to the provident fund and to be credited to every member's account. Every member also will pay to the provident fund an amount equivalent to more than eleven per cent of his monthly emolument.

Paragraph 7 of this letter of 29 June, 1952, from Chevrat Haovdim fixes a seven-hour work day for intra-urban and a seven-and-a-half-day for inter-urban drivers, five days a week with one hour less on Fridays and on the day of the eve of religious holidays. For all other workers in the bus co-operatives, Chevrat Haovdim fixed the work-day at eight hours and one hour less on Fridays and on the day of the eve of holidays. Drivers may use a quarter of an hour of their working time "for preparing the vehicle, etc." Overtime pay for the first two hours includes a twenty-five per cent supplement and fifty per cent pay for Sabbaths (which includes Saturday night and the nights of religious holidays) includes a seventy-five per cent supplement. All those on night shifts—10 p.m.–5 a.m.—receive a twenty-five per cent supplement.

Paragraphs (10), (11) and (12) of the aforementioned Chevrat Haovdim letter also prescribes the following annual vacations with full pay; 28 days for members with a seniority of over ten years; 18 days for those with over five and up to ten years' seniority; and 12 days for those with five years' seniority or less. There is a proviso that all who were members when the State was established receive 28 days' annual vacation with full pay. In addition to annual vacations with full pay, members also receive an annual cash vacation allowance equivalent to their vacation period. Members also are entitled to one month per year sick leave with full pay.

Paragraph (13) of the Chevrat Haovdim letter prescribes the payment by the bus co-operatives of the all-inclusive Histadrut dues (which include Kupat Cholim) for their respective members and supply their respective members with work clothes (a uniform) and shoes.

The following are extracts from an open letter to the Minister of Transport, which the Jerusalem Post of 28 June, 1956 published as an advertisement.

Open Letter to the Minister of Transport

"Sir,

At 5 p.m. on Tuesday, 26 June, our representatives agreed to postpone the transport strike in the light of assurances given by the secretariat of the Chevrat Haovdim to solve the problem of bus fares within a few days. Four hours later on the same day, you, sir, made an announcement.

"This announcement 'contains theoretical and factual inaccuracies . . .'

"(*a*) Your statement that the requested rise in fares will increase our income by 10 million pounds . . . our demands have resulted from the Government's economic policy in raising the costs of essentials, such as fuel, tyres, taxes, etc., as well as the Histadrut wage policy. The additional income . . . will only . . . cover expenses incurred as a result of the above factors.

"(*b*) Simultaneously with the presentation of our demands for a rise in rates last February, and subsequently, we have . . . submitted all the requested material to your staff . . . they . . . visited our offices for . . . checking . . . and control of every balance-sheet and required document. Furthermore monthly reports . . . of our financial activities are submitted to your office. Our balance-sheet of 31 March, 1956, has not yet been . . . completed.

"(*c*) The conclusions of the Zohar Committee (upon which you base your claim that payments were not made in accordance with the agreement) proved to be an incorrect approach to the transportation problem, in addition to many errors in calculation. These findings were also recognized by the Histadrut representatives and the former Minister of Transport by the mere fact of his last approval of the increased rates. And this despite the committee's conclusions. Payment to members was made in accordance with the decisions of the trade union. It is surprising then to hear, from you, statements which invalidate the authority of the trade union based on conclusions of the committee which entered an area not under their terms of reference. *It is unheard of that in solving the economic problem of an enterprise the standing (standard) of the workers be jeopardized.* (Original underlined.)

"(*d*) . . . The Ministry of Transport is the authority fixing transport fares, every change was subject to regulations acceptable to the Ministry, but not always acceptable to us.

"At the beginning of 1955 the Minister of Transport decided that once a year this office would investigate transport fares in the light of the changes in general costs. *Our recent claims were submitted for your consideration in accordance with this decision.* (Original underlined) . . . the Governmental Ministerial Committee for Economic Affairs . . . in opposition to the above mentioned decision, and after four months of investigation, suggested that the problem be submitted to a special committee.

"(*e*) *It is not the Ministry of Transport which has granted us the franchise for bus transportation. We have earned and maintained this right through 25 years of sweat, toil and blood. But for our earnest endeavour . . . the State would not be blessed with such a modern public transportation system . . . we have been left to struggle for the import of every single bus and each spare part while thousands of private cars and taxis, as well as lorries were imported without much difficulty. The lack of official response to the activities of the taxis, paralleling our services, contradicts the claim of our monopoly rights.* (Original underlined.)

"(*f*) The Minister's office controls all our activities; the fixing of fares, as well as all decisions as to routes, timetables, etc. His representatives actively participate in the control of the Depreciation Fund as well as in the Financial Committee, etc.

"(*g*) We have stated that a partial increase in fares will be unfair to rural areas and border settlements. This statement (without any obligation to accept the offer) was made in the light of your announcement which informed us that a fare increase of 5 per cent would be permitted on routes which do not cover their cost of operation. This primarily refers to rural areas and border settlements and goes to show that we did not ignore public opinion when we rejected this proposal, *but this was the clear result of the Minister's approach.* (Original underlined.)

"(*i*) Important public persons in the economic spheres of the country have more than once declared that the fares are among the lowest in the world. . . . The high taxes levied by the Government on transportation requirments is the main burden of the population. . . . *It is only in the power of the Government to lighten this* burden. It is true that we are an essential public service. It would therefore be *justified if this service be granted the same financial assistance given to other transport services.*" (Original underlined.)

Signed
Egged (Eshed), Dan, Hamekasher

On 1 July, 1956,[117] the Merkaz Haco-operatzia secretariat met the representatives of the bus co-operatives to discuss their application for an increase in bus fares. S. Goren explained that since transportation was a primary public service subject to Government and other public control, every request for increased fares raised "special difficulties". But, according to Mr. Goren, an increase in bus fares

> "has much less influence on the cost of living index than has the price of vegetables and fruit." Yet the Ministry of Transport must worry about "the uninterrupted maintenance of this service" which, in Mr. Goren's opinion, is "cheaper and more efficient, in spite of all the room for improvements and extensions, than all other public services and undertakings".

He agreed that, in the prolonged negotiations, the Ministry of Transport showed less flexibility while the bus co-operatives displayed considerable patience and a sense of responsibility. But Mr. Goren advised the bus co-operatives not to use their last means—a strike.

A. M. Weisbrot replied that none of the bus co-operatives or their members really wanted to rush into a strike, but they were being forced into this undesirable step.

A. Hochman challenged the Government's threat to call up all strikers into Army service, which it did not do when the railway workers stopped work.

A. Davidson stated that their members received the Histadrut scale of remuneration, plus the small differential which the Histadrut committee of four considered justifiable. The bus co-operatives also distributed part of their gross annual surpluses among the wage workers with seniority who had permanent status. The cost calculations of bus fares were based on such general conditions of work (work hours, social security allowance, etc.) conducive to the efficiency of the bus services.

Zvi Lehman wanted Merkaz Haco-operatzia to take an unequivocal stand against a strike.

The bus co-operatives were paying for their mistake in not reviving the special transportation division which was attached to Merkaz Haco-operatzia. Primarily they were fighting for the very existence of the bus co-operatives and not for an increase in bus fares. He recommended:

(*a*) The avoidance of any decision to strike.
(*b*) The suggestion of a decrease of IL.50 a month must be considered when fixing the remuneration for members.
(*c*) Members and non-members in the bus co-operatives should receive the same cost of living supplement.
(*d*) Merkaz Haco-operatzia's decision should be given the maximum publicity.
(*e*) Merkaz Haco-operatzia Secretariat, jointly with a special committee to be appointed, should deal with all problems of the bus co-operatives.

E. Hendel notes that the global amount of the supplements which the co-operatives pay to the members for their investment in the share capital and for their responsibility in the management, is only five per cent more than the total amount of the supplements which the bus co-operatives distributed among their senior permanent wage workers.

B. Giladi states that the success of the strike depends on whether there are real possibilities of obtaining results; and of ensuring a favourable public reaction. Both possibilities seemed very improbable. Therefore, more effective results could be obtained by patient negotiations and enlisting the joint support of Chevrat Haovdim and Merkaz Haco-operatzia.

A. Tzwick notes that they must bear in mind that all the economic ministries unanimously endorsed the suggestion of the Minister of Transport for a five per cent increase in bus fares. The bus co-operatives belong to the same family ("you are in the same house") and nobody declares a strike in his own home (i.e., against their Government).

Y. Ritov notes that the question of the organization of the division for transportation co-operatives was a purely internal matter for Merkaz Haco-operatzia. Chevrat Haovdim discussed this question and gave "its blessing for the organization of this division." Zvi Lehman stresses that the status of the division depends entirely on whether the co-operatives will unequivocally accept its authority and not vice versa.

P. Shamgar claims that all road transport groups, including those road transport co-operatives whose membership are restricted to kibbutzim and moshavim, as well as the Histadrut-sponsored and non-sponsored non-co-operative road transport groups, wish to join the new division of Merkaz Haco-operatzia.

The joint meeting of the secretariat, and the representatives of bus co-operatives affiliated to Merkaz Haco-operatzia, 1956, decided:

1. To support the decisions of the Chevrat Haovdim representative on the management of Egged (Eshed) who, after carefully examining the accounts jointly with the auditing department of Merkaz Haco-operatzia, concluded that the increased costs of materials and of labour required an increase in bus fares by nine per cent plus another two per cent for the retroactive period.
2. To oppose "with all their strength" a strike and to insist that the bus co-operatives, together with the representatives of Merkaz Haco-operatzia and Chevrat Haovdim, persist in their efforts, through the accepted channels, until their justified demands were met.
3. That the secretariat of Chevrat Haovdim should appoint a special committee to examine the differences of opinion between the Egged (Eshed) management and Chevrat Haovdim representatives on the management about the calculations.

The Histadrut Central Committee, though prepared to persist in its negotiations until the Government had complied with the equitable demands of the bus co-operatives, issued a stern warning that if the bus co-operatives disregarded the prohibition to strike, this would be considered a breach of the discipline which the Histadrut demanded from every member.

Report of the Zackai Committee to enquire into the cost accounting of the bus co-operatives submitted to the Minister of Transport 16 August, 1956

On 15 July, 1956, the Minister of Transport appointed an enquiry committee on bus fares[118] and asked it to complete its work by 7 August, 1956. *Inter alia,* its terms of reference authorized the committee

"to examine the cost calculations of the bus co-operatives and to test, scrutinize and to express an opinion as to what would be an equitable increase in bus fares.

"The committee is free to fix its own plan and scope of work and to examine all the material relating to the problem. . . ."

The thirteen-page report (mimeographed) is signed only by the chairman. It includes the letter of appointment (and terms of reference); just over four pages of text (double spacing); and the proposed monthly budgets for the inter-urban bus co-operative Egged (Eshed) and for the intra-urban bus co-operative Dan (Tel Aviv), together with explanations of the calculations.

The report also includes the aforementioned letter of 29 June, 1952

(A40/27/MM) (referred to earlier on page 233) from Chevrat Haovdim to the management of Egged (Eshed), signed by Z. Onn (copy to Merkaz Haco-operatzia), giving the findings of a sub-committee of Messrs. A. Reiss and S. Zan-Bar appointed by the Histadrut committee of three, dealing with the question of Egged (Eshed). Paragraph 16 of the agreement between Egged (Eshed) and Chevrat Haovdim prescribes that the central committee will appoint a special committee to define the wages and fringe benefits of the workers. The Histadrut Central Committee after discussing with the management committee of Egged (Eshed) the sub-committee's recommendation, will then make its decisions. In all their memoranda and other announcements, the bus co-operatives persistently claimed that they based and that they wished to continue to base their calculations on the letter of 29 June, 1952, from Chevrat Haovdim.

The report of the enquiry committee on bus fares refers to its open meetings to hear the evidence of the representatives of the bus co-operatives and of the Ministry of Transport, and also to twenty closed meetings at which the committee examined the written material that the bus co-operatives, the Ministry of Transport and others had submitted and to "hear the evidence of experts in various fields", including independent licensed auditors who submitted analyses and summaries of the bus co-operatives' balance-sheets and revenue and expenditure accounts.[119]

The enquiry committee, in their conversations with representatives of the bus co-operatives, tried to verify (confirm), as far as this was possible, the correctness and reliability of their accounts and cost calculations. In its report, the enquiry committee notes that the time fixed for the submission of its findings makes it impossible for them to include in their report "all the various ramifications of the problems."

The enquiry committee reached the following conclusions:

1. General assumptions about the conditions of work for the members of the bus co-operatives:

   (*a*) The most useful way to ensure the maximum stability and to minimize uncertainty and crises in the future of the bus co-operatives is to accept as "a basis for the remuneration and conditions of work for their members" those principles which the Histadrut craft union has fixed plus a reasonable return on the member's participation in the share capital of the respective bus co-operatives plus an allowance for the member's participation in the management and responsibility for their respective co-operatives. Therefore the enquiry committee based its calculations on the basis of the Chevrat Haovdim letter of 29 June, 1952 (given on the preceding pages).

   (*b*) The committee did not approve the scale of emoluments which the bus co-operative suggested because these were based on a "perverted and unauthorized interpretation" of the decisions of Chevrat Haovdim. Similarly the committee did not approve of the point (bonus) system for the "effort" and "premium" supplements which Egged (Eshed) had introduced. However, it recognized the importance of instituting a system of rewards to encourage "the workers of the bus co-operatives" to greater efforts to increase their productivity and efficiency. An organization, such as the Institute of Productivity, should be requested to prepare a plan along these lines.

(*c*) The enquiry committee accepted the 7½ hours (net) workday for the members of the bus co-operatives which the Histadrut-authorized bodies had fixed previously.

(*d*) The committee considered it preferable that the supplement to be paid to members "for participation in management and responsibility" should be fixed in relationship to "the value of a share". This should replace the procedure which the Histadrut committee recommended in June 1952 to pay 20 per cent of the basic monthly emolument and of the cost of living allowance. The committee also fixed evaluation of the members' participation in a bus co-operative's capital at IL.8,000, which, when allowing for depreciation of the purchasing power of the currency, was much more than most members actually invested. The committee further concluded that the annual dividend or interest which a bus co-operative pays to the members on their investment in the capital of the respective bus co-operative should not exceed thirteen per cent on IL.8,000, or about IL.87 per month.

2. Allocations for depreciation.

(*a*) It is of primary interest to the public, the bus transportation system and the bus co-operatives, that the equipment and property of the bus co-operatives be "maintained, improved and renewed".

(*b*) The cost accounting system which the committee suggests is intended primarily

> "to ensure the replacement of all the vehicles of the bus co-operative which have not yet been fully depreciated . . . and to replace all the vehicles . . . with Diesel buses which are cheaper, better, and larger (have more sitting and standing place)".

(*c*) The allocation of depreciation for vehicles which already has been fully written off, should be discontinued "since it is an unecessary burden on the bus fares. . . ."

(*d*) The investments in additional equipment must keep pace with the increases of population. The bus co-operatives should use for this purpose the entire amount which new members pay into the capital etc. and such funds as they can obtain from private and public sources, including the Government and other public bodies.

3. Other items in the calculation of bus fares.

(*a*) The committee in its efforts to verify the figures which the bus co-operatives submitted could "not always accept" the explanations of the co-operatives.

(*b*) The committee used as a basis the actual costs during the last year plus such increases as it considered reasonable in the light of the higher costs of certain items and of services.

4. Calculation of increased costs.
   (*a*) The committee estimated the attached monthly budget on the probable figures for August, 1956.
   (*b*) The committee notes that it was unable to prepare concrete suggestions for a uniform accounting system (including cost accounting) to be used by all bus co-operatives. Such a system should make it possible to calculate bus fares in the light of changes which occur from time to time. The bus co-operatives also should be obliged to

   (i) submit reports to the Ministry of Transport regularly and on fixed dates;
   (ii) prepare their annual budgets in advance; and
   (iii) review and bring up to date the budgets concurrently.

ENQUIRY COMMITTEE'S ESTIMATE OF EXPENDITURE FOR EGGED (ESHED) (2,100 MEMBERS AND 1,525 WAGE WORKERS)[(a)]

Total—Monthly IL.2,802,100. Annual IL.33,613,500.
2,100 Members receive IL.1,089,700 or an average gross monthly emolument of over IL.505 per member

	IL.
1. Basic emolument plus seniority & family allowances plus cost of living allowances.	609,000
2. Overtime[(b)]	154,200
3. Supplement for participation in and responsibility for management of the co-operative.	110,000
	873,200
4. Other supplements (provident fund; holiday allowance; day allowance; clothing allowances; Histadrut dues).	216,500
Total for members	1,089,700

(*a*) Egged's (Eshed) budget for wage workers and apprentices (based on April 1956) was calculated for 1,600 wage workers and apprentices. In July only 1,450 were reported to be working for Egged (Eshed).

(*b*) The introduction of a work-day of 7½ hours net adds another 132½ hours per member per year or a total of 278,250 hours a year for all members. The committee deducted the 278,250 hours from the 508,200 hours overtime which Egged (Eshed) included, leaving a balance of 229,950 hours. The committee then estimates that there will be 99,550 overtime hours per month @ IL.1·550 per hour or IL.154,225.

AVERAGE MONTHLY EMOLUMENTS PER MEMBER (IN IL.)

		Recommended
(a)	Basic emolument	100
	Seniority and family allowance	26
	Cost of living allowance	128
		254
	Additional cost of living allowance (in case of further increases in cost of living index)	37
	Total of (a)	291
(b)	20 per cent of (a)	58
(c)	1/12 of thirteenth month	20
(d)	Provident fund (Co-operatives participation)	38
(e)	Vacation allowance	8
(f)	Histadrut dues	6
(g)	National Social Insurance (obligatory)	9
(h)	Clothing	5
(i)	Day allowance	11
(j)	Overtime (see note (b) above)	73
	Total	519

NON-MEMBERS (WAGE WORKERS AND APPRENTICES). THE 1,525 WAGE WORKERS WOULD RECEIVE IL.451,200 OR IL.300 GROSS PER MONTH PER WORKER.

	IL.	IL.
Wages (13 months)	356,599	
Overtime	38,220	
Pension Fund and vacation allowance	39,133	
	433,952	
Other	17,248	
Total for Non-Members		451,200

MONTHLY MAINTENANCE COSTS OF VEHICLES ETC.

	IL.		IL.
Fuel	405,000		
Tyres & Inner tubes	100,000		
Spare parts	206,000		711,000
Depreciation (calculated on a ten-year life at replacement value of IL.35,000 for a bus)		232,700	
Licences for buses, Government and municipal taxes		90,000(c)	
Repairs, garages & miscellaneous expenses		47,600	
Insurance		31,500	
Rent		28,000(d)	

Allowances to drivers for losses on fares (includes IL.1,000 to ticket sellers)	18,500[e]	
Printing of Tickets	9,000	
Miscellaneous expenses for and on account of members and others (holidays, gifts, severance allowances, sport, entertainment, etc.)	18,900	476,200
Other expenses		73,000
		1,711,400

	IL.
(*c*) Licences	40,000
Fees to municipalities and institutions	45,000
Police reports, accidents etc.	5,000
	IL.90,000

	IL.
The Committee estimates Egged (Eshed) pays annually to Local Authorities	166,000
Government trade tax	150,000
Histadrut, Mapai & other taxes	106,000
Merkaz Haco-operatzia	42,000
Increased costs requested by bus co-operatives	75,000
	IL.539,000

(*d*)

	Annually IL.	
New stations	123,000	
Rental of stations	183,000	
Offices	26,000	332,000

(*e*) During the year April, 1955 to March 1956, the actual bill for losses was reported as IL.220,400 or 1½ per cent of the total revenue from the sale of tickets by the drivers. The committee considers one per cent of sales during work hours and half of one per cent of sales after work hours.

DAN BUS CO-OPERATIVE (TEL AVIV)
PROPOSED MONTHLY BUDGET

Total: Monthly IL.1,242,900; Annual IL.14,914,800

916 Members	IL.
1. Basic Emoluments (13 months) plus seniority and family allowance[f]	287,400
2. Overtime	67,000
3. Supplement for participation in and responsibility for management	48,300
4. Other (provident fund, holiday, clothing and maintenance allowances, Histadrut dues)	62,000
	464,700

(*b*) Wage Workers (Number not stated)		
Wage plus cost of living and other allowances		197,600
Allowances for holidays, provident fund, clothing and National Insurance, Histadrut fees		92,900[g]
		290,500
(*c*) Maintenance of vehicles		
1. Fuel	187,000	
2. Tyres and inner tubes	31,000	
3. Spare parts	66,000	284,000
4. Depreciation (ten years, replacement value, IL.35,000 a bus)		86,000
5. Licences for vehicles and fees to local authorities & Government, Histadrut, Mapai and other Institutions	47,500	
6. Outside repairs and garage & miscellaneous expenses	14,000	
7. Insurance (including third party insurance)	14,000	
8. Rent	7,000	
9. Allowance to drivers for losses on fares	9,000	
10. Printing of tickets	5,000	
11. Miscellaneous expenses on account of members and others (holidays, gifts, etc.)	7,900	104,000
(*d*) Other Expenses		12,300
		1,241,900

(*f*) Monthly Emoluments per Member		
Basic emolument	100	
Seniority & family allowance	26	
Cost of living allowance	128·300	
	254·300	
Cost of living allowance (June 1956)	12·500	
Additional cost of living allowance (10 per cent of basic emolument and of cost of living allowance)	22·850	
	289·650 × 916 members	IL.265,300
Thirteenth Month		22,100
		IL.287,400

(g) Holiday supplements (6 per cent of wages)	IL.11,900
Overtime	40,000
Provident fund (10 per cent of wages)	19,800
National Insurance (2·9 per cent of wages)	5,700
Other (co-operative's figures accepted)	15,500
	IL.92,900

Recommendations of Committee about Increase of Bus Fares

1. The committee unanimously recommends permission for Dan and Hamekasher bus co-operatives to raise their fares by 8·2 per cent and Egged by 6·4 per cent.

Committee's Calculations for Dan

		IL.
1. Revenue (according to auditor's report for 1955-56 (April-March))		13,902,000
2. Rebates		155,000
3. Interest on investments, etc.		49,000
4. Miscellaneous		6,000
5. Difference between 10 per cent increase in fares and Government subsidies for period October, 1955, to March, 1956		120,000
		14,232,000
6. Committee's proposed budget of expenses	14,914,800	
7. Less revenue	14,232,000	
	686,800	

The committee notes that in spite of its many requests, Hamekasher Bus Co-operative, Jerusalem, did not submit and the Ministry of Transport did not have sufficient data for estimating this co-operative's budget. The oral evidence and data which Hamekasher submitted were inadequate. The committee recommends the same rate of increase of fares for Hamekasher as it proposes for Dan since both bus co-operatives "furnish an identical service". If and when Hamekasher submits the data required, the Committee recommends review of the rate of increase suggested for this co-operative.

Committee's Calculations for Egged (Eshed)

	IL.
1. Revenue according to auditor's report 1955-56 (March-April)	32,169,500
2. Interest	53,000
3. Difference between the increase of fares by 10 per cent and Government subsidies for period October, 1955 to March 1956	508,000
	32,739,500

4. Less one per cent for loss of revenue*		327,000
5. Committee's budget for expenditures	33,613,500	
6. Gross revenue	32,403,500	
	1,210,000	

2. A permanent Government authority, made up of official and non-official members, should be attached to the Ministry of Transport and advise on all road transportation problems.
3. Immediate arrangements should be made for a Governmental authority to print all tickets for all of the bus co-operatives. This would facilitate the control of the revenue of the bus co-operatives, which the Committee has recommended.
4. The many written and oral complaints about the uncleanliness, overcrowding, timetables, etc., should receive more expeditious attention.

The spokesman of the bus co-operatives described (Haaretz, 26 July, 1956) as an unprecedented intervention by the Government in the internal management of co-operatives, the letter which the Ministry of Transport sent to every member of the bus co-operatives. It was an attempt to undermine the authority of the bus co-operatives. The bus co-operatives should not relinquish the right of every worker to use the weapon of a strike to preserve his standard of living.

The bus co-operatives rejected the offer of the Ministry of Transport of an increase of bus fares by five per cent, and threatened to stop all bus services. The bus co-operative's spokesman was referring to the letter the Minister of Transport, (Mr. M. Carmel, a member of Achdut Haavoda) sent on 20 July, 1956, to every member of the three bus co-operatives, explaining that neither the Government nor the Ministry of Transport questioned

> "the co-operative pattern of the bus services or the aptitude of the members to organize the bus transportation in the country . . . (and) for carrying public responsibility". The Minister's letter further notes that there are both subjective and objective reasons "for the blemishes and shortcomings of the bus co-operatives which the Ministry of Transport jointly with the co-operatives must help to correct."

The Minister's letter also notes that the licensing of additional carriers (bus transportation companies) would ferment a bus fare war, and that this would precipitate confusion and disorganization on the roads which could be bad for all concerned. On the other hand, the Government could not permit the bus co-operatives to enjoy the *de facto* monopoly unless it exercised effective comprehensive control (including the fixing of bus

* Inter-urban travel is sensitive to economic and other changes (security of roads from attacks by Arab infiltrators, etc.). Therefore the committee notes that it deducted one per cent for loss of revenue during the fluctuation.

fares) over the bus services. Otherwise, the consumers might consider themselves unprotected against abusive practices.

The Government, in fixing bus fares, the Minister's letter explains, must make sure that a member of a bus co-operative will enjoy a reasonable remuneration and also a reasonable return on his participation in the co-operative's capital. By allocating adequate depreciation, the bus co-operatives will be able to renew their equipment and improve the quality of the bus services. But in the interests of the consumers the authorities must also protest against and cannot sanction onerous bus fares. The Government must have the final authority to fix the bus fares. On the other hand, the management of the respective bus co-operatives will enjoy the maximum opportunity to submit and to explain to the Ministry of Transport their calculations of the bus fares.

The Minister's letter, which was sent to every member of the bus co-operatives, also notes that one of the most serious obstacles to be overcome is the public's loss of confidence in the bus co-operatives. The enemies of the co-operative pattern of bus transport will exploit the situation and prepare the ground for replacing bus co-operatives with other patterns. The prevailing atmosphere of a lack of confidence also is a favourable breeding ground for exaggerated rumours about "the enrichment" and "about the creamy emoluments". The Government control of the bus services and bus fares will enable the bus co-operatives to regain the public's confidence. And only the Government can consider the interests of both parties when fixing bus fares.

The public rejection by the bus co-operatives of the fares which the Government fixed and the threat of a complete stoppage of all bus transportation was additional evidence to the public of the co-operative's disregard of the Government's authority. The Minister's circular letter then reiterated that the Government, in deciding on a five per cent increase in bus fares, had considered the wage scale, conditions of work, and such fringe benefits as sick leave and vacations with pay, participation in Provident and Pension Fund, etc., which the Histadrut defined. The Ministry of Transport also included in the calculations of the bus fares an allowance for members' participation in the actual management. It gave due consideration to the actual revenue and expenditures of the bus co-operatives during the past year.

The closing paragraphs of the Minister of Transport's letter sounds a warning that if the members of the bus co-operatives continued to consider only their personal benefits and convenience, it was bound to jeopardize their status and livelihood as well as the public transportation system. Therefore, the Minister of Transport asked the members

> "to consolidate and to ensure the status of the bus co-operatives in the future; . . . to deepen their roots in the public mind and to win the sympathy of the consumers. It is in the interests of every member of every bus co-operative and also of the bus service that the Government should play a permanent role in fixing bus fares. The managements of

the bus co-operatives have *de facto* turned down the five per cent increase in fares which the Government fixed and effective on 1 July, 1956. Therefore the Government has appointed an *ad hoc* independent official committee to examine the calculations and submit within the shortest period its conclusions. Let us hope that the conclusions of the committee will help with a solution which the problem merits."

A leader in Hameshek Hashitufi, of 17 July, 1956, admits the rights of the bus co-operatives on the basis of past performance. On the other hand, one cannot base the present and the future only on the past. The development and the problems of the bus co-operatives must be considered in the light of the new conditions and of the role and place which the bus co-operatives play in the economy of Israel as a whole and not only in respect of the bus co-operatives' role as one of the economic weapons of the labour sector. Since the basic principle of the Histadrut-sponsored WPSTS is that these must be both employer and employee (unlike the consumers movement which can perform only services as distributors), they do not have the choice which a theoretician of the co-operative movement has described as whether to be "a rat among rats" or a "bird among birds" or both together. In the case of bus co-operatives, the dilemma not infrequently arises when the status of "rats" is stronger than that of "the birds".

It is to be regretted that the leaders and managers of the bus co-operatives either do not understand or have consciously ignored the fact that in the case of bus co-operatives (like other economic undertakings of a public character) every deviation from its ethos must bring the bus co-operatives in conflict with the general interests. Though not authorized to decide whether and to what extent the claims of the bus co-operatives in the present controversy about higher fares and other claims, are justified, there can be no difference of opinion that the activities of the bus co-operatives must be subject to "public" supervision and control. The services of the bus co-operatives are as much the concern of the community as they are of the members. And the Government, Municipalities and other local authorities or Histadrut bodies represent the public interests. The Minister of Transport is justified in his determination to control the printing of all bus fare tickets and also in looking into the decision of the bus co-operatives to divide their resources among the members. The measures taken to exercise the right of control are not directed against the "independence" or "autonomy" of the management of the respective bus co-operatives; and the need to take such measures would not have arisen had the public control been efficient and adequate. Any compromise about the present problems means that it will take longer to resolve these in the future.

After meeting on 16 or 17 July, 1956, the public committee to enquire into the cost calculations of the bus co-operatives, the three bus co-operatives "Egged (Eshed)", "Dan" and "Hamekasher" wrote a letter to the committee which, *inter alia*, refutes the opinion "expressed from time to time by various parties that the co-operative pattern for bus transportation is no longer tenable. These opinions have spread among the public the illusion that it would be better if the bus services were transferred to another authority."

In this letter (date not given), the three bus co-operatives explain that the co-operative pattern for bus transportation prevails in Israel because "no other redeemer was found for this function". Nobody fixed this pattern for bus transportation in advance. Only groups of workers could provide and maintain the bus service since this required a considerable degree of chalutziut and risk. It was only natural for the small groups to integrate and then "find their way to co-operation and to the Histadrut". The letter also stresses that public bodies and third parties, including the present Minister of Transport, rejected the allegation that the co-operative pattern of bus transportation had failed. The Minister had stated publicly "that it would not be equitable to conclude that it should be changed. . . . Nevertheless we (i.e. the bus co-operatives) do not desire to impose on the public the existing framework".

The joint letter to the Minister of Transport acknowledged[120] the public character of bus services and spelled out the extent of the *de jure* public control (in addition to fixing bus fares) which they considered justifiable, such as monthly reporting to the Ministry of Transport on Ministry forms; the Ministry's supervision of the routes and timetables; the participation of the Ministry's representatives and also of those from other Government Ministries and Committees that dealt with bus transportation in the control, etc. The letter also referred to the authority which the Histadrut exercised through Chevrat Haovdim and the latter's representatives on the Management Committees of the bus co-operatives and on the governing organs of such bodies as Merkaz Haco-operatzia.

The letter further noted that the members' emoluments, which the bus co-operatives "fixed with the approval of Chevrat Haovdim" included supplements, social security, and a special payment for the members' participation in the management. Except for increases in cost of living allowances which the Government fixed, there had been no change since 1952. But "for various and technical reasons", the letter explained, Chevrat Haovdim had not yet acted on the application of the bus co-operatives of 6 October, 1952, to increase the basic emolument for members from IL.100 to IL.125 per month.[121] The joint letter also promised to confirm in writing that the bus co-operatives pay their wage workers the scale of salaries which the Histadrut craft unions fixed. Since the increase in bus fares for at least five years had lagged behind operational costs, the letter noted, the bus co-operatives had a very large cumulative operational deficit which the committee should take into consideration when fixing the bus fares.

"In the calculations submitted more recently to the Ministry of Transport we failed to include the operational deficits from previous years.

And we noted only operational deficits which are likely to occur as a result of the increased costs." The best way of ensuring "an accurate and objective method for calculating bus fares on various routes, and which would relieve both the Government and ourselves from prolonged negotiations every time there was an increase in the cost of living and of wages . . ." was for the Ministry of Transport to act on their request to define the procedure for calculating an index for bus transportation costs.

This would require the introduction in all bus co-operatives of a uniform accounting system, statistical tabulations and reporting. Finally, the letter noted that two other problems which required almost immediate attention were

(*a*) the reduction of the types of vehicles which would simplify the problems of spare parts; and
(*b*) the improvement of the relations of the bus co-operatives with the Government and with the public.

Schedule One to the Joint Letter of Bus Co-operatives sent to the Committee to enquire into cost accounting of bus fares, 1956 (date of letter not given).

EGGED (ESHED)—MANPOWER—30 JUNE, 1956

	Members	Non-members	Total
1. Drivers	1,373	215	1,588
2. Administration			
(*a*) Traffic	150	35	185
(*b*) Ticket sellers	57	128	185
(*c*) General (office and accounting)	158	123	281
(*d*) Vehicles, equipment and supplies	128	69	197
3. Garages (skilled, unskilled and apprentices)	147	659	806
4. Services (cleaning buses, watchmen etc.)	12	129	141
5. Parcel services (clerks, drivers and porters)	19	90	109
6. Others	20	7	27
Total	2,064	1,455	3,519
On leave with pay (over a month)	34	1	35
Indefinite Long Leave	26	8	34
	2,124	1,464[a]	3,588[a]

[a] 135 non-members of Egged (Eshed) work on a contract basis as *de facto* unregistered commandites

STRIKE OF BUS SERVICES 22-30 AUGUST, 1956

The following excerpts from a leader in Shituf (August 1956) "Transportation Strike" are in line with the decisions of a joint meeting of the secretariats and the representatives of the bus co-operatives affiliated to Merkaz Haco-operatzia. (It seems that the bus co-operatives did not feel themselves bound by the decisions.)

"The bus co-operatives' demands are justified in so far as these fall within the framework which the representatives of Merkaz Haco-operatzia and Chevrat Haovdim jointly approved (committee of four). But this in no way justifies the strike. Only complete disillusionment and the loss of the faculty to think could induce this 'declaration of war against the Yishuv, the Government, and the Histadrut. For tens of years we have tried to inculcate the idea that bus transportation exists for the community and not *vice versa*; that it is not for the bus co-operatives to impose their authority on the public but *vice versa*. And that a public service which has a concession must depend on negotiations and on its power of persuasion and may not use any other method to achieve its demands . . . and the public must judge whether the requests are justified or not. To the extent that Government represents the public, the Government is the judge. And the bus co-operatives can and should continue to press their demands and try to obtain redress if they think that they have been wronged by the Government's mistaken judgment. Otherwise you destroy from under your feet the basis of public service which is part of a concession. It is a pity that all our efforts to explain this thoroughly to the bus co-operatives before the strike have failed. . . ."

According to the report in L'Chavereinu,[122] (27 October, 1956, pp. 1-18; 59-67) the nine-day general strike of bus transport, 22-30 August, 1956, occurred 25 years after the first general strike (1931), in which Arab and Jewish bus drivers were united. The bus co-operatives declared that they were fully aware of the fact that

"it will have serious results in their relationship . . . with those bodies that deal with our problems and on the procedure in dealing with transportation problems in the future.

"It is hoped that our discussion with the Histadrut about wages, and fringe benefits, will start in a few days. The aim will be to spell out (define) the basis so clearly as to leave no possibilities for differences in interpretations 'from time to time' and the concomitant complications.

"It is also hoped that the Ministry of Transport jointly with us and without any delay, will start to fix the procedure for calculating bus fares. This has been previously agreed to between the Government and ourselves."

The management of the bus co-operatives attributed the serious deterioration in their financial position during the first eight months of 1956 to the "appreciable rise in prices which considerably increased the expenses". Yet, they could not increase the bus fares. The operational deficits on the one hand, and the capital investments for buildings and renewal of vehicles on the other hand, made it impossible for the bus co-operatives to meet their obligations. Work on the central garage in the north and on the new bus stations continued. A hundred of the 150 buses ordered in England had arrived (30 were already in service). Negotiations were continuing for the financing of the purchase of another 200 buses.

An article in the aforementioned issue of L'Chaveireinu, 27 October, 1956, by A. Bialostotsky, presented the Egged (Eshed) version about the developments which forced it to take the undesirable strike decision. Dan joined Egged (Eshed), but Hamekasher in Jerusalem, at the last moment, did not. He notes that if the Ministry of Transport, when calculating bus fares, had agreed to include the IL. 62 per month for the period to March 1957 per member for participation in and responsibility for management, Egged (Eshed) as a *quid pro quo* was prepared to include a global amount in the budget for this purpose which was equivalent to IL.45 (and not IL.62) times the total membership.

> "At a chance meeting, the Minister of Transport advised one of our members that at the end of 1956 he may, provided the revenue of the co-operative does not cover the expenses, cover half of the IL.62. There would have been no strike had the Minister promised to cover the entire amount (IL.62) in the event that the expenses exceeded the revenue."

Late in the evening of 21 August, 1956, according to this article, the Histadrut Central Committee made a three-point suggestion, viz., that the Histadrut would

(*a*) support the co-operatives' demand that the members' gross emoluments shall not be reduced by more than IL.45-50 a month over the present scale:

(*b*) intervene with the Government to devise a procedure mutually acceptable to the Government and the bus co-operatives to ensure punctual payments to the members of the co-operatives; and

(*c*) help the bus co-operatives to obtain from the Government and other sources the financing which they needed.

However, notes Mr. Bialostotsky, the Minister of Transport would not accept the suggestion that bus fares should be reviewed annually and linked to the cost of living index. On the other hand, the bus co-operatives would not accept the Minister's proposal (made after five months' negotiations, from February to June 1956) for a five per cent increase in bus fares. He alleges that the Chevrat Haovdim representative in the management of the Egged (Eshed) considered that an 11 per cent increase was justified. However, this was before the price of fuel increased and the cost of living index rose by 10 points, which together were equivalent to an increase of 2·9 per cent in expenses. The article further notes that the staffs of the Ministry of Transport and of Merkaz Haco-operatzia endorsed an eleven per cent increase in bus fares which the bus co-operative requested. The Minister of Transport would not budge from his proposal for a five per cent increase and appointed another *ad hoc* committee that allegedly was loaded with people from the local labour councils. This committee recommended an increase of 6½ per cent in bus fares; that Egged (Eshed) should make further economies which would have reduced the monthly emoluments per member by IL.107, and also pare other operating expenses, including the allocation for depreciation. If the co-operatives acted on these suggestions, the Minister of Transport would authorize an increase in bus fares by 8·1 per cent. The Histadrut, which on previous occasions had been active in this question, "was completely passive". Mr. Bialostotsky reiterates that the strike weapon was directed not against the public; it was intended as a warning to the Government that it could not impair the rights of a large group of workers or destroy their co-operatives without creating unrest.

He blames the general hostility towards the bus co-operatives on the lack of an appreciation and unwillingness to reward chalutziut. Generally speaking there is a spirit of jealousy and envy of the members of the bus co-operatives who, after many years of labour, have improved and consolidated their position.

The public, incited by the press and radio, was hostile during the first three days of the strike. Then, according to Mr. Bialostotsky, the public's hostility turned into disillusionment and a general feeling that the bus fares were not excessive when compared with other essentials and that "the services are not so bad".

The strike was called off only after the Ministry of Transport withdrew its previous stand. In his letter to Egged (Eshed) of 30 August, 1956, the Minister of Transport, according to the article, agreed *inter alia* that

(*a*) Egged (Eshed) as of 1 September, 1956, may increase the bus fares by 8·1 per cent and include in the monthly emoluments to its members during the 1955-56 budget year, IL.62 per month per member more than the amount which the Ministry's costs accounting schedule fixed. The Government believes that the revenue will exceed the estimates. This, together with an increase in efficiency, will cover the extra IL.62.

(*b*) The Government will cover, in such manner as it will find right, such operational deficit as will result from this additional payment of IL.62. Should the estimates which the Ministry of Transport made for any items of expenditure prove to be inadequate, and provided that the revenues of Egged (Eshed) will be insufficient to meet the shortage, the Ministry will cover the differences.

The report in the issue of L'Chaveireinu (27 October, 1956) also gives the Egged (Eshed) version about Hamekasher's decision not to participate in the general strike. For six months the three bus co-operatives (Egged (Eshed); Dan and Hamekasher) maintained a united front. On 21 August, 1956 (i.e. one day before the strike fixed for 22 August, 1956) the Histadrut

Central Committee which had been authorized to deal with the bus co-operatives, was discussing a compromise proposal to reduce the gross monthly emoluments to members by only IL.45-IL.50 and not by IL.102 which the Zackai Committee had suggested. The Hamekasher representative (Mr. Lichtman) favoured the compromise. But, on the evening before the strike was to start it was clear that the Minister of Transport and other members of the Economic Ministries Committee (a sub-committee of the Cabinet) would not accept the compromise which the Histadrut Central Committee proposed. On the evening of 21 August, 1956, at a joint meeting of the Councils of the three bus co-operatives, Mr. Lichtman, the Hamekasher representative, spoke against a strike. He returned to Jerusalem to a general meeting of Hamekasher members which, to the surprise and disappointment of everybody, decided to break the united front. Hamekasher, according to this version in L'Chaveireinu, refused to permit representatives of Egged (Eshed) and of Dan to address a general meeting of Hamekasher members. Relations were broken off, including the mutual arrangements between the three bus co-operatives which permitted Hamekasher members to travel free on the buses of the other two bus co-operatives. The article notes that the rank and file of Hamekasher members were unhappy about the break in the united front and that this is reflected in the last paragraph of the resolutions of Hamekasher's general meeting expressing support for the demands of Egged (Eshed) and of Dan.

The article draws the following main conclusions from this episode:

1. The Histadrut, jointly with the bus co-operatives, should define a procedure for fixing the emolument to members of the bus co-operatives which would minimize the chronic friction with the public who persistently abused the members of the bus co-operatives because their earnings exceed "the accepted framework". The article reiterates the "chronic allegation that the basic emolument of IL.100 fixed in 1953 for members of bus co-operatives is less than the basic wage of IL.143 which was fixed for grade AA metal workers though these have not invested their money and do not carry the responsibility for management.[123]
2. The Ministry of Transport should agree to link bus fares (and/or Government subsidies) with increased costs and fix "a transportation basket" of items to be considered for calculating costs. The respective Ministries also should obtain for the bus co-operatives from the Government an annual allocation of foreign exchange for replacement of vehicles. The article refers to the Government's unexpected decision "last year"—when a purchasing commission of the bus co-operatives was advised that "because of a shortage of foreign exchange" the allotment of foreign exchange has been cut in half, i.e. for the purchase of only 250 instead of 500 buses for all the bus co-operatives.
3. The relationships with the public and especially with those using the buses must be improved.

Mr. Sobelman, in the same issue of L'Chaveireinu, of 27 October, 1956 (writing in a sarcastic vein), suggests that the bus co-operatives should influence their members to put vociferous demands for the nationalization of the bus services.

"Since this (nationalization) will come sooner or later, and if we wish to look at things from a long range point of view, this is their duty (after the strike) to shake off the responsibility for a Government service. . . . Then there will be no more hard bargaining about bus fares; no need to declare strikes or for public enquiry committees. But transportation will become a Garden of Eden in the country . . . the nationalized bus transportation will serve a valuable and important role in the development of the country and it will carry many responsibilities. Its only rights will be the publication of the bus fares."

Mr. Sobelman includes in his article a verbatim transcript of his conversation on 24 August, 1956, (at 1 p.m.) with the Minister of Transport who made a surprise visit to the central bus station (presumably in Tel Aviv):

Replying to the Minister's questions, Mr. Sobelman stated that he came to Israel 32 years before and had been a member of a bus co-operative for 15 years. The Minister asked: "Why do not the members revolt against the management, which is leading the undertaking to destruction (waste)". Mr. Sobelman allegedly answered: "I am surprised at this question by a Minister. a member of the Labour Party. Furthermore", Mr. Sobelman continued, "I explained to him that the co-operative pattern is very democratic; there are annual elections and that the rank and file of the members to a man stand behind the management." The Minister then asked Mr. Sobelman's opinion about the spirit during the strike. "I answered that his predecessor (the previous Minister of Transport), though opposed to the co-operative pattern, had succeeded in improving the relationships between the users of the buses and the drivers and had helped the bus co-operatives to acquire new vehicles.

"You on the other hand, to our regret, have succeeded in making the atmosphere turbid and in creating an artificial link between us and the public. I draw special attention to your radio address which was used to reiterate the familiar misrepresentations. The wheels of transportation were silenced because the Ministry of Transport did not use ordinary common sense." Answering the Minister's question what would be the end of it all, Mr. Sobelman replied: "Since the Minister has for the first time in 20 years (actually it was 25 years) succeeded in bringing bus transportation to a standstill, I, therefore, have come to think that there is no place for bus co-operatives. You, as Minister, would be doing a good service to the State and to the public if you would take measures to nationalize the bus service. Rebellious and antagonistic bus co-operatives must not be permitted to become the single power on the roads. Then there will be no need to appoint committees. We, as ordinary workers, will be defended by the Histadrut and the craft union and the travelling public will be patient and will refrain from persistent criticism and complaints. And when the public will become incensed they will direct this only against the Government and not against the bus service, and not against the co-operative that is presently and constantly subjected to slander by the public." According to Mr. Sobelman, the Minister befittingly replied that the bus co-operatives are desirable (beautiful) and should be continued. But then the Minister declared that "I should explain to the management that they cannot dictate the terms to the Government which they want and I told him that there has never been a case of a driver who charged even one pruta (a tenth of a cent) more than the Government-prescribed bus fare."

Mr. Sobelman argues sarcastically that since bus transport has been described as so profitable a business "for thousands of members" it cannot be less profitable to the Government. Therefore the Government

> "should not find it difficult to find the resources to pay for the acquisition of such a pleasant and orderly enterprise established over a period of several decades, with a widespread service, modern garages and workshops, stations and parking space; a staff for planning and carrying on with the traffic; departments for manpower, accounting, etc. . . . And we will continue to drive on the roads . . . and many enterprising newspapers in the State will raise paeans of praise about the voluntary dedication and effort of Egged members who are working for the State bus system."

This issue of L'Chaveireinu, of 27 October, 1956 (pp. 60-67), also reproduces some of the articles about the bus strike which appeared in the dailies of all parties. An introductory note to these excerpts draws attention to the fact that from the beginning of the strike only "Haboker" (the daily of the General Zionists) did not display a hostile attitude towards the striking co-operatives and did not accept the communiques of the Ministry of Transport as "the Law from Mount Zion".

Haboker, of 21 August, 1956, writes:

> "Ultimately the Ministry of Transport will have to sit down with the representatives of the strikers and arrive at some compromise about a suitable increase in bus fares. Therefore, why not do so without a strike."

This article argues that the increases in expenses justified the decision of the Committee of Economic Ministries to offer an increase in bus fares by 8·1 per cent for Egged (Eshed) and 9·9 per cent for Dan and Hamekasher. These increases were larger than those which the Zackai enquiry committee suggested.

> "These increases do not cover the increase in basic emolument and the last increase in the cost of living supplement. There is also the appreciable increase in the price of fuel and spare parts. . . . If the Histadrut insists that the bus co-operatives must increase the wages of their wage

workers, it is clear . . . that members' emoluments also must be increased. . . . The Histadrut and the Government must seek more practical (useful) ways how to avoid an additional increase in bus fares. . . ."

Generally speaking, the newspapers, during the strike competed in their protests against the striking co-operatives and in urging the Government "to put an end to monopolies; to enforce the emergency laws or to nationalize the bus co-operatives". The replies of the bus co-operatives which had to be published as paid advertisements, told the Government: "If you don't give us the possibilities to exist, take over and manage the transportation yourselves." This seemed to put a stop to the suggestions for nationalization and gradually to change public opinion. Since nationalization of the bus services would increase costs on account of bureaucratic management, and because of the indifferent attitude of the Government employee "towards the traveller and the property, there was pressure on the Minister of Transport to find a way out through negotiations with the bus co-operatives".

When, after the strike, there was a new wave of complaints against the new bus fares, the Minister of Transport had to issue an official explanation. The Press, in general, were of the opinion that the bus co-operatives had achieved what they had sought at the beginning.

According to an article in Maariv (afternoon daily) by the ex-manager of Egged (who was director-general of the Ministry of Transport for about a year) the bus co-operatives had achieved even more than they had sought. In a broadcast, the Minister of Transport asked the public not to adopt a bitter attitude towards the co-operative members and "denied the slander about the enrichment of the members of these co-operatives". Some papers omitted this sentence from their reports. The article in L'Chaveireinu (27 October, 1957) asks the staff of the Ministry of Transport, if an increase in bus fares was unavoidable, why was it necessary to create such a storm "against us and to misrepresent us to the public?"

Yaakov Shaanan's letter to Haaretz (3 September, 1956) notes that a member of a bus co-operative is both a wage worker and an investor in the undertaking. Therefore, in addition to wages he is also entitled to a reasonable return on his capital. Those who think it wrong to have permitted the bus co-operatives to accumulate so much capital may be right. But it is impossible to turn back the clock and to sequester the property which the bus co-operatives have "not illegally" accumulated. He questions the sincerity of the declarations of the bus co-operatives calling for nationalization or whether these are reactions to "influence and pressure". At all events, if bus transportation is nationalized, the State will have to pay

"many millions for the property, and every member will receive a significant amount. And the total emoluments of an ex-member of a co-operative, i.e. the monthly income from such an investment plus the gross monthly earnings which consolidated undertakings in Israel pay, will exceed the gross earnings which anybody has mentioned."

Mr. S. Eyal, in Herut, of 27 August, 1956, writes about the dangers of nationalizing bus transportation.

> "Dan and Egged (Eshed) are not alarmed by the possibilities of transferring to the Government their deficits. The dangers of the threat of nationalization becoming a reality are more serious for the public" than they are for the members of the bus co-operatives.
>
> The waste and inefficiency of the bus co-operatives which are reported, Mr. Eyal notes, are less than that of Government-owned and managed services which the taxpayers cover. The article gives some examples, such as the costs of nationalizing the Palestine Electric Company. He thinks that the real reason for the strike is not so much the amount or rate of increase of bus fares as the desire of the ex-brigadier general (Minister of Transport) to compel the bus co-operatives to surrender.
>
> "The Minister of Transport's relentless attacks on the strikers creates the impression of a war being waged against enemy number one of Israel who must be subdued at any price." The Government unjustifiably labels the members of Egged (Eshed) and of Dan "Enemies of the People".

On the other hand, Mr. Eyal thinks that it is difficult to justify the bus co-operatives because they have not always sufficiently considered the public and have relied too much on their monopolistic position. It seems ridiculous for the Government, at a time when there is a wave of demands for increases by skilled workers in general, to insist that the members of the bus co-operatives accept a cut by IL.50 monthly of their emoluments. Had the Government acted on previous occasions about the increase of members' emoluments in Egged (Eshed) and Dan, then the Government would be justified in intervening now. For years the members of the bus co-operatives have been receiving large emoluments and have become accustomed to a certain standard of living, common "in a period of inflation and rising prices". And only a month ago the Knesset approved an appreciable increase in salary for its members and for Ministers.

Haaretz, of 22 August, 1956, *inter alia*, has the following observation on a comparative table in the article on emoluments of Egged (Eshed) members. Economic circles generally agree that it is preferable to calculate the amount to be paid for the participation in management and responsibility for the society's affairs as 20 per cent of the monthly basic wage of a grade AA driver plus the cost of living supplement, than to fix such compensation as a certain percentage return on the member's respective investment in a bus co-operative. The recommendations of the Zackai Enquiry Committee to increase the net work-day from seven to seven-and-a-half hours has an appreciable effect on the earnings of a member of Egged (Eshed), because this increase in net work-hours will decrease the amount of a member's overtime pay. The public enquiry committee also did not approve of the point or premium system which Egged (Eshed) uses. But the committee of economic ministries found that the Zackai Committee had erred in calculating the cost of living supplement and that it had calculated the budget for a calendar year (January-December) and not for the fiscal year April to March.

Chanan Yosef's article[124] in Al Hamishmar (Mapam daily) (date not given but written after the strike was called off, 30 August, 1956) castigates the "lack of flexibility of both parties and pleads for improvements in the service and for more and closer supervision of the bus co-operatives by the Government and by the Histadrut. To forestall any potential stoppage of this vital service in the future, there must be far-reaching changes in the character of the supervision of the bus co-operatives. These must unequivocally accept the authority of the Histadrut, of which they are members; and of the Government which represents the public. The possibility of the Government and the Histadrut participating in the capital of the co-operatives must be carefully considered. This would give a more tangible basis for Government's and Histadrut's decisive voice in the management of the bus co-operatives. The pattern of the most suitable organization for this kind of relationship must be formulated without delay. And the suggestion for a standing public advisory committee on transportation must be seriously considered. He rejects, however, at this stage, the suggestion of the Right-wing to nationalize the bus transportation system.

> "And finally . . . the members of the bus co-operatives are entitled to a fair remuneration as well as a return on their investments in the undertaking, but not more than this. More recently, a queer spirit is perceptible among the members of the bus co-operatives; this emanates from the . . . speculators, the snare to become rich. While we must combat this spirit, at the same time we must remember that the members of the bus co-operatives are not to be considered as part of the economic parasites in the economy. They are working people and all incitements against the members of the co-operatives must be repelled."

The founders meeting of the division for transportation co-operatives was held on 23 October, 1956. Representatives of the three bus and of the 20 road haulage co-operatives affiliated to Merkaz Haco-operatzia were present. Mr. Zvi Lehman, the representative of Chevrat Haovdim on the management of Egged (Eshed), and Mr. Uri Alpert, a Histadrut representative in Egged (Eshed), also attended the meeting.

Y. Ritov noted that the immediate functions of this division were to

(*a*) act as the representative of the transport co-operatives in all their external relationships;
(*b*) lay the foundations for a uniform accounting and statistical system for the bus and for the road haulage co-operatives;
(*c*) fix a procedure for the cost accounting of bus fares and cartage rates, and these always must be open for inspection;
(*d*) organize public relations; and arrange the purchases of spare parts from first sources.

The representation on the management committee of the division would be apportioned on the basis of the membership of each of the three bus co-operatives, and the total membership of the road haulage co-operatives. In this way Egged (Eshed) would have three representatives; Dan two; Hamekasher one; road haulage co-operatives two; and Merkaz Haco-operatzia three.

M. Weisbrot stated "there is no *raison d'être* for our existence" (the division) unless it is formally recognized and accepted by the Chevrat Haovdim Secretariat.

Y. Ritov read a letter from the Chevrat Haovdim Secretariat welcoming "the establishment of the division". A committee was dealing with the question of uniform accounting, statistical and reporting systems for the bus co-operatives and another committee, which the Minister of Transport had appointed to make a general study of the division, had started negotiations with Chevrat Haovdim for the appointment of a committee to draft regulations about emoluments, employment, etc., for all Histadrut-sponsored road haulage co-operatives, including those not affiliated to Merkaz Haco-operatzia.

M. Maliskovitz (Egged (Eshed)) notes that he had previously asked the Merkaz Haco-operatzia Secretariat whether the Histadrut Executive Committee recognized the division. The Histadrut-sponsored non-co-operative road haulage sector and the Histadrut-sponsored agricultural co-operatives that also transport goods for others were not represented at this meeting.

M. Libai (Dan) agrees that they "will succeed only if we function within Histadrut and not within an empty shell".

P. Shamgar wants the division to include all the Histadrut-sponsored road haulage firms, including non-co-operatives. Otherwise the Histadrut-sponsored road haulage sector will never achieve the status which the bus co-operatives in Israel have attained.

A. Hochman (Secretariat—Egged (Eshed)) and others complain about the small representation accorded to the co-operatives on the ad hoc committee, which the Minister of Transport appointed to enquire into the problem of road haulage in general, and on a second ad hoc committee appointed to enquire into emoluments and other problems of bus co-operatives.

The meeting appointed a committee to prepare the data for submission to the aforementioned two public committees.

EMOLUMENTS AND CALCULATIONS OF BUS PRICES

The management[125] explained to the Fifth Council Meeting of Egged (Eshed), 2 March, 1958, that according to "the agreement between (it) and the Ministry of Transport in the middle of 1956-57", the co-operative's revenue and expenditures will be estimated at the end of every fiscal year and the Government would then grant a subsidy to cover the operational deficit. The Government covered the 1956-57 deficit of Egged

(Eshed) and also authorized an increase of fares by 7·8 per cent which was intended to cover the co-operative's estimated 1957-58 operational deficit of over IL.2 million. "We hold a document from the Ministry of Transport to this effect." But, the report notes, the Government refused to honour its undertaking because Egged (Eshed) had not fixed the emoluments of its members in accordance with the conclusion of the Zackai Committee, of 26 August, 1956.

> "We served notice in advance that we considered the conclusion of the Zackai Committee as binding only for one year, 1956/57" March/April. The Ministry of Transport and the Histadrut "had promised us that they would find a way for calculating the bus fares before the end of 1956-57. And the Histadrut also promised to find a solution by that time for the problem of emoluments of members."

In the meantime the cost of living increased by 3·2 per cent, insurance by 100 per cent, etc. When in April 1957, it seemed clear that the question of how to calculate bus fares and wages would not be resolved, we started negotiations for a Government subsidy for 1957-58. The Government withdrew its authority for the 7·8 per cent increase of bus fares and withheld the subsidy which it promised would continue until Egged (Eshed) would reintroduce the 1956-57 scale of emoluments for its members. "This is something which we certainly cannot do. There is no precedent in the country for a reduction of wages . . . when prices continue to rise. . . ."

The management of Egged (Eshed) notes that in spite of the co-operative's persistent prodding throughout 1957, the Histadrut had not yet submitted its proposals about the new scale of emoluments for members, which is "the main problem underlying the differences between the co-operative (Egged (Eshed)) and the Histadrut". In December 1957, Egged (Eshed) could not wait any longer, and decided to put into effect a decision made in October 1957, to increase "the basic emolument" of its members. Had the Histadrut made a decision, and even "if it had not been entirely satisfactory", Egged (Eshed) would have accepted it and then requested an early hearing for an appeal. Egged (Eshed) considered the additional payments which it had made to its members "as an advance". In April, 1958, five months after Egged (Eshed) had started paying the additional remuneration to members, the general secretary of the Histadrut invited Egged (Eshed) to a meeting. To demonstrate the desire for a solution, a special meeting of the Council of Egged (Eshed) decided to freeze the payment of the increase in the emolument.

> "But to our regret, and contrary to the agreement to this effect, we were not asked to appoint our representative on the Wages Committee which the Histadrut had appointed. Apparently this was a misunderstanding. We still hope to be invited to the deliberations of the Wages Committee. . . . We expect an equitable decision which will then make . . . it possible to re-establish normal relationships between us and the Histadrut bodies. . . ."

The management of Egged (Eshed) then asked the Government why it paid subsidies on certain vegetables direct to all farmers or through the co-operatives, irrespective whether the farmers were efficient or inefficient, or their production costs stable. Yet, in the case of the bus co-operatives, the staff and/or the committees of the Ministry of Transport delve into such questions as economies, and efficiency, and then reduce subsidies. If the bus co-operatives increase the emoluments of their members and/or introduce incentive payments, the Government refuses to honour its undertaking to grant subsidies. Why is the remuneration which the bus co-operatives pay to their members treated differently from the farm prices, which farmers realize for subsidized produce?

The management of Egged (Eshed) labels as inaccurate the Minister of Transport's report to the Knesset "that the members (i.e. of the bus co-operatives) had divided among themselves public funds which had been earmarked for the renewal of vehicles."

The development fund, according to Egged (Eshed) management's report, has made available IL.13,745,000 for all bus co-operatives since 1953. During this period Egged (Eshed) spent "in cash over IL.15 million" and for 1958-59 assumed obligations for an additional IL.6 million, though the Ministry of Transport's estimated budget for Egged (Eshed) included less than IL.2·8 million for this year. The Ministry of Transport also refused to approve the increase which Egged (Eshed) suggested in the annual global amounts for depreciation, which would expedite the modernizing of equipment and "assure better and more comfortable service for the public".

L'Chavereinu[126] reprinted a copy of a leader in "LaMerchav" of 11 June, 1958 (the daily of the Achdut Haavoda Party and Hakibbutz Hameuchad) which referred to Mr. Davidson's statement at a press conference in Tel Aviv in early June, 1958 (date not given) that Egged (Eshed) since 1949 invested, for the purchase of 741 buses, IL.8 million in excess of the amounts of Government loans for this purpose. The leader notes that it is normal business procedure to use surpluses for development and expansion.

> "Egged (Eshed) disposes its surpluses as it pleases and then uses public funds for expansion. Every private business would choose, like Egged, to pass on to the public the entire risk. When fixing the bus fare, the Government ensures a very reasonable emolument for members which includes a liberal return on the members' investment in the capital of the respective bus co-operative; the full maintenance of the buses and of the garages; and a depreciation fund for renewal of equipment. And if all of this does not suffice, the Government makes available grants and loans for increasing the co-operative's vehicles and improving the public services."

The leader in LaMerchav then refers to Egged's decision to increase by IL.110 per month the emolument for every member. This additional emolument is an open breach of the directive from the Government and the Histadrut, and Egged (Eshed) is doing everything possible to have this payment recognized as a *fait accompli.* It is inconceivable that the Government "as the trustee of public funds" should in these circumstances be expected to increase its subsidies to Egged (Eshed). A distinction should be made in the character of the relationships between Egged (Eshed) and the Government and of those between Egged (Eshed) and the Histadrut. *De facto* there is no difference between Egged (Eshed) and any private business. The leader in LaMerchav thinks that the Histadrut should no longer permit Egged (Eshed) to use the word co-operative "in vain". Egged (Eshed) also fixes the amount which new members have to pay into its share capital on the basis of "supply and demand". (According to Mr. A. Ehrenfeld, head of the national traffic department, and quoted by Davar of 22 July, 1958, Egged (Eshed) has 2,100 wage workers, 400 apprentices and 2,400 members.)

Summary—Report of the Committee to Enquire into the Structure of Emoluments for Members of Bus Co-operatives

The Report of the Committee to Enquire into the Wage Structure for the Members of Bus Co-operatives, dated 11 August, 1958, (mimeographed eight pages, single spacing) was accompanied by a letter of the same date and signed by Mr. M. Bar-Tal, the chairman of the committee. The other members of the committee were Messrs. U. Alpert; M. Libai; Y. Meshel; I. Nimri; A. D. Lichtman (Hamekasher); Chaim Fletcher; A. Davidson; A. Mazor (Dan); A. Tzwick; I. Duchovni; L. Cantor. (The Egged (Eshed) representatives participated only in the last stages of the enquiry).

All the Bar-Tal Committee's recommendations were retroactive to 1 April, 1958, and the Histadrut Central Committee was requested to appoint a standing committee to follow up the implementation of the Bar-Tal recommendations. The chairman of the committee, Mr. Bar-Tal, noted that all the recommendations constituted one inseparable unit to be accepted and implemented. On the day that these recommendations are effective, all other existing practices in force, in all or any of the bus co-operatives (except those specifically noted in the report), would be annulled at once, irrespective whether or not these were mentioned in the conclusions. In other words, the conditions of work and emoluments (remuneration) in effect in the future would be only those which were defined in the Bar-Tal Committee's conclusions.

Messrs. A. Davidson (Egged (Eshed)) and D. Lichtman (Hamekasher) expressed their agreement with the committee's conclusions. But they asked that the bus co-operatives be not asked to deviate from existing practices, such as the composition of the basic emolument, supplement for seniority and the special payment for participation in management of the bus co-operative and for overtime pay. They also asked for an increase in the *per diem* allowance for meals, etc.

The chairman's letter accompanying the report notes that the committee, on the

> "basis of the existing price structure and conditions of work, came to the conclusion that as long as the present conditions of work continue, the demand of the bus co-operatives for an increase in emoluments should not be approved. . . . The committee considers its conclusions as a one and indivisible unit and under no circumstances are they to be considered as separate items. Any deviation in this respect will create an imbalance of the internal structure and the results will be contrary to the committee's intentions. To prevent this undesirable development, the committee suggests that a standing official committee should be established to follow up the application of (its conclusions) and to adjudicate any problems which may arise out of its conclusions."

The recommendations of the report were:

1. The basic emolument of all members of the bus co-operatives should be increased from IL.134 to IL.155. This is a basic daily emolument of IL.5·960 for 26 work days a month.
2. In addition to the basic emolument, the members should also receive the following supplementary payments:

   (*a*) Seniority, at the rate of IL.4 per month for every year's service and for a maximum period of ten years[127];
   (*b*) cost of living allowance "in accordance with the general practice in the State";
   (*c*) family allowance of IL.6·640 for a wife, and IL.5·960 for each child up to a maximum of three children, up to the age of 20½ (the age limit used to be 18).

3. The supplementary payment for a member's effort and participation in the management and responsibility of the bus co-operative, is fixed at 20 per cent of the basic emolument; plus cost of living allowance; plus seniority payment; plus family allowance.
4. Every member of a bus co-operative will receive an extra month's emolument (thirteenth month), which will be paid in two equal instalments at Pesach (Passover) and Rosh Hashana (New Year). This thirteenth month's emolument includes the basic emolument, plus the three supplementary payments mentioned in paragraph 2.
5. All members of bus co-operatives who are assigned to managerial positions will receive an extra supplementary payment of IL.35 per month as long as they continue in these assignments.
6. The supplementary payments which Egged (Eshed) and Dan bus co-operatives now pay for effort must be discontinued. But the bus co-operatives may request the respective authorized Histadrut and Government organs to enquire into and to make recommendations on how to increase efficiency and productivity p.m.h. per member.
7. The net work-day will be seven and seven-and-a-half hours for mem-

bers on the intra-urban and inter-urban routes respectively, except on Fridays and the eve of holidays, when the work-day is six and six-and-a-half hours respectively.

8. Members assigned to office or to garage work are subject to the same regulations regarding daily working hours as are applicable to those doing similar work in non-co-operative enterprises.
9. The daily working hours of members who are 50 years of age and over and working as drivers, and of members 55 years of age and over doing other work, is one hour less respectively than the prescribed work-day (per para. 7).
10. Pools of any kind for working hours are not permissible.
11. Overtime is permissible only when this is unavoidable. And overtime pay will be paid to a person only for the actual overtime worked and on the following basis. All overtime premiums are based on the basic wage plus the three supplementary payments listed in (2).

    For the first two hours of overtime the premium is 25 per cent; for overtime in excess of the first two hours the premium is 50 per cent; and for overtime on Saturday night and/or on the nights of the expiration of other holidays, the premium is 75 per cent.

    All members working on the shifts between 10 p.m. and 6 a.m. receive a premium of 25 per cent.

    "If because of work arrangements a driver, in accordance with the provisions of the ordinance on work hours and rest (1951), must interrupt his work for three or more hours, he shall receive extra compensation at the rate of IL.1·500 per work-day."
12. At the beginning of every month the management of every bus co-operative will fix the timetable for work, including overtime for the current month. And the management of every bus co-operative must submit a monthly report to a designated "authorized body" about the concurrent overtime.
13. The annual vacation with pay is:

    (*a*) A minimum of twelve and a maximum of 28 work-days.
    (*b*) Beginning with the fourth year of membership, a member receives an additional two work-days per year.
    (*c*) Members receive the grants for their annual holidays with full pay on the following basis: the first five years, for six-10 days work; from six to nine years—12 days; and from 10 years and over—14 days. The amount of these cash holiday grants, which are to be paid direct to the member, shall be fixed on the basis of the rates prevailing in the rest houses for visitors which Histadrut-sponsored agricultural settlements run.

14. Sick leave with pay shall be on the following basis: One month per year with the right of cumulative sick leave with pay for nine years, subject to a medical certificate from Kupat Cholim.[128]

During the five-year transitory period as from August 1958, a member of a bus co-operative, in case of a prolonged illness, will be allowed a maximum of 60 days' sick leave with pay in advance. Such sick leave shall be deducted in instalments within the five-year transitory period.

Two members of Merkaz Haco-operatzia are to enquire into and submit a report to an authorized committee about the cumulative sick leave which every member of the respective bus co-operative now has to his credit.

15. If because of an accident in the course of work, a member of a bus co-operative does not report for work for three consecutive work-days, he is entitled to pay for only the third day. If the enforced idleness exceeds three consecutive work-days, then the member shall receive full pay for the entire period of his enforced idleness. In the event of semi-incapacity, a bus co-operative will assign the respective member to such work as the Kupat Cholim will prescribe and will not permit the respective disabled member to work overtime.

The bus co-operative will pay to their respective incapacitated members the difference between the equivalent of the full basic emolument, plus the three supplementary payments (authorized in paragraph 2), plus pay for the thirteenth month, and the amount of compensation which the respective member may receive from any source. In the event of a member becoming fully incapacitated, the aforementioned arrangement shall continue for four years. If the disabled member has not withdrawn his participation in the society's capital, he will receive the supplementary payment for investment and participation in management and responsibility of the bus co-operative. Beginning with the fifth year of the member's total incapacity for work, the bus co-operative will pay the equivalent of the basic remuneration, plus the three supplementary payments authorized in paragraph 2, plus the pay for the thirteenth month, less the pension or any other compensation which such member receives from any other sources. The respective members may retain any one time lump sum compensation which he receives from any source. In the event of death as a result of the accident the co-operatives pay to the widow and/or other heirs an amount equivalent to sixty per cent of the total pension to which the member was entitled.

The pension fund transfers to the respective bus co-operative the amount standing to the credit of the incapacitated member whose membership in the pension fund is discontinued. Should the incapacitated member recover and return to work, his membership in the pension fund is renewed and the respective bus co-operative refunds to the pension fund the amount which it received and also pays its participation in the pension fund, together with interest for the respective period, for such a member.

The bus co-operatives shall carry accident insurance for all their respective members.

16. Every bus co-operative will establish a pension fund. The resources of the existing provident funds and other similar funds, which are

to be liquidated, must be transferred to the new pension funds of the respective bus co-operatives. The pension funds of the bus co-operatives must credit the account of every member with the amount of his respective share in the resources of the existing provident and other similar funds.

Every month the bus co-operative will pay into the respective member's account in the new pension fund an amount equivalent to 13¼ per cent of his basic emolument, plus the three supplementary payments referred to in paragraph 2; plus one-twelfth of the pay for the thirteenth month. Every member of a bus co-operative for the present, will assign to the new pension fund three per cent of the total of all the aforementioned items.

The Histadrut Central Committee will seek the recommendation of an actuary about the disposition of the resources of the old provident and other similar funds and also of the new pension funds. One-and-a-half per cent of the participation by the bus co-operative and the respective member in the pension fund respectively plus another 0·4 per cent of these participations will be used for the obligatory payments to the national social insurance. The bus co-operative will recover the 0·4 per cent by withholding the equivalent from all payments which it makes to any of its members. The pension fund will deduct from the pension payable to any member of a bus co-operative the amount which such member receives directly from the national social insurance. All pensions are calculated on the basis of basic emolument, plus the three supplementary payments mentioned in paragraph 2; plus the emolument for the thirteenth month. Every bus co-operative also arranges a death insurance of IL.3,000 for every member, and beginning with the fourth year after the pension fund of the respective bus co-operative has been operating, it begins to pay the premium for the life insurance of every member.

17. Payment to Widows. During the first year after the death of a member the respective bus co-operative pays to the widow, irrespective of cause of death, the full emoluments, including all allowances of the deceased member. After the first year the co-operatives pay to the widow of the deceased member such pension as the pension fund regulations prescribe.
18. Only those members on jobs directly concerned with the actual traffic (drivers, stewards, supervisors, controllers, foremen and wireless operators) shall be entitled to a uniform daily allowance of IL.1·200 for intra-urban and IL.1·600 for inter-urban routes and the respective daily allowances are payable only for the days when the members are on duty. Costs of daily allowances constitute one of the items in the calculation of transportation costs.
19. A bus co-operative may not pay, directly or indirectly or in any manner, any part of any member's personal income tax.
20. Drivers purchasing bus tickets for resale to passengers are entitled to a commission of one-and-a-half per cent on the gross value of the

tickets which they purchased.[129] Drivers who, in addition to driving, also sell bus tickets to passengers are entitled to receive a two per cent commission on their gross purchases of tickets. This commission is considered as compensation for the time which the drivers use for the purchase and sale of tickets and which is not considered as part of the prescribed net work-day.

Only those members who complete their work between 10 p.m. and 6 a.m. may be credited with the equivalent of an additional quarter of an hour as compensation for time lost returning home from work. And in all such cases, the last station is considered as the place of employment.

21. Those members of bus co-operatives called up for any military service in accordance with the law of the country will continue to receive full emoluments, except for pocket-money which a member receives from the Army. When called up for military service the member must assign and/or transfer to his respective bus co-operative all amounts, including allowances for maintenance, which he receives for Army services from the Army and/or any other sources.
22. The committee asks the Histadrut Central Committee to decide whether the bus co-operatives may continue to pay the subscriptions for newspapers for all their members.
23. The bus co-operatives may furnish their members in kind or in cash with the following items: Summer, one pair of shoes; two pairs of trousers; two pairs of socks; three shirts and one hat annually. Winter, a work suit bi-annually. The clothing allowances, if not issued in kind, shall be calculated on the basis of "Ata" (textile mill) prices.
24. The committee has noted that it is the general practice of the bus co-operatives to:

    (*a*) distribute to all their members before Pesach and before Rosh Hashana one bottle of liqueur; brandy (cognac) and wine;
    (*b*) give free travelling passes to the members' wives; and to children until they marry or up to the age of 25, and to two parents of a member;
    (*c*) make special grants of IL.50 for marriage; IL.50 for the birth of a child and IL.25 for a barmitzvah.

25. Every member of a bus co-operative is entitled to the following extra (additional) leave with full pay, viz. one work-day on marriage; the birth of a child; marriage and/or barmitzvah of a child; and, in the case of death, for the prescribed mourning period.

Haaretz, 25 February, 1960. Mr. P. Ginzburg (director-general of the Ministry of Transport) at a news conference in Jerusalem on 24 February, 1960, allegedly said:

"An increase by 16·3 and 12·3 per cent (in bus fares) will go into effect on 16 March, 1960 for the intra- and inter-urban routes respectively.

Government subsidies were discontinued as from the beginning of 1960 and the bus co-operatives will have to carry themselves."

Mr. Ginzburg also allegedly said that the Government had arranged to pay compensation for the operational losses in January and February of 1960 because the bus co-operatives did not receive any Government subsidies and were not permitted to increase the bus fares in these two months. The Government subsidies (IL.5·8 million) during the fiscal year 1958-59 (April to March), according to Mr. Ginzburg, covered nearly nine per cent of the gross expenditures of the bus co-operatives for that year. He estimated Government subsidies to the bus co-operatives for April to December 1958, to be more than IL.6 million, or about eleven per cent of the total expenditures of the bus co-operatives for that period. The bus co-operative Hamekasher (Jerusalem) would continue to receive Government subsidies after 16 March, 1960, when the new fares were effective because otherwise the bus fares would have to be increased by 18-20 per cent (instead of by 16·3 per cent). For Hamekasher, the Government subsidies will cover the gap between the actual increase in costs and the increases in bus fares authorized.

The aforementioned issue of Haaretz carries a report about the press conference in Tel Aviv arranged by Mr. Yitzchak Ben-Aharon, the Minister of Transport, on 24 February, 1960, in connection with "Public Transport Day" organized by the Dan bus co-operative in Tel Aviv. Haaretz reported that the Minister said:

"I hope that during my administration the Knesset will enact legislation which will change public transport into a national asset of the state as has been done in the case of the land, mines and water resources in the country."

The Minister of Transport is also alleged to have said that the proposed Government authority for public transport would lease the assets as a concession and the concessionnaire, an autonomous body, would activate the assets on such conditions which the Government would define. The Minister is also reported to have announced that the question of bus fares would again be considered on 1 January, 1961. He was dissatisfied with the fact that the bus fares are fixed by a Ministry of Transport, whose Minister is a political appointee. Under such conditions there cannot be complete objectivity, that is, freedom from political pressure. "I have come to the conclusion . . . that a body of neutral economists should deal with this question which is the procedure used in fixing the cost of living allowance. We will not revert to the system of subsidies because the services (i.e. bus) should carry themselves."

Excerpts from an article, "The Bus Tariff Mess", the Jerusalem Post, Friday,[130] October 20, 1961:

"Our economic editor analyses the transport co-operatives' demands.

"For some reasons, which are not so mysterious, the facts and figures unearthed by the Public Authority for Bus Tariffs have been kept strictly confidential until now.[131]. . . There is not the slightest justification for such an undemocratic procedure. Public knowledge is not likely to alter data referring to the business year ending March, 1960, on which all the deliberations up to date are based. Nor can the *sub judice* argument be invoked in a case where the Authority's members are supposed to act, not as unbiased judges, but as a committee *safeguarding the public will.* (Original underlined).

". . . In the year 1959-60 Egged's (Eshed's) operating revenue was IL.49m., that of Dan IL.22m., and that of Hamekasher IL.6m. The aggregate amount spent by the Israel public on bus traffic and ancillary services in that year was IL.78m. In the past year Egged's revenue rose to IL.58m. and Dan's to over IL.26m., bringing the aggregate amount to over IL.90m. In the current year the amount will certainly top IL.100m., even if the bus fares are maintained at their present level. Of this total no more than five to eight per cent is accounted for by tourist and other special revenue such as parcel despatch.

"An increase of bus fares by 25 per cent—the lowest limit of the co-operatives' present claims—would burden consumers, therefore, with an additional expenditure of IL.25m. a year. . . .

"The bus fares were stable from September 1956 to March 1960, due to large-scale subsidy payments, which amounted to almost 20 per cent of the co-operatives' traffic proceeds. When these subsidies were discontinued in March, 1960, the fares were increased by an average of 13 per cent. In the beginning of 1961, another increase of 12·5 per cent was approved by the Public Authority as a preliminary measure, subject to subsequent reappraisal. The current rates are therefore already 25·5 per cent higher than two years ago, and approval of the co-operatives' minimum demand would mean a rise by 50 per cent in a period of two years, whide the c.-o.-l. index advanced by only 11 per cent, and the building cost index by about 15 per cent.

The Bank of Israel Report

"A computation in the Bank of Israel report shows that, calculated in stable money terms, revenue per bus kilometre declined by nine per cent, and revenue per bus-seat by five per cent, between 1955 and 1960. This decline, however, must be considered together with an increase of 58 per cent in the total bus kilometrage, and of 48 per cent in the total number of bus-seats, while bus service expenses rose by only 42 per cent, largely due to the change-over from petrol to Diesel engines and to higher labour efficiency. The bus co-operatives' total labour force increased by only about 20 per cent during that period. (The number of the co-operatives' members rose by about 30 per cent, due to the Histadrut's pressure and the number of hired hands by 15 per cent) (parenthesis used in original).

". . . In the case of Egged . . . the report shows that running operational expenses (fuel, tyres, spare parts and so on) amounted to IL.12m. in 1959-60; repairs (outside Egged's own garage) and other operational costs to IL.6m., and depreciation to IL.4·2m. If the office and general expenses are also included, we arrive at IL.24·5m., i.e. just 50 per cent of the revenue of 42 per cent of the expenditure.

"Dr. Ofir, the Authority's deputy chairman, has pointed out, however, that several exaggerations have crept into the above figures due either to improper accounting practices or to a lavish scale of spending which cannot be considered as representing genuine costs, e.g., in computing the depreciation amount and the cost of spare parts, the scrap value of used vehicles and parts has been unduly neglected. Some expenses of a capital nature have been treated as costs.

"In the overheads, over IL.0·25m. was included for advertisements and public relations, another IL.0·25m. for receptions and for staff's cafeterias, almost IL.0·3m. for members' income-tax, and IL.0·2m. for 'sport', 'culture', 'educational fund for members' children', etc. If all these items are taken together, the above cost figures must be reduced by about IL.2m. and to less than 40 per cent of the total expenditure. . . . (original underlined).

Finance Charges

"Another two per cent of Egged's expenditure (IL.1m.) was used in the year under review for 'finance charges', but—Dr. Ofir recommended—this should also be excluded from the service's cost account, because the amount of loans on which this interest was paid (IL.11·5m.) just balances the total of Egged's 'unauthorized' expenditure during the stable fare-period (March, 1956, to December, 1959), of which 40 per cent went on excessive members' emoluments. Had these amounts been kept by the co-operative, argues Dr. Ofir, it would not have been forced to resort to borrowing; if interest must be paid, it should be charged to the members' account, since they profited from the excessive disbursements, and not to the bus passengers.

"The bulk of the expenditure—about IL.34m. (if the above corrections in accounting are duly made) i.e. almost 60 per cent of the total—was made in respect of wages and other labour emoluments of the co-operative's members and hired employees . . . 'The accountants' statement shows that the hired employees received in 1959-60 about IL.7·7m. (namely IL.5·1m. in wages and salaries, IL.1m. in overtime pay and the rest in social benefits).' (Parenthesis used in original.)

Egged Member—IL.10,000

"This leaves the Egged members with about IL.26m., or over IL.10,000 a year per member, of which straight wages accounted for just one-half, overtime pay for one-fifth, and the rest in various other payments in cash and kind. It is, of course, this amount which is the principal bone of contention at present. Already in 1959-60 it accounted for fully 45 per cent of the company's total expenditure, and included about eight per cent (ca. IL.5m.), not approved by the authorities. Since then, however, its relative importance has increased further. For the past year additional wages and some for the hired labour amount to about IL. 0·5m., while over IL.6m. have been claimed for members under various categories. As for the present year, the situation is indicated by the fact that the above figures for members' annual income in 1959-60 equal the amount of the membership admission fee, which has now risen to IL.14,000 (i.e. by 40 per cent in two years). (Parenthesis in the original.)

Clouding the Issue

"The discussion concerning this point has been complicated by references to technical details. . . . Three major points should, however, be kept in mind in this respect.

"Firstly, it is the unauthorized expenditure by the bus co-operatives for the benefit of their members which has resulted in their accounting deficits in recent years. In the case of Egged, for example, the IL.4·2m. 'deficit' of 1959-60 would not have been incurred had the company not included in its expense accounts excessive overtime pay, leave pay, free newspapers, tax payment for members' accounts, interest for members' benefit and similar items. . . .

"Secondly, one important element included in the authorized pay for members is the 20 per cent addition to the ordinary wage (including c.o.l., family and seniority allowances) which members receive on account of 'self-sustained enterprise'. This addition may or may not have been justified when the bus co-operatives were financed by their members' investments, and when a rudimentary competition (involving some risk element) existed at least in the bus traffic. Today, however, the co-operatives' monopoly position is unassailable, and their income is virtually guaranteed by the State, while their members' share in the financing of their assets is negligible. In Egged's case, for example, the IL.28m. assets were financed entirely by loans and other debts to banks, suppliers, and, to a great part, indirectly to the State, with the IL.12·4m. of share capital and reserves completely eaten up by continuous 'deficits' i.e. by unauthorized pay disbursements. Dr. Ofir in his report to the Authority already suggested a renewed discussion of this issue, pointing out that even if one agrees to the members earning a 12 per cent yield on the value of their shares, this would still be much less than what they get under the present system.

"Thirdly, one should bear in mind that the current discussion—though touching upon matters of expenditure—is intended to fix the business tariff, while leaving the co-operatives to manage their financial affairs at their own discretion. The co-operatives are thus left in a position to create facts which the controlling authority cannot altogether neglect. Under such a system, the co-operatives, will naturally get the upper hand in any bargaining. The least that must be done in order to remedy this situation, of course, is to lay down some fixed starting points, such as has been attempted by Dr. Ofir in his analysis of the 1959-60 accounts. Only if a start is made can there be any further progress in clearing up the bus tariff mess."

CHAPTER SIX

Reorganization of the Services

The following are excerpts from the debate at the Mapai Congress of 14 May, 1958 (second session).[132]

Pinchas Lavon (Histadrut general secretary) considered the present organizational structure of bus transport unsuitable for the present needs of the State. This was not meant as a reflection or deprecation of the generally acknowledged heroic and self-sacrificing services of the bus co-operatives and their members. But "it is not permissible for any group of workers to have a monopoly over any vital public or economic service in the state. Just as it is inconceivable that the workers should enjoy a monopoly at the port or over electric power, so it is impossible to permit the present pattern of bus transport to continue. A decisive vein in public and economic life cannot be left to the domination of the . . . members of co-operatives."

Mr. Lavon then quotes his statement made at a meeting of the Histadrut Executive Committee in December 1949, which at the time was discussing the problem of bus transport.

"We can excuse the general tendency to neglect the equipment and the economy, since bus co-operatives always tended to think that their only purpose is the distribution of accumulated resources among their members. We all considered this bad and as a serious matter from the point of view of the economy. But because of the conditions then prevailing we had to put up with it. And for many years we were . . . fully aware of the difficulties and complications created by the use of wage labour, yet we put up with it. . . . But what was possible yesterday is not feasible today. What was justifiable yesterday—from the broad national point of view—is unjustifiable today. It is not a question whether they distributed this or that amount, or whether they did this out of Provident Funds or as housing loans . . . 'the kernel of the sin is that this pattern of organizational structure (i.e. co-operative) permits a hundred, two hundred or five hundred people to be the owners of property which has a basic national value . . .'." He considers the ownership by the workers of such national public services as electricity, railways, ports, and bus transport as "anti-socialistic".

Zeev Onn supported Mr. Lavon, especially in the case of Egged (Eshed) because it is an inter-urban service. It is true that eight years ago

the Histadrut "after a long and serious debate did not accept the proposal for the establishment of a public utility corporation; and . . . the Histadrut urged and made possible the merger of the three inter-urban bus co-operatives into Egged (Eshed). . . . And I must say that the members justified the confidence placed in them. They looked after their economy and its efficient management. And they were able by their management to maintain lower bus fares than in all other countries. . . .[133] But on the other hand they disappointed us in one essential and decisive matter from the social-public point of view, viz., that the supervision (control) of the bus co-operatives failed."

Mr. Onn also dwelt on the continuous distribution by the bus co-operatives of their resources among their members. In spite of its persistent efforts during the last six to seven years, the Histadrut had failed to convince the members of the bus co-operatives that they alone did not have the right to dispose of the funds. Mr. Onn had come to the conclusion that there was no other way than to transfer the inter-urban bus service to a Government-owned or controlled public utility company which would have the full co-operation of the members and the wage workers of the bus co-operatives.

Uri Alpert described the members' approach as "a dangerous social and public conception". He asked for a partnership of the Government, Chevrat Haovdim, and the members and wage workers of the bus co-operative. The admission of any other partners into the public utilities transport company should be subject to the agreement of the Mapai Central Committee.

E. Hendel (member of Egged (Eshed) management) complained that the various Mapai bodies dealing with bus transportation never asked for the opinion of their colleagues (Mapai members) on the governing bodies of Egged (Eshed). Nobody could deny the relatively greater efficiency of the bus co-operative compared with other patterns of organization "in the execution of work; maintenance of the property and in minimizing waste since the members regard themselves as the owners and, therefore, responsible for the undertaking." He attributed the deficiencies prior to that to "objective factors" and described the improvements during the last three or four years. There was still much to be done in the way of improvement. He referred to the multiple control of every aspect of the bus co-operatives activities; and noted that the only outstanding problem was that of basic emolument for members, which was last fixed in 1952. He emphatically denied that the bus co-operatives deviated from the Histadrut decisions during the six years, but during the last year the bus co-operatives could reduce the tension of their members only by deviating from the Histadrut decisions. For this the Histadrut must share the blame since it had not found a solution for the problem of the basic emolument for members. On the basis of experience in other nationalized undertakings, he thought that a change in the organizational pattern of bus transportation would reduce the efficiency and productivity, etc., of the members and the non-members of the bus co-operatives. He considered Mr. Lavon's proposal "as a *de facto* liquidation of the bus co-operatives in particular, and in the course of time also the weakening of the WPSTS movement in general". He cautioned against haste and urged further negotiations.

Y. Ritov called for unequivocal self-criticism and urged a thorough enquiry into the concentration of power in a very small group—the danger of "one ruler . . . I am for a thorough house cleaning reaching the highest level ('floor')." There should be a second study to find out why "infatuation" for and a positive attitude to the co-operative pattern in general has vanished. Histadrut-sponsored credit co-operatives have nearly all been liquidated; its sponsored housing co-operatives are on their last legs; the Histadrut-sponsored consumers co-operatives are next in line; and the process may even reach the kibbutz sector. The WPSTS movement,

> "to which I am closest, is on the operating table and the surgeons do not like the body which is under their scalpels." They say that "Merkaz Haco-operatzia is under the complete control of the transportation and service societies. It is also possible to say "that the Histadrut Executive Committee is under the complete dictatorship (authority) of those from Solel Boneh and Hamashbir. . . . In the course of tens of years the Histadrut has invested only IL.200,000 in WPSTS, all in the purchase of shares of Kupat Haco-operativim. And half this amount represents profits from the WPSTS."

According to Mr. Ritov the proposal to establish

> "a bus transport company for the benefit of the public" was discussed for some months by various committees and "between various people." Yet neither "the members of the bus co-operatives who belong to Mapai or the head of the Transport Division of Mapai who is acting for Merkaz Haco-operatzia and Chevrat Haovdim, have been consulted."

This individual is a member of Mapai and also of the Mapai Merkaz. Mr. Pinchas Lavon interceded: "Can you substantiate this statement?" Mr. Ritov replied: "Yes," and he continued by saying that nobody even discussed this matter with him except about a formal reply which had to be made to some items which appeared in the press.

P. Lavon: "Did nobody meet you and Goren?"

Mr. Ritov replied:

> "Nobody spoke with me and I am head of the division for transportation co-operatives as the Chevrat Haovdim representative." He noted that his original proposal was that the Histadrut and the bus co-operatives should be equal partners in the public utility bus transportation

> corporation. But now he suggested "a partnership of the State, the Histadrut, etc." Mr. Lavon, when quoting from his own statement at the meeting of the Histadrut Executive Committee in December 1949, omitted the following sentence: "Best of all from every point of view would be if the entire property of the bus co-operatives could be transferred to the Histadrut. I also would compromise on a 51 or 50 per cent share for the Histadrut." Of course Mr. Lavon was entitled to change his opinion. Mr. Ritov then referred to his statement at the December 1949 meeting, "I am for a partnership between the bus co-operatives and the Histadrut. I discussed this frequently with the bus co-operatives and they were on the verge of agreeing."

Mr. Ritov was inclined to think that the bus co-operatives would accept this proposal now. Either the Histadrut agree to a partnership with the bus co-operatives and not with "the members of the bus co-operatives", or it would not participate at all in such a public bus transportation corporation.

Mr. Ritov at a later session of this Mapai Congress, made the following personal declaration:

> "Mr. P. Lavon, answering my question, stated that he was not responsible for the reports in 'Haaretz' and other newspapers about his proposal for the public ownership of the bus transport services. Actually eight years ago Mr. Lavon had proposed public ownership of bus transportation. I told him that basically I accept the proposal, but we should discuss the plan. I also told him that I am for a partnership limited to the Histadrut and its sponsored bus co-operatives, but we will discuss this further in a special conversation. At the suggestion of G. Josephtal,* I persistently proposed that the meeting should be held; but it did not take place. This was the only negotiation between the head of the division for co-operative transportation of Merkaz Haco-operatzia (i.e. Mr. Ritov) and the Histadrut about the fate of the bus co-operatives and the service societies."

The following resolution of the Egged (Eshed) management on 1 July, 1958, is found in L'Chaveireinu (July 1958):

> "The management of Egged (Eshed) sees no reason for changing the structure of the bus co-operatives and it is opposed to entering into any kind of partnership. The management decides to inaugurate a campaign among the public and the public institutions, to explain the advantages, from the point of view of the public and the State, of continuing the co-operative bus transportation system, and that a change in the organizational structure will impair the rights and usefulness of the undertaking."

Davar (22 July, 1958) reports on an excursion of journalists to Upper Galilee on 21 July, 1958, in which members of the management of Egged (Eshed) and representatives of the Ministry of Defence participated.

Z. Weiser is reported to have belittled the claim that the proposal of the Histadrut General Secretary could "resolve the transportation problem in the country or bring about improvements or relief." Mr. Weizer is further reported to have said that under the conditions in Israel there is no substitute for the co-operative structure (presumably of bus transportation) which has proved its effectiveness during all the years of its existence. In answer to journalists' questions, Mr. Y. Goren, the director of Egged (Eshed) public relations department and "other members of the management", allegedly said that the co-operative Egged (Eshed) "continuously integrates members from the ranks of the wage workers on the basis of their personal suitability."

Mr. Eliyahu's article (L'Chaveireinu, 15 July, 1958) notes that the proposals at the Mapai Congress "present serious dangers for a number of economic bodies in the country, including those for public transportation". He considers the present trend as a revival of a similar state of thinking among certain Histadrut circles to turn over the transport services to the Government and to the Municipalities. "This dangerous approach preaches that the time is past for chalutziut, voluntary effort, and self-production; the Government will supply everything. . . ."

The article then notes that "over a long period all the articles published have a political slant and an undisguised purpose to magnify the inefficiency of their bus services". The closing paragraph of Mr. Eliyahu's article castigates those who argue that Histadrut and Government supervision is not enough.

> "And even if we accept this assumption as being correct, are the bus co-operatives responsible for this? There is not another body which has been or is subject to so much control, auditing and supervision by so many bodies (auditing departments of the Histadrut and Merkaz Hacooperatzia; Chevrat Haovdim; the Government auditor; the Ministry of Transport, etc.). . . . We do not object to control and to suggestions for mending weaknesses. We will accept and carry out these to the extent that we find the reforms logical and beneficial. But under no circumstance will we willingly agree to destroy the hard labour of many years. . . . And . . . no body or institution can carry out anything against our will. . . ."

Yitzchak Goren (head of public relations for Egged (Eshed)) in the same issue of L'Chaveireinu (15 July, 1958, pp. 5-6) deals mainly with the question of public control. The opening paragraph reads: "Not even the sworn adversaries of Egged (Eshed) have ever complained about the inefficiency of its activities. All agree that the organization is flexible and efficient. The productivity is high; significant improvements have occurred in the traffic arrangements."

He quotes the Minister of Transport in the course of the debate in the Knesset on 24 March, 1958, on the budget of his ministry as having said: "During recent years Government control over the bus co-operatives has grown and encompasses financial, management and equipment services."

According to Mr. Goren, the monopoly which Egged (Eshed) enjoys *de facto* is confined to the routes to unpopulated sectors with bad roads, etc. On the profitable routes Egged (Eshed) must meet the competition of the railway, whose deficits the taxpayers cover, and the inter-urban limousine (taxi services). The Government subsidies also covered the operational deficits of the bus co-operatives.

Referring to a leader in Haaretz, of 20 June, 1958, on "Government Supervision, not Nationalization", which it reprinted, L'Chaveireinu notes that the general secretary of the Histadrut proposed a jointly owned public utility bus corporation because he did not want the bus co-operatives to be the sole arbiters of the country's bus service. The Haaretz leader also thinks that it is not right for "the Histadrut alone to accept the full authority of any service on which the entire community relies and notes that the new company, which the Histadrut general secretary suggested should replace the bus co-operatives, would enjoy the monopoly. In view of the "prevailing opposition among wide circles in the community to the present monopoly, the leader adds, this may be more politically expedient for the Histadrut and the Mapai. But, for the individual, it is unimportant whether the monopolies are the bus co-operatives, the Histadrut, the Government or the large municipalities. If a bus transport monopoly is bad, changing the monopolist does not alter the fact that a monopoly exists. What the public, generally speaking, objects to is that the monopolist exploits his position, not the monopoly *per se.* True, notes the leader in Haaretz, there are many advantages, technical, administrative and financial, to centralization which, *per se*, need not be harmful to the public.

> "There is no doubt that the bus co-operatives basically meet the needs of the consumers, and that there is no need for a change of ownership in order to correct such deficiencies. . . ." If the members of the bus co-operatives become a minority shareholding group in a governmental public corporation "there is no certainty that they will continue to maintain the same degree of concern and interest over the vehicles, etc."

The "Haaretz" leader adds that the unsatisfactory aspects of the bus services could be resolved if the Ministries of Finance and of Transport controlled and checked more stringently the financial reports which the bus co-operatives submit. This would enable the Government to fix an equitable policy with regard to the "pay envelope" of the members of the bus co-operatives. It is not likely that the mere change of organizational structure would decrease the extent of Government financial assistance required for the renewal of the vehicles, equipment, etc., or that there would be fewer strikes.

L'Chaveireinu (15 July, 1958) reprints a leader from the evening daily Maariv, which alleges that the Histadrut "favours the new plan" because:

1. It believes that the bus co-operatives distributed "millions of pounds among their members" which should have been used for vehicle improvements, etc.

2. It is wrong for any one group to have a monopoly over such a vital public service as bus transport.
3. Experience has shown that control alone is insufficient "to resolve the problem".
4. A joint partnership of the Government, public bodies and the bus co-operatives will better ensure the public interest.

The Maariv leader then proceeds to answer the aforementioned reasons mainly by quoting Mr. A. Davidson, a member of the management, and the heads of the finance department of Egged (Eshed).

(*a*) "No enterprise managed by wage workers will give the public the same advantages (such as relatively low fares; high standard maintenance, etc.) as one managed by independent workers" (workers who own and manage the enterprise).

(*b*) The internal regulations about conditions of work in the co-operative provides for a more rational division of work; fuller exploitation of manpower; and a higher productivity per man-hour. And this minimizes the need for overtime pay.

(*c*) Reports about the gross monthly emoluments for members of Egged (Eshed) (IL.700 a month) are exaggerated. "Every organized worker of every enterprise receives fringe payments" said Mr. Davidson, "but there isn't any hue or cry". And, according to Mr. Davidson, the Histadrut insisted on Egged (Eshed) discontinuing the payment of IL.150 overtime pay to members per month although this amounted to less than the cost of an extra full time staff.

L'Chaveireinu (July 1958) also reprints a leader from "Herut" (11 June, 1958), "In the Shadow of Nationalization".

The introductory paragraph of this leader admits the shortcomings of the bus co-operatives in the past and praises the considerable improvements during the last year. It describes the proposal of the Histadrut general secretary as "the New Deal" and as a threat of nationalization. It asks why the general secretary deals only with this monopoly and does not speak about the other Histadrut-sponsored monopolies. The main reason for singling out the bus co-operatives, according to the leader, is because

> "the members of these co-operatives no longer accept unreservedly the authority of the Mapai . . . this was reflected in the strike which Egged (Eshed) and Dan declared and which the Histadrut opposed. . . . Under the prevailing atmosphere in the country it is premature to talk about the nationalization of bus services."

The leader refers to the other nationalized undertakings in difficulties, such as the Potash Company, the copper smelting works "Timna", which must be saved, and to Mr. Davidson's statements that

(*a*) the Government subsidies (of Egged (Eshed)) do not exceed two per cent of their gross expenditures.

(*b*) The co-operative decided in October 1957, to increase the remuneration of its members by IL.54 per month, since the Histadrut had not acted on the thrice repeated request to associate its (Egged (Eshed)) representatives with the Histadrut Committee on Wages Policy.

The longest (pp. 57-59) of the documents (in L'Chaveireinu, July 1958) is the reply of the public relations department of Egged (Eshed) to Eliezer Hacohen's article in Al Hamishmar (18 June, 1958). The introductory paragraph of Mr. Goren's reply describes Mr. Hacohen's article as "one more" of "the exaggerated accusations" against the bus co-operatives. It was not what it purported to be, viz., "a concrete and practical analysis" of the bus transportation problems. Mr. Goren, however, agreed with Mr. Hacohen's closing remarks "that the picture is not complete and all inclusive and that there is room for debate and more clarity. . . ." While he described Mr. Hacohen's solution as "defeatist", he accepted Dr. Walter Preuss' explanations about the "sins of youth" of the bus co-operatives during the pre-State period, such as the distribution of their resources among members which created a "certain mishandling of its assets" (e.g. the vehicles and other property).

> "During that particular period (i.e. its infancy) bus co-operatives were the only possible pattern of organization, because there was no possibility of attracting private capital for a branch which was subject to potential dangers, both for its property and workers. With honour and success the bus co-operatives assumed the national task of ensuring the Yishuv with its own transport services under all circumstances. And not infrequently did they (i.e. the bus co-operatives) save Jewish communities under conditions which involved considerable risk for their members and their property. . . ."

Mr. Goren writes that most of the Yishuv has a deeply entrenched "anti-co-operative" conception which helped to embitter the atmosphere against the services of the bus co-operatives. Generally speaking, the Yishuv ignored such factors as the rapid and large increase in population; difficulties in acquiring vehicles and spare parts because of the shortage of and therefore, control of foreign exchange, etc. It seemed to Mr. Goren that somebody was interested in intensifying these preconceived prejudices.

Competition with taxis, railways, and other media, according to Mr Goren

> "constitute one of the main causes of the chronic operational deficit shown on the accounts of the bus co-operatives, and the reason why the Ministry of Transport has appropriated millions to cover part of these".

The Ministry of Transport is delaying the payment of the subsidies, because the bus co-operatives decided to increase the monthly emoluments of their members. This has increased operational deficits. Does Mr. Hacohen think that the transfer of ownership of the bus co-operatives to another body, will deter the members and "workers" from demanding higher wages? Mr. Goren then discusses the extent and effectiveness of the control by Government and other bodies. This is almost a verbatim repetition of other articles, etc., that concludes with the question: "Would a change in ownership change much in this respect?"

Mr. Goren refutes Mr. Hacohen's imputation that the co-operative ethos, in general, and the Co-operative Societies Ordinance in Israel in particular, proscribe the use of wage labour. Mr. Goren does not deny the seriousness of the global and relative increase of wage labour in the bus co-operatives. He attributes the ineffectiveness of the counter-measures against the use of wage labour, to the seasonal variations in load traffic; the scarcity of holders of AA bus driving licences who can meet the inflexible high standards of Egged (Eshed); and the strict enforcement and the literal interpretation of equal remuneration for all members, irrespective of the physical disabilities etc., which develop among the members in the course of time. Referring to Mr. Hacohen's suggestion that the shares of the bus co-operative should be negotiable and subject to the law of demand and supply, Mr. Goren notes that the Co-operative Societies' Ordinance and co-operative principles proscribe this.

Finally, referring to Mr. Hacohen's suggestion about nationalization and improvements, Mr. Goren notes that the nationalization of the Palestine Electric Corporation was followed by a doubling of the electricity rates. He asks what guarantee there is that bus fares will not be increased appreciably after the nationalization of the bus services and without any corresponding improvement of the services.

> "The present pattern of bus service is the most convenient for both the public and those working in the co-operatives. For years the members of the bus co-operatives have been subjected to a most serious incitement and smear campaign. The member (of a bus co-operative) carries a load of trying work and a nervous strain under most difficult conditions of work. And the fringe benefits which he enjoys are no better than those . . . which many skilled wage workers in various branches receive. Yet the members prefer a co-operative framework. . . . Turning bus services upside down will not breed any good or comfort to the public at large and it is almost certain that the results will be bad."

Shituf (August-September 1958, p. 4) reports that Chevrat Haovdim appointed a committee to examine in detail the proposal for nationalizing bus transport. This committee would submit its recommendations to the Chevrat Haovdim management, and would undoubtedly appreciably influence the fate of the bus co-operatives and "in one form or another also will influence the entire WPSTS movement".

The members of the committee were Messrs. A. Khoushi (Chairman—Mayor of Haifa and head of Haifa Labour Council); U. Alpert (Chevrat Haovdim); Y. Arnon (Director-General, Ministry of Finance); Baram (Secretary, Labour Council, Jerusalem); Goren (Merkaz Haco-operatzia);

Eliezer Hacohen (Mapam, member Kibbutz Beit Alfa); Z. Hering (member, Histadrut Central Committee); Zitelni (executive committee of the labour council, Tel Aviv); I. Yalon (executive committee of the labour council, Haifa); Surkis (chairman of local council, Kfar Saba); A. Tzwick (Merkaz Haco-operatzia); R. Tzimand (Haoved Hatzioni); and Y. Ritov (Merkaz Haco-operatzia). The first two paragraphs of the letter of appointment sent to every member of the Committee are given below.

"Chevrat Haovdim secretariat decided to set up a public utility company for bus transport which will include the Government, local authorities, the Histadrut, etc., and the members and the permanent non-member workers of the bus co-operatives.

"The committee set up to implement the decision will enquire into the procedure for setting up this public service corporation and clarify the problem with the Government; obtain the views of the members and of the permanent workers of the bus co-operatives; and will formulate and submit a proposal to Chevrat Haovdim."

The following are extracts from a report on the conversation between representatives of Merkaz Haco-operatzia and the bus co-operatives, 2 and 14 July, 1958. "The Co-operative Transportation and its Future", with Y. Ritov, presiding.

A. Hochman (Egged (Eshed)) referred to the chairman's brief and vague opening remarks and asked Mr. Ritov whether he wished to hear "just talk" or real facts.

Mr. Ritov replied that without any intention to restrict the speakers, the exchange of views would be fruitful if the participants made practical suggestions about the future course of action.

S. Atzmon (Dan) noted that those present were representatives elected by their respective bus co-operatives. Irrespective of what the others may do, he could not express any view without first discussing the question with Dan's Council. Mr. Ritov's statement that "this is a frank (open) conversation" should not exclude the right not to speak. It would be preferable "from various points of view" for the representatives of the bus co-operatives to first discuss the questions between themselves and with the members of their respective bus co-operatives.

A. D. Lichtman (Hamekasher) observed that "ostrich politics is sometimes useful." Therefore, he was prepared to facilitate the work of the committee which Chevrat Haovdim had appointed to report on the changes in the organizational pattern of bus transport. He felt certain that the committee after it had studied the material "would surrender its mandate". The views of the members of the bus co-operatives were so clear that there was no need for their representatives at this meeting first to submit the question to their Councils which would only confirm the members' reply of "No". "The members and we want to continue the bus co-operatives which we established at the Histadrut's request."

L. Cantor (Egged (Eshed)) questioned whether those who convened the meeting were authorized to do so. The terms of reference of the Chevrat Haovdim committee were clear. Even though this committee and all its members were bound by the Chevrat Haovdim decision, every bus co-operative could submit its views and supporting data. This meeting could discuss only one question, viz., "how to put into effect the decisions of the Chevrat Haovdim secretariat".

A. Tzwick (Merkaz Haco-operatzia) disagreed with Mr. Cantor's doubts about the authority to convene the meeting. The decision of Chevrat Haovdim was still under discussion and had not yet been confirmed. Even after the Chevrat Haovdim decision was confirmed, the bus co-operatives should meet to fight and not to discuss the decisions. Those invited to the meeting were experienced and knowledgeable people, and everyone should express his and not his respective co-operative's views. It was, he thought, regrettable that such a meeting on a larger scale was not convened before Chevrat Haovdim's opinion and decision had crystallized. He criticized the assumption "that the Chevrat Haovdim committee will be unsuccessful and nothing will be changed". He personally disagreed with the Chevrat Haovdim decision because it must lead to the disappearance of bus co-operatives. But the bus co-operatives must be prepared to carry out the Histadrut's decision even if they disagreed with it; for if they opposed any changes in their organizational pattern, then "we have missed the bus". He thought that "Egged (Eshed) is largely responsible for the proposal to transfer bus services to another authority". If the bus co-operatives had really been sincere in their declarations that they are ready to accept, co-operate and help to carry out genuine control by the Histadrut, they would not have reached this state of affairs. It is an illusion that a change in the person of the general secretary of the Histadrut or of the Chevrat Haovdim would lead to a "*status quo ante*". The question was not whether changes were needed but "how to make the changes". It should not be impossible to devise the suitable legal pattern for the new organization. And "if the bus co-operatives will submit constructive proposals, it is unlikely that Chevrat Haovdim Committee would ignore these."

S. Goren thought the meeting would be worth while if it convinced only one of the representatives, "as for example Mr. Lichtman", that it is no longer possible for the bus co-operatives to continue without any changes in their pattern. "Whether the bus fare will increase or decrease by a *grush* (0·6 of a cent) is no longer the important question. At some later date the historian will decide and distribute the blame. They must discuss 'tomorrow and not yesterday'."

There is almost unanimity of opinion that the bus co-operatives cannot remain the sole owners of the bus services. In the past, the bus co-operatives accepted the Histadrut authority only when it suited them. Mr. Goren states that as a member of Chevrat Haovdim Committee he is interested in the opinion of this meeting about the implementation of the plan of Chevrat Haovdim.

Mr. Maliskovitch asked Mr. Goren: "Why did you not ask for the opinion of the bus co-operatives before 'the decisive verdict?'"

Mr. Goren referred Mr. Maliskovitch to the Egged (Eshed) Council discussion about its unilateral decision to increase the members' emoluments.

A. Davidson (Egged (Eshed)) replied that the bus co-operatives did not agree to any change in their structure because the members "do not wish to become wage labourers . . . we accept the co-operative as our way of life . . . we introduced equality in everything, also in emoluments. . . ." He then repeated the allegations that the Histadrut had failed to use effectively its right of control and that its representatives, perhaps not intentionally, were persistently absent from those Management Committee meetings which discussed questions relating to Merkaz Haco-operatzia and to Noa. It was his conviction that no other branch justified its existence as much as the bus co-operatives "in every way and in every form, from the point of view of efficiency, security and supplying a public service". He asked why the bus co-operatives should not object to decisions taken for political reasons, which they considered erroneous. They had considerable experience in bus transport and therefore it was their duty to state frankly and unequivocally that they opposed any changes in the bus co-operatives pattern which were "not in the interest of the State, the public and the members". They refused to share the responsibility for the bus service with others; all deficiencies in the future would be ascribed to their "bitterness, etc." He was especially bitter about the persistent threats to which the members of the bus co-operatives are subjected, viz.

> "if you don't like it you may go your own way and we will give you bonds as compensation for the assets of the bus co-operatives which the company will take over. . . . Wage workers in the garages of the bus co-operatives may strike when the co-operatives refused their requests for a glass of milk gratis or because they desire to start work at 9 a.m. and not at 7.30 a.m. But the members of bus co-operatives may not strike 'to protect their vital interests'."[134]

I. Maliskovitch disagreed with Mr. Goren's belief that they must accommodate themselves to the decision of Chevrat Haovdim. He did not recall any conference which discussed the changes in the pattern or the elimination of the bus co-operatives. The negative attitude towards the bus co-operatives started in 1948 when the question of the "reforms" was raised. It was not true that the co-operatives made any major decisions such as fixing bus fares, timetables, etc., without the approval of the Government and the Histadrut.

L. Cantor (Egged (Eshed)) stated that ten years ago Mr. Lavon, who at the time was general secretary of the Histadrut, suggested the plan which Chevrat Haovdim had now approved and refuted the allegation that Chevrat Haovdim and/or Mr. Lavon now pressed this because "the members have misbehaved (are not good boys)." Mr. Lavon argues that the concentration of the ownership of the bus transportation in the hands of the co-operatives is a luxury which the State cannot afford. Mr. Cantor admits that he has always urged that bus transport service must be in the hands of a public body, and asks the bus co-operatives to accept in principle the Chevrat Haovdim decision.

A. D. Lichtman (Hamekasher) considered it strange that the founders of the WPSTS movement at a meeting in a building belonging to the WPSTS (Merkaz Haco-operatzia) were asking meekly but unequivocally for the liquidation of the bus co-operatives. He described the allegation that the bus co-operatives alone are the masters of bus transport as an "unadulterated lie".

Mr. Yavniel thought Mr. Lavon had underestimated the difficulties. On the other hand, Messrs. Davidson and Lichtman had oversimplified the question. The bus co-operatives did not accept unequivocally all the supervision. On the contrary, they opposed and completely disregarded the supervision and unjustly accused the Histadrut for neglecting them. "I believe in authority accompanied by financial participation."

Z. Weiser thought that the bus co-operatives should welcome the establishment of a joint authority since "this would be a defensive wall for them and would free you from the need of haggling about the cost plus plan and subsidy system. It was a pity that the bus co-operatives did not support Mr. Ritov who was the first to suggest a fifty-fifty partnership between the Histadrut and the bus co-operatives".

A. Hochman asked: "Are we still living in the age when they marry the girl without asking her?" With all due respect to Mapai and the Histadrut, he was a member of both, he rejected a decision taken without even asking the opinion of those who were most directly concerned. One can be just as extreme in introducing innovations as in preserving fossilization. His opposition to the changes of the pattern of bus co-operatives was not based on "love" or "sentiment;" or on reward due for past performances and good behaviour. He could not understand why Mr. Lavon thought that "the present system at times is in conflict with the State's needs and that it no longer meets the needs of the State."

Everyone agreed that the bus co-operatives had succeeded; continued to provide cheap and efficient services; and that they answered the call to open additional routes whenever and wherever they were needed. Does the Histadrut question the accounts and other data which the bus co-operatives submit? As wage workers of the new corporation they will not hesitate to strike. But, as owners of their respective bus co-operatives the members will think twice before striking and losing revenue and the public's confidence.

E. Hendel praised Merkaz Haco-operatzia for calling this meeting and supported those who do not accept any pattern other than a co-operative "which for us is a form of life no less than is the kibbutz for its members. Perhaps 'we sinned' in increasing the emoluments of the members". But is this "sin" a reason for eradicating the bus co-operatives? Does not our decision to discontinue the additional emoluments prove that we accept "authority"? He asked why the Histadrut does not liquidate kibbutzim and its other sponsored "co-operative sectors" that have sinned.

Y. Kitzis (Merkaz Haco-operatzia) admonished the attitude of the bus co-operatives at the meeting. ". . . Your behaviour helps those who wish to carry out the decisions. You should submit your proposal. It is not enough to say that everything is in order. There were many mistakes and many sins. . . . Prepare clear proposals about control, wages and about authority (of the Histadrut). And circulate these among the institutions and the public." This will help, in the event of the bus co-operatives appealing against the decision of Chevrat Haovdim, in the first instance to the Histadrut Executive Committee and also, if necessary, to the Histadrut Council.

Y. Borowsky thought that it was an "illusion" to think that the members of the bus co-operatives will approve the Chevrat Haovdim decision. The liquidation of the bus co-operatives will lead to the disappearance of the entire Histadrut-sponsored co-operative movement. He accused the leaders of Merkaz Haco-operatzia of abandoning the front. As members of the Histadrut, the bus co-operatives and their members should carry their fight to the rank and file of the Histadrut. He was sure that the Histadrut will not use force to kill the bus co-operatives.[135]

N. Yisraeli agreed with those who thought that they had lost the first battle but not the war. However, he regretted the sharpness of Mr. Hochman's reaction to Mr. Yavniel's suggestion about a partnership between the bus co-operatives and the Histadrut. There is room for a free debate about the pattern of bus co-operatives most suitable for the nurture in which they live. Neither the Histadrut, the party (Mapai), nor Mr. Lavon criticized the "efficiency, organizational ability", of the co-operatives; therefore why debate these questions? He criticized those leaders of Merkaz Haco-operatzia who were sure that the impact of a change in the pattern of the bus co-operatives would lead to their *de facto* extinction and eventually to the disappearance of the entire Histadrut-sponsored co-operative movement. Mr. Yisraeli thought that Mr. Lavon, in insisting on the participation of the workers in the management of the respective Histadrut-sponsored non-co-operative undertakings, was *de facto* furthering the co-operative movement. "True this is co-operation without ownership (of means of production), without responsibility and without soul." He accused the Histadrut of "loving co-operation but hating the co-operatives". He noted:

1. The rules which were prepared when the bus co-operatives were small, need basic changes to meet the requirements of a bus co-operative which has thousands of members.
2. The scope of the Government and of Histadrut authority should be more clearly defined.
3. Only a merger of Egged (Eshed) with Dan and Hamekasher "from wall to wall" will enable the bus co-operatives to speak one common language.

Y. Ritov closed the meeting 14 July, 1958, with the following statement:

"Merkaz Haco-operatzia decided to convene the meeting for an exchange of views. At a more or less suitable time we may convene a meeting of the Council. I am not worried or concerned very much when this meeting will be held."

A one-page unsigned article "Co-operation without Equality" (Hameshek Hashitufii, 17 October, 1958, pp. 392-3) refers to the report of the "Bar-Tal Wage Committee". It states that the report would abolish equal emolument for all members, a practice which dates from the organization of the first bus co-operatives. The public never really knew the exact amount of emolument paid to a member, and the rank and file of members of the bus co-operatives were not aware of all their rights, etc., "which the management cooked up for them". *De facto*, the bus co-operatives have a monopoly, and the users of the buses have to pay for every increase in the members' emoluments. The users of the buses also provide the resources of the provident and pension funds which the three bus co-operatives that merged into Egged (Eshed) have distributed among their members. The Bar-Tal Wage Committee's recommendations will make it unnecessary for the members of the bus co-operatives to contribute anything to the provident and pension funds of Egged (Eshed) which replace the three funds that were liquidated. And for "tactical" reasons the Bar-Tal Wage Committee also had to retain such fringe benefits as allowances for clothing, special paid holidays, grants for members' children on various occasions, etc.[136] which, the article notes, workers in no other undertakings enjoy. The Bar-Tal Wage Committee justifies its action by the general thesis that one must never surrender "any fringe benefits". Having achieved such fringe benefits, the article notes, has made the members of the bus co-operatives dizzy with success and has generated a clear tendency among the members to remove the shackles of Merkaz Haco-operatzia and the "Histadrut chains". Therefore, Chevrat Haovdim began to question whether there was any *raison d'être* for the bus co-operatives to continue to enjoy the Histadrut's "honoured patronage". The possibilities of Chevrat Haovdim exercising authority and control over the Histadrut non-co-operative undertakings are greater than those over the bus co-operatives whose members have been estranged from "economic and social authority". This is the genesis of the idea of a public utility transportation corporation as a substitute for the bus co-operatives. It has been suggested that this is only a tactical step, a means of exerting pressure which enabled the Histadrut to re-establish its authority over the bus co-operatives. But, what is disconcerting, is that Chevrat Haovdim has not yet devised an effective type of control of the social and economic aspects of Histadrut-sponsored co-operatives which could help to maximize their economic usefulness and their returns from the investment and yet preserve the labour social code.

"Co-operation, and especially WPSTS, has experienced a serious economic setback and a social contamination." This gave co-operation a bad name and brought on the agitation to give the co-operatives a "bill of divorce". The "Bar-Tal Report" has shown the need for a more basic investigation. "One blood transfusion will not resurrect the WPSTS Movement."

The article adds that the Bar-Tal Wage Committee, by abolishing the principle of equal emoluments for all members, irrespective of the type of work, has removed the last vestige of the social aspects of co-operation in the bus co-operatives. This is "an ideological defeat" though it is undoubtedly an important "strategic" achievement. The arrangement will not appreciably help to change the bus co-operative into a genuine Histadrut mould; sooner or later there will be no escape from the necessity to change over unequivocally from the co-operative to the administrative form of a Histadrut undertaking. A revival of proposals for the nationalization or for the participation of public bodies in the bus service *must be considered as a real possibility*. (Original underlined).

Yaakov Ben Ari's article[137] does not differentiate between commercial companies and public utility corporations in which the Government and/or local authorities participate and in which the returns on shares are limited. He considers that

"the 'question of questions' is whether the various blemishes (such as wage labour; unauthorized distribution of funds among members; financial manipulations; insufficient consideration of the public interest, etc.) which were uncovered in the bus co-operatives are embedded in their pattern (organizational structure) and therefore are unavoidable."

Generally speaking, the positive aspects in the bus co-operatives are no less, if not more, than their misdemeanours. While not condoning the general strike (1956) of the bus co-operatives, this was the only strike in their 30 years of operations. Unlike the stoppage of the railway services "several weeks ago", the strike of the bus co-operatives was preceded by prolonged negotiations. A public corporation owned bus system will not make the bus services *per se* less monopolistic. There also are no grounds for assuming that there will be less "protection" (patronage), and smaller operational deficits in a public transport corporation owned jointly by the Government and the local authorities than there has been in the nationalized railways.

Anybody who offers a so-called "ideal solution" for bus transportation is deceiving the public. Mr. Ben Ari doubts whether the mere fact that the Government, local authorities and the Histadrut held 60 per cent of the voting shares in a public transport corporation, would in itself eliminate internal strifes and conflicting interests in such a diversified economy as bus transport. The bus co-operatives having a 40 per cent interest can become a serious and troublesome factor. If the intention of the architects of the plan is to convert the bus co-operatives into "Government tools", this is bound to create unexpected repercussions in the economy and among the public. Since the bus co-operatives would not voluntarily agree to relinquish their present status, the Knesset would be obliged to enact special legislation which would be strongly tainted with nationalization and create apprehension among not a few of the Mapai leaders.

Mr. Ben Ari then referred to the Histadrut's approval of the Bar-Tal Wage Committee's recommendation that the bus co-operatives must replace equal basic emolument and fringe benefits for all members with a graded scale of basic emoluments based on type of work, seniority, number of dependents, etc. The bus co-operatives would display less rigid ("holier than the Pope") attitudes towards equal basic remuneration for all if the members were not suspicious that the purpose of the Histadrut was to create a social stratification within the bus co-operatives. The Histadrut, on the other hand, was confident that after the Knesset elections (September 1959) Egged (Eshed) also would follow the example of Dan and Hamekasher and accept the Bar-Tal Wage Committee's proposals. Egged (Eshed) was aware of the important role which the Government and the Histadrut can and do play in making available financing for the bus co-operatives.

Mr. Ben Ari labelled the changes which the Khoushi Committee suggested as "far reaching but not far sighted". The plan changed the members of the bus co-operatives into shareholder workers who receive a return on their investments and it does not really insist on the admission of the wage workers as members by the bus co-operatives. Since the liquidation of the bus co-operatives already had been decreed, it was better for the members to retrieve their investments and not to accept any responsibility for the management of bus transport in the future.

The following is an extract from Mark Segal's article (Jerusalem Post, 26 December, 1958), "Compromise Possible over Future of Bus Co-operatives."

> "Despite pressure from the Histadrut, the co-operatives cling to their system of equal pay for all—from managers to garage hands. They claim that if this system goes in favour of grading according to skill and job, so will mutual responsibility and that the share will just become 'the right to hold a job down.' Similarly, their methods of electing managers straight from behind the driver's wheel or garage would be impossible under a graded wage system.
>
> "The pros and cons of the present system through the eyes of co-operative key men were admirably summed up in a speech by Mr. Ritov before the Afro-Asian Seminar on Co-operation recently:
>
> Pros: "Members have an interest and incentive in their work resulting in high personal efficiency and a real sense of responsibility, reduction of waste, and a willingness to work at all times, out of hours, and in times of emergency."
>
> Cons: "A high percentage of hired labour undermines co-operative principles; inadequate provision for reserves and depreciation in order to maintain high earnings; excessive dependency of the management on the goodwill of members, especially near election time; and frequent changes in management, leading to disruption of administrative work."

Conclusions of the Khoushi Committee appointed by Histadrut to enquire and report on the organization of the bus services in Israel—Khoushi Report—end 1958

A one-page handout (press release) of the public relations department of Mapai, dated January 1959, and reproduced in Davar, of 14 January, 1959, gives the date of the report as 12 December, 1958. This release did not include the minority proposals of E. Hacohen (Mapam); and of S. Zitelni and A. Tzwick (Achdut Haavoda) and of D. Tzimand (Haoved Hatzioni). Shituf[138] published the complete text of the Khoushi conclusions and recommendations, including the three dissenting opinions. According to the text of the report in Shituf, the committee had seven long meetings and heard the extensive evidence of the authorized representatives of the three bus co-operatives; Mr. Moshe Carmel, the Minister of Transport; and that of the representatives of the wage workers employed by the three bus co-operatives.[139]

The introductory paragraph to the committee's conclusions published in Shituf refers to the considerable attention and time which the Government, the Histadrut, and local authorities, gave to the problem of the bus services. It also records, with appreciation, the services which the bus co-operatives have rendered and to the "material and personal losses which the bus co-operatives suffered in the interests of Israel and the Yishuv". But, with the geographical expansion and dispersal of colonization and the considerable increase of the population, there was a growing feeling that this "sensitive and vital service should not remain in the hands of the bus co-operatives as a monopoly". The dissatisfaction was reflected in the intensification of public pressure that the bus co-operatives should be subjected to the maximum supervision by Governmental and public authorities. The bus co-operatives did not act on the many suggestions to mend their ways; and *de facto* did not give the Histadrut representatives appointed by the Chevrat Haovdim to the Management Committees that measure of authority which their rules prescribed. Therefore, it became evident that only a basic change in the ownership of the means of transportation can ensure an orderly, efficient, cheap, and convenient bus service for "the masses of travellers."

On 18 June, 1958, Chevrat Haovdim Secretariat decided "that a public utility bus service corporation owned jointly by the Government, public bodies, and the members and the permanent non-member workers of the bus co-operatives should be established", and that a special committee should enquire into the procedure for setting up such a corporation.

After this special committee appointed by the Histadrut to enquire and report on the bus co-operatives in Israel had discussed the question with the Government and with the members and permanent non-member workers of the bus co-operatives, it decided that it should formulate and submit its proposals to the secretariat of Chevrat Haovdim.

Accordingly, this committee submitted the following conclusions:

1. It is indispensible that the ownership and the operation of the means

of bus transportation should be vested in a public utility corporation which embodies the principle of democratic representation of the public that uses this vital service. The bus co-operatives should admit most of their permanent wage workers as members with equal rights in every respect, and the bus co-operatives will be partners in the corporation. For the present, one countrywide and two regional public corporations for the bus services should be organized.

(*a*) In the countrywide corporation, the Government, the Histadrut, and Egged (Eshed) will each have a 50; 10 and 40 per cent interest respectively.
(*b*) In the first regional corporation for the routes which Dan bus co-operative now services, the Government; the local authorities jointly of the respective communities which the regional corporations services; the Histadrut; and Dan will each have a 30; 20; 10 and 40 per cent interest respectively.
(*c*) In the second regional corporation for the routes which Hamekasher services in the Jerusalem region; the Government; the Histadrut; the Jerusalem Municipality; and the local authorities jointly of the respective communities serviced, and Hamekasher will each have a 30; 10; 20; and 40 per cent interest respectively.
(*d*) Additional corporations will be established, as and when needed.
(*e*) If any of the bus co-operatives do not accept most of their respective wage workers as members, the participation allotted to the respective co-operative will be divided *pro rata* between that co-operative and its respective wage workers.

2. After the share capital of a bus co-operative has been refunded in full, all its immovable and movable property shall be transferred to the respective public corporation in which it will participate.
3. Each of the participants in any of the three public corporations will pay (10 per cent cash and 90 per cent in guaranteed undertakings to be amortized within ten to fifteen years) its *pro rata* share of

(*a*) the amount which is needed to refund the members' participation in the capital of the respective bus co-operatives and
(*b*) the working capital which the particular corporation will need.

4. Each corporation will select the most able, experienced and technically equipped members of its respective participating bus co-operatives, for the focal positions in the day-to-day management. Those in managerial posts are to be directly responsible and subject to the decision of the Management Committee of the respective corporation.
5. Each of the public bus service corporations in the country will have "appropriate representation" on a national council which will look after the co-ordination and efficiency of the bus transportation services in the entire country and arrange for mutual help. The national council will prepare its regulations which, *inter alia*, will define the

operational procedure, functions, and authority of the various public bus transportation corporations.

6. It would be desirable if, simultaneously with the establishment of the first three public corporations, the Government also would appoint a national council whose function would be to co-ordinate the railway, bus, and road haulage services of the entire country.

Minority recommendations (found in the text of the committee's report published in Shituf, January 1959, pp. 28-29).[140]

(A) E. Hacohen (Mapam) recommended that the majority report should become effective only if the bus co-operatives do not "rectify the serious blemishes in the bus co-operative pattern . . ." within the year. This was suggested because the representatives of the bus co-operatives have repeatedly expressed their loyalty and their belief in the advantages of the co-operative principles and of the co-operative pattern. The managements of the bus co-operatives have also declared that they can get their members' agreement for the following changes:

(*a*) The bus co-operatives will admit as members "hired drivers; workers in the garages and in the other services". It will then be possible to abolish the prevailing practice of equal emoluments for all members of the bus co-operatives and to introduce the craft union scale of wages. All members will enjoy the same fringe benefits.

(*b*) The participation of all members in the capital of a bus co-operative will be the same and will be fixed as the equivalent of 3-4 months' emolument (average) to members. Wage workers admitted as members may pay their participation in the capital of the respective bus co-operative in instalments. In addition to the prescribed minimum participation of a member in the bus co-operative's capital, every member will be periodically credited with his *pro rata* share of the net surplus and other divisible funds of the respective bus co-operative, and there would be no limit to the global amount of such credits refundable to the members, from time to time. On the withdrawal of a member from the bus co-operative, his credit in the refundable reserves, etc., will be revalued and then paid to him.

(*c*) The general meeting of a respective bus co-operative, at which Chevrat Haovdim has the deciding vote, shall decide on the distribution of all net surpluses, including the amount which is to be credited pro rata to every member's account.

(*d*) Government control will cover every facet of the operations of bus services. The bus co-operatives also will loyally, persistently and unequivocally accept and comply with the authority of the Histadrut and of Chevrat Haovdim in everything which pertains to safeguarding "the principles of the Chevrat Haovdim and the Histadrut-sponsored WPSTS". Chevrat Haovdim will actively co-operate with the bus co-operatives in adjusting their respective bus services to the needs of the expanding economy of the State and in accordance with the needs and welfare of the users of these services.

Should the bus co-operatives fail to carry out fully the aforementioned conditions, the majority proposals (of the Khoushi Committee) will have to be carried out. The property of the respective bus co-operatives will then be evaluated

"by a committee of independent experts. This evaluation will be used as the basis for fixing the capital structure and the participation of the partners in the respective public service transport corporations. . . ."

(B) Shmuel Zitelni and Arye Tzwick, Achdut Haavoda.

The first paragraph of their minority recommendations reiterates the positive achievements and contributions and the loyalty, under all conditions, of the bus co-operatives; and the

"considerable improvements of the bus transportation service in the course of years as the result of the combined efforts of the workers (members and non-members); the Government;" and, more especially, of the Histadrut.

The second paragraph refers to the serious blemishes of the bus co-operatives over a period of years, such as the "deviations from the principle of Histadrut-sponsored co-operatives" and the complete evasion of Government control and instructions.

The third paragraph defines the two "obligatory principles to improve the position and to prevent the breakdown of the co-operative pattern of bus services".

1. The bus co-operatives and their members must accept unequivocally the authority of the Histadrut with regard to everything which pertains to

    (*a*) the admission of members;
    (*b*) the working conditions of non-members;
    (*c*) fixing the nominal value of a member's share and
    (*d*) the participation of a new member; conditions of work; control etc.

2. All bus transportation services must be subject to planning, and the comprehensive control by the Government in all matters relating to administration, operation, economy, finances, bus fares; etc.

The fourth paragraph repeats the praise of the advantages of the co-operative pattern for all concerned, and the fifth paragraph asks the Government

"as the only licenser of buses" to define by law "the principles and conditions for operating the bus services, which are to be embodied in the licence given to the bus co-operatives for a fixed period, and also the requirements for the renewal of the licence when it expires. . . ."

The sixth paragraph asks for rigid enforcement of Histadrut authority, which is necessary to ensure the preservation of the two fundamental principles of the bus co-operatives, "first and foremost" that wage labour should be appreciably reduced and ultimately eliminated and that the bus co-operatives must admit the wage workers as members with equal rights with the other members.

The seventh and eighth paragraphs ask for

1. The appointment of an official committee, that would include the representatives of the bus co-operatives, to examine the regulations about the admission of new members.
2. The establishment of a special fund which would grant loans to enable those wage workers accepted as members, to pay their participation in the share capital of the respective bus co-operatives.

The ninth and last paragraph of these minority recommendations notes the considerable improvements in the management and services, etc., of the bus co-operatives and in the effective control by the Government, etc. Therefore, the pattern of bus co-operatives should continue.

(C) Mr. Tzimand's (Haoved Hatzioni) minority recommendation, reported in one paragraph, suggested that the bus co-operatives should continue for another two years. He gives the same reasons and asks that they should be subjected to the same conditions as those included in the other two minority reports (A and B above). If the two-year transitional period proves unsuccessful, the suggestion for setting up a public bus transportation corporation, or another pattern which will ensure public authority over the bus services, should be considered.

The following are extracts of a 2,000 word statement to the "Khoushi Committee" by Mr. A. Mazor of the "Dan" management and published as an advertisement in The Jerusalem Post, 26 December, 1958.

The Public's Welfare Demands Co-operative Transport

"The turning point came in 1952 when imports of new buses were permitted, after four years of next to no activity, or at best very restricted activity in regard to the renewal of the transport fleet. At this juncture new buses should have been allocated to permit Dan's expansion as fast as possible in order to close the wide gap between the insistent demands for service and our limited possibilities. This course was not adopted however, and even after this date, imports of new buses remained limited . . . for the improvement of services to the public.

"Ever since the establishment, in 1953 of our 'Fleet Replacement Fund' and the lifting of Government restrictions on the import of buses, we have devoted our major efforts and the greater part of our investments to the renewal of our vehicles. I think that I would not be exaggerating if I said that what 'Dan' accomplished in this field, and 'Egged' and 'Hamekasher' too, could serve as an example for the country as a whole. . . . For the major part of our expenditures for new buses came from liabilities which we undertook, above and beyond the limits set in our depreciation fund, and not included in the calculation of bus fares at the time . . .

Changes in "Dan"

"Progress was not limited only to equipment renewal. It also expressed itself in the improvement in bus routes, travelling conditions and auxiliary services.* . . . We are fully cognizant of improvements still needed, but at the same time we fully believe that we are doing the utmost in our power in this field, and we would be wrong to adopt an exaggerated attitude of self-accusation. . . ."

The Co-operative—The Secret of Our Strength

". . . The basis of our rejection of the organizational changes proposed in the public transport system is our firm belief that the co-operative form . . . is the only form which can provide the maximum service to both the public and the Government, under the special conditions existing in Israel.

We are certainly not claiming that no other company could provide public transport services, but it is absolutely clear to us and should be to everyone else that no other companies, or other organizational set-up, would possess the same operational ability that we have, and that these would be lacking in the basic attributes needed for the running of a public transport system.

We see in the establishment of a new public transport organization, the end of our co-operative framework, and the destruction of the basic principles on which we have built our organization over the decades. . . . Our most deep-seated apprehensions are that such a basic change in our present organizational structure, accompanied as it most surely will be by changes in internal personal and administrative relations, will result in a profound change in the co-operative transport system. . . . No other organizational form will ever possess the same strength, drive, devotion and perseverance which the co-operative form has shown in the past.

The results of any such change would be worse and not better than those we have achieved as a result of our present co-operation structure.

* The seating capacity of our buses was increased (from an average of 37 to 45 per bus). Our range of service was expanded (from 30 routes in 1948 to 77 in 1958). Frequency of bus departures was increased on all routes (up to one bus every three minutes on main routes). The sale of tickets was moreover both on buses and at the various bus stops; and the sale of bus-journey cards introduced. A special service was introduced to and from work for the employees of large firms. Scores of station shelters were put up.

> Fares will not be lower; efficiency will not be higher; and neither the State nor the public will benefit, as they haven't benefited from the recent upheavals in other spheres.
>
> On the other hand, we foresee the public transport system becoming a pawn of the various political interests. . . . Political appointments will replace democratic election of management bodies; political factionalism will replace the present atmosphere of comradeship and creativity; management and operational activities will be conducted under the pressure of the voter and not for the public's welfare.
>
> In all fairness, however, we admit that there is full justification for a greater extent of Government supervision over the public transport services, and the Government has a complete right to enlarge its control over the direction of our activities. . . . The Minister of Transport, Mr. Moshe Carmel, recently said in the Knesset: "Government supervision of the transport co-operatives has grown in the past few years. It now encompasses their economic, financial, administrative and operational activities."

Davar[141] reports that the conference of the three bus co-operatives on 13 January, 1959, referred to the Khoushi Committee's recommendations as a "decree of apostasy" ("renunciation") or "an act of suicide". "We will sweat and they will have the say."

The bus co-operatives are reported to have told the Histadrut Executive Committee, which had the final say on the Khoushi Committee's recommendations: "nobody can force us into a partnership with somebody else". This report in Davar adds that the opposition of the bus co-operatives would make it impossible to carry out the committee's conclusions and that, therefore, the bus co-operatives doubted whether the Histadrut would confirm the committee's recommendations.

This issue of Davar also reports what it describes as the reaction of the three bus co-operatives.

> Mr. Davidson (Egged (Eshed) Management) estimated the value of the share capital and of the property of the three bus co-operatives as IL.40 and IL.80 million respectively. If the committee's recommendations were put into effect, the existing cheap community service run without public money, would be replaced by a public service which would be administered as other well-known Government public services. He also noted that the Government Co-operative Advisory Council decided to counsel the Histadrut not to confirm the Khoushi Committee's conclusions because this would destroy the bus co-operatives.
>
> Mr. Lichtman (Hamekasher Management) declared that the bus co-operatives were not fighting the Histadrut, but a miscalculation which would be damaging to the interests of all concerned. He considered the changes made in the management of Solel Boneh *de facto* were only "a change of the mezuzot."[142] But the changes proposed for the bus co-operatives affect the actual ownership and content of the undertakings.

Mr. A. Mazor (Dan management) was derisive about the advantages of the managerial procedure suggested for the public bus service corporations. Dan is now managed by a committee of three, while under the new plan "two buses will be insufficient to carry all the members of the enlarged and involved management". He thought that there was a veiled contradiction between the often repeated praises describing the achievements of the bus co-operatives and the committee's conclusions.

Davar[143] also reported that the Histadrut Executive Committee on 15 January, 1959, discussed the Khoushi Committee's conclusions. Mr. Pinchas Lavon (then the general secretary of the Histadrut), summing up the first stage of these decisions, is reported to have asked

> "the members of the bus co-operatives to forget once and for all the period when a small monopolistic group of members ruled over the bus services. . . . On the other hand, the internal structure of the corporation suggested by the committee need not be considered as final. Changes are possible in the *pro rata* participation of the various partners (bodies)."

Referring to the report that the bus co-operatives had declared that there is no power which could impose a partnership on them, Mr. Pinchas Lavon is reported to have warned the bus co-operatives not to use this offensive tone.

> "Are you members of the Histadrut or effendis?" he asked them. The Government and the Histadrut can impose their views on the bus co-operatives. . . . "I am aware of the efforts invested in the bus co-operatives but . . . you have not lost anything from this. And why this offensive tone?"

Mr. Lavon allegedly also said that the public was entitled to enquire into the use of the "chattel" which the public entrusted to the bus co-operatives. He found it difficult to reconcile the language of the declarations of the bus co-operatives with a genuine desire to continue their membership in the Histadrut. The general secretary referred to, but did not give the content of the conclusions of the two Achdut Haavodah members (Messrs. Zitelni and Tzwick) (summarized in the preceding pages) on the Khoushi Committee and castigated the Minister of Transport for permitting his affiliation to the Achdut Haavodah "to bemuddle (confuse) his attitude". Referring to the conclusion of the third Mapam member (Mr. E. Hacohen) on the committee (also summarized in the preceding pages), Mr. Lavon is reported to have said that in view of past experience, it would be impossible to believe that the bus co-operatives would make good any of their promises or agreements. The Histadrut, as in the past, would be compelled to continue to waste time and energy. Mr. Lavon accused the bus co-operatives of trying to confuse public opinion by labelling the Khoushi Committee's conclusions as the nationalization of the bus transportation services. He described the attitude of the leaders of the bus co-operatives as "electioneering", courting popularity with their members. Mr. Lavon then noted that in the past, the Histadrut killed the effort of the previous Minister of Transport to restrain the bus co-operatives, by proposing to license competition on the same routes. The Histadrut also extricated the bus co-operatives out of the "messy strike". He labelled the accusation that the Histadrut and/or the Khoushi Committee wanted to liquidate the bus co-operatives as "a gross misrepresentation". Histadrut and Government control were not and could not be effective unless all parties "sit as one body".

A. Khoushi expressed doubts whether bus co-operatives that employ so many permanent wage workers can be genuinely co-operative in character, spirit and action.

A. Davidson asked for action on the committee's conclusions to be postponed since the bus co-operatives were prepared to accept the authority of the Histadrut on all questions and also to make far-reaching concessions about the admission of their wage workers as members.

Mr. Lieberman (representative of wage workers in the bus co-operatives) is reported to have declared that all 3,000 wage workers, irrespective of their political affiliation, supported the Khoushi committee's conclusions. Though the wage workers contributed as much as the members to the achievements of the bus co-operatives, they were assigned to the "least respected" type of work. Non-member drivers were given the worst buses and assigned to the most difficult routes. The families of non-members, unlike those of member drivers, did not enjoy free bus tickets.

A leader in Shituf[144] "On the Future of the Bus Co-operatives" notes the following questions still to be answered:

> "What will the Histadrut and the organized labour sector do to preserve co-operative bus transportation? And what are the assurances that in the process of carrying out the (Khoushi Committee's) conclusions, the bus co-operatives will not be swallowed and that the significant co-operative achievement, unique in our time which has raised our status in the world co-operative movement, will not be destroyed? What will be done to forestall a potential fatal shock to the entire (Histadrut-sponsored) co-operative structure in the country, urban and rural?"

The first part of the leader in Hameshek Hashitufi (27 January, 1959 pp. 40-41) "A Re-examination of Co-operation" deals with the Khoushi Committee's conclusions. Is it a contradiction to describe the bus co-operatives as an extraordinary achievement of the co-operative movement in Israel when addressing the outside world and on the other hand to criticize and then to replace the bus co-operatives by nationalized bus transportation? The fact that the Histadrut-sponsored WPSTS, credit and consumers co-operative movements have been, relatively speaking, signally successful (by comparison with other countries) does not preclude the possibility that some members have tried to adulterate the credo of co-operation and "to consider themselves as the lords of important sectors of life in the State". This has happened in the case of the bus co-operative; a group of members who sit at the steering wheels of the buses, hold the steering wheels of the bus co-operative and mould the pattern of bus services in the country. The bus co-operatives enjoy a monopoly and they exploit without restraint these concessions only for their own benefit. They interpret co-operation as the right to benefit from an unrestrained monopoly for selfish interests; this is an adulteration of the co-operative principle. Everybody should assist the Histadrut general secretary's efforts to uproot this wild grass so widespread in the Histadrut-sponsored co-operative movement. Including the bus co-operatives within the framework of an efficient and suitable public transportation system need not impair the interest of the drivers, ticket sellers, etc., who wish to continue as co-operatives even though these will be subject to a more effective and practical control. Co-operative ideology must not be used as a veil for monopolistic purposes and/or interpreted as "absolute exclusiveness and unbridled domination by a group of members over the entire public". This leader closes with the following paragraph:

> "Co-operation is not meant to be a blind and unyielding preservation of the *status quo*, irrespective whether it is good or bad or whether it is carrying out its mission or whether those who are carrying out the mission have sinned, or have falsified or forged the ideals entrusted into their hands. Co-operation is not an ethos which may be interpreted in accordance with the tastes of those who are putting it into effect and intended to serve only their narrow interests. Co-operation is meant to be genuine joint activity in the general interests and it is not . . . intended to serve individuals whose interests do not always coincide with public interests."

Nathan Ben Nathan (staff economist of Davar) (30 January, 1959) in the introductory paragraph of his article "The Struggle for the Soul of the Co-operatives" notes that he is not joining these publicists

> "who have done their best to cover up the basic fact that the bus co-operatives do enjoy a monopoly which yields a good income to their members who, therefore are naturally interested that this should continue. . . . During the ten years (of struggle with the recalcitrant bus co-operatives) the Histadrut has not excelled in its determination . . . to impose its authority on the bus co-operatives. The fact that the Histadrut leadership accepted the many and petty compromises which the bus co-operatives offered . . . accounts to not a small extent for the vein of cynicism widespread among youth. . . . The self-deception in accepting the assumption that the bus co-operatives are prepared to accept effective control by the Histadrut collapsed a half year ago, after all efforts to carry out the control failed. And in May 1948 the Chevrat Haovdim secretariat decided that a public utility corporation for bus transportation service should be established."

Mr. Ben Nathan further notes that the bus co-operatives are exploiting the fact that the Khoushi Committee's conclusions have become a political football and are not being considered on their merits. Therefore, the bus co-operatives insist that only the Knesset is authorized to decide this question. Supporting the school which insists that the foundation stone of the WPSTS Movement is self-labour, he refers to the late Prof. Franz Oppenheimer's conclusions "that every co-operative which uses wage labour must ultimately be changed into a limited company".[145]

According to Mr. Ben Nathan, the bus co-operatives have the same number of wage employees as members, 3,500 of each. And experience has demonstrated that it is equally bad to give a co-operative a monopoly over any economic sector as it is to give it to a non-co-operative. It is useless for the bus co-operatives to remonstrate at Histadrut meetings that they have not exploited their monopolistic status. He also accepts the allegation that the bus co-operatives have treated the wage employees unfairly and shabbily by giving them the most difficult and unpalatable assignments, etc.

Mr. Ben Nathan writes that management elected by "thousands of members in the syndicalist spirit which can be overthrown any hour by elections, is bound to be unstable. . . . A distinction must be made between democracy and demagogy".

He accuses Mapam and Achdut Haavoda that in order to get votes they conveniently forget that they have urged Chevrat Haovdim persistently to insist on a fifty per cent share of all the votes in a co-operative since this is a means of preserving its public character. Even if the Khoushi Committee had recommended nationalization (which it had not) Mr. Ben Nathan would see nothing wrong in this. Since when have Labour Parties rejected nationalization of monopolistic undertakings? And "we have learnt from years' experience" that Government and/or Histadrut supervision cannot be a substitute for actual participation in Histadrut-sponsored co-operatives, and in local authorities. Ways of evading external bureaucratic control can always be found. This is much less likely, in the case of actual participation in management as part owners.

> "In the public utility corporations which the (Khoushi) Committee proposes, the only difference in the status between the wage workers and the members of the co-operatives will be that the latter will get a return on their investments. There will be no more exploitation by one worker of another worker."

According to Davar[146] the Histadrut Merkaz on 18 January, 1959, approved the conclusions and recommendations of an ad hoc committee of three (Messrs. Meshel; Haskin and Talmon) about the working conditions, including wages, for the workers in the bus co-operatives. The more important changes in the terms of employment for wage workers in the bus co-operatives which became effective on 1 February, 1959, are:

(*a*) Increased allowance for convalescence for wage workers with 10 or more years' seniority.

(*b*) The wives and children of wage workers with a seniority of five and more years in any of the bus co-operatives to have the same privileges of free travel as the families of members of the respective bus co-operatives.
(*c*) Increased allowances for dependents of all wage workers and also of the seniority supplementary payment for wage workers with five or more years' seniority.
(*d*) Wage workers with seniority of five or more years, who are admitted as members of the respective bus co-operative, to receive a severance allowance.
(*e*) Equitable distribution of jobs among members and non-members alike.
(*f*) It is mandatory for a bus co-operative to ensure promotion of its wage workers "on the basis of ability, aptitudes and the character of their jobs (functions)".
(*g*) The same work-day for all drivers, members and non-members; and those non-members who work in traffic and other services to receive a daily allowance.
(*h*) All wage-workers, like the members of the respective bus co-operatives, are entitled to special grants for marriages; births; etc. Wage workers with five or more years seniority are entitled to the same allowances when called up for reserve military service as those given to members.
(*i*) If it is the practice of a bus co-operative to pay the fee for the drivers' licence of member drivers, it will also pay for the non-members' licence.

The Jerusalem Post, Editorial, 13 September, 1960, Bus Co-operatives v. the Histadrut

"All that can be said about the bus co-operatives has been said on numerous occasions. Whether their argument is with their public, the passengers, or whether it is with the Histadrut or with the Ministry of Transport, the bus co-operatives seem in the long run to have their own way.

"When Mr. Lavon became the head of the Histadrut again, he did not hide his intention to compel the co-operatives to join in a partnership with the State, the Histadrut, and the municipalities, thus assuring public control of a vital public service. But nothing happened.

"The present controversy is not between the public and the transport co-operatives. The public is not interested whether the drivers are co-owners or simply paid workers. But, for the Histadrut, control over the bus companies is a primary concern.

"The compromise which the Histadrut accepted on Sunday was, in fact, reached on the co-operatives' terms. The bus companies are more powerful than they seem to be. . . . The co-operatives, which have emerged as one of the powers that control the country, will leave no stone unturned to avoid state control.

"The success of the bus co-operatives has been all too great. It may be true that under the prevailing conditions, only a co-operative can run a public transport concern successfully. But it is not for the public good, in the long run, that one particular group of men, who happen to run a vital service, should think that what is good for them is good for the country.

"The moral defeat suffered by the Histadrut in handling the dispute is perhaps more important than anything else. If the Histadrut cannot keep the companies within the bounds of co-operative ethics, nobody can."

CHAPTER SEVEN

Minutes, Reports and Activities

The Third Congress in November 1934 was devoted almost entirely to the problem of the employment of wage labour, which, according to the report of Merkaz Haco-operatzia Secretariat, if not completely uprooted "will destroy all our work and will disrupt and demolish the WPSTS from inside". The problem of wage labour was most acute in the industrial workers co-operatives for building materials. Merkaz Haco-operatzia expelled three WPSTS and the Histadrut dropped the members of these because they did not carry out the Histadrut's decision that part of the operating surplus of the WPSTS should be distributed among the wage workers. The Secretariat's report to the Third Congress also notes that WPSTS were asking new members to pay exorbitant share capital participation and were distributing these funds among the old members. It referred to "the trade in the shares (rights or credits) in bus co-operatives", and "old experienced drivers who do not have LP.700-800, and asked Merkaz Haco-operatzia why the Histadrut does not take measures to enable them to join one of the bus co-operatives". The report suggests that "when fixing the value of the members' rights, we should consider the investments which the respective co-operatives had made; the improvements, the hardships in the past, etc., etc."[147]

The manager of Egged Bus Co-operative agreed that trading in rights is the "stumbling block" of the WPSTS and "only if we know how to suppress our lust, to stamp out this evil devil called rights, will we survive".

He supports the demand of the vatikim that their employment and livelihood etc. when they are old or become partially or totally incapacitated, should be secured. Where necessary, members are entitled to special consideration such as shorter hours, less strenuous work, pensions, etc. But they must battle against those who join the co-operative at the opportune time with the intention to sell their rights to the highest bidders (the "vultures"), and also against those members who insist upon distributing the surplus reserves instead of using the resources to improve the services without having to borrow. He criticizes another delegate whom he characterizes as "a Histadrut orator about Histadrut ideals" who argued that there is no great harm "in accepting only LP.200 or LP.250 ($800-1,000) more than the value of the share . . . and distributing these profits (i.e. the extra payments) among the members". Pointing to the dais the manager of Egged continues: "It is these whom I accuse and who sit at the table—Merkaz Haco-operatzia, Chevrat Haovdim, the Histadrut, the party (Mapai). These are aware of (see) all this and yet answer 'amen'. I accuse them of inaction, weakness and cowardice. . . ."

A member of the secretariat replied that the manager of Egged had no right to criticize the "excessive prices which other WPSTS were demanding as long as his own home (Egged) was not in order". Egged was asking new members to pay "many times the par value of the shares" and did not help Merkaz Haco-operatzia to fight this disease. He considered it criminal for any WPSTS to ask new members to pay six times the amount which other members had paid.

A member of an inter-urban bus co-operative said: "If Merkaz Haco-operatzia had declared war on the three or four WPSTS that started to speculate in members' shares, other WPSTS would have joined the battle."

He accepted the secretariat's formula for fixing the amount which a new member should be required to pay as his share in the society's capital. But he objected to the distribution among the members of the difference between the amount which new members paid and the amount which the member who is selling his right to a new member had paid. The members will begin to think that their main source of revenue are these windfall profits and not their emoluments.

Some speakers, including members of the Merkaz Haco-operatzia Central Committee, suggested that the amount which new members paid should not exceed by more than 20 to 25 per cent the par value of the share (or any other unit of participation). Other speakers wished to leave the problems in the hands of a regulatory committee that would consider each case on its merits, and use as the "yardstick" seniority of service, the real balance-sheet value of the share plus depreciation of property, etc. Only one delegate at the Third Congress (November, 1934) suggested eradicating the unco-operative practice by prohibiting it.

One delegate asked why a member of a housing co-operative is free to dispose of or to sub-let his apartment or house at any price[148] whereas a member of a WPSTS is condemned if he sells his participation for more than he paid for it. Actually the member of the WPSTS has contributed and suffered more than has the member of the housing co-operative.

The Third Congress of Merkaz Haco-operatzia reiterated that self-labour is the cornerstone of WPSTS and it asks the "sinners" to change their ways. It instructs Merkaz Haco-operatzia to take immediate action to arrange the question of purchase and transfer of "rights" and at the same time protect the rights of the members. Merkaz Haco-operatzia must prohibit all speculation in and any demands for inflated prices for a unit of participation (shares).

S. Gorochowsky (Goren) told the Fourth Congress of Merkaz Haco-operatzia, of 16 June, 1938, that non-members account for 27 per cent of the entire labour force of 3,095 in all the affiliated WPSTS, a slight increase in the percentage over 1934. The increase of non-member workers in the bus co-operatives was from 12 to 34 per cent of their total labour force and was directly related to the garages which the larger bus co-operative societies have opened. Inasmuch as the skilled workers and office staff are probationers, Mr. Gorochowsky notes "that actually we are approaching a solution of the question of wage labour.[149]

Y. Ritov notes that "there are craft unions which complain bitterly at meetings about the wage labour (in WPSTS) and yet they are the first to press the WPSTS to use wage workers, even when Merkaz Haco-operatzia thinks that such wage labour is not essential". He suggested:

> Firstly, that a small number of WPSTS that have to work and compete under special conditions may, "with the approval of the authorized bodies", use seasonal or incidental wage labour. Provided that such wage labour share in the operational profit of the respective WPSTS.
>
> Second, the reactivation of the special tribunal which was set up to consider appeals and complaints.
>
> Third, the rules of every WPSTS should give the Chevrat Haovdim one half of the seats in its management. If these representatives of Chevrat Haovdim will identify themselves with every aspect of the activities of the respective WPSTS "they will gain the confidence of and influence the members and in this way help to deal with the solution of the question of wage labour".

A delegate who has been a member and manager of one of the larger co-operative joineries stated that only a WPSTS which works for a permanent clientele and/or during the period when it is mainly engaged in preparing stocks can maintain itself on the basis of self-labour.

A delegate from a bus co-operative explains why the abolition of all wage labour, especially in road haulage co-operatives is impossible. Those against wage labour in the WPSTS (and in the kibbutzim) he notes, consider that the differentiation in the kind of work between member and non-member is a very serious deviation from the co-operative principle of "equitable distribution". From an economic point of view, members of a road haulage co-operative should not clean the vehicles and should leave this to apprentices. Otherwise, members' requests for change of jobs will multiply and a continuous and large turnover is bad for the co-operative's property. ". . . We will introduce equality in conditions of work and in the tasks of all workers when the Histadrut does this in its institutions." He reminds the Congress that for years members of bus co-operatives received LP.6 a month and that the bus co-operatives invested all surpluses in equipment and for consolidating their financial position. "Are we not entitled to compensation for this?" Histadrut organs pay allowances for seniority and severance pay to those released. "Why are we not entitled to compensation for our seniority?" (i.e. the vatikim).

A delegate of a bus co-operative said that if garage workers and others have to be accepted as members, the bus co-operatives would have to do away with the principle of equal emolument for all members irrespective of type of work. "And in my opinion a co-operative without equality among the members is not a co-operative."[150]

A delegate from Haifa states that 60 per cent of employees in the garages of the bus co-operatives were non-members. This could not be justified and "many of the skilled workers in the garages could have been admitted as members . . . were it not for the opposition of the craft unions who contend that in the time of unemployment, the unemployed should be employed."

The delegate of another bus co-operative (one of the big three bus co-operatives that in 1951 merged into Egged (Eshed), said that the WPSTS would go bankrupt if they could not use seasonal wage labour. The WPSTS must insist that the participation of a new member in the WPSTS capital must cover the full cost, at the price prevailing when admitted, of the equipment needed for a worker, and also allow for some compensation for the financial and physical sacrifices and "the many years of efforts and suffering" of those who already are members.

An ex-member of a moshav who joined a bus co-operative five years ago, while generally supporting the previous speaker, objected to the distribution among the old members of any part of the moneys which the new members pay.

One delegate gave the following example to support the allegation that the Histadrut and its sponsored projects, like Solel Boneh, compelled the WPSTS to use wage labour. After many months of unemployment "we received a contract for LP.160 on condition that we use hired labour for 60 per cent of this work. We were advised that if the co-operative refused to employ hired labour it would not get any part of the work."

The delegate from a co-operative machine shop in Haifa (established in 1918) asked why Merkaz Haco-operatzia and/or the Histadrut expelled the smaller WPSTS (like his) for using wage labour and yet did not expel the bus co-operatives. The co-operative of which he is a member, used wage labour not because the members did not want to do "the unclean and unskilled labour". But because, unlike the transportation and other WPSTS, their co-operative has the problem of seasonal work and of cycles of employment and unemployment. If Solel Boneh and other Histadrut-sponsored bodies would give the same consideration to their co-operative as do the private contractors and if Merkaz Haco-operatzia did more to help train skilled workers, the problems of wage labour would be less troublesome.

One delegate suggested that those WPSTS that are not competitive without wage labour should become Histadrut administered enterprises.

Another delegate noted that experience has demonstrated that it is definitely possible for WPSTS to be competitive without using wage labour. It depends entirely on the will. This delegate asked for a resolution which obligates the affiliated WPSTS to obtain "the prior approval of an authorized body (institution) as a condition for using wage labour."

A veteran Histadrut co-operator thinks that the high percentage of wage labour which bus co-operatives use in their garages is as justified as is the wage labour which the Co-operative Wholesale Society in England uses on its boats and on its tea plantations in Ceylon. He asks "which is better, that the bus co-operative should send their buses to private garages which use unorganized labour or to establish well equipped garages which the Histadrut more or less controls. Why the commotion because 60 or more per cent of the labour force (in the garages of the bus co-operatives) are wage workers?"

He pleads for a realistic human and evolutionary approach to this question.

A vatik of the Histadrut-sponsored co-operative movement suggested that the wage workers in the garages of the bus co-operatives should be organized into commandites. The bus co-operatives would retain the ownership of the equipment, etc. and the commercial and financial administration of their respective garages.

The secretary of the labour-sponsored co-operative committee in Haifa reports that those WPSTS in the Haifa region that are discharging wage workers will not be permitted to re-employ them "when the times change and the work increases". This should help reduce the extent of wage labour which cannot be abolished with a "stroke of the pen". And like the kibbutzim, WPSTS should be permitted to use seasonal wage workers provided these will enjoy the same working conditions as the members.

Another member of Merkaz Haco-operatzia Central Management Committee notes that having two classes of workers in a WPSTS—members and wage labourers—is contrary to the Histadrut conception of "Jewish self-labour". While not asking for an immediate ban on wage labour, the WPSTS movement should openly declare that wage labour is a blemish which must be rooted out. This problem cannot be solved by the repetitious mumbling of the word

> "co-operation" which "is based on self-labour and not on the exploitation of your fellow men. Only when we will stop acting as small shopkeepers . . . and will know how to evaluate the long term policy . . . will the word co-operative . . . have its full content. And a solution for the question of the amount of the financial participation by new members must be found".

Today an individual who arrived in Israel "yesterday or the day before", and came to the country because of "need", and not as a convinced Zionist, can join a WPSTS because he can pay the LP.800 participation required. But a vatik with 15-20 years' experience is excluded because he cannot pay the admission fee. Such candidates can join a kibbutz because national institutions provide the land and loans for housing, equipment, etc. Why are there no such facilities for the qualified skilled people without means who want to join WPSTS?

The Fourth Congress of Merkaz Haco-operatzia, of 16 June, 1938, reconfirms that self-labour is the principal essence of a WPSTS and asks Merkaz Haco-operatzia to continue its war against wage labour until it has been completely uprooted. The Congress asks that if Merkaz Haco-operatzia authorizes a WPSTS to use wage labour, this should be subject to the strictest regulations and profit sharing with the wage workers.

The Congress considers the establishment of partnership between WPSTS and Histadrut-sponsored bodies as one of the positive solutions for wage labour. The desirability of organizing co-operatives of workers (commandites) especially of those employed in the garages of the bus co-operatives, as a way for resolving the question of wage labour, should be explored.

The Congress also instructs the Council of Merkaz Haco-operatzia to devote one of its meetings in the near future to a thorough discussion of wage labour.

The report of Merkaz Haco-operatzia for 1938-42 notes that one of the oldest road haulage co-operatives, Hovala, which was organized in 1923 and serviced the Palestine Potash Company's northern plant (near Jericho), was expelled from Merkaz Haco-operatzia because it used a relatively excessive number of wage workers. This was a difficult decision, the report adds, because the co-operative during the Arab disturbances between 1936 and 1939 had performed heroic services and lost several members on the very dangerous Jerusalem-Jericho road.

The twenty-page chapter on wage labour in this report (212 pp) starts with the following sentence: "Many are the tricky problems of the WPSTS which have economic and especially social dangers. The most serious is wage labour . . . the crucial question is whether our WPSTS should continue within the framework of their founder, Chevrat Haovdim, or God forbid should be outside."

The regulations included as part of the resolutions of the Fourth Congress, of Merkaz Haco-operatzia, 16 June, 1938, prescribe *inter alia*:

1. A Histadrut-sponsored WPSTS should be approved only if "it . . . will be able to do all the work with its own manpower".
2. The use of seasonal and temporary hired labour may be authorized "in exceptional cases . . . by the local labour councils with the knowledge of Merkaz Haco-operatzia".
3. Profit sharing for all wage workers is obligatory for all WPSTS.
4. The Third Congress of Merkaz Haco-operatzia (November 1934) in two resolutions confirmed

   (*a*) Merkaz Haco-operatzia Secretariat's decision to expel those WPSTS ("rebels and dissenters") that used wage labour and
   (*b*) that the primary basis of WPSTS is "self-labour".

Between June 1938 and the end of September 1941 there was an absolute and relative increase in the total number of wage workers in the WPSTS, from 832 and about 27 per cent to 1,130 and more than 36 per cent of the entire labour force. War orders account for 170-175 or 15 per cent of the 1,130 wage workers. This is the kind of wage labour which is "without doubt permissible".

About two to three per cent of the 1,130 wage workers at the end of September 1941 are probationers; three per cent were unemployed forced on the WPSTS by the local labour councils, and 43 per cent (486) wage workers are used by the bus co-operatives in their garages. In other words the apprentices, temporary wage workers on war orders, probationers for membership, garage workers and the unemployed directed to the WPSTS account for about 49 per cent of all wage workers.

The report also notes that a census recorded in the summer of 1941 showed that 20 per cent of the wage workers were apprentices. Merkaz Haco-operatzia considers that it is the duty of every co-operative to employ apprentices but in the spirit which the labour leader, Mr. Berl Katzenelson, defined at the Fourth Congress of the Histadrut in 1934:

> "There is a difference between apprentices and wage workers. . . . The wage worker in a WPSTS is an entirely negative manifestation. But this is not so in the case of apprentices. A practical school must be used for the children and for the immigrants. The conditions and the period of apprenticeship must be appropriate; and . . . the apprentice must not be moved from place to place. The employment of apprentices under appropriate conditions is not a deviation from the principles of co-operation."

The report comes to the conclusion that the use of wage labour in the garages of bus co-operatives is unnecessary because the bus co-operatives either can contract out the work to garages or help to organize the wage workers in the garages into co-operatives (commandites). Wage labour in the garages of the bus co-operatives is "a magnificent thorn in the body of the Histadrut". The report adds that there is evidence that the use of wage labour is an important factor in the spread of anti-WPSTS feeling. It is essential to clarify the definition of apprentice and to fix precisely the kinds of work for which apprentices may be used. Included in this problem, are the duration, hours of employment, wages, what happens after the completion of apprenticeship, and public supervision. The report suggests that a WPSTS employing apprentices and the Merkaz Haco-operatzia should each appoint one or two members whose duty it will be to take special interest in apprentices. And the report endorses the demand of the WPSTS that children of members must enjoy priority for a fixed percentage of the apprenticeships in the respective WPSTS. It rejects the demands of the Histadrut-sponsored youth movement (Hanoar Haoved) that all apprenticeships be distributed on the basis of merits. It notes "that since nobody denies the rights of the members of the moshavim ovdim to integrate their sons in their holdings, why should the members of the WPSTS be deprived of this right."

The report suggests that the following amendments and clarifications should be introduced into the labour code about probationers.[151]

1. Merkaz Haco-operatzia should be designated as the authorized institution for all questions relating to WPSTS.
2. The total minimum and maximum duration of the initial and subsequent probation periods should be increased.
3. The right to engage "experts" as wage workers should be cancelled.
4. The clause dealing with appeals should specifically prescribe the instance of final appeal; the grounds on which a probationer may be rejected. And the sanctions which can and/or may be imposed on a WPSTS which disregards decisions, etc., should be clearly defined.

S. Goren (formerly Gorochowsky) in his opening address at the Fifth Congress on 7-9 April, 1949, refers to the question of wage labour. "We (Merkaz Haco-operatzia) encountered difficulties with the problem of wage labour. Solving this (problem) required considerable efforts by the Histadrut and ourselves . . . the problem of wage labour to all intents and purposes has ceased to be a social problem. If we are to prevent the return (of wage labour) and its penetration within this sector we and the Histadrut will have to be on guard."[152]

The secretariat's report for 1938-49 to the Fifth Congress of Merkaz Haco-operatzia, between 7 and 9 April, 1949, summarizes the negotiations (from the end of 1941 to June 1946) about wage labour in the WPSTS, between the bus co-operatives and Merkaz Haco-operatzia on the one hand, and between Merkaz Haco-operatzia and the Histadrut on the other hand. Some "important WPSTS advised" Merkaz Haco-operatzia that they would boycott the Fifth Congress if the latter would make a binding decision about wage labour, and if Merkaz Haco-operatzia asked the Histadrut and Chevrat Haovdim to help to resolve this question. While some service and industrial workers co-operatives also used wage labour on a large scale, this question was most pressing in the bus co-operatives. Therefore, the bus co-operatives were invited to the tripartite negotiations, between Merkaz Haco-operatzia, Chevrat Haovdim and the Histadrut.

After the first meeting with the bus co-operatives on 10 April, 1942, the Histadrut Executive Committee submitted and publicized the following proposals which Chevrat Haovdim had prepared (referred to as the seven-point proposal).

1. In any dispute between WPSTS and members of the Histadrut and its institutions or any non-Histadrut body, the Histadrut's decision is binding.
2. A small joint sub-committee would fix the procedure for liquidating wage labour in the affiliated WPSTS before the end of World War Two.
3. A permanent representative of Chevrat Haovdim on the Management

Committee of an affiliated WPSTS would have the same rights as "all other members of the committee" jointly.

4. Merkaz Haco-operatzia would continue to control the budgets of its affiliated WPSTS.
5. The WPSTS would pay the full amount of the Histadrut dues for their respective members.
6. The terms of employment for the wage workers in the affiliated WPSTS are to be as favourable as those for wage workers in other places of employment. Until such time as wage employment will be abolished in the WPSTS, a small committee will formulate special rules for the implementation of this section.
7. The Histadrut's approval is required if a WPSTS decides that a new member has to participate in the society's capital with an amount which exceeds the par value of such participation.

The Histadrut also reconfirmed section five of the *Chukat Haavodah Hashitufit* (co-operative employment regulations) which the Histadrut Congress had approved, viz.,

> "The temporary employment of wage workers in exceptional cases, and only on a seasonal and temporary basis, may be authorized by a special joint committee made up of representatives of Chevrat Haovdim, Merkaz Haco-operatzia and the local Labour Council."

The representatives of the bus co-operatives advised the committee that it would submit the seven-point proposal to every affiliated bus co-operative. Merkaz Haco-operatzia insisted that except for the last part of the seventh point (paragraph), the seven-point programme summarizes the actual practice. But the representatives of the bus co-operatives argued that the enforcement of the seven-point programme *de facto* changes the autonomous co-operatives into "chattel mortgagees of the Histadrut". On 29 June, 1942, when the Alamein crisis in North Africa was very serious, the negotiations were interrupted.

The secretariat's report to the Fifth Congress notes that the bus co-operatives exploited this crisis to set up their own transportation secretariat, completely independent of Merkaz Haco-operatzia; discontinued paying their dues to Merkaz Haco-operatzia and started discussing the establishment of their own audit union. Shortly thereafter, four of the seven bus co-operatives formally joined a federation of transportation co-operatives; the other three bus co-operatives became *de facto* members. According to the secretariat's report, practically the entire eleven hours of the second meeting of the joint committee of the Histadrut, Chevrat Haovdim and Merkaz Haco-operatzia, with the representatives of the bus co-operatives to discuss the seven-point programme, was concerned with "the question of the secessionist organization". When closing this second meeting its chairman, Mr. David Remez, announced "that the Histadrut insists on the immediate liquidation" of the new federation of transport (bus) co-operatives. A few more official and non-official meetings of the joint committee failed to break the deadlock about the question of wage labour. Merkaz Haco-operatzia, after discussing the problem with its other affiliated WPSTS, appointed in September 1942 an *ad hoc* committee "to enquire into the status of wage labour used by its affiliated societies, other than bus societies, and vested this committee with the responsibility for the eradication of wage labour". But insurmountable obstacles were uncovered and nothing was achieved.

At the end of 1942 Merkaz Haco-operatzia suggested that the local labour councils should deal with the elimination of wage labour in the WPSTS. In early 1943, the wage workers in the WPSTS organized and started to press their demands to be admitted as members of their respective WPSTS and press for the improvement of their working conditions. Merkaz Haco-operatzia intensified the pressure on its WPSTS to eradicate wage labour and to counteract the demagogues ". . . whose goal was to exterminate the foundations" of these co-operatives. The secretariat's report to the Fifth Congress also notes that the attitude of the labour councils and also of the affiliated WPSTS made it difficult for the joint parity committees to function. In December, 1943, the Histadrut accepted the suggestion of Merkaz Haco-operatzia and appointed an *ad hoc* committee[153] "to deal with the problems of the WPSTS in a practical way", and approved the following terms of reference which Merkaz Haco-operatzia secretariat suggested for this committee.

1. Plan for the elimination of wage labour in bus co-operatives.

    (*a*) Every bus co-operative able to operate only with self-labour must dismiss all wage workers and undertake not to re-introduce wage labour.

    (*b*) A bus co-operative unable to operate without wage labour, firstly must establish a partnership with the Histadrut, with equal rights for both partners in every respect.

    Second, operational surpluses will be distributed between the members of the co-operative of workers (the commandite) and the wage workers, *pro rata* to the respective number of work-days. Third, as the volume of work becomes fixed (consolidated) the co-operative will accept the wage workers as members. Fourth, part of the operational surpluses which were not distributed (as in the second point), will be used to help pay the participation in the capital of the respective co-operative for such wage workers who are accepted as members. Fifth, if the partnership between the co-operative and the Histadrut is dissolved, those wage labourers employed in the respective joint undertakings, who are prepared to accept Histadrut supervision may organize and register as an autonomous co-operative.

2. Road haulage co-operatives.

    (*a*) Since it is now impossible for the road haulage co-operatives to accept all their wage workers as members, the co-operatives should transfer to a Histadrut-sponsored economic body such part of the surpluses earned from the use of wage labour, calculated on the basis of the number of work-days of the wage workers.

(*b*) The fund created per 2(a) will be used to help to pay the participation in the respective road haulage co-operative's capital of those wage workers accepted by the respective road haulage co-operative as members on the basis of their technical suitability and seniority and to the extent that the economic position of the respective road haulage co-operative has been consolidated.

(*c*) For the purpose of fixing the operational surplus of a road haulage co-operative, precise definitions are needed:

(i) compensation to members;
(ii) depreciation;
(iii) the unit of participation in the co-operative's capital;
(iv) consolidation of a co-operative's economic position.

(*d*) A road haulage co-operative must accept as members those wage workers who started to work for the respective co-operative at least one year before the start of World War Two and continued uninterruptedly for three successive years during the war. A special committee will decide whether the economic condition of the respective road haulage co-operative warrants the immediate admission of more wage workers as members. One of the suggestions which should be considered is whether to convert the garages of the respective transportation co-operatives into separate and autonomous co-operatives based on self-labour or whether to organize the garages as a partnership of a co-operative of the workers of the respective garage (commandite) and a Histadrut-sponsored economic body.

The secretariat's report refers to an incident in the summer of 1942 which further embittered the negotiations. On the advice of income-tax experts it had been decided in principle that every transport co-operative should turn over all its immovable and movable property to a subsidiary co-operative. Before the details were cleared, the bus co-operatives already had registered and transferred their respective properties to subsidiaries whose rules, unlike those of most WPSTS, did not prescribe special rights for Chevrat Haovdim. The Histadrut did not accept the explanations of the WPSTS about this omission. More serious was the fact that the Registrar of Co-operatives did not follow the accepted unwritten procedure of obtaining the opinion of the Merkaz Haco-operatzia, as the audit union for WPSTS, before registering the rules of the subsidiary co-operatives. The secretariat's report describes as "evasive" the Registrar's reply as to why he acted in this way. The Histadrut, through Chevrat Haovdim, on 23 January, 1944, submitted to the Registrar "at his request" proposals on how to safeguard the social aspects of WPSTS. The secretariat's report notes that the bus co-operatives "rightly" took exception to the fact that

Chevrat Haovdim did not send them a copy of the proposals.[154] The bus co-operatives alleged that the secret negotiations confirmed their views that the Histadrut wished "to rule, and to treat them as chattels and to force them on their knees". Merkaz Haco-operatzia argued that Chevrat Haovdim's proposals, which the bus co-operatives rejected after three weeks of debate, embody the principles which the Histadrut previously had approved.

Chevrat Haovdim's memorandum of 24 January, 1944, to the Registrar included the following recommendations:

(*a*) Audit unions should have more influence over their affiliated co-operatives' decision about the amount which new members have to pay into the capital and about the allocation of the surpluses. The audit unions also should enjoy the right to veto "such decisions which they consider are potentially injurious to the healthy development of the respective co-operatives or are a departure from co-operative principles.

(*b*) Every existent active co-operative must immediately join an audit union and a new co-operative must join an existing audit union within one year after registration.

(*c*) Decisions to withdraw from an audit union should require the approval at a general meeting by a three-fourths majority of the members of the respective co-operative, at which the pros and cons have been set forth by the members and by the representatives of the respective audit union. Any decision to withdraw from the audit union becomes effective two years from the date of the general meeting of the respective co-operative at which the decision was taken.

(*d*) Officially approved public organizations which are interested in advancing co-operation should be eligible for membership and such a member should be authorized to cast up to half the votes at all general meetings of the respective co-operatives.

According to the secretariat's report, Chevrat Haovdim was prepared to consider amendments to its aforementioned memorandum. This did not help, and four of the seven bus co-operatives (names of the bus co-operatives not given) withdrew from the division for bus co-operatives of Merkaz Haco-operatzia and also withdrew their representatives from the management of this division.

The report on the proceedings of the Fifth Congress notes that Berl Katzenelson, David Remez, David Ben-Gurion and Mrs. Golda Myerson (now Golda Meir) attended a meeting on 1 February, 1944, to discuss the memorandum which Chevrat Haovdim had submitted to the Registrar of Co-operatives. Some of Berl Katzenelson's remarks at this meeting, given in the report, are quoted below:

"It seems to me that the bus co-operatives are now on a decline and the problem is how to prevent these from being destroyed. . . . In spite of serious disappointments . . . I remain a devotee (Chasid) to co-operation —including the bus co-operatives. I am opposed to the nationalization of bus transportation. I consider co-operation, with all its defects, as a large national undertaking. Transportation on foundations similar to those in Israel is not found in any other country. . . . It is not coincidental that the bus service was the child of national considerations and that its very marked development is attributable to the . . . Histadrut. And it could not exist one day without the Histadrut . . . it is a fact that all of the property is yours. The Histadrut is interested in . . . the integration of immigration, and in appropriate arrangement of the country's affairs; labour relations and the prevention of exploitation. If you are not prepared for all these, you will have the competition from new and more worthy co-operatives, which are more national, Zionist, public and Histadrut minded.

"The question is not the extent of the Histadrut authority over you but the extent of your ties to the Histadrut. . . . You argue that actually it is the member and not the wage worker who is exploited. If this is the case do you continue to use wage labour in order to prove that he is not being exploited. . . . This debate cannot bring any blessing. Suppose the bus system was divorced from (outside of) the Histadrut; that you are not restricted about the use of wage labour and you are completely free of the partnership with the Histadrut. Have you any idea how the battle of the wage workers will develop against you? . . . The Histadrut's main interest, which takes precedence even over the abolition of wage labour, is that the co-operative must not be closed to new immigration, war veterans, or to any type of additional members. The Histadrut also is interested in the quality of the service. While I believe and wish to support the idea that in our country the organized producer is a more important factor than is the productive power of the consumer, nevertheless the producer must have respect for the consumer. Therefore you must give good service.

"I look on you as children of the Histadrut, you have established a Histadrut economic enterprise of great importance. But its importance lies in the fact that it is a movement, that it is tied to the national economy. This identification is the educational foundation of the bus co-operatives in the country. And remember, you must make firm decisions, which are most important for the Histadrut and for co-operation. Decide, therefore, with a full sense of responsibility."[155]

But this conversation was not continued, and the secretariat's report to the Fifth Congress of Merkaz Haco-operatzia notes that the bus co-operatives persisted in their objections to the proposals which Chevrat Haovdim had submitted to the Registrar for safeguarding the social aspects of the Histadrut-sponsored co-operatives. Efforts made at the Sixth Histadrut Congress, of 28 January-2 February, 1945, to find a *modus vivendi* with the bus co-operatives were unsuccessful. And this Congress adopted the following resolutions:

"The Histadrut will no longer tolerate within its midst what amounts to *de facto* exploitation of wage labour by its members. The Sixth (Histadrut) Congress instructs the Histadrut Executive Committee to enforce the decisions about the liquidation of wage labour, previously adopted and published; and to draw all the consequences arising from this decision of the Sixth (Histadrut) Congress in the case of every co-operative which does not carry out (accept) its (Congress) decisions."

The only item on the agenda of the extraordinary meeting of the Histadrut council on 23 March, 1945 was wage labour in the co-operatives (presumably bus co-operatives). Mrs. Myerson (now Meir) reported to the Council that "there was a genuine desire among the members of the bus co-operatives to remain in the camp and not to secede. Three of the seven bus co-operatives (Jerusalem, Tel Aviv and the one serving the suburbs in the Haifa Bay district) had signed contracts; two were about to sign and the negotiations with two others were continuing."

According to the Secretariat's Report the basis of the contract was the Sixth Histadrut Congress decision of 2 February, 1945, viz., that

(*a*) there was no place in the Histadrut for a co-operative which exploited wage labour;
(*b*) the liquidation of wage labour must not be implemented by discharging the wage workers; and
(*c*) the procedure for the liquidation of wage labour must not culminate in the destruction of the respective economic undertaking.

The Histadrut Council at its extraordinary meeting, of 23 March, 1945, approved the committee's report (submitted by Mrs. Myerson) about the agreement with the five bus co-operatives and it decided to refer to the Histadrut arbitration tribunal any bus co-operative which does not sign the agreement by 15 May, 1946.

On 14 May, 1946, the Histadrut Executive Committee fixed the terms of employment (including the fringe benefits) for the permanent wage workers in the WPSTS and the procedure for accepting them as members.[156]

The secretariat's report to the Fifth Congress of 7-9 April, 1949, then notes that on 27 June, 1946, the sub-committee which the Histadrut appointed to implement the Histadrut decisions about wage labour in WPSTS decided to dissolve. Its functions were taken over by local committees having one representative each appointed by the chairman of the Histadrut Executive Committee; Merkaz Haco-operatzia; and the respective local labour councils. A WPSTS could not accept any temporary wage labour without the express approval of the respective local committee. The bus co-operatives returned to the folds of Merkaz Haco-operatzia and on 15 September, 1946, an agreement was concluded for setting up a central committee for bus co-operatives as an ancillary to Merkaz Haco-operatzia. The Management Committee and the secretariat of this ancillary organ would include an equal number of representatives of the Chevrat Haovdim and of the bus co-operatives. Unresolved differences of opinion between the representatives on the above mentioned Central Committee would be referred to Merkaz Haco-operatzia in the first instance and to the Histadrut Executive Committee in the last instance.

L. Weisbrot (Egged) told the Fifth Congress, of Merkaz Haco-operatzia (7-9 April, 1949), that the local labour councils forced the WPSTS to employ wage workers, especially during periods of unemployment.

> "The founders (of the bus co-operatives) did not think about and were not interested in the exploitation of their fellow beings." Egged's decision to turn over the garage to Solel Boneh was not actuated by the profit motive. In the course of time wage labour became a serious problem which embittered their life. He refutes the allegation that the members consider their bus societies "only as a place of employment".

Another delegate to the Fifth Congress considered it unfair that the Histadrut asks only the members of the bus co-operatives to share their savings with others. The bus co-operatives are ready to accept new members but the Government, the Histadrut and national institutions should help the new members to pay their participation in the bus society's capital which he notes is high.

A. Kitzis (third member of the Secretariat of the Merkaz Haco-operatzia) notes that those who objected to the bus co-operatives distributing among their vatikim the difference between the nominal and real value of the shares and/or part of the entrance fees which new members pay, were revolutionists and reactionaries. "Nobody will give away what belongs to him especially if he has derived this from his own work, unless it will be taken from him by force. . . . A man who has worked 20 or 25 years is entitled to a part of the surplus which his work has helped to create."

A number of delegates cited examples of pressure by local labour councils on WPSTS to employ wage labour and provide better conditions than the workers in the parallel non-co-operative undertakings. The labour councils also insist that the wage workers should receive the same fringe benefits as do the members of the respective WPSTS. Not a few wage workers, especially women, do not wish to become members of WPSTS.[157]

Mr. Shechter, a delegate from the largest road haulage co-operative, "Shelev", reported that the children of the older members are not enthusiastic about the suggestion for the integration of immigrants.[158]

Mr. B. Lin (Chevrat Haovdim delegate) replied that only on one occasion did the labour councils ask the bus co-operatives to employ wage labourers. He attributes the increased use of wage labour by the bus co-operatives in more recent years to their economic needs. He gives as an example the Egged garage which uses considerable wage labour.

The Fifth Congress, of 7-9 April, 1949, instructs Merkaz Haco-operatzia to continue in its efforts to minimize the extent of wage labour in the affiliated WPSTS and to safeguard the special conditions of employment for wage workers which the Histadrut organs have approved. It instructs

Merkaz Haco-operatzia, with the co-operation of the Histadrut Executive Committee, to establish and to maintain a permanent apparatus to minimize the use of wage workers and to safeguard their interests.

The secretariat's report to the Second Council meeting of Merkaz Haco-operatzia 24-25 May, 1950, refers to the chronic irritant of wage labour and to the closely allied problems of equal pay for all members; the participation by new members in WPSTS capital; and whether the rights of new members to the accumulated reserves, open and hidden, should be limited. Inasmuch as the Jewish Agency will not supply long term, low interest loans for the purchase of the minimum equipment, etc., which the WPSTS have to acquire for new members, the report argues that it is preferable to earmark the accumulated open and hidden reserves for the old members rather than to keep new members out because they cannot pay the participation in the capital, and large entrance fees which the respective WPSTS requires. Closed WPSTS must lead to their extinction.

The report considers that equal emoluments for all members is a way for maintaining the closed co-operative ("an instrument of lock outs"). "If all members receive the same emolument . . . the WPSTS insist that the skill of every new member should be such as to warrant paying him the maximum salary. This *de facto* closes the co-operatives" to new members.

Equal emoluments also increase the production costs and the number of marginal producers because there is no incentive.

One member of the staff of Merkaz Haco-operatzia keeps an eye on the use of wage labour and co-operates with a special committee for the elimination of wage labour, the chairman of which is a representative of the Histadrut control committee on which representatives of Merkaz Haco-operatzia and the local labour councils sit.

The few members of the council who referred to the secretariat's suggestion to change the policy of equal emoluments for all members disagreed since experience has demonstrated that differential emoluments precipitate most of the internal friction in the WPSTS.

In April 1954, Merkaz Haco-operatzia appointed a committee of nine (Mr. Ritov of the Merkaz Haco-operatzia secretariat attended all meetings) to enquire into and report on the question of the financial participation of members accepted by WPSTS affiliated to Merkaz Haco-operatzia. The Management Committee of Merkaz Haco-operatzia on 21 March, 1955, started to debate the committee's report (Shituf, March-April, 1955, pp. 24-25), which noted that wage labour was a serious question in only 10 per cent of the affiliated WPSTS (including Egged (Eshed) and Hamekasher). But this 10 per cent of the WPSTS' accounted for 50 per cent of the membership and for 55 per cent of the wage workers in all affiliated WPSTS. Furthermore, this group of 10 per cent includes

> "the most developed and consolidated WPSTS on which, to a very large degree, the future of the WPSTS movement depends." The committee also reported that "in most of the affiliated WPSTS they did not find

any relationship between the freezing of membership and the specific problems of the amount of participation prescribed for new members. However, the committee suggests that the affiliated WPSTS should continue to consult the standing committee of Merkaz Haco-operatzia that deals with the question of (financial) participation by new members . . . as and when applicants present themselves to the respective WPSTS."

The *ad hoc* committee of nine found that a second group "of several tens of WPSTS," that together with private or public capital, are the joint owners of workshops and factories, use a very appreciable number of wage workers. And that in the course of time the principle of self-labour in these joint undertakings became a fiction (imaginary). The committee thinks that this group of WPSTS also should be considered separately.

The *ad hoc* committee of nine also notes that the wage labour of five bus co-operatives (3,000) account for 40 per cent of their total labour force. According to its report, these bus co-operatives are prepared to admit as members those hired drivers who hold a bus driver's licence, and to permit these new members to pay their financial participation in instalments. But the bus co-operatives insist that they should have the right to fix the amount of the participation of a new member on the basis of a realistic evaluation (replaceable value) of their property (including goodwill). The *ad hoc* committee, on the other hand, recommended that the participation of new members in the capital of the bus co-operatives should not exceed 25 times the monthly gross emolument (includes cost of living allowance and all fringe benefits) to a member of the respective bus society at the time when the applicant is admitted. (A new member accepted in March 1955 by Egged (Eshed) on this basis would have to pay IL.7,700 ($4,400) in one or more instalments).

The *ad hoc* committee of nine also stressed that in the case of another nine per cent of the WPSTS affiliated to Merkaz Haco-operatzia, the question of the amount of participation by new members in the respective WPSTS' capital is the decisive reason for these having become closed co-operatives and that this stimulates the liquidation of WPSTS. For this group of WPSTS the committee recommends that every member should be required to hold at least one share with a nominal value, and members may acquire as many additional shares on which they will receive a guaranteed return. But all members will have only one vote each. The plan was suggested by Mr. Ritov.

The management's report to the meeting of the Council of Egged (Eshed), on 19 and 21-22 September, 1955, stated that acting on the advice of the Histadrut, Solel Boneh in the near future will return the garage which Egged (Eshed) had leased to Solel Boneh. The Histadrut also decided that Egged (Eshed)

(*a*) must retain the 63 workers who were employed in the garage when it was transferred to Solel Boneh;

(*b*) give priority to the other workers in this garage, if and when Egged (Eshed) will hire additional staff for the garage.

The management's Report to the Council of Egged (Eshed) notes that in the period between 1 April and 1 August, 1955, there was an increase in drivers from 1,480 to 1,536 and a decrease in the total labour force from 1,785 to 1,748.

According to the report of the proceedings of this council meeting, Egged (Eshed) had organized a subsidiary company, "Chevrat Hatachanot", which had taken over the construction, etc., of Egged (Eshed) stations throughout the country. Egged (Eshed) held all the IL.200,000 shares in this company which its members had purchased. A contract drafted by a special committee defines the relationship between Egged (Eshed) and the company which was to be signed in the near future.[159] The participation of every old member in the share capital of Egged (Eshed) was revalued and fixed at IL.8,000. And the tens of new members already "admitted in principle" will arrange to pay a similar amount. But Egged (Eshed) has yet to decide how much members leaving will receive as a refund of their participation in the co-operative's capital.

S. Goren explains that the meeting of the Management Committee of the division for industrial workers co-operatives of Merkaz Haco-operatzia on 12 December, 1958, was convened primarily to discuss the recommendations of the "committee on integration (of additional members) . . .". He said: "I consider this meeting decisive for the future existence of the WPSTS movement. This I say on the basis of my thirty years' experience in this field and in this house (Merkaz Haco-operatzia building)."

He noted that they are far from having been "completely successful" in their co-operative goal. This is equally true of other Histadrut-sponsored co-operative sectors. "I never thought that it would be possible to do away with all wage labour . . . but we cannot permit the present situation to continue, because this is leading to the liquidation of the WPSTS movement. . . . Since wage labour is an emasculation and perversion of the conception of equity (equality)."

He considers the principle of equal emolument for all members as a perversion of the definition of equity (equality). No economy can exist on the basis of a system of emoluments which *de facto* provide the maximum reward to "all members without exception". Such a WPSTS cannot compete with other plants in the same branch which have longer workdays and a differential wage scale. He is especially concerned because most of the vatikim are approaching the age group of 55 years and over. With the introduction of wage labour the old co-operatives have declared a *de facto* lock-out of new and younger members. Generally speaking, there is "much talk about the elimination of wage labour, but very little has been achieved mainly because of a fear to face the ultimate consequences".

The three years' effort to resolve the question of a member's participation in a WPSTS capital also has been unsuccessful. For instance, the co-operative workshops in the metal industry report a decrease by five members and an increase by 150 wage workers during the last five years. The same unsatisfactory development is found in the co-operative joineries and in practically every other branch. Though very anxious that the industrial workers co-operatives admit new members, Mr. Goren does not think that it will be possible to carry out in full the proposal of the *ad hoc* committee about the elimination of wage labour. But he does accept the basic principle of a consistent increase of membership of WPSTS. And it must be made abundantly clear that if the WPSTS fail to comply with the Histadrut's directives to minimize wage labour and to fix a reasonable amount for new members' participation in their capital, that this will affect the extent of the Histadrut's financial assistance to the WPSTS. And "95 per cent of our co-operatives, even the large ones, cannot get along without Histadrut help."

The Management Committee of the division for industrial workers co-operatives of Merkaz Haco-operatzia then considered the following proposals (some of which have been amended) of the *ad hoc* committee on the integration of additional members.

(*a*) The division for industrial workers co-operatives of Merkaz Haco-operatzia should immediately initiate the steps necessary for gradually replacing wage labour through the admission of additional members.

(*b*) The number of new members which every WPSTS must admit shall not be less than 25 per cent of the wage workers which it used during the last year.

(*c*) A plant jointly owned by another party and a co-operative of workers, and if the number of wage workers exceed half the number of the members of the workers co-operative, the latter must admit 25 per cent of all wage workers as members.

(*d*) A WPSTS should have the right to discharge wage workers with a seniority of three or more years who refuse to join the co-operative. If the co-operative turns down a wage worker having three or more years' seniority, the respective worker should enjoy a special status in the co-operative.

(*e*) The division for industrial workers co-operatives of Merkaz Haco-operatzia must arrange that every affiliated industrial workers co-operative using wage labour should distribute part of its annual surplus among these.

(*f*) The division for industrial workers co-operatives should facilitate the admission of additional members by helping its affiliated WPSTS to obtain increased financing; training the youth, and arranging courses for the new members, etc.

(*g*) The secretariat should convene a special meeting of the Council of Merkaz Haco-operatzia and should arrange for its affiliated WPSTS to accept a thousand additional members in the next two years. Prior to the council meeting, Merkaz Haco-operatzia should arrange for the general meeting of every affiliated WPSTS and regional meetings of groups of WPSTS.

(*h*) A five-member committee, appointed by the division for industrial workers co-operatives, after studying the position should fix the quota of new members for each affiliated WPSTS. It also should supervise the enforcement of the quotas. The Management Committee of the division will adjudicate any appeal of an affiliated WPSTS about its quota and apply sanctions against an affiliated WPSTS that does not fill its quota of new members.

A. Tzwick, unlike Mr. Goren, wants Merkaz Haco-operatzia, in principle, to have the right to fix the amount of a new member's participation for every affiliated WPSTS. And a special joint committee of the three divisions should deal with their respective affiliated co-operatives. He gives four main reasons why WPSTS have accepted so few new members.

1. Lack of desire ("I fear that this will continue").
2. Merkaz Haco-operatzia did not help sufficiently to ensure the enforcement of its decision.
3. The two-pronged policy of the Histadrut—asking the WPSTS to liquidate wage labour and at the same time permitting plants jointly owned by a Histadrut-sponsored body and a co-operative of workers to employ wage labour.
4. During one period the Histadrut leaders argued that the integration of immigrants as workers should have precedence over the liquidation of wage labour.

Zvi Lehman is apprehensive that in line with the general trend of the recommendations of the *ad hoc* committee on integration[160] that Merkaz Haco-operatzia and its divisions will be "maximalist" in debate and "minimalist" in the enforcement of decisions. They must define the procedure for implementing the recommendations and the application of sanctions. He agrees with Mr. Goren that Merkaz Haco-operatzia should not become involved in an endless debate about the amount of the members' participation in the capital, since there are so few applicants who are ready to pay the large amounts which the respective WPSTS have fixed, especially in the case of the "run down WPSTS". There is still a considerable field for elucidating the problems to the rank and file of members of the old and new WPSTS affiliated to Merkaz Haco-operatzia.

Mr. Yavnieli is more concerned about the decrease (thinning out) of WPSTS than about the use of wage labour which in his opinion will determine the fate of the WPSTS. He would welcome the establishment of 50 new WPSTS, each with 15 members and 12 wage workers. The main problem is to provide work for the immigrants. It is equally important to make certain that the wage workers' interests are not prejudiced and that they receive part of the profits.

Chaim Benyovitz also thinks that every WPSTS is in the best position to fix the amount of a new member's participation in its capital in the light of the prevailing situation and conditions. The discussion and the decision about the number of new members which a WPSTS should accept must be individualized.

Mr. Goldberg describes Mr. Yavnieli's reaction as a "defeatist attitude", viz., that they accept the situation and do not try to mend it. This must lead to the disappearance of the WPSTS movement. Either they should make a desperate effort to change conditions or liquidate the WPSTS movement by converting the 50 most profitable WPSTS into limited companies. Had they taken action ten years ago, even if that would have reduced the number of WPSTS, the WPSTS movement would not have reached the present impasse. There is no question that the wage workers would join their respective WPSTS if they were convinced that otherwise they could be discharged. And if the wage workers are given a voice in the management without becoming a member of the WPSTS, why should they join?

K. Cohen confirms that better situated WPSTS have accepted very few new members. In accepting wage workers, they have contributed their share to the integration of immigrants. Unless the use of wage workers is immediately curtailed and their percentage relationship to members is decreased, the WPSTS movement will disappear. A sub-committee appointed by the Histadrut Executive Committee to check wage labour in WPSTS includes some of the members of the management of the unemployment fund which advances loans to enable WPSTS to increase their wage labour force. Without a defined and unified policy from the top, results cannot be expected. He asks Merkaz Haco-operatzia to appoint a committee that will fix the amount of a new member's participation, case by case, in the light of the situation of the respective WPSTS at the time.

M. Lam ascribes the marked hesitancy of WPSTS to accept additional members to

(*a*) unsatisfactory experience in the past;
(*b*) emoluments to members exceeding the wages of wage workers; and
(*c*) the hesitancy of Merkaz Haco-operatzia to use its authority and its refusal to individualize the treatment of its affiliated WPSTS.

Rachel Perry wants the value of a member's share fixed once and for all. Otherwise, a WPSTS may be compelled to accept additional members and to require only nominal participation in the respective WPSTS capital.

S. Goren is reported as having said that

"we came to this meeting in order to change certain practices . . . I also say that this is not an attempt to do away with all wage labour. The . . . decrease in the percentage of wage labour . . . in the global labour force . . . is not a final solution but it does establish a more acceptable and healthier relationship. . . . All our intervention with regard to fixing the amount of a member's financial participation has failed. Therefore there is no other choice than to leave it to every WPSTS to settle this question. . . . And I gather from the speakers' remarks that the majority of the Management Committee (of the division for industrial workers co-operatives of Merkaz Haco-operatzia) favour the recommendation of the *ad hoc* committee. . . . We will have to sit down and talk with the labour council in every region. Because without them we cannot succeed in our goal."

Mr. Goren told the Sixth Council Meeting of Merkaz Haco-operatzia on 12 January, 1959, that the management committee of the division for industrial workers co-operatives[161] devoted two sessions, on 2 and 24 December, 1958, to the question of wage labour.

"The problem of wage workers is especially serious in the WPSTS of the metal branch . . . in some of these co-operatives there are more wage workers than there are members . . . two wage workers for every member. . . . This is a very sad picture."[162]

The decision of the management committee of the division of industrial workers co-operatives calls for the admission of a thousand additional members within the next two years. The division is determined to enforce the decision "even if it will be necessary to apply sanctions". An *ad hoc* committee will examine and fix the procedure and quota of additional members which each and every affiliated industrial workers co-operative has to accept.

Mr. Goren notes that the industrial workers co-operatives do not accept the proposal of Merkaz Haco-operatzia about the participation of the new members in the capital of the respective WPSTS, i.e., that every member has one voting share with a nominal value and any member may acquire an unlimited number of non-voting dividend bearing preference shares. The industrial workers co-operatives argued

"that if an acceptable solution will be found for the participation in the capital for new members and for a refund of participation to members leaving, the gates of the co-operative will be opened for new members. I did not believe this and I believe it still less today. . . . In the light of past experience . . . we came to the conclusion that this (i.e., participation of new members in the capital) is a question for direct negotiations between the member and the respective WPSTS. Any other procedure is doomed to failure. Merkaz Haco-operatzia's only concern is that the . . . participation of the new members (in a co-operative's capital) should remain with the respective co-operative and should not be distributed among the old members."

Mr. Goren, replying to the contention by the industrial workers co-operatives that

"it is difficult to find suitable members," said "it seems to me, that the mere fact that because an individual has been used to being a wage worker for some time, is no reason for disqualifying him for membership. . . . But the decision must be left to the WPSTS. Other methods tried out in recent years have failed."

A. Tzwick notes that the 60 co-operatives affiliated to the division for service co-operatives have 1,000 members and 400 wage workers. He attributes the relatively small percentage of wage workers in the global labour force to the fact that "these (the service co-operatives) do not attract people from the economic point of view and also do not have the possibilities of offering large scale employment." There are certain service co-operatives with more wage workers than members. He thinks that the increased use of wage labour is directly related to the demand on the co-operatives a few years ago

"to provide employment for war veterans, new immigrants, the unemployed. . . . I cannot say that all the service co-operatives, without exception, do not wish to accept new members. There are some whose very existence depends on the admission of new members, but there are no applicants (nobody to integrate)". Those relatively few new immigrants who decide to join the WPSTS "as the only way out", choose the consolidated WPSTS "of which—to our regret—there are not many". And in these the amount fixed for a new member's participation is beyond the reach of those few who wish to join. Therefore "if we agree to give the co-operatives complete freedom of action to fix the participation of new members . . . the co-operative will become a commercial business".

B. Lin (Histadrut Executive Committee) agreed to leave the question of participation in the WPSTS capital to negotiations between the co-operative and the respective new members. "Unless an obligatory solution (reply) is found for this question . . . it will be impossible to . . . reduce the number of wage workers and it will certainly be impossible to do away with all wage labour in the WPSTS."

In the case of the bus co-operatives there is the additional difficulty that every candidate must be "within a specified age group and have an A.A. bus driver's licence". If these continue to be the unalterable qualifications there is no real hope of reducing, let alone abolishing wage labour in the bus co-operatives "in our days".

A. Davidson refutes Mr. Lin's criticism because the bus co-operatives require an A.A. driver's licence as a condition for membership. The co-operative must be able to rotate members' jobs as the need arises. The Histadrut Executive Committee at a plenary session decided that the garage which Solel Boneh had run with wage workers should be returned to Egged (Eshed). And now the Histadrut complains "that we employ wage labour". He agrees that the bus co-operative should not use non-members for driving posts and perhaps also for certain other skilled jobs and for senior staff appointments.

A. Mazar notes that in the light of the increase of the membership of

Dan from 500 to 1,100 and of Egged (Eshed) from 1,300 to 2,000 within "a relatively short time, he cannot understand the complaints about wage labour in the bus co-operatives."

Y. Ritov told the Seventh Council Meeting of Merkaz Haco-operatzia on 3 September, 1959, that the working conditions of wage workers in the bus co-operatives, "a beloved child of the public", is a chronic irritant and engenders conflicts with the wage workers and at times also strikes. The "Chaskin Committee", made up of representatives of Chevrat Haovdim; the craft union; Merkaz Haco-operatzia; the bus co-operatives and the wage workers, has just about summarized its conclusions. The Histadrut also has appointed a special committee, Meshel Committee, to consider the appeals of the bus co-operatives and of their wage workers against the recommendation of the Chaskin Committee. After several months of negotiations, the Meshel Committee fixed the scale of emoluments for the members and for the wage workers of bus co-operatives. "I think that in no other place of employment are the conditions as favourable as those fixed for the wage workers" in the bus co-operatives.

Though the bus co-operatives accepted "hundreds of members this year (1958-59)" these still use 2,000 wage workers, Mr. Ritov said. But the Histadrut wants the bus co-operatives to accept all their wage workers as members. The question of an increase of new members is closely tied to the amount which these must pay to the bus co-operatives. There is an old oral agreement that the amount should be the equivalent of 28 months' gross emoluments which a member receives, IL.10,500, and that wage workers with at least two years' seniority are eligible for a discount of IL.1,000. The secretariat of the division for bus and road haulage co-operatives have approved, subject to confirmation by Chevrat Haovdim, the request of the bus co-operatives that the payments by new members should be linked with the cost of living index.

Zeev Onn considers the problem of wage workers in the WPSTS as very serious, especially in the bus co-operatives in which the number of wage workers and of members are about the same. The WPSTS must create "a genuine spirit of equality between the members and the wage workers". If, as is the case in Haargaz and Egged (Eshed), wage workers with eight to ten years' seniority continue to enjoy fewer rights than do the members, there is a real danger that such WPSTS "will explode".

S. Stenger differentiates between seasonal and permanent wage labour and thinks that the reduction and elimination of wage labour must be "step by step and planned". But "those WPSTS in which most of the permanent labour staff are wage workers should not be tolerated".

M. Yavnieli (Haargaz) notes that years of experience have demonstrated that the smaller WPSTS can get along without wage labour and that equal emoluments for all members is feasible. Medium size WPSTS need a variable labour force and number of apprentices and equal emoluments for all members is ruinous. Large industrial workers co-operatives can operate profitably only if they can regulate their labour force to their needs by the use of wage labour. These large establishments should be changed into partnerships between the co-operative of workers (commandites) and Chevrat Haovdim. He thinks that Haargaz is an example.

A. M. Davidson notes that much has been said in this and at other meetings about the bus co-operatives. But a concrete proposal has not been made. The *ad hoc* committee which the Council (12 January, 1959) appointed has not submitted any proposal. Therefore, he suggests that one other inter-WPSTS committee

> "should formulate and submit a new code or procedure for the admission of wage workers as members a month before the Sixth Congress is convened. A wage worker who reaches a certain grade of skill either should join or leave the respective WPSTS. . . . Between April, 1958, and August, 1959, Egged (Eshed) accepted 387 new members and of these, 155 were from its permanent wage labourers. But there is no doubt that a large co-operative and apparatus like Egged (Eshed) cannot do without wage labour. . . ." He thinks that "a differential emolument system would destroy the internal structure of the WPSTS . . . shake its moral foundations . . . and therefore should be avoided by all possible means".

The Eighth Council, of 29 September, 1959, supports the decisions of the Merkaz Haco-operatzia secretariat to reduce appreciably the imbalance in the relationship between the number of wage workers and the number of members and the council directs the affiliated WPSTS to carry out the decisions.

H. Zackai at the meeting of the division for industrial workers co-operatives, of 21 May, 1960, explains the psychological aspects about the admission of new and young members which invariably creates apprehension among the vatikim that "in the course of time they will be thrown out". This accounts for the tendency for the WPSTS to become closed co-operatives and to use more wage labour which in more recent years has led to their bankruptcy. Wage labour without exploitation is impossible, and therefore industrial workers co-operatives which cannot operate profitably without wage labour should be forced to change into another pattern.

Zvi Lehman notes that the industrial workers co-operatives have 1,500 members and 1,750 wage workers. The 1,750 include 150 apprentices; 450 seasonal workers; and 250 women in various branches.

> "Does anyone suggest that we accept these three categories as members?" he asked. There are 150-200 wage workers who do not wish to become members for the present. Therefore "the serious problem is one of only 700 wage workers and there really is no justification for not accepting these as full members. But we should not speak about 1,750."

S. Goren finds Mr. Lehman's calculations as "over simplified". Even if the Histadrut accepted the principle that a WPSTS may use wage workers provided that these do not exceed the number of members, the Histadrut and Merkaz Haco-operatzia would still have to expel "not a small number of WPSTS". Merely because it is difficult to merge the two generations is not a reason why "fathers and sons" should not be members of the same co-operative. There are already WPSTS all of whose members are invalids and yet these have not accepted additional members.

Y. Barzilai (Merkaz Haco-operatzia) notes that generally speaking "a co-operative plant which maintains discipline and good social relationships has no financing difficulties. A bank will not assist a co-operative in which there are unsatisfactory internal relationships".

There are industrial workers co-operatives that have not admitted new blood for 25 years. Do not their members realize that they have aged and the infusion of new blood will ameliorate and consolidate their co-operatives?

A. Frumerman (Achdut, bakery branch) notes that wage labour is unavoidable because there are no applicants for membership. Their co-operative accepted two of the four wage workers of their branch as members. But within a year they had to get rid of them to prevent the complete economic and social collapse of this branch. He still thinks that with effective and persistent educational work, youth could be attracted to WPSTS. And he suggests that every WPSTS which uses wage labour should have four or five apprentices.

Yaacov Cohen (Merkaz Haco-operatzia) notes that in many of the WPSTS that use wage labour there are groups who adopt the attitude of employers towards these and block the acceptance of new members.

M. Ofner (Achva, printing co-operative) thinks that they must reconcile themselves to the use of wage labour "within certain limits as a hurdle which they cannot jump". Admittedly, only young members can safeguard the interest of the old members; but *de facto* one must consider the conflict between the younger members and the vatikim. More thorough screening of applicants probably would reduce potential inter-member conflicts.

D. Harel (Ketef, soap and detergents) reports that their co-operative cannot attract new members as it cannot pay the craft union rate for parallel work and they are four months in arrears in the emoluments.

P. Golobovitz (Ilan, one of the oldest co-operative joineries) thinks that the differences between the young and the vatikim, which is both psychological and economic, are very serious and involved, and that both groups "cannot live and work under one roof as equals with equals and with full understanding". "It seems to me that there is no solution for this problem," he added.

H. Goldberg (Merkaz Haco-operatzia) speaks as one who has spent most of his days in a WPSTS and rejects the assumption that the employment of wage labour is a transgression of principles of the Histadrut. The section in the Histadrut constitution about the exploitation of one's neighbour was drafted when there was no WPSTS movement. Wage labour cannot be eliminated without the agreement of the WPSTS, and it would be unjust to expel a WPSTS from the Histadrut merely because it uses wage labour.

Y. Zeidenberg (Namlit, building materials, Haifa Bay) notes that their co-operative has members in the age group 60 and over, and does not use any wage labour. Yet they are competitive and earn their livelihood. Their only need is more working capital.

D. Weiss (Naalei Artzeinu, shoe co-operative, Jerusalem) states if he and others like him had again to choose a pattern of life, they probably would prefer not to be "exploiters" in a WPSTS. Times have changed and have influenced the pattern of the WPSTS that undoubtedly "in spite of their sins" have achievements to their credit. One must adjust experiments to the realities of the day. At one time their co-operative abolished all wage labour and accepted as members the apprentices recruited from Hanoar Haoved, the Histadrut-sponsored youth movement. At present the young people argue that it is more advantageous to continue as wage workers.

Y. Levy (Naalei Artzeinu) states that the members are aging and that their co-operative must have new blood. Yet, only one of the eight wage workers accepted the invitation to join. The others did not wish to pay their participation in the co-operative's capital.

S. Goren reported to the Eleventh Council Meeting, of 12 December, 1960, that the joint Chevrat Haovdim-Merkaz Haco-operatzia committee had agreed on a plan for the elimination of wage labour to the mutual satisfaction of all parties. There were separate and parallel discussions with the bus co-operatives "and at times the relationship between the bus co-operatives and the Histadrut were almost at breaking point". There is reason to assume and to believe that "the (bus) co-operative will carry out the agreement" and that at the end of two years the number of wage workers will not exceed 20 per cent of the total labour force. (At the end of 1964 the three bus co-operatives had 5,216 members and 1,444 non-members, including apprentices.)

Y. Ritov calls 1960 outstanding

> "in the history of our co-operatives . . . in the struggle for a solution for wage labour . . . since it was decided to change the status of wage workers to members . . . over a thousand men and women in the three bus co-operatives (Egged 530; Dan 387; Hamekasher 70-80)[163] have been admitted as members and additional quotas will be fixed for 1962, etc. The question will be fully resolved within a shorter period than that which Histadrut fixed."

Only in the bus co-operatives have the wage workers pressed their demand to be admitted as members. This he attributes to the fact that the economic opportunities seem more favourable in the bus co-operatives than in the other categories of WPSTS.

> "When we ask (approach) a small or medium size industrial workers or service co-operative to admit wage workers, the reply is that this depends on the renewal or replacement of equipment, the increase of credits and the consolidation of their indebtedness; and the provision

of loans to enable the applicant to pay his participation . . ." (for membership).

Mr. Ritov reports that in the last two or three months the industrial workers co-operatives and the service societies have accepted 45 people as full members and 47 as probationers, "whose confirmation as full members is only a technical question". The road haulage co-operatives were the first to agree to admit most of their wage workers provided Merkaz Haco-operatzia would help the wage workers to pay in cash their participation in the capital of the respective co-operatives. There is some hope that Merkaz Haco-operatzia will succeed in arranging this financing.

There are some industrial workers co-operatives and service societies in which the wage workers appreciably exceed the number of members. In some of the co-operatives in these two groups the members account for 25 per cent of the respective total labour forces. These WPSTS have not shown any willingness to resolve the question of wage labour "even within a period of four years". It seems that the only recourse is to expel them (from Merkaz Haco-operatzia) subject to their right of appeal to the secretariat of Chevrat Haovdim. But it is improbable that the appeals committee of Chevrat Haovdim will grant the appeal of the respective co-operatives.

A. Tzwick attributes the extensive use of wage workers to the failure of Merkaz Haco-operatzia to deal effectively with this problem at the very outset. They must completely destroy the plague and continue as a movement or they can "make peace" with the offenders, and face the gradual degeneration and the ultimate disappearance of the WPSTS movement. He rebukes those who deal with this question "light heartedly", and who invariably point to wage labour in the kibbutzim and moshavim "as an alibi, because they are ignorant of the fact that the Histadrut-sponsored agricultural settlements" encourage the wage labourers and give them every opportunity and every inducement to become full members without any reservations or equivocations. Not a few WPSTS have become so accustomed to wage labour that they think that their very existence depends on this. WPSTS in which wage workers do all the hard labour and unskilled work and receive much smaller emoluments than do members, "had lost their public value and Histadrut content and are only private partnerships. The WPSTS, in spite of deviations, can still be used as a dam to bridge the feelings of insecurity and moral disintegration . . . the most immediate task is to uproot the wild grass, the plague of wage labour."

Chaim Zackai notes that *de facto* the fight against wage labour concerns 25-30 WPSTS affiliated to Merkaz Haco-operatzia. But these 25-30

> "account for 80 per cent of our consolidated WPSTS (original underlined) and I do not have the feeling that we have the necessary unequivocal resistance for this."

Experience thus far has shown that the consolidation fund has not been an effective agent. Slogans such as[164] "the open gate" alone cannot resolve the problem. Even if Merkaz Haco-operatzia had functioned more effectively, or if wage labour were discontinued, he doubts whether this would have appreciably influenced the status and prevented the decline of the WPSTS movement. His final remark is "what then is the real (truthful) answer".

Yehoshua Ron (Dan Bus Co-operative) refutes the assumption that a wage worker if admitted as a member "can become rich". True, an additional emolument of IL.50-100 a month makes it possible to "raise a little" his standard of living and enables him to give his children more schooling. But this is not "becoming rich". When admitted as a member in 1935, the LP.450 which he had paid into Dan's capital was real money ("full weight in coins"). Today the participation of a new member is equivalent to one-third of the purchase price of a bus. Where can they obtain the money to cover the "millions of pounds which have to be invested for the additional buses needed for the increase in membership?" He refutes the statement that members do not do any of "the dirty work . . . there is no dirtier work than driving a bus[165]. . . and there are other difficult jobs which they are not prepared to turn over to others".

M. A. Davidson (Egged (Eshed)) states that the introduction of a graded scale of emoluments for members will weaken (jeopardize) and not bolster the co-operative aspects. They prefer to continue "as one family whose main goal is to obtain jointly the maximum from their labour". And "he who enriches himself through co-operation is not a co-operator". They want that "equal division among the members of the revenue and the elimination of the conception of suitable and unsuitable work for members should be introduced into all WPSTS."

The WPSTS, like kibbutzim, cannot and should not be asked to accept every applicant for membership.

> "If we (bus co-operatives) had known that we would have to accept all wage workers, we would not have accepted them as wage workers. . . . This is why we said that the bus co-operatives cannot accept permanent wage workers. If it is proposed to obligate the co-operatives (it is not clear whether Mr. Davidson means only bus co-operatives or all WPSTS) to widen their framework by admitting the wage workers, then the co-operatives should have the right to choose the wage workers."

The WPSTS are interested in admitting wage workers whom they have selected after screening. On the other hand, Mr. Davidson does not share the general view that admission of more members compels the WPSTS to look for budgets or colonization loans ("taktsivim"). If he did not believe in the unlimited creative and productive power and efficiency of the members he would have declared that there is no *raison d'être* for the existence of the WPSTS. He, therefore, warns the members that the continuity of their co-operatives depends on a limited use of wage labour and defining a procedure for admitting wage workers as members. He asks the Histadrut to accept the following conception or interpretation of self-labour, viz., "that it is confined to those skilled operations which require a specified standard of skill". Excessive rigidity in this matter must lead to subterfuges (equivocations) and co-operatives must and should not "resort to subterfuges".

The Eleventh Council, of 12 December, 1960, expressed its full agreement with the decisions of the Chevrat Haovdim secretariat about wage labour in WPSTS (co-operatives) and instructs the secretariat of Merkaz Haco-operatzia, in close co-operation with the secretariats of the respective divisions, to try (to work) to achieve these.

Decisions of Sixth Congress of Merkaz Haco-operatzia, 15-16 July, 1962, about Wage Labour.

1. The elimination of wage labour is a condition *sine qua non* for ameliorating the social aspects and for the economic consolidation and the persistent development of the WPSTS.
2. The Congress notes that during the last two years there has been a marked advance in dealing with the question of wage labour and that hundreds of wage workers have been admitted by the bus and other WPSTS.
3. The Congress considers the above as the first step for the final solution of wage labour in the WPSTS and directs the secretariat of Merkaz Haco-operatzia and the management of their divisions (industrial co-operatives; transport co-operatives and service societies) to continue their efforts to clarify to their respective affiliated WPSTS the social and economic dangers of wage labour and that they should take all the necessary steps to resolve the problem within three years. The Congress also directed the secretariats of its respective departments to take steps against the "closed co-operative" trend and the non-admission of new members by many WPSTS.
4. Wage workers who will be accorded the right to join as members of WPSTS are requested to express their agreement to do this. Wage workers who refuse to join as members of their respective WPSTS for reasons which are not considered as reasonable to those who are authorized to deal with this question, will lose their right of employment in the respective WPSTS.
5. A condition for all WPSTS that may be organized is the unequivocal acceptance and practice of self-labour and the prohibition of any wage labour.
6. The use of temporary or seasonal labour that may be needed for the orderly maintenance of established WPSTS requires the approval of the secretariat of Merkaz Haco-operatzia. The use of such labour will be limited both as to time and number.
7. WPSTS that will not accept and carry out the aforementioned decisions about the elimination of wage labour and/or will not admit wage workers as members, will be denied financial and organizational assistance from the Histadrut-sponsored bodies, and may also be expelled from Chevrat Haovdim. The Histadrut also will take disciplinary measures against them.

The resolutions also include the following note:

The standing committee of the Sixth Congress also submitted the following proposals about members' participation in the share capital and emoluments for members. But in view of the difference of opinion within the committee during the general debate, the Presidium of the Congress suggested to the Congress not to vote on these proposals and to request Merkaz Haco-operatzia again to discuss these.

1. A member's participation in a respective WPSTS will be fixed by the secretariat of Merkaz Haco-operatzia subject to the approval by the secretariat of Chevrat Haovdim after joint discussion with the Chevrat Haovdim.
2. In fixing a member's participation in the capital of a respective WPSTS, only two factors are to be considered,
   (*a*) the property and
   (*b*) the general commercial status of the respective WPSTS.
3. The amount of participation is the same for a member being admitted and for a member who leaves his respective society.
4. When fixing the amount of participation the assets of the respective WPSTS are evaluated by an assessment committee appointed by the secretariat of Merkaz Haco-operatzia. The assessment committee shall include one representative each of the department to which the respective WPSTS is attached and a member of the auditing department of Merkaz Haco-operatzia, and one expert.
5. The aforementioned net value of the property shall be divided into a number of shares of the same denomination and these will constitute the capital of the respective WPSTS. The assessment committee may increase or decrease the nominal amount of a share but not by more than 30 per cent and the revised nominal amount shall constitute the amount of every member's participation (share) in the respective WPSTS.
6. The assessment committee's conclusion requires the confirmation of Merkaz Haco-operatzia and that of the secretariat of Chevrat Haovdim.
7. A member who leaves his respective WPSTS within one year after his admission is entitled to a refund equivalent to the amount of the nominal value of a share which was fixed when he was admitted, irrespective of any changes which may have taken place in the commercial position of the respective WPSTS. This section does not apply to those organizing a new WPSTS.
8. The probation period of a member is not considered when fixing the one-year period of membership of a respective member. The date of the decision to admit to membership and the date when membership ceases are considered when fixing the period of membership of a respective member.
9. With a view to facilitating the admission of new members, and subject to the agreement of Merkaz Haco-operatzia and confirma-

tion by the secretariat of Chevrat Haovdim, the shares may be split but the total number may not exceed four times the original number. A new member admitted must acquire only one of the shares after the split.

10. A member of a WPSTS who holds more than one share as a result of the split (in the ninth paragraph above) only enjoys the same rights as a member with one share. But a member may receive a dividend not exceeding four to six per cent per annum of the par value of the split shares. The secretariat of the division to which the respective WPSTS belongs will, from time to time, fix the dividend within the maximum limits of four to six per cent and the division's decision is to be considered as final. There can be no appeal against the decision.
11. The refund of the nominal value of the shares held in accordance with paragraph 9 and 10 are subject to the same conditions as the refund of a single share which a member holds.
12. The policy is for every member to hold one share each and for every member to enjoy the same rights, irrespective of the number of shares he holds. Every member shall have the right to acquire additional shares.
13. A member's liability for the society's debts in case of liquidation is the same, irrespective of the number of shares of the respective society which he holds.
14. In the case of a member leaving, the number of shares which he holds does not affect the consideration of any claims which the member has against the WPSTS.
15. With regard to questions to which sections (seven) and (nine) refer, the parties concerned may appeal against the decisions of Merkaz Haco-operatzia to the secretariat of Chevrat Haovdim.
16. WPSTS having many members of various skills shall fix the emoluments on the basis of skill and proficiency. But the fringe benefits, including participation in surpluses, shall be the same for all members.

SUMMARY OF PROPOSALS[166] FOR THE LIQUIDATION OF WAGE LABOUR IN WPSTS AND IN THE LABOUR (HISTADRUT-SPONSORED) COLONIZATION

Section C, divided into three parts, deals with WPSTS. The opening sentence of the first part declares that every Histadrut-sponsored WPSTS, including new ones, must operate only with self-labour.[167] The wage workers should be the first candidates for membership to be considered. It will be the responsibility of Histadrut bodies to transfer to other places of employment wage workers who refuse to apply for membership of the respective co-operatives in which they are now employed.

The second part of the section of the resolutions referring to WPSTS defines the principles for the participation in the share capital of respective WPSTS which it is hoped "should facilitate the integration of additional members". Every member of a WPSTS should have one share and that Chevrat Haovdim "on the basis of an opinion expressed by Merkaz Haco-operatzia will fix the nominal value of the share". Chevrat Haovdim jointly with Merkaz Haco-operatzia and with the help of an expert may re-evaluate the share capital of a respective WPSTS. Any surplus resulting from a re-evaluation of the share capital of a respective WPSTS made in connection with the carrying out of the new procedure about share capital (referred to above), shall be dealt with in the following manner: After allocating part of the surplus to reserves, etc., which are needed to improve the economic position of the respective WPSTS, the balance of such surplus shall be credited to the accounts of the old members in such manner as Chevrat Haovdim and Merkaz Haco-operatzia jointly shall fix, provided that the amounts allocated to members, remain with and are used by and for the respective WPSTS. Merkaz Haco-operatzia, subject to confirmation by Chevrat Haovdim, will define the conditions, etc., for refunding to a member who leaves his share of the surplus and also his participation in the new share capital in the respective WPSTS. In the event of the liquidation of a WPSTS, any assets remaining, after refunding to the members their participation in the old and new share capital and of other divisible funds of the respective WPSTS, become the property of Chevrat Haovdim.

B. Repetur who disagreed with some of the above provisions made the following suggestion: After allocating part of any annual surplus to depreciation and to replacement funds, 25 per cent of the balance of the surplus remaining shall be divided equally among all members; 50 per cent should be allocated to indivisible reserves of the respective WPSTS and 25 per cent should be allocated to a fund which will be used for making refunds to members who leave (in addition to their participation in the capital and divisible funds of the respective WPSTS). The amount which a member receives from this special fund shall be fixed on the basis of the number of years' membership in the respective WPSTS. In the case of a WPSTS that employed wage labour and whose capital is re-valued, Chevrat Haovdim shall appoint a committee to fix the amount of the surplus resulting from the re-evaluation of the old share capital of the respective WPSTS which should be used to pay for the shares of wage workers who are admitted as members. A member leaving a WPSTS shall not receive any interest on his share in the capital and in refundable reserves.

The three-paragraph part of the resolutions is also applicable to partnership between a WPSTS, Chevrat Haovdim, and private capital. Generally speaking, a plant owned jointly by Chevrat Haovdim and a WPSTS will operate on the basis of self-labour. The share of a WPSTS in such a partnership will be fixed on the basis of the membership, i.e. the manpower of the respective WPSTS. If wage labour is used in a plant jointly owned by a WPSTS and Chevrat Haovdim, any balance of the surplus remaining, after payment of dividends to the WPSTS and Chevrat Haovdim on the shares which they have in the respective plant, will be divided between the two partners *pro rata* on the basis of the number of members of the co-operative and the number of wage workers. Chevrat Haovdim will fix how much of its share of the aforementioned surplus it will use for the expansion of the respective WPSTS.

Messrs. Lin and Repetur of the committee suggested a ban on any partnerships between a WPSTS and private capital.

The fourth and final part of the section of the resolutions about WPSTS which the committee wants the Histadrut Council to approve, deals with the question of equal basic emoluments plus fringe benefits according to the accepted practices for all members of all WPSTS. Those WPSTS, such as transport co-operatives, in which the basic wages of all members are graded on the basis of skill, shall also continue to maintain the reserve which enables the co-operative to fix equal emoluments and fringe benefits for all members. But in cases of large co-operatives whose economy requires the employment of people with varied skills and with various degrees of skill, a wage scale based on skill shall be permissible, provided that these WPSTS will maintain the principles which have been fixed, one share per member of the same value, equal duties and obligation in the work and in the management of the co-operative, fringe benefits and rights to participate in the surplus.

B. Repetur dissented with the exclusion of the special cases of big co-operatives from the principle of equal emolument in every respect for every member.

CHAPTER EIGHT

Forecasts about the Future of the WPSTS

S. Goren asked the delegates at the Fifth Congress of Merkaz Haco-operatzia, 7-9 April, 1949, to remember that there is no future for the WPSTS "unless we become a movement; only if every WPSTS and every member in it will feel himself as a member of a movement . . . a desire to be an agent of the movement. There is no future for the members and for the development of their undertakings unless they feel that they are a part of . . . the Labour movement of the country. . . ."

On 29 November, 1956, 13 and 20 December, 1956 and 3 January, 1957, the secretariat of Chevrat Haovdim discussed in some detail the future of WPSTS in Israel[168]

S. Goren reported that about 250 WPSTS were affiliated to Merkaz Haco-operatzia, and that about 7,000 or 58 per cent of their total labour force of 12,000 are members. The 5,000 non-members include "several hundred apprentices". The industrial workers' co-operatives, and the road haulage and bus co-operatives, each have a total labour force of 5,500, and the service societies have 1,000. The bus co-operatives have the largest number—absolutely and relatively—of non-member workers.

Because of "the economic changes in the country as a whole", the fatalities until now (150 affiliated WPSTS) were more numerous than the number anticipated for the "250-260 WPSTS that Merkaz Haco-operatzia sponsored in 1949 and 1950". Other reasons for the high rate of liquidation, according to Mr. Goren, was the lack of screening, the lack of occupational training of the immigrants, and the "under capitalization" of the new WPSTS established. Kupat Haco-operativim did not have the resources adequately to finance either the pre-State or post-State WPSTS. Chevrat Haovdim supplied about half the paid-up share capital which Kupat Haco-operativim had invested in undertakings jointly owned by affiliated industrial workers co-operatives and the Histadrut.

Mr. Goren referred to the unsuccessful struggle to combat wage labour which has such destructive effects on the WPSTS. A number of "successful" WPSTS that had used wage labour had "divided the resources among the members" and were liquidated. A partnership of the Histadrut with industrial workers' co-operatives has been an effective preventive against the spread of this practice and has helped to maximize the members' interest both in the development of the joint undertaking and in their respective co-operative commandites. In a capitalist economy it is difficult to limit a WPSTS to self-labour "because it is constantly subject to market fluctuations . . .". They also have come to the conclusion that Merkaz Haco-operatzia cannot sufficiently help, advise and direct its affiliated WPSTS because it does not have the means to maintain a large enough staff of instructors to visit every affiliated society "once every two or three months". The complete dependency of Merkaz Haco-operatzia on its member co-operatives is neither desirable nor healthy, especially if it hopes to influence such aspects as "internal member-relationships". Since Merkaz Haco-operatzia has started to cover part of its budget out of the all inclusive (embracing) tax which WPSTS members pay to the Histadrut, it has been able to expand its services. Mr. Goren thinks that no part of the budget of Merkaz Haco-operatzia should be covered by the direct contributions of its affiliated WPSTS and/or their members.[169]

Mr. Goren asks whether Chevrat Haovdim endorses the view of not a few Histadrut leaders, more especially those of the craft unions and some Histadrut co-operators, that in view of the admitted defects, difficulties and failures, the WPSTS movement

> "is too heavy a burden on the Histadrut and that it should no longer be encouraged." These . . . consider a WPSTS as "the private business of a group of members". There is a sector within the Histadrut which "is actually ashamed of the responsibility which the Histadrut has for the WPSTS and that the WPSTS does not belong within the Histadrut framework."

Mr. Goren argued that Merkaz Haco-operatzia "is not a central (organisation) of WPSTS". Those responsible for the activities of Merkaz Haco-operatzia consider themselves "as performing this task for the Histadrut." The Histadrut must decide whether the time has come to discontinue WPSTS. A question, which remains unanswered and unresolved, is "how, generally speaking, one creates a labour economy. Should the workers be required to do this themselves or must somebody do it for the workers?" He defines socialism as an economy of the workers which the workers build and manage and enjoy the fruits of their own labour. Merkaz Haco-operatzia insists that if the Histadrut considers it worth while to foster the WPSTS, then it must translate this desire into real action, viz., to finance and to provide a substantial budget for organization, instruction and guidance. He claims that half the WPSTS liquidated during the last two or three years could have been saved if these had been guided adequately. Mr. Goren's closing remark was:

> "I have discussed the matter in a general way but have not touched . . . the question of bus co-operatives, about which I have much to say . . . I am not too popular with bus co-operatives. . . . Nevertheless even admit-

ting the negative and problematic aspects of the bus co-operatives . . . the positive and the bright spots are much larger than the marked negative and deviative aspects. And we must safeguard this co-operative economy."

Y. Ritov then said that the larger absolute and relative fatalities of WPSTS than of other types of co-operatives have their roots in the fact that most of the WPSTS were established in the post-State period. He criticizes the Co-operative Societies Ordinance which prescribes seven members as the minimum for a WPSTS. However, the Government (i.e. the Registrar) does not always insist on the liquidation of a WPSTS whose membership falls below seven. It was to be expected that many WPSTS (as well as non-co-operative workshops and factories), which were established in the period of peak Government rationing and control, would be liquidated when a seller's changed into a buyer's market. Though many WPSTS disappeared "we rescued several thousand (people) from degeneration and introduced them to a productive life".

Mr. Ritov thinks that the Histadrut is duty bound not only to renew its help but also to "return the crown to the WPSTS". It is regrettable that

> "more and more sectors of Histadrut-sponsored co-operatives are being converted into administered bodies and that the co-operative basis of the Labour movement is being removed."

Referring to the many complaints about the bus co-operatives, Mr. Ritov allegedly said:

> "I do not know whether these (i.e. WPSTS) have more problems and deviationists than have other Histadrut-sponsored co-operatives and the Histadrut-administered undertakings. . . . We should see the positive and not only the negative in the WPSTS."

According to Mr. Ritov, the main slogan of the Histadrut annual drive for funds in the U.S.A. is its sponsored co-operatives, and especially the WPSTS. He asks why WPSTS do not enjoy the same status within the Histadrut in Israel. For some years none of the funds which the Histadrut has collected abroad have been allocated for Kupat Haco-operativim.

S. Blas thinks that WPSTS which grade remuneration for the members are more likely to succeed. "This is not ideal but it is better and can be arranged if the Histadrut and a co-operative of workers jointly own the undertaking."

Zeev Onn cannot understand why the Government, the Jewish Agency and the Histadrut have singled out the WPSTS as being unworthy of support. It was true that the Joint Reconstruction Fund established in 1948 had advanced over a million pounds to immigrants who joined WPSTS. Only IL.30,000 has not been repaid. The fund was liquidated and the collections distributed *pro rata* among those who provided the money. A committee of four of which he is a member "three years ago devoted considerable time to a basic study of the WPSTS and for various reasons (no details given) we failed".

A. Zabarsky (joint manager of the Workers Bank Ltd.) reiterates his conviction that the Histadrut-sponsored co-operative movement in Israel had to and will continue to develop in its own pattern and procedures. "We are a Labour Commonwealth (Chevrat Haovdim). From the outset we mapped broader goals for ourselves." The industrial workers' co-operative is the most ideal for small and medium sized factories and workshops in light industry, provided, and this has not been the case, they enjoy adequate financing. The stability of management in the WPSTS can be assured only if half the votes are vested in Chevrat Haovdim, and it effectively uses this right. He suggests that the reconstruction fund should be re-established as a permanent financial instrument.

B. Lin doubts whether additional resources can really help the pre-State WPSTS and some of the post-State WPSTS. Except in the case of the bus co-operatives, very few of the young members of the WPSTS are the children of members because the vatikim do very little to encourage such a development. He describes the partnership of co-operatives with the Histadrut in such undertakings as Haargaz as a failure, because the use of wage labour and other undesirable practices continue.

B. Repetur (Achdut Haavodah) agrees with Messrs. Goren and Ritov that the Histadrut has done much less for its sponsored WPSTS than it has for its other sponsored economic sectors. And like Mr. Onn, he is seriously concerned with the so-called "administered economy". The Histadrut is destroying the little which remains of the WPSTS movement, which admittedly has certain weaknesses. He considers the WPSTS and the small factories in the kibbutzim, "in spite of the doubts and apprehensions about these", as absolutely essential for the conditions in Israel. "But if the Histadrut and Chevrat Haovdim will reconcile themselves to the use of wage labour in the WPSTS, these will sooner or later cease to be co-operatives."

He urged Chevrat Haovdim to adopt an uncompromising attitude towards self-labour (presumably in WPSTS and in the factories in the kibbutzim) and to stress that the interests of the group have priority over those of the individual.

Y. Tzimand said that he had close contact "with the human material for whom the WPSTS were organized". He feels that liquidation would have been unnecessary for "an appreciable number of WPSTS" if a more intensive effort had been made. Members of WPSTS have a much deeper sense of independence than do those working in the Histadrut-sponsored administered industry. But this cannot be a reason for condemning all administered industry, any more than the failure to eliminate all wage labour justifies the doing away with WPSTS.

Mrs. Senta Josephtal feels that the future of the WPSTS movement (like that of the kibbutz movement) depends on a youth movement that has been conditioned for integral co-operation. She unequivocally rejects the suggestion that light industry in Israel should be based on home industry as it is in Japan, even though the organizational pattern of this home industry is "co-operative".

A. Razi (manager of Choma) believes that the WPSTS movement can expand only if the Histadrut (or some other institution) jointly with the workers co-operatives (commandites) own and manage the plant. This pattern can better develop a sense of responsibility among the workers than administered plants. He thinks there is also the possibility of using such commandites as subsidiaries for larger industrial establishments.[170]

Y. Chorin (managing director, Yakhin, a Histadrut-sponsored labour contractor and management body) thinks that the joint ownership of the means of production by a WPSTS with a Histadrut-sponsored body is contradictory to the principles of WPSTS, the reason being that the Histadrut would have to play an effective and active role in the administration of these jointly owned plants. *De facto*, such a joint arrangement is only a more advanced stage of an "administered economy".

Y. Efter (general manager, Hamashbir Hamerkazi, Histadrut-sponsored co-operative wholesale society) noted that he voted against the conversion of the Histadrut-sponsored credit co-operatives into branches of the Workers Bank Limited because this was a retrogressive step and harmful to the co-operative movement as a whole. On the other hand, he favours only such WPSTS that do not deviate from the basic principles, even if this means a contraction of the WPSTS movement. A plant having 100 members and 200 wage workers is not a WPSTS. He also opposes any partnership of WPSTS with private capital. Merkaz Haco-operatzia should confine its activities to organization, control and guidance of small and medium size co-operative plants and Hamashbir Hamerkazi, Solel Boneh and Yakhin should deal with the larger Histadrut-sponsored industrial undertakings. He favours one central marketing agency for all products from all Histadrut-sponsored WPSTS and other industrial undertakings.

S. Eshet favours large and small WPSTS, whose members can do all the work "from the beginning to the end".

Y. Ritov disagrees with the suggestions that the WPSTS pattern is suitable only for small undertakings which agree not to expand (grow). This would limit the life of a WPSTS to the anticipated life span of the group of members who started it.[171] Mr. Ritov cites the case of the co-operative silicate brick factory, a closed co-operative whose members are in the older age groups, whose productivity has decreased, and the plant was about to shut down. He notes that there is as much specialization in some small plants as in larger factories. Merely because there were successes as well as failures in middle size and large WPSTS it is not sufficient reason for concluding that only medium or large plants are suitable soil for WPSTS. There are cases of privately owned plants which were saved from complete failure by their conversion into WPSTS, and there are also WPSTS that were saved by becoming private undertakings. He would welcome younger blood for Merkaz Haco-operatzia if this will help the WPSTS movement.

S. Goren's closing remarks at the Chevrat Haovdim meeting of November and December, 1956, and January 1957, noted that "a WPSTS is entitled to encouragement and help". Merkaz Haco-operatzia always advocated differential remuneration to members according to skill, provided that all members would be entitled to the same scale of fringe payments and to an equal share in the divisible surpluses. Lack of sufficient capital more than anything else prevents the expansion of individual WPSTS and of the WPSTS movement. He asks whether the Histadrut prefers a WPSTS like "Kesher" which still has twelve members as it did 33 years ago when it started, or a co-operative which started in 1932 with four members and today has hundreds of members and wage workers.[172] All the problems basically amount to only one large problem—how to create an economy in which the workers will be the owners and managers and carry the responsibilities. He discards the idea of an administered economy, especially if it is intended as the only pattern.

An unsigned article in March 1957, on the "Future of WPSTS"[173] draws attention to the increase from 118 in 1948 to 250 WPSTS in 1957, and to the liquidation of 190 WPSTS having a labour force of 1,500 (members and non-members), in which IL.1·5 million had been invested. It notes that Mr. Ritov, the general secretary of Merkaz Haco-operatzia, at a conference with Chevrat Haovdim, reported that there was no screening of applicants or a thorough investigation of the economic possibilities of various branches. "Merkaz Haco-operatzia has depended on the unimplemented promises of the Minister of Finance and on the hope that the Histadrut will not bury them." (WPSTS)

Time has demonstrated that the policy of immediate employment of the immigrants was a greater social-economic danger than would have been the delay resulting from the screening of members and of the industrial branches and insisting on an appreciable financial participation by the members. Mr. Ritov takes comfort from the "ups and downs" of WPSTS—especially of the construction and "conjucture" societies in Italy and France, "the classic schools for producers co-operatives". In spite of these "ups and downs, co-operation continues forever".

The article notes that a basic analysis of the reasons for the crisis in the WPSTS movement has not been made and it asks how much of the IL.1·5 million invested in the 190 WPSTS that have been liquidated was squandered? Should additional funds be used for bolstering existing or for establishing new WPSTS? The focal problem is whether and to what extent the investments created productive units which have prospects of continuity, and not whether those financing the WPSTS have incurred losses. While the failure of 190 WPSTS raises serious doubts about the advisability of continuing investments in WPSTS, the significance of this aspect should not be over-stressed. Of decisive importance is to resolve the problem of the optimum size (number of employees) for a WPSTS. The hope of WPSTS becoming "a movement for the masses" was unduly emphasized. "Only a small WPSTS can maintain its pure co-operative character." The article concluded that to a considerable extent the crisis in the WPSTS movement was "an economic crisis of small undertakings that cannot compete with larger enterprises and maintain themselves, let alone expand, in a volatile and changing market."

While it was not the purpose of the article to discuss the effects of the expanded use of wage labour by the WPSTS, it was certain that the employment of wage workers has contributed "to the expansion and commercial success of WPSTS". As the total permanent labour force increases, more wage labourers became members, and this strengthened the "co-operative garin (kernel)", and helped to consolidate large units with strong co-operative foundations. The WPSTS movement in Israel should find ways and means to further bolster the healthy economic units and "such funds as become available should not be given to weak WPSTS (bodies)".

On 15-16 February, 1957, about eighty people active in the WPSTS movement met.[174]

Y. Ritov asked the WPSTS movement to give up its isolationism which threatens its existence. It should "open its gates to the new immigrants" among whom there are suitable people for the establishment of new WPSTS and who also qualify for admission to the existing WPSTS. The older WPSTS should send their members who should also act as instructors for the new WPSTS and to the central organizational and financial organs of Merkaz Haco-operatzia.

S. Goren criticizes those WPSTS whose members stress an improved standard of living as being more important than increased productivity (p.m.h.). "The WPSTS must reduce overhead and labour costs—improve the equipment . . . and quality, and reduce production costs. The WPSTS will then be more competitive on the export market and better able to integrate additional members."

M. Ofner (Achva printing co-operative, Jerusalem) thinks that an agreement about the procedure for fixing the value of a share, especially in the pre-State WPSTS, must precede the admission of additional members. He does not accept the low or popular price share ("people's share") which Mr. Ritov suggested as the solution. The WPSTS have passed "the peak of its crisis" and are on the "road of constructive creation. Our discouragement in certain fields stimulated by the negative manifestations in the life of the older WPSTS should not deter us from establishing new WPSTS by exploiting on a wide scale the positive in our societies."

S. Goldman denies that there is a lack of young people in the WPSTS who can qualify as members, or that the human material in the WPSTS is inferior to that in moshavim and kibbutzim.

A. Yisraeli warns the WPSTS not to become "a sacrifice on the altar of die-hard co-operation" and that they should not ignore the changes which the new conditions have simulated, even though these may "taint the old time principles of democracy and freedom. . . . Such (patterns of) democracy and freedom which imperil the economic stability and the co-operative undertaking can no longer be part of the co-operative ethos."

Y. Borowsky (Egged) thinks that Merkaz Haco-operatzia and the Histadrut jointly should concentrate on bolstering and expanding the potentialities of the existing small and medium size WPSTS. And "the large undertakings (i.e. WPSTS) will find their own way".

A. Yerushalmi (Imun) thinks that the first step is to introduce such internal changes as the evaluation of a member's share, increase the term of office of the Management Committee from one to three or even four years; and introduce a graded scale of remuneration for members.

I. Wuntch (Haargaz) criticizes "the leaders of the WPSTS movement for allowing themselves to be dragged into a defeatist frame of mind . . . and for their excessive tolerance of serious deviations . . . from certain principles which heretofore were regarded as holy".

Y. Podisuk (Levanon) thinks that Merkaz Haco-operatzia must have a larger staff of

> "mobile instructors to help both large and small WPSTS" to condition their members to the realities of the time. Where necessary, the instructors should take over temporarily the administration of a respective co-operative, even for an extended period. "Merkaz Haco-operatzia is still the authority which the rank and file accept and only its representatives can resolve the complicated questions in the WPSTS."

S. Goldman considers the economic and social aspects of WPSTS as inseparable and interwoven. He divides the affiliated WPSTS in three categories, most of which fall within the first two:

(*a*) WPSTS consolidated and rooted to the life and the economic realities of the country and unshakable in their adherence to the co-operative way of life which they have chosen.
(*b*) Those that could be like (*a*) if their economic position were improved.
(*c*) Several tens of affiliated WPSTS that are struggling very hard for their existence and have become discouraged with the co-operative way of life. These "cannot continue unless they can get working capital, new equipment, additional space, etc." This requires hundreds of thousands of pounds which are not available.

Generally speaking, Mr. Goldman ascribes the improvement in the Histadrut's attitude (and of its sponsored bodies) towards WPSTS to the deficiencies in the Histadrut-sponsored administered economy. The affiliated WPSTS will have to do their share to ensure this revival of goodwill.

Eliahu Razi discussed the integration of the new immigrants, many from European communist satellite countries. He warns against sending these to weak and unconsolidated WPSTS because this creates the double danger that these WPSTS may go to the rocks and that the immigrants will not be integrated. Their conception of the WPSTS pattern differs from that prevailing in Israel. The immigrants from the satellite communist countries consider the equipment in the WPSTS as inferior to that to which they were accustomed. On the other hand, these immigrants are frightened by the measure of responsibility which the members must carry for their respective WPSTS. The immigrants must be screened as to character, past experience, skill, etc., and should be distributed among a selective group of WPSTS. In spite of the risks, new WPSTS should be established, even though the resources are insufficient for adequate equipment. A few larger WPSTS should feed work to smaller WPSTS.

S. Goren's theme at the Fourth Council of Merkaz Haco-operatzia of 8 May, 1957 was "An examination of our methods in the light of the actualities."[175] He reiterates his confidence in WPSTS and his lack of confidence from a long range point of view, in the Histadrut-sponsored administered plants. He agrees with Mr. Ritov that the isolationism of the WPSTS is enemy number one of the WPSTS movement. The unavoidable aging of members has not been counter-balanced by "a continuous stream of young and reinvigorating forces", which is the best insurance for continuity. He disagrees with Mr. Ritov's assumption that the renewed mass immigration is an omen that the WPSTS movement is out of the slump. The industrial workers co-operatives, especially the older ones, are deteriorating and degenerating. They have fenced themselves in with an "atomic wall" and are on the verge of "crumbling to pieces. These co-operatives have not added one member in the eighteen months since Merkaz Haco-operatzia summed up the discussion and approved resolutions about the evaluation of the shares". Only the bus co-operatives are fed by a constant stream of new and young blood. He still maintains that equal basic payment for all members does not spur the members to increase their productivity (p.m.h.) and improve the quality of the products.

Zeev Onn told the Fifth Council of Merkaz Haco-operatzia of 2 March, 1958, that the main difference between a member of a kibbutz or a moshav and a member of a WPSTS is that the latter does not think that his children will continue in his footsteps. Members of WPSTS want their children to attend universities, and on the other hand, they are in constant dread that new members will create unemployment for the old members.

B. Lin at the Sixth Council of Merkaz Haco-operatzia, of 2 January, 1959, notes that during the last decade the membership of WPSTS has increased by 75 per cent and the number of wage workers by 227 per cent. This "raises a serious question about the future of the WPSTS in general. . . . But one must face such serious and stark realities as the indifference, if not the animosity of the post-State immigrants to any kind of joint effort; that most of the WPSTS have not the equipment to stand up against the mechanized industry in the country. And there is also the difficulty in checking the consistent increase of wage labour. WPSTS members should not at one and the same time be workers and employers. . . . With the possible exception of the bus co-operatives very few, if any, children of the members in the WPSTS carry on what the parents have started. Therefore it seems impossible to assure the continuity of the WPSTS."

H. Goldberg said that the time is ripe for Merkaz Haco-operatzia to establish a youth department and to foster the admission of members' sons into their parents' respective WPSTS on special conditions, such as not having to be put on waiting lists and granting them a discount on their participation in the society's capital. A special member of the staff of Merkaz Haco-operatzia should organize garinim in the trade schools.

"The face of the WPSTS movement will change if we will admit young people."

S. Goren told the Seventh Council of Merkaz Haco-operatzia of 3 September, 1959: "We have not succeeded in integrating additional members into the existing WPSTS or in establishing new WPSTS." Only the co-operative workshops for building materials agreed to admit new members, but there were no applicants. While Merkaz Haco-operatzia will continue with a policy of persuasion, "it will not be deterred from applying sanctions". Generally speaking, he was apprehensive whether

> "the existing WPSTS, even those consolidated, will maintain their position", unless
>
> (*a*) these are supported by a large and expanded WPSTS movement,
> (*b*) there is a revolutionary change within the WPSTS, and
> (*c*) the members begin to consider their society not only "as a place of work but as a source of livelihood". He also asks the Histadrut "to change its attitude towards the industrial workers' co-operatives, and not to consider these only as the private business of a number of members. . . ." "We cannot expand unless the Histadrut considers this movement as its child" and will encourage labour youth who do not choose agricultural colonization, to join the WPSTS movement. Otherwise the WPSTS will remain in cold storage and this would contribute "to the constant decline of its status in the country's economy".

A. Tzwick submits a rather pessimistic report about most of the affiliated consumer service co-operatives. These have 1,000 members and 500 wage workers. He complains that the Council of Merkaz Haco-operatzia does not pay sufficient attention to the "problem of problems, viz. the continuity of its WPSTS", mainly due to a lack of identification with the co-operative ethos (ideology). The uncertainty of the continuity applies not only to the service co-operatives but the entire WPSTS movement. The WPSTS do not attract people because the economic conditions in the non-co-operative (private) and in the Histadrut-sponsored administrative sector are better than are those in the parallel WPSTS. And he asks why the "exemplary" bus co-operatives, which account for half the total membership of the WPSTS affiliated to Merkaz Haco-operatzia, have not recognized the need to help resolve the problem of the industrial workers and the service co-operatives.

Y. Ritov said that in spite of the crises and the decrease of the number of affiliated WPSTS from 400 to 230[176]

> "I believe unqualifiedly that the future of WPSTS . . . is both good and significant (large) . . . Life is the same everywhere. The comparative data for 1951 and 1958 which I have shows that the WPSTS movement in Italy and France also have their ups and downs. . . . While the total labour force (in the WPSTS) in Italy and in France remained the same

the total labour force (in the WPSTS) in Israel increased from 12,000 to 14,000."[177]

Mr. Ritov adds that Merkaz Haco-operatzia have received concrete plans for organizing groups from Hanoar Haoved, the Histadrut-sponsored youth movement, into WPSTS. "While I do not know what the actual results will be, the fact that there were proposals is of considerable importance." This is tied up with some special problems, such as who will replace members in those groups when they are called up for the obligatory two-and-a-half years military service, and what will be the fate of these after completing Army service. Mr. Ritov was sure "that in co-operation with Hanoar Haoved we will be able to resolve these difficulties. . . ."

If Merkaz Haco-operatzia had enjoyed real support and help from the State and the Histadrut and "if these will put their shoulders to the wheel", ex-service men could prove to be a "significant potential source of human material" for the WPSTS. In spite of the past and relatively few successes, Mr. Ritov thought that there was no room for despondency about the possibilities of organizing immigrants into WPSTS, but "we did not have the financial means for the development of the WPSTS and we do not have a budget for Merkaz Haco-operatzia, therefore the (unsatisfactory) results are not surprising. . . . Without straw we cannot make bricks. . . . We could establish and maintain WPSTS if we had the IL.6,000-IL.8,000 needed for every immigrant. . . ."

S. Stenger refutes the statement that the WPSTS is not a movement. Is not this council meeting the best proof that there is a WPSTS movement? He cautions the council that achievements alone are not sufficient to ensure the growth and continuity of the WPSTS movement. Is it not their mutual interest that the best WPSTS should second their best members as instructors for the weaker WPSTS? "Even a strong WPSTS which concentrates only on the economic aspect and disregards the social aspects is doomed to degeneration." They must prepare

(*a*) a competent organizational and instructional staff, made up entirely of members from the existing WPSTS; and
(*b*) plans for the social and economic consolidation of the existing WPSTS and for the expansion of the movement.

Y. Borowsky (Egged (Eshed)) notes that the liquidations appreciably exceed the registration of new WPSTS.

Y. Ritov was the first of three members of Merkaz Haco-operatzia secretariat to reply to the general debate[178] He considers as "the pivotal problem" how to save the weak WPSTS, "not a few in number". Second, the WPSTS sector is no longer "dynamic" and it is not integrating new immigrants. Third, there is a lack of inter-WPSTS mutual aid. As an example he notes that the three bus co-operatives and Haargaz have not sponsored and fostered secondary industrial workers and service co-operatives, such as co-operatives of upholsterers, carpenters, printers and tailors, that could supply part of the needs of these large societies. "And Egged

(Eshed) has flouted our (Merkaz Haco-operatzia) decision and has established its own printing shop. . . ." Mr. Ritov then cites the failure of the older printing co-operatives to second a single instructor for a new co-operative printing works for immigrants, and that the Namlit co-operative for building materials refused to establish a branch near Nazareth. The establishment of a branch of an existing WPSTS is potentially less risky than organizing a new WPSTS. Mr Ritov thinks that the position of no other movement is as critical as is that of the WPSTS movement.

"At every meeting, orally and in writing, we castigate ourselves and others. But we also accept external criticism provided it emanates from a real interest and is accompanied by real help. . . . Nothing can be done without money. . . . We wanted not the establishment of the Teeus Company but more funds for Kupat Haco-operativim, which it could use for new WPSTS for immigrants, Hanoar Haoved and other groups."

N. Lifshitz (Chevrat Haovdim) thinks that Merkaz Haco-operatzia could get help if they presented their requests "in an orderly form". The company Teeus would give 20-25 per cent, and the Government Development Fund the balance of the funds required for the establishment and equipment of industrial workers co-operatives for a thousand people in the development zones. "I objected to giving the money to Kupat Haco-operativim." He could not understand why a movement with 4,200 members was unable to provide people to establish "three, five or ten industrial workers co-operatives" in the development zones, not even a nucleus of 20 from their younger members.

S. Goren confirms that the funds of the Teeus company may be used only for projects in the development zones. Mr. Goren agreed that the company should start by establishing some factories on the pattern of Histadrut-sponsored administration projects which later could be turned over to industrial workers co-operatives. The general question of the WPSTS movement is one for the Histadrut and not the company to deal with. With regard to the unfulfilled promise of Chevrat Haovdim to Kupat Haco-operatavim, Mr. Goren said: "I could read to you the exchange of correspondence between me and the secretary of Chevrat Haovdim about this matter."

Zeev Schiff's article in 1960 on "The Bankruptcy of the Co-operative Movement"[179] is "directed only to the Histadrut-sponsored WPSTS that are affiliated to Merkaz Haco-operatzia". The "aging and impending social and, in many cases also, economic bankruptcy" cannot be attributed to the fact that the WPSTS movement is half a century old. Few of the WPSTS established during the post-State period were still active at the end of 1958, in spite of "the very appreciable amounts of public and private funds which were made available since the establishment of the State for the establishment of the new WPSTS".

About 250 of the WPSTS which Merkaz Haco-operatzia helped to establish since the establishment of the State in May, 1948, have been liquidated. According to Mr. Schiff, most of these post-State WPSTS were not competitive and had to be liquidated after Government rationing and price control were first curtailed and then discontinued. He refers to the unsuitability of the post-State immigrants for the WPSTS pattern of life which "sooner or later" must lead to a serious conflict between the co-operative ethos and "the desire of the individual to exploit the common till as much as possible".

The affiliated WPSTS, especially the industrial workers' co-operatives, refused to co-operate with those who were ready to help them raise their technological standards. Therefore, it is not surprising that only relatively few of the industrial workers and of the service co-operatives are competitive with the non-co-operative plants in parallel branches. The spread of wage labour, Mr. Schiff considers as evidence of "the lack of social cohesion in the WPSTS". And he refers to the "schizophrenic" attitude of the leaders to this problem, who on the one hand persist in championing self-labour, and on the other hand either ignore the existence of the problem or confine their action to resolutions. "It is their (the leaders) opinion that in the economic realities of Israel it is impossible to beat this problem."

That Merkaz Haco-operatzia has had to deal with the problem of wage labour almost since its inception in 1928, is reflected in the resolutions of four Congresses of Merkaz Haco-operatzia between 1933 and 1949 and the resolutions of the Histadrut Congresses since 1945, calling "for the abolition of all wage labour without delay". This, he describes as "lip service to the ethos of the Histadrut-sponsored co-operatives", because the Histadrut is fully aware of the fact that if they really put into effect their resolutions, they would have to expel tens of WPSTS from the Histadrut.

Mr. Schiff concludes "that the prospects of the WPSTS movement for the future, either from a social or economic point of view, are not very promising". Co-operation is no longer "a magic word", not even for the weaker strata of wage workers, because "the wage and the fringe benefits in the general (non co-operative) employment fields are very attractive".

M. Shamner in December 1960 reports[179] that affiliated to the division for bus and road haulage co-operatives of Merkaz Haco-operatzia are

(*a*) thirteen urban road haulage co-operatives that have 416 members and 193 wage workers and

(*b*) nine rural road haulage co-operatives which service 171 labour agricultural settlements that have a labour force of 700, of whom about 200 are wage workers. The 193 wage workers in the 13 urban road haulage co-operatives include 44 drivers; 59 workers in the garage; 17 porters; 31 clerks, etc.; eight temporary and part-time and 34 apprentices. The 44 drivers will be the first to be admitted as members of their respective societies; but Mr. Shammer notes they are unable to make the initial payments on account of their participation in the respective societies' capital.

The 22 urban and rural road haulage co-operatives have "about a thousand lorries" and do an annual business of about IL.20 million. Mr. M. Shamner criticizes the public works and low cost housing departments of the Ministry of Labour because they do not "distribute their work evenly over the twelve months of the fiscal year" (April-March). This would enable a more normal exploitation of the vehicles and of the manpower of the road haulage co-operatives. Since the Government discontinued price control in 1956, the prices for hauling remained static "and even declined". The railways can cut their prices "because the state treasury covers the deficits". And the semi-Government road haulage company Tovala can afford to cut prices because it enjoys a monopoly in the development districts "and most favourable conditions for the import of vehicles".

The Ministry of Finance, urged by the Ministry of Transport, made available for the road haulage co-operatives credits amortizable within thirty months for the import of lorries and also had agreed to permit them to pay the import duty within 21 months after the lorries arrived. But the Ministry of Finance did not grant any credits for the replacement of vehicles in 1959-60, and insisted that the import duty had to be paid within 18 months from the date the lorries arrived. For 1960-61 the Ministry of Finance has allocated $350,000 and $200,000 for imports of lorries from the U.S.A. and Europe respectively, and Chevrat Haovdim made available IL.550,000 during the three years 1958-59 to 1960-61 for the replacement of vehicles.

The Ministry of Transport appointed an *ad hoc* advisory committee on road haulage on which all sectors in the road haulage industry are represented. This committee suggested:

1. A standing committee of the Ministry of Finance should discuss annually whether to permit the imports of additional vehicles, and to what extent and the types.
2. A new road haulage agent should be licensed only if it has suitable vehicles to carry a minimum of a hundred tons; that the area which it proposes to service does not have adequate hauling facilities and that the applicant has "the technical know-how".
3. Replacement of all pre- 1942 models should enjoy priority rights for import licences and should be given credits on convenient terms to cover the replacement costs.
4. The citrus growers, construction contractors, and others who do not hold licences for commercial road haulage should be prohibited from carrying any goods for third parties.
5. The Government should fix minimum rates for haulage and that the law with regard to delayed payment of wages should apply to payments due for road haulage.

The Report of the Registrar of Co-operatives for 1960 notes that, generally speaking,

> "not a few of well informed co-operators are sceptical about the possibilities or even the rights of existence of WPSTS. The appreciable number of negative manifestations among the WPSTS, such as the

materialistic transformation; isolation (closed societies); wage labour, etc., has engendered among many a feeling of uncertainty about the future of the WPSTS movement in Israel." The Registrar asks "whether this pessimistic forecast is justified and has a real basis? Nobody will deny that the WPSTS in our country has to no small extent disappointed even its loyal devotees. But . . . have we made it possible for the WPSTS to exist? Did those who *de facto* determine the fate of joint economic enterprise adequately support (show the proper attitude) the movement? There is no doubt that the WPSTS suffered from under-capitalization and serious inadequate credit facilities and lack of co-operation of the Histadrut-sponsored economic organs, including co-operatives. . . . And yet the WPSTS in spite of chronic under-capitalization and financing difficulties have displayed a high standard of efficiency and productivity. And cannot one assume that the performance of the movement, had it had the necessary means, would have been much better, not only from the point of view of the individual members of the WPSTS, but also from the point of view of the country's economy?"

The Registrar notes that in any discussion about the future of the WPSTS, one must consider that the emphasis in Israel in the immediate future will be shifted from agriculture to industry. The expansion of the large heavy industrial plants will be simultaneously supplemented with medium and small light industry, which should provide the "fertile soil for the growth (flowering) of WPSTS, since experience has demonstrated that the average investment required is less than for non-co-operative plants. There is no reason for concluding (saying) that since unsatisfactory deficiencies have been uncovered in the WPSTS, the movement has no future, even in the immediate future."

The Registrar however stresses that the reality of his forecast depends very much on those in the Histadrut who define its economic policies and also on whether the movement simultaneously takes steps "to eradicate the blemishes, first and foremost wage labour".

Abraham Hochman's article early in 1961 discusses briefly the measures which would improve what he describes "a paradoxical situation" and could ensure the future of the WPSTS movement.[180] The Government and the Histadrut organs use "every opportunity to proclaim their positive attitude towards and stress the important role reserved for co-operation in developing a normal economy and social relationship within the State". Yet, Mr. Hochman asks, why must the WPSTS movement struggle for its very existence ("soul") and what measures can be taken to ameliorate the depression? Placing the entire blame on "objective factors" could only end in "disappointment, apathy and carelessness". True, they should not disregard the influence of economic conditions; but on the other hand "we have not done enough to ameliorate and to rectify the conditions in those fields where the influence of external objective factors is either very limited or non-existing". Mr. Hochman asks the next (Sixth) Congress of Merkaz Haco-operatzia of 15 and 16 July, 1962, to consider the following.

Organized and directed co-operative education and commercial, technical and administrative guidance are two of the most neglected fields. The liquidation of a large number of WPSTS can be traced to social and economic degeneration; to the intensification of the problem of wage labour, to the efforts "one way or the other" to get rid of the authority of the Histadrut; and the absence of any feeling among the WPSTS and their members that they constitute a social movement "worthy of its name". He describes the supervision and co-operative educational activities of Merkaz Haco-operatzia as "ineffective, haphazard . . . unsatisfactory both from the public point of view and the benefits which the WPSTS derive". The follow-up to ensure that the respective WPSTS are effectively carrying out the commercial and administrative measures which they have been instructed to take, is casual and not persistent. He calls for more effective auditing of the current and annual accounts of the affiliated WPSTS, with Merkaz Haco-operatzia exercising its authority more effectively. This requires the early completion of the reorganization of the internal structure of Merkaz Haco-operatzia, including its auditing department.

Of special importance, is a change in the archaic conception that the WPSTS pattern is suitable only for "small social-economic units; a conception that is especially harmful "to the future" of the WPSTS movement. Small WPSTS may be useful for "certain branches under certain conditions". But "we must accommodate ourselves to the view that under the new conditions there is at best only a very limited economic possibility for small undertakings which "are neither workshops nor factories". They (Merkaz Haco-operatzia) should concentrate on establishing large plants and amalgamating the small plants in various branches. "This is the order of our day (era)."

Mr. Hochman calls on WPSTS to depend on themselves and not on others for the financial resources. And "to reinforce our justified demands we must prove that we have exploited our own resources, strengthened our own financial organ, Kupat Haco-operativim, so that it can help existing and new WPSTS . . . integrate more members."

Mendel Singer's article[180] on "Stabilization of the Israeli Mould as a Chalutz Nation" quotes from the address of the Prime Minister Mr. David Ben-Gurion at the second session of the Fourth Knesset to the effect that "in no other country has the expansion of the WPSTS, relatively speaking, been on the same scale as in Israel. And this field of co-operation . . . has won for Israel an international reputation and serves as a magnet for the young generation in the new countries in the continents close to us."[181]

However, Mr. Singer notes that with all due respect to the evaluation by the Prime Minister the development of the WPSTS movement in Israel

> "does not satisfy us. In my opinion this growth of the WPSTS in Israel is more the *by-products* (*results*) *of a reflex than of the activation of the awakening forces which accompany the revival of our people in its home-*

land and the exploitation of the appreciable hidden opportunities of this branch (of co-operation) in the economy of the State during the period of mass immigration which we were privileged to have during this era." (Original underlined.)

The article notes that the WPSTS movement integrated as members only 8,000 or 0·8 per cent of the million immigrants who arrived during this period.[182] Yet the WPSTS have served as an "ideal vehicle (channel)" for making productive the penniless unskilled immigrants and instilling them with the principle of mutual aid. That the WPSTS movement integrated "such an insignificant percentage" can, according to Mr. Singer, be interpreted as reflecting the inaptitude of the WPSTS movement (i.e. Merkaz Haco-operatzia) and justifies the dissatisfaction with their achievements. If they wish to prevent a further deterioration and ensure its continuity the WPSTS movement must take measures to extend and intensify "co-operative identification" of the rank and file already within the WPSTS. And identification must be translated into inter-co-operative mutual aid and contact, without which a genuine WPSTS movement is impossible.

Mr. Singer complains that the contact between the WPSTS movement in Israel and the forces outside of Israel always have been indirect, through third parties who are not actually members of the movement. This must be changed, and "the forces who speak in our name should be those who live, work and are unequivocally dedicated to the WPSTS movement. This is the best guarantee that they can influence those whom they address with the same belief."

Menashe Ofner[183] writes about the considerable lag in the rate of development of industrial workers and of service co-operatives and the rate of expansion of the Israeli economy, because Histadrut circles consider "WPSTS as an historical anachronism, something that has outlived its usefulness". Only "the large Histadrut-sponsored and administered industries, majestic establishments" are able to integrate "tens of thousands of immigrants as workers'. This school thinks that the WPSTS pattern and ethos cannot contribute much to this enormous task of expanding the Israeli economy. He thinks that since the administration of the Histadrut-sponsored administered plants "is bureaucratic and technological", this "opens the road for a revival of . . . WPSTS (the glory of co-operation). . . . But admittedly the WPSTS, because they are small economic units, cannot be considered as an alternative to the large Histadrut and national economy."

Mr. Ofner questions whether the transfer of the property and means of production from the members of the WPSTS to Chevrat Haovdim "is in itself a cure for the problems of the social aspects of co-operation and for safeguarding its public character".

He argues that because of its social character and as long as the members in the WPSTS retain the ownership and administration, these are "public property". Any outside (foreign) body introduced to the WPSTS must lead "sooner or later" to the destruction of self-management, autonomy and the freedom of the members. The ownership by the members of the WPSTS' property engenders a feeling of personal security and mutual aid.

An article "A Refreshing Wind (spirit) in the WPSTS", signed Y. Ben, refers to an ever rising interest by outsiders in the WPSTS in Israel. These include students from African and Asiatic countries; articles in the press abroad by co-operators who have seen the wonders of co-operation in Israel, etc. On the other hand, the WPSTS is not "a mass movement" and has failed to attract new people in Israel. The article refers to the great hopes aroused by the increase of WPSTS affiliated to Merkaz Haco-operatzia between 1948 (115 with a labour force of 5,564) and 1950 (368 affiliated WPSTS with a labour force of 9,527). But at the end of 1960 the affiliated WPSTS had dwindled to 203 but the total labour force had increased to 13,724. The total labour force of the transportation co-operatives had doubled.

The article notes that the one bright spot is the evidence of some interest in WPSTS by those in the Hanoar Haoved. More than 600 of these are working in 34 WPSTS all over the country, "a proof that there is a future for the WPSTS . . . and it is especially encouraging that the awakening has occurred where in the past it was least pronounced". According to the article, the new public relations policy has contributed much to this development.

Extracts of views expressed by S. Goren (Merkaz Haco-operatzia) and Zeev Tzur, a member of the Shapiro Committee, to enquire into the future of the WPSTS in Israel.[184]

"Public attention was recently drawn to the state of co-operatives here when the head of the Haifa meat skinners' co-operative murdered the head of the competing group and then committed suicide. This led to the Haifa slaughtering business being taken over by the municipality and the appointment of a Histadrut enquiry committee headed by the eminent lawyer, Yaakov Shimshon Shapiro. The committee not only found Co-operative Centre officials guilty of negligence but put forward a series of proposals for its reform. The Centre (Merkaz Haco-operatzia) reacted by blasting the committee. After nearly a year, the report is still pigeon-holed. The only action taken by the Centre's officials has been some changes in the secretariat and the disconnection of the Co-operative Audit Union from the Centre. Hitherto the Centre's officials had acted as their own auditors.

"Mr. Goren prefaced his remarks by reminding us that he was no longer actively engaged in running the Centre which he helped found in the 1930s. He . . . devotes his time to Teeus, the Industrial Development Corporation for new areas. We met him in the informal atmosphere of his office, with his secretary walking in and out, telephones ringing all the time. . . .

"Mr. Goren's reply to a general question on the future of co-operatives (i.e. WPSTS) was to talk of the tempo of their development being dependent on the aid they get from public funds. Because of full employment and a shortage of skilled labour, he does not anticipate a trend towards co-operatives. The Co-operative Centre's Fund can supply capital which a worker, however hard he tries, would never be able to save. . . . Mr. Goren . . . points to the excellent business acumen and organizational ability of the bus co-operatives as a model with which to compare any private concern.

"The interview with Mr. Tzur took place in the secretariat room of Achdut Haavodah's head offices. . . . The former Deputy Agriculture Minister is now political secretary of his party. We talked over a green baize-covered conference table.

"Mr. Tzur believes that as much public capital as is required should be put at the disposal of the co-operatives. He sees them as weakening due to the decreasing desire of urban workers to assume economic responsibility. Viewing the balance sheet of producers' co-operatives in the world as a whole, Mr. Tzur admits that it does not present a very optimistic picture. 'Either they failed economically because they could not compete with the big firms, or they failed socially in that they became exploiters of other men's labour'. He regrets that a similar trend has emerged in Israel. Mr. Tzur, however, believes that industrial co-operatives could perhaps provide the answer to the question of livelihood for Jewish artisans wishing to immigrate from the free countries.

"After noting that co-operation had succeeded in transportation, Mr. Tzur raised the question of hired labour. As far as he knows, the average ratio is one-and-a-half hired hands to every member. 'This is because there is no education to co-operation, no preparation for common responsibility. The trend here is towards more centralization, whilst co-operatives require decentralization. . . .' The prevalence of hired labour not only created tension between members and employees but it weakened the moral fibre of the members. 'If the co-operatives do not abolish hired labour, then they are finished,' he declared emphatically.

"Mr. Goren is sceptical as to whether the co-operatives could ever dispense with employed labour. 'We must allow a measure of flexibility in the matter of hired labour. . . . An economic unit must adjust to the fluctuations of the market and not the other way round,' . . . For him the crux of the matter is keeping the ratio of workers to members down. 'If in the old days, 30 members employed ten workers, it wasn't so bad, but if today ten members take on 30 employees, that is another matter. I confess we have done too little to maintain the ratio.'

"The question of where the line is drawn between a co-operatively-managed firm and an ordinary business company, led to the case of the Haargaz plant, with its 100 members and 600-700 workers. The co-operative also owns a share in the Amcor industrial corporation. Mr. Goren said: 'If the ratio was smaller it would present no problem. But you know it cannot go on like this.' If they refuse to accept more employees as members and insist on keeping out new men, then they cannot stay within the co-operative framework. This applies to all co-operatives. If they refuse to accept public control they must be shut down. The last phrase was said with more emphasis than conviction. . . .

"Mr. Tzur objected strongly to members holding more than one share 'otherwise it becomes like any other shareholding concern'. . . . Mr. Tzur felt that this was ridiculous, 'there is no need for Haargaz to be a partner in such a large concern as Amcor. Let them concentrate on one plant but not the entire lot with its 1,300 employees.' Hakibbutz Hameuchad economic policy maker believed that in so far as producers' co-operatives were concerned there was need to give Chevrat Haovdim a direct say in their affairs. Wherever these co-operatives enjoy monopolies, 'that invites trouble' and there must be proper public control, Mr. Tzur believes. This comment came after Mr. Tzur had agreed that these co-operatives prosper mainly because of the powerful backing they get from the Histadrut, and therefore the Histadrut should have a say in what they do. This opinion was supported by Mr. Goren as well.

"The powerful bus co-operatives are a different matter altogether. Both Mr. Goren and Mr. Tzur expressed their satisfaction, not only with the business success of these co-operatives, but also with their service. Mr. Tzur insisted that the Transport Ministry (Achdut Haavodah) exercised sufficient control while Mr. Goren said the bus co-operative gave good service at low fares and were accepting an increasing number of employees as members. He compared the bus co-operatives' monopoly with the bus concession granted in New York City and with regulated air lines.

"If hired labour was such a bad thing in urban co-operatives, what about the kibbutz movement? . . . 'I distinguish between the single kibbutz and the corporate movement,' he answered, adding sharply that Hakibbutz Hameuchad would resist any attempt to force it to merge its construction concern with Solel Boneh.

"Discussing the Shapiro Committee and its report, Mr. Tzur described it 'as a most daring document' . . . 'I assumed that now was a wonderful opportunity for the Histadrut to embark upon social and organizational surgery in the co-operatives. . . . Our proposals for reforms in the Co-operative Centre are still awaiting implementation; perhaps I console myself by saying that they can still be carried out. I hope that the subject will be tackled at the forthcoming Histadrut Council.' "

Six months later (18 October, 1963) the Jerusalem Post published the opinion of its economic editor about the "preparations for the forthcoming Histadrut Congress scheduled Council to discuss the problems of "Labour Economy". The title of the article is "Reforming Co-operatives" and it included the following comments of the Economic Editor about the WPSTS movement:

"The problem of urban productive co-operatives, which was discussed at the last of the three public meetings, was economically the least weighty, for the time is long since past when co-operation was an important factor in Israel industry. Today production co-operatives account for about 2·5 per cent of the total urban labour force (ca. 14,000 people), and their share is progressively declining. For the socialist object of non-exploitation, however, the problem of hired labour here is no less crucial, perhaps even more so, than in rural settlements, for here the employers are neither communal bodies to which the hired hands are outsiders, nor individual farmers, segregated in their village, but fellow-workers, mixing with the wage-earners on an equal footing, yet enjoying a preferential status on account of their capital investment. As urbanization advances the problem is becoming more acute because co-operatives are a convenient form of combining resources for small and medium enterprises, thus making possible the productive absorption of youth and new immigrants without turning them into hired hands. This, incidentally, is another reason—in addition to its ideological motives—why the Histadrut has always supported production co-operatives, and why it has adopted a new expansion programme (envisaging an investment of IL.10m. a year for the next three years) to cope with the needs of increased immigration. But how can action in this field be justified if the co-operatives themselves turn employers? The economic incentives for such a development are all too obvious, but no less obvious is the fact that co-operation cannot succeed without overcoming them.

"Indeed, the past ten years have witnessed not only a decline in the number of production co-operatives (partly due to mismanagement and failures, but partly also because successful enterprises spurned co-operative status) but also an exacerbation of internal conflicts. While the number of members increased only by 11 per cent in that period, the number of employees soared 40 per cent, and now almost equals that of members. Moreover, while in 1951 a member's average wage was 1·2 times that of a hired hand, it is now 2·2 times as high, apart from steep differences in many marginal benefits.

"The Histadrut could not go on supporting the principle of co-operation without making up its mind on which side of the fence it stood, and it has somewhat belatedly come out in support of the wage-earners, as befits its primary function as a trade union.

"The Onn Committee, appointed to deal with the question, has recommended that every co-operative either dismiss or accept as full members all hired workers who have been employed more than three months. The Histadrut would provide those who are dismissed with alternative employment. New co-operatives would not be allowed to hire employees at all. Though an exception would be made for the yetzivim, a certain category of veteran employees who benefit from special status, this point is not of basic importance, for they are few.

"Another suggested reform would split up members' shares in the co-operatives—some of which are currently worth IL.25,000 and more—into two components, so as to make it easier for the hired workers to join. The share proper—i.e. the entrance fee—would be no higher than one or two years' wages. In addition, members leaving the co-operative would be able to take their full share in any appreciation of the co-operative's assets, or at least a substantial part of it, and possibly also receive interest or dividends on this 'excess capital'.

"Lastly, some co-operatives may be allowed to depart from the principle of wage equality, and to maintain differentials, retaining equality only in voting.

"The reform thus outlined seems to be radical and practical enough to have a fair chance of approval, even though its implementation would probably result in a number of co-operatives leaving the Histadrut's fold. It might even give a fillip to establishment of new co-operatives. Yet, the basic problem involved—the relative rigidity of the co-operatives' capital and labour resources—will of course remain unsolved, and their competitive position in a rapidly shifting economy will even be weakened. In order to offset that, the reform programme also envisages a battery of financial and institutional assistance for the co-operative enterprises, including a special credit and investment fund, a fund for loans to would-be members, a Histadrut concern for sharing know-how and management, an audit union of course, a court of appeal, etc.

The co-operatives may thus do away with their hired labour, but will they be able to function independently? Will they not be viable only at a big cost in hidden subsidies? Past experience shows that grants of official and non-official monopolies, often actively supported by the Histadrut, has spoiled co-operatives at least as much as has hired labour."

In fact, it was the reason for the big profits and the hired worker's resultant envy. No reform of the co-operatives can, therefore, be complete without attacking this basic evil.

NOTES TO BOOK FIVE

(1) The following table appears in the Report of the Registrar of Co-operatives for 1962.

WPSTS AFFILIATED TO MERKAZ HACO-OPERATZIA—1962

Type WPSTS	Total Turnover IL.000	Emoluments in IL.000 Members	Non-Members	Total	No. Membs	No. Non-Membs	Per Memb* IL.	Per Non-Memb* IL.
Industrial	62,425	9,495	7,746	17,241	1,455	2,113	543	305
Service	24,853	5,118	2,547	7,665	911	745	468	285
Transport	136,768	45,345	15,527	60,872	5,375	4,090	703	316
Total	224,046	59,958	25,820	85,778	7,741	6,948		

* Includes Apprentices.

(2) The writer's close contacts with WPSTS in Israel (1925-57) do not confirm Dr. Zweig's statements.

(3) Review of International Co-operation, Vol. 50, No. 1, January 1957, pp. 14-20. "Workers Productive Societies in Israel"—Ermano Mondini, Sec. International Co-operative Alliance (I.C.A.—Auxiliary Committee of Workers' Co-operatives and Artisan Societies).

(4) Mr. Mondini is mistaken because this tendency or policy for closed co-operatives already was evident in the 1930s in not a small number of the WPSTS, especially in co-operative printing and bus societies, and in the co-operative workshops manufacturing "specialities".

(5) Shituf, October 1955, pp. 18-20.

(6) CENSUS OF WPSTS IN JULY 1926

Branch	Entire Country No. Societies	Entire Country No. Workers (Members & Non-Members)	Tel Aviv No. Societies	Tel Aviv No. Workers
Metal	20	135	9	57
Joineries	8	144	2	75
Transportation	6	230	5	210
Printing	3	112	2	97
Building Materials	6	56	3	25
Leather	6	36	3	14
Wearing Apparel	6	32	2	18
	55	745	26	496
Others	21	190	13	65
Total	76	935	39	561

(7) Drom Yehuda, the second Bus Co-operative to register on 16 April, 1930, serviced the area south of Tel Aviv; Egged, registered on 15 February, 1934, and the fourth Chavir (name later changed to Shachar) registered on 8 June, 1937, which serviced Haifa and Galilee. These three merged in 1951 into the present Egged (Eshed), registering first as a partnership and on 14 April, 1953, as a co-operative. The bus co-operative Hamekasher registered on 22 June, 1931, continues to service Jerusalem and its suburbs. (Early in 1967 Hamekasher amalgamated with Egged (Eshed.))

(8) Shituf, April, 1958. Thirty Years of Merkaz Hacooperatzia—by Mr. Abraham Dickenstein. He notes that the members of this volunteer Committee of Four were Moshe Shertok (later known as Moshe Sharett, Minister of Foreign Affairs, 1948 to 1956, and Prime Minister 1954 to 1955, who died in 1965); Yisrael Garfunkel (later known as Guri); Leib Feinstein (later known as Shefer) and Abraham Dickenstein.

(9) The first members of this Central Co-operative Committee included Yosef Aaronovitz* who was the Joint Manager of the Workers' Bank Ltd.—1922-32; Eliahu Golomb*; Y. Efter (General Manager of Hamashbir Hamerkazi since it was registered in 1934); Abraham Dickenstein and Mr. I. Brudni (name changed to Bareli)* Joint Manager of Workers' Bank Ltd. (1926-56).

(10) The rules of not a few WPSTS require their members to sign an undertaking to the effect that for a specified period, generally two years, after they leave they will not compete with the respective co-operative directly or indirectly within its area of operation. Most of these undertakings include a heavy penalty in case of a breach of this undertaking. According to the report of the Registrar of Co-operative Societies for 1921-37, "this clause may cause much hardship to members . . . it has on the other hand kept societies together and has served as a deterrent to unscrupulous members".

Most of the WPSTS still adhere to the practice, dating from the very early twenties, to pay full remuneration to members who are permanently or temporarily invalided. These payments generally are made out of special provident funds of the respective co-operatives. Working men's compensation and other Government and Histadrut regulations have reduced considerably the financial burdens of the WPSTS. In the early years, the advances were paid to members only after the co-operative had covered all other expenses, except depreciation, and only to the extent that cash was available. A WPSTS which adheres to this basic principle does not have balance sheet operational losses such as the several million pounds which the annual accounts of the bus co-operatives show. The following observations in the Registrar's Report for 1921-37 are also applicable today (1963) as then to the bus co-operatives and to some of the larger industrial workers' co-operatives.

> "Committees of Management . . . are under constant pressure by members to allot less for amortization, depreciation and reserves and to distribute as much as possible in wages. The outcome . . . has been that in some societies members have been . . . paying themselves higher wages than is justified by their trading returns . . . in identical industries or services . . . the scale of wages differs considerably in accordance with the trade returns."

(11) Kupat Poalei Eretz Yisrael (KAPAI) was organized by the Federation of

Jewish Socialist Workers—Workers of Zion (Brith Hapoalim Haivrim Hasotzialistim, Poalei Zion) in Cracow, West Galicia, in December 1908. The organization started operations in Israel early 1912. Though organized and financed by a political labour party, KAPAI worked with all groups. The general purpose of the organization was to assist in rooting the Jewish workers

> "economically and culturally to the country. The plan of work was to be adapted to the needs of life and of the work . . . it was to operate for the workers, but it was also to get the workers in the country to participate in the activities undertaken on their behalf."

KAPAI raised about $317,000—about 60 per cent—in the United States. Nearly 75 per cent of the entire amount was raised between October 1922 and March 1925. The statement of expenditure includes one item which can be considered as assistance to co-operatives, loans of $27,500 to kibbutzim and individuals. The following items of expenditure: $41,000 in connection with a warehouse for machines and tools, $75,000 for urban undertakings and $70,000 for labour institutions may have been used in part for WPSTS.

The activities of KAPAI in Israel fall into three periods, 1912-14; 1915-20 and 1921-24. *De facto* the management was in the hands of the Histadrut. Among the more important activities of KAPAI was the establishment of employment exchanges and information bureaux in the largest Jewish centres; the financing of public works in Jerusalem, Tel Aviv and Haifa during periods of unemployment; and the organization and financing of the first mobile labour contract groups for building and construction. (These groups, *inter alia,* worked on the first buildings of the Technion in Haifa.) KAPAI also helped to organize and finance the first co-operative machine workshop and carpentry, both in Haifa, and encouraged the tailors, printers and shoemakers to organize co-operatives.

In 1921 the KAPAI organized a drive in the United States for all kinds of machines, equipment and tools which were brought to Israel and distributed to workers, artisans and farmers. KAPAI engaged instructors, taught the recipients how to use and maintain the machines, including those for agriculture and miscellaneous purposes, and the equipment for carpenters' shops.

During the period 1922-27, the prevailing opinion within the Histadrut was in favour of having its Office for Public Works (Misrad L'avodot Tziburyot) organize the workers into labour contracting societies for building and construction of roads and that Mashbir should organize the industrial workers and the service societies, because "it had to market their products". The groups were too dependent on Solel Boneh and on KAPAI for technical guidance and administration. The managers and the members of WPSTS made little or no effort to improve the quality of their products or increase their productivity p.m.h.; and since the KAPAI and the Misrad L'Avodot Tziburiot and its successor Solel Boneh supplied the equipment, raw materials and working capital, the WPSTS made no effort to accumulate their own capital.

(12) Review of International Co-operation, Vol. 50, No. 1, January, 1957, Dr. Erwin Langeludeky, Hamburg, writes:

> "There are 60,000 transport operators for road haulage and about 5,000

for inland water transport in the Federal Republic of Germany. The drive to preserve the existence of individual transport enterprises and recognition of the economic importance of collaboration caused transport operators to organize both inland water transport and road haulage . . . co-operatives, all affiliated to the Auditing Union of German Transport Co-operatives (Pruefungs Verband der Deutschen Verkehrsgenossenschaften e. V.) Hamburg.

". . . fifty years ago co-operative organizations for inland water transport were found in East Prussia, Schleswig, Pomerania, along the Elbe, the Rhine, the Ruhr, the Main and other German waterways. In ports . . . Hamburg, Bremen, Stettin, Erden, . . . sailors had also organized themselves co-operatively . . . there were others (co-ops) for the provision of credit and for underwriting shipping insurance, as well as burial clubs and benevolent funds. . . .

"The owners of small tugs and motor boats joined together to procure for their members the necessary forward and return consignments and to ensure the most orderly transport arrangements in the interests of the consigning agencies and the recipients. . . . Owners of small tug boats have joined tug boats co-operatives designed to arrange tug contracts for their members . . . on the Rhine there are ferry co-operatives which handle tourist traffic as well as the ferries. Co-operative organizations have been established also among coastal shippers, whilst in Bremen and Bremerhaven there are storage co-operatives.

"The various types of co-operatives . . . negotiate transport orders for their members . . . looking after the general interests of the ship owners . . . finance transportation and assist owners in getting equipment and fuel . . . watch their business interests . . . make themselves responsible for shipping repairs and protecting ship owners' interests with the shore authorities . . . co-operatives are . . . the 'economic home' of the owners, who bring . . . all their economic problems and financial worries. . . .

"Former sea captains . . . have formed co-operatives . . . for guarding foreign vessels while unloading in port. Some co-operatives . . . have erected loading appliances, trans-shipment facilities, granaries and warehouses. . . .

"In the Federal Republic of Germany, including West Berlin, there are . . . about thirty inland waterway co-operatives. . . . The total volume of turnover of the Inland Water Co-operatives in 1955 was DM.92 million.

"The function of the co-operatives in short distance haulage is mainly to apportion bulk commissions amongst members, to settle accounts with the consignors and to arrange for advanced payments to the road transport contractors for work done. Small contracts are not handled by these co-operatives to any great extent . . . these short distance road transport co-operatives . . . (arrange) the removal of rubble . . . transportation of milk. . . . The co-operatives not only finance the transportation, but provide an excellent insurance system and help their members with repairs and the buying of fuel, obtaining spare parts and other requirements.

"Co-operatives are responsible for arranging the financial details of long distance goods haulage . . . retaining the transportation tax and forwarding it to the financial authorities . . . ensuring that the loads are fully insured. . . .

"To ensure a better and safer transport service it was necessary for the long distance haulage contractors to have lorry yards . . . to guard vehicles, to assemble and store goods, to give accommodation to drivers and to maintain and repair vehicles. . . . Fourteen (lorry yards) have been erected by co-operatives . . . there are (also) about eighty load distribution offices sponsored by co-operatives.

"The large road transport co-operatives are affiliated to a Federal Central Road Transport Co-operative with its headquarters in Frankfurt-on-Main. . . . At the present moment in Western Germany there are about sixty road transport co-operatives functioning. . . . The consignors too . . . have joined in co-operatives . . . making their loading problem simpler. . . . Co-operatives . . . have also got a footing in the tanker transport field.

"In the public transport sector omnibus co-operatives are active and they operate fixed route traffic as well as providing for tourist traffic and holiday transport with inclusive charges for hotels, meals, etc. More recently the transport requirements of workers in industrial areas are being provided through co-operatives. In the taxi and car hire business . . . co-operatives . . . provide commissions for their members through taxi ranks. They also . . . make joint purchases on their (members') behalf. . . ."

(13) At the end of 1931, under the leadership of S. Gorochowsky (now Goren) of Merkaz Haco-operatzia and Hasan Sidki, the Arab and Jewish drivers staged a general strike. The Mandatory Government then agreed to meet the drivers' demand that it should pursue a more stringent policy concerning the issue of licences for new routes; permit a larger number of buses on the existing routes; and decrease the high duties on petrol.

(14) The members of the transportation co-operatives, like the chalutzim who joined the kibbutzim and the moshavim ovdim, were part of the "elite" in the Yishuv. The material and spiritual contribution of these transportation co-operatives and their losses in lives and of property during the three decades (1919-48) of almost continuous civil strife and ambushes have been publicized less than have the contributions of the kibbutzim and the moshavim ovdim in the defence of the Yishuv.

(15) According to the Registrar's Report for 1921-37 "competition had been eliminated until what is virtually a monopoly in passenger transport had been obtained".

(16) The following is an excerpt from the Report:
"Co-operative Movement in the United States in 1925 (other than Agricultural)", U.S. Department of Labour, Bureau of Labour Statistics, Bulletin No. 437, March 1926, prepared by Miss Frances Parker.

"The Workers Producers' Movement is the least developed of the types studied and shows the least indication of future expansion. This type of society is subject to the special handicaps that

1. the groups forming them are usually small, and to start a business generally requires more capital per member than the average working man has at his disposal;
2. even though the members be skilled in their line of work they are usually inexperienced in the sale of their products and must often resort to hiring outside assistance for marketing the output;

3. the manager is, as a rule, chosen from among the workers themselves, a feature which, while democratic, may lead to difficulties in discipline, as the member-worker is apt to feel that he is as good as the manager (who holds office only by the members' pleasure) and to resent taking orders from him; and
4. if the business is financially successful there is the temptation to restrict the number of members who must share in the profits of the business, and if additional labour is needed, to secure this by hiring workers instead of taking in new members."

(17) The Registrar in his Report for 1921-37 notes that "looking at it from a purely co-operative point of view (use of non-member labour) is definitely an undesirable practice which should be eliminated."

Mr. N. Verlinsky, who has been General Manager of Merkaz Tnuva for three decades, has either overlooked or does not know that the philosophy of co-operation has always stressed the materialistic as well as the social aspects of co-operatives, and that co-operatives must run on a business-like basis. The Tnuva (Book Six) has from the very outset stressed the material interests of the producers; its members not infrequently have been accused of forgetting the consumers' interests and generally the social aspects of co-operation.

(18) Prior to the enactment of the new Co-operative Societies Ordinance (1933) and Regulations (1934), Audit Unions were not recognized.

(19) Judging by the developments in the period 1934-1963, either Mr. Brudni asked too much of ordinary human beings, even of good Labour Zionists, or Merkaz Haco-operatzia and/or the Histadrut has not been equal to the task.

In this connection the following excerpts from an unsigned article in Shituf, March 1958, commemorating the thirtieth birthday of Merkaz Haco-operatzia, is of interest.

> "From then and until the present Merkaz Haco-operatzia has marched alone in the path of affliction, without encouragement and assistance. The Workers Bank did *not* (original underlined) create the special fund for the needs of the WPSTS; the Histadrut Executive Committee did not make the annual allotments out of the funds collected abroad . . . Hamashbir Hamerkazi did not pay any special attention to the marketing of the produce of WPSTS . . . and during the last decade the Government Treasury persistently said no (to the requests of Merkaz Haco-operatzia)."

The article also notes that what Merkaz Haco-operatzia needed mostly was a "friendly Histadrut climate and more than the broken promises of financial help", and that the Histadrut affiliated craft unions considered the WPSTS as a kind of "semi-bourgeois whirlpool within the labour movement, in the class war". The few kind words of some of the Histadrut leaders were drowned by the persistent flood of criticism of "even the very pattern of WPSTS" and of "its insignificant achievements".

In the early years, Merkaz Haco-operatzia prepared an annual detailed report about the administration and special problems of every affiliated WPSTS. These reports were made available to banks and other parties working with the WPSTS. Since about 1945, if such reports were prepared, these are no longer available. Merkaz Haco-operatzia blames the co-operatives for the considerable delay in the audit and preparation of the annual accounts. According to the Auditing Department and Management of the Merkaz Haco-operatzia, the delay is caused by differences among the members in the WPSTS with regard to disposal of surpluses and the evaluation of assets.

According to a report of the Auditing Department, *Shituf*, April 1959, p. 29, the situation had improved considerably "during the six months ending 31 March, 1959".

(20) The Report of Merkaz Haco-operatzia notes that with the abolition of food rationing and price control, the 27 affiliated WPSTS in the food industry probably will be unable to compete with the larger and better equipped factories, which also grant liberal credit terms. The consumers do not appreciate the better quality of the merchandise of the co-operative bakeries. It is also becoming increasingly difficult for the food processing co-operatives to sell to the consumers' co-operatives.

(21) Shituf, August-September 1953, p. 2.

(22) Shituf, July 1953, p. 27.

(23) L'Chavereinu (published by Egged (Eshed)), September 1953, pp. 5-17, of which pp. 12-16 are tables on revenue, expenditure, costs of rolling stock, prices of fuel, spare parts, etc., and on bus fares.

(24) L'Chavereinu, November 1953, pp. 14-16.

(25) Hameshek Hashitufi, 20 October 1953, the organ of Consumers' Co-operatives.

(26) The writer of the leader probably refers to "La Regie Co-operative" by Bernard Lavergne, 1927. Relatively few co-operators, even the theoreticians of the Co-operative Movement consider the socialized undertakings described in this book as co-operatives.

(27) An anonymous article in Shituf, February-March 1954, gives the following explanation for the larger gross remuneration per member:

> "While a member's remuneration is higher than that of a wage worker, a member, especially in a small or medium-size WPSTS, is not only a worker but also carries more responsibility (than does the wage worker). He exerts himself, his earnings also include interest on his investment in the respective WPSTS and an allowance for risk and overtime."

(28) Shituf, February-March 1954, p. 6. In 1960 Mr. M. Carmel was appointed Minister of Transport.

(29) The article does not give the share of the road haulage co-operatives in this as 80 per cent, but according to other sources, all road haulage co-operatives accounted for about 70 per cent of the goods transported by lorries.

(30)

Goods Transport	Haulage in 1,000 ton kilometres		
Railways	90,310	303,139	70,867
Lorries and other means[(a)]	430,000	540,000	410,000
	520,310	843,139	480,867

(*a*) Other means include small quantities by coastal shipping, part of which is done by one co-operative.

(31) Shituf, October 1954, pp. 20-23.

(32) Practically the same problems were discussed at all meetings. Apparently the regional meetings had no fixed agendas and the addresses of the members of the secretariat of Merkaz Haco-operatzia occupied most of

the time. The observations of the members of the Management Committee at the regional meetings were more restrictive and individualistic.

(33) This statement probably refers to the Histadrut directive that the co-operative bakeries were not to join the strike of bakeries, though most of the members of the co-operative bakeries accepted the view that a general strike of all bakers was the only way of forcing the Government to approve an increase in the price of bread.

The workers, including those of the co-operative of workers, which is a partner in the Haargaz Company, staged a sit-down strike because a bus co-operative had not awarded to the Haargaz Company the entire contract for the bodies. The bus co-operative stated that it had been its practice for many years to divide its orders for bodies.

The Histadrut and the respective craft union ruled that it was natural for co-operatives to give their contract to other co-operatives, but the respective co-operative workshop had to demonstrate its ability to complete the work in accordance with accepted standards of work and within the period specified in the contract.

(34) Pecher, Dr. M., A Study of the Health of Jewish Drivers in the Transport Co-operatives of Israel—Released by the Occupational Hygiene Commission and Hamerkaz Hachaklai.

(35) The Co-operative Societies Ordinance, 1933, (Book One) empowers the Registrar

(*a*) to accept the audits of registered audit unions in place of audits by Government-licenced auditors and

(*b*) to issue special licences to one or more employees of the respective audit unions to audit and to prepare the annual accounts of their member co-operatives.

(36) The diamond cutting and polishing industry was started in Israel about 1940. In 1944 Merkaz Haco-operatzia started organizing the diamond workers into co-operatives (commandites). The Histadrut and Kupat Haco-operativim established workshops and assumed the responsibility for getting the raw material and merchandising the finished product. Within a few years all the diamond workers co-operatives and the joint undertakings were liquidated.

(37) The Histadrut acted favourably on the second suggestion, which had been under consideration for some years.

(38) About three years after this Council Meeting an article in Haaretz, 12 February, 1952, alleged that the balance-sheets and the details about their activities which bus co-operatives submitted to the "approved authorities" and "for public information" concealed important details. In reply to the writer's letter of 17 February, 1952, asking for the observations of Merkaz Haco-operatzia on these allegations, one of the auditors of the Auditing Department of Merkaz Haco-operatzia replied on 11 March, 1952: "Admittedly the bus co-operatives during the last two years have done (things) which are contrary to the opinion of Chevrat Haovdim. The Histadrut Executive Committee discussed these cases and took suitable action. But we point out that the WPSTS did not exclude any data and figures from their balance sheets."

The writer of the article in Haaretz and the auditor of Merkaz Haco-operatzia fail to mention that all the five bus co-operatives had transferred to subsidiary corporate bodies, wholly owned by their members, nearly all their property, i.e. equipment, vehicles and buildings. Over a period of years, it was exceptional for the balance-sheets of these bus co-operatives to include a note to this effect. These subsidiaries have since been liquidated and the bus co-operatives repurchased their assets, paid the owners of the subsidiaries, i.e. the members of the bus co-operatives, a much higher price for their shares than that which the members had paid. Furthermore, the co-operatives for a number of years paid to their subsidiaries, i.e. themselves, what appeared to be excessive charges for managerial services.

(39) The Secretariat's Report to the Council of 24-25 May, 1950, also notes that Merkaz Haco-operatzia had to discontinue the technical service for its affiliated societies since

> "a one man (an engineer) department could not do effective work. An all-embracing technical staff was needed . . . for technical training, supervision, and planning; to deal with equipment, estimates, and plan for establishing new WPSTS. . . . This requires a large staff and an appreciable budget."

(40) The Secretariat's Report's summary of the negotiations about the "reform" of the bus co-operatives does not unequivocally admit that Merkaz Haco-operatzia and Chevrat Haovdim had approved the re-evaluation of the assets and of the capital and reserves and permitted the bus co-operatives to distribute several million pounds among the members. According to the Secretariat's Report the negative decision of the Histadrut Executive Committee reflects faulty co-ordination within the Histadrut, and also creates the impression that the negotiations which Merkaz Haco-operatzia carried on, with the approval of Chevrat Haovdim, were limited to the amendments of the rules of the bus co-operatives about the special status of Chevrat Haovdim and were not concerned with the financial "reform."

(41) Mr. Zeev Onn, of Chevrat Haovdim, was a member of the special committee which submitted to the Histadrut Executive Committee a report on the bus co-operatives. Mr. Onn and his colleagues sought to avoid at all costs the secession from the Histadrut of such an influential financial sector as the bus co-operatives. Therefore they do not distinguish between the Histadrut-sponsored co-operatives and the Histadrut-owned and administered undertakings. It seems that they were unwilling or unable to understand that the co-operative pattern is not the most suitable form for all economic enterprises under all conditions.

(42) On 24 August, 1953 the representatives of 50 of the 65 co-operative bakeries decided to set up a fund of IL.100,000 for mutual aid to modernize their equipment; for the central purchase of flour and of other commodities; and generally to strengthen the societies. The co-operative bakeries were to pay in IL.25,000 within one year. This special fund was registered as a company which started to operate at end of 1953. It was reported that these 65 co-operative bakeries had 600 members and 400 wage workers (including only 10 apprentices).

(43) Shituf, October 1957, Problems Requiring Solution, pp. 4-6. "One Co-operative is Liquidated and Another is Consolidated."

(44) Shituf, January-February 1958.

(45) The decision of Chevrat Haovdim early in 1958 to organize the special Company, jointly with the Government, to establish industries in the development zones includes a paragraph to the effect that "it will encourage the organization of co-operative undertaking and/or partnerships between co-operatives of workers and the new company, Teeus". The company also will establish and directly administer industrial plants with the ultimate aim of transferring these, in part or in whole, to WPSTS.

(46) Shituf, April 1958, pp. 49-50. Mr. Pinchas Zomer has some doubts ("impure thoughts") about the reorganization of Merkaz Haco-operatzia and about the attitude of Teeus to the WPSTS movement. The many who "were invited and accepted the invitation to express their views on these two questions" included very few of those actually working and dealing with the individual affiliated WPSTS. Those who work with the WPSTS are interested in the essence (content) and not in the organizational structure of Merkaz Haco-operatzia; they are interested in the economy, members, and problems of the WPSTS, and not in "the framework" with which they are linked and in which they are active. The individual member of a WPSTS will judge the desirability and efficiency of the reorganization plan only after he can judge whether the "autonomous divisions and their respective governing bodies will more efficiently guide and give more comprehensive practical assistance to the person dealing with and responsible for the respective WPSTS than has been the case prior to the reorganization of Merkaz Haco-operatzia. Since the Chevrat Haovdim secretariat prepared and approved the reorganization plan, those working with the WPSTS

> "believe that the Histadrut and its various bodies will from now on guide and give all the help which the individual societies and the WPSTS movement need to solve their problems." Mr. Zomer emphasizes that he is thinking first and foremost of help "not from the higher organs of the Histadrut and Chevrat Haovdim but from the local workers councils; the branches of the Workers Bank; the projects on which Solel Boneh is engaged; Hamashbir Hamerkazi and the consumers' co-operatives, the Histadrut-sponsored bodies."

(47) Shituf, July 1957, p. 15, "Partnerships between WPSTS and Private Enterprises", in Israel. Summary of a memorandum submitted to the International Co-operative Alliance on the status of the WPSTS in the middle of 1957.

> "Shortage of operating and investment capital forces us from time to time to come to an arrangement for partnership with private capital; especially the transfer to the employees organized as co-operatives of a going concern, or a partnership with the previous employers." All such arrangements are subject to the approval of Chevrat Haovdim and the share of the industrial workers co-operatives in the plants may not exceed 50 per cent of the capital and of the votes in the respective plant. Experience has demonstrated that in many instances such partnerships create internal "antagonisms and deviations against which the undertaking cannot successfully stand up." On the one hand, the industrial workers co-operatives depend too much on the private owners, i.e. on their experience and connections, and therefore the

members of the co-operatives do not fully utilize and take advantage of self-management. This is to the disadvantage of the undertaking. On the other hand, the members of the workers co-operatives cannot reconcile themselves to the special privileges which the private owners enjoy. "This is the source of misunderstanding, irritation and strife, which lead to the liquidation of the partnership . . . and even of the undertaking. . . ."

(48) The Sixth Congress was convened on 15-16 July, 1962. The Background Material for and the Proceedings of the Congress were not summarized. See Shituf, May-June and July-August, 1962.

(49) A joint meeting of the Merkaz Haco-operatzia secretariat with some members of the preparatory committee for the Sixth Congress accepted the proposal and decided that the Sixth Congress should be convened in April 1960, "and that the date should be fixed in consultation with the secretariat of Chevrat Haovdim."

(50) On 31 December, 1958, the members constituted only 53 per cent of the global labour force in all affiliated WPSTS.

(51) On 31 December, 1958, the bus co-operatives had over 2,900 wage workers (including apprentices).

(52) Mr. Tzwick probably refers to the insistence in 1951 by Mapai and the Government in which it was the dominant factor, that it was the patriotic duty of the kibbutzim and moshavim to employ the immigrants as wage workers.

(53) It seems to the writer that Mr. Tzwick, perhaps unconsciously, is twisting and misinterpreting the Histadrut's request, which was not to eliminate but to minimize wage labour by admitting most of the wage workers as members. The problem of wage labour in the WPSTS is not comparable with that in kibbutzim and moshavim. The moshavim, and more especially the kibbutzim, offer every possible concession for wage workers to join as members. On the other hand, the WPSTS, generally speaking, place all kinds of obstacles, such as relatively large initial payments, which they justify with the argument that the WPSTS have received relatively little financial assistance from the Government, the Jewish Agency and public institutions. Mr. Tzwick, one of the founders and ex-member of a large and important kibbutz in the Emek, is not unaware of these facts He also misinterprets Mr. Onn's suggestion about the autonomy of the divisions, ignoring the fact that Chevrat Haovdim will have adequate representation on all the governing bodies of the respective autonomous divisions, and that Chevrat Haovdim representatives enjoy special rights, such as the power of veto and/or the postponement of action on not a few questions.

(54) This is the Histadrut-sponsored Industrial Bank, a subsidiary of Ampal. Another speaker at this Council Meeting identified the undertaking as the Solel Boneh.

(55) Differentiation between members and non-members not given.

(56) A workshop in a kibbutz which markets its products, and/or a kibbutz transport service which also caters to outsiders, is an organic part of the kibbutz and its economy, and with very few exceptions, are not registered as separate corporate bodies. The workshops, etc. in not a few kibbutzim do not pay their way and are carried by agricultural or other branches which have operating surpluses.

(57) Co-operatives consider any price maintenance, whether wholesale or retail, as an unfair trade practice which is harmful to the interests of the consumers.

(58) London Sunday Times, 11 April, 1954, Hugh Trevor-Roper, who made an on-the-spot study of Israel, wrote:

"Consider, for example, the Histadrut (the General Federation of Labour in Israel)." The Histadrut is "the most powerful, most monopolistic trade union faced by any Government in the world.

"The Histadrut began as a co-operative institution to organize and finance Jewish enterprise under, and sometimes against, the Mandate; it is now a huge and efficient system disposing of vast resources, organizing welfare services, controlling and financing agriculture and industry, fixing prices and wages, and managing, as a party, the best run municipalities. It is the universal trade union, the only union to which the vast majority of the population may and all Government employees belong. Theoretically it is controlled by the Labour Zionist Party (MAPAI), but in fact, owing to its huge membership and economic power, it controls that party, and through it, the State.

"One of its directors sought to explain to me that the Histadrut is really quite inoffensive in politics. 'The present Government of Israel,' he said 'is a coalition Government. I (for he spoke like the late Ernest Bevin) would prefer a straightforward majority Government by the Labour Party. Nevertheless, the Histadrut will tolerate this Government. To tolerate implies the power not to tolerate. It is because of its latent power, not its present policy, that Israeli Liberals sometimes view the Histadrut with alarm, and sceptics describe its vast new offices in Tel Aviv as the Kremlin.'"

(59) Fifteen million cases were exported during the 1939-40 season.

(60) The report does not explain why Merkaz Haco-operatzia could not restrain the co-operative from investing in a new building and branches with exquisite furnishings and equipment, which is described as "a very large jump from a deep cave to a high roof." The restaurant had occupied a "small room, very badly furnished from every point of view". Purchasing supplies on credit and borrowing funds at exorbitant interest rates for capital investments plus a mounting operational deficit resulted in the complete destruction of this co-operative. It is reported that the expenditure of interest amounted to 2-3 per cent of the gross revenue. The Management was continuously involved in financial combinations, and neglected the administration. Waste of food was excessive, labour productivity was very low, and the equipment was not maintained. But the report fails to mention that the unsecured creditors were forced to compromise and suffered appreciable losses.

(61) This hope was not realized.

(62) The main source of income of Merkaz Haco-operatzia (1938-42) was a one per cent levy on the gross emoluments paid to members and non-members by every affiliated WPSTS. This levy was later changed to three per thousand of gross revenue for any year, plus LP.1 per member per year. Every WPSTS when joining Merkaz Haco-operatzia pays a one-time levy equivalent to three per cent of their paid-up share capital and two per cent of their reserves. The miscellaneous sources of revenue of

Merkaz Haco-operatzia were management fees from its subsidiaries, NOA and Kupat Haco-operativim, and from its Insurance Deparement.

(63) STATUS OF SPECIFIED ITEMS FOR WPSTS AFFILIATED TO MERKAZ HACO-OPERATZIA (Amounts in LP.000)

Item	1938 *LP*	1948 (Estimate) *LP*
Capital & Reserves	375	3,000
Investments (Immovables, Movables)	548	**5,162**
Gross Business for the Year	451	3,964
Wages Paid (to members and non-members) during the Year	392	4,400

The official exchange rate was $4 and $2.80 in 1938 and 1948 respectively.

(64) Israel was still without a Constitution at the end of 1966.
(65) This analysis has proved erroneous.
(66) Farmers in the moshavim ovdim and also in the kibbutzim had accepted into their homes many thousands of immigrants, especially Aliyat Hanoar. The cost for maintaining Youth Aliya exceeded the payments which the moshavim and the kibbutzim received for this service.
(67) This refers to the textile factory in Beit Dagon (near Tel Aviv) whose Arab owners had left Israel. The Custodian of Absentee Owners Property sold the textile mill to Hamashbir Hamerkazi and the purchase price was allegedly too small.
(68) Another 300 war veterans were organized into new WPSTS.
(69) The secretary of Merkaz Haco-operatzia spent most of his time at committee meetings and, therefore, heard very little of the general debate. This may explain why his reply was rhetorical and verbose and contained little of constructive value.
(70) Had not yet been enacted by the end of 1964.
(71) The Secretariat's Report to the Second Council Meeting (24-25 May, 1950) cites the following two examples of the conversion of private establishments into industrial workers co-operatives. In 1944 a factory for elevators, (passenger; goods and dumb) scales etc., was opened with eleven workers. Differences between the shareholders made it possible for the workers to acquire half the ordinary voting shares. The founder of the plant, an engineer, kept the other half. This co-partnership co-operative producer society also has a one-third financial interest, which carries with it one-half of the voting shares, in a subsidiary company for making elevators.

A second example is a large glass factory (Gavish, Rishon-le-Zion) in which the workers first purchased a half interest and then increased this to 75 per cent. The former owner retained the other 25 per cent and was active in the business.

(72) These included a large restaurant each in Haifa, Jerusalem, and Tel Aviv; a small restaurant each in Beersheba, Netanya and Tiberias; a co-operative which has a summer vacation home in Jerusalem and a winter vacation home in Tiberias; two medium-size hotels in Haifa; a medium-size hotel in Tel Aviv, which was bought in 1950, and a small hotel each in Jerusalem and Beersheba. And most of the twelve co-operative restaurants and hotels have become commandites. A company, Merkaz Hamisadot, was registered with a capital of IL.20,100. Chevrat Haovdim holds the 100

founder shares, with a nominal value of IL.100, and has half the votes at the general meeting and on the management committee of the company. The three co-operative restaurants in Haifa, Jerusalem and Tel Aviv together have a half interest and the Kupat Haco-operativim the other half. In the event of liquidation all the assets remaining after payment of all the company's liabilities will be transferred to Chevrat Haovdim.

The company is the registered owner of all the property of all the co-operative restaurants, except of the one in Tel Aviv; it appoints the administration and half the management committee of these co-operatives, and adjudicates all differences within a management committee of any co-operative. Nearly all the members in the co-operative restaurants are women. Except for some fringe benefits (social security provisions) the conditions of employment for members and non-members are the same. Therefore, according to the secretariat's report, there are very few wage workers who wish to become members. There is also a large turnover among the members. In the case of the co-operative restaurants in Jerusalem and Haifa, Merkaz Haco-operatzia reports that the productivity is declining since most of the members are over 50 and there is a relatively higher percentage of illness than there is in the co-operatives with a predominantly male membership.

(73) The Secretariat's Report expresses apprehension that the large fully mechanized non-co-operative shoe factory to be opened in Jerusalem at the end of 1950 is a potential danger for this co-operative.

(74) The writer, at the time, directed the activities of the Foreign Loans Department of the Ministry of Finance. The charges in the Secretariat's Report are unfounded and without substance.

75) An unsigned article "If Choma will Fall" (Hameshek Hashitufi, 13 December, 1956, pp. 433-34) reports that eight plants in which Choma has invested (in share capital and in loans) employed 277 people and the value of their gross production in 1955 was IL.4,222,500. Should this institution fall by the wayside another Histadrut-sponsored body, probably Kupat Haco-operativim, will carry on. But the disappearance of one of the first independent economic bodies which Chevrat Haovdim established, would be regrettable. Choma gave priority to the establishment of middle size factories in the post-State immigrant localities and to saving weak industrial workers co-operatives, either by acquiring these or affording them the possibility of continuing. Chevrat Haovdim had promised to invest IL.250,000 in Choma's registered capital of IL.500,000. Chevrat Haovdim transferred to Choma six factories which needed immediate assistance. It invested only IL.87,000 during the first year (1951) and the balance, IL.163,000, during the next four years.

(76) The second session of the Eighth Mapai Congress on 16 May, 1958 decided that the bus service must be organized as a public service (utility) company jointly owned and managed by the Government and other public interests and by the members and the workers of the respective bus co-operatives. The Mapai Congress instructed its members on the Histadrut Executive Committee to draft a plan which, after it had been discussed with the Mapai members who are on the management of Merkaz Haco-operatzia and of the bus co-operatives, should then be submitted to the Histadrut Executive Committee. Government agreement also should be sought. The Mapai Congress also expressed the opinion that the Govern-

ment should set up an official Committee to enquire into every facet of the motor transportation economy, with a view to reducing the operating costs.

(77) This refers mainly to changing the industrial workers co-operatives into labour contracting societies that do not own any of movable and immovable property of the respective plants in which they work.

(78) See table on p. 374.

(79) Mr. Kitzis refers to a story about Napoleon who was asked how he could suffer his confinement on St. Helena and not commit suicide. Napoleon allegedly replied that he still had hopes of repairing the mistakes which he had made in his life-time. "But I will not do anything which I cannot mend."

(80) Mr. Goren notes that this is equally true for non-co-operative industry.

(81) ROAD ACCIDENTS—NO. OF ACCIDENTS AND RATE PER 100,000 INHABITANTS (corrected figures)

	1959	1960
1. Total No. of Accidents	21,157	19,373
2. No. of Accidents involving Casualties	8,255	8,356
3. Total Casualties	10,738	10,542
4. Total killed	200	176
5. Total Seriously Injured (sent to hospital)	2,140	1,868
6. Slightly Injured	8,398	8,498
Accidents per 100,000 Inhabitants		
7. No. of accidents	1,026	920
8. No. of Accidents involving casualties	400	394
9. Total Casualties	521	497
10. Total Killed	10	8
11. Total Seriously Injured (sent to hospital)	104	89
12. Slightly Injured	407	400

Statistical Abstract of Israel 1959-60, No. 11, Table 7, p. 219, and 1962, No. 13, Table 10, p. 277.

(82) Mr. Hovne is an official of the Ministry of Labour & Social Security. These are extracts from the English text of a report in Hebrew released by the Ministry of Labour and Social Security, Israel, in 1951 (mimeographed). The unpublished English text which Mr. Hovne made available to the writer is not too satisfactory. There are some differences between the Hebrew and the English texts; none of these significant. The original wording of the text has been used except in a few instances where clarity required minor changes in construction and terminology. This is one of the best reports on the bus transportation system known to the writer, though he does not agree with Mr. Hovne's reasoning or conclusions. The explanatory notes were added by the writer.

(83) Davar, 26 June and 6, 10, 16, 28, 30 July; and 6 and 7 August, 1953, Mr. Shabatai used Eshed and not Egged (Eshed) the full name. These eight articles by Mr. Shabatai are one of the best sources about bus co-operatives, both from the general and co-operative point of view. They are written in a light satirical and at times, humorous style. But this does not detract

(78) STATUS OF BUS CO-OPERATIVES AFFILIATED WITH MERKAZ HACO-OPERATZIA

	Unit	1951	1954[c]	1957[c]	1959[c]	1961[d]
1. All Bus Co-operatives affiliated with Merkaz Haco-operatzia		5	3	3	3	3
2. Buses (Yearly Average)		1,422	1,662	1,790	2,011	2,223
3. Seating Capacity (Yearly average)		46,625	56,882	65,768	81,488	101,220
4. Average Number of Seats per Bus		33	34	37	41	
5. Journeys (regular services[a])[d]	1,000	7,570	7,490	8,676	11,775	
6. Kilometres run (regular services)[d]	1,000km	83,000	81,000	92,500	122,823	
7. Revenue (regular services)[b]	IL. 1,000	13,581	37,318	55,696	71,385	104,801[e]
8. Revenue per Bus per kilometre (regular services)	Pruta	164	461	602	581	

(*a*) A return journey is calculated as two runs.
(*b*) Including Defence Stamp Taxes.
(*c*) The number of bus co-operatives were reduced after 1951 because three merged in Egged (Eshed).
(*d*) Shituf July-August 1962, p. 22, Report to Sixth Congress of Merkaz Haco-operatzia.
(*e*) Shituf April 1961; March 1962.

from Mr. Shabatai's realistic approach which is based on a wide knowledge of original sources. In some respects, these eight articles are more enlightening and paint a more accurate picture than the report "The Bus Service in Israel" by Avner Hovne.

(84) The reference was to a housing project for members of the Dan bus co-operative, on the outskirts of Tel Aviv. The houses which some of the members were building were (unjustly) described as "palaces".

(85) About 400 bus co-operatives in Mexico controlled half or more of the passenger traffic in certain districts in Mexico. Mr. Shabatai writes "that the three important encyclopedias which I searched did not describe transportation co-operatives similar to those in Israel." Mr. Shabatai apparently did not use the right source.

(86) Mr. Shabatai also notes that Mr. Zeev Onn (Chevrat Haovdim) after his trip abroad had remarked, "These (co-operators abroad) are very critical, and in particular of our bus co-operatives."

(87) One of the leaders of Egged (Eshed) allegedly replied: "If they think that we do not understand, why doesn't somebody, for example Merkaz Haco-operatzia, instruct us about this."

(88) If this is an accurate report, then there appears to be some confusion. Co-operative principles do not prohibit the use of wage labour. At best, in the case of WPSTS, the use of wage labour may be considered as an unorthodox practice. There is no principle involved in paying high remuneration to members provided this is not accompanied by exploitation. Strictly speaking, there are no wages in WPSTS. There is a distribution of the difference between gross revenue and gross expenditures. The net surplus is the surplus remaining after providing for reserves, depreciation, etc. As for withdrawal of funds, a co-operative, including a WPSTS, may have divisible and non-divisible reserves, etc. But the bus co-operatives distributed money which was not even actually available; they distributed book surpluses which were created by revaluation of assets, especially equipment, in terms of costs of replacement.

(89) This extract lends some support to the view that the Histadrut Executive Committee heard about the "reform" only when it was asked formally to confirm something which the bus co-operatives, with the approval of Merkaz Haco-operatzia and some members of Chevrat Haovdim Secretariat, had already approved.

(90) Mr. Shabatai mentions his conversation with Mr. Joseph Canaan, an economic reporter on the Histadrut daily, "Davar" who a few months previously had asked (Eshed) why they pay all their drivers a daily maintenance allowance of 750 prutot. Surely most of the drivers could eat at home or bring their lunch as do most of the workers in other industries. Eshed's evasive reply, according to Mr Canaan, was that "members working out of town spend more than the daily allowance (paid by the co-operative) for food". Mr. Canaan said that he had also enquired and received unsatisfactory answers about the equal allowances to every member for clothing (though they are free to dress as they please) and for holidays, culture, etc. According to the Chevrat Haovdim representative on the daily management of Egged (Eshed), the Histadrut knows about these supplements but has not approved them.

(91) About half of Mr. Karni's article is used for citing quotations out of context; and poking fun at both Mr. Shabatai and Mr. Canaan.

(92) Mr. Baer devotes much of the article to the intelligence and cultural level

of the members of the bus co-operatives, their services and bravery during the period of the Mandate, World War Two and the War of Liberation. He stated that were it not for the bus co-operatives, road transportation would have been crippled after the Mandatory Government left Israel. Also that the buses are less crowded and faster today than they were before.

(93) Mr. Handler's article in the main is a repetition of the arguments used by Mr. Levita and by others about the reasons for the deficiencies of certain routes; the competition between the buses and the trains; the high bus fares; control; overtime pay; etc. And Mr. Handler's article, like the other articles in L'Chavereinu about Mr. Shabatai's articles, also relies very much on poking fun at Mr. Shabatai (and other intellectuals) who obtain their information and criticism from encyclopedias, wrong text books, etc. Mr. Handler hammers away at the fact that bus fares in Israel are lower than of private (capitalist) transportation companies in other countries, on the basis of distances, etc., and also those of nationalized transportation services, which are not efficient.

(94) The letter is mainly a repetition of Mr. Handler's allegation. Mr. Weitzer starts with a eulogy of Mr. Shabatai as a balanced, far-sighted writer with a penetrating yet simple style and language, "beautiful and understood by all", and that Mr. Shabatai has a "deep knowledge about transportation. . . . As far as I know you never attended a school for transportation either in Israel or abroad. . . ."

(95) L'Chavereinu (August 1953), September 1953 (pp. 41-43). Generally speaking Mr. Ritov's reply is unconvincing and practically devoid of any factual data. It is written in a flowery style, rich in similes and in paeans of praise of the activities of Merkaz Haco-operatzia.

(96) L'Chavereinu, November 1953, pp. 43-44. This is a bill of complaints to support his condemnation of Merkaz Haco-operatzia (and by implication also of Mr. Ritov) which, as far as the bus co-operatives are concerned, is a "prostrate (powerless) body".

(97) In a P.S. Mr. Ritov draws attention to his article about WPSTS in a special economic supplement of "Hador" (the Mapai daily which discontinued in 1956) of 10 July, 1953, and which included the following paragraph.

". . . Of course there are many justified complaints about the bus co-operatives, but there are also many misrepresentations and much insolence. And these obscurities confused those who were dealing with the question. Is it permissible to ignore the fact that during the last three years there were no possibilities of doubling the equipment required to keep pace with the one hundred per cent increase in population? And are only the drivers to blame for the altercations between the public and the drivers which, in a measure, are caused by the babel of language of the immigrants?" But the problem remains that of adjusting the bus transportation to the mutual benefit of the public and those serving it.

(98) The bus co-operatives "Dan" in Tel Aviv and "Hamekasher" in Jerusalem though outside the combine, together with Eshed established a united front *vis-à-vis* the Government and the public, and in most questions also *vis-à-vis* the Histadrut. Hamekasher amalgamated with Egged (Eshed) early 1967.

(99) The voluntary liquidation of the three bus co-operatives which merged into Egged (Eshed) was not completed until 1958. The name acknowledged the seniority and status of Egged, and Eshed is made up of the first letters of the three societies—(E(gged), Sh(achar) and D(rom Yehuda).

(100) *De facto* the rules of the new co-operative Egged (Eshed) include nearly all the modifications which Eshed had suggested and which the Histadrut allegedly had approved, but which the *ad hoc* Committee of Three on Bus Transportation had rejected.

(101) Section 31 of the Regulations of the Co-operative Societies Ordinance, 1933, empowers the Registrar or his appointee to approve the value of the amounts due to a member of the WPSTS at the time of his withdrawal from the society or of his death. The society must make all payments within twelve months from the date the respective membership ceases.

(102) The agreement of 9 January, 1952, provided that the society shall pay interest on the 25 per cent of the surplus which is allocated to the divisible reserves for members and also that the society's reserves should be used for

(*a*) remuneration and social security supplementary allocations to members;
(*b*) allocations for the members' provident and pension funds; and
(*c*) allocations for depreciation fund (according to the accepted norms).

(103) Parshot Dan (Story of Dan)—"Thirty Years of Public Transportation in Israel", February 1956 (p. 128), by Moshe Lavi, published in commemoration of the tenth anniversary of Dan on 25 December, 1955. This pamphlet contains interesting historical material about the background and early days of passenger transport co-operatives and the merger of these into the present bus co-operatives. The following table (page 70 of pamphlet) shows the status of Ichud Regev prior to their organic merger in 1945. These figures also reflect the effects of the Arab disturbances 1936-39.

	Hamaavir			Ichud Regev		
	1935	1939	1945	1935	1939	1945
Labour Force (members and non-members)	347	353	366	189	169	222
Number of buses	87	136	165	95	80	79
Number of fares carried during year (in millions)	32·9	29·3	52·3	7·3	4·6	8·4
Gross annual revenue (in LP.000)	154	146	594	99·4	48·5	267

Dan Bus Co-operative has a *de facto* monopoly of the internal bus traffic in Tel Aviv-Jaffa and of the traffic between Tel Aviv-Jaffa and the suburbs up to and including Petah Tikva. Dan's buses serve a population of 700,000, approximately 35 per cent of Israel's population. During the first decade since it was organized (an amalgamation of three bus co-operatives) and registered in December 1945, Dan's equipment increased from 244 to 354 buses (including 166 Diesel), according to an article by the Minister of Transport, Yitzchak Ben Aharon (Shituf October 1955).

DAN BUS CO-OPERATIVE

Year	Labour Force	Buses Petrol	Buses Diesel	Fares Carried (millions)
1945	688	244	—	8·1
1949	1,032	304	14	12·4
1952	1,596	321	97	19·0
1955	1,905	288	166	21·8

The Government Statistical Abstract, 1962, reports that on 21 May, the total population of

(*a*) Tel Aviv-Jaffa was 386,079;
(*b*) and that of Tel Aviv District (including 20 communities) was 685,400 (all Jewish except for 2,800); 35·7 and 2·8 per cent of the Jewish and Arab population in Israel respectively.

Dan had a labour force of 2,690 (at the end of 1960) on 79 routes; its buses had 23,731 seats. In 1959-60 Dan's 625 buses covered 35·5 million kilometres and carried 24·3 million passengers. The gross revenue was IL.22·4 million.

(104) *De facto* this danger is considerably minimized because many of those in office are re-elected. More recently, especially in Egged (Eshed) where there was a revolt of the younger generation, re-election is not a certainty. The Co-operative Societies Ordinance, 1933, does not prescribe either a minimum or maximum term of office and also permits staggered term of office.

(105) In 1953 and 1954 there were four serious strikes of wage workers employed by the Dan Bus Co-operative, especially by those employed in the co-operative's garages.

(106) Aaron Davshi's article (pp. 105-108) "In the Cultural Paths of Dan" contradicts this completely negative statement.

(107) This article is a sharp rejoinder to the young members and presents the case of the vatikim with more emotion than reality.

(108) Leviticus XXVI and Deuteronomy XXVIII.

(109) There is an aphorism that a successful co-operative or Co-operative Movement is one which has accommodated itself to the environment and at the same time has adapted the environment to its needs.

(110) The Municipal Council unanimously decided to appoint as an enquiry committee its Municipal Traffic Committee, the three members Messrs. A. Kublanov, M. Eden and D. J. Jacobi. On 26 February, 1950, the council decided that Mr. Jacobi should be chairman of the committee. The chairman alone questioned most of the witnesses. All but five of the 32 hearings were public and three of the five exceptions discussed policies and tax principles.

The stencilled report (113 foolscap pages, double spacing, text plus statistical and other appendices) is one of the best and frankest documents of its kind to which the writer had access. But it remained the unknown or forgotten soldier in the battle between the Histadrut-sponsored bus co-operative Hamekasher and the public. According to paragraph 6, page 5 of the report, the legality of the committee has been questioned. The report refers to the committee's decision merely to note the refusal of Hamekasher to submit balance-sheets, statistical data, the complaint file, etc. Since the legality of the appointment of the committee is in doubt,

> "we cannot ask the council to appropriate funds. . . . The root of the problem is that the municipality is not an autonomous body authorized to do everything which it considers necessary and desirable . . . the (municipality) may not do anything which is not included within the framework of its obligations and powers embodied in the (respective) legislation . . . and the law has not yet empowered municipalities to deal with transportation and also has not given them any specific authority to appoint an enquiry committee or to represent their (respective) inhabitants, *vis-à-vis* the Government. Nevertheless, the municipality is empowered to do everything needed—for the security of her (respective geographical) region."

The Committee decided that though it was its duty to continue with its work, it would not ask for special appropriations. The Committee used the part-time services of a few members of the municipality's regular staff.

(111) Hamekasher at the end of December 1963 had 180 buses with 6,703 seats, and a labour force of 517 (members and non-members). During 1959-60 this bus co-operative covered 7·5 million kilometres on 25 routes; carried 47 million passengers; and its gross revenue was IL.4·7 million.

The Statistical Abstract of Israel, 1962, reports that on 22 May, 1961, the Jerusalem district had a population of 187·7 thousand and of these 167·4 lived in Jerusalem.

(112) The Committee was appointed on 7 November, 1954, and the letters of appointment with the terms of reference are dated 25 November, 1954.

(113) According to Haaretz of 13 December, 1954, the representative of the "Dan" Bus Co-operative (Tel Aviv) told the Committee of Nine on 12 December, 1954, that unless an interim increase of bus fares by 25 per cent was approved, which the Minister of Transport and the representatives of the Ministry of Finance allegedly had promised, Dan could not continue to operate.

(114) The Report (mimeographed) is addressed to the Minister of Transport. It has five single-space foolscap sheets plus two detailed estimated budgets for 1955-56 (April-March) for the three bus co-operatives Egged (Eshed), "Dan" and "Hamekasher". These estimates were prepared by a sub-Committee and then amended and approved by the Committee as a whole.

(115) The Report does not give the number of these meetings; the number of the oral witnesses or their views, and also gives no indication of the type of written material submitted to the Enquiry Committee or from whom it was received.

(116) At a press conference, the Ministry of Transport circulated the following data about the increase in the costs of the various items between 23 February and 7 October, 1954.

PERCENTAGE INCREASES BETWEEN 23 FEBRUARY AND 7 OCTOBER, 1954 REPORTED FOR THE BUS CO-OPERATIVES

Item	Egged(Eshed)	Dan	Hamekasher
1. Fuel, Cost of Living Index	6·7	6·7	6·7 (b)
2. Social Insurance (effective March 1954) based on estimated costs of IL.8000 for Egged, IL.4000 for Dan & IL.800 for Hamekasher—per month	0·4	0·4	0·4
3. Total of 1 plus 2	7·1	7·1	7·1
4. Less reserve earmarked on 16 April, 1954 (3)	3·0	3·0	3·0
5. Cost of Living Index (increase)	1·5	1·5	1·5
6. Increase in bus fares (rounded off)	1·6	0·3	1·1
7. Increase of weekly fare tickets	1·5	1·5	1·5
8. Total of 4 plus 5 plus 6 and 7	7·6	6·3	7·1
Paid out to members for increase in Cost of Living	3·6 (a)	4·6 (a)	

(*a*) IL.39·320 contributed by 1960 members equals IL.77,067·2, which is equivalent to 3·6 per cent of the gross estimated expenses (IL.2,135,000) in February 1954.

(*b*) IL.50·200 contributed by 840 members equals IL.42,168, which is equivalent to 4·6 per cent of gross estimated expenses (IL.909,000) in February, 1954.

(117) Shituf, July 1956.

(118) Letter of appointment 15 July, 1956 from the Minister of Transport, to seven members of Committee. Judge Dr. Nathan Ben-Zackai, Chairman; Messrs. Mordechai Ish Shalom (secretary, Labour Council, Jerusalem); Chaim Baili; Efraim Ben Artzi; Shmuel Zitelni; Shlomo Rozen and Nachum Shamir.

Except for the chairman, all are Histadrut members and working for the Histadrut or Histadrut-sponsored institutions. Four are members of Mapai and one each of Mapam and Achdut Haavodah.

(119) The minutes of these 20 closed meetings were not available to the writer.

(120) The letter fails to mention the failure of the bus co-operatives to co-operate and to comply with the measures which the controlling bodies recommended and the ineffectiveness of the control to date, which Mr. Avner Hovne mentions in his study (Chapter Four).

(121) The letter does not mention that *de facto* the bus co-operatives have paid their members a basic monthly emolument exceeding the authorized IL.100.

(122) L'Chavereinu, 27 October, 1956, (pp. 1-18; 59-67).

(123) L'Chavereinu No. 35, July 1958. This harping on the basic emolument seems a conscious design to confuse the entire issue. The problem is gross payments made to members and not the basic emolument

which, generally speaking, at the time constituted one-third or less of the gross payment to a member (take home pay).

(124) Mr. Chanan Yosef, does not mention the persistent protests against the Government, the Histadrut, and also at times against the "rif raf who use the buses" which Egged (Eshed) has carried on through their internal monthly bulletin; meetings of its members, etc. One of the cartoons in L'Chavereinu, of October 1956 (p. 67), depicts a conversation between two Egged members standing in front of their bus and reading the same newspaper.

> "Have you read that the Government has approved $40,000 for the import of 200 taxis?" The second member replies "Why was the annual quota of buses to be imported decreased from 500 to 200?" The first member replies: "What do you think, are they (taxi owners) not entitled to some reward for their efforts during the bus strike?"

(125) L'Chavereinu No. 34, May 1958.

(126)(The article (L'Chavereinu, 15 July, 1958) repeats the story of the trials and errors of the bus co-operatives and of their achievements, in spite of the difficulties, especially since the merger of the three bus co-operatives into Egged (Eshed) (1951), a period of unusually large immigration, and on the other hand abnormal shortages of spare parts, tyres, foreign currency, etc., without which it was impossible to improve the services.

(127) The maximum at that time (August 1958) was IL.20 per month for seniority. The bus co-operatives asked for 25 per cent.

(128) At that time—a member of a bus co-operative was entitled to sick leave with pay of 42 work-days per year; combined annual vacation and sick leave without any limitations about the cumulative period or the need to submit a medical certificate.

(129) Most buses are manned only by a driver.

(130) Histadrut-sponsored companies have a substantial financial participation and a substantial block of voting shares in the Jerusalem Post.

(131) A copy of the 17-page report, dated 22 August, 1961, (stencilled—double space) was sent to the writer on 29 November, 1962. The letter accompanying the report notes "Of course no part is for publication". The report is signed by the Chairman of the Sub-Committee, Dr. Zvi Ofir.

(132) Shituf, May 1958, pp. 26-32.

(133) Another speaker described this as an incorrect statement if the bus fares are considered in terms of workers' wages, that is in terms of working time required to earn the equivalent of a bus fare.

(134) The members of the bus co-operative who reject the plan could receive Government bonds of the new Company.

(135) Borowsky's prognosis has been proven correct (1964).

(136) One of the basic principles of WPSTS is that the members as owners and managers of the means of production also enjoy the right to dispose of the revenues. Therefore, the allowances to which this article in Hameshek Hashitufi objects, *per se* are not contrary to a basic co-operative principle. But "if such allowances" are unwise from a financial point of view then, third parties—the Government and/or the public—must exercise their authority. Monopolistic exploitation of any kind and by any pattern of economic enterprise is wrong. But this cannot justify the abolition of the co-operative pattern or fostering anti-co-operative sentiment. The social and/or economic desirability of a certain pattern of

economic undertaking—co-operative or non-co-operative—must not be confused with or judged by the malfunction or application of certain principles.

(137) One of Mr. Ben Ari's main arguments is that the possibilities of sharp practices in a commercial company is almost unlimited. The Public Transportation Corporation, which the Khoushi Committee suggests, would restrict the transfer of shares, voting rights, etc. The article seems very political and slanted.

(138) Shituf, January 1959 (pp. 26-29).

(139) The writer was unable to obtain a copy of the proceedings of these meetings and of the material which was submitted to the Committee.

(140) Initially the Left-wing Socialists mercilessly criticized Mapai because it had agreed to increase the gap between the lowest and highest grades of civil servants and to supplementary payments for those with academic and professional degrees. Mr. Hacohen's support for a graded scale of remuneration for the members of the bus co-operatives was said to have been prompted by the elections to the new Knesset to be held in September, 1959.

(141) Davar, 14 January, 1959.

(142) A mezuza is a container fixed on the doorposts containing a page with Deuteronomy, Chapter 6, verses 4 to 9, and Chapter 11, verses 13 to 17.

(143) 16 January, 1959.

(144) Shituf, January 1959. The closing paragraph of this leader could be interpreted as disagreement with the Khoushi Committee's conclusions.

This closing paragraph is directed to all the sectors of the Histadrut-sponsored Co-operative Movement, not only the WPSTS, and more especially the bus co-operatives.

(145) Mr. Ben Nathan does not identify the source of his quotation. The writer on several occasions discussed this very aspect with the late Prof. Franz Oppenheimer, both in Israel and abroad. And Prof. Oppenheimer never expressed the view quoted. It is a fact, however, that the use of wage labour was an important and, in the opinion of some, one of the main reasons for the collapse of such communitarian movements in the U.S.A. as the Shakers, Inspirationalists and the Perfectionists. And this may be the reason why the Hutterites who do not use wage labour are still an active movement with a history of about 150 years.

(146) Davar, 19 January, 1959.

(147) The remedy compromises a co-operative principle that the accretion in assets belongs to all members irrespective of the length of time they have been members and as long as they remain members of the respective co-operative. This is why the value of a share or unit of participation in the capital of a co-operative remains at par—the amount which the member actually paid. In periods of inflation a co-operative may increase the value of a unit of participation or may increase the minimum number of shares or units of participation which every member is required to hold. But the co-operative does not reward older members for hardships which they have suffered in the past. The manager of the bus co-operative in Jerusalem correctly noted that "the member belongs to the co-operative but the co-operative is not the property of the members". Co-operatives may and do pay a fixed or variable, but nominal interest on shares or units of participation. One of the reasons why co-operatives generally limit the maximum of shares of participation for any one

member is because it does not wish a member to consider himself mainly as an investor in his co-operative. The anti-co-operative compromise which the secretary of Merkaz Haco-operatzia suggested at the Third Congress is the "bad seed", which may lead to the disappearance of the WPSTS movement.

(148) In 1934 the Histadrut had not yet decided to require that all its sponsored housing co-operatives must register all their property in the name of the respective societies, and that the members are only tenants, and also that only the co-operatives and not the members may dispose of a part or all of a flat or house of a member who withdraws or is expelled from the respective co-operative.

(149) This forecast was inaccurate and premature. The position at the end of 1964 was worse than at the end of 1937.

(150) The co-operative principle of equality refers to equality of opportunity and equitable distribution. It is not the purpose of co-operatives to do the impossible, i.e. to introduce equality in every respect. For instance, every member has one vote but not every member has the same influence on the other members. The goal of co-operation, except for all inclusive integrated co-operatives like kibbutzim, is not economic equality in the sense of equality in earnings, ownership of property, etc. There are, however, some WPSTS, and especially the commandites in France, that distribute the earnings equally among all members. But generally speaking, WPSTS, including the co-partnership productive societies in England, fix payments to members on the basis of skill, seniority, number of dependents, and in some cases, productivity.

(151) The labour code includes the following regulations about applicants for membership in WPSTS:

1. A probation period of a wage worker may be prolonged to more than two months only if the WPSTS advises the authorized body that it definitely considers the particular worker as a probationer.
2. The maximum extensions of the probation period (over the two months as in (1)) is five months. (In 1960 a probation period of up to 18 months was permissible.)
3. Only with the express approval of the authorized institution, may the number of probationers exceed 50 per cent of the membership of the respective WPSTS at any time.
4. A special Committee of the authorized body shall examine semi-annually the extent to which the WPSTS can integrate additional members. Additional members shall be selected, on the basis of seniority, from those probationers who have worked at least four months in the respective WPSTS.
5. Applicants who have been rejected may appeal to the authorized body which is not obliged to give its reasons for a negative decision on the appeal. The authorized body may instruct a WPSTS not to accept during "a specific period" additional wage workers.
6. Wage workers who do not wish to become members may not be employed by the respective WPSTS for more than two years.
7. If after an investigation it is decided that the size of the labour force of a WPSTS must be reduced, then members who were accepted during the two years immediately preceding the decision, shall be the first to be dropped.

(152) A serious deterioration in the position regarding wage labour started within six months of this statement.

(153) Representing the Histadrut—Messrs. Chazan, Tabenkin, Lubianiker (who later became known as Lavon), Kol, Remez* and Mrs. Meyerson (now Meir). Representing Merkaz Haco-operatzia—Messrs. Goren, Kitzis and Ritov.

(154) It is not clear how the bus co-operatives obtained a copy of the Chevrat Haovdim proposals.

(155) Is this not the attitude of Soviet Russia, Yugoslavia, Poland, Albania, Bulgaria and Hungary where the co-operatives became and remain agencies which carry out Government economic, social and to some extent also the political policies?

(156) The agreement prescribed that for a period of three years as from January 1946, a 15 per cent increase in basic salary and cost of living allowance was to be substituted for profit sharing by the permanent wage workers in the bus co-operatives. But the profit sharing plan was applicable to all wage workers in other WPSTS. The Solel Boneh was instructed to take over "as soon as possible" the legal ownership of the Egged garage.

(157) This is especially the case in the co-operative restaurants, nearly all of whose members are women. These have both an absolute and relatively higher turnover of membership than any other type of WPSTS.

(158) The rules of nearly all primary transportation co-operatives prescribe priority for the children (including sons-in-law) and other blood relations over other applicants for membership.

(159) The report to this Council Meeting also notes that by the end of 1955, Egged (Eshed) will take possession of the building which it has acquired in Haifa, in which all the co-operative's offices will be housed, and that Egged (Eshed) also plans to put up an office building in Tel Aviv.

(160) Mr. Lehman noted that wage workers constitute 67 per cent of the labour force in the co-operative workshops in the metal branch; 55 per cent in the co-operative joineries; 41 per cent in construction and 29 per cent in the co-operative printing shops in which the percentage of member-workers has increased.

(161) The division for industrial workers' co-operatives included 170 societies with 4,000 workers, between 55 and 58 per cent of whom are non-members. Representatives of affiliated WPSTS constitute the majority on the Management Committee of this division.

A report of Merkaz Haco-operatzia on industrial workers and service co-operatives, February, 1960, Table 1 and 2, p. 60, notes that the 158 industrial workers' co-operatives have a total labour force of 3,780 workers (members and non-members) and that the 22 co-operatives in metal and electrical branches account for 1,062 and the 48 co-operative bakeries for 606.

(162) Mr. Goren gives the following figures which differ from those published by Merkaz Haco-operatzia on 31 December, 1958 and given in brackets below.

Branch of Industrial Workers' Co-operatives	Members	Wage Workers
Metal[a]	323 (314)	668 (675)
Joineries	135 (143)	167 (182)

Building Materials	128 (79)	89 (65)
Printing	121 (152)	156 (183)
Leather	66 (78)	105 (87)
Textile & Clothing	52 (48)	31
Foodstuffs	61 (52)	29 (22)

[a] The metal branch includes Haargaz which manufactures citrus cases; bodies for lorries and buses; metal office furniture, etc. The Haargaz co-operative jointly and equally with Kupat Haco-operativim, own and operate the Haargaz Company.

(163) At the end of 1964 the three bus co-operatives had 5,216 members and 1,444 non-member workers (including apprentices). Mr. Ritov refers to the valuable contribution made by Mr. A. Davidson of Egged (Eshed) in the discussions about wage labour and also praises "all the members of the management committees of the three bus co-operatives . . . whose approach was basically positive."

(164) F. W. Deacon (The Brutal Friendship, Mussolini, Hitler and the Fall of Italian Fascism) uses the very descriptive phrase "shop-soiled baggage of ideological catchwords" for a slogan (pp. 62-63). Published by Weidenfeld & Nicholson, London 1962.

(165) Extract from "The Roots of Heaven", Romain Garry, p. 1,031. Waitari of the Outes tribe explaining to Saint-Denis why he joined the rebellion against France. "Look here, my friend, for three years I was a conductor in Paris. I recommend it during rush hours; it gave me what you might call a knowledge of human nature, a good, solid knowledge, which prompted me to change sides and go over to the elephants. I hope that that'll do for you, as an explanation."

(166) A twelve-page pamphlet issued by the Histadrut Executive Committee in August 1963, "for the Labour Colonization Convention in Tel Aviv on 1 September, 1963".

(167) There is a note that the rights of permanent employees who may be permitted to continue as wage workers will be safeguarded. No details are given. The following note appeared in the "Jerusalem Post" of 14 February, 1963.

> TEL AVIV.—The Histadrut has arranged loans totalling IL.1·5m. to enable hired hands employed by the bus co-operatives to become members. This was reported to a recent meeting of the Histadrut Central Committee by Mr. Avigdor Eshet, who has the job of co-ordinating the elimination of hired labour in co-operatives.
>
> He noted that Hamekasher took in 67 hired hands as members, in keeping with the number set by the Histadrut. Egged accepted 450 out of 530 and Dan only took in 230 out of 375 candidates.
>
> Egged has 3,300 members and 783 employees, compared to 1,100 employees and 2,259 members in 1960. Dan has 578 employees compared to 1,640 members (in 1960 the ratio was 760 to 1,258), and Hamekasher has 133 hired men and 316 members (140 to 229 members).
>
> Mr. Benny Atlas, of the Dan management, explained that because there was little difference between the wages of hired men and members, the former were now less eager to join the co-operative. He argued against lowering the co-operative's stringent health and age standards,

and added that it will continue to insist on its right to judge candidates' social adaptability.

(168) Shituf, January 1957 (pp. 3-9) and February 1957 (pp. 3-14).

(169) This is a unique, co-operative point of view. The main reason for the establishment of audit unions was the desire of the co-operatives to be completely independent of outside forces. However, the co-operative movements in some countries, such as in Great Britain and in India, do not require audit unions to do the official annual audit and confine their functions to educational, advisory and supervisory activities.

(170) Mr. A. Razi, a veteran of the Histadrut, wrote on 8 June, 1955, to the writer, that if the fate of the WPSTS movement in Israel is not to be that of its counterpart in Europe, then it must try to weave new paths and introduce radical constitutional and structural changes in the old and new co-operative undertakings (WPSTS).

"It seems to me that the full co-operative ownership of the means of production which is the basis of a WPSTS has not achieved the desired goal, in spite of the excellent human material that joined the first co-operatives (WPSTS).

"Within Chevrat Haovdim opinion is crystallizing about the need, on the one hand, of bolstering the public control of all WPSTS, and on the other hand the importance of increasing the workers' participation in the Histadrut-sponsored administered undertakings."

(171) The suggestion was that a WPSTS should not expand if such expansion will require the use of wage labour.

(172) Is this not a question whether one prefers the advantages of genuine co-operative production or prefers the glamour of large WPSTS in which the co-operative aspect is the forgotten soldier.

(173) Shituf, March, 1957 (pp. 10-18).

(174) Shituf, April 1957 (pp. 11-13).

(175) Mr. Goren's address was mainly a repetition of his statement at the joint meeting of Merkaz Haco-operatzia with the secretariat of Chevrat Haovdim on 29 November, 1956, about the future of the WPSTS.

(176) WPSTS AFFILIATION TO MERKAZ HACO-OPERATZIA, AUDIT UNION OF HISTADRUT-SPONSORED WPSTS.

	1951	1958	1961	1962
Total number	387	226	204	202
Workers Producers Societies		142	122	117
Service Societies		56	53	58
Transport—Goods & Passenger		28	27	26
Total Members		6,674	7,446	7,741
Total non-Members (includes apprentices)	13,131	6,014	7,050	6,948

According to the report of the Registrar of Co-operative Societies there were 251 active WPSTS at the end of 1962. And of these 201 were affiliated to Merkaz Haco-operatzia, 21 to Hapoel Hamizrachi Audit Union and 29 were unaffiliated.

The 21 WPSTS affiliated to Hapoel Hamizrachi at the end of 1962 (including two for transportation and one for services) had 160 members and 200 wage workers. The total of their own funds amounted to IL.169,000 and the total business in 1962 exceeded IL.3½ million. Hapoel Hamizrachi has allocated IL.125,000 for the establishment of WPSTS for religious youth.

(177) Mr. Ritov does not mention that wage workers account for practically the entire increase in Israel and that the WPSTS in Italy and France have relatively few wage workers.

(178) All three speakers were repetitious; skirted around the issues and seemed to rely on cliches and not on naked realities. Therefore, only a very short summary was made of their closing remarks.

(179) Shituf, December 1960.

(180) Shituf, January 1961.

(181) The Prime Minister also referred to the increase of the WPSTS in Israel since 1947 from 115 to 219; their labour force (members and non-members) from 5,334 to 13,341; their capital and reserves from less than IL.2 million to nearly IL.20 million (at official exchange rates $5·6 million and $11·2 million).

(182) The number and the percentage of the employable immigrants of working age is important.

(183) Hameshek Hashitufi, 15 September, 1961, 18 (521).

(184) The Jerusalem Post, 19 April, 1963, Extracts from the article "Co-operation, or Capitalism".

BaHistadrut No. 9-10, September-October, 1962 includes the Shapiro Report of 16 October, 1962 (pp. 84-113), and photostat copies of the signatures of the five members of the Shapiro Committee. This issue also publishes the précis of the discussions by the Histadrut Merkaz (Central Committee) on 21-22 October, 1962 (pp. 114-147). Messrs. Y. Ritov, the secretary of Merkaz Haco-operatzia, and A. Milak, of the Haifa Labour Council, participated in these meetings. Haaretz, of 31 October, 1962, publishes an exchange of the reactions of Mr. Ritov to the report and the Committee chairman's reply to Mr. Ritov. The writer has not summarized this report.

Sources

WPSTS-sources used for Analysis of Minutes of Governing Bodies of Merkaz Haco-operatzia and of the Council of the Egged (Eshed) Bus Co-operative and Reports on Activities of Merkaz Haco-operatzia.

First Congress, June, 1930 } Records of these two
Second Congress, 12 January, 1933 } Meetings were not found.
Third Congress, November, 1934 (date of meeting not given).
Report of the Proceedings, p. 40, published by Merkaz Haco-operatzia 1935(?).
The reports of the secretariat of Merkaz Haco-operatzia and the resolutions of the Third Congress cover nine and three pages respectively of the proceedings and the general debate covers 28 pages of the published proceedings. Of these, 18 pages report the remarks of ten delegates from the affiliated WPSTS and ten pages to the comments of four (of the seven) representatives of the staff and Central Committees of Merkaz Haco-operatzia who participated in the Third Congress.

Fourth Congress 6 June, 1938.

The report of the Fourth Congress, held on 16 June, 1938, published by Merkaz Haco-operatzia is unusually detailed. It includes the list of the 93 delegates from 62 WPSTS affiliated to Merkaz Haco-operatzia. Nine other affiliated WPSTS did not participate. There is no information about the basis for the distribution of the delegates among the three types of WPSTS shown in the following table. Egged, the oldest and the largest of the bus co-operatives, had eight delegates and the other three bus co-operatives, Hamekasher, Ichud Regev, Darom Yehuda, each had five.

AFFILIATED WPSTS WHOSE DELEGATES ATTENDED THE FOURTH CONGRESS OF MERKAZ HACO-OPERATZIA, 16 JUNE, 1938.

Type of WPSTS	No.	No. Delegates
Transportation (passenger & road haulage)	19	43
Industrial Workers Co-operatives	23	32
Service Co-operatives	20	18
Total	62	93

The report of the proceedings of the Fourth Congress includes financial and statistical data for 73 WPSTS and a note that seven WPSTS affiliated to the Merkaz Haco-operatzia did not submit the data. Forty-nine of the 73 societies were registered as co-operatives between 1933-1938 (13 in 1935, the year in which the largest number of immigrants, most of them from Nazi countries, arrived in Israel).

About 20 member delegates and four Histadrut officials participated in the general debate. The resolutions in the report on the proceedings of the Fourth Congress cover about nine pages. Apparently the committee on resolutions either disregarded or disagreed with the delegates' sharp criticism of the auditing, supervision and educational (culture) activities of Merkaz Haco-operatzia.

Report on the Activities of Merkaz Haco-operatzia 1938-1942 (p. 200) prepared for the Fifth Congress of Merkaz Haco-operatzia (7-9 April, 1949).

The Secretariat's report for 1938-1949 (p. 112) stresses that the desire to prevent a rift between the WPSTS affiliated to Merkaz Haco-operatzia and the Histadrut was the main reason for the eleven years' interval between the Fourth and Fifth Congresses. At the end of 1941 a committee was appointed to prepare suggestions for resolving the problem of wage labour, which were to be submitted to the Fifth Congress in January 1942. The Congress was postponed from month to month because the committee negotiating with the WPSTS about wage labour could not make headway. Important WPSTS advised Merkaz Haco-operatzia that "they could see no possibilities of resolving the question of wage labour during the war (i.e., World War Two), and they would not participate in the Congress if it were asked to take a definite stand on this question." This crisis led to other crises and Merkaz Haco-operatzia, at the request of the Histadrut, postponed the Fifth Congress from month to month.

None of the WPSTS delegates at the Fifth Congress 7-9 April, 1949, accepted the explanations given by Merkaz Haco-operatzia or the Histadrut representatives about the eleven-year interval between Congresses. Nor did they see any value in a Council which met only three times during eleven years. The delegates of a printer's co-operative in Haifa noted that "the Histadrut during the same period had convened two Congresses and had arranged general elections. A public movement cannot function without public backing and our public backing is the Congress and Council of WPSTS," A delegate of "Shachar" bus co-operative (which allegedly was the first to abolish wage labour) was sure that Merkaz Haco-operatzia could have accomplished more in all fields, including the sphere of wage labour, "if there were not such long intervals between the congresses."

The Report on the Proceedings of the Fifth Congress (7-9 April, 1949) published by Merkaz Haco-operatzia in the autumn of 1950 included a detailed report of the general debate. But the financial and the statistical data and description of the WPSTS movement are sparse. The three interesting and useful innovations in the report on the proceedings of the Fifth Congress are

1. the inclusion of the general debate on the resolutions submitted;
2. a classified directory of the 307 WPSTS affiliated to Merkaz Haco-operatzia at the end of the 1949 and

3. photographs and short biographical sketches of the 63 members of WPSTS who had died in the eleven years between the Fourth and Fifth Congresses, 1938-1949, most of them in action in World War Two and in the War of Liberation, 1948-49.

The 12-page introduction to the proceedings of the Congress summarizes the developments since the Fifth Congress. The report to the Fifth Congress by the secretary on behalf of the Secretariat of Merkaz Haco-operatzia covers 58 pages, and the general debate 71 (including six pages of the discussion of resolutions submitted.) The four papers delivered at the Congress, two on social insurance and co-operation and one each on the place of co-operation in the economy of the country and Chevrat Haovdim and co-operation, covers 21 pages.

Since its election in April, 1949, the Council has met six times. As far as the writer was able to determine, there were no stenographic records of the proceedings of these meetings. Mr. Lush of the Secretariat of Merkaz Haco-operatzia makes short notes (or summaries) of some of the debates and also records the budgets and the decisions. The reports about some of the Council meetings were published in Shituf; the pages of Shituf are pasted in the minute book and are considered as the official minutes.

The fifth Congress elected a Central Management Committee (Merkaz) of 32 members, half from the list submitted by Chevrat Haovdim and half from the WPSTS affiliated to Merkaz Haco-operatzia. The Merkaz meets monthly and is considered an enlarged secretariat. Most of the minutes of these meetings include only the decisions. Short summaries of some of the merkaz meetings are published in Shituf.

First Meeting of the Council 14 July, 1949. (The Council elected on the last day of the Fifth Congress (9 April, 1949).

Shituf, August-September, 1949, pp. 14-24, of which 3½ pages summarizes the general debate and the reports and replies by the Secretariat and staff of Merkaz Haco-operatzia. This issue of Shituf also has the second part of a report of a conference of new co-operatives held on 30 June, 1949. The first part is in Shituf, June-July, 1949.

The report of the proceedings of the Fifth Council Meeting does not give the number present. There were three items on the agenda.

1. An oral summary by the secretary of the secretariat about the activities of Merkaz Haco-operatzia since the Fifth Congress.
2. Supervision and audit by Merkaz Haco-operatzia of its affiliated WPSTS;
3. Insurances of the property and social insurance for members of the affiliated WPSTS. (Prof. Benenson had presented to the Fifth Congress 29 April, 1949, a plan for social insurance).

Second Council Meeting 24-25 May, 1950.

Shituf, June-July, 1950, pp. 1-28. The secretariat's report uses 15 pages;

another report and the general debate each six pages and the resolutions one page). There is no information about how many participated in this meeting.

The Second Council Meeting like the first Council (14 July, 1949) was mainly concerned with the problems of the bus co-operatives. A number of the WPSTS elected members on the Council complained about this and also about the failure to carry out the promise made at the first Council Meeting that the secretariat would circulate its report before the meeting. Six of the thirteen elected members of the council represented bus co-operatives and their observations take up more than four of the six pages of Shituf's report on the general debate. Most of the observations of four of the five appointed representatives on the Council were about the problems of bus transportation.

Mr. Y. Ritov, the secretary of Merkaz Haco-operatzia, explains that it was decided to use a public hall for this council meeting, which is a departure from the usual practice. This will make it possible for more members of WPSTS, other than members of the Council, to hear the discussions and will also help to publicize the reports presented, discussions and resolutions. He said that since the status of the WPSTS "reflects (is a window pane for) the continuous revolution . . . the growing achievements, the events deserve such publicity."

Third Council Meeting, 12 September, 1951.

Shituf, September, 1951, pp. 12-18. This short and unsatisfactory summary does not report the general debate at this meeting. Merkaz Haco-operatzia advised the writer that this summary is the only available record of the proceedings of this Council, held fifteen months after the previous Council Meeting (24-25 May, 1950). Several Congresses had instructed the Secretariat of Merkaz Haco-operatzia to convene the Council at least every six months. The only item on the agenda, in addition to the secretariat's oral report, was Kupat Haco-operativim, the financial subsidiary.

Council of Egged (Eshed) 21 June, 1954—L'Chavereinu, June 1954, pp. 10-12. The report publicizes only the resolutions which "were all adopted unanimously." Not even a summary is given of the debate in which 22 participated.

Council of Egged (Eshed) 15/16 September, 1954.

L'Chavereinu, November, 1954, pp. 34-39. The editor notes that the report of the council meeting are "flash minutes" recorded by Mr. Nathan Harari. Eight delegates from Chevrat Haovdim participated at this meeting, two from Merkaz Haco-operatzia; one each from the Labour Councils in Haifa and Jerusalem and one from the Craft Union. The other three are described as an engineer; an individual who deals with "transportation problems;" and the secretary co-ordinator of the delegates (from Chevrat Haovdim).

Council of Egged (Eshed) 16 March, 1955.
L'Chavereinu, May 1955, p. 2.
Council of Egged (Eshed) 8-9 June, 1955.
L'Chavereinu, June, 1955, pp. 1-4 and 14-30; and July, 1955, pp. 13-26.
Council of Egged (Eshed) 19 September, 1955.
L'Chavereinu, October 1955, pp. 1-33.
Council of Egged (Eshed) 22-23 September, 1955.
L'Chavereinu, November, 1955, pp. 1-2 and 8-37; and December 1955, pp. 35-36.
Council of Egged (Eshed) 25 June, 1957.
L'Chavereinu, August, 1957, pp. 1-3.
Council of Egged (Eshed) 15-16 July, 1957.
L'Chavereinu, August, 1957, p. 43.
Merkaz Haco-operatzia Division for Transport Co-operatives.
Founders Meeting, 23 October, 1956.
L'Chavereinu, 4 November, 1956—unsigned article, pp. 38-40.

This division, organized before the reorganization of Merkaz Haco-operatzia, had a short and ineffective life. The division for transportation co-operatives includes the three bus co-operatives (Egged (Eshed), Dan, and Hamekasher); 21 road haulage co-operatives; Ofir (the only sea transport co-operative; and one taxi co-operative (Nesher). The co-operatives in this division account for 58 per cent of the total labour force (members and non-members) in all WPSTS affiliated to Merkaz Haco-operatzia.

Fourth Council Meeting of Haco-operatzia 8 May, 1957 (six years after the previous meeting 12 September, 1951).
Shituf, May, 1957, pp. 9-19.

Mr. Ritov's address "Signs of a New Epoch" was in the main an apology for the deluge of bankruptcies of WPSTS; the apathetic atmosphere in the WPSTS movement, etc. The report of the proceedings of this council meeting includes only "selected extracts from the general debate."

First Meeting of the Management Committee of the Division for Transport Co-operatives, 25 February, 1958.
Shituf, March, 1958.
Report on Activities of Merkaz Haco-operatzia, 1948-1958.

This report of 72 pages, published in February, 1960, was prepared for the Sixth Congress of Merkaz Haco-operatzia, which was to have met in March, 1960, and was postponed on the instructions of Chevrat Haovdim. Chevrat Haovdim ordered the postponement, four days before the date fixed for the opening of the Congress 25 April, 1961.*

* The Sixth Congress of Merkaz Haco-operatzia was held on 15-16 July, 1962. Background material for the Sixth Congress, Shituf, May-June, 1962, carries a two-page leader (pp. 1-2) about the Sixth Congress and eight articles (background material of debates (3-21). The last article (by Arieh Gifman) (pp. 16-21) is a good statistical presentation about the WPSTS for the years 1948-1961.

Age Grouping	Percentage	Country of Birth	Percentage	Seniority	Percentage
30 and Under	4·0	Europe	79·7	Five Years & Less	16·0
31—40	17·3	Middle East	6·3	6—10	8·0
41—50	36·7	Born in Israel	14·0	11—20	54·0
51—60	34·0			21—30	15·3
Over 61	8·0			Over 30	6·7
	100·0		100·0		100·0

The report, 1948-1958, was prepared by L. Lush and edited by Y. Ritov. It has thirteen sections of text (including a two-paragraph (pp. 5-6) Introduction). The fourteenth section (pp. 59-68) includes the statistical tables and the fifteenth section (pp. 69-72) is a directory of the WPSTS affiliated to Merkaz Haco-operatzia on 1 January, 1960, divided into

(*a*) industrial workers co-operatives;
(*b*) bus and road haulage co-operatives;
(*c*) service societies.

Sections (*a*) and (*c*) are subdivided according to branches.

The introduction gives the dates for the five previous congresses of WPSTS which include one held prior to the organization of Merkaz Haco-operatzia.

First: June, 1930, delegates for 27 WPSTS with a total labour force (members and non-members) of 700.

Second: January, 1933, delegates for 39 WPSTS with a total labour force (members and non-members) of 1,100.

Third: December, 1934, delegates for 74 WPSTS with a total labour force (members and non-members) of 3,000.

Fourth: June, 1938, delegates for 73 WPSTS with a total labour force (members and non-members) of 3,000.

Fifth: April, 1949, delegates for 128 WPSTS with a total labour force (members and non-members) of 5,700.

Only the statistical material has been summarized. The proceedings are published in Shituf, July-August 1962 (pp. 5-86). This issue of Shituf also carries a three-page unsigned leader (pp. 1-3), "After the Sixth Congress" and a short article (pp. 86-87) signed by Mendel Senger, "Protests about the Procedure of the Sixth Congress and the Result". Only the resolutions pp. 74-78 are summarized.

The Introduction to the Report on the Proceedings describes the Sixth Congress 15-16 July, 1962, as "entirely satisfactory from every point of view—contents and form". The greetings to the Congress are given on pp. 5-16 and the opening address by the General Secretary of Merkaz Haco-operatzia, Y. Ritov, are given on pp. 17-33. His report includes the following data about the 305 voting delegates and 16 delegates from that many WPSTS without voting rights. The 321 delegates included 65 from bus co-operatives: 44 from road haulage co-operatives; 143 from industrial workers co-operatives and 69 from service societies. The following data about the delegates is in percentages. Of those of the 86 per cent not born in Israel, 89·3 per cent were pre-State and 10·7 per cent post-State immigrants.

Fifth Council Meeting, Merkaz Haco-operatzia, 2 March, 1958 (first council meeting in the new building of Merkaz Haco-operatzia opened in September, 1957).

Shituf, April, 1958, pp. 14 to 38, "Excerpts from Minutes."

S. Goren opening the meeting lists three items for the agenda:

1. Reorganization of Merkaz Haco-operatzia.
2. New Government-Histadrut sponsored company, Teeus, for the industrialization of the development zones.
3. The Convening of the Sixth Congress of Merkaz Haco-operatzia.

First Meeting of the Management Committee for Industrial Workers Co-operatives, 4 March, 1958.

Shituf, April, 1958, p. 55.

Meeting of the Management Committee, 12 December, 1958.

Shituf, January, 1959.

Meetings of the Management Committee of the Division for Industrial Workers Co-operatives of Merkaz Haco-operatzia, 2 December, 1958.

The inadequate published report of the proceedings of this meeting clearly reflects an attitude of "let well enough alone". The report permeates a "fatalistic" approach to the problem of wage labour and the question of the new members' participation in the capital of the industrial workers co-operatives.

First Meeting (Plenary Session) of the Management Committee of the Division for Industrial Workers Co-operatives, 19 January, 1959.

Shituf, February-March, 1959, pp. 43-45.

Sixth Council Meeting, Merkaz Haco-operatzia, 12 January, 1959.

Shituf, February-March, 1959, pp. 17-31.

Special meeting of road haulage co-operatives, 24 February, 1959.

Shituf, February-March, 1959, pp. 40-42.

Seventh and Eighth Council Meeting, Merkaz Haco-operatzia 3 and 29 September, 1959.

Shituf, October-November, 1959, pp. 3-32.

Ninth Council Meeting, 4 May, 1960.

Shituf, June, 1960, pp. 3-32.

Meeting of the Division for Industrial Workers Co-operatives of Merkaz Haco-operatzia, 21 May, 1960.

Shituf, July-August, 1960, pp. 8-20.

Division for Service Co-operatives of Merkaz Haco-operatzia, 6 June, 1960.

Shituf, July-August, 1960.

The published report of this meeting includes only "selected extracts" from the general debate.

Tenth Council Meeting, Merkaz Haco-operatzia, 27 June, 1960.

Shituf, July-August, 1960, pp. 5-7.

The brief published report notes that the 1960 budget of Merkaz Haco-operatzia was sharply debated.

Eleventh Council Meeting, 12 December, 1960.

Shituf, January-February, 1961, pp. 20-27.

There were three items on the agenda:

1. Sixth Congress of Merkaz Haco-operatzia;
2. code for adjudicating differences;
3. wage labour.

Only "Extracts from the General Debate" are included in the published report of the proceedings.

GLOSSARY EXPLANATORY NOTE

For the localities, the spelling of the Ministry of Posts Telephone Directory, English Edition is used.

In all other cases the transliterations of the Hebrew terminology are phonetic, following the Sephardi pronunciation used in Israel. For example the Ashkenazi Hebrew pronunciation for rumours is *Shmuos*, while while the Sephardic pronunciation is *Shmuot*.

The *ch* in such words as *Ch*evrat Haovdim and *Ch*uka is pronounced like the *ch* in Rei*ch*. Most difficult were the transliterations of the names of individuals and I request the reader's indulgence for any mistakes. The Hebrew nomenclature is used for kibbutz(im), kvutza(ot), moshav (im) and the different sectors of the kibbutz and of the moshav movements, and most of the central co-operatives and the major central organizations.

The literal translation of the Hebrew word "Chuka" is law or statute. It is also used to denote the Constitution, Regulations, Rules and Codes. Therefore, when the word "Chuka" is used, the translation is generally given in parentheses.

The Hebrew word "Tnua" literally means movement, motion or traffic. However, this word is frequently used when referring to a sector of the co-operative movement and to the sub-sectors of the kibbutz and moshav movements. The word "tnua" is also used in the possessive form together with one or more other words as for example, Tnuat Hapoalim (The Labour Movement), Tnuat Hamoshavim is used for the Moshav Movement as a whole and as the name of the main federation of the Moshavim.

Wherever in the main text of the book an asterisk is to be found after a man's name, without a following footnote, it indicates that he was deceased before the series went to press (August 1964).

Glossary

1. Aliya	Immigration (lit. ascension) to Israel
2. Chalutz (*pl.* chalutzim)	Pioneer(s)
3. Chalutziut	Pioneering
4. Chaver (chavera) chaverim (chaverot)	Member(s) of any co-operative; also comrade(s), companion(s)
5. Chavura (Chavurot)	Generally used in the 1920s for mobile construction contracting groups
6. Chevra	1. A corporate body other than a co-operative 2. The Society as such, or a community, in the sociological sense
7. Chok (chukim)	Law; statute
8. Chuka (chukot)	Law; regulations; internal code(s); rule(s); ethos (depends on context)
9. Eretz Yisrael or Eretz Israel	Land of Israel
10. Garin (garinim)	Literally kernel(s), embryo or nucleus of a kibbutz or a moshav or of a workers producers co-operative
11. Galut	The Diaspora
12. Hapoel Hamizrachi	The religious labour party. Sponsor of Hakibbutz Hadati and its affiliated kibbutzim

13. Hashomer Hatzair	Left-wing socialist party, sponsor of Hakibbutz Haartzi and of its affiliated kibbutzim
14. HeChalutz	Pioneer organization in the Diaspora
15. Histadrut (Hahistadrut Haklalit shel Haovdim Haivrim B'Eretz Yisrael)*	General Federation of Jewish Labour in Israel, also a Federation of individuals or of organizations
16. Kupa	Safe or cash till, also used to designate a financial institution (such as Kupat Haco-operativim of the Workers Producers Co-operatives Transportation and Service Societies)
17. Maki (Miflaga Kommunistit Yisraelit)	Israeli communist party
18. Mapai (Mifleget Poalei Eretz Yisrael)	Party of Israel workers, right-wing labour socialist party. Sponsor of Ichud Hakvutzot V'Hakibbutzim and its affiliated kibbutzim
19. Mapam (Mifleget Poalim Meuchedet)	Party of united workers, united left-wing socialist party
20. Moetzet Hapoalot	Histadrut-sponsored council of working women
21. HaNoar HaOved	Histadrut-sponsored youth movement
22. Poalei Zion	Workers of Zion Socialist Labour Party that fused with Achdut Haavoda and organized the Mapai
23. Sabra	Prickly pear, used for native-born Jewish Israeli
24. Shikun	Housing and housing development (project)

25. Tnua (*pl.* Tnuot)	A movement; kibbutz movement (Tnuat Hakibbutzim); moshav movement (Tnuat Hamoshavim)
26. Vatik (vatikim)	Originally used for the founders generally of the pre-State kibbutzim, moshavim and moshavot. Later used for all who joined the kibbutzim and moshavim before or immediately after they were organized. Vatikim is used for the old-timers but is not a synonym for the older age groups. The derivative vetek is used for seniority
27. Yishuv	In the pre-State era it was used for the Jewish community in Israel. It is at present used to disignate a locality, more particularly an agricultural settlement and its population

* The Histadrut is a federation of the individual workers most of whom also are members of Labour political parties. The seats on the Histadrut organs, excluding its Executive Committee (Vaad Hapoel) are apportioned *pro rata* on the basis of the affiliation of the individual members of the Histadrut with the various labour parties that put up their own lists of candidates for office in the Histadrut. If for instance party A receives one-fourth of the total votes cast by members of the Histadrut in the election of delegates to a respective Histadrut Congress, party A members constitute one-fourth of the main governing organs (except for the Executive Committee) and of the main standing and *ad hoc* committees of the Histadrut. Davar is the Histadrut daily.

A Note on Hebrew Grammar

by David M. Jacobs

In order to help those readers unfamiliar with the Hebrew language to understand the structure of the many names of organizations to be found in this book, the following grammatical notes are appended.

The definite article

The definite article is "ha-" which is prefixed not only to the noun, but to all qualifying adjectives. For example the word for "worker" is "poel" and for "pioneering" is "chalutzi" thus "the pioneering worker" becomes "hapoel hachalutzi".

Formation of the plural

Normally masculine nouns form their plurals by adding "-im" and feminine nouns by changing the "-ah" of the feminine ending to "-ot". Thus "chaver" (f. chaverah) means "comrade" or "member". "The pioneering comrades" will be "hachaverim hachalutziim" or in the feminine "hachaverot hachalutziot".

The construct case

The Hebrew language has no genitive case instead it uses a grammatical form known as the construct case. If you wish to say "an association of workers", the word for association will go into the construct (meaning association of) while the word workers will remain in the nominative. The word for "association" is "agudah" which is feminine and the construct is formed by changing the mute final "h" of the feminine to "t" so that "an association of workers' becomes "agudat poalim". However the construct cannot take a definite article which is instead taken by its connected noun, thus "the association of workers" becomes "agudat hapoalim". The masculine singular of the construct is the same as the nominative. For example "meshek" is "farm" thus "the comrade's farm" becomes "meshek hachaver". The masculine plural of the construct ends in "-ei" thus "the farms of the comrade" becomes "mishkei hachaver". The feminine plural of the construct is the same as the nominative thus "the associations of women pioneering workers" would be "agudot hapoalot hachalutziot". Occasionally however the construct is not used and the word "shel" meaning "of" is used in its stead.

And

The word for "and" is a prefix "v' " or before certain consonants "u" Thus "the worker and the comrade" is "hapoel v'hachaver".

Vowel change

It will be noticed that there are sometimes internal vowel changes when words change their grammatical form.

General Bibliography

Workers' Producers Transport Service Societies (WPSTS)

Breslavsky Moshe—Tnuat Hapoalim Haaretz-Yisraelit (The Israeli Labour movement). Publishing house of Hakibbutz Hameuchad, Israel, 1955. Hebrew

Gdud Haavodah—Kovetz (Compendium). Mitzpa Publishing Company, Tel Aviv, 1932. Hebrew

The Histadrut—Report of the Third Congress, 1927. Hebrew

Hovne Avner—Report on the Bus Transportation Service. The relation between the co-operative form of monopoly and social control. (English text of the Hebrew report released by the Ministry of Labour and Social Insurance), Jerusalem, 1951. English

Kovetz Haco-operatzia—Compendium about Co-operation. (First Issue.) Merkaz Audit Union Credit Co-operatives (non-Histadrut), Tel Aviv, 1927. Hebrew

Kurland Samuel—Co-operative Palestine. The story of the Histadrut. The National Committee for Labour Palestine, New York, 1947. English

Lavergne Bernard—La Regie Co-operative. Librarie, F. Alean, Paris, 1927. French

Lloyd F. A.—The Co-operative Movement in Italy. The Fabian Society, George Allen and Unwin Ltd., London, 1925. English

Merkaz Haco-operatzia—Haco-operatzia Hayatzranit V'Hasherutit Shel Haovdim B'Eretz Yisrael (Central Organ for Histadrut-sponsored WPSTS in Israel), 1933. Hebrew

Meshek Haovdim 1958-62 (The Labour Economy). The Institute for Economic and Social Research, Vaad Hapoel (Executive Committee), the Histadrut, June, 1963. Hebrew

Poisson Ernest—The Co-operative Republic (English Edition). The Co-operative Union Ltd., Holyoake House, Manchester, 1925. English

Preuss Walter—Co-operation in Israel and the World (English Edition). Rubin Mass, Jerusalem, 1960. English

Report of the Registrar of Co-operative Societies on Developments during the Years 1921-1937, Jerusalem, 1938. English

Report of the Co-operative Department (Typescript), 1934-1946. Prepared by the Co-operative Department of the Mandatory, 1946. English

Shabatai K.—Bus Co-operatives, Davar, Eight Articles, 26 June; 6, 10, 16, 28, 30 July; 6 and 7 August, 1953. Tel Aviv. Hebrew

Shnaton HaHistadrut (Histadrut Year Book), Education and Cultural Centre Executive Committee. The Histadrut, Tel Aviv, 1963. Hebrew

Woolf Leonard S.—Co-operation, The Future of Industry. George Allen and Unwin, London, 1919. English

Zweig Ferdynand—The Israeli Worker. The Herzl Press and Sharon Books, New York, 1961. English

Official Exchange Rates in Terms of U.S.A. Currency

Sterling (£1)	**U.S. $**	
1920-29	5.00	
1923-24	4.33-4.65	
1925 (January to April)	4.75	
1925 (May)-1930	5.00	Return to Gold Standard
1931 (September)-1932	3.30-3.90	
1933-1938	5.00	Return to Gold Standard
1938 (End)	4.67	
1939 (September)	4.03	
1949 (September)	2.80	

Palestine and Israel

1. Until 1 November 1927, the Egyptian Pound (EL) was the currency and the exchange rate was 2½ per cent above Sterling.
2. 1 November 1927, the Palestine Pound (LP) was introduced and had the same value as Sterling.
3. IL (Israel Pound):

(*a*) 8 October 1948 to August 1949	IL.1 = LP.1
(*b*) September 1949 to January 1952	IL.1 = $2.80
(*c*) February 1952 to December 1953	Three rates for IL.1: $2.80; $1.40 and $1.00
(*d*) May 1953 to December 1953	Fourth rate for IL: IL.1 = $0.55
(*e*) January 1954 to January 1962	$1 = IL.1.80
(*f*) February 1962 to November 1967	$1 = IL.3.00
(*g*) November 1967	$1 = IL.3.50

Immigration Periods

Aliya: Immigration Periods	*Standard Jewish Encyclopedia*	*Other Sources*
First	1882-1903	1882-1903
Second	1904-1914	1904-1918
Third	1919-1923	1919-1923
Fourth	1924-1931	1924-1929
Fifth	1932-1940	1930-1936
Sixth	1941-1947	1939-1940
Seventh		1940-1947
Eighth		1948-1954

List of High Commissioners

1920-1925	Sir Herbert Louis Samuel (later 1st Viscount Samuel)
1925-1928	Field Marshal Sir Herbert Charles Onslow Plumer (later 1st Viscount Plumer)
1928-1931	Sir John Robert Chancellor
1931-1938	General Sir Arthur Grenfell Wauchope
1938-1944	Sir Harold MacMichael
1944-1945	Field Marshal John Standish Surtees Prendergast Vereker 6th Viscount Gort
1945-1948	General Sir Alan Gordon Cunningham

Government Census of Population (31 December 1965)

Statistical Abstract of Israel 1966—The Central Bureau of Statistics—Jerusalem, Israel. Table B/8 (p. 29); Table B/9 (p. 30).

		All	**Jewish**
Total Number of Settlements		875	771
Total Population[(a)]		2,598,400	2,299,100
Urban	No. Settlements	76	72
	Population	2,126,700	2,031,700
Rural	No. Settlements	799	699
	Population	471,700	267,400
Kibbutzim	Number	230	230
	Population	80,700	80,600
Moshavim[(b)]	Number	343	343
	Population	120,000	119,600
Moshavim Shitufiim			
	Number	22	22
	Population	4,800	4,700

(a) All population figures are given to the nearest hundred.

(b) Includes both moshavim ovdim and moshavim olim.

Index